EGON RONAY'S

COCA-COLA GUIDE

GOOD FOOD IN PUBS & BARS

Establishment research is conducted by a team of full-time professional inspectors, who are trained to achieve common standards of judgement with as much objectivity as this field allows. Their professional identities are not disclosed until they seek information from the management after paying their bills. The Guide is independent in its editorial selection and does not accept advertising, payment or hospitality from establishments covered.

Egon Ronay's Guides
Second Floor, Greencoat House
Francis Street, London SW1P 1DH

Editorial concept Moyra Fraser
Copy editor Lorraine Roche
Chief copywriter Peter Long
Research editors Coreen Williams Helen Perks Nicola Graham
Head of Editorial Barbara Littlewood
Publisher William Halden

Design Carole Thomas & Associates
Illustrations Linda Clark
Cover design Spero Communications Design Ltd
Marketing and Sponsorship Consultants Spero Marketing Consultancy Ltd

Cartography by Geoprojects (UK) Ltd. All road maps are based on the Ordnance Survey Maps, with the permission of the Controller of HM Stationery Office.
 Town plans by Intermap PS Ltd, Reading

Distributed in the United Kingdom by the Publishing Division of The Automobile Association, Fanum House, Basingstoke, Hampshire RG21 2EA and overseas by the British Tourist Authority, Thames Tower, Black's Road, London W6 9EL.

ISBN 0 86145 6289

AA Ref-50898

Typeset in Great Britain by Tradespools Ltd, Frome, Somerset
Printed by Hazell Watson & Viney Ltd, Aylesbury,
a member of the BPCC printing group

C·O·N·T·E·N·T·S

continued overleaf

C·O·N·T·E·N·T·S

H·O·W T·O U·S·E T·H·I·S G·U·I·D·E

GOOD BAR FOOD

We include establishments where our team of professional inspectors found excellent-quality bar food. Such pubs are indicated by the word **FOOD** printed in the margin alongside the entry. Reference may also be made to the pub's restaurant, but our chief concern has been with bar food.

Two typical dishes are listed, with prices valid at the time of our visit. Prices may, however, have risen a little since then.

We indicate when bar food is served and also any times when food is not available, but recent changes in the licensing laws may mean that some establishments are open for meals for longer hours than those stated in the entry.

Those establishments serving outstanding food are indicated by a star alongside the description.

GOOD ACCOMMODATION AT PUBS

We also inspected the accommodation, and those pubs recommendable for an overnight stay are indicated by the letters **B & B** in the margin alongside the entry.

We list the number of bedrooms, and a symbol shows the minimum price (including VAT) for bed and a full cooked breakfast for two in a double room:

£A	**over £50**
£B	**£41–50**
£C	**£30–40**
£D	**under £30**

If residents can check in at any time, we print ***all day***; if check-in is confined to certain hours or if it's advisable to arrange a time when booking, we print ***restricted***.

PUBS WITH ATMOSPHERE

Pubs recommended as pleasant or interesting places for a drink rather than for their bar food or accommodation are indicated by the letter **A** alongside the entry.

CHILDREN WELCOME

Those pubs we suggest as suitable for families are ones that have a room or indoor area where children are allowed, whether eating or not. Many pubs welcome children if they are eating bar food and some pubs make a feature of outdoor play areas, but readers should note that these are not the qualifications on which we base our category. Restrictions on children staying overnight are mentioned in the entries.

H·O·W T·O U·S·E T·H·I·S G·U·I·D·E

DRAUGHT BEERS AND CIDER

We indicate whether an establishment is a free house or brewery-owned. After the ▮ symbol we list the names of a number of beers, lagers and cider available on draught. We print ***No real ale*** where applicable.

OPENING TIMES

Opening hours vary throughout the country. Some pubs have a six-day licence. Any regular weekday closure is given in the entry. As most pubs close at some time during Christmas and New Year, it's advisable to check during that period.

ORDER OF LISTING

London entries appear first and are in alphabetical order by establishment name. Listings outside London are in alphabetical order by location within the regional divisions of England, Scotland, Wales, Channel Islands and Isle of Man.

MAP REFERENCES

Entries contain references to the map section at the end of the book, or to the town plans (see Contents list).

S·Y·M·B·O·L·S

FOOD	Recommended bar food
B & B	Recommended for accommodation
A	Recommended for atmosphere
★	Outstanding bar food
LVs	Luncheon vouchers welcome
Credit	Credit cards accepted
(rocking horse symbol)	Suitable for families
(tankard symbol)	On draught
(cheese symbol)	Good cheese (see p. 34)
(wine glass symbol)	French wine pubs (see p. 43)
£A–D	Cost of B & B

Of pubs and elephants . . .

In these days of pubs open all hours, masquerading as restaurants, with tables laid for food rather than pints, and with more waitresses than barmaids, you might think it would be difficult for us to decide what really qualifies as a pub and therefore competes for a place in this Guide.

But this is not the case. However good the food and excellent the service, we know, as soon as we walk in, whether it deserves that unique British description 'pub' on just one criterion – the 'feel' of the place. There's something about the atmosphere, the welcome, the cheerfulness that gives pubs their particular appeal and distinguishes them from wine bars, restaurants or bistros.

As Lord Denning once said: he would have great difficulty describing an elephant but he would know one when he saw it.

Pubs will have to battle to keep their identity. One obvious result of the new law will be pressure on them to become all-day fun palaces and fast-food centres. Let's hope that landlords remind themselves of their heritage and, like the elephant, never forget.

A woman's place?

Yet there are other threats to the pubs' traditional role, threats which feed on the weakness from within their own ranks.

This year, for the first time for many years, our team of inspectors has been enhanced by the recruitment of a woman. She is quiet, business-like and well qualified. Visiting hundreds of pubs in every area of the country over the past 18 months has taught her also to recognise a pub by its 'feel'.

Sadly, she has also had to learn to recognise hostility and rudeness. This has not been from customers, or from landlords but from the group which – to a man – would appear the most unlikely: the landladies and the barmaids.

Some landladies apparently still resent other women on their own using pubs and, furthermore, go out of their way to make it obvious. And, it seems, the further north you travel, the worse this resentment becomes, and if the lady behind the counter is over 40 years old she is more likely to be hostile.

Typically, in a pub on the Scottish border, Elizabeth ordered her lunch and sat down at the only chair vacant, at a table with an elderly man. When they had finished their meal the landlady asked the man if he would like coffee, yet completely ignored Elizabeth. She then brought the coffee and again ignored her.

Further south, when Elizabeth went into one lounge bar, two men standing at the bar moved aside to allow her to order. The landlady barely smiled and, when Elizabeth asked for a menu, she simply pointed to the end of the bar. The men were so embarrassed at the rudeness that one went to fetch it. The menu, as it happened, was equally uninviting and our inspector left shortly afterwards.

'It's strange,' says Elizabeth, 'how the two go together. If the welcome and the atmosphere in the pub are all wrong then invariably so is the food'.

If the fortunes of pubs are to thrive then they must welcome women who are on their own. Hotels have already recognised the business-woman traveller as a growing market. When women are driving many thousands of miles a year, particularly through country areas, pubs provide an ideal place to pause, enjoy a meal, make a phone call and visit the loo. Yet women are unlikely to stop if they expect to be unwelcome.

Perhaps the last word on the subject, at least for this year, was provided by another inspector: 'Speaking as an Australian,' he said, 'I find the pubs in this country are absolutely wonderful in their treatment of women.'

Goodbye Mr Chips

Another group of people made to feel unwelcome in far too many pubs is the elderly. The youngest inspector in the team reports that this year he has been angered at the treatment he has seen retired people receiving.

'So often I hear staff talking down to elderly people, treating them as though they were a nuisance. Yet in many pubs, particularly in the middle of the week, retired people represent 90 per cent of the customers.'

The main attraction for the retired in pubs is lunch but, too often, pubs are failing to provide the sort of meal they want. The food arrives in mounds, always surrounded by chips. And standards are usually lower at lunchtime than in the evening although prices remain the same.

The inspector's experience is shared by many of the elderly. Recently, a reader asked us to use our influence with pubs. 'The over sixties', wrote the lady from Berkshire, 'enjoy pub lunches but are put off by the size of portions and the everlasting presence of chips. When we ask for a smaller serving we are invariably told: "it's standard". Don't pubs realise how nauseated we feel when presented with a plate groaning with enough food to satisfy a student or a long-distance lorry driver'.

Let's just hope that, with extended hours, landlords and landladies will have more time to cater for these customers — women, even if they are on their own, and pensioners, even if they don't look hungry.

They may not have been part of the pubs' tradition, but they could represent the future.

William Halden
PUBLISHER

THE PUB OF THE YEAR AWARD

The three pubs described below are the finalists for the 1988 award and the winner will be announced at the launch of the Guide

■

The Pub of the Year award is a hand-painted and gilded octagonal decanter by Mason's Ironstone, engraved with the name of the winner, who will retain it. The runners-up will receive similar decanters.

■

As in previous years, the main criteria for the award are a very high standard of bar food and a pleasant, congenial atmosphere.

■ QUEEN'S HEAD, *NEWTON* ■

For more than 20 years the Short family have been running this charmingly old-fashioned pub. There is no hint of pretension either in the decor or in the food, which is deliciously simple and simply delicious: satisfying soups, home-cooked meats in wholemeal bread, a splendid evening buffet and cheeseboard.

■ Black Bull Inn, *Moulton* ■

This popular pub is well worth a lunchtime visit, both for its hospitable, relaxing ambience and also for its straightforward but excellent bar snacks. Soups, sausages, steaks and pan-fried sole are typical fare, and there's a good selection of prime English cheeses. Eating areas include an old Pullman carriage.

■ Wykeham Arms, *Winchester* ■

Everything you could want in a pub you'll find here – smashing food, excellent beer, wines by the glass and bonhomie dispensed liberally by the Jamesons and their splendid staff. The three bars generate a tremendous atmosphere, and the bedrooms, too, are comfortable and full of character.

The Early Days

The story of BACARDI rum starts more than a century and a quarter ago in Cuba. Don Facundo Bacardi y Maso, a wine merchant, succeeded in perfecting a process for distilling and blending from molasses, a spirit that was so mellow, light and pure that it could be sipped straight.

It was natural that the light, dry taste of BACARDI rum should soon find favour with American visitors to Cuba. In 1898 a US Army Lieutenant celebrating Cuba's independence from Spain tried mixing BACARDI rum with the latest soft drink from America, Coca-Cola. Today Bacardi and Coke or 'Cuba Libre' has grown to be the most popular way of enjoying BACARDI rum around the world.

Three years later, a US mining engineer working in the Daiquiri mines in the Sierra Maestra mountains created an icy cocktail of white BACARDI rum and lime juice – the famous Daiquiri.

BACARDI rum
and a little imagination!

The One Bottle Bar

Invariably asked for by name in bars throughout the world, BACARDI rum is so versatile, it's been called the 'one bottle bar'. The ideal base for hundreds of refreshing drinks, it's now increasingly drunk with orange juice, tonic, lime or lemonade. Many enjoy it straight with a little ice or mixed as a Daiquiri, a long drink or short drink – it can even be enjoyed in a warming punch or hot with tea and coffee.

Why not try these:

BACARDI Cocktail

According to a famous ruling of the New York Supreme Court in 1936, a genuine BACARDI Cocktail can only be made with BACARDI rum. Simply add a teaspoonful of Grenadine to the BACARDI Daiquiri recipe, shake well with ice and strain into a glass.

BACARDI Original Daiquiri

To recreate the original taste of a BACARDI Daiquiri add 1½ measures of BACARDI rum to 1 measure of lemon or lime juice. Add 2 or 3 teaspoonsful of sugar according to taste, and stir well. Serve with plenty of ice, or alternatively make the drink up in a shaker, add some ice cubes, shake well and strain into a cocktail glass.

O·U·T·S·T·A·N·D·I·N·G ★B·A·R F·O·O·D★

The following list highlights a select number of pubs where our inspectors judge the food to be of particularly high quality. The gazetteer entries for these establishments carry a star symbol.

ENGLAND

BRIGHTLING, E Sussex: **Fullers Arms**
BURTON, Wilts: **Plume of Feathers**
DARTMOUTH, Devon: **Cherub Inn**
FALMOUTH, Corn: **Pandora Inn**
FOSSEBRIDGE, Glos: **Fossebridge Inn**
FULKING, W Sussex: **Shepherd & Dog**
GREAT WALTHAM, Essex: **Windmill**
GRIMSTHORPE, Lincs: **Black Horse Inn**
HASLEMERE, Surrey: **Crowns**
KIRKBY STEPHEN, Cumb: **King's Arms Hotel**
LITTLE WALDEN, Essex: **Crown Inn**
MAIDENSGROVE, Oxon: **Five Horseshoes**
MALMESBURY, Wilts: **Suffolk Arms**
MONKSILVER, Som: **Notley Arms**
MOULTON, N Yorks: **Black Bull Inn**
NEWTON, Cambs: **Queen's Head**
OLD DALBY, Leics: **Crown Inn**
PITTON, Wilts: **Silver Plough**
SHAMLEY GREEN, Surrey: **Red Lion**
SHENINGTON, Oxon: **Bell**
SPEEN, Bucks: **Old Plow Inn**
STANTON HARCOURT, Oxon: **Harcourt Arms**
STAPLETON, Co Durham: **Bridge Inn**
STUCKTON, Hants: **Three Lions Inn**
WINCHESTER, Hants: **Wykeham Arms**
YATTENDON, Berks: **Royal Oak**

SCOTLAND

TARBERT, S'clyde: **West Loch Hotel**

WALES

LLANFIHANGEL CRUCORNEY, Gwent: **Skirrid Inn**
LLOWES, Powys: **Radnor Arms**

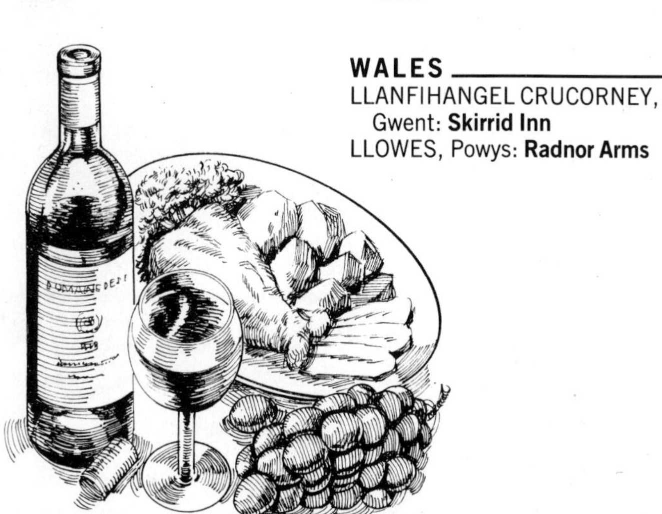

PUBS FOR FAMILIES

LONDON

Anchor, SE1
Bull's Head, W4
Cask & Glass, SW1
City Barge, W4
Cock Tavern, EC1
George Inn, SE1
Glasshouse Stores, W1
Goat, W8
Grenadier, SW1
Jack Straw's Castle, NW3
Mayflower, SE16
Museum Tavern, WC1
Old Ship, W6
Paxton's Head, SW1
Prospect of Whitby, E1
Samuel Pepys, EC4
Shepherd's Tavern, W1
Ship, SW14
Slug & Lettuce, N1
Spaniards Inn, NW3
Swan Tavern, W2
White Horse on Parsons Green, SW6
Ye Olde Windmill Inn, SW4

ENGLAND

AINSWORTH, **Duke William Inn**
ALFOLD CROSSWAYS, **Napoleon Arms**
ALFRISTON, **George Inn**
ALSAGER, **Manor House**
ALSWEAR, **Butchers Arms**
APPLEBY, **Royal Oak Inn**
APPLETREEWICK, **Craven Arms**
ARMATHWAITE, **Duke's Head Hotel**
ASCOT, **Stag**
ASHBURTON, **Exeter Inn**
ASHBURY, **Rose & Crown**
ASHWELL, **Bushel & Strike Inn**
ASKHAM, **Punch Bowl**
ASKHAM, **Queen's Head Inn**
ASKRIGG, **King's Arms Hotel**
ASTON CANTLOW, **King's Head**
ASWARBY, **Tally Ho**
BAINBRIDGE, **Rose & Crown Hotel**
BAMFORD, **Rising Sun Hotel**
BANTHAM, **Sloop Inn**
BARBON, **Barbon Inn**
BARNARD CASTLE, **Red Well Inn**
BASSENTHWAITE LAKE, **Pheasant Inn**
BATHAMPTON, **George Inn**
BEAUMARIS, **Liverpool Arms**
BEAUWORTH, **Milbury's**
BEER, **Anchor Inn**
BEETHAM, **Wheatsheaf Hotel**
BELFORD, **Blue Bell Hotel**
BELSAY, **Highlander Inn**
BERKELEY ROAD, **Prince of Wales Hotel**
BEWDLEY, **Black Boy Hotel**
BIBURY, **Catherine Wheel**
BIDDENDEN, **Three Chimneys**
BIDFORD-ON-AVON, **White Lion Hotel**
BINFIELD, **Stag & Hounds**
BISHOP WILTON, **Fleece Inn**
BLAKESLEY, **Bartholomew Arms**
BLEDINGTON, **King's Head Inn**
BLETCHINGLEY, **Whyte Harte**
BOOT, **Woolpack Inn**
BORTONWOOD, **Fiddle I'th Bag Inn**
BOSTON, **New England Hotel**
BOURTON-ON-THE-HILL, **Horse & Groom Inn**
BOWLAND BRIDGE, **Hare & Hounds**
BOX, **Chequers Inn**
BRATTON, **The Duke**
BREDWARDINE, **Red Lion**
BRENDON, **Stag Hunters Hotel**
BRIDGNORTH, **Falcon Hotel**
BRIDGWATER, **Admirals Landing**
BRIDPORT, **Bull Hotel**
BRIDPORT, **George Hotel**
BRIGHTLING, **Fullers Arms**
BRIGHTWELL BALDWIN, **Lord Nelson**
BRIGHTON, **Black Lion Hotel**

continued on page 22

Coca-Cola

CHICKEN CRUNCH

Good food is more fun with Coke.

Coca-Cola

MEXICAN CHILLI

Good food is more fun with Coke.

BRISTOL, **Jolly Cobblers**
BROADCHALKE, **Queen's Head**
BROCKTON, **Feathers Inn**
BROME, **Oaksmere**
BROMHAM, **Greyhound**
BROOM, **Broom Tavern**
BUCKLER'S HARD, **Master Builder's House Hotel**
BURFORD, **Bull Hotel**
BURNHAM-ON-CROUCH, **Ye Olde White Harte Hotel**
BURTON, **Plume of Feathers**
BURTON UPON TRENT, **Riverside Inn**
BURWASH, **Bell Inn**
CAMBRIDGE, **George Inn**
CANTERBURY, **Falstaff Hotel**
CAREY, **Cottage of Content**
CARTHORPE, **Fox & Hounds**
CARTMEL FELL, **Mason's Arms**
CASTERTON, **Pheasant Inn**
CASTLETON, **Castle Hotel**
CASTLETON, **Moorlands Hotel**
CERNE ABBAS, **New Inn**
CHADDLEWORTH, **Ibex**
CHAGFORD, **Globe Inn**
CHALE, **Clarendon Hotel**
CHARLBURY, **Bell at Charlbury**
CHARLTON VILLAGE, **Hurrow**
CHEDWORTH, **Seven Tuns**
CHENIES, **Bedford Arms Thistle Hotel**
CHESTER, **Ye Olde King's Head**
CHICHESTER, **Nags**
CHICKERELL, **Turk's Head**
CHIDDINGFORD, **Swan**
CHIEVELEY, **Blue Boar Inn**
CHILHAM, **Woolpack**
CHIPPING NORTON, **Crown & Cushion**
CHIPPING NORTON, **Fox Hotel**
CHISELHAMPTON, **Coach & Horses**
CHORLEYWOOD, **Sportsman Hotel**
CHRISTOW, **Artichoke Inn**
CHURCH ENSTONE, **Crown Inn**
CHURCHSTOW, **Church House Inn**
CIRENCESTER, **Crown**
CLANFIELD, **Clanfield Tavern**
CLARE, **Bell Hotel**
CLEARWELL, **Wyndham Arms**
CLIFTON HAMPDEN, **Barley Mow**
COCKWOOD, **Ship Inn**
COLEFORD, **Speech House Hotel**
COLESBOURNE, **Colesbourne Inn**
COLESHILL, **Coleshill Hotel**
COLLYWESTON, **Cavalier Inn**
COLN ST ANDREWS, **New Inn**
CONSTABLE BURTON, **Wyvill Arms**
CORSHAM, **Methuen Arms Hotel**
COXWOLD, **Fauconberg Arms**
CRANBORNE, **Fleur-de-Lys**
CRAZIES HILL, **Horns**
CROSCOMBE, **Bull Terrier**
CROYDE, **Thatched Barn Hotel**
CUCKFIELD, **Kings Head**
DAMERHAM, **Compasses Inn**
DARRINGTON, **Darrington Hotel**
DARTMOUTH, **Royal Castle Hotel**
DEDHAM, **Marlborough Head**
DERSINGHAM, **Feathers Hotel**
DEVIZES, **Bear Hotel**
DORNEY, **Palmer Arms**
DRIFFIELD, **Bell Hotel**
DUDDINGTON, **Royal Oak Hotel**
DUMMER, **The Queen**
DUNWICH, **Ship Inn**
EAST DEAN, **Tiger Inn**
EAST DEREHAM, **King's Head Hotel**
EASTERGATE, **Wilkes Head**
ELKSTONE, **Highwayman Inn**
ELSLACK, **Tempest Arms**
ELTERWATER, **Britannia Inn**
EMPINGHAM, **White Horse**
ESKDALE, **Bower House Inn**
ETTINGTON, **Houndshill**
EVERCREECH JUNCTION, **Natterjack**
EWEN, **Wild Duck Inn**
EWHURST GREEN, **White Dog Inn**
EXFORD, **Crown Hotel**
EYAM, **Miners Arms**
EYAM, **Rose & Crown**
FAIRFORD, **Bull Hotel**
FALMOUTH, **The Pandora Inn**
FARINGDON, **Bell Hotel**
FAUGH, **String of Horses**
FEN DRAYTON, **Three Tuns**
FENNY BENTLEY, **Bentley Brook Inn**

FIDDLEFORD, **Fiddleford Inn**
FINDON, **Snooty Fox Bar**
FINGEST, **Chequers Inn**
FITTLEWORTH, **Swan**
FONTHILL BISHOP, **King's Arms**
FORD, **White Hart at Ford**
FORTY GREEN, **Royal Standard of England**
FOSSEBRIDGE, **Fossebridge Inn**
FOTHERINGHAY, **Falcon Inn**
FOVANT, **Cross Keys Hotel**
FOVANT, **Pembroke Arms**
FOWLMERE, **Chequers Inn**
FOWNHOPE, **Green Man**
FRADLEY, **Fradley Arms Hotel**
FRAMPTON MANSELL, **Crown Inn**
FRILFORD HEATH, **Dog House**
FRISKNEY, **Barley Mow**
FYFIELD, **White Hart**
GIBRALTAR, **Bottle & Glass**
GOLDSBOROUGH, **Bay Horse Inn**
GOMSHALL, **Black Horse**
GOOSTREY, **Olde Red Lion Inn**
GOSBERTON, **Five Bells**
GREAT CHISHILL, **Pheasant Inn**
GREAT RYBURGH, **Boar Inn**
GREAT STAINTON, **King's Arms**
GREAT WOLFORD, **Fox & Hounds**
GRETA BRIDGE, **Morritt Arms Hotel**
GUISBOROUGH, **Fox Inn**
GUISBOROUGH, **Moorcock Hotel**
HALFORD, **Halford Bridge Inn**
HALLATON, **Bewicke Arms**
HAMBLEDEN, **Stag & Huntsman Inn**
HARRIETSHAM, **Ringlestone Inn**
HARROGATE, **West Park Hotel**
HATHERLEIGH, **George Hotel**
HAWKHURST, **Tudor Arms Hotel**
HAYTOR VALE, **Rock Inn**
HELFORD, **Shipwright's Arms**
HELMSLEY, **Feathers Hotel**
HELSTON, **Angel Hotel**
HENLEY-ON-THAMES. **Little Angel**
HEXWORTHY, **Forest Inn**
HIGHCLERE, **Yew Tree Inn**
HINDON, **Lamb at Hindon**
HOLT, **Old Ham Tree**
HOLYWELL, **Ye Olde Ferry Boat Inn**
HOLYWELL GREEN, **Rock Hotel**
HONLEY, **Coach & Horses**
HOPE, **Poachers Arms**
HORRINGER, **Beehive**
HORTON, **Horton Inn**
HORTON IN RIBBLESDALE, **Crown Hotel**
HUBBERHOLME, **George Inn**
HUNTINGDON, **Old Bridge Hotel**
KERSEY, **Bell Inn**
KETTLEWELL, **Racehorses Hotel**
KEYSTON, **The Pheasant**
KINETON, **Halfway House**
KINGSCOTE, **Hunters Hall Inn**
KINGSTON, **Juggs**
KINGSWINFORD, **Summerhill House Hotel**
KINTBURY, **Dundas Arms**
KINVER, **Whittington Inn**
KIRKBYMOORSIDE, **George & Dragon**
KIRK LANGLEY, **Meynell Arms Hotel**
KNAPP, **Rising Sun**
KNIGHTWICK, **Talbot Hotel**
KNOWL HILL, **Bird in Hand**
LACOCK, **Red Lion at Lacock**
LAMBERHURST, **George & Dragon**
LANCASTER, **Farmers Arms Hotel**
LANCHESTER, **Kings Head**
LANCING, **Sussex Pad Hotel**
LANGDALE, **Pillar Hotel, Hobson's Pub**
LANGHAM, **Noel Arms**
LANREATH, **Punch Bowl Inn**
LEAFIELD, **Old George Inn**
LEDBURY, **Feathers Hotel**
LEDBURY, **Verzons Country House Hotel**
LEDBURY, **Ye Olde Talbot Hotel**
LEDSHAM, **Tudor Rose**
LEDSTON, **White Horse**
LEEK, **Three Horseshoes Inn**
LEIGH ON MENDIP, **Bell Inn**
LEOMINSTER, **Royal Oak Hotel**
LICKFOLD, **Lickfold Inn**
LIFTON, **Arundell Arms**
LIMPLEY STOKE, **Hop Pole Inn**
LINCOLN, **Wig & Mitre**
LINTON, **Windmill Inn**
LITTLE LANGDALE, **Three Shires Inn**

continued on page 26

WEPPES' AND THE FOUNTAIN DEVICE ARE REGISTERED TRADE MARKS OF SCHWEPPES INTERNATIONAL LIMITED.

LITTLE WASHBOURNE, **Hobnails Inn**
LONG COMPTON, **Red Lion**
LONG MELFORD, **Crown Inn Hotel**
LONG MELFORD, **Hare Inn**
LONGFRAMLINGTON, **Granby Inn**
LOWDHAM, **Springfield Inn**
LOWER PEOVER, **Bells of Peover**
LOWER WOODFORD, **Wheatsheaf**
LOWESWATER, **Kirkstile Inn**
LOWICK GREEN, **Farmer's Arms**
LUDLOW, **Angel Hotel**
LURGASHALL, **Noah's Ark**
LYDDINGTON, **Marquess of Exeter**
LYDFORD, **Castle Inn**
LYONSHALL, **Royal George Inn**
MADINGLEY, **Three Horseshoes**
MALHAM, **Buck Inn**
MALTON, **Green Man Hotel**
MANACCAN, **New Inn**
MARHAMCHURCH, **Bullers Arms**
MARKET DRAYTON, **Corbet Arms Hotel**
MARKET WEIGHTON, **Londesborough Arms**
MARLBOROUGH, **Sun Inn**
MARSHSIDE, **Gate Inn**
MATTINGLEY, **Leather Bottle**
MELLOR, **Millstone Hotel**
MERE, **Old Ship Inn**
METAL BRIDGE, **Metal Bridge Inn**
METHERELL, **Carpenters Arms**
MIDDLEHAM, **Black Swan**
MIDDLETON STONEY, **Jersey Arms**
MIDHURST, **Angel Hotel**
MILDENHALL, **Bell Hotel**
MINSTER LOVELL, **Old Swan Hotel**
MOLESWORTH, **Cross Keys**
MONKSILVER, **Notley Arms**
MONTACUTE, **King's Arms Inn**
MORETON-IN-MARSH, **Redesdale Arms Hotel**
MORVAL, **Snooty Fox Hotel**
NANTWICH, **Lamb Hotel**
NASSINGTON, **Black Horse Inn**
NEEDHAM MARKET, **Limes Hotel**
NETLEY, **Prince Consort**
NETTLECOMBE, **Marquis of Lorne**
NEWARK, **Robin Hood Hotel**
NEWTON, **Queen's Head**
NEWTON, **Red Lion Inn**
NEWTON, **Saracen's Head**
NEWTON-IN-BOWLAND, **Parkers Arms Hotel**
NORTH BOVEY, **Ring of Bells**
NORTH CERNEY, **Bathurst Arms**
NORTH PETHERTON, **Walnut Tree Inn**
NORTH WOOTTON, **Crossways**
NORTHIAM, **Six Bells**
OAKWOODHILL, **Punchbowl Inn**
OCKLEY, **King's Arms**
ODIHAM, **George Hotel**
OLD DALBY, **Crown Inn**
OLLERTON, **Dun Cow**
ONECOTE, **Jervis Arms**
OSWALDKIRK, **Malt Shovel Inn**
OVINGTON, **Bush Inn**
OXFORD, **Perch**
PELYNT, **Jubilee Inn**
PEMBRIDGE, **New Inn**
PENDOGGETT, **Cornish Arms**
PENSHURST, **Spotted Dog**
PEPPARD COMMON, **Red Lion**
PETWORTH, **Angel**
PHILLEIGH, **Roseland Inn**
PICKHILL, **Nag's Head**
PIN MILL, **Butt & Oyster**
PITTON, **Silver Plough**
PLUMLEY, **Smoker Inn**
POCKLINGTON, **Feathers Hotel**
POOLE, **Inn in the Park**
PORLOCK WEIR, **Anchor Hotel & Ship Inn**
PORT GAVERNE, **Port Gaverne Hotel**
POWERSTOCK, **Three Horseshoes Inn**
PRIORS HARDWICK, **Butchers Arms**
PULBOROUGH, **Waters Edge**
PULVERBATCH, **White Horse**
PYRTON, **Plough Inn**
RAMSBURY, **Bell at Ramsbury**
RINGMORE, **Journey's End Inn**
RINGWOOD, **Original White Hart**
RIPON, **Unicorn Hotel**
RISPLITH, **Black-a-Moor Inn**

ROCHESTER, **Redesdale Arms Hotel**
ROCKCLIFFE, **Crown & Thistle**
ROTHERWICK, **Coach & Horses**
RUNNING WATERS, **Three Horse Shoes**
RUSTHALL, **Red Lion**
SAFFRON WALDEN, **Eight Bells**
ST MARGARETS-AT-CLIFFE, **Cliffe Tavern**
ST MAWES, **Rising Sun Inn**
ST NEOTS, **Chequers Inn**
SALISBURY, **Haunch of Venison**
SANDON BANK, **Seven Stars Inn**
SANDSIDE, **Ship Inn**
SANDWICH, **Fleur-de-Lis**
SCOLE, **Crossways Inn**
SCOLE, **Scole Inn**
SEAHOUSES, **Olde Ship Hotel**
SEDGEFIELD, **Dun Cow Inn**
SEMLEY, **Benett Arms**
SEVENOAKS, **Royal Oak**
SHALFLEET, **New Inn**
SHAVE CROSS, **Shave Cross Inn**
SHELLEY, **Three Acres Hotel**
SHENINGTON, **Bell**
SHEPPERTON, **Anchor Hotel**
SHEPPERTON, **King's Head**
SHEPPERTON, **Thames Court**
SHEPPERTON, **Warren Lodge**
SHEPTON MALLET, **Kings Arms**
SHIPLAKE, **Baskerville Arms**
SHIPSTON-ON-STOUR, **Bell Inn**
SHIPSTON-ON-STOUR, **White Bear**
SHIPTON-UNDER-WYCHWOOD, **Shaven Crown Hotel**
SILK WILLOUGHBY, **Horseshoes**
SKIDBY, **Half Moon Inn**
SLAIDBURN, **Hark to Bounty Inn**
SLEIGHTS, **Salmon Leap**
SMARDEN, **Bell**
SMARDEN, **Chequers Inn**
SNAINTON, **Coachman Inn**
SNETTISHAM, **Rose & Crown Inn**
SOUTH DALTON, **Pipe & Glass**
SOUTH LEIGH, **Mason Arms**
SOUTH ZEAL, **Oxenham Arms**
SOUTHWOLD, **Crown Hotel**
STAFFORD, **Swam Hotel**
STAMFORD, **Bull & Swan Inn**
STAMFORD, **Crown Hotel**
STAMFORD, **George of Stamford**
STANFORD DINGLEY, **Old Boot Inn**
STANTON HARCOURT. **Harcourt Arms**
STAPLE FITZPAINE, **Greyhound Inn**
STAPLETON, **Bridge Inn**
STARBOTTOM, **Fox & Hounds**
STAVELEY, **Royal Oak**
STAVERTON, **Sea Trout Inn**
STEWKLEY, **Swan**
STOCKBRIDGE, **Grosvenor Hotel**
STOKE LACY, **Plough Inn**
STOKE ST GREGORY, **Rose & Crown Inn**
STONY STRATFORD, **Bull Hotel**
STONY STRATFORD, **The Cock Hotel**
STRATFORD-UPON-AVON, **Slug & Lettuce**
STRETTON, **Ram Jam Inn**
STUCKTON, **Three Lions**
SUTTON, **Anne Arms**
SUTTON, **Sutton Hall**
SUTTON-UPON-DERWENT, **St Vincent Arms**
SYMONDS YAT WEST, **Old Court Hotel**
TALKIN VILLAGE, **Hare & Hounds Inn**
TARRANT MONKTON, **Langton Arms**
TEDDINGTON, **Clarence Hotel**
TEMPLE GRAFTON, **Blue Boar**
TERRINGTON, **Bay Horse Inn**
TESTCOMBE, **Mayfly**
TIMPERLEY, **Hare & Hounds**
TOMARTON, **Compass Inn**
TREBARWITH, **Mill House Inn**
TROUTBECK, **Mortal Man**
TUTBURY, **Ye Olde Dog & Partridge**
TWICKENHAM, **Prince Albert**
TWICKENHAM, **White Swan**
UPPER ODDINGTON, **Horse & Groom Inn**
UPTON GREY, **Hoddington Arms**
UTTOXETER, **White Hart Hotel**
WALKERN, **White Lion**
WALTHAM-ON-THE-WOLDS, **Royal Horseshoes**
WALTHAM ST LAWRENCE, **Bell**
WANSFORD, **Haycock Hotel**

continued on page 29

WANSTROW, **King William IV**
WARENFORD, **Warenford Lodge**
WARK, **Battlesteads Hotel**
WARMINGTON, **Wobbly Wheel Inn**
WARMINSTER, **Old Bell Hotel**
WARWICK-ON-EDEN, **Queen's Arms Inn**
WASDALE HEAD, **Wasdale Head Inn**
WASHINGTON, **Frankland Arms**
WATERINGBURY, **Wateringbury Hotel**
WATH-IN-NIDDERDALE, **Sportsman's Arms**
WELFORD-ON-AVON, **Shakespeare Inn**
WEOBLEY, **Red Lion Hotel**
WEST ILSLEY, **The Harrow**
WEST LAVINGTON, **Wheatsheaf Inn**
WEST LULWORTH, **Castle Inn**
WEST WITTON, **Wensleydale Heifer**
WESTBURY, **Reindeer Inn**
WESTON, **White Lion**
WESTWOOD, **New Inn**
WETHERBY, **Alpine Inn**
WHATCOTE, **Royal Oak**
WHITEWELL, **Inn at Whitewell**
WHITNEY-ON-WYE, **Rhydspence Inn**
WICKHAM, **Five Bells**
WILMCOTE, **Swan House Hotel**
WIMBORNE ST GILES, **Bell Inn**
WINCHAM, **Black Greyhound Hotel**
WINCHCOMBE, **George Inn**
WINCHELSEA, **Winchelsea Lodge Motel**
WINCHESTER, **Wykeham Arms**
WINFORTON, **Sun Inn**
WINFRITH NEWBURGH, **Red Lion**
WINKLEIGH, **King's Arms**
WINKTON, **Fisherman's Haunt Hotel**
WINSFORD, **Royal Oak Inn**
WINSLOW, **Bell Hotel**
WINTERTON-ON-THE-SEA, **Fisherman's Return**
WITHINGTON, **Mill Inn**
WITHYBROOK, **Pheasant**
WITNEY, **Red Lion Hotel**
WOBURN, **Black Horse Inn**
WONERSH, **Grantley Arms**
WOODBRIDGE, **Bull Hotel**
WOODHALL SPA, **Abbey Lodge Inn**
WOOLER, **Tankerville Arms**
WOOLHOPE, **Butchers Arms**
WOOLVERTON, **Red Lion**
WYE, **New Flying Horse Inn**
WYKEHAM, **Downe Arms**
YARMOUTH, **Bugle Hotel**
YATTENDON, **Royal Oak**

SCOTLAND

ANSTRUTHER, **Craw's Nest Hotel**
ANSTRUTHER, **Smugglers Inn**
ARDENTINNY, **Ardentinny Hotel**
BUSBY, **Busby Hotel**
CASTLE DOUGLAS, **King's Arms**
COMRIE, **Royal Hotel**
DYSART, **Old Rectory Inn**
EDDLESTON, **Horse Shoe Inn**
EDINBURGH, **Cramond Inn**
EDINBURGH, **Rutland Hotel**
FOCHABERS, **Gordon Arms Hotel**
GLAMIS, **Strathmore Arms**
GLENDEVON, **Tormaukin Hotel**
GLENFINNAN, **Stage House Inn**
INGLISTON, **Norton Tavern**
INVERMORISTON, **Glenmoriston Arms**
KILLIN, **Clachaig Hotel**
KIPPEN, **Cross Keys Inn**
LEWISTON, **Lewiston Arms**
LINLITHGOW, **Champany Inn**
LOCHGAIR, **Lochgair Hotel**
LOCK ECK, **Coylet Inn**
LYBSTER, **Bayview Hotel**
MELROSE, **Burts Hotel**
MELROSE, **George & Abbotsford Hotel**
MOFFAT, **Balmoral Hotel**
MOFFAT, **Black Bull**
MUIR OF ORD, **Ord Arms Hotel**
NEW ABBEY, **Criffel Inn**
SPEAN BRIDGE, **Letterfinlay Lodge Hotel**
TARBERT, **West Loch Hotel**
TURRIFF, **Towie Tavern**
ULLAPOOL, **Argyll Hotel**
WEEM, **Ailean Chraggan Hotel**

WALES

ABERGAVENNY, **Llanwenarth Arms Hotel**
BEAUMARIS, **Liverpool Arms Hotel**
BETWYS-YN-RHOS, **Ffarm Hotel**
BODFARI, **Dinorben Arms Inn**
CARDIGAN, **Black Lion Hotel**
CÊNARTH, **White Hart**
CHEPSTOW, **Castle View Hotel**
COWBRIDGE, **The Bear**
CRICKHOWELL, **Bear Hotel**
CRICKHOWELL, **Nantyffin Cider Mill Inn**
EAST ABERTHAN, **Blue Anchor**
FELINDRE FARCHOG, **Salutation Inn**
FELINGWN UCHAF, **Plough Inn**
FFAIRFACH, **Torbay Inn**
HAY-ON-WYE, **Old Black Lion**
LLANARMON DYFFRYN CEIRIOG, **West Arms Hotel**
LLANDISSILIO, **Bush Inn**
LLANDOVERY, **King's Head Inn**
LLANFIHANGEL CRUCORNEY, **Skirrid Inn**
LLANFRYNACH, **White Swan**
LLANGOLLEN, **Britannia Inn**
LLANGORSE, **Red Lion**
LLANNEFYDD, **Hawk & Buckle Inn**
LLANTILIO CROSSENNY, **Hostry Inn**
LLANTRISSENT, **Royal Oak Inn**
LLOWES, **Radnor Arms**
LLYSWEN, **Griffin Inn**
MENAI BRIDGE, **Gazelle Hotel**
MONMOUTH, **Queens Head Hotel**
MUMBLES, **Langland Court Hotel**
NOTTAGE, **Rose & Crown**
PEMBROKE, **Old King's Arms Hotel**
PENMAENPOOL, **George III Hotel**
PENYBONT, **Severn Arms**
RAGLAN, **Beauford Arms Hotel**
SHIRENEWTON, **Carpenter's Arms**
TRECASTLE, **Castle Hotel**
WHITEBROOK, **The Crown at Whitebrook**
WOLF'S CASTLE, **Wolfe Inn**

CHANNEL ISLANDS

PLEINMONT, **Imperial Hotel**
ST ANNE, **Georgian House**
ST AUBIN'S HARBOUR, **Old Courthouse Inn**

ISLE OF MAN

PEEL, **Creek Inn**

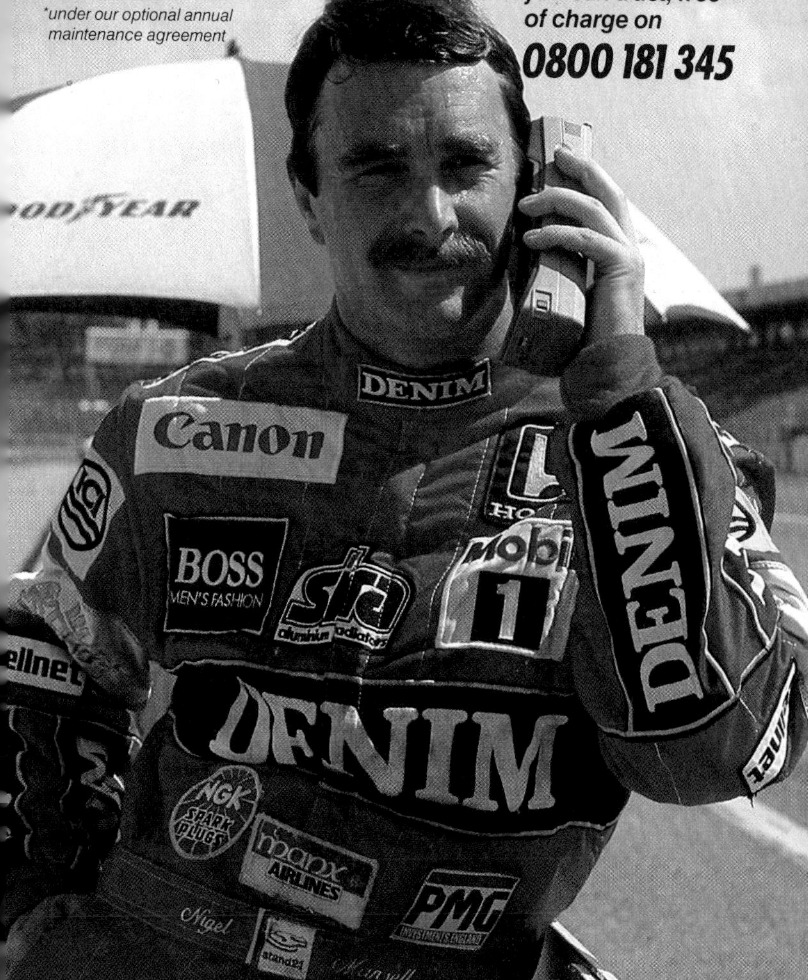

DENIM
Canon
BOSS
MEN'S FASHION
1
DENIM
DENIM
NGK
SPARK PLUGS
AIRLINES
PMG
INVESTMENTS ENGLAND
Nigel
Mansell
stand21

APPROVED for connection to telecommunication systems specified in the instructions for use subject to the conditions set out in them
SECURICOR
COMMUNICATIONS

Accredited Retailer
Cellnet
THE CELLPHONE NETWORK

The Dairy Crest Symbol of Excellence

Wherever you see this sign, you will be entering a restaurant, pub or cafe where the quality and presentation of cheese on the menu is excellent.

The inspectors for Egon Ronay's Guides will have paid a visit and decided to award the Dairy Crest Symbol of Excellence for the high standard of cheese available – whether presented on a cheeseboard or included in a meal or snack.

As Britain's leading manufacturer of cheese, Dairy Crest Foods has joined with Egon Ronay's Guides to acknowledge those catering establishments who are applying the highest standards of quality and presentation to the cheeses they offer. These are identified in three major 1988 Guides: the Hotel and Restaurant Guide, the Just A Bite Guide and the Pub Guide.

So, wherever you see the Symbol of Excellence, you will enjoy guaranteed quality of:

- TASTE – through expert selection, handling and storage
- VARIETY – through imaginative use of traditional, new and local cheeses
- PRESENTATION – through the use of colour, texture and shape to give a mouth-watering display
- INFORMATION – through the caterer's knowledge and understanding

Where you find English cheeses at their best, you will be sure to find Dairy Crest's own excellent cheeses, such as the famous Lymeswold range, the reduced-fat Tendale range and the full selection of English and Welsh traditional cheeses and prize-winning Cheddars and Stilton.

OUTSTANDING CHEESEBOARDS

LONDON

Admiral Codrington, SW3
Lamb & Flag, WC2

ENGLAND

BEDFORD, Beds: **Park**
BIDDENDEN, Kent: **Three Chimneys**
BRIDPORT, Dorset: **George Arms**
CHENIES, Herts: **Bedford Arms**
CORTON, Wilts: **Dove at Corton**
DODDISCOMBSLEIGH, Devon: **Nobody Inn**
DORCHESTER-ON-THAMES, Oxon: **George Hotel**
EMPINGHAM, Leics: **White Horse**
FOSSEBRIDGE, Glos: **Fossebridge Inn**
GREAT WALTHAM, Essex: **Windmill**
GRIMSTHORPE, Lincs: **Black Horse Inn**
HATHERLEIGH, Devon: **George Hotel**
HILDENBOROUGH, Kent: **Gate Inn**
HORLEY, Surrey: **Ye Olde Six Bells**
HUNTINGDON, Cambs: **Old Bridge Hotel**
KNIGHTWICK, H & W: **Talbot Hotel**
LEDBURY, H & W: **Feathers Hotel**
LEVINGTON, Suffolk: **Ship**
LITTLE LANGDALE, Cumbria: **Three Shires Inn**
LONGPARISH, Hants: **Plough Inn**
MELMERBY, Cumbria: **Shepherds Inn**
MOULTON, N Yorks: **Black Bull**
OLDBURY-ON-SEVERN, Avon: **Anchor Inn**
PHILLEIGH, Corn: **Roseland Inn**
PITTON, Wilts: **Silver Plough**
PLYMOUTH, Devon: **Unity**
PYRTON, Oxon: **Plough Inn**
SAFFRON WALDEN, Essex: **Eight Bells**
SHALFLEET, I of W: **New Inn**
SONNING-ON-THAMES, Berks: **Bull Inn**
SOUTHWOLD, Suffolk: **Crown**
STAMFORD, Lincs: **George of Stamford**
STAPLE FITZPAINE, Som: **Greyhound Inn**
STEEPLE ASTON, Oxon: **Red Lion**
STRETTON, Leics: **Ram Jam Inn**
STUCKTON, Hants: **Three Lions**
TARRANT MONKTON, Dorset: **Langton Arms**
TESTCOMBE, Hants: **Mayfly**
THAMES DITTON, Surrey: **Albany**
TIMPERLEY, Ches: **Hare & Hounds**
WASHBROOK, Suffolk: **Brook Inn**
WEOBLEY, H & W: **Red Lion Hotel**
WHITNEY-ON-WYE, H & W: **Rhydspence Inn**
YATTENDON, Berks: **Royal Oak**

SCOTLAND

GLASGOW, S'clyde: **Babbity Bowster**

WALES

BABELL, Clwyd: **Black Lion Inn**
BEAUMARIS, Gwynedd: **Ye Olde Bull's Head**
CENARTH, Dyfed: **White Hart**
CHEPSTOW, Gwent: **Castle View Hotel**
FELINGWM UCHAF, Dyfed; **Plough Inn**
HAY-ON-WYE, Powys: **Old Black Lion**
LLANDISSILIO, Dyfed: **Bush Inn**
LLOWES, Powys: **Radnor Arms**
LLYSWEN, Powys: **Griffin Inn**
WHITEBROOK, Gwent: **The Crown at Whitebrook**

THE GLENFIDDICH*GUIDE TO THE SEVEN DEADLY SINS.

*THE ULTIMATE TEMPTATION.

 6. AVARICE.

W·A·T·E·R·S·I·D·E P·U·B·S

LONDON

Anchor, SE16
Angel, SE16
Bull's Head, W4
City Barge, W4
Dickens Inn, E1
Dove, W6
Grapes, E14
Mayflower, SE16
Old Ship, W6
Prospect of Whitby, E1
Samuel Pepys, EC4
Ship, SW14
Trafalgar Tavern, SE10

ENGLAND

ARMATHWAITE, Cumbria: **Duke's Head Hotel**
BATHAMPTON, Avon: **George Inn**
BEDFORD, Beds: **Embarkment Hotel**
BEER, Devon: **Anchor Inn**
BIDFORD-ON-AVON, Warwicks: **White Lion Hotel**
BLEDINGTON, Oxon: **King's Head Inn**
BRENDON, Devon: **Stag Hunters**
BRIDGWATER, Som: **Admiral's Landing**
BUCKLER'S HARD, Hants: **Master Builders House Hotel**
BURNHAM-ON-CROUCH, Essex: **Ye Olde White Harte Hotel**
BURTON UPON TRENT, Staffs: **Riverside Inn**
CAMBRIDGE, Glos: **George Inn**
CAREY, H & W: **Cottage of Content**
COCKWOOD, Devon: **Anchor Inn**
COCKWOOD, Devon: **Ship Inn**
DARTMOUTH, Devon: **Royal Chase Hotel**
ELSLACK, N Yorks: **Tempest Arms**
ESKDALE, Cumbria: **Bower House Inn**
EXFORD, Som: **Crown Hotel**
FALMOUTH, Corn: **The Pandora Inn**
FEN DRAYTON, Cambs: **Three Tuns**
FORD, Wilts: **White Hart at Ford**
FOSSEBRIDGE, Glos: **Fossebridge Inn**
HELFORD, Corn: **Shipwright's Arms**
HOLYWELL, Cambs: **Ye Olde Ferry Boat Inn**
HORLEY, Surrey: **Ye Olde Six Bells**
HUBBERHOLME, N Yorks: **George Inn**
HUNTINGDON, Cambs: **Old Bridge Hotel**
KETTLEWELL, N Yorks: **Race Horses Hotel**
KINTBURY, Berks: **Dundas Arms**
KNIGHTWICK, H & W: **Talbot Hotel**
LAMBERHURST, Kent: **George & Dragon Inn**
LANGDALE, Cumbria: Pillar Hotel, **Hobson's Pub**
LITTLE LANGDALE, Cumbria: **Three Shires Inn**
LLANFAIR WATERFINE, Shrops: **Red Lion Inn**
LOWESWATER, Cumbria: **Kirkstile Inn**
MARSHSIDE, Kent: **Gate Inn**
METAL BRIDGE, Cumbria: **Metal Bridge Inn**
MONKSILVER, Som: **Notley Arms**
MURCOTT, Oxon: **Nut Tree Inn**
NEEDINGWORTH, Cambs: **Pike & Eel**
NEWENDEN, Kent: **White Hart**
NEWTON-IN-BOWLAND, Lancs: **Parkers Arms Hotel**
NORTH CERNEY, Glos: **Bathhurst Arms**
NORTH DALTON, Humb: **Star Inn**
ONECOTE, Staffs: **Jervis Arms**
OVINGTON, Hants: **Bush Inn**
OXFORD, Oxon: **Perch**
PIN MILL, Suffolk: **Butt & Oyster**

continued on page 38

iners offer you a second Card. Free.
hat you do with it is your business.

This is an offer of two Diners Club cards for you.
One has Business Account marked on it. And that's exactly what it's for. The second card is for your personal expenses.
You get a two-part statement each month. One cheque settles both bills.
The second card doesn't cost you any extra.
Needless to say, your Diners Club Cards are acceptable at more than 1 million establishments around the World, wherever you do business.
Diners Club are the first and only card to offer two cards. If you'd like to know how two cards are better than one, telephone 01-930 2755.
Diners Club International
Diners Club International
3643 2613 0011
J N TRAVERS
BUSINESS ACCOUNT
iners
eans business
(and pleasure).

POOLEY BRIDGE, Cumbria: **Crown Hotel**
PORLOCK WEIR, Som: **Anchor Hotel & Ship Inn**
PORT GAVERNE, Corn: **Port Gaverne Hotel**
PULBOROUGH, W Sussex: **Waters Edge**
ST MAWES, Corn: **Rising Sun Inn**
SANDSIDE, Cumbria: **Ship Inn**
SEAHOUSES, Northumberland: **Olde Ship Hotel**
SENNEN COVE, Corn: **Old Success Inn**
SHEPPERTON, Middlesex: **King's Head**
SHEPPERTON, Middlesex: **Thames Court**
SHEPPERTON, Middlesex: **Warren Lodge**
STOCKBRIDGE, Hants: **Vine**
TESTCOMBE, Hants: **Mayfly**
THAMES DITTON, Surrey: **Albany**
TREBARWITH, Corn: **Mill House Inn**
TWICKENHAM, Middlesex: **White Swan**
UMBERLEIGH, Devon: **Rising Sun**
WANSFORD, Cambs: **Haycock Hotel**
WASDALE HEAD, Cumbria: **Wasdale Head Inn**
WATH-IN-NIDDERDALE, N Yorks: **Sportsman's Arms**
WHITEWELL, Lancs: **Inn at Whitewell**
WHITNEY-ON-WYE, H & W: **Rhydespence Inn**
WINKTON, Dorset: **Fisherman's Haunt Hotel**
WITHINGTON, Glos: **Mill Inn**
WITHYBROOK, Warwicks: **Pheasant**
WIXFORD, Oxon: **Three Horseshoes**

SCOTLAND

ARDENTINNY, S'clyde: **Ardentinny Hotel**
CANONBIE, D & G: **Riverside Inn**
EDINBURGH, Loth: **Cramond Inn**
KILLIN, Central: **Clachaig Hotel**
LOCH ECK, S'clyde: **Coylet Inn**
MAIDENS, S'clyde: **Bruce Hotel**
SPEAN BRIDGE, H'land: **Letterfinlay Lodge Hotel**
TARBERT, S'clyde: **West Loch Hotel**
TAYVALLICH, S'clyde: **Tayvallich Inn**

WALES

ABERGAVENNY, Gwent: **Llanwenarth Arms Hotel**
CENARTH, Dyfed: **White Hart**
CRICKHOWELL, Powys: **Nantnffw Cider Mill**
LLANARMON DYFFRYN CEIRIOG, Clwyd: **West Arms Hotel**
LLANGORSE, Powys: **Red Lion**
MENAI BRIDGE, Gwynedd: **Gazelle Hotel**
PENMAENPOOL, Gwynedd: **George III Hotel**
PENYPONT, Powys: **Severn Arms**

CHANNEL ISLANDS

PLEINMONT, Guernsey: **Imperial Hotel**
ST AUBIN'S HARBOUR, Jersey: **Old Court House Inn**

ISLE OF MAN

PEEL, I of M: **Creek Inn**

AN
EGON RONAY'S
GUIDE
ONLY INCLUDES
THE BEST.
LIGHT-DRY
CARTA BLANCA
RUM
Ron
BACARDI
Superior
Nassau, Bahamas
Coca-Cola

WILLIAM GRANT & SONS LTD

SCOTCH WHISKY DISTILLERS

Whisky can be divided into two broad categories, Malt Whiskies and Blended Whiskies.

Malt whisky is made only from malted barley – soaked, spread out on the malting floor to germinate and finally dried in a peat-fired kiln – and distilled twice in traditionally shaped copper pot stills.

Blended whisky, first made in the 19th century, is a newcomer compared with malt. It is made from grain whisky, produced from various cereals, by a modern method of continuous distillation, then blended with a number of malt whiskies. A blend can consist of from 15 to 50 different whiskies. Blended whisky is drunk by 17 million people in the UK alone, and is, moreover, the world's most popular spirit.

Each individual malt matures and peaks at its own special pace; some reach perfection after 8 years, others may need 12, 15 or 30 years. The distiller's art is to know when the peak is reached and to bottle at that moment.

The art of distilling malt whisky, the traditional drink of the Scottish Highlander, has been practised in Scotland for well over 500 years. The whole traditional process from malted barley to bottle, can be seen at the Glenfiddich Distillery, where the whisky is distilled, matured and bottled at its own distillery.

The Glenfiddich Distillery is owned by William Grant & Sons, an independent family company, which celebrates its Centenary this year.

OUTSTANDING FRENCH WINE LISTS

LONDON

Bull's Head, W1
White Horse on Parsons Green, SW6

ENGLAND

ALSAGER, Ches: **Manor House**
APPLEBY, Cumbria: **Royal Oak Inn**
BEAULIEU, Hants: **Montagu Arms Hotel**
BEAUWORTH, Hants: **Milbury's**
BIDDENDEN, Kent: **Three Chimneys**
BRIGHTLING, E Sussex: **Fullers Arms**
BRIGHTWELL BALDWIN, Oxon: **Lord Nelson**
CHILGROVE, W Sussex: **White Horse Inn**
CLARE, Suffolk: **Bell Hotel**
DODDISCOMBSLEIGH, Devon: **Nobody Inn**
DORCHESTER-ON-THAMES, Oxon: **George Hotel**
FALMOUTH, Corn: **The Pandora Inn**
FINDON, W Sussex: **Snooty Fox Bar**
FOTHERINGBURY, Northants: **Falcon Inn**
FOWLMERE, Cambs: **Chequers Inn**
HUNTINGDON, Cambs: **Old Bridge Hotel**
KINTBURY, Berks: **Dundas Arms**
LANCING, W Sussex: **Sussex Pad Hotel**
MAYFIELD, E Sussex: **Rose & Crown**
MOULTON, N Yorks: **Black Bull Inn**
OAKWOOD HILL, Surrey: **Punch-bowl Inn**
PORT GAVERNE, Corn: **Port Gaverne Hotel**
SAFFRON WALDEN, Essex: **Eight Bells**
SAFFRON WALDEN, Essex: **Saffron Hotel**
SCOLE, Norfolk: **Crossways**
SHELLEY, W Yorks: **Three Acres Inn**
SHIPSTON-ON-STOUR, Warwicks: **White Bear**
SHIPTON-UNDER-WYCHWOOD, Oxon: **Lamb Inn**
SOUTHWOLD, Suffolk: **The Crown**
STAPLE FITZPAINE, Som: **Greyhound Inn**
STEEPLE ASHTON, Oxon: **Red Lion**
STUCKTON, Hants: **Three Lions**
TIMPERLEY, Ches: **Hare & Hounds**
WHITEWELL, Lancs: **Inn at Whitewell**
WOBURN, Beds: **Bell Inn**
YATTENDON, Berks: **Royal Oak**

SCOTLAND

CANONBIE, D & G: **Riverside Inn**
EDDLESTON, Borders: **Horseshoe Inn**
INVERMORISTON, H'land: **Glenmoriston Arms**
WESTER HOWGATE, Loth: **Old Howgate Inn**

WALES

BABELL, Clwyd: **Black Lion Inn**
CHEPSTOW, Gwent: **Castle View Hotel**
CRICKHOWELL, Powys: **Nantyffin Cider Mill Inn**
WHITEBROOK, Gwent: **The Crown at Whitebrook**

WE STILL HOLD POLL POSITION.

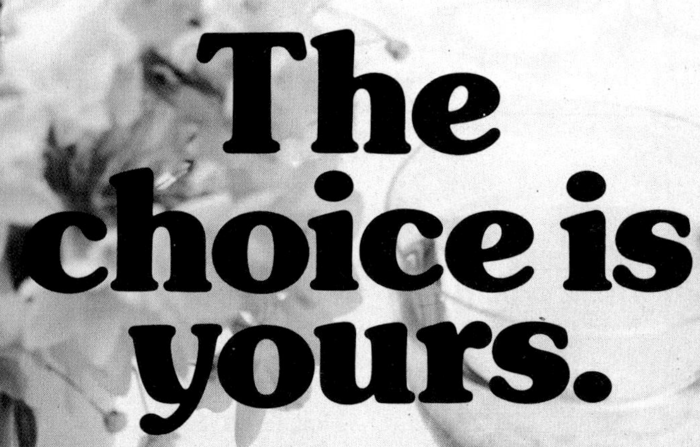

At home you choose Flora for all the right reasons. You enjoy its light, delicate taste and you know it's made with pure sunflower oil, which is high in essential polyunsaturates, low in saturates, low in cholesterol.

Today you can also choose Flora when eating out because it's now available in portion packs at all the best restaurants in town.

L·O·N·D·O·N P·U·B·S B·Y A·R·E·A·S

BAYSWATER & NOTTING HILL

Slug & Lettuce, W2
Swan Tavern, W2
Victoria, W2
Windsor Castle, W8

BLOOMSBURY & HOLBORN

Lamb, WC1
Museum Tavern, WC1
Princess Louise, WC1
Ye Olde Mitre Tavern, EC1

CHELSEA

Admiral Codrington, SW3

CITY

Black Friar, EC4
Cock Tavern, EC1
Fox & Anchor, EC1
Hand & Shears, EC1
Railway Tavern, EC2
Samuel Pepys, EC4
Ye Olde Dr Butler's Head, WC2
Ye Olde Watling, EC4

COVENT GARDEN

Lamb & Flag, WC2
Nag's Head, WC2
Nell of Old Drury, WC2
Salisbury, WC2

EAST LONDON

Dickens Inn, E1
Grapes, E14
Prospect of Whitby, E1

FLEET STREET

Old Bell Tavern, EC4
Printer's Devil, EC4
Seven Stars, WC2
Ye Olde Cheshire Cheese, EC4
Ye Olde Cock Tavern, EC4

KNIGHTSBRIDGE

Grenadier, SW1
Paxton's Head, SW1

MAYFAIR & MARYLEBONE

The Audley, W1
Prince Regent, W1
Red Lion, W1
Shepherd's Tavern, W1

NORTH & NORTH-WEST LONDON

Albion, N1
Eagle, N1
Flask, N6
Jack Straw's Castle, NW3
Slug & Lettuce, N1
Spaniards Inn, NW3

ST JAMES'S

Red Lion, SW1
Two Chairmen, SW1

SOHO & TRAFALGAR SQUARE

Glasshouse Stores, W1
Sherlock Holmes, WC2
Tom Cribb, SW1

SOUTH-EAST LONDON

Anchor, SE1
Angel, SE16

continued on page 49

George, SE1
Mayflower, SE16
Trafalgar Tavern, SE10

SOUTH-WEST LONDON

Ship, SW14
Sun Inn, SW13
White Horse on Parsons Green, SW6
Ye Olde Windmill Inn, SW4

VICTORIA & WESTMINSTER

Albert, SW1
Cask & Glass, SW1
Slug & Lettuce, SW1
Two Chairmen, SW1

WEST LONDON

Bull's Head, W4
City Barge, W4
Dove, W6
Goat, W8
Greyhound, W8
Old Ship, W6

THE FIAT GUIDE TO SUCCESSFUL MOTORING

Fiat main and service dealers are strategically situated across the United Kingdom to offer comprehensive sales, servicing and repair facilities together with an abundant availability of spares and accessories.

At the time this guide is going to press we have 369 dealerships, as shown in the list below, bringing the stylish Fiat range close to home and ensuring you can easily contact us wherever you are.

To learn of any possible new appointment nearer to you please contact the Fiat Information Service, Dept ER87, PO Box 39, Windsor, Berks SL4 3SP. Telephone: 07535 56397 or call free on Linkline (0800) 521581

★ denotes Service Only Dealer

ENGLAND

AVON

Bath **MOTOR SERVICES (BATH) LTD** Circus Pl. 0225 27328
Bristol **AUTOTREND LTD** 724-726 Fishponds Road. 0272 659491
Bristol **BAWNS (BRISTOL) LTD** 168-176 Coronation Rd. 0272 631101
Clevedon **JEFF BROWNS (CLEVEDON)** Old Church Rd. 0272 871211
Weston-Super-Mare **JEFF BROWNS (LYMPSHAM)** Bridgwater Rd. 0934 72300/72696
★ *Thornbury Bristol* **SHIPPS OF THORNBURY** Midland Way. 0454 413130

BEDFORDSHIRE

Bedford **OUSE VALLEY MOTORS** 9 Kingsway. 0234 64491
Biggleswade **OWEN GODFREY LTD** 91-119 Shortmead St. 0767 313357
Billington **D & J AUTOS LTD** The Garage, Leighton Buzzard Rd. 0525 383068
Luton **BLACKABY & PEARCE (LUTON) LTD** Poynters Rd. 0582 67742

BERKSHIRE

Goring-on-Thames **COURTS GARAGE (GORING)** 42 Wallingford Rd. 0491 872006
Maidenhead **SOUTH BERKSHIRE MOTOR CO LTD** 264-270 Windsor Rd. 0628 71628
Newbury **BLACK AND WHITE GARAGE** Hermitage Rd, Cold Ash. 0635 200444
Reading **JACK HILL (READING) LTD** Chatham St. Multi-Storey Car Park. 0734 582521
Windsor **ANDREWS OF WINDSOR** 110 St. Leonards Rd. 0753 866108

BUCKINGHAMSHIRE

Amersham **AMERSHAM MOTORS LTD** Chesham Rd, HP6 5EX. 02403 22191
Aylesbury **AMERSHAM MOTORS** Stoke Rd. 0296 81181
Beaconsfield **MAURICE LEO LTD** 15 Gregories Rd. 049 46 6171
Bourne End **CARCHOICE LTD** Station Rd. 06285 22606
Gerrards Cross **BURWOODS GARAGE LTD** Oxford Rd. Tatling End. 0753 885216
High Wycombe **DESBOROUGH MOTOR CO LTD** 41 Desborough Ave. 0494 36331
Milton Keynes **ELMDENE MOTORS LTD** Townsend Thoresen Auto Centre, Unit 15, Erica Rd. 0908 320355

CAMBRIDGESHIRE

Cambridge **HOLLAND FIAT CENTRE** 315-349 Mill Rd. 0223 242222
March **CARL PORTER LTD** Causeway Garage, The Causeway. 0354 53340/55956
Peterborough **PETERBOROUGH AUTOS** Midland Rd. 0733 314431
St Ives **OUSE VALLEY MOTORS** Station Rd. 0480 62641

CHESHIRE

Chester **HERON** Mountview, Sealand Rd. 0244 374440
★ *Congleton* **ROBIN HOOD GARAGE** West Heath. 0260 273219
Crewe **COPPENHALL GARAGE LTD** Cross Green. 0270 583437
Macclesfield **MOSS ROSE MOTORS LTD** London Rd. 0625 28866
Northwich **STATION ROAD GARAGE (NORTHWICH) LTD** Station Rd. 0606 49957
Warrington **WILLIAM MARTYN GARAGES LTD** Wilderspool Causeway. 0925 50417

CLEVELAND

Middlesbrough **MARTINS LONGLANDS** Longlands Rd. 0642 244651
Stockton-on-Tees **WENTANE MOTORS LTD** 100 Yarm Lane. 0642 611544

CORNWALL

Newquay **TOWER OF NEWQUAY** Tower Rd. 0637 872378/877332
Pensilva **MARSH'S (GARAGES)** Princess Row. 0579 62595
Truro **W.H. COLLINS & SON (MOTORS) LTD** Kenwyn Mews. 0872 74334

CUMBRIA

Carlisle **GRIERSON & GRAHAM (CARLISLE) LTD** 33 Church St, Caldergate. 0228 25092
Flimby **DOBIE'S GARAGE** Risehow. 0900 812332
★ *Kendal* **CRAIGHILL & CO LTD** 113 Stricklandgate. 0539 20967/8
Keswick **KESWICK MOTOR CO LTD** Lake Rd Garage. Sales: 0596 72534
Barrow-in-Furness **COUNTY PARK MOTORS,** County Park Industrial Est., Park Rd. 0229 36888

CO DURHAM

Consett **TRAVELWISE** Delves La. 0207 502353
★ *Crook* **BROOKSIDE GARAGE LTD** New Rd. 0388 762551
Darlington **E. WILLIAMSON (MOTORS) LTD** 1-7 Woodland Rd. 0325 483251 Parts: 0325 55850
Sacriston **FULTONS OF SACRISTON,** Woodside Garage, Witton Rd. 0385 710422.

DERBYSHIRE

Derby **KEN IVES MOTORS (DERBY) LTD** 574-576 Burton Rd, Littleover. 0332 369723
Chesterfield **WOODLEIGH MOTOR SALES LTD** 300 North Wingfield Rd, Grassmoor. 0246 850686
Heanor **NAVIGATION GARAGE (HEANOR)** Loscoe Rd. 0773 717008
Kegworth **J.C.S. GARAGES LTD** Station Rd, Kegworth. 050 97 2523
★ *Wirksworth* **WIRKSWORTH SERVICE GARAGE** Derby Rd. 062 982 2143

DEVON

Barnstaple **NORTH DEVON MOTOR CO** Pottington Ind Est. 0271 76551
Exeter **SIDWELL STREET MOTORS LTD** 85-88 Sidwell Street. 0392 54923
Newton Abbot **QUAY GARAGE FREDDIE HAWKEN LTD** The Avenue. 0626 52525/6
★ *Okehampton* **F J GLASS & CO (1981) LTD** 57 Exeter Rd. 0837 2255
Plymouth **MUMFORDS OF PLYMOUTH** Plymouth Rd. 0752 261511
Sidmouth **CENTRAL GARAGE (SIDFORD) LTD** Crossways, Sidford. 039 55 3595

DORSET

Bournemouth **CAFFYNS P.L.C.** 674-680 Wimborne Rd, Winton. 0202 512121
Weymouth **OLDS** 172 Dorchester Rd. 0305 786311

ESSEX

Basildon **H.W.S.** Roundacre, Nethermayne. 0268 22261
Buckhurst Hill **MONTROE MOTORS** Epping New Rd. 01-504 1171
Colchester **D SALMON CARS LTD** Sheepen Rd. 0206 563311
Frinton-on-Sea **POLLENDINE MOTORS LTD** 132 Connaught Ave. 02556 79123

Harlow **MOTORSALES (HARLOW) LTD**
Elizabeth Way, Burnt Mill. 0279 412161
Hutton **HUTTON GARAGES LTD**
661 Rayleigh Rd. 0277 210087
Little Waltham **MATTHAMS FIAT CENTRE,** Braintree Rd. 0245 361731
Romford **McQUIRE MOTORS LTD**
229-307 Collier Row La. 0708 66806
Southend-on-Sea **BELLE VUE MOTORS LTD** 460-464 Southchurch Rd. 0702 64945
Westcliff-on-Sea **H W STONE MOTOR CO**
684 London Rd. 0702 715181

GLOUCESTERSHIRE

Cheltenham **DANEWAY MOTOR CO LTD**
84 Bath Rd. 0242 523879
Cirencester **PAGE & DAVIES LTD**
10 Love La. 0285 69112/3
Stroud **PAGANHILL SERVICE STATION LTD** 105 Stratford Rd. 04536 4781
Gloucester **WARNERS MOTORS LTD**
Quedgeley Garage, Quedgeley. 0452 720107
★*Wotton-under-Edge* **WOTTON MOTOR CENTRE LTD**
Gloucester St. 0453 842240

GREATER MANCHESTER

Ashton-under-Lyne **PREMIER MOTOR CO**
Manchester Rd, Mossley. 04575 67121
Bolton **KNIBBS (BOLTON) LTD**
Kay St/Higher Bridge St. 0204 386306
Bury **BLACKFORD BRIDGE CAR SHOW LTD** 701 Manchester Rd, Blackford Bridge. 061-766 1346
Leigh **SMALLBROOK SERVICE STATION**
Smallbrook La. 0942 882201/891939
Manchester **KNIBBS (MANCHESTER) LTD** Midland Street Garage, Ashton Old Rd. 061-273 4411
Oldham **KNIBBS (OLDHAM) LTD**
23-37 Lees Rd. 061-624 8046
Rochdale **KNIBBS (ROCHDALE) LTD**
Queensway. 0706 33222
Stockport **KNIBBS (STOCKPORT) LTD**
West End Garage, Heaton La. 061-480 6661

HAMPSHIRE

Aldershot **CLEVELAND CARS LTD**
Ash St, Ash. 0252 313033
Andover **CLOVER LEAF CARS (ANDOVER)** Salisbury Rd. 0264 61166
Basingstoke **CLOVER LEAF CARS (BASING)** London Rd (A30). 0256 55221
Fareham **DIBBEN MOTOR CO LTD**
244 West St. 0329 286241
Lymington **STATION GARAGE LYMINGTON** Station St. 0590 77771
Portsmouth **CANNON GARAGES (PORTSMOUTH) LTD**
117 Copnor Rd. 0705 691621
Ringwood **WELLS RINGWOOD**
Salisbury Rd. 04254 6111
Southampton **SEWARDS**
Rushington Roundabout, Totton Bypass. 0703 861001

HEREFORD & WORCESTER

Evesham **BRIGHTS GARAGE**
3 Cheltenham Rd. 0386 2301
Hereford **GODSELL'S (HEREFORD) LTD**
Bath St. 0432 274134
Kidderminster **STANLEY GOODWIN MOTORS LTD** Worcester Rd. 0562 2202
Worcester **BOWLING GREEN GARAGE (POWICK) LTD** Powick. 0905 830361
Bromsgrove **NEALE'S GARAGE (1985) LTD** 2-12 Station St. 0527 72071

HERTFORDSHIRE

Croxley Green **CROXLEY GREEN MOTORS LTD** 185 Watford Rd. 0923 55511
Hemel Hempstead **SHAW & KILBURN LTD**
Two Waters Rd. 0442 51212
Hitchin **SERVAL (HITCHIN) LTD**
Ickleford. 0462 54526
Knebworth **LISLES MOTOR REPAIRS LTD**
London Rd, Woolmer Green. 0438 81 1011
St Albans **L.A.P. GROUP**
2 Beech Rd, Marshalswick. 0727 50871

HUMBERSIDE

Driffield **GEORGE WILLIAMSON (GARAGES) LTD**
82-84 Middle St. South. 0377 43130
Grimsby **ERIC C. BURTON & SONS LTD**
Station Garage, Wellowgate. 0472 55951
★*Goole* **J WARDLE & SON LTD**
Boothferry Rd, Howden. 0430 30388
Hull **A B MOTOR CO OF HULL LTD**
96 Boothferry Rd. 0482 506976 & 54256
Hull **JUBILEE GARAGE**
Holderness Rd. 0482 701785
Scunthorpe **BRUMBY SERVICE GARAGE LTD** The Fiat Centre, Normanby Rd. 0724 861191

ISLE OF WIGHT

Sandown **HODGE & CHILDS LTD**
Station Av. 0983 402552

KENT

Ashford **ASHFORD MOTOR CO**
Chart Rd. 0233 22281
Beckenham **BRUTONS OF BECKENHAM LTD** 181 Beckenham Rd. 01-650 0108/9/ 01-650 3333
Bexleyheath **BELLWAY MOTORS KENT**
303/307 Broadway. 01-301 0420
Brasted **MANNERING BROTHERS**
Brasted Garage, High St. 0959 62540/64497
Bromley **THAMES**
96 Bromley Hill. 01-460 4646
Canterbury **MARTIN WALTER LTD**
41 St. George's Pl. 0227 763800
Deal **CAMPBELLS OF DEAL LTD**
6 The Marina. 0304 363166
Farnborough **FARNWAY SERVICE LTD**
2 Church Rd. 0689 50121
Gillingham **AUTOYACHTS LTD**
171 Pier Rd. 0634 28133
★*Gravesend* **MARTINS GARAGE**
50 Singlewell Rd. 0474 66148
★*Ham Street* **ANNINGS MARSH ROAD**
Nr. Ashford. 023 373 2275
Hythe **RAMPART GARAGE**
15-17 Rampart Rd. 0303 67088
Maidstone **UNION MOTORS**
29 Union St. 0622 55403
★*Margate* **S & S MOTORS**
10-12 Park La. 0843 227778
Orpington **GODDINGTON SERVICE STATION,** 318 Court Rd. 0689 20337
Ramsgate **S & S MOTORS LEVERPOINT LTD** Willsons Rd. 0843 593465
★*Sittingbourne* **J G BURGESS & CO**
Ufton Lane Garage. 0795 23815
Swanley **FOREMAN BROS LTD**
London Rd. 0322 68411
Tunbridge Wells **G.E. TUNBRIDGE LTD**
319 St John's Rd. 0892 511522

LANCASHIRE

Accrington **MICHAEL O'SULLIVAN**
Rising Bridge Garage, Blackburn Rd. 0706 225321
Blackburn **BARKERS**
King St. 0254 52981
Burnley **KNIBBS (BURNLEY) LTD**
Parker St. Kingsway. 0282 58271
Colne **EAGLE SERVICE STATION**
Stonebridge Works, Windybank. 0282 863254
Lancaster **G & L CAR SERVICE LTD**
Wheatfield St. 0524 39857
Preston **LOOKERS GROSVENOR MOTORS LTD**
306-310 Ribbleton La. 0772 792823
Wigan **WILLIAM MARTYN (WIGAN) LTD**
Great George St. 0942 826390

LEICESTERSHIRE

Earl Shilton **SWITHLAND MOTORS LTD**
42 Wood St. 0455 4411
Leicester **TRINITY MOTORS (D.R. WATTAM) LTD**
47 Blackbird Rd. 0533 530137
★*Market Harborough* **BADGER BROTHERS** 109 Main St. Lubenham. 0858 66984
Melton Mowbray **ROCKINGHAM CARS LTD** Manor Garage, Mill St. 0664 60141
Wigston **KILBY BRIDGE MOTORS LTD**
Kilby Bridge. 0533 881109/886264

LINCOLNSHIRE

Boston **LONDON ROAD GARAGE**
200 London Rd. 0205 55500
Grantham **WILLSONS OF GRANTHAM LTD Spittlegate Level. 0476 74117**
Lincoln **MINSTER CARS**
316-322 Wragby Rd. 0522 34805
Louth **BURTONS OF LOUTH,**
Legbourne Rd. 0507 607555
★*Rippingale* **WILLSONS OF RIPPINGALE**
Windmill Garage, Bourne. 077 835 777
Skegness **D R M MOTORS**
Beresford Ave. 0754 67131
Sleaford **RALPH DEAR**
Greylees Garage, Grantham Rd. 05298 674

LONDON

London E4 **ALLEN BRIGGS (MOTORS) LTD** 47-59 Chingford Mount Rd. 01-527 5004/5
London N7 **CONTINENTAL MOTOR CENTRE LTD** Campdale Rd. 01-272 4762
London N12 **LINDSAY BROTHERS LTD**
920 High Rd. 01-445 1022
London N17 **BRUCE MOTOR GROUP**
127 Lordship La. 01-808 9291
★*London NW1* **HUNTSWORTH GARAGES LTD**
24-28 Boston Pl. 01-724 0269/ 01-723 8782
★*London NW10* **MARN SERVICE CENTRE** 854 Coronation Rd. 01-961 2377/ 01-965 7001
London NW11 **PAMSONS MOTORS LTD**
761/3 Finchley Rd. 01-458 5968/8384
London SE9 **CLIFFORDS OF ELTHAM**
Well Hall Rd. 01-850 3834
London SE18 **WOOLWICH MOTOR CO,**
160-170 Powis St. 01-854 2550
London SE19 **S.G. SMITH MOTORS LTD**
Crown Point Service Station, Beulah Hill. 01-670 6266
London SE23 **PREMIER MOTORS (FOREST HILL) LTD**
163/167 Stanstead Rd. 01-291 1721
London SW12 **BALHAM AUTOS**
147 Balham Hill, SW12 9DL. 01-675 6744/5/6/7
London SW15 **A.F. TANN LTD**
96-98 Upper Richmond Rd. 01-788 7881
London SW19 **SPUR GARAGE LTD**
39 Hartfield Rd. Sales: 01-540 3325
London W1 **FIAT MOTOR SALES LTD**
62-64 Baker St. 01-486 7555
London W12 **MARN WEST LONDON**
370-376 Uxbridge Rd. 01-749 6058/9
London W11 **RADBOURNE RACING LTD**
1a Clarendon Rd. 01-727 5066

MERSEYSIDE

Birkenhead **FIRS GARAGE (WIRRAL) LTD**
Claughton Firs, Oxton. 051-653 8555
Formby **ALTCAR AUTOS LTD**
Altcar Rd. 070 48 73342
Heswall, Wirral **J STUART & CO (GARAGES) LTD**
Chester Rd. 051-342 6202
Southport **MILNER & MARSHALL LTD**
89-91 Barth Street North. 0704 35535
St. Helens **FORWARD AUTOS**
Gaskell St. 0744 21961
Liverpool **STANLEY MOTORS (LIVERPOOL) LTD**
243 East Prescot Rd. 051-228 9151
Liverpool **CROSBY PARK GARAGE LTD**
2 Coronation Road, Crosby. 051-924 9101
Liverpool **LAMBERT AUTOS LTD**
Custom House, Brunswick Business Park. 051-708 8224

MIDDLESEX

Ashford **ASHFORD MANOR MOTORS**
102 Fordbridge Rd. 07842 50077
Hampton Hill **SUPREME AUTOS (HAMPTON HILL) LTD**
7-11 Windmill Rd. 01-979 9061/2
Norwood Green **FIRST COUNTY GARAGES LTD**
Norwood Rd. 01-571 2151
Wembley **FIAT MOTOR SALES LTD**
372 Ealing Rd. 01-998 8811
West Drayton **PRIORS,**
127 Station Rd. 0895 444672

THE FIAT GUIDE TO SUCCESSFUL MOTORING

Whitton **SPEEDWELL GARAGE (WHITTON) LTD** 53/55 High St. 01-894 6893/4
Wraysbury **CONCORDE GARAGE (WRAYSBURY)** 31 Windsor Rd. 078481 2927/2815

NORFOLK

★*Aylsham* **WATT BROTHERS** Norwich Rd. 026 373 2134
King's Lynn **DENNIS MARSHALL LTD** Scania Way. 0553 771331
Norwich **POINTER MOTOR CO LTD** Aylsham Rd. 0603 45345/6
★*Norwich* **ANGLIA AUTO CENTRE,** Barford. 060 545 501
Norwich **WOODLAND CAR SALES LTD** Salhouse Rd. 0603 37555/6
Scole **DESIRA MOTOR CO LTD** Diss Rd. 037 9740741
Sherringham **EARLGATE MOTORS LTD** 41 Cromer Rd. 0263 822782
Great Yarmouth **DESIRA MOTOR CO LTD** North Quay. 0493 844266

NORTHAMPTONSHIRE

Corby **ROCKINGHAM CARS LTD** Rockingham Rd. 0536 68991
Kettering **GRADY BROTHERS (KETTERING) LTD** Britannia Rd. 0536 51 3257
Kilsby, Nr. Rugby **HALFWAY GARAGE (1986) LTD** Crick Cross Rds. 0788 822226
Northampton **MOTORVOGUE LTD** 74 Kingsthorpe Rd. 0604 714555
Rushden **ROCKINGHAM CARS LTD** John St. 0933 57500

NORTHUMBERLAND

Hexham **MATT CLARK LTD** Tyne Mills. 0434 603013/603236
Stakeford **T LIDDELL & SON** Milburn Terrace. 0670 815038

NOTTINGHAMSHIRE

Newark-on-Trent **ELLIOTS GARAGE (NEWARK)** Sleaford Rd. 0636 703405
Nottingham **BRISTOL STREET MOTORS (SHERWOOD) LTD** 323-333 Mansfield Rd. 0602 621000
Ruddington **J C S GARAGES LTD** Manor Park Garage, Wilford Rd. 0602 844114 & 844164
Sutton-in-Ashfield **J.J. LEADLEY LTD** Downing St. 0623 515222
Worksop **BARRATT MOTORS LTD** 7 Newcastle Ave. 0909 475124

OXFORDSHIRE

Banbury **WHITE HORSE GARAGE (BANBURY) LTD** 21-27 Broad St. 0295 50733
Henley-on-Thames **BELL STREET MOTORS (HENLEY) LTD** 66 Bell St. 0491 573077
Oxford **J D BARCLAY LTD** Botley Rd. 0865 722444
Witney **M A WILKINS** 1a Bridge St. 0993 3361/2
Wantage **MELLORS OF CHALLOW LTD** Faringdon Rd. 023 57 2751

SHROPSHIRE

Shrewsbury **WAVERLEY GARAGE LTD** Featherbed La, Harlescott. 0743 64951
Telford **T J VICKERS & SONS** Trench Rd, Trench. 0952 605301

SOMERSET

Bridgwater **STACEY'S MOTORS** 48 St John St. 0278 424801 & 423312
Minehead **MINEHEAD AUTOS LTD** 37-39 Alcombe Rd. 0643 3379/3238
Street **RIZZUTI BROTHERS** West End Garage. 0458 42996
Taunton **COUNTY GARAGE (TAUNTON) LTD** Priory Ave. 0823 337611
Yeovil **ABBEY HILL MOTOR SALES** Boundary Rd, Lufton Trading Est. 0935 29111

STAFFORDSHIRE

Chasetown **SPOT OF CHASETOWN** Highfields Rd. 054 36 5544
Newcastle-under-Lyme **B S MARSON & SONS** Deansgate Garage, Keele Rd. 0782 622141
Stafford **BOSTONS OF MILFORD** 16 The Green, Milford. 0785 661226
Stoke-on-Trent **PLATT'S GARAGE (LONGTON) LTD** Lightwood Rd, Longton. 0782 319212/3/4
★*Uttoxeter* **SMITHFIELD ROAD GARAGE LTD** Smithfield Rd. 08893 3838

SUFFOLK

Beccles **BRAND (MOTOR) ENGINEERS LTD** Ringsfield Rd. 0502 716940
Bury St Edmunds **DESIRA MOTOR CO LTD** Mildenhall Rd. 0284 3280 & 3479
Ipswich **STATION GARAGE** Burrell Rd. 0473 690321
★*Leiston* **AVENUE SERVICE STATION** King George's Ave. 0728 830654
Needham Market **TURNER'S (NEEDHAM MARKET) LTD** 30 High St. 0449 721212

SURREY

Camberley **MARN CAMBERLEY,** 71 Frimley Rd. 0276 64672
Cheam **GODFREY'S (SUTTON & CHEAM) LTD** 50 Malden Rd. 01-644 8877
Croydon **THAMES** 115 Addiscombe Rd. 01-655 1100
Englefield Green **SAVAGE & SON (MOTOR ENGINEERS) LTD** Victoria St. 0784 39771
Epsom **H F EDWARDS & CO LTD** 4 Church St. 03727 25611
★*Farnham* **FRENSHAM ENGINEERING CO** Shortfield, Frensham. 025125 3232
Guildford **A.B.C. GUILDFORD,** Pilot Works, Walnut Tree Close. 04835 75251
Kenley **MARN KENLEY** 60 Godstone Rd. 01-660 4546
New Malden **LAIDLER MOTOR CO LTD** 69 Kingston Rd. 01-942 6075
Reigate **COLIN CRONK,** Showroom: 87/89 Bell St. RH2 7AN. 0737 223304
Wallington **BALHAM AUTOS (WALLINGTON)** 208 London Rd. 01-647 5527/8
Weybridge **TONY BROOKS LTD** Brooklands Rd. 09323 49521
Woking **TONY BROOKS LTD** College Rd, Off Maybury Hill. 04862 20622 & 21222

EAST & WEST SUSSEX

Brighton **TILLEYS (SUSSEX) LTD** Showroom: 100 Lewes Rd. 0273 603244
Burgess Hill **TILLEYS (SUSSEX) LTD** Chandlers Garage, London Rd. 044 46 43431
Chichester **CITY SALES CENTRE** Chichester By-Pass (A27), Kingsham 0243 782478
Eastbourne **CENTRAL MOTOR CO,** 38 Ashford Rd. 0323 640101
East Grinstead **FELBRIDGE GARAGE** Eastbourne Rd. Sales & Service: 0342 24677
Horsham **WILSON PURVES LTD** Brighton Rd. Sales: 0403 61821/65637
Hailsham **G.F. SHAW LTD** Cowbeech. 0323 833321
★*Isfield* **ROSEHILL GARAGE** Isfield, Nr. Uckfield. 082575 313/445
Pulborough **FLEET GARAGE (FITTLEWORTH) LTD** Fittleworth. 079 882 307 & 244
Shoreham-by-Sea **KEEN & BETTS (SHOREHAM) LTD** Church Wood Dr. 0273 461333
St. Leonards-on-Sea **ST LEONARDS MOTORS LTD** Church Wood Drive 0424 53493
Wadhurst **EATON BROS** Forge Garage, Beech Hill. 089288 2126
Worthing **P D H (GARAGES) LTD** Downlands Service Station, Upper Brighton Rd. 0903 37487

TYNE & WEAR

Gateshead **BENFIELD MOTORS,** Lobley Hill Rd. 091 490 0292
Newcastle-upon-Tyne **BENFIELD MOTORS LTD** Railway St. 091 2732131
Sunderland **REG VARDY LTD** 16-18 Villiers St. 091 510 0550
Whitley Bay **WHITLEY LODGE MOTOR CO** Claremont Rd. 091 2523347

WARWICKSHIRE

Balsall Common **CARSTINS LTD** 324 Station Rd. 0676 33145
Nuneaton **RESEARCH GARAGE (NUNEATON) LTD** Haunchwood Rd. 0203 382807
Warwick **GRAYS GARAGE LTD** Wharf St. 0926 496231

WEST MIDLANDS

Birmingham **COLMORE DEPOT LTD** 35 Sutton New Rd, Erdington. 021-350 1301
Birmingham **COLMORE DEPOT LTD** 979 Stratford Rd, Hall Green. 021-778 2323
★*Clent* **HOLY CROSS GARAGE LTD** Bromsgrove Rd. 0562 730557
Coventry **SMITH & SONS MOTORS LTD** Roland Ave, Holbrooks. 0203 667778
Marston Green **MARSTON GREEN GARAGE** 32 Station Rd. 021-779 5140
Solihull **TANWORTH GARAGE LTD** The Green, Tanworth in Arden. 056 44 2218
Tipton **CALDENE AUTOLAND** Burnt Tree 021-520 2411
Walsall **SPOT OF WALSALL,** 44A Ward St. 0922 32911
West Bromwich **COLMORE DEPOT LTD** Birmingham Rd. 021-553 7500/7509
Wolverhampton **A N BLOXHAM LTD** The Fiat Centre, Raby St. 0902 57116

WILTSHIRE

Chippenham **WADHAM STRINGER (CHIPPENHAM) LTD** 21 New Rd. 0249 655757
★*Marlborough* **SKURRAYS** George La. 0672 53535
Salisbury **CAFFYNS** 194 Castle St. 0722 336668
Swindon **SKURRAYS** Drove Rd. 0793 20971

YORKSHIRE

Barnsley **S.A. SNELL (BARNSLEY) LTD** 436-440 Doncaster Rd, Stairfoot. 0226 206675
Bradford **WEST YORKSHIRE MOTOR GROUP** Keighley Rd, Frizinghall. 0274 490031
Bradford **JCT 600** The Italian Car Centre, Sticker Lane. 0274 667234
Castleford **AIRE AUTOS LTD** Lock La. 0977-515806
Doncaster **R ROODHOUSE LTD** York Rd. 0302 784444
Halifax **MAYFIELD GARAGE (HALIFAX) LTD** Queens Rd. 0422 67711/3
Harrogate **CROFT & BLACKBURN LTD** Leeds Road, Pannal. 0423 879236
Huddersfield **GALWAY SMITH OF HUDDERSFIELD** 4 Queensgate. 0484 548111
Keighley **WEST YORKSHIRE MOTOR GROUP** Alkincote Street, Tanfield. 0535 667621
Leeds **JCT 600 (LEEDS) LTD** Spence La. 0532 431843
Leeds **WHITHEAD & HINCH LTD** South Broadgate Lane, Horsforth. 0532 585056
★*Malton* **BENTLEYS GARAGE** Amotherby. 0653 3616
Mirfield **THORNTON MOTORS OF DEWSBURY LTD** Calder Garage, 117 Huddersfield Rd. 0924 498316

★*Northallerton* **TIM SWALES (CAR SALES) LTD**
Clack Lane Garage, Osmotherley.
060 983 263/666
Ripon **CROFT & BLACKBURN LTD**
Harvester House, Kirkby Rd. 0765 4491/4
Rotherham **DEREK G PIKE & CO**
126 Fitzwilliam Rd. 0709 361666
Scarborough **MISKIN & KNAGGS LTD**
Manor Rd. 0723 364111/3
Selby **PARKINSON'S GARAGE LTD**
Hambleton. 075 782 396
Sheffield **G T CARS**
Suffolk Rd. 0742 21370/21378/22748
Wakefield **PICCADILLY WAKEFIELD LTD**
Bradford Rd. 0924 290220
York **PICCADILLY AUTO CENTRE LTD**
84 Piccadilly. 0904 34321

SCOTLAND

Aberdeen **CALLANDERS GARAGE (AUTOPORT) LTD**
870 Great Northern Rd. 0224 695573
Ayr **ROBERT McCALL LTD** Galloway Avenue 0292 260416
Bathgate **J & A BROWNING LTD** 11 East Main Street 0501 40536
Brechin **KAY'S AUTO CENTRE,**
18 Clerk St. 03562 2561
Coatbridge **R J CROSS LTD**
Sales: 206 Bank St, ML5 1EG. 0236 35774
Dollar **STEWART BROTHERS**
28-34 Bridge St. 025 94 2233/4
★*Dumbarton* **DUNCAN McFARLANE & SON** 96 Church St. 0389 63689
Dumfries **CENTRAL CAR SALES**
77 Whitesands. 0387 61378
Dundee **MACALPINE MOTORS**
MacAlpine Rd. 0382 818004
Dunfermline **FLEAR & THOMSON LTD**
128-138 Pittencrieff St. 0383-722565/6
Edinburgh **CROALL & CROALL**
Glenogle Rd. 031 556 6404/9
Edinburgh **HAMILTON BROTHERS (EDINBURGH) LTD** 162 St. Johns Rd. 031 334 6248
Falkirk **ARNOLD CLARK AUTOMOBILES LTD**
Falkirk Road, Grangemouth. 0324 474766
Forres **DICKSON MOTORS (FORRES) LTD** Tytler St. 0309 72122/3
Glasgow **RITCHIES**
393 Shields Rd. 041 429 5611
Glasgow **PEAT ROAD MOTORS (JORDANHILL) LTD**
120 Whittingehame Drive, Jordhanhill. 041 357 1939
Gourock **MANOR VEHICLE (TURIN) LTD**
92 Manor Crescent 0475 32356
Hamilton **JAMES J NICHOLSON LTD**
136 Strathaven Rd. 0698 284606
Hawick **BORDER MOTOR CO**
12 Havelock St. 0450 73881
Invergordon **SEAFIELD MOTORS (INVERNESS) LTD**
Scotburn Road, Kildary. 086 284 2552
Inverness **DONALD MACKENZIE LTD**
62 Seafield Rd. 0463 235777/8
Parts: 0463 232285
Irvine **HARRY FAIRBAIRN LTD**
Ayr Rd. 0294 72121
Kilmarnock **GEORGE BICKET & CO LTD**
67-79 Campbell St, Riccarton.
0563 22525/6
★*Lanark* **J & J FERGUSON**
Wellgatehead. 0555 3106
Leven **LINKS GARAGE (LEVEN)**
Scoonie Rd. 0333 27003
Oban **HAZELBANK MOTORS LTD**
Stevenson St. 0631 66476
Paisley **HAMILTON BROS LTD**
Ralston Garage, 255 Glasgow Rd.
041-882 9901
★*Paisley* **LOCHFIELD GARAGE**
4-8 Lochfield Rd. 041-884 2281
Perth **MACALPINE OF PERTH,**
St. Leonards Bank. 0738 38511
Peterhead **CLYNE AUTOS**
Seaview, St. Fergus. 077 983 258
★*Pitscottie by Cuper* **D.H. PATTERSON MOTOR ENGINEERS**
Burnbank Garage. 033482 200
★*Rutherglen* **McKECHNIE OF RUTHERGLEN**
77 Farmeloan Rd. 041-647 9722/5915
St. Boswells **ST. BOSWELLS GARAGE**
St. Boswells 08352 2259/3475
Stirling **HAMILTON BROTHERS LTD**
44 Causeway Head Rd. 0786 62426
Tranent **WILLIAM B COWAN LTD**
The Garage Elphinstone 0875 610492

WESTERN ISLES

★*Stornoway* **KIWI'S GARAGE (STORNOWAY) LTD**
Bells Rd. 0851 5033

ORKNEY ISLES

Kirkwall **J & M SUTHERLAND**
Junction Rd. 0856 2158

SHETLAND ISLES

Aith **AITH AUTOS LTD**
Aith by Bixter. 059 581 230
Lerwick **AITH AUTOS LTD**
9 Blackhill Industrial Estate. 0595 3385/4450

WALES

Pwllheil **PULROSE MOTOR SERVICES LTD** Ala Rd. 0758 612827
Abergele **SLATERS EUROCARS LTD**
Marine Road, Pensarn. 0745 822021/823387
Wrexham **N & G DICKENS LTD**
Border Service Station, Gresford.
097-883-6262
Cardigan **B.V. REES**
Abbey Garage St. Dogmaels. 0239 612025
Carmarthen **WILLIAM DAVIES & SONS**
Central Garage, St. Catherine St.
0267 236284
Aberystwyth **EVANS BROS**
Royal Oak Garage, Llanfarian.
0970 61 2311/2
Kilgetty **STEPASIDE GARAGE LTD**
Carmarthen Rd. 0834 813786
Builth Wells **PRYNNE'S SERVICE STATION LTD** Garth. 059 12 287
Abergavenny **CLYTHA MOTOR CO**
Merthyr Road, Llanfoist. 0873 6888
★*Blackwood* **A.J. STEVENS & SONS**
High Bank Garage, Fairview. 0443 831703
★*Cwmbran* **C.K. MOTOR CO (SOUTH WALES LTD)**
10/11 Court Road Industrial Estate.
06333 72711
Newport **L.C. MOTORS**
121 Corporation Rd. 0633 212548/598892
Bridgend **T.S. GRIMSHAW (BRIDGEND) LTD** Tremains Rd. 0656 2984
Cardiff **T.S. GRIMSHAW LTD**
Fiat House, 329 Cowbridge Road East.
0222 395322
Llanishen Cardiff **YAPP'S GARAGES LTD**
Fidlas Rd. 0222 751323
★*Merthyr Tydfil* **CYFARTHFA MOTORS LTD** Cyfarthfa Rd. 0685 5400
★*Tonyrefail* **VALLEY MILL MOTORS**
Gilfach Rd. 0443 670742
Swansea **MOORCROFT MOTORS LTD**
54 Sway Road, Morriston. 0792 75271
Aberdare **WILSON CAR SALES (ABERDARE) LTD**
Canal Road, Cwmbach. 0855 875577/883717

NORTHERN IRELAND

Omagh **GLENPARK MOTORS**
62 Gortin Road, Co. Tyrone. 0662 46521
Armagh **ARMAGH GARAGES LTD**
Portadown Rd. 0861 524 252
Ballymena **YOUNG'S (BROUGHSHANE) LTD** 11 Raceview Road, Broughtshane.
0266 861380/861497
Ballymoney **MODEL CAR MART**
Model Rd. 026 56 63275
Banbridge **ANNAGH MOTORS (BANBRIDGE) LTD**
51 Church St. 082 06 24495
Bangor **JAMES THOMPSON**
135-141 Bryansburn Rd. 0247 463911
Dungannon **FRANCIS NEILL MOTORS (DUNGANNON) LTD**
1 Ranfurley Rd. 086 87 22552
Enniskillen **T & T TOWN & COUNTRY CARS LTD** Sligo Rd. 0365 22440
Holywood **TERENCE McKEAG**
36-38 Shore Rd. 0232 28900/1
Lisburn **DORNAN'S SERVICE STATION (LISBURN) LTD**
22 Market Pl. 08462 77412
Portadown **ANNAGH MOTORS WORKS**
Mahon Industrial Estate, Mahon Rd.
0762 332552
Newry **N.W. KEHOE & SONS**
18 Patrick St. 0693 3193/66500
Belfast **BAIRDS CARS**
7-9 Boucher Rd. 0232 247770
Belfast **B.A.S. (MOTORS) LTD**
45-47 Rosetta Rd. 0232 491049/491676
Belfast **DICK & CO (BELFAST) LTD**
43 Mallusk Road, Newtownabbey.
0232 342511
Belfast **W.J. BELL & SON**
40-50 Townsend St. 0232 241394
Comber **T.J. CHAMBERS & SON (BELFAST) LTD**
31-37 Mill Street, Comber. 0247 873565
Downpatrick **D.S.C. CARS**
10/12 Church Street, Downpatrick.
0396 2858/4322

CHANNEL ISLANDS

Guernsey **GT CARS**
Les Banques Garage, St. Sampsons.
0481 47838
Jersey **BEL ROYAL MOTOR WORKS LTD**
Bel Royal, St. Lawrence. 0534 22556

EUROPE'S DRIVING FORCE

LONDON

Admiral Codrington

FOOD 17 Mossop Street SW3
MAP 13 B5
01–589 4603
Parking limited

Bar food 12–3 & 6.30–10.30
No bar food Sat & Sun eves

Landlords Melvyn & Irene Barnett
Brewery Bass
Bass; Charrington IPA; Worthington Best Bitter; Guinness; Carling Black Label; Tennent's Extra; Lamot; cider.

The gas-lit bar and plant-filled patio provide an appealing choice of rendezvous for snacking at this friendly Victorian pub. At lunchtime, follow soup or potted shrimps with, say, shepherd's pie, a steak or mixed grill – adding fish and chips if it's a Saturday, a traditional roast on Sunday. Similar, more formal evening choice. Sandwiches, salads and cheese always available on request.
Typical prices Garlic mushrooms £2.25 Steak & kidney pie £3.45
Credit Access, Amex, Diners, Visa **LVs**

Albert

A 52 Victoria Street SW1
MAP 13 C4
01-222 5577
Parking difficult

Landlord Eric Jones
Owner (Chef & Brewer) London Host
Webster Yorkshire Bitter; Watney Combes Bitter, Stag; Holsten; Budweiser; Fosters.

Determined survivor of a bygone age, this sturdy redbrick Victorian pub is dwarfed by towering modern office blocks. Although the large, plush, open-plan interior has been modernised, many of the original features live on in engraved glass panels and windows, lofty ceilings, carved woodwork and a big solid wood bar, to give a real traditional pub look. Drinkers might perhaps heed the set of old prints depicting the evils of alcohol.
Credit Access, Amex, Diners, Visa

Albion

FOOD 10 Thornhill Road N1
MAP 12 D1
01-607 7450
Parking limited

Bar food 12–2.30
No bar food eves & all Sun

Landlords Michael & Shirley Parish
Brewery Hamden Hosts
Ruddles County; Webster Yorkshire Bitter; Watney Special, Coombes Bitter; Holsten; Fosters; cider.

A charming Victorian pub notable for its lovely flower displays. The regular bar menu of fish and chips, quiche and sandwiches is backed up by daily specials such as oxtail soup, salt beef (Monday and Friday), sausage toad and chicken, bacon and mushroom casserole. Good sweets, too, like rhubarb crumble or bread and butter pudding. Patio and garden.
Typical prices Salt beef £3.25 Steak & kidney pudding £3.25
Credit Access, Visa

Anchor

A Bankside, 34 Park Street SE1
MAP 11 D4
01-407 1577
Parking ample

Landlord Debby Jelffs
Free house
Courage Best Bitter, Directors; John Smith's Yorkshire Bitter; Guinness; Kronenbourg; Hofmeister; cider.

A smart patio with tables right on the waterside makes fine weather drinking a delight at this historic Southwark pub. On this spot in 1666 the original Anchor's customers watched the Great Fire reflected in the waters of the Thames. Nearby stood the Globe theatre and the notorious Clink prison. Beautiful panelling, characterful beams and a minstrels' gallery grace the interior of the present Georgian building, which has several atmospheric bars.
Credit Access, Amex, Diners, Visa **LVs**

Angel

A 101 Bermondsey Wall East SE16
MAP 11 D4
01–237 3608
Parking ample

Landlord Nick Parker
Owner THF
Courage Best Bitter, Directors; John Smith's Yorkshire Bitter; Guinness; Kronenbourg; Hofmeister; cider.

Superb views across the river towards Tower Bridge, the City and beyond have attracted a host of notable regulars down the centuries, from Laurel and Hardy to Captain Cook and Samuel Pepys – Judge Jeffries reputedly announced executions here, too. Monks from Bermondsey Priory originally built a tavern here in the 15th century. Today's brick-built pub has a sensitively modernised interior, nautically themed with photos of sailing ships. Terrace.
Credit Access, Amex, Diners, Visa **LVs**

The Audley

FOOD 41 Mount Street W1
MAP 12 B3
01-499 1843
Parking difficult

Bar food 11–2.45 & 5.30–10 (till 10.30 in summer)
Landlords Chris & Hilary Plumpton
Free house
Webster Yorkshire Bitter; Ruddles County; William Younger's Scotch; Carlsberg; Budweiser.

Recent refurbishment has not altered the period charm of this busy pub, where ornate ceilings and much darkwood give a Victorian feel to the bar. Salads and sandwiches are the things to order – roast turkey, smoked salmon, mixed seafood, roast beef, ham carved off the bone in generous portions. All this can be enjoyed at the counter or at a comfortable table.
Typical prices Roast beef salad £6.65 Smoked salmon sandwich £2.95
Credit Access, Amex, Diners, Visa

Black Friar

A 174 Queen Victoria Street, EC4
MAP 12 D3
01–236 5650
Parking difficult

Landlords Mr and Mrs McKinstry
Owner J.W. Nicholsons Ltd.
Adnams Bitter; Bass; Tetley Bitter; Boddingtons Bitter; Guinness; Castlemaine; Löwenbräu; cider.

Admirers of Art Nouveau will enjoy the turn of the century decor – intricately carved woodwork, marble and mother of pearl inlay, stained glass windows and bas reliefs of friars – which gives a unique charm to this unusual wedge-shaped pub dating back 300 years and handsomely modernised by the Victorians. Summer drinks can also be enjoyed in the forecourt.

Prices given are as at the time of our research and thus may change.

Bull's Head

A Strand-on-the-Green W4
MAP 11 A5
01–994 1204
Parking limited

Landlords Mr & Mrs R.D. Smart
Owner London Host
Watney Combes Bitter; Webster Yorkshire Bitter; Guinness; Carlsberg; Holsten Export.

Pretty, countrified Strand-on-the-Green at Chiswick is the delightful setting for this popular pub dating back to the 17th century. Its chief claim to historical fame is that it was on more than one occasion used by Oliver Cromwell as his headquarters during the time of the Civil War. There's a relaxing panelled bar and, for summer drinking, the terrace overlooking the Thames is a sought-after spot. Children are welcome lunchtime only.
Credit Access, Diners, Visa

Cask & Glass

FOOD 39 Palace Street SW1
MAP 13 C4
01-834 7630
Parking difficult

Bar food 12–3 & 5.30–10
No bar food Sun
Closed Sun eve

Landlords R. & M. Beatty
Owner Chef & Brewer
Watney Special; Webster Yorkshire Bitter; Carlsberg.

A sandwich and a half of bitter (no pints sold) is the usual order at this pretty little corner pub presided over by kindly Mr & Mrs Beatty. Generously filled brown bread sandwiches – cheese, turkey, ham, chicken, corned beef and egg salad – are made in advance for the lunchtime trade, to order in the evening. Hot sausage sandwiches and salads are also available. Outside tables.
Typical prices Cream cheese sandwich 95p Egg salad sandwich 95p
Credit Access

City Barge

A Strand-on-the-Green W4
MAP 11 A5
01–994 2148
Parking limited

Landlords Mr & Mrs Hitchings
Brewery Courage
Courage Directors, Best Bitter; Guinness; Hofmeister; Kronenbourg; Miller Lite; cider.

Hard by the Thames at pretty Strand-on-the-Green, this pleasant pub still has a good deal of period charm although a wartime bomb necessitated a good deal of rebuilding. There are two bars, one of which is contemporary in style, and a terrace on the towpath for al fresco drinking. The name is gained from the Lord Mayor's staff barge, which was moored nearby in former times. Children's play area in the conservatory.
Credit Access, Visa

Cock Tavern

FOOD Poultry Avenue, Central Markets, EC1
MAP 12 D3
01-248 2918
Parking limited

Bar food 5.30–3 & 5–10
Closed Sat, Sun & Bank Hols

Landlord Alan Burrows
Free house
Young Special; Charles Wells Bombardier; Courage Best; Red Stripe; cider.

A cellar pub right in the heart of Smithfield Market, notable for its excellent food and long opening hours. Breakfast, served from 5.30 am, offers anything from kippers to kidneys, from toast to a T-bone steak. Grills, roasts, game birds and salt beef sandwiches are lunchtime favourites. There's a short selection of dishes of the day, and a cold table too.
Typical prices Hot salt beef sandwich £1.40 T-bone steak £9
Credit Access, Amex, Diners, Visa **LVs**

Dickens Inn

A St Katharine's Way E1
MAP 11 D4
01-488 9936
Parking ample

Landlord Adrian Hyde
Free house
Dickens Special; Courage Best, Directors; Oliver's Bitter; Guinness; Kronenbourg; cider.

Right in the heart of St Katharine's Dock redevelopment area, this popular pub is an 18th-century warehouse that was moved some 70 yards from its original location and reconstructed in the style of a balconied inn. The timber shell, ironwork and many other features are original, and the decor, including antique marine bric-a-brac, is very much in keeping with the period. It's on three floors, with a terrace.
Credit Access, Amex, Diners, Visa **LVs**

Dove

A 19 Upper Mall W6
MAP 11 A5
01–748 5405
Parking difficult

Landlord Brian Lovrey
Brewery Fuller Smith & Turner
■ Fullers ESB, London Pride; Guinness; Fullers K2 Lager; Heineken.

Tucked away in a narrow Georgian alley on the river between Chiswick Eyot and Hammersmith Bridge, this pleasant 17th-century pub boasts many historic connections. Nell Gwynne drank here, as did A.P. Herbert, who featured it in his novel *The Water Gypsies*, and James Thomson wrote *Rule Britannia* in one of the upper rooms. Beamed ceilings, bare wood floors and a delightful terrace overlooking the river are the attractions today. **LVs**

Eagle

A 2 Shepherdess Walk N1
MAP 10 D3
01-253 4715
Parking difficult

Closed Sun

Landlord Mr L. Deadfield
Brewery Charrington
■ Charrington IPA; Bass; Toby Bitter; Guinness; Carling Black Label; Tennent's Extra; cider.

Immortalised for ever in the popular ditty 'Pop Goes the Weasel', this is the Eagle where the money went after its customers had popped the weasel (i.e. after they had pawned their possessions). In former times it was a popular variety theatre, and among the many famous performers who appeared on stage here was the much-loved vaudeville star Marie Lloyd.
Credit Access, Visa

Flask

A 77 Highgate West Hill N6
MAP 10 C2
01–340 3969
Parking ample

Landlord Mrs G. Light
Brewery Taylor Walker
■ Taylor Walker Bitter; John Bull Bitter; Ind Coope Burton Ale; Guinness; Löwenbräu; Castlemaine XXXX; cider.

A characterful 17th-century pub which is one of the landmarks of Hampstead. Inside, the bars are cosy and panelled, and there is a forecourt for al fresco drinking in the summer. Former patrons include Dick Turpin, who reputedly hid in the cellars, and William Hogarth, who used to paint there. It gained its name from the flasks of Hampstead spa water it used to dispense.
Credit Access, Amex, Visa **LVs**

Fox & Anchor

OD 115 Charterhouse Street, EC1
MAP 12 D2
01–253 4838
Parking limited

Bar food 6.30 am–2.30 pm
No bar food eves
Closed Sat, Sun, Bank Hols & 1 wk Xmas

Landlord Seamus O'Connell
Brewery Taylor Walker
■ Taylor Walker Bitter; Burton Ale; Friary Meux Bitter; Guinness; Castlemaine; Löwenbräu; cider.

As you might expect from its proximity to Smithfield market, first-class meat tops the bill at this handsome late-Victorian pub. The day starts with hearty breakfasts from 6.30 am to noon, then it's a feast of chump chops, steaks and superb sausages, plus steak and kidney pie, soup, salads and sandwiches, with home-made apple pie for afters. Patio for summer drinks.
Typical prices Mixed grill £6.75 Sirloin steak £6.85
Credit Amex, Visa **LVs**

George Inn

A 77 Borough High Street, Southwark SE1
MAP 11 D4
01-407 2056
Parking difficult

Landlord John Hall
Brewery Whitbread
Flowers Original; Wethered Bitter; Greene King Abbot Ale; Guinness; Fremlins; Stella Artois; cider.

Built on the site of a much older inn of the same name in 1677, the George is London's last surviving galleried inn and, until the 1880s, enclosed three sides of a courtyard where Shakespeare's plays were once performed. Oak panelling, beams and leaded windows abound, and the downstairs coffee room features the old box-paid compartments which were universal until mid-Victorian times. Patio for outdoor drinking in the summer.
Credit Access, Amex, Diners, Visa **LVs**

Glasshouse Stores

FOOD Brewer Street W1
MAP 12 C3
01-734 4771
Parking difficult

Bar food 11.30–2.30 & 5.30–10.30
No bar food Sun

Landlords Robert & Christine Cook
Brewery Taylor Walker
Taylor Walker Best Bitter; Burton Ale; Guinness; Skol; Löwenbräu.

Frequently busy but rarely too crowded, so you can snack in relative comfort at this Edwardian-style Soho pub, whose most notable feature is its ornate bar ceiling. Snacks cover a standard spread, from sandwiches and salads to hot lunchtime dishes such as lasagne, chilli or steak and kidney pie. Vegetable dishes such as leeks in white sauce or vegetable provençale, but no puds.
Typical prices Duck in orange sauce £2.10 Steak pie £2.10
Credit Access, Amex, Visa

Goat

FOOD 3a Kensington High Street W8
MAP 13 A4
01–937 1213
Parking limited

Bar food 11–2 (Sun from 12) & 5.30–9
No bar food Sun eve

Landlords Jane & Stuart Davies
Free house
Webster Yorkshire Bitter; Younger's Bitter, IPA; Guinness; Carlsberg; Holsten Export; cider.

Dating from 1771, this tiny pub stands opposite the private driveway leading to Kensington Palace. In the long, narrow bar you can tuck into simple, enjoyable fare like fluffy quiche and salad, ploughman's, sausages, lamb pie or beef and pasta bake. Limited choice Sunday lunchtime. Children are welcome in the bar at lunchtime only.
Typical prices Beef & Guinness pie £2.95 Lamb & leek pie £2.95
Credit Access, Amex, Diners, Visa

Grapes

A 76 Narrow Street E14
MAP 11 D4
01–987 4396
Parking limited

Landlord Frank Johnson
Brewery Taylor Walker
Taylor Walker Bitter; Ind Coope Burton Ale; Friary Meux Bitter; Guinness; Löwenbräu.

This little 16th-century pub in a favoured position close to the Thames – in the heart of the rapidly changing dockland area – is a pleasant place in which to enjoy a peaceful drink. It has a long history of association with literary and dockland life and is believed to have been the model for the 'Six Jolly Fellowship Porters' in Charles Dickens' novel *Our Mutual Friend*. Patio for summer drinks.
Credit Access

Grenadier

A 18 Wilton Row, SW1
MAP 13 B4
01-235 3074
Parking difficult

Landlord Mr A. R. Taylor
Owner London Hosts
Ruddles County; Webster Yorkshire Bitter; Watney Combes Bitter; Guinness; Holsten; Carlsberg; cider.

Once the officers' mess for the Grenadier Guards, and also once frequented by the Duke of Wellington, this famous pub built in 1802 stands in a quiet cobbled mews, its position signalled by a smart sentry box outside. The military theme continues within, and in the small but very cosy bar you can enjoy a pint of well-kept ale or one of the long-serving barman's justly popular Bloody Marys.
Credit Access, Amex, Diners, Visa

Greyhound

OOD 1 Kensington Square W8
MAP 13 A4
01-937 7140
Parking limited

Bar food 12–2 & 5.30–10, Sun 12–1.15 & 7–10
Landlord Mr J. Dougall
Free house
Charles Wells Bombardier, Eagle Bitter; Green King Abbot Ale; Webster Yorkshire Bitter; Guinness; Fosters; cider.

Built in 1899, this friendly pub faces a pretty square just moments from High Street Kensington. The bar food is very reasonable and covers quite a good range, from sandwiches, cold pies, Scotch eggs and simple salads to hot specials like Somerset sausage casserole or spicy stuffed peppers. Tables outside in fine weather. No sweets. Traditional roast available Sunday.
Typical prices Trawlerman's pie £2.95 Smoked salmon £3.50
Credit Access, Visa

Hand & Shears

A 1 Middle Street EC1
MAP 12 D2
01–600 0257
Parking difficult

Closed Sat, Sun & 1 wk Xmas
Landlord Mr Latimer
Brewery Courage
Courage Directors, Best Bitter; Guinness; Hofmeister; Kronenbourg; Tennent's Pilsner; cider.

The original 12th-century pub became a popular haunt for tailors from nearby Cloth Fair; consequently, the Guild of Merchant Tailors allowed the pub to use its hand and shears emblem as an inn sign. Less cheerful customers were condemned prisoners from Newgate who were allowed a last drink here. The present building is late Georgian–early Victorian, with a horseshoe-shaped bar and panelled walls hung with medical cartoons.

Jack Straw's Castle

A North End Way NW3
MAP 10 B2
01–435 8374
Parking ample

Landlords Brian & Alva Hillyard
Brewery Charrington
Charrington IPA; Bass; Worthington Best Bitter; Guinness; Tennent's Extra; Carling Black Label; cider.

Standing high on Hampstead Heath, near the Round Pond, this eye-catching, weatherboarded pub takes its name from Wat Tyler's second-in-command during the Peasants' Revolt of 1381. The haunt of highwaymen in Elizabethan days and later frequented by Victorian artists and writers – including of course Dickens who often stayed here – the old castle was damaged in the 1940 blitz and completely rebuilt in the 1960s.
Credit Access, Amex, Diners, Visa

Lamb

A 94 Lamb's Conduit Street WC1
MAP 12 D2
01–405 0713
Parking limited

Landlord Mr R. Whyte
Brewery Young
■ Young Bitter, Special, Winter Warmer; Guinness; John Young London Lager, Premium Lager; cider.

Charles Dickens used to live just round the corner from this warmly inviting pub and was a familiar figure in the cosy bar. Victorian cut-glass snob screens are a noteworthy feature; as are the walls which are covered with a fascinating collection of sepia photographs of Victorian and Edwardian stars of theatre and music hall. There's also a small patio for fine-weather drinking.
Credit Access, Visa **LVs**

Lamb & Flag

FOOD 33 Rose Street WC2
MAP 12 C3
01–836 4108
Parking difficult

Bar food 12–2.30 & 5.30–9, Sun 12–1.30 & 7–10

Landlord Terry Archer
Brewery Courage
■ Courage Best Bitter, Directors; John Smith's Yorkshire Bitter; Guinness; Kronenbourg; Miller Lite; cider.

Cheese is king at this famous old pub, where customers frequently spill out from the tiny bars on to the street. Somerset Brie and blue Cheshire along with stalwarts like Stilton, Cheddar, Caerphilly and sage Derby can all be enjoyed with baguettes or slices of delicious hot bread. There's also the odd hot lunchtime dish.
Typical prices Ploughman's lunch £1.80 Two cheese ploughman's £3

Mayflower

A 117 Rotherhithe Street SE16
MAP 11 D4
01–237 4088
Parking ample

Landlord Mr Emslie
Owner Vintage Inns
■ Charrington IPA; Bass; Guinness; Carling Black Label; Tennent's Lager; cider.

It was while drinking at this hostelry in 1611 that the captain of the Mayflower received his assignment to transport the Pilgrim Fathers to the New World. Customers leading less eventful lives can still enjoy the latticed windows, black beams and nautical memorabilia, not to mention the jetty with splendid views over the Thames. Although the upper floor was destroyed by a wartime bomb, restoration has been faithful to the 17th-century original.
Credit Access, Amex, Diners, Visa

Museum Tavern

A 49 Great Russell Street WC1
MAP 12 C3
01–242 8987
Parking difficult

Landlord Mr C. Lawton
Free house
■ Greene King IPA, Abbot; Brakspear Special; Ruddles County; Guinness; Carlsberg; Fosters; cider.

An eye-catching corner pub opposite the British Museum to which many notables, including Karl Marx, have come to quench their bodily thirst after satisfying the spiritual one in the Reading Room across the road. The large, bustling bar is a monument to Victorian extravaganza, with ceiling-mounted fans, carved wood, stained and frosted glass and gilded columns. There is an excellent range of well-kept real ales.
Credit Access, Amex, Diners, Visa

Nag's Head

A 10 James Street WC2
MAP 12 C3
01–836 4678
Parking difficult

Landlords Mr & Mrs Grant
Brewery McMullen
McMullen Country Bitter, AK Mild; Guinness; McMullen Steingold, Hartsman; cider.

These days the clientele at this 18th-century pub, close to the Royal Opera House, tends to be the fashionable theatre-going crowd, but in former times it provided a welcome haven for Covent Garden market porters taking an early-morning break from their duties. The bar decor is Edwardian-style, with etched mirrors, plush fabrics and, adorning the walls, opera and ballet playbills.
Credit Access, Visa **LVs**

Nell of Old Drury

A 29 St Catherine Street WC2
MAP 12 D3
01–836 5328
Parking difficult

Closed Sun

Landlord Maurice Dunphy
Brewery Courage
Courage Directors Bitter, Best Bitter; John Smith's Bitter; Guinness; Kronenbourg; Hofmeister; cider.

The eponymous Nell is of course the famous Nell Gwynne, good friend of Charles II and, in her earlier and more obscure days, purveyor of fruit to the patrons of the Theatre Royal opposite the pub. The pub's long connection with the theatre world is demonstrated by the playbills which adorn the walls of the simply-furnished bar. Playwright Richard Sheridan was apparently an habitué of this historic establishment.

Old Bell Tavern

A 95 Fleet Street EC4
MAP 12 D3
01-583 0070
Parking difficult

Closed Sat eve & Sun

Landlord Mrs N. Healy
Free house
Old Bell Bitter; Wadworth 6X; Tetley Bitter; Boddingtons Bitter; Guinness; Castlemaine XXXX; Löwenbräu; cider.

An old Fleet Street tavern which has long been a popular watering hole for journalists and printers, those most famous denizens of the area. The builders of the Wren church of St Bride's next door once found it a handy place to quench their thirst, too. The surroundings are simple to the point of plainness, but the real ales are exceptionally well kept and are a great attraction.

Old Ship

A 25 Upper Mall W6
MAP 11 A5
01–748 3970
Parking difficult

Landlord Mrs M. McCormack
Brewery Watney Combe Reid
Watney Combes Bitter; Watney Combe Reid Stag; Webster Yorkshire Bitter; Guinness; Budweiser; Fosters; cider.

A well-maintained, white-painted building with a 400-year-old history that makes it the oldest pub on this stretch of the Thames. The bars, with traditional pub furniture, are decorated with a riot of nautical objects including rowing sculls and blades. The overall effect is one of warmth and comfort, enhanced by a roaring log fire in winter. The riverside patio is an added attraction in the summer.

Paxton's Head

A 153 Knightsbridge SW1
MAP 13 B4
01–589 6627
Parking difficult

Landlord George Redgewell
Owner H.H. Finch & Co.
Ind Coope Burton Ale, Special; John Bull Bitter; Double Diamond; Guinness; Skol; Löwenbräu; cider.

This popular pub is named after Sir Joseph Paxton, designer of the conservatory at Chatsworth and the famous Crystal Palace which stood a few hundred yards from the pub. The Victorian-style interior is much more recent, but there is plenty of atmosphere to the bar, with its green velvet seats and mahogany walls adorned with delightful etched mirrors. Downstairs, one of the old cellars is now a simple, exposed-brick bar.
Credit Access, Amex, Diners, Visa

Prince Regent

FOOD 71 Marylebone High Street W1
MAP 12 B2
01–935 2018
Parking limited

Bar food 11–2.30 & 5.30–9
No bar food Sun

Landlords Tim & Jill Beesley
Brewery Charrington
Charrington IPA; Bass; Worthington Best Bitter; Tennent's Extra; Guinness; Carling Black Label; cider.

An engaging pub where the atmosphere is cosy but lively. The spacious bar houses portraits and caricatures of the Prince Regent and a valuable collection of fine old cheese dishes. An appetising array of food is on offer, including hot dishes such as lasagne, chicken cacciatore and pork dijonnaise and, for cold snacks, quiches, cold meats and filled rolls. Terrace.
Typical prices Ploughman's £2.50 Chilli con carne £2.75
Credit Access, Amex, Diners, Visa

Princess Louise

A 208 High Holborn WC1
MAP 12 C3
01-405 8816
Parking limited

Landlord Ian Phillips
Brewery Vaux
Vaux Samson; Wards Sheffield Best Bitter; Greene King Abbot Ale; Brakspear Bitter; Guinness; Tuborg Pilsner; cider.

A real gem of the late Victorian era, this friendly, bustling pub has almost all its original features preserved in the large ground-floor bar, which is invariably thronged at lunchtime with local office workers. Its barewood floors, splendid etched mirrors, ornate moulded ceilings and fin-de-siècle tiles give it enormous character, while an added attraction is an excellent selection of real ales, placing it firmly in the 'drinking pub' category.
LVs

Printer's Devil

A 98 Fetter Lane EC4
MAP 12 D3
01–242 2239
Parking difficult

Closed Sat lunch & all Sun

Landlord Mr Collyer
Brewery Whitbread
Whitbread Best Bitter, Trophy; Wethered Bitter; Flowers IPA, Original; Greene King Abbot Ale; Guinness.

The very name, meaning a printer's apprentice or errand boy, has acquired a certain anachronistic charm since Fleet Street ceased to be the hub of the press world, but this is still a popular haunt for print workers who remain in the area. The main bar has a fine display of artefacts relating to their craft: rare old books, woodcuts, models of printing presses and satirical caricatures. There is also a public bar, a rarity in the city.
Credit Amex, Diners, Visa

Prospect of Whitby

A 57 Wapping Wall E1
MAP 11 D4
01–481 1095
Parking difficult
Landlord Trevor Chapman
Owner London Hosts
Watney Stag, Combes Bitter; Webster Yorkshire Bitter; Ruddles County; Guinness; cider.

Probably the best-known and best-loved of London's riverside pubs, featuring on every tourist agenda. In former times it was the haunt of smugglers and thieves, while more reputable clients included Turner and Whistler, who painted river scenes from here, and Charles Dickens, no doubt gathering material on London lowlife. Judge Jeffreys came to sup here, favouring the unusual after-dinner entertainment of watching pirates being hanged.
Credit Access, Amex, Diners, Visa

Railway Tavern

A 15 Liverpool Street EC2
MAP 11 D4
01–283 3598
Parking difficult
Closed eves from 9pm & all Sat, Sun & Bank Hols
Landlord Mr Hanley
Brewery Whitbread
Flowers Original; Wethered Bitter; Brakspear Bitter; Boddingtons Bitter; Guinness; Stella Artois.

A busy, popular pub near to Liverpool Street Station which is a shrine for train spotters. It is liberally endowed with memorabilia of the bygone days of steam; photographs and a model of one of those great locomotives of the past. Other railway artefacts, including crests of 19th-century railway companies, abound. Even the uninitiated will enjoy the atmosphere, while train buffs will find much to discuss.
Credit Access, Amex, Diners, Visa

Red Lion

OD 23 Crown Passage, Pall Mall SW1
MAP 13 C4
01-930 8067
Parking difficult
Bar food 12–3 & 5.30–11
Closed Bank Hol Mons
Landlord Michael McAree
Brewery Watney Combe Reid
Ruddles County; Webster Yorkshire Bitter; Guinness; Budweiser; Fosters.

A welcoming and very popular pub tucked away in a passage off Pall Mall. The trade in bar food is brisk, with most people opting for the excellent selection of home-made pies (chunky chicken, steak and kidney, gammon and mushroom). There's a good choice of salads including Scotch roast beef, prawn or ham and a tasty quiche. Also, a variety of sandwiches, but no starters or sweets.
Typical prices Chunky chicken pie £3.10 Beef & ale pie £3.95 **LVs**

Red Lion

A 1 Waverton Street W1
MAP 13 B4
01-499 1307
Parking difficult
Landlord David Butterfield
Owner London Hosts
Webster Yorkshire Bitter; Watney Combes Bitter; Ruddles County; Guinness; Fosters; Holsten Export; cider.

Built in 1723 to accommodate the builders constructing Chesterfield House, the home of Lord Berkeley, this cosy pub was the headquarters of the US Airborne Division during World War II. Today, its darkly panelled interior, rustic plain wooden floor, leaded windows and old pub prints, together with its small, cosy gas log fires, make it a favourite haunt of many. The little front patio with its benches and barrel tables is very popular in summer.
Credit Access, Amex, Diners, Visa **LVs**

Salisbury

A 90 St Martin's Lane WC2
MAP 12 C3
01–836 5863
Parking difficult

Landlord David Suter
Owner Clifton Inns
■ Ind Coope Burton Ale; Taylor Walker Bitter; John Bull Bitter; Guinness; Löwenbräu; Castlemaine XXXX; cider.

David Suter is the new landlord at this ornate late-Victorian pub in the heart of theatreland. A favourite meeting place before the curtain rises, the lavishly authentic bars provide just the right atmosphere with their moulded ceilings and darkwood panelling, gilded statuettes, engraved glass screens and plush velvet seating. The clientele, too, can often be just as colourful.
Credit Access, Amex, Diners, Visa

We publish annually so make sure you use the current edition.

Samuel Pepys

A Brooks Wharf, 48 Upper Thames Street EC4
MAP 11 D4
01–248 3048
Parking difficult

Closed Bank Hols
Landlord Mr Spencer
Brewery Charrington
■ Charrington IPA; Bass; Stones Bitter; Guinness; Carling Black Label; Tennent's Pilsner, Extra; cider.

Facing Bankside, this atmospheric drinking pub is in fact an accurate representation of a 17th-century inn, skilfully constructed in an old warehouse on the Thames. The flagstoned cellar bar has a nautical theme, recalling Samuel Pepys' lesser-known time as Secretary to the Navy, and there are fascinating extracts, too, from his celebrated diary. Watch the river life roll by from the verandah.
Credit Access, Amex, Diners, Visa

Seven Stars

A 53 Carey Street WC2
MAP 12 D3
01-242 8521
Parking difficult

Closed Sat, Sun & Bank Hols
Landlord Mr J.A. Crawley
Brewery Courage
■ Courage Best Bitter, Directors, JC; Guinness; Hofmeister; Kronenbourg; Stella Artois; cider.

Betwixt the Law Courts and Lincoln's Inn Fields is this tiny gem of a pub, much frequented by members of the legal profession. The pub was first licensed in 1602 and bears an interesting 17th-century fire mark on the exterior wall. The little bar – always busy – is enlivened with Spy cartoons of distinguised members of the Bench and Bar. The rear entrance to the Law Courts is nearby, giving rise to the expression 'to be in Carey Street', meaning to be bankrupt.

Shepherd's Tavern

A Hertford Street W1
MAP 13 B4
01–499 3017
Parking difficult

Landlords Mark & Meroulla Lindley
Owner London Hosts
■ Ruddles County; Watney Combes Bitter; Webster Yorkshire Bitter; Guinness; Holsten Export; cider.

Quaint Shepherd's Market is the setting for this fine old pub which dates back 300 years. A popular haunt of tourists and business people alike, it has mellow pine panelling and pebbled glass bow windows. The telephone is housed in a splendid sedan chair which belonged to the Duke of Cumberland, younger son of George II and vanquisher of Bonnie Prince Charlie at Culloden in 1746.
Credit Access, Amex, Diners, Visa **LVs**

Sherlock Holmes

A 10 Northumberland Street, WC2
MAP 13 C4
01-930 2644
Parking difficult

Landlords Eddie & Joan Hardcastle
Brewery Whitbread
Whitbread Best Bitter; Samuel Whitbread Strong; Abbot Ale; Flowers Original; Guinness; Heineken.

Fans of Sherlock Holmes flock to this cheerful pub that started life as the Northumberland Arms in the days when the great detective's creator Sir Arthur Conan Doyle used to drink here. It glories in the distinction of a mention in *The Hound of the Baskervilles*, and even non-devotees will be fascinated by the collection of Holmes memorabilia and early instruments of forensic science. Pavement with tables and chairs for outdoor drinking in the summer.
Credit Access, Amex, Diners, Visa

Ship

A 10 Thames Bank, Riverside SW14
MAP 11 A6
01–876 1439
Parking ample

Landlord Mr A.G. Davidson
Owner Gateway Hosts
Watney Combes Bitter; Ruddles County; Webster Yorkshire Bitter; Guinness; Holsten Export; Fosters; cider.

This agreeable pub, with a history going back to Elizabethan times, is *the* place to be on Boat Race day, when enthusiastic patrons throng its pleasant riverside terrace conveniently opposite the winning post. Inside is a cosy bar, warmed in winter by a genuine log fire, where old paddles and sculls hang from the ceiling, and trophies from various rowing events and mementoes from the Oxford v Cambridge contests are proudly displayed. Garden.
Credit Access, Amex, Diners, Visa

Slug & Lettuce

OOD 47 Hereford Road W2
MAP 12 A3
01–229 1503
Parking limited

Bar food 12–2.30 & 7–10.15, Sun 12–1.30 & 7–9.45

Landlord Chris Bromley
Brewery Watney, Combe & Reid
Ruddles County; Webster Yorkshire Bitter; Watney Combes Bitter; Guinness; Holsten Export; Budweiser; Carlsberg; cider.

The atmosphere is young and lively at this Victorian pub offering a comprehensive range of appetising food. A selection from the blackboard might include garlicky mushrooms with bacon or smoked mackerel and pitta, followed by beef and Guinness casserole or tagliatelle carbonara. Nice sweets like chocolate and Cointreau mousse. Patio.
Typical prices Salmon fishcakes with hollandaise sauce £4.50 Lamb chop with Cumberland sauce £4.75
Credit Access

Slug & Lettuce

OOD 1 Islington Green N1
MAP 12 D1
01-226 3864
Parking difficult

Bar food 12–2.30 & 7–10.15, Sun 12–1.15 & 7–9.30
Landlord Richard Davis
Brewery Watney Combe Reid
Ruddles County; Combes Bitter; Webster Yorkshire Bitter; Guinness; Fosters; Holsten; cider.

The cooking is consistently enjoyable at this large, bustling Victorian pub very much geared towards food. The daily changing blackboard menu is imaginative, and has something for everyone: cream of lettuce soup, hot vegetable platter, tagliatelle napoletana, lamb's kidneys with a brandy sauce. A good selection of cheeses and sweets. Outside tables.
Typical prices Suprême of chicken with avocado & garlic £4.75 Chicken livers with port £2.45

Slug & Lettuce

FOOD 11 Warwick Way SW1
MAP 13 C5
01–834 3313
Parking difficult

Bar food 12–2.15 & 6.30–10.15
No bar food Sun

Landlord Hugh Corbett
Brewery Watney Combe Reid
Ruddles County; Webster Yorkshire Bitter; Watney Combes Bitter; Carlsberg; Holsten; Budweiser; cider.

Getting a table can be a gamble at this lively, very popular pub-cum-bistro, where the accent is on fast food. Home-made soup, and egg and bacon baps provide light bites. More substantial fare ranges from smoked haddock in white sauce or spicy sausage to salads and deep pan quiches. Finish with cheese and fruit or a tempting sweet. The restaurant upstairs offers a wider choice of dishes.
Typical prices Tagliatelle £2.50 Chicken livers & bacon £2.50 **LVs**

Spaniards Inn

A Spaniards Road NW3
MAP 10 B2
01–455 3276
Parking ample

Landlord David Roper
Owner Vintage Inns
Charrington IPA; Bass; Stones Bitter; Guinness; Carling Black Label; Tennent's Extra; Pilsner; cider.

Dick Turpin started his legendary ride to York from this famous old weather-boarded pub near Hampstead Heath and in the 18th century, too, bands of Gordon rioters paused here for refreshment while on a fire-raising sortie. These days there's much more convivial company to be found in the popular beamed bars that have changed little over the years, and in the attractive garden, scene of the tea party in Dickens' *Pickwick Papers*.
Credit Access, Visa **LVs**

Sun Inn

A 7 Church Road, Barnes SW13
MAP 11 A5
01–876 5893
Parking ample

Landlords Len & Jan Harris
Brewery Taylor Walker
Taylor Walker Bitter; Ind Coope Burton Ale; Tetley Bitter; Guinness; Löwenbräu; Castlemaine XXXX; cider.

An 18th-century pub with a much more venerable bowling green at the back on which, according to legend, Drake and Walsingham taught Elizabeth I to play bowls. The pub's position overlooking Barnes pond and common is echoed in the interior, which sports historical pictures of Barnes in the 18th century, while horse brasses and low-beamed ceilings add to the period charm. Terrace.

Swan Tavern

FOOD 66 Bayswater Road W2
MAP 12 A3
01-262 5204
Parking limited

Bar food 11–2.30 & 5.30–10.30, Sun 12–1.45 & 7–10

Landlord Mr D. C. Stone
Free house
Tetley Bitter; Webster Yorkshire Bitter; Friary Meux Bitter, Fosters; Carlsberg; cider.

A traditional, white-painted pub on busy Bayswater Road, its large terrace filled with tables, benches and parasols. The bar food is very decent, comprising an assortment of home-made pies, hot sausages and the very popular turkey casserole, plus quiches, cold turkey, ham and simple well-made salads. Children are admitted to the back bar. Patio.
Typical prices Steak & kidney pie £2.50 Turkey casserole £2.50

Tom Cribb

A 36 Panton Street SW1
MAP 12 C3
01-839 6536
Parking limited

Landlord Patricia Cook
Brewery Charrington
▮ Charrington IPA; Bass; Worthington Best Bitter; Guinness; Stella Artois; Tennent's Extra; cider.

Tom Cribb, one-time champion barefist boxer, retired from the ring in 1811 to run this corner pub – then known as the Union Arms – opposite the Comedy Theatre. The walls of its cosy wood-panelled bar are covered with posters recording his famous fights and there are numerous other old prints and drawings with a boxing theme. Its genuine pubby atmosphere keeps it high in the popularity stakes and in fine weather tables and parasols hug the narrow pavement outside. **LVs**

Trafalgar Tavern

A Park Row, Greenwich SE10
MAP 7 D3
01-858 2437
Parking ample

Landlord Elvyn Thomas
Owner Gateway Hosts
▮ Ruddles County; Watney Combes Bitter; Webster Yorkshire Bitter; Ben Truman; Guinness; Carlsberg; cider. 🍷

The Thames laps against the walls of this substantial pub, which dates from 1837. On the first floor there's a fine period ballroom and a bar arranged as the forecastle of a sailing ship (only in use on Sunday mornings). The main bar downstairs has a nautical flavour, with oil paintings of an admiral (not Nelson!) and an old sailing ship. Old fireplaces, jugs and bottles add to the atmosphere.
Credit Access, Amex, Diners, Visa

Two Chairmen

A 39 Dartmouth Street SW1
MAP 13 C4
01–222 8694
Parking difficult

Closed Sat eve & all Sun
Landlord Penny Allcorn
Owner Clifton Inns
▮ King & Barnes Sussex Bitter; Webster Yorkshire Bitter; Ruddles County; Guinness; Fosters; Carlsberg; cider.

Eighteenth-century gentlemen would summon sedan chairs to take them to this agreeable tavern, then a popular coffee house. A sign depicting two sedan chairmen hangs outside, and there's a fine mural on the same theme in the mellow panelled bar. An open fire keeps the whole place snug in winter, while in finer weather tables, chairs and parasols are set out on the pavement. **LVs**

Two Chairmen

A Warwick House Street, off Cockspur Street *SW1*
MAP 13 C4
01–930 1166
Parking difficult
Closed Sunday.

Landlord James O'Hare
Brewery Courage
▮ Courage Best Bitter, Directors; John Smith's Yorkshire Bitter; Guinness; Hofmeister; Kronenbourg; cider.

Built in 1683 and reconstructed some 200 years later in Queen Victoria's reign, this popular little drinking pub near Trafalgar Square is named after the sedan chairmen who plied their energetic trade in the City during the 17th and 18th centuries. The bar is very atmospheric and most appealing, its panelled walls being lined with fascinating prints of London life. Well-kept Courage beers. **LVs**

Victoria

A 10a Strathearn Place W2
MAP 12 A3
01–262 5696
Parking difficult

Landlords Mr & Mrs Byrne
Brewery Charrington
Charrington IPA; Bass; Stones Bitter; Guinness; Carling Black Label; Tennent's Extra; cider.

Queen Victoria apparently called into this fine old pub after she had officially opened nearby Paddington Station, though it's doubtful that she propped up the splendid bar counter. An ornate plaster ceiling, etched mirrors and mahogany panelling are complemented by traditional furnishings, and memorabilia of Victoria and Albert line the walls. The upstairs Gaiety Theatre bar is to be transformed into a champagne bar. Patio. **LVs**

White Horse on Parsons Green

FOOD 1 Parsons Green SW6
MAP 11 B5
01–736 2115
Parking limited
Bar food 12–2.30 & 5.30–9.30
Closed 1 wk Xmas

Landlord Sally Cruickshank
Brewery Vintage Inns
Bass; Hook Norton Best Bitter; Charrington IPA; Highgate Mild; Carling Black Label; Guinness; cider.

Tutored wine tastings, hearty weekend breakfasts and a well-chosen selection of wines are just three of the appealing features of this 19th-century pub. There's an appetising cold food display, while hot dishes might include spinach and leek flan and chicken and mushroom vol-au-vent. Delicious hot puds. Traditional Sunday lunch. Children are welcome lunchtimes only.
Typical prices Pasta & mushroom sauce £2.60 Chocolate banana bread & butter pudding £1.10

Windsor Castle

A 114 Campden Hill Road W8
MAP 11 B4
01-727 8491
Parking limited

Landlord Mr A. J. Owen
Brewery Charrington
Charrington IPA; Bass; Guinness; Carling Black Label; Tennent's Extra; cider.

One of the few truly old-fashioned, unspoilt pubs left in London. To feel its true charm catch it before the crowds arrive – if you can, for it's immensely popular. The simple wood panelling of the two homely small bars with their wooden settles will soon make you forget you're in the great metropolis. The larger, oak panelled bar follows the simple tradition in decor. In summer the lovely high-walled garden is famous as a drinking haunt and a sun trap.
Credit Visa **LVs**

Ye Old Dr Butler's Head

A Mason's Avenue, Coleman Street EC2
MAP 11 D4
01–606 3504
Parking difficult

Closed eves from 8.30pm & all Sat, Sun & Bank Hols

Landlords Nigel & Caroline Field
Free house
Tolly Cobbold Original; Courage Directors; Webster Yorkshire Bitter; Guinness; Kronenbourg; Tuborg; cider.

A pub founded in 1610 by Dr William Butler, royal physician to James I and firm believer in the medicinal properties of alcohol. Today his prescription is still being followed here, mostly by convivial crowds of City workers who throng the sawdust-strewn bar. Venerable black beams, antique brewery mirrors, traditional (and genuine) Georgian wood panelling and gas lights all add to the historical charm.
Credit Access, Amex, Diners, Visa

Ye Olde Cheshire Cheese

A 145 Fleet Street EC4
MAP 12 D3
01–353 6170
Parking difficult

Closed Sat & Sun

Landlord Mr L. Kerly
Free house
■ Samuel Smith's Old Brewery Bitter, Museum Ale; Pilsner.

Journalists, lawyers and tourists gather today to drink at this renowned Fleet Street pub. Once a favourite tippling place of Dr Johnson's, it was rebuilt in 1667 after the Great Fire of London. An authentic 17th-century atmosphere pervades the tiny bars; an open fire in winter, sawdust-strewn floors, a panelled stairway and a narrow courtyard (for summer drinks) all add to its tremendous period charm.

Ye Olde Cock Tavern

A 22 Fleet Street EC4
MAP 12 D3
01–353 3454
Parking difficult

Closed Sat, Sun & Bank Hols

Landlord Robin White
Owner London Hosts
■ Ben Truman Best Bitter, Bitter, Special Mild; Guinness; Holsten Export; Carlsberg; Fosters.

Built in 1549, both the Plague and the Great Fire in 1666 bypassed this venerable tavern. Literary and theatrical associations are strong: Goldsmith, Sheridan, Garrick and Irving were all customers, while Pepys used it as a rendezvous for illicit liaisons, Dickens ate his last public meal here, and Alfred Lord Tennyson mentioned it in verse. A splendid gilded cock guards the entrance and there is a superb Tudor chimneypiece.
Credit Access, Amex, Diners, Visa

We welcome bona fide recommendations or complaints on the tear-out pages for readers' comments.

They are followed up by our professional team but do complain to the management.

Ye Olde Mitre Tavern

A 1 Ely Court, Ely Place, Holborn EC1
MAP 12 D3
01–405 4751
Parking difficult

Closed Sat, Sun & Bank Hols

Landlord Michael Kennedy
Brewery Ind Coope
■ Ind Coope Burton Ale; Friary Meux Bitter; Tetley Bitter; Löwenbräu; Castlemaine XXXX; Skol; cider.

Tucked down an alleyway between Hatton Garden and Ely Place, this enchanting little pub dates from the 18th century. The Mitre Tavern was originally built on this site by the Bishop of Ely for his servants. It was later used as a prison and as a Civil War hospital, but its present brand of hospitality is much in contrast. The two characterful bars have a great deal of charm, with darkwood panelling and fine old seating. Patio.

Ye Olde Watling

A 29 Watling Street EC4
MAP 11 D4
01-248 6252
Parking difficult

Landlord Mr D. Firth
Brewery Charrington
Bass; Charrington IPA; Young Bitter; Toby Bitter; Guinness; Carling Black Label; cider.

Just around the corner from the atmospheric church of St Mary Aldermary and on London's oldest street, this richly historic hostelry once furnished the workers on St Paul's with lodging and sustenance. The passing of more than 300 years has made little impression on the evocative ground floor bar which still bears the black beams, leaded windows and arched doorways of that bygone age. The upstairs bar, Wren's Room, has a cosy Victorian feel.
Credit Access, Amex, Diners, Visa

Ye Olde Windmill Inn

B & B South Side, Clapham Common SW4
MAP 11 C6
01-673 4578
Parking ample

Landlord Mr P. Nazer
Brewery Young
Young Bitter, Special, Winter Warmer (winter only), London Lager, Premium; Guinness; cider.

ACCOMMODATION **13 bedrooms £C**
Check-in all day

Once a prominent coaching inn, this sturdy pub by Clapham Common makes a convenient overnight stopping place for motorists. Bedrooms are smartly modern, with neat fitted furniture, colour TVs and tea-makers. One has an en suite bathroom, the rest shower units and washbasins. The spacious bars boast some fine wood panelling and stained glass, and there are two outside drinking areas. *No children overnight. No dogs.*
Credit Access, Visa

AN EGON RONAY'S GUIDE FOR FREE!

Dear Reader,

We need your help please.

EGON RONAY'S GUIDES would like to know more about you.

To enable us to continue to publish the kind of Guides that you enjoy, please fill in this questionnaire. Simply tick the appropriate boxes or write in the spaces provided, and as a token of our appreciation, we will send you a complimentary copy of **Egon Ronay's Guide to Healthy Eating Out**.

Thank you.

Barbara Littlewood
Editor

NB. Your replies will, of course, be treated in the strictest confidence.

1 Where did you obtain your copy of this guide from?

☐

2 Which other guide books, if any, do you own?

☐

☐

3 How do you *prefer* to pay for:

A restaurant meal? ☐

An hotel bill? ☐

4 Which credit or charge cards, if any, do you own?

Access ☐ Visa ☐

American Express ☐ Other ☐

Diners ☐ None ☐

5 Which newspaper do you read most often:

On a weekday? ☐

On a Sunday? ☐

6 Do you own a car phone?

Yes ☐ No ☐

If not, are you considering buying a car phone in the future?

Yes ☐ No ☐

7 Are you:

Under 35 ☐ Male ☐

35 – 54 ☐ Female ☐

55+ ☐

8 What is the total annual income for your household?

Under £5,000 pa. ☐

£ 5,000 – £ 9,999 pa. ☐

£10,000 – £14,999 pa. ☐

£15,000 – £19,999 pa. ☐

£20,000 or over ☐

Name and address

☐

☐

☐

BUSINESS REPLY SERVICE
Licence No. BZ501

2

The Automobile Association
Marketing Research Department
PO Box 50
BASINGSTOKE
Hampshire
RG21 2BR

ENGLAND

AINSWORTH — Duke William Inn

FOOD Well Street, Nr Bolton
MAP 3 C4 *Greater Manchester*
Bolton (0204) 24726
Parking ample

Bar food 12–2 & 7–9.30
No bar food Sat lunch, Mon, Tues & Thurs eves & all Sun

Landlords Basil & Ann Coller-Brown
Brewery Whitbread
■ Whitbread Trophy; Chesters Best Mild, Light; Stella Artois; Heineken; Heldenbrau; cider. *No real ale.*

The atmosphere is intimate and friendly at this homely little pub dating back to 1724. The straightforward menu offers a good choice of food, capably cooked by Ann Coller-Brown and served at the table by pleasant waitresses. You might start with soup of the day, followed by gammon steak or steak and kidney pie. Finish with a delicious crumble. Portions are generous.
Typical prices Chicken & vegetable soup 40p Roast shoulder of lamb £2.75

ALFOLD CROSSWAYS — Napoleon Arms

FOOD Nr Cranleigh
MAP 6 D3 *Surrey*
Loxwood (0403) 752357
Parking ample

Bar food 11.45–1.45 & 6.45–9.45

Landlords Wilf & Mary Forgham
Free house
■ Webster Yorkshire Bitter; Ruddles Rutland Bitter; Fullers London Pride; Carlsberg; cider.

Set back from the A281, with a pretty patio and pond out front, this low, white-painted pub is very much a family affair. The Forghams' son does the cooking, offering an extensive choice of familiar snacks as well as full meals that might start with soup or frogs' legs and move on to, say, chicken chasseur, roast beef or a curry. Traditional Sunday lunch menu available.
Typical prices Smoked mackerel salad £2.40 Vegetable curry £2.70
Credit Access, Amex, Diners, Visa

ALFRISTON — George Inn

B & B High Street, Nr Polegate
MAP 6 E4 *East Sussex*
Alfriston (0323) 870319
Parking difficult

Landlords Terri & Tony Bond
Brewery Phoenix
■ King & Barnes Sussex Bitter; Webster Yorkshire Bitter; Watney Special Mild; Ben Truman; Guinness; Holsten; cider.

***ACCOMMODATION* 8 bedrooms £B**
Check-in all day

Smuggling was once rife in this area and it's easy to imagine this fine old timber-framed inn playing its part. Blackened beams, sturdy wall timbers and a large inglenook fireplace characterise the bar. Upstairs, sloping corridors, low beams and panelling maintain the atmosphere but the simple, well-kept bedrooms, five with en suite bathrooms, have modern comforts like TV and tea/coffee making facilities. Garden. *No children under five overnight. No dogs.*
Credit Access, Amex, Diners, Visa

ALREWAS — George & Dragon

B & B Main Street, Nr Burton upon Trent
MAP 5 B1 *Staffordshire*
Burton upon Trent (0283) 790202
Parking ample

Landlords Ray & Mary Stanbrook
Brewery Marston, Thompson & Evershed
■ Marston Pedigree, Burton Bitter; Guinness; Marston Pilsner Lager; Stella Artois; cider.

***ACCOMMODATION* 16 bedrooms £C**
Check-in all day

A busy, popular inn standing in a village between Lichfield and Burton upon Trent. The accommodation is alongside in the Claymar Motel as well as five new rooms in a recently built extension; all offer private facilities. Accessories include TVs, direct-dial phones, radio-alarms, tea-makers and trouser presses. There's also a garden and a children's play area. Accommodation closed one week Christmas. Children are welcome overnight.
Credit Access, Visa

ALSAGER — Manor House

D B

Audley Road, Nr Stoke-on-Trent
MAP 3 C4 *Cheshire*
Alsager (093 63) 78013
Parking ample

Bar food 12–2 & 7.30–10 (Sun till 10.30)

Landlords Mr & Mrs A. Cottingham
Free house
Tetley Bitter; Ind Coope Burton Ale; Skol; Löwenbräu; Castlemaine XXXX; cider.

Just five miles from the M6 is this impressively refurbished red-brick inn, sensitively combining period character and modern comfort. The spacious lounge bar and smart cocktail bar are attractively beamed and low-ceilinged. Fish and seafood are the menu's specialities, with lemon sole, fillet of plaice and hot seafood platter typical choices. At lunchtimes there's a welcoming cold buffet and other choices – available all day – include soups, pâtés, sandwiches and a daily roast. Finish off with the excellent fruit salad. Traditional Sunday lunch menu.
Typical prices Ploughman's platter £1.85 Prawn sandwiches £2.70

ACCOMMODATION **28 bedrooms £B**
Check-in all day

The top class accommodation at this inn has now been extended with the completion of a new wing comprising 20 bedrooms. All rooms have handsome fitted units, excellent beds and pretty covers, direct-dial phones, tea-makers, and lots of extras. Each has its own well-equipped bath/shower room. Modernised older rooms still feature characterful oak beams. Patio. *No dogs.*

Credit Access, Amex, Diners Visa

ALSWEAR — Butchers Arms

B

Nr South Molton
MAP 9 B1 *Devon*
Bishop's Nympton (076 97) 477
Parking ample

Landlords Peter & Jean Gannon
Free house
Bass; Usher Triple Crown; Flowers Original; Whitbread Best Bitter; Guinness; Tuborg Pilsner; cider.

ACCOMMODATION **3 bedrooms £D**
Check-in restricted

Peter and Jean Gannon offer a warm welcome to their cosy little 18th-century pub on the A373 just south of South Molton. Gleaming brasses and a log fire give a golden glow to the homely lounge bar, while the locals gather in the public bar, which leads into the popular pool room. There's also a skittles alley. The three neat, homely bedrooms are spotless and offer good, simple accommodation; one room has en suite facilities. Garden.

Changes in data may occur in establishments after the Guide goes to press.

Prices should be taken as indications rather than firm quotes.

APPLEBY — Royal Oak Inn

FOOD
B & B

Bongate
MAP 3 C2 *Cumbria*
Appleby (0930) 51463
Parking ample

Bar food 12–2 & 6.30–9, Sun 12–1.30 & 7–9

Landlords Colin & Hilary Cheyne
Free house
McEwan's 70/–; Webster Yorkshire Bitter; Guinness; McEwan's Lager; Beck's Bier; cider.

A most attractive black and white coaching inn; its exterior noteworthy for the delightful dormer windows. Within, the focal point is the welcoming main bar, characterfully decked out with antiques, brassware and oak beams to give a real old world atmosphere. There's also a cosy little snug. Bar food covers a fair span of dishes and the cooking here is honest and enjoyable. Tasty tomato and celery soup and chicken liver pâté are typical starters, and to follow there's a choice of excellent steaks, as well as langoustines in garlic butter and other more adventurous dishes. To finish, you might try the delicious orange fool.
Typical prices Chicken paprika £3.25 Mexican beef tacos £2.95

ACCOMMODATION **7 bedrooms £C**
Check-in all day

Fair-sized bedrooms are simple but attractive – tasteful colour schemes and a selection of good books give a homely feel. All bedrooms have colour TVs and tea-makers, and three have well-equipped bathrooms. There's a pretty residents' lounge and a terrace for summer drinks.

Credit Access, Amex, Diners, Visa

APPLETREEWICK — Craven Arms

A

Burnsall, Nr Skipton
MAP 4 D3 *North Yorkshire*
Burnsall (075 672) 270
Parking ample
Landlords Gordon & Linda Elsworth
Free house
Tetley Bitter; Theakston Best Bitter, Old Peculier; Younger's Scotch; Guinness; Tuborg Gold; cider.

Gordon and Linda Elsworth offer a warm welcome to walkers of this beautiful countryside who stop off in need of refreshment. Situated off the beaten track amongst the rolling hills of this splendid national park, between Burnsall and Bolton Abbey, their 300-year-old pub oozes charm and character, from its slate roof exterior to the huge fireplace that dominates the bar, where polished copper utensils hang jauntily from the beams. There's also a cosy little snug and a garden.

ARMATHWAITE — Duke's Head Hotel

B & B

Front Street, Nr Carlisle
MAP 3 C2 *Cumbria*
Armathwaite (069 92) 226
Parking ample
Landlords Bob & Betty Cuthbert
Brewery Whitbread
Whitbread Castle Eden, Trophy, Best Bitter, Best Mild; Heineken; cider.

ACCOMMODATION **7 bedrooms £D**
Check-in all day

Bob and Betty Cuthbert are the amiable hosts at this modest, pebbledash pub, which stands near an imposing stone bridge over the picturesque river Eden. Simple overnight accommodation is provided in seven traditionally furnished bedrooms which all have candlewick bedspreads, washbasins and tea-makers and share two well-kept public bathrooms. Downstairs, the public and lounge bars have a cosy, mellow appeal and there's a pleasant walled garden for summer drinks.

ASCOT **Stag**

D 63 High Street
MAP 7 C3 *Berkshire*
Ascot (0990) 21622
Parking ample

Bar food 11–2.30 & 5.30–10.30

Landlords Mr & Mrs T. McCarthy
Brewery Friary Meux
Friary Meux Best Bitter; John Bull Bitter; Guinness; Castlemaine XXXX; Skol; cider.

Home-made wholemeal pasta is just one of many good things produced by Ann McCarthy in this friendly pub. Filled jacket potatoes are another popular choice, along with burgers, salads, made-to-order sandwiches and specials like chicken and ham pie. To round off a tasty meal there are homely sweets like apple and cherry crumble. Limited Sunday menu. Pavement tables.
Typical prices Vegetable chilli & brown rice £4 Granary bread & butter pudding £1 **LVs**

ASHBURTON **Exeter Inn**

A West Street
MAP 9 C2 *Devon*
Ashburton (0364) 52013
Parking ample

Landlords Mr & Mrs Billington & Mr & Mrs McNichol
Free house
Bass; Hall & Woodhouse Badger Best; Flowers IPA; Tetley Bitter; Guinness; Carlsberg Export; cider.

Former patrons of this quaint old inn in the centre of town include Francis Drake and Walter Raleigh. The low beamed bar areas with their sturdy rustic furniture and old stone fireplaces provide plenty of old-world atmosphere as the setting for a quiet drink. There's also a very useful children's room, and a pretty walled garden which provides a secluded corner for summer drinking.

ASHBURY **Rose & Crown**

D
B
Nr Swindon
MAP 7 B3 *Oxfordshire*
Ashbury (079 371) 222
Parking ample

Bar food 11–2.30 & 6–11, Sun 12–2 & 7–10.30

Landlord Marcel Klein
Free house
Charrington IPA; Worthington 'E'; Toby Bitter; Stones Bitter; Guinness; Tennent's Extra; Carling Black Label; cider.

About 4 miles from junction 15 of the M4, this whitewashed village pub serves excellent bar food. Alsace-born proprietor-chef Marcel Klein presents a versatile menu, including perhaps a tasty well-seasoned coarse pâté and a succulent baked ham cooked with white wine. Traditional favourites range from steak and kidney pie to sausages with bubble and squeak. Flavoursome, stock-based soups and spicy turkey curry are also very popular. Vegetarian dishes available on request, and there's a roast for Sunday lunchtimes. Vegetables are carefully cooked; puddings slightly disappointing. Drinks can be enjoyed in the comfortable lounge bar or in the noisier public bar-cum-games room which offers plenty of local colour.
Typical prices Turkey & ham pie £2.60 Cotswold hot pot £1.95

ACCOMMODATION **11 bedrooms £C**
Check-in all day

The 11 bedrooms are simply furnished in modern style, with pretty floral fabrics. All have satellite TVs and teamakers. Three nicely kept bathrooms are shared; two rooms have private facilities. Garden and patio.

Credit Access, Amex, Diners, Visa

ASHWELL — Bushel & Strike Inn

FOOD

Mill Street, Nr Baldock
MAP 7 D1 *Hertfordshire*
Ashwell (046 274) 2394
Parking ample

Bar food 12–2 & 7–10

Landlords Sandy & Tony Lynch
Brewery Wells
Wells Eagle Bitter, Bombardier, Silver Special; Guinness; Red Stripe; Talisman; cider.

A fine selection of good-quality bar food is always on offer at the Lynchs' hospitable village pub. As well as the splendid cold table display, there are exciting starters to choose from including fresh paw paw filled with cottage cheese and bacon, with possibly succulent spare ribs or creamy fish pie to follow. Super puds include a yummy banana cake. Garden.
Typical prices Herring roes on toast £2 Fish & bean stew £3.75
Credit Access, Amex, Diners, Visa

ASHWELL — Three Tuns Hotel

FOOD
B & B

High Street
MAP 7 D1 *Hertfordshire*
Ashwell (046 274) 2387
Parking ample

Bar food 12–2 & 6.30–10.30 (Sun 7–10)

Landlord Elizabeth Harris
Brewery Greene King
Greene King Abbot Ale, IPA, Mild; Guinness; Kronenbourg; Harp; cider.

Set in the heart of a pretty little village a mile or so from the A505 Baldock–Royston road, this two-storey, brick built inn with a large garden is very much the hub of Ashwell's social life. The bar is a warm and inviting spot in which to enjoy tasty snacks at both the lunchtime and evening sessions. Consult the blackboard for a daily-changing selection that might typically include fish pie, filled jacket potatoes, home-made soup and some delicious casseroles. There are ploughman's, salads and sandwiches, too, as well as pleasant sweets like apple strudel, plus a traditional roast on Sundays.
Typical prices Lamb hot pot £3.95 Venison pie £4.25

ACCOMMODATION **11 bedrooms £D**
Check-in all day

Prettily decorated bedrooms, including four in a nearby Victorian house with their own shower cubicles, are individually furnished to a high standard, and many feature interesting antiques. All have TVs and tea and coffee makers, and share three carpeted public bathrooms. *No dogs.*

Credit Access, Amex, Diners, Visa

Prices given are as at the time of our research and thus may change.

ASKHAM — Punch Bowl

FOOD
B & B

Penrith
MAP 3 C2 *Cumbria*
Hackthorpe (093 12) 443
Parking ample

Bar food 12–2 & 7–9.30

Landlord Diana Zalk
Brewery Whitbread
Castle Eden; Whitbread Trophy, Mild; Guinness; Heineken; Stella Artois; cider.

The M6 is only ten minutes away, but this 17th-century, sporting inn enjoys a peaceful setting in a delightfully unspoilt village. The bar has lots of character, with beams and a log-burning stove, and it's a great favourite locally. Bar food spans an imaginative range, from subtly spiced curried apple soup and houmus with pitta bread to chicken Kiev, Chinese-style spare ribs and the very tasty minced beef cobbler with its dumpling-type crust. Sandwiches, salads and well-kept English cheeses

are available for lighter bites, and there are some nice puddings such as peach meringue or lemon ice-cream cake. A traditional Sunday lunch menu is also available during the winter.
Typical prices Clam fries £2.95 Steak & kidney pie £2.95 ⊜

ACCOMMODATION **5 bedrooms £D**
Check-in restricted

The five bedrooms, decent-sized doubles or twins, are simply but tidily furnished; all share a well-kept public bathroom, and there's always plenty of hot water. Tea-making facilities are provided. Good housekeeping. Patio.

Credit Access

ASKHAM — Queen's Head Inn

& B

Nr Penrith
MAP 3 C2 *Cumbria*
Hackthorpe (093 12) 225
Parking ample

Landlords John & Anne Askew
Brewery Vaux
Wards Mild, Sheffield Best Bitter; Lorimer's Best Scotch; Vaux Mild; Guinness; Tuborg Pilsner; cider.

ACCOMMODATION **6 bedrooms £C**
Check-in all day

This proud old coaching inn has much to offer, including its own model railway. Enjoy a drink in the distinctive atmosphere of the public bar – overhead beams, oak tables and a fireplace dating back to 1682 – or try out the comfortable lounge bar or homely residents' lounge with TV and video. Bedrooms, delightfully furnished and thickly carpeted, share two nicely-kept bathrooms equipped with shower cubicles. Patio. *No children under seven overnight. No dogs.*

ASKRIGG — King's Arms Hotel

& B

Market Place, Wensleydale
MAP 4 D3 *North Yorkshire*
Wensleydale (0969) 50258
Parking ample

Landlords Mr & Mrs R. Hopwood
Free house
Younger's No 3, Scotch; Newcastle Exhibition; McEwan's 80/-, Tartan Bitter, Lager; cider.

ACCOMMODATION **10 bedrooms £D**
Check-in all day

Askrigg was used as the setting for the television series 'All Creatures Great and Small', and some scenes were filmed in this charming 17th-century coaching inn. The main bar features a huge inglenook and some original saddle hooks, while the panelled lounge bar boasts handsome period furnishings. Bedrooms – with more fine pieces, including several splendid beds – are kept in excellent order, and each has its own en suite bathroom. Courtyard.
Credit Amex, Diners

ASTON CANTLOW — King's Head

A

Bearley Road, Nr Stratford-upon-Avon
MAP 7 A1 *Warwickshire*
Stratford-upon-Avon (078 981) 242
Parking ample

Landlords Mr & Mrs Saunders
Brewery Whitbread/Flowers
Flowers IPA, Original, Best Bitter; Whitbread Best Bitter; Stella Artois; Heineken; cider.

The Saunders offer the warmest of welcomes at this lovely old black and white half-timbered village inn, where Shakespeare's parents held their wedding breakfast in 1557. Fresh flowers decorate the heavily beamed main bar with its wooden settles and original flagstones, and there's a cosy snug next to the large open fireplace. Drinks can also be enjoyed in the garden on sunny days.

ASWARBY — Tally Ho

B & B

Nr Sleaford
Map 6 D1 *Lincolnshire*
Culver Thorpe (052 95) 205
Parking ample

Landlords Rachel & Christopher Davis
Free House
Bateman Best Bitter; Adnams Bitter; Stella Artois; Ayingerbräu; cider.

***ACCOMMODATION* 6 bedrooms £D**
Check-in all day

Delightful owners contribute to the pleasure of the stay in this 200-year-old pub, which lies south of Sleaford alongside the A15. The spacious bar is in the original building, while the former stable block houses the simple and attractive overnight accommodation. The carpeted bedrooms have cane and pine furniture and are smartly kept, and the beamed pair on the top floor are particularly pleasing. All rooms have TVs, tea-makers, and private bath or showers. Garden.

AXMOUTH — Ship Inn

FOOD

Church Street, Nr Seaton
MAP 9C2 *Devon*
Seaton (0297) 21838
Parking ample

Bar food 12–2 & 7.30–9 (till 10 in summer)
No bar food Fri eves in winter
Landlords Jane & Christopher Chapman
Brewery Devenish
Devenish Wessex, Cornish Original; cider.

A small village pub, parts of which date back to the 14th century. Local patrons include fishermen and gamekeepers, who help keep the kitchens supplied; wild duck and pheasant are available in season and fresh fish is always on the menu. Snacks include fried whitebait and mushrooms on toast; evening meal could be honey roast duck or local sole. Good puds, too. Garden.
Typical prices Seafood lasagne £2 Wild duck casserole £4

BAINBRIDGE — Rose & Crown Hotel

B & B

Nr Leyburn
MAP 3 C3 *North Yorkshire*
Wensleydale (0969) 50225
Parking ample

Landlord Penny Thorpe
Free house
Younger's Scotch; John Smith's Bitter, Magnet; McEwan's 80/-; Guinness; Carlsberg.

***ACCOMMODATION* 13 bedrooms £C**
Check-in all day

Dating back to the 15th century, this fine old coaching inn dominates the village green. The Bainbridge horn – traditionally blown to guide lost travellers – is to be found in the panelled entrance hall and a welcoming atmosphere pervades throughout. There's a lounge bar, a cosy snug, a public bar and a residents' lounge. Immaculate bedrooms are prettily furnished; most have private bathrooms – all have tea-makers and TVs. Patio.
Credit Access, Visa

BAMFORD — Rising Sun Hotel

B & B

Hope Road, Hope Valley
MAP 4 D4 *Derbyshire*
Hope Valley (0433) 51323
Parking ample

Landlords Anne Longstaff & Michael Humphries
Free house
Mansfield Bitter, Mild, Marksman, Lager; *No real ale.*

***ACCOMMODATION* 13 bedrooms £B**
Check-in all day

Outside Bamford on the A265, this cheerful half-timbered inn enjoys fine views of the surrounding Peak District. Comfortable bedrooms (including two luxurious mini-suites) are all furnished with deep-pile carpets and pretty fabrics. All offer TVs, tea-makers, radio-alarms and direct-dial telephones. Six have en suite bathrooms, the rest shower cabinets. Beamed and traditional public rooms include a spacious popular main bar. Garden.
Credit Access, Amex, Visa

BANTHAM **Sloop Inn**

&B
Nr Kingsbridge
MAP 9 B3 *Devon*
Kingsbridge (0548) 560489
Parking limited

Landlord Neil Girling
Free house
Usher Best Bitter; Bass; Flowers Best Bitter; Worthington Best Bitter; Guinness; Stella Artois; cider.

ACCOMMODATION **5 bedrooms £D**
Check-in restricted

It's only 300 yards across the dunes to the sea from this appealing 16th-century inn, famous once as a smugglers' base. The several interconnecting bars have a good deal of old-world charm, and one area, with counters made from old rowing boats, has a distinctly nautical feel. Prettily decorated bedrooms, equipped with TVs and tea and coffee making facilities, are kept neat and perfectly shipshape. Four have good, up-to-date en suite bathrooms. Patio.

BARBON **Barbon Inn**

&B
Nr Kirkby Lonsdale
MAP 3 C3 *Cumbria*
Barbon (046 836) 233
Parking ample

Landlord Mr K. Whitlock
Free house
Theakston Best Bitter, Old Peculier; Younger's Scotch; Carlsberg; cider.

ACCOMMODATION **9 bedrooms £C**
Check-in all day

Enjoy a peaceful rural setting amid some superb scenery between the Lakes and the Dales. This old white-washed coaching inn is well cared for throughout; china plates decorate the walls of the homely little bar, which also features a carved settle, and there are chintzy armchairs and gleaming brasses in the comfortable lounge areas. Prettily papered bedrooms (one boasts a four-poster) are all equipped with TVs and tea-makers. Garden
Credit Access, Visa

BARNARD CASTLE **Red Well Inn**

OD
Harmire Road
MAP 4 D2 *Co Durham*
Teesdale (0833) 37002
Parking ample

Bar food 11.45–1.45 & 7–9.30

Landlords Mike & Liz Rudd & Anne & Ken Thompson
Free house
John Smith's Bitter, Tawny Scotch, Magnet; Guinness; Hofmeister; Kronenbourg; cider.

On the B6278 just outside town, the cheerful lounge bar of this family-run pub provides a convivial setting in which to enjoy Mike Rudd's excellent cooking – chicken and asparagus pancake, spare ribs in an orange and cider sauce or deep-fried mushrooms among lighter bites, with main course choices such as pork fillet in a creamy pineapple sauce or trout with almonds.
Typical prices Hot smoked mussels £2.35 Sizzling pepper pot £3.65
Credit Access, Visa

BARTLOW **Three Hills**

OD
Nr Linton
MAP 7 D1 *Cambridgeshire*
Cambridge (0223) 891259
Parking ample

Bar food 12–1.45 & 7–9.30

Landlords Sue & Steve Dixon
Brewery Greene King
Greene King IPA, Abbot Ale; Kronenbourg.

A bright and friendly, well-maintained pub offering a choice of good honest bar snacks including several vegetarian dishes. Enjoyable daily specials such as moist, home-made duck liver pâté or tuna and asparagus quiche top up a regular menu ranging from assorted ploughman's and pizzas to roast chicken, fish and steaks. Banana split, sorbets and sometimes pavlova are among the nice puds on offer. Garden.
Typical prices Seafood pancake £3.40 Steak & red wine pie £3.60

BASSENTHWAITE LAKE — Pheasant Inn

FOOD
B & B

Nr Cockermouth
MAP 3 B2 *Cumbria*
Bassenthwaite Lake (059 681) 234
Parking ample

Bar food 11–1.45
No bar food eves

Landlords Mr & Mrs W.E. Barrington-Wilson
Free house
Theakston Best Bitter; Bass; Guinness; Carlsberg Hof; Danish Light.

Five minutes' walk from Bassenthwaite Lake (and close to the A66) this attractive old whitewashed inn has great character. Three appealing lounges are furnished with fine old sofas and armchairs and the old-fashioned bar is delightfully atmospheric. A simple menu offers soup, quiche and ploughman's, plus lots of tasty bites served with brown bread and butter: salmon mousse, smoked trout or mackerel, Parma ham with melon, smoked chicken, asparagus mayonnaise, and cottage cheese and pineapple salad. Children are welcome in the bar Monday to Saturday.
Typical prices Potted shrimps £2.50 Cumberland sausage platter £2.30

***ACCOMMODATION* 20 bedrooms £A**
Check-in all day

Beds get turned down in the impeccably clean bedrooms, all of which have en suite facilities. Their fresh white decor and plain light carpets set off the pleasing wood furniture and attractively patterned fabrics. Early morning tea and shoe cleaning are offered. Excellent breakfast and good housekeeping. Garden. Accommodation closed two days Christmas. *No dogs.*

BATHAMPTON — George Inn

FOOD

Mill Lane, Bath
MAP 7 A3 *Avon*
Bath (0225) 25079
Parking ample

Bar food 12–2 & 6–9.30 (Sun from 7)

Landlord Walter John Hall
Brewery Courage
Courage Best Bitter, Directors; John Smith's Yorkshire Bitter; Guinness; cider.

Cross the old tollbridge from the A4 to this lovely creeper-clad 15th-century inn alongside the picturesque Kennet and Avon canal. The many lounge areas with their exposed beams and open fires do full justice to the setting, and the food is excellent: home-prepared ham and salt beef for ploughman's or salads, garlic mushrooms, salmon quiche, sautéed lamb, and a really regal queen of puddings. Patio and garden.
Typical prices Beef curry £3.10 Beef in Stilton & red wine sauce £4.20

BEAULIEU — Montagu Arms Hotel

FOOD
B & B

MAP 5 C4 *Hampshire*
Beaulieu (0590) 612324
Parking ample

Bar food 12–2 (Sun till 1.45) & 7.30–9.30
No bar food Sun & Mon eves

Landlord Nicholas Walford
Free house
Wadworth 6X; Usher Best Bitter; Webster Yorkshire Bitter; Guinness; Carlsberg; Holsten Export; cider.

A monks' hostelry before it became a coaching inn, this comfortable creeper-clad hotel is found near the abbey and the National Motor Museum. A tempting range of wholesome home-made fare is offered in the attractively refurbished pub-like bar (now known as The Wine Press at Beaulieu). The hot choice embraces tasty soups, pizzas, meat and vegetable pasties, steaks and filled jacket potatoes, supplemented by hearty blackboard specials like roast lamb and fish pie. Lighter bites include

colourful open sandwiches and salads with cold meats or smoked fish, while strawberry cheesecake and kiwi fruit mousse are typically appealing sweets. Full restaurant menu available.
Typical prices Chicken Kiev £5.25 Smoked salmon & prawn open sandwich £3.25 ⊖

ACCOMMODATION **26 bedrooms £A**
Check-in all day

Inviting bedrooms are furnished in traditional style (some boast four-posters) and all offer TVs, direct-dial phones and well-equipped bathrooms. There's a spacious residents' lounge and amenities include laundry service and a garden.

Credit Access, Amex, Diners, Visa

BEAUWORTH — Milbury's

A Nr Cheriton
MAP 5 C3 *Hampshire*
Bramdean (096 279) 248
Parking ample

Landlords Len & Jan Larden
Free house
Gales HSB; Flowers Original; Wadworth 6X; Wethered Bitter; Guinness; Stella Artois.

An attractive tile-hung pub buried deep in the Hampshire countryside. Dating from approximately 1700, it has been sympathetically restored to its original style, with flagstoned floor, beamed ceilings and an old brick inglenook fireplace. An unusual feature is the huge old treadwheel (designed to be worked by a man) that lowers a bucket into a 300-foot well. The atmosphere is friendly and there are real ales available. Garden.
Credit Access, Diners, Visa

BECKLEY — Abingdon Arms

OD Nr Oxford
MAP 7 B2 *Oxfordshire*
Stanton St John (086 735) 311
Parking ample

Bar food 12.15–2 & 7.15–10
No bar food Sun eve in summer

Landlords Mr & Mrs H. B. Greatbatch
Free house
Wadworth 6X; Hall's Harvest Bitter; John Bull Bitter; Guinness; Löwenbräu; Skol.

This handsome stone pub has comfortable traditional bars and a large, pretty garden. Mrs Greatbatch's cooking is a big attraction, and her summer menu concentrates on tempting cold dishes like prawns créole, poached salmon salad, ploughman's and quiches. Winter brings warming fare like fish soup, sweetbreads, game pie and curry. Gâteaux and tarts for pudding.
Typical prices Roast beef & salad £3.25 Smoked chicken £3.50 ⊖

BEDFORD — Embankment Hotel

B The Embankment
MAP 7 C1 *Bedfordshire*
Bedford (0234) 61332
Parking limited

Landlord Mr Bradnam
Owner Toby Restaurants
Charrington IPA; Worthington Best Bitter; Toby Bitter; Carling Black Label; Tennent's Pilsner, Extra.

ACCOMMODATION **20 bedrooms £B**
Check-in all day

A half-timbered building set at a discreet distance from the bustle of the town centre on a broad stretch of the Ouse. Overnight accommodation is of a high standard. All rooms are spacious and neatly decorated in pleasant contemporary style and equipped with a good range of extras including TVs, telephones, trouser presses and teamakers. Almost all rooms have up-to-date en suite facilities. Children accommodated. *No dogs.*
Credit Access, Amex, Diners, Visa

BEDFORD **Park**

FOOD 98 Kimbolton Road
MAP 7 C1 *Bedfordshire*
Bedford (0234) 54093
Parking ample

Bar food 12–2
No bar food eves & all Sun

Landlords Bob & Janet Broomhall
Owner Charles Wells
Wells Bombardier, Eagle Bitter, Noggin; Guinness; Red Stripe; Kellerbrau; cider.

A little way outside the city centre, this substantial mock-Tudor pub is just the place to come for the perfect ploughman's. Every lunchtime (except Sundays) a wonderful display of more than 30 British cheeses is available to choose from in the handsome beamed bar. Home-made soup and a hot dish such as spaghetti bolognese or chilli con carne are also on offer. Garden.
Typical prices Ploughman's £2.25 Filled jacket potato £1.65
Credit Access, Amex, Diners, Visa

BEER **Anchor Inn**

B & B Fore Street
MAP 9 C2 *Devon*
Seaton (0297) 20386
Parking limited

Landlord David Boalch
Free house
Flowers, IPA; Hall & Woodhouse Badger Best, Tanglefoot; Guinness; Stella Artois; Heineken; cider.

ACCOMMODATION **9 bedrooms £C/D**
Check-in restricted

Some of the bedrooms enjoy fine sea views at this pleasant pub in a small fishing village. Neat, bright and homely, all the rooms offer TVs and tea-makers and five have modern en suite bathrooms. Children are welcome during the lunchtime session in the extensive bar area, and there's a comfortable reception-lounge and a beer garden overlooking the sea. Accommodation closed one week Christmas. *No children under ten overnight. No dogs.*
Credit Access, Visa

BEETHAM **Wheatsheaf Hotel**

B & B Nr Milnthorpe
MAP 3 C3 *Cumbria*
Milnthorpe (044 82) 2123
Parking ample

Landlord Mrs F. Miller
Free house
Thwaites Bitter; Stones Bitter; Younger's Scotch; Bass Mild; Guinness; Carlsberg; cider.

ACCOMMODATION **7 bedrooms £C**
Check-in all day

Black and white gables and leaded windows lend a distinctive air to the Miller family's popular old pub just off the A6. The three beamed bars are splendidly traditional, and residents also have an attractive upstairs TV lounge. Pleasant well-kept bedrooms, with TVs and tea and coffee making facilities, all have their own bathrooms, five of them en suite. Excellent housekeeping and maintenance add to the hospitable charm.
Credit Access, Amex, Diners, Visa

BELFORD **Blue Bell Hotel**

B & B Market Street
MAP 2 D5 *Northumberland*
Belford (066 83) 543
Parking ample

Landlords Carl & Jean Shirley
Free house
Newcastle Exhibition; McEwan's Scotch; Drybrough Scotch, Heavy; Carlsberg; cider. *No real ale.*

ACCOMMODATION **15 bedrooms £B**
Check-in all day

In a charmingly unspoilt country town less than a mile from the A1, this handsome, 18th-century coaching inn has a solid, traditional appeal. The atmospheric main bar is most welcoming, with its copper-hooded hearth; next door the popular public bar offers darts and pool. Comfortable, good-sized bedrooms (one with a four-poster) all have private bathrooms, TVs, tea-makers and radio-alarms. There is also a pleasant lounge. Good housekeeping. Patio.
Credit Access, Amex, Diners, Visa

BELSAY — The Highlander Inn

FOOD

Hygham Dykes
MAP 4 D2 *Northumberland*
Belsay (066 181) 220
Parking ample

Bar food 11.30–2.30 & 6.30–9.30

Landlord Mr S. Carmichael
Brewery Newcastle Brewery
Newcastle Bitter, Exhibition; Younger's No. 3; Guinness; Beck's Bier; McEwan's Lager; cider.

A warm-hearted Geordie atmosphere and appetising food attract the crowds to this converted farmhouse, now an appealing roadside pub with smart cheerful bars and welcoming staff. A handsome cold display featuring cooked meats, pies and salads, is complemented by daily changing dishes such as pork chop normande, soup, sandwiches and home-made sweets.
Typical prices Haggis & neaps £2.20 Chicken with almonds £2.70
Credit Access, Amex, Visa **LVs**

Any person using our name to obtain free hospitality is a fraud.

Proprietors, please inform Egon Ronay's Guides and the police.

BENENDEN — King William IV

FOOD

The Street
MAP 6 E3 *Kent*
Benenden (0580) 240636
Parking ample

Bar food 12–2 & 7.30–9.30
No bar food Mon eve & all Sun

Landlords Nigel & Hilary Douglas
Brewery Shepherd Neame
Shepherd Neame Masterbrew, Hurlimann Sternbrau; Guinness; Shepherd Neame; Steinbock Lager; cider.

A most appealing tile-hung pub with an inglenook fireplace, old beams and fresh flowers in the lounge bar. There are some exotic dishes on offer on the ever-changing menu as well as more standard fare – first course might be Senegalese soup, smoked trout pâté or chilli tacos, while main courses include moussaka and a nicely made fish pie with garlic crumble. Garden.
Typical prices Javanese curry £3.25 Chicken mornay £3.25
Credit Access, Amex, Diners, Visa

BERKELEY ROAD — Prince of Wales Hotel

B & B

Nr Berkeley
MAP 7 A2 *Gloucestershire*
Dursley (0453) 810474
Parking ample

Landlords Mr & Mrs D.K. Taylor
Free house
Wadworth 6X; Marston Pedigree; Ansells Bitter; Gibbs Mew Bishop's Tipple; Guinness; Castlemaine XXXX; cider.

***ACCOMMODATION* 9 bedrooms £C**
Check-in all day

The Taylors offer a warm welcome to their friendly, well-run hotel, which was named at the Prince's own suggestion in about 1870. There's an inviting, traditional lounge bar, a well-used function room and restaurant. The bedrooms are double-glazed, thickly carpeted and furnished in solid contemporary style. All have colour TVs, direct-dial phones and tea and coffee-makers; seven have well-equipped private bathrooms. Garden.
Credit Access, Amex, Diners, Visa

BEWDLEY — Black Boy Hotel

FOOD
B & B

Kidderminster Road
MAP 5 B2 *Hereford & Worcester*
Bewdley (0299) 402119
Parking ample

Bar food 12–2
No bar food eves or Sun

Landlord Mr A.R. Wilson
Free house
Mitchells & Butlers Brew XI, Springfield Bitter; Tennent's Pilsner; Carling Black Label; cider.
No real ale.

An early Georgian town house and a characterful medieval building combine in this fine inn, whose club-like bar is a popular spot at lunchtime when homely snacks are served. Sandwiches, seafood platters and cold meat salads make tasty light bites, while more substantial offerings include fish or cottage pies and rich braised oxtail. Simple sweets and good cheeses to finish. Evening meals and traditional Sunday lunch available in the restaurant.
Typical prices Oxtail casserole £3.25 Fish pie £1.60

ACCOMMODATION **28 bedrooms £C**
Check-in all day

Bedrooms in the Georgian section are very spacious, and some ground-floor rooms open out on to the garden. Fifteen offer well-equipped private facilities, and ten have TVs. Residents can also watch TV in the two lounges, or retire to the peace of the reading-room. Personal service includes an early morning tea-tray complete with newspaper – a most welcome touch, and typical of the old-fashioned service here.

Credit Access, Amex, Visa

Our inspectors never book in the name of Egon Ronay's Guides; they disclose their identity only after paying their bills.

BIBURY — Catherine Wheel

FOOD
B & B

MAP 7 A2 *Gloucestershire*
Bibury (028 574) 250
Parking ample

Bar food 12–2 & 7–10, Sun 12-1.30 & 7–9.30

Landlord Bill May
Brewery Courage
Courage Best Bitter; John Smith's Yorkshire Bitter; Simmonds Bitter; Guinness; Kronenbourg; Hofmeister; cider.

In a charming village setting, this Cotswold-stone inn has considerable period charm with its heavy beams, massive walls and old wooden benches. Log fires warm the cosy bar, and there's a separate room for families as well as a pretty garden. Hearty, traditional snacks range from home-made soup and crusty bread, sandwiches, ploughman's and roast beef salad among lighter bites to more substantial dishes such as local trout or sirloin steak and sausages. The blackboard features daily specials – perhaps liver and onions or a good steak and mushroom pie – and there's favourite bread and butter pudding to finish.
Typical prices Bibury trout with chips & peas £4.20 Bread pudding £1.30

ACCOMMODATION **2 bedrooms £D**
Check-in restricted

The two double-glazed bedrooms have been attractively refurbished and feature duvets and smart white wardrobes, plus remote-control colour TVs. They share a large, well-equipped bathroom which has a separate shower cubicle.

We welcome complaints and bona fide recommendations on the tear-out pages for readers' comments. They are followed up by our professional team. Please also complain to the management instantly.

BIDDENDEN — Three Chimneys

OD

MAP 6 E3 *Kent*
Biddenden (0580) 291472
Parking ample

Bar food 11.30–2 & 6.30–10, Sun 12–1.30 & 7–10

Landlords Mr & Mrs C.F. Sayers
Free house
Adnams Bitter; Harvey Best Bitter; Goacher Maidstone Ale; Fremlins Bitter; Marston Pedigree; Stella Artois; cider.

Beams, an open fire and bare brick walls give this unspoilt pub plenty of character. The blackboard menu offers interesting items such as pear and Stilton tartlet, spinach and pork terrine or carrot and tarragon soup as starters, with rabbit casserole or lamb meatballs as a main course. Good cheeses, and homely sweets like plum crumble or walnut flan. Garden.
Typical prices Chicken breast in cream & artichoke sauce £4.45 Nutty treacle tart £1.35

BIDFORD-ON-AVON — White Lion Hotel

& B

High Street
MAP 7 A1 *Warwickshire*
Stratford-on-Avon (0789) 773309
Parking ample

Landlords Barry & Hilary Coomber
Free house
Everards Old Original; Newcastle Bitter; Samuel Smith's Old Brewery Bitter; McEwan's Export; Tuborg; Heineken; cider.

ACCOMMODATION **15 bedrooms £C**
Check-in all day

Owners Barry & Hilary Coomber personally run this sturdy white-painted hotel, which stands by an old stone bridge on the banks of the Avon. Bedrooms (eight with en suite shower/bathrooms) are of a decent size, with central heating, colour televisions and mainly modern furnishings. The honeymoon suite features a four-poster bed. The cosy bar is a popular place with locals, and there's a riverside terrace and mooring.
Credit Access, Amex

BINFIELD — Stag & Hounds

A

Forest Road
MAP 7 C3 *Berkshire*
Bracknell (0344) 483553
Parking ample

Landlord Mr B. Howard
Brewery Courage
Courage Directors, Best Bitter; Guinness; Miller Lite; Hofmeister; Kronenbourg; cider.

Dating back over 600 years, this historic pub was once a royal hunting lodge and stood right in the heart of Windsor Great Forest: outside remains the stump of the ancient elm that marked the centre of the forest. Low ceilings, open fires and a wealth of blackened beams characterise the five snugs, all of which have a very cosy atmosphere. Gleaming horse brasses and a collection of thimbles decorate the pleasant lounge bar. Garden.
Credit Access

BISHOP WILTON — Fleece Inn

& B

Nr York
MAP 4 E3 *Humberside*
Bishop Wilton (075 96) 251
Parking ample

Landlords Colin & Joan Hague
Free house
Younger's Tartan Bitter; John Smith's Bitter, Old Tom; Tetley Bitter, Mild; Guinness; cider.

ACCOMMODATION **4 bedrooms £D**
Check-in all day

By the village green, this sturdy, redbrick inn is run in friendly, welcoming fashion by Colin and Joan Hague. The four cheerful bedrooms furnished in a variety of styles share a well-kept bathroom and all have cosy duvets and washbasins. Guests can watch TV in the homely, beamed residents' lounge and there's a convivial bar. A carefully cooked breakfast is served in the little dining area. *No children under 12 overnight. No dogs.*

BISHOP'S WALTHAM — White Horse

FOOD

Beeches Hill
MAP 5 C4 *Hampshire*
Bishop's Waltham (048 93) 2532
Parking ample

Bar food 12–2 & 6.30–10
No bar food Mon eve

Landlords Arthur & Carol Noot
Brewery Whitbread
Samuel Whitbread Strong Ale; Flowers Original; Wethered Bitter; Guinness; Stella Artois; cider.

Take the Beeches Hill turning off the B3035 on the edge of town to reach this cheerful little low-beamed inn. Choose the home-cooked rabbit pie, cheese bake or chilli con carne, with roly poly and custard to follow for the really famished. Snackers can opt for various ploughman's with crisp French or granary bread and salads. Garden with children's play area.
Typical prices Home-made Stilton soup £1 Home-made steak & kidney pie £1.95

BLACKPOOL — Grosvenor Hotel

FOOD

Cookson Street
MAP 3 B3 *Lancashire*
Blackpool (0253) 25096
Parking difficult

Bar food 12–2.30
No bar food eves, Sun lunch (except mid summer), also last 2 wks June

Landlord John McKeown
Brewery Bass
Bass, Cask Bitter, Dark Mild; Stones Bitter; Guinness; Carling Black Label; cider.

Portions are generous at the McKeowns' cheerful Victorian pub where the down-to-earth menu is justly popular. Soup, home-smoked fish, burgers, grills and omelettes are supplemented by tempting daily specials such as goulash, beef bourguignon, hot pot, Hawaiian-style pork and a chunky meat and potato pie. Homely sweets include a juicy apple and sultana pie.
Typical prices Lasagne £2 Seasonal fruit pie 60p

We welcome bona fide recommendations or complaints on the tear-out pages for readers' comments.

They are followed up by our professional team but do complain to the management.

BLAKESLEY — Bartholomew Arms

B & B

Nr Towcester
MAP 7 B1 *Northamptonshire*
Blakesley (0327) 860292
Parking ample

Landlord Mr C. E. Hackett
Free house
Marston Pedigree; Newcastle Bitter; McEwan's Export; Guinness; Beck's Bier; Carlsberg Export; cider.

ACCOMMODATION **6 bedrooms £D**
Check-in all day

Only about ten minutes' drive from Silverstone, this friendly pub is a popular pit stop on motor racing weekends, and the village is also a centre for soapbox racing, as shown by photographs in the public bar. The bars are filled with a variety of bric-a-brac, from model ships to firearms. Six well-kept bedrooms with TVs and washbasins are decorated in traditional style with bold floral bedspreads and simple light colour schemes. There's a garden for summer drinking.

BLEDINGTON — King's Head Inn

OD & B

The Green, Nr Kingham
MAP 7 B2 *Oxfordshire*
Kingham (060 871) 365
Parking ample

Bar food 11.45–2 (Sun 12–1.30) & 7–10.15
No bar food Sun eves

Landlords Mr & Mrs M. Royce
Free house
Wadworth 6X; Hook Norton Best Bitter; Hall's Harvest Bitter; Guinness; Löwenbräu; Castlemaine XXXX; cider.

A 15th-century pub in a most delightful setting overlooking a splendid village green with its rambling brook complete with a large number of friendly ducks. The bar has a wealth of old-age charm, with low ceilings, beams and an inglenook fireplace. The bar menu offers a good choice of enjoyable and well-prepared dishes such as vegetable soup, spicy sausages or garlic mushrooms, followed by chicken pie, kidneys bordelaise, tagliatelle with chicken and mushrooms or rabbit casserole. There are sandwiches, too, at lunchtime. Good home-made sweets such as treacle tart. An interesting à la carte restaurant menu is available in the evening.
Typical bar prices Kidneys Bledington £3.25 Aubergine & tomato gratin £2.75

ACCOMMODATION **3 bedrooms £C**
Check-in all day

The cottagy bedrooms have plenty of character, with sloping ceilings, beams, white furniture and pretty fabrics. All have good-sized en suite bathrooms, TVs, tea and coffee-makers and trouser presses. Patio, terrace and garden. *No dogs.*

BLETCHINGLEY — Whyte Hart

& B

High Street
MAP 7 D3 *Surrey*
Godstone (0883) 843231
Parking ample

Landlord Geoff Parsons
Brewery Allied
Ind Coope Burton Ale; Friary Meux Bitter; John Bull Bitter; Guinness; Skol; Löwenbräu; cider.

ACCOMMODATION **9 bedrooms £C**
Check-in restricted

Neatly done out in black and white, this 600-year-old inn stands on the main street. Inside, everything has a delightfully mellow patina, from the well-worn brick floor in the entrance to the traditional furnishings and burnished brass in the bar. Bedrooms have pretty matching curtains and bedcovers; four functionally fitted rooms have en suite facilities; traditionally furnished rooms share two public bathrooms. Tiny TV lounge and garden. *No dogs.*
Credit Access, Amex, Diners, Visa **LVs**

BLICKLING — Buckinghamshire Arms Hotel

& B

Nr Aylsham
MAP 6 F1 *Norfolk*
Aylsham (0263) 732133
Parking ample

Landlord Nigel Elliot
Free house
Adnams Bitter; Greene King Abbot Ale, IPA; Flowers Original; Guinness; Carlsberg Hof; cider.

ACCOMMODATION **3 bedrooms £B**
Check-in all day

Two of the bedrooms at this fine, 17th-century inn have splendid views of nearby Blickling Hall – a dramatic sight when floodlit. Comfortable four-posters add to the period charm of the spacious bedrooms; all rooms have armchairs in which to watch TV, plus tea-makers and mineral water. The shared bathroom is well-kept and boasts an old-fashioned bath. Open fires warm the two friendly bars, one tiny. Garden. Children welcome overnight.
Credit Access, Amex, Diners, Visa

BOOT — Woolpack Inn

B & B Eskdale, Holmbrook
MAP 3 B3 *Cumbria*
Eskdale (094 03) 230
Parking ample

Landlords Fred & Ann Fox & Bernard & Elaine Dickinson
Free house
Younger's Scotch, IPA; Guinness; Carlsberg; Harp; cider.

ACCOMMODATION **7 bedrooms £D**
Check-in all day

A friendly atmosphere is immediately apparent on entering this inn, where the public bar is a popular place for walkers to catch their breath after tackling Hardknott pass. There is also a cosy bar and chintzy lounge for residents. The appealing bedrooms have period-style furniture, electric blankets and tea/coffee making facilities; four have shower cabinets en suite and there's also a neat bathroom. Garden. Children's play area. *No dogs.*
Credit Visa

BOSTON — New England Hotel

B & B Wide Bargate
MAP 6 D1 *Lincolnshire*
Boston (0205) 65255
Parking ample

Landlord Chris Dyson
Free house
John Smith's Bitter, Old Tom; John Courage; Hofmeister.

ACCOMMODATION **25 bedrooms £B**
Check-in all day

Standing proudly in the heart of the town, this red-brick hotel offers a high standard of accommodation – eight rpoms have recently been upgraded. All rooms have smart fitted units and are equipped with direct-dial phones, TVs, radios and plenty of writing space – plus hairdryers, mini-bars and trouser presses in the two executive rooms. Each room also has its own smartly tiled bathroom. Downstairs there's a spacious panelled lounge bar.
Credit Access, Amex, Diners, Visa

BOURTON-ON-THE-HILL — Horse & Groom Inn

B & B Nr Moreton-in-Marsh
MAP 7 A1 *Gloucestershire*
Blockley (0386) 700413
Parking ample

Landlords Mr & Mrs J.L. Aizpuru
Brewery Bass
Bass; Toby Bitter; Worthington Best Bitter; Carling Black Label; cider.

ACCOMMODATION **3 bedrooms £D**
Check-in all day

Colourful hanging flower baskets bedeck the attractive Cotswold stone exterior of this rustic pub. The comfortable stone-walled public and lounge bars are adorned with horsy prints, reflecting the Basque landlord's love of English racing, while upstairs three well-kept bedrooms, equipped with washbasins and with en suite bathrooms, offer a comfortable overnight stay. There is a pretty garden and lovely Cotswold views. *No children under ten overnight. No dogs.*

BOWDON — Griffin Tavern

FOOD Stamford Road, Nr Altrincham
MAP 3 C4 *Cheshire*
061-928 1211
Parking ample

Bar food 12–2.30 & 7–10.30
No bar food Sun & Mon eves

Landlords Tony & June Lee
Owners Chef & Brewer
Wilson Great Northern, Mild; Webster Yorkshire Bitter; Guinness; Carlsberg; cider.

A former church meeting house, this spacious 200-year-old pub is today extremely smart and welcoming. In the open-plan bar there's a lunchtime food counter with a choice of salads based on cold meats, quiche and smoked mackerel, soup and pâté, and hot dishes such as beef stroganoff and Mexican chicken. Grills, too, simple sweets and a traditional Sunday roast. Patio.
Typical prices Steak and kidney pie £2.60 Cheese platter £1.35
Credit Access, Amex, Diners, Visa

BOWLAND BRIDGE — Hare & Hounds

& B

Grange-over-Sands
MAP 3 C3 *Cumbria*
Crosthwaite (044 88) 333
Parking ample

Landlords Peter & Barbara Thompson
Free house
Tetley Bitter, Mild; Guinness; Skol; cider.

***ACCOMMODATION* 9 bedrooms £D**
Check-in all day

Dating back to 1600, this fine old inn enjoys a peaceful valley setting. The spacious, softly lit main bar makes an atmospheric spot for a quiet drink, and prettily decorated bedrooms in the original building also have considerable appeal. They share two modern bathrooms, while remaining rooms – located above the pool room bar – have en suite showers. Colour TVs and tea and coffee making facilities are standard throughout. Garden.

BOX — Chequers Inn

OOD
& B

Market Place
MAP 7 A3 *Wiltshire*
Box (0225) 742383
Parking limited

Bar food 12–2.30 & 7–9.30

Landlords Kenneth & Jackie Martin
Brewery Usher
Usher Founder's Ale, Best Bitter, PA; Webster Yorkshire Bitter; Guinness; Holsten; cider.

Nestling in the market place of a largely unspoilt village, this characterful stone-built pub was around in Cromwell's day and was an important changing post in coaching days. The present landlords couldn't be more charming or hospitable, Kenneth dispensing bonhomie in the bar and Jackie producing snacks to delight one and all. Ploughman's, burgers and lasagne are popular quickies, while other choices might include steak and kidney pie cooked in Guinness, moussaka or a super game pie. Simply prepared trout and a vegetarian special such as courgette and hazelnut bake show a trend towards healthy eating. Sweets range from ice cream to apple flan. Best choice in the evenings.
Typical prices Liver and bacon £2.95 Treacle tart £1.30

***ACCOMMODATION* 1 bedroom £D**
Check-in restricted

Heavy beams and a sloping floor characterise the double bedroom, where floral prints brighten the decor and home comforts include a television and a teamaker. There's a well-kept en suite shower. Terrace. *No dogs.*

Changes in data may occur in establishments after the Guide goes to press. Prices should be taken as indications rather than firm quotes.

BRANSCOMBE **Masons Arms**

FOOD
B & B

Nr Seaton
MAP 9 C2 *Devon*
Branscombe (029 780) 300
Parking ample

Bar food 12–1.45 & 7–9.30

Landlord Mrs J.B. Inglis
Free house
Bass; Hall & Woodhouse Badger Best, Tanglefoot; Guinness; Carlsberg; Tennent's Lager; cider.

A scenic drive through wooded valleys brings you to this charming old creeper-clad inn set amidst attractive terraced gardens. An enormous log-burning fire warms the beamed and slate-floored bar, and provides the heat for the split roasts offered on Thursday lunchtimes throughout the winter. Alternative options range from fresh local fish, Cumberland sausages and tagliatelle in Stilton cream sauce to delicious open sandwiches and ploughman's with locally baked bread. Try the hot apfelstrudel for dessert. Traditional Sunday lunch.
Typical prices Lamb sweetbreads in sour cream sauce £3.20 Seafood platter £3.90

***ACCOMMODATION* 20 bedrooms £C**
Check-in all day

Exposed beams add to the appeal of attractively furnished bedrooms (some in nearby ancient cottages), which include a particularly fine room in the main building with a huge half-tester and swish modern bathroom. Most have private facilities, and the views are delightful. A chaise longue and chesterfields make the residents' lounge particularly inviting.
Credit Access, Visa

BRATTON **The Duke**

B & B

Nr Westbury
MAP 7 A3 *Wiltshire*
Bratton (0380) 830242
Parking ample

Landlords Mick & Justine Considine
Brewery Usher
Usher Founder's Ale, Best Bitter; Webster Yorkshire Bitter; Guinness; Fosters; Carlsberg; cider.

***ACCOMMODATION* 5 bedrooms £C**
Check-in all day

A pleasant village pub on the B3098 with a spacious, comfortable bar and lounge boasting characterful black beams. There is also a peaceful garden and a patio for al fresco drinking. The five good-sized bedrooms (two with a view over the garden) are warm and homely, and have modern fitted units, radio-alarms, TVs and tea-makers. They share two well-kept modern bathrooms. Children are welcome in the bar lunchtime only. *No dogs.*
Credit Access, Amex, Visa

BRAY **Crown Inn**

FOOD

High Street
MAP 7 C3 *Berkshire*
Maidenhead (0628) 36725
Parking ample

Bar food 12.30–2.30
No bar food eves

Landlords Mr H. Whitton & Mr M. Ashcroft
Brewery Courage
Courage Best Bitter; Guinness; Hofmeister; Kronenbourg.

Old-world charm and tasty lunchtime bar snacks prove an irresistible combination at this smart black and white high street pub. Highlights of the changing blackboard menu include pâté, roast lamb, cottage pie and lovely home-made flans like prawn and tomato. Splendid treacle tart for afters. On Saturday filled rolls only, and a barbecue in the garden on Sunday.
Typical prices Cheese & asparagus flan £2.85 Chicken curry £3.25
Credit Access, Amex

BREAGE — Queen's Arms

B & B

Nr Helston
MAP 9 A3 *Cornwall*
Helston (032 65) 73485
Parking ample

Landlords Mr & Mrs V.M. Graves
Brewery Cornish Breweries
Devenish Cornish Original, John Devenish Dry Hop, Falmouth Ale; Guinness; Grünhalle Gold; Heineken; cider.

ACCOMMODATION **2 bedrooms £D**
Check-in all day

The Graveses offer a warm and friendly welcome to their traditional village pub. The two bars decorated with photographs of the Fleet Air Arm, have unfussy furnishings and open fires and are popular with the locals. The bedrooms are small and clean, with simple furniture, washbasins, tea and coffee-makers and TVs, and they share a large, spotlessly clean carpeted bathroom which also has a shower cubicle. Garden. *No children under 14 accommodated overnight. No dogs.*

BREDWARDINE — Red Lion

B & B

MAP 5 A2 *Hereford & Worcester*
Moccas (098 17) 303
Parking ample

Landlord Mr M. Taylor
Free house
Bass; Allbright Bitter; Mitchells & Butlers DPA; Carling Black Label; cider.

ACCOMMODATION **10 bedrooms £C**
Check-in all day

Shooting parties and fishermen swap yarns in the homely lounge and beamed bar of this 17th-century red-brick inn overlooking one of the most beautiful parts of the Wye valley. Main-house bedrooms have old-world charm, but modernists will prefer those in the outbuildings, which have central heating, practical whitewood furniture and modern bathrooms. Garden. Accommodation closed end October–March except for party bookings.
Credit Access, Amex, Diners, Visa

BRENDON — Stag Hunters Hotel

B & B

Nr Lynton
MAP 9 C1 *Devon*
Brendon (05 987) 222
Parking ample

Closed Mon–Fri (Jan–mid Mar)

Landlords John & Margaret Parffrey
Free house
Usher Best, Triple Crown; Golden Hill Exmoor Ale; Webster Yorkshire Bitter; Guinness; Carlsberg; cider.

ACCOMMODATION **21 bedrooms £C**
Check-in all day

Enjoying a lovely setting by the East Lyn River, this sturdy inn provides a good base for guests wishing to explore Lorna Doone country. A log-burning stove warms the beamed lounge bar and there's a spacious public bar plus two lounges for residents' use (one with TV). Simple, spotlessly kept bedrooms all offer tea-makers and seven have neat private facilities. Accommodation closed January–mid March. Garden.
Credit Access, Amex, Diners, Visa

BRERETON GREEN — Bears Head Hotel

B & B

Nr Sandbach
MAP 3 C4 *Cheshire*
Holmes Chapel (0477) 35251
Parking ample

Landlord Mr Tarquini
Free house
Bass; Burtonwood Best Bitter; Guinness; Carlsberg; Carling Black Label; cider.

ACCOMMODATION **24 bedrooms £B**
Check-in all day

A classic 17th-century pub within a few miles of the M6. Gleaming horse brasses, wooden beams, open fires, a haphazard arrangement of little bars and even some wattle and daub cannot fail to please. Fifteen vividly decorated bedrooms are in the main building; they have modern furniture, telephones, radios, TVs, tea/coffee-makers and private facilities. Nine rooms in an annexe, including a honeymoon suite, are similarly equipped. Patio. *No dogs.*
Credit Access, Amex, Diners, Visa

BRIDGNORTH — Falcon Hotel

B & B

St John Street, Lowtown
MAP 5 A2 *Shropshire*
Bridgnorth (074 62) 3134
Parking ample

Landlord Mr A.R. Owen
Brewery Mitchells & Butlers
Mitchells & Butlers Brew XI; Springfield Bitter; Carling Black Label; cider. *No real ale.*

ACCOMMODATION **17 bedrooms £C**
Check-in all day

Close to the bridge over the Severn, this agreeable old coaching inn offers unfussy and comfortable accommodation. Well-kept bedrooms with light, airy colour schemes have practical modern furniture and traditional style fabrics. Three have private facilities and the rest share four public bathrooms; and all have TV. The spacious bar is very cosy, embellished by knick-knacks and pieces of period furniture – just the place for a nightcap.
Credit Access, Amex, Diners, Visa

BRIDGWATER — Admirals Landing

FOOD

Admirals Court, The Docks
MAP 9 C1 *Somerset*
Bridgwater (0278) 422515
Parking ample

Bar food 11–2.15 & 5.30–9
Landlord Mr P. Wood
Free house
Tetley Bitter; Ind Coope Burton Ale, John Bull; Wadworth 6X; Guinness; Skol; cider.

This huge, friendly pub, a converted warehouse with a delightful waterside patio, really draws the lunchtime crowds. Favourites like ham and eggs, chicken with chips, grills and omelettes feature alongside a cold buffet (lunchtime only) and specials like lasagne and good home-made soup – perhaps beef and vegetable. Lighter snacks include crusty filled rolls and jacket potatoes.
No children evenings.
Typical prices Liver & bacon £1.75 Bread & butter pudding 70p

BRIDPORT — Bull Hotel

B & B

34 East Street
MAP 9 C2 *Dorset*
Bridport (0308) 22878
Parking ample

Landlords Terleski family
Free house
Eldridge Pope Royal Oak; Hall & Woodhouse Badger Best; Bass; Palmer BB; John Smith's Yorkshire Bitter; Carlsberg Export.

ACCOMMODATION **16 bedrooms £D**
Check-in all day

Once a posting house on the coach run from Hendon to the South-West, this solidly built hotel in the centre of Bridport continues to provide a convenient overnight stopping place. Half the simply furnished bedrooms have their own bathrooms as well as tea and coffee making facilities and TVs and there's also a residents' lounge. Downstairs, there's a cosy, welcoming bar, a family room and a patio for drinking outdoors in fine weather.
Credit Access, Visa

BRIDPORT — George Hotel

FOOD
B & B

4 South Street
MAP 9 C2 *Dorset*
Bridport (0308) 23187
Parking ample

Bar food 12–2.15 & 6.30–10
No bar food Sun (except eves July & Aug)
Landlord John Mander
Brewery Palmer
Palmer IPA, Best Bitter, Tally Ho; Guinness; Eldridge Pope Faust Pilsner; Shilthorn.

An austere frontage belies the relaxed Bohemian atmosphere inside this delightful pub. A happy blend of tradition and flair give a civilised but unpretentious feel to the two cosy, beamed bars where a range of enjoyable bar snacks is to be had. Light bites include croque-monsieurs, omelettes, toasted sandwiches and smoked fish pâté, while heartier appetites will be satisfied by the day's pie (which might be steak and kidney, pigeon or rabbit), moussaka or goulash. Traditional tarts and puddings,

and excellent quality, well-chosen English cheeses to finish. Children are welcome in the dining room whether eating or not, but not in the saloon bar.
Typical prices Fish & mushroom pie £1.85 Welsh rarebit £1.45 ☺

***ACCOMMODATION* 3 bedrooms £C**
Check-in all day

The modest but comfortable bedrooms are furnished with some wonderfully old-fashioned pieces, with modern additions such as colour TV and a selection of magazines. They share a homely, well-equipped bathroom. Accommodation closed one week Christmas.

BRIGHTLING — **Fullers Arms**

FOOD
Oxley Green, Nr Robertsbridge
MAP 6 E3 *East Sussex*
Brightling (042 482) 212
Parking ample

Bar food 12–2 & 7–10
Closed Mon except Bank Hols

Landlords John & Sheila Mitchell-Sadd
Free house
Fremlins Bitter; Adnams Bitter; Harvey Best Bitter; Guinness; Stella Artois; Heineken; cider.

★ Built in the early 19th century and named after John Fuller, an eccentric local MP and folly builder, this pub is in an attractive setting and a huge open fire warms the patrons in winter months. There is an extensive list of excellent bar food, all prepared on the premises from fresh, wholesome ingredients. There are more than 20 main dishes, among them a range of pies made with wholemeal pastry, including chicken and mushroom and turkey and ham, mouthwateringly cooked; there is vegetable lasagne, quiches and ten vegetable side dishes such as cheesy leek and potato bake and ratatouille. Don't leave without sampling the delicious home-made sweets – four different chocolate puddings are on offer, plus spotted dick and many more. A very good choice of English wines by the glass or bottle, is also on offer. Garden. ★
Typical prices Chicken casserole £3.25 Beef dumpling stew £3.50 Steak & kidney pie £3.50 Blackcurrant & apple crumble £1.25 ☺

BRIGHTON — **Black Lion Hotel**

B&B
London Road, Patcham
TOWN PLAN *East Sussex*
Brighton (0273) 501220
Parking ample

Landlords Mr & Mrs Colin Patey Johns
Brewery Beard
Harvey Best Bitter, XXXX Old Ale, XX Mild; King & Barnes Festive; Flowers Best Bitter; Carlsberg; cider.

***ACCOMMODATION* 15 bedrooms £B**
Check-in all day

A very spruce brick, stone and pebble-dash pub built in the late 19th century, and situated in a village on the A23, a few miles from Brighton. It's a pleasant place for an overnight stop and, with central heating in every room, a warm one. Large colour TVs, radios and telephones are also provided, and only two rooms lack private facilities. There are two plush bars and a big garden with wooden trestle tables and giant play animals for children.
Credit Access, Amex, Diners, Visa **LVs**

BRIGHTON — The Greys

FOOD

105 Southover Street, off Lewes Road
TOWN PLAN *East Sussex*
Brighton (0273) 680734
Parking ample

Bar food 12–2.30 & Sat 7–9
No bar food Sun & all eve except Sat

Landlords Mike Lance & Jackie Fitzgerald
Brewery Whitbread
Flowers Original; Wethered Bitter, Winter Royal; Stella Artois; Guinness; Heineken; cider.

Mike Lance is the jovial front-of-house man at this lively, popular pub, leaving the cooking in the capable hands of Jackie Fitzgerald. Lunches include creamy soups and jacket potatoes, local fish specials such as skate with capers, and appetising vegetarian dishes. Special Saturday night menu, otherwise evening meals by arrangement only.
Typical prices Pasta with tomato, vegetable & yoghurt sauce £2.30 Avocado with smoked chicken £2.25
Credit Visa

BRIGHTWELL BALDWIN — Lord Nelson

FOOD

Nr Watlington
MAP 7 B2 *Oxfordshire*
Watlington (049 161) 2497
Parking ample

Bar food 12–2 & 6.30–10
Closed Mon (except Bank Hols)

Landlords Barry Allen & David & Muriel Gomm
Free house
Brakspear Bitter; Webster Yorkshire Bitter; Carlsberg; Cider.

Good food is a watchword of this pretty, stone-built pub opposite the village church. Sandwiches, steak and kidney pie, chilli con carne and breaded chicken are traditional favourites, or you can start with scampi meunière or seafood pancake, followed perhaps by wiener schnitzel or chicken in prawn and asparagus sauce. Traditional roast for Sunday lunch. Irresistible puds. Patio.
Typical prices Pork Trafalgar £5.95 Raspberry meringue glacé £1.95
Credit Amex, Visa

BRISTOL — Jolly Cobblers

FOOD

20 King Street
TOWN PLAN *Avon*
Bristol (0272) 26872
Parking limited

Bar food 12–2.30
No bar food eves

Landlords C.L. Giorgione & A.B. Jacobs
Free house
Wadworth 6X; Bass; Courage Best Bitter; Theakston Best Bitter; Kronenbourg; Carlsberg.

This old ale house, is opposite the Old Vic and close to Bristol's floating harbour. Crowds flock here at lunchtime for good hearty fare: turkey, steak and kidney pies, Hungarian goulash, chicken curry and a daily roast, as well as cold meat and salads. Vegetables are liberally dispensed and helpings are enormous. The upstairs restaurant provides further choice in the evenings.
Typical prices Lasagne £2.60 Pâté maison £1.80
Credit Access, Amex, Diners, Visa **LVs**

BROAD CHALKE — Queen's Head

B & B

Nr Salisbury
MAP 5 B3 *Wiltshire*
Salisbury (0722) 780344
Parking ample

Landlord Mr B. E. Lott
Free house
Webster Yorkshire Bitter; Wadworth 6X; Ringwood Best Bitter; John Smith's Yorkshire Bitter; Guinness; Hofmeister; cider. *No real ale.*
***ACCOMMODATION* 4 bedrooms £C**
Check-in all day

Set among the peace and beauty of the Chalke Valley, this immaculate little inn has a history that spans six centuries. The main house, containing bars and restaurant, oozes old-world atmosphere with its heavy beams and rough stone walls. Accommodation, in a separate block, is contrastingly modern, and all rooms offer abundant space, warmth and amenities (phones, remote-control TVs, smart private bathrooms, teamakers). Patio. *No dogs.*
Credit Visa

BROADWELL — Fox Inn

OD B

Moreton-in-Marsh
MAP 7 B1 *Gloucestershire*
Cotswold (0451) 30212
Parking ample

Bar food 12–1.45 & 7–8.45
No bar food Tues eve & Sun

Landlords Denis & Debbie Harding
Brewery Donnington
Donnington BB, SBA; Carlsberg; cider.

Denis and Debbie Harding are the charming hosts of this splendidly traditional stone pub on the village green. Beams, flagstones and rough stone create a rustic setting in which to enjoy some tempting cooking. Typical items on the blackboard menus (which change daily) range from home-made soup, pâté or perhaps avocado mousse for starters, to imaginative hot dishes such as roast pork with a peach sauce, seafood in a brandy and tarragon sauce and spicy devilled chicken. Booking is essential in the evenings.

Typical prices Country pigeon & beef casserole £3.75 Lamb Nepalese £3

***ACCOMMODATION* 2 bedrooms £D**
Check-in restricted

The two characterful bedrooms, furnished in a simple traditional style are quiet and comfortable. Homely touches include tea-makers and TVs, and the rooms share a large, well-kept bathroom. Garden. Accommodation closed one week at Christmas and last week January. *No children under 14 overnight. No dogs.*

Credit Access, Visa

Any person using our name to obtain free hospitality is a fraud.

Proprietors, please inform Egon Ronay's Guides and the police.

BROCKTON — Feathers Inn

A

Nr Much Wenlock
MAP 5 A2 *Shropshire*
Brockton (074 636) 202
Parking ample

Landlords Mr & Mrs Robinson
Free house
Holden Black Country Bitter; Mitchells & Butlers Springfield Bitter, Mild; Carlsberg; cider.

Old-world charm is much in evidence at the Robinsons' delightful 14th-century roadside pub in a quiet village setting about four miles from Much Wenlock. A superb inglenook fireplace dominates the bar area, which also features a giant pair of blacksmith's bellows which are used as a drinks table. Also of interest are the many attractive ornaments, pieces of china and gleaming brass and silverware. Patio for outdoor drinking.

BROME — Oaksmere

FOOD
B & B

Nr Eye
MAP 6 F2 *Suffolk*
Eye (0379) 870326
Parking ample

Bar food 12–2 & 7–10

Landlords Mike & Bill Hasted
Free house
Adnams Bitter; Courage Directors, Best Bitter; Guinness; Kronenbourg; Hofmeister; cider.

A long, tree-lined drive leads to this delightful 16th-century country mansion, once a rectory, which has a splendidly characterful bar with ancient beams, log fires and a brick-lined well. Snacks, always available, cover a good range and are well-prepared from fresh ingredients: tasty soups (with good granary bread), pâté, sandwiches and chargrilled steaks, with daily specials like carbonnade of beef and aubergine créole adding a touch of variety. Enjoyable sweets include a good sherry-soaked trifle.
Typical prices Vienna steak £4.25 Chicken & leek pie £3.75

ACCOMMODATION **5 bedrooms £B**
Check-in all day

The five spacious bedrooms are all superbly individual and stylish, with tasteful decor and period furnishings. All have tea-makers, clock-radios and carpeted modern bathrooms (four en suite). Summer breakfasts are served in the vine-shaded Victorian conservatory. There are some 200 acres of parkland featuring some fine topiary.

Credit Access, Amex, Diners, Visa

BROMHAM — Greyhound

FOOD

Nr Chippenham
MAP 7 A3 *Wiltshire*
Bromham (0380) 850249
Parking ample

Bar food 12–2 & 7–10

Landlords George & Morag Todd
Free house
Wadworth 6X, IPA; Flowers Best Bitter; Bass Special; Guinness; Carling Black Label; cider.

Jovial George and Mo Todd impress their infectious brand of humour on this happy village pub whose beams are covered with bric-a-brac. A menu drawing on many cultures ranges from clam fries, taramasalata, shashlik, crab Bombay and chicken Verluccio to sambal udang and saddle of lamb, and there are daily specials – including a vegetarian dish – sandwiches (lunchtime only) and sweets. Garden.
Typical prices Pork 'things' £4 Pavlova £1.80

BROOK — Dog & Pheasant

FOOD

MAP 6 D3 *Surrey*
Wormley (042 879) 3364
Parking ample

Bar food 12–2.15 & 7–10.30, Sun 12–1.45 & 7–10

Landlord John Keary
Brewery Allied Lyons
Ind Coope Burton Ale; Friary Meux Bitter; Benskins Bitter; Tetley Bitter; Castlemaine XXXX; Löwenbräu; cider.

Excellent bar snacks keep business brisk at this friendly old pub on the A286, and the customers regularly spill over from the beamed bars into the garden. Traditional pub grub includes ploughman's and a variety of jacket potatoes. A little more unusual: deep-fried calamari rings with a garlicky mayonnaise dip. Sunday roast lunch and a full dinner menu are also available.
Typical prices Home-made beefburgers & chips £2.25 Shepherd's pie £2.25
Credit Access, Visa

BROOM — Broom Tavern

OD

High Street, Nr Alcester
MAP 7 A1 *Warwickshire*
Stratford-upon-Avon (0789) 773656
Parking ample

Bar food 12–2 & 7–10

Landlords Gienek & Liz Zdanko
Brewery Whitbread
Flowers Original, Best Bitter; Whitbread Best Bitter; Guinness; Heineken; Stella Artois; cider.

The long regular menu and daily specials provide abundant choice at this attractive village pub. Dutch pâté or garlic mushrooms could precede gammon, a seafood platter or chicken in an excellent cream and prawn sauce. French bread sandwiches and salad platters are also popular. Children's portions on some items, and there's a Sunday roast in winter. Garden.
Typical prices Lasagne & Broom salad £3.60 Salmon & prawn pie £4.70
Credit Visa

BUCKLER'S HARD — Master Builder's House Hotel

B

Beaulieu, Brockenhurst
MAP 5 C4 *Hampshire*
Buckler's Hard (059 063) 253
Parking ample

Landlord James Dolan
Brewery Allied Lyons
Ind Coope Burton Ale; Hall's Harvest Bitter; John Bull Bitter; Castlemaine XXXX; Löwenbräu; Skol; cider.

***ACCOMMODATION* 23 bedrooms £C**
Check-in all day

Once the home of master shipbuilder Henry Adams, this 18th-century hotel has grounds extending down to the Beaulieu River. One bar stands right on the waterfront, while those in the original building are heavily beamed and traditional. Accommodation ranges from sturdily furnished rooms with river views in the main house (one has its own bathroom) to cheerfully modern and with showers in the extension. There's a homely residents' lounge. Garden.
Credit Access, Amex, Diners, Visa

BURCOT — Chequers

OD

Mr Abingdon
MAP 7 B2 *Oxfordshire*
Clifton Hampden (086 730) 7771
Parking ample

Bar food 12–2 & 6.30–10
No bar food Sun eve

Landlords Michael & Mary Weeks
Brewery Usher
Usher PA, Founder's Ale; Webster Yorkshire Bitter; Guinness; Carlsberg; Hosten; cider.

A 16th-century thatched pub on the A415 where Michael and Mary Weeks offer charming hospitality and a consistently high standard of cooking. The extensive choice of food covers two blackboards: taramasalata or fennel and tomato savouries, followed by beef and basil lasagne or Tunisian lamb. Finish with Disaster cake or a hot sweet pancake. Garden.
Typical prices Savoury pancakes £2.35 Pork ginger & pineapple £4.80
Credit Access, Visa

We welcome bona fide recommendations or complaints on the tear-out pages for readers' comments.

They are followed up by our professional team but do complain to the management.

BURFORD — Bull Hotel

FOOD
B & B

High Street
MAP 7 B2 *Oxfordshire*
Burford (099 382) 2220
Parking limited
Bar food 12–2 & 7–9.30
Landlords Clive & Edwina Nicholls
Free house
Wadworth 6X, Farmers Glory, IPA; Younger's Tartan; Guinness; Löwenbräu.

Visitors to this exceptionally charming old inn in the town centre can enjoy good bar food in the historic atmosphere of a building nearly 600 years old. The two traditional bars – one pleasantly dim with darkwood panelling, the other lighter and overlooking the high street – are both warmed by log fires. Bar snacks include soup, sandwiches, pâté and ploughman's, as well as hot croissants filled with garlic prawns, while Guinness and vegetable casserole, grills and deep-fried cod feature among hot dishes. Vegetarians are catered for with non-meat burgers and cashew nut roast. Children's menu. Traditional roast Sunday lunch. Terrace.
Typical prices Game pie £4.25 Mussels in cream & garlic £3.45

ACCOMMODATION **14 bedrooms £C**
Check-in all day

The neat and clean bedrooms, two with four-poster beds and magnificent fireplaces, have lots of charm and owners are slowly decorating to improve facilities. All rooms have TVs and decent old-fashioned furniture. Ten have functional en suite bathrooms. There's a huge upstairs residents' lounge.
Credit Access, Amex, Diners, Visa

BURFORD — Inn For All Seasons

B & B

The Barringtons
MAP 7 B2 *Oxfordshire*
Windrush (045 14) 324
Parking ample
Landlords John & Jill Sharp
Free house
Hall & Woodhouse Badger Best; Wadworth 6X; Löwenbräu; Carlsberg; cider.

ACCOMMODATION **9 bedrooms £A**
Check-in all day

Heavy beams, stone walls, original flagstones and open fires characterise the welcoming public areas of this 17th-century coaching inn standing three miles west of Burford on the A40. There's a splendid garden, too, which can be admired from the comfort of the residents' lounge. Cottagy, well-kept bedrooms (front ones are double-glazed) all have TVs, tea-makers and attractive modern bathrooms. *No children under ten overnight. No dogs.*
Credit Access, Amex, Visa

BURNHAM-ON-CROUCH — Ye Olde White Harte Hotel

B & B

The Quay
MAP 6 E3 *Essex*
Maldon (0621) 782106
Parking limited
Landlords Lewis family
Free house
Tolly Cobbold Bitter; Adnams Bitter; McEwan's Export; Stones Bitter; Guinness; Carling Black Label; cider.

ACCOMMODATION **15 bedrooms £D**
Check-in all day

Situated in the centre of town, this 400-year-old free house has its own jetty where visitors can enjoy a pint while watching the yachts in the estuary. A nautical theme runs through the bars, where open fireplaces, old settees and shiny brass, paint a canvas of mellow charm. Homely bedrooms – top ones with sloping ceilings and dormer windows – include seven with private bathrooms. There's also a simple lounge with TV.

BURTON — Plume of Feathers

OD
& B

Nr Chippenham
MAP 7 A3 *Wiltshire*
Badminton (045 421) 251
Parking ample

Bar food 12–2 & 6.45–9.45

Landlords Mr & Mrs P. Bolin
Brewery Usher
Usher Best Bitter, Founder's Ale, Triple Crown; Guinness; Carlsberg; cider.

***ACCOMMODATION* 2 bedrooms £D**
Check-in all day

★ Some surprises are in store at this 16th-century village pub whose traditional appearance belies an unusual and imaginative menu which includes authentic oriental dishes. These are inspired by the Bolins' years in the Far East, where they learned the secret of such delights as the subtle Sinhalese chicken curry served with perfect rice and delicious side dishes, and the Indonesian-style buffet that is a popular feature of Sunday lunchtimes. Meanwhile the less adventurous can feast on home-made soups, ploughman's, seafood lasagne and an honest steak and kidney pie. Bought-in sweets include a splendid sachertorte. ★

Typical prices 10oz sirloin steak £6 Broccoli Marie Rose £2.65 Garlic mushrooms & prawns £3.35 Sweet & sour pork £2.95

Two spacious, pretty bedrooms with practical modern furnishings and restful colour schemes cater for overnight guests. Each has a tiled shower room well supplied with soft towels.

BURTON-UPON-TRENT — Riverside Inn

& B

Riverside Drive, Branston
MAP 5 B1 *Staffordshire*
Burton-upon-Trent (0283) 511234
Parking ample

Landlord Bruce Elliott-Bateman
Brewery Burton Inns Ltd
Marston Pedigree, Burton Bitter; Bass; Löwenbräu; Marston Pilsner Lager; Tennent's Lager; cider.

***ACCOMMODATION* 22 bedrooms £B**
Check-in all day

A beautiful location on the banks of the river Trent is one of the attractions of this pleasant inn, parts of which date from the 16th century. The splendid bar has pink velour seating and beaten copper tables and you can stroll out on to a patio in summer. The bedrooms have fitted units, soft autumnal decor, floral bedcovers with matching curtains, and compact bathrooms. All have teamakers, TVs and telephones. There's also a simple residents' lounge.
Credit Access, Amex, Visa

BURTONWOOD — Fiddle i'th Bag Inn

OD

Alder Lane, Nr Warrington
MAP 3 C4 *Cheshire*
Newton-le-Willows (092 52) 5442
Parking ample

Bar food 11.30–3 & 6.30–10.30

Landlords Don & Jean Roy
Brewery Greenall Whitley
Greenall Whitley Local Bitter, Festival, Mild; Watneys Export Gold; Guinness; Grünhalle; cider.

Reputedly a favourite haunt of local poachers in bygone days, this comfortable, well-maintained pub knows how to cater for hearty appetites. Try the lunchtime cold buffet featuring succulent home-roasted topside of beef, or hot pot served with pastry and red cabbage. For lighter snacks there are nice sandwiches and omelettes. Traditional Sunday lunch. Splendid garden.
Typical prices Steak pie 2.75 Lamb curry £3.55
Credit Access, Amex, Visa

BURWASH — Bell Inn

B & B

High Street
MAP 6 E3 *East Sussex*
Burwash (0435) 882304
Parking ample

Landlords Maureen & Bruce Townend
Brewery Beard
Harvey XXXX, Best Bitter; Fremlins Bitter; Stella Artois; Carlsberg; cider.

ACCOMMODATION **5 bedrooms £D**
Check-in restricted

An attractive inn, dating back to the 17th century. The comfortable bar is cheered by a log fire, and is a meeting point for many locals, with darts and quiz games on the weekly agenda. Accommodation is simple, but comfortable enough, and all bedrooms have washbasins and tea-makers. The shared bathroom is spotless. Low oak beams and sloping floors make the oldest room in the building especially appealing. Nice views from the patio. *No dogs.*
Credit Access, Visa

CALLINGTON — Coachmakers Arms

FOOD
B & B

Newport Square
MAP 9 B2 *Cornwall*
Liskeard (0579) 82567
Parking limited

Bar food 12–1.45 & 7–9.30

Landlords Sandy & Jon Dale
Free house
Bass; Stones Bitter; Worthington Best Bitter, 'E', Mild; Guinness; Tennent's Pilsner; cider.

Sandy and Jon Dale are the amiable hosts at this gleaming white-painted inn, built some 300 years ago when coachbuilding was the leading local industry. The beamed bar with its wooden settles and barrel drinks tables is a pleasant spot to enjoy some sound home cooking – and there's live piano music as an added attraction at weekends. Sandwiches, soup and steaks are all staples, supplemented by daily specials like fresh fish, hearty casseroles and popular pasta dishes, with simple sweets like apple pie to finish. Traditional Sunday lunch menu also available.
Typical prices Chilli con carne £2.25 Lasagne & salad £2.75

ACCOMMODATION **4 bedrooms £C**
Check-in all day

Four neat, centrally heated bedrooms with pine fitted units offer colour TVs, tea-makers and radio-alarms. All have carpeted private facilities (one with bath, the rest showers only) and the largest room boasts its own patio complete with garden furniture.
Credit Access, Visa

Our inspectors never book in the name of Egon Ronay's Guides; they disclose their identity only after paying their bills.

CAMBRIDGE — George Inn

FOOD

MAP 7 A2 *Gloucestershire*
Cambridge (045 389) 270
Parking ample

Bar food 12–2 & 7–10 (Fri & Sat till 10.30)

Landlords Ray & Annette Whiteley
Brewery Whitbread
Flowers Original; Whitbread Best Bitter; Guinness; Heineken; Stella Artois; cider.

A canalside terrace, splendid garden and numerous bars provide ample eating space at this much-modernised inn. Crunchy tuna bake, pâté and devilled kidneys are typical snacks, and for larger appetites, there are omelettes and vegetarian specials, chicken curry, fisherman's pie, and a summer cold table. Children's menu, and playground. Sunday roast available in winter.
Typical prices Garlicky mushrooms £1.75 Chicken breast £4.25
Credit Access, Amex, Diners, Visa

CANTERBURY — NEW ENTRY — Falstaff Hotel

& B

St Dunstan's Street
MAP 6 F3 *Kent*
Canterbury (0227) 462138
Parking ample

Landlord Rolf Walter Steinmetz
Owner Whitbread Hotel & Leisure Services
Flowers Best Bitter; Fremlins Bitter; Whitbread Best Bitter; Stella Artois; Heineken.

***ACCOMMODATION* 24 bedrooms £A**
Check-in all day

Pilgrims were among the early guests at this 15th-century inn just outside the West Gate. Sympathetic modernisation has preserved the old-world charm of the beamed lounge and a magnificently panelled function room; there's also a large, softly-lit bar. Bedrooms, both those in the original building and in a modern extension, have smart darkwood furniture, many useful extras, and good carpeted bathrooms. Two have splendid four-posters. Patio. *No dogs.*
Credit Access, Amex, Diners, Visa

CAREY — Cottage of Content

& B

Hereford
MAP 5 A2 *Hereford & Worcester*
Carey (043 270) 242
Parking ample

Landlords Mike Wainford & Glyn Johns
Free house
Hook Norton Best Bitter; Worthington Best Bitter; Marston Burton Bitter, Pedigree, Pilsner Lager; cider.

***ACCOMMODATION* 3 bedrooms £C**
Check-in restricted

An attractive 500-year-old pub in an idyllic setting by a small humped bridge over a tributary of the river Wye. Inside, the tiny bars have plenty of atmosphere, with dried hops suspended from the beams, open fires and old settles. Three homely bedrooms have attractive old furniture, armchairs and pleasing decor. All have carpeted modern bathrooms (one not en suite), and tea and coffee making facilities. Good maintenance. Terrace.
Credit Access, Visa

CARTHORPE — Fox & Hounds

OOD

Nr Bedale
MAP 4 D3 *North Yorkshire*
Thirsk (0845) 567433
Parking ample

Bar food 12–2 & 7–10
Closed Mon
Landlords Bernadette & Howard Fitzgerald
Free house
Cameron Lion Bitter, Strongarm; Younger's Scotch; Guinness; Cameron Hansa; McEwan's Lager; cider.

A lovely, well-run village pub that's full of character. Fresh, home-cooked fare includes Stilton and onion soup, pâté or fresh mussels; tempting main dishes such as paella, rabbit and Guinness pie and rack of lamb. Desserts include luscious profiteroles or a traditional apple pie, and vegetarian dishes are available on request. There's a roast lunch on Sundays and service is friendly and efficient.
Typical prices Lemon sole £3.95 Barbecued spare ribs £2.25

CARTMEL FELL — Masons Arms

OOD

Strawberry Bank, Nr Grange-over-Sands
MAP 3 C3 *Cumbria*
Crosthwaite (044 88) 486
Parking ample

Bar food 12–1.45 & 6–8.45 (Sun from 7)
Landlord Mrs H. Stevenson
Free house
McEwan's 70/-, 80/-; Jennings Bitter; Guinness; Beck's Bier; Kronenbourg; cider.

Spectacular lakeland views are enjoyed by this converted coach house and the prospect within is attractive too, with beams, flagstones and open fires providing a cosy setting for soup, salads, sandwiches and exotic daily specials such as Italian fennel bake, Russian vegetable pie and blue cheese lasagne. Traditional afters include spotted dick and a gorgeous bread and butter pudding. Terrace.
Typical prices Coachman's casserole £4.50 Fruit crumble £1.20

CASTERTON — Pheasant Inn

B & B Nr Kirkby Lonsdale
MAP 3 C3 *Cumbria*
Kirkby Lonsdale (0468) 71230
Parking ample
Landlord Mr D. Hesmondhalgh
Free house
Thwaites Bitter, Mild; Younger's Scotch; Tuborg; Beck's Bier; cider.
ACCOMMODATION **10 bedrooms £C**
Check-in all day

A pleasant little patio for summer drinking fronts this neat pebbledash pub. On cooler days, the mock-beamed bar with its copper-topped tables and red plush seating makes a cosy alternative. Four of the ten bedrooms are traditionally furnished (one boasts a four-poster), the rest have white fitted units. TVs and teamakers are standard, and all offer smart, modern bathrooms. There's a comfortable lounge for residents' use.

CASTLETON — Castle Hotel

B & B Castle Street
MAP 4 D4 *Derbyshire*
Hope Valley (0433) 20578
Parking ample
Landlord Jose Luis Rodriguez
Brewery Bass North
Stones Bitter; John Smith's Yorkshire Bitter; Guinness; Carling Black Label; Tennent's Pilsner; cider.
ACCOMMODATION **10 bedrooms £B**
Check-in all day

The ruins of Peveril Castle look down on this welcoming old inn with its old blackened beams, uneven flagstones and creaky staircases. Recent extension and refurbishment have provided all rooms with en suite facilities. Furnishings are traditional (some four-posters) and rooms are comfortable and well equipped with direct-dial phones, TVs and videos, tea-makers and mini-bars. There are two pleasant bars and a lounge bar. Patio and garden. *No dogs.*
Credit Access, Amex, Diners, Visa

CASTLETON — Ye Olde Nag's Head

FOOD
B & B Cross Street
MAP 4 D4 *Derbyshire*
Hope Valley (0433) 20248
Parking ample
Bar food 12–2.30 & 7–10.30
Landlords Mr & Mrs G. Walker
Free house
Stones Bitter, Mild; Tennent's Pilsner Extra; Carling Black Label; cider.

Situated in a delightful village at the heart of the Peak District, this well-kept former coaching inn has a friendly, welcoming feel. In the comfortable bar, heated by a cheerful open fire in winter, there's a fair selection of wholesome snacks, from hearty home-made soup and fresh dressed crab to salads, sandwiches on white or rye bread, prawn-stuffed cod, steaks and the joint of the day. Ice creams, sorbets and fresh cream gâteau round things off. Decent reliable cooking with flavours to the fore. There's also a restaurant, and a traditional roast on Sundays.
Typical bar prices Joint of the day & vegetables £3.25 Pâté-filled mushrooms in savoury sauce £2.20

ACCOMMODATION **8 bedrooms £B**
Check-in all day

Housekeeping is immaculate, and bedrooms offer deep-pile carpets and handsome dark-wood reproduction furniture. Direct-dial phones, TVs and tea-makers are standard. All rooms now have en suite bathrooms. Good breakfasts. *No dogs.*

Credit Access, Amex, Diners, Visa

CASTLETON — Moorlands Hotel

& B

Nr Whitby
MAP 4 E2 *North Yorkshire*
Castleton (0287) 60206
Parking ample

Landlords Kenneth & Glynis Gowland
Free house
John Smith's Magnet; Guinness; Hofmeister; cider. *No real ale.*

ACCOMMODATION **10 bedrooms £C**
Check-in all day

Right in the heart of the North Yorkshire Moors, both business people and holidaymakers are well catered for at this small, family-run hotel. There are lovely views from the neat cheerful bedrooms, with pretty floral curtains and practical fitted units and wardrobes. Six have en suite facilities, while the remainder share two well-maintained bathrooms. Downstairs there is a simple yet homely lounge, a small TV room, and a spacious friendly bar. Decent breakfasts.

CAVENDISH — Bull

OOD
& B

High Street
MAP 6 E2 *Suffolk*
Glemsford (0787) 280245
Parking ample

Bar food 12–1.45 & 6–9
No bar food Sun–Wed eves

Landlords Lorna & Mike Sansome
Brewery Adnams
Adnams Old (Oct–Apr), Bitter; Carling Black Label; cider.

Charmingly cosy and welcoming behind its red-brick facade, this homely old pub on the high street offers enjoyable home cooking in its mellow beamed bar. Winter-warming soups like leek, parsley and watercress or chicken and vegetable. Steak and kidney pie and casseroled dishes such as beef bourguignon typify the robust fare on offer, and you can enjoy the delicious home-cooked ham in sandwiches, salads or ploughman's platters. Sweets like apple crumble and treacle and ginger tart have a definite English slant, and there's a traditional Sunday lunch menu also available.

Typical prices Chicken in cream & white wine sauce £3 Lasagne £2.50

ACCOMMODATION **3 bedrooms £D**
Check-in restricted

The three neatly kept bedrooms with beams and simple white furnishings share a bathroom and compact shower room. Residents can watch TV in the ground-floor lounge, and there's a garden and patio for fine-weather drinks. Children are welcome overnight.

Our inspectors never book in the name of Egon Ronay's Guides; they disclose their identity only after paying their bills.

CERNE ABBAS — New Inn

& B

14 Long Street, Dorchester
MAP 9 D2 *Dorset*
Cerne Abbas (030 03) 274
Parking ample

Landlords Brian & Maria Chatham
Brewery Eldridge Pope
Eldridge Pope Royal Oak, Dorset Original IPA, Dorchester Bitter; Faust Pils, Export; cider.

ACCOMMODATION **5 bedrooms £D**
Check-in restricted

This slate-roofed pub built in the 16th century is a comparative newcomer in a village with a thousand years of history. Originally an abbot's home and later a courthouse and coaching inn, it's a friendly, comfortable place. The five bedrooms, all with TVs and tea and coffee making facilities, are neat and simple; they share two public bathrooms full of greenery. There's a cosy, many-nooked bar, along with a family room and an attractive garden.

CHADDLEWORTH — Ibex

FOOD

MAP 7 B3 *Berkshire*
Chaddleworth (048 82) 311
Parking ample

Bar food 12–2 & 7–9.30

Landlord Collin Brown
Brewery Courage
Courage Best Bitter, Directors; Guinness; Hofmeister; cider.

The talk is of horses and racing at this picturesque little village inn in stables and gallops country. Soup can be followed by a steak and kidney pie, grilled trout or lasagne, and for lighter appetites there are roast beef or smoked salmon salads, ploughman's, rolls and freshly made sandwiches. Hungry horses can finish with apple pie or treacle tart. Garden.

Typical prices Ibex meat pie £3.25 Beef in red wine £3.75

CHAGFORD — Globe Inn

B & B

High Street
MAP 9 B2 *Devon*
Chagford (064 73) 3485
Parking ample

Landlords Gerald & Polly Catterall
Free house
Whitbread Best Bitter, Trophy; Bass; Guinness; Skol; Carlsberg; cider.

ACCOMMODATION **4 bedrooms £C**
Check-in all day

The four bedrooms at this 18th-century Dartmoor inn are large and comfortable, with nice views of the church and hills beyond. Furnishings are traditional mixed with pine, and all rooms have TVs and tea-makers (fridge for milk), plus smart modern bathrooms. The lively public bar is home to several darts teams, and there's a lounge bar with horse-racing prints and photos. Hearty breakfasts. *No children under five overnight.*

Credit Access, Visa

CHALE — Clarendon Hotel

B & B

MAP 5 C4 *Isle of Wight*
Isle of Wight (0983) 730431
Parking ample

Landlord John Bradshaw
Free house
Burt Light Bitter; Whitbread Best Bitter, Strong Country; Flowers Original; Guinness; Stella Artois; cider.

ACCOMMODATION **13 bedrooms £C**
Check-in all day

A quiet situation and sweeping coastline views as far as the Needles are among the attractions at this 17th-century coaching inn. There's a quiet reading room and the adjoining pub has plenty of atmosphere, with timbers salvaged from shipwrecks. The pretty bedrooms are individually decorated, some being compact and cottagy while others are more grand, with period furniture. All have colour TVs and tea-making facilities plus nice thoughtful touches; eight have en suite bathrooms.

CHARLBURY — Bell at Charlbury

B & B

Church Street
MAP 7 B2 *Oxfordshire*
Charlbury (0608) 810278
Parking ample

Landlord David Jackson
Free house
Wadworth 6X; Younger's IPA; Guinness; Beck's Bier.

ACCOMMODATION **14 bedrooms £A**
Check-in all day

David Jackson is currently renovating his lovely inn which dates back to 1700. Its cosy flagstoned bar is dominated by a magnificent inglenook, and there's a small residents' bar and spacious first-floor lounge. Nearly all main building bedrooms have now been restyled with pastel shades and good quality fittings, while those in the converted stable have en suite facilities and are in an attractive cottage style. All rooms have phones and TVs. Patio.

Credit Access, Amex, Diners, Visa

CHARLTON VILLAGE **Harrow**

FOOD

142 Charlton Road, Shepperton
MAP 7 C3 *Middlesex*
Sunbury (0932) 783122
Parking limited

Bar food 12–2.30
No bar food eves & Sun

Landlord Mr R. John
Brewery Watney
Ruddles County; Webster Yorkshire Bitter; Ben Truman; Guinness; Carlsberg; Fosters.

Reputedly the oldest inhabited building in Middlesex, this lovely thatched cottage has a lot of charm. It's busy at lunchtime, when crowds throng the beamed bars to enjoy the good food. A blackboard announces familiar favourites like quiche, jacket potatoes, shepherd's pie and a roast. Simple starters and sweets, plus sandwiches (the sole Saturday choice). Garden.
Typical prices Shepherd's pie £2 Chicken & ham pie £2.50 **LVs**

CHEDWORTH **Seven Tuns**

A

Cheltenham
MAP 7 A2 *Gloucestershire*
Fossebridge (028 572) 242
Parking ample

Closed Mon lunch in winter

Landlords Mr & Mrs B. Eacott
Brewery Courage
Courage Directors, Best Bitter; John Smith's Yorkshire Bitter; Guinness; Hofmeister; John Smith's Lager; cider.

In a peaceful village, an idyllic country pub approached along winding, leafy lanes. From its creeper-clad exterior to the two cosy bars, it exudes the rustic charm of nearly 400 years. The cottagy, beamed lounge with its high-backed wooden settles is nicely complemented by a public bar (also used as a family room) hung with scenes of Chedworth's rural past. A games room and a lovely garden with its own stream are added attractions.

CHELSWORTH **Peacock Inn**

B & B

Nr Hadleigh
MAP 6 E2 *Suffolk*
Bildeston (0449) 740758
Parking limited

Landlords Mr Marsh & Mrs Bulgin
Free house
Greene King IPA, Abbot Ale; Mauldon's Bitter; Adnams Bitter; Norwich Bitter; Guinness; Carlsberg; Kronenbourg; cider.

ACCOMMODATION **5 bedrooms £C**
Check-in all day

An idyllic 14th-century inn, popular for its comfortable accommodation (book in advance) and for its real ales. The delightful character of the bar – heavy oak beams, cosy settle seats and giant inglenook fireplace – is reproduced in the cottagy-style bedrooms, all with period dressing tables. Rooms (four with double beds) also have TVs and tea/coffee-makers. One shared bathroom. Garden. Accommodation closed three days Christmas. *No children under ten overnight. No dogs.*

CHENIES **Bedford Arms Thistle Hotel**

FOOD
B & B

Nr Rickmansworth
MAP 7 C2 *Hertfordshire*
Chorleywood (092 78) 3301
Parking ample

Bar food 12.30–2 & 7–10

Landlord Gerard Virlombier
Free house
Younger's No. 3, Scotch, Tartan; McEwan's Export; Guinness; Beck's Bier.

Imaginative and varied snacks are served in the two mellow, traditional bars of this handsome Elizabethan-style roadside hotel. There's a choice of over 30 different sandwiches (including avocado with prawn and tasty hot salt beef on rye with dill pickle, mustard and potato salad), as well as delicious daily specials as diverse as moules marinière and spare ribs, roast guinea fowl and boiled brisket with carrots, dumplings and pease pudding. Simple sweets (chocolate mousse, trifle) and a fine cheeseboard.

Typical prices Soft herring roes on toast £4.20 Sauté of kidneys with rice £4.40

ACCOMMODATION 10 bedrooms £A
Check-in all day

Smartly furnished bedrooms are of a decent size and provided with everything from direct-dial telephones and colour TVs to trouser presses, hairdryers and dressing gowns. All have splendidly fitted bathrooms en suite. There's an invitingly chintzy lounge and a pleasant garden.

Credit Access, Amex, Diners, Visa

CHESTER — Ye Olde King's Head

B

48 Lower Bridge Street
MAP 3 C4 *Cheshire*
Chester (0244) 24855
Parking limited

Landlords Richard & Jane Casson
Brewery Greenall Whitley
Greenall Whitley Original Bitter, Local Bitter; Guinness; Grunhalle Lager, Export Gold; cider.

ACCOMMODATION 8 bedrooms £B
Check-in all day

Built in 1520 as a private home, this half-timbered inn within minutes of the Rows and the river Dee was first licensed in 1717. Major refurbishment has greatly increased its comfort but has not spoilt its period charm. The welcoming, beamed bar is traditional in character. Delightfully cosy, cottagy bedrooms, with black beams and sloping ceilings, have pretty floral colour schemes, teamakers and attractive modern bathrooms (five with shower only). *No dogs.*
Credit Access, Amex, Diners, Visa **LVs**

CHICHESTER — Nags

OD
B

3 St Pancras
MAP 5 C4 *West Sussex*
Chichester (0243) 785823
Parking ample

Bar food 12–2 & 7–9
No bar food Sun eves

Closed 1 Jan & 25, 26 & 30 Dec

Landlord John Speleers
Brewery Whitbread
Strong Country Bitter; Flowers Original; Whitbread Best Bitter; Guinness; Stella Artois; Heineken; cider.

An attractive half-timbered facade graces this town-centre pub. Victorian atmosphere is strong in the oak-panelled bar and there is a high standard of food at the carvery and buffet. Succulent meats, pies, quiches and interesting salads are on offer, while a blackboard menu lists daily specials which might be lasagne, grilled trout and beef bourguignon. Evenings and Sunday lunchtimes bring a hot carvery of roasts and a more exotic special such as guinea fowl or poussin chasseur. Sweets are both tempting and adventurous.
Typical prices Beef curry £2.50
Sherry trifle 80p

ACCOMMODATION 11 bedrooms £C
Check-in restricted

Good quality carpets and handsome woodwork are immediately apparent on entering the extremely comfortable and spacious bedrooms. They are decorated with pretty, coordinating fabrics and all have TVs. Two have shower cubicles, one an en suite bathroom, while the rest share three well-kept public ones. Patio. Accommodation closed 1 January and 25, 26 & 30 December. *No children under eight overnight. No dogs.*

Credit Access, Amex, Diners, Visa **LVs**

CHICKERELL — Turk's Head

B & B

6 East Street, Weymouth
MAP 9 D2 *Dorset*
Weymouth (0305) 783093
Parking ample
Landlords John & Kath Hutchinson
Brewery Devenish
John Devenish; Carlsberg.
ACCOMMODATION **5 bedrooms £C**
Check-in all day

Sensitive modernisation has retained the old-world charm of this 18th-century village hotel near to the coast. The stone-walled, beamed bar combines seafaring and Tudor themes, while there is a popular skittle alley and a patio for al fresco drinkers. Upstairs, the bedrooms are modern, with quality furnishings and decor. All have colour TV, tea/coffee making facilities and up-to-date en suite bathrooms. Good housekeeping throughout.
Credit Access, Amex, Visa

CHIDDINGFOLD — Crown Inn

FOOD
B & B

The Green
MAP 6 D3 *Surrey*
Wormley (042 879) 2255
Parking ample

Bar food 12–2 & 7–9
No bar food Sat & Sun eves
Landlords Mr & Mrs Bosch
Brewery Wiltshire
Adnams Bitter; Brakspear Bitter; Young Special (summer); Carlsberg.

The Crown Inn is one of the oldest recorded pubs in England, having been established in 1383, and its picture-postcard setting on the village green makes its charm irresistible. The oak-beamed bar, with its inglenook fireplace, is an atmospheric room in which to enjoy the simple bar snacks – sandwiches (including home-baked ham), ploughman's, croque-monsieur and a hot dish of the day. The tiny restaurant, dominated by an open-fired grill, offers fixed-price two-course meals every evening except Sunday. Traditional Sunday roast.
Typical prices Stilton & walnut pâté £2.20 Roast beef salad £4.50

ACCOMMODATION **8 bedrooms £B**
Check-in all day

Records show that Edward VI stayed here and it's possible Elizabeth I did, too. Consequently there are two rooms named after the monarchs, with regal four-poster beds and oak beams. The other bedrooms are in a tastefully-built 1950s annexe and have pine furniture and floral wallpaper. All have private bathrooms, TVs, phones and tea-makers. Terrace and garden. *No dogs.*

Credit Access, Amex, Diners, Visa

CHIDDINGFOLD — Swan

FOOD

Petworth Road
MAP 6 D3 *Surrey*
Wormley (042 879) 2073
Parking ample

Bar food 12–2 & 7–10.30
No bar food Sun eve
Landlords Jackie & Neil Bradford
Brewery Friary Meux
Friary Meux Bitter; Tetley Bitter; John Bull Bitter; Guinness; Skol; Löwenbräu; cider.

Neil Bradford is in charge of the cooking at this attractive, tile-hung village pub, offering a wide range of sound, home-cooked fare. Garlicky grilled mussels, steaks, roast chicken and omelettes are all available, as well as more elaborate dishes from the restaurant menu – perhaps venison in red wine, monkfish provençale or asparagus-stuffed chicken breast en croûte. Traditional Sunday lunch menu available.
Typical prices Lamb Kiev en croûte £6.25 Lasagne £2.50

CHIEVELEY — NEW ENTRY — Blue Boar Inn

B North Heath
MAP 7 B3 *Berkshire*
Newbury (0635) 248236
Parking ample

Landlord Mr N. Norton
Free house
John Arkell Bitter; Usher Best Bitter; Morland Best Bitter; Wadworth 6X; Carlsberg; Kronenbourg; cider.

ACCOMMODATION **16 bedrooms £C**
Check-in all day

Oliver Cromwell stayed in this charming 16th-century thatched inn overlooking the Berkshire Downs. Today the main bar still has a warm old-fashioned feel. Bedrooms, including ten brand new additions, are comfortable, plainly furnished and have direct-dial phones, TVs and coffee-makers. All have tidy bathroom/shower units. Older rooms are in a converted stable block and one has a four-poster. Terrace. *No children under five overnight. No dogs.*
Credit Access, Amex, Diners, Visa **LVs**

CHILGROVE — White Horse Inn

ƆD Nr Chichester
MAP 5 C4 *West Sussex*
East Marden (024 359) 219
Parking ample

Bar food 12–2
No bar food eves
Closed Mon, 3 wks Feb & 10 days Oct

Landlords Barry & Dorothea Phillips
Free house
Antelope Ale; Ben Truman; Guinness; Carlsberg.

In a pretty position beneath the South Downs, this handsome old inn offers a short but appealing selection of lunchtime bar fare. In summer there are excellent smoked salmon sandwiches, cold cuts and salads, in winter some tasty hot dishes. There's also a good restaurant (lunchtime and evening) with an outstanding wine cellar. Patio.
Typical prices Prawn salad £3.95
Oxtail traditional style £3.95

CHILHAM — Woolpack

ƆD High Street
B MAP 6 E3 *Kent*
Canterbury (0227) 730208
Parking ample

Bar food 12-2 & 7–10
Landlord John Durcan
Brewery Shepherd Neame
Shepherd Neame Master Brew Bitter; Hurlimann Sternbrau; Guinness; Shepherd Neame Steinbock Lager; cider.

Once inside this former coaching inn you can really sense its 400-year-old history. Hops adorn the oak beamed bar, where a huge inglenook fireplace and pew seating add to the atmosphere. Here, cooked meats served with plentiful vegetables from the adjacent Carvery restaurant can be enjoyed, or you can choose a snack from the blackboard menu. There are ploughman's, plus hot dishes such as beef pie and gammon steak. Round things off with a simple sweet like crème caramel, chocolate fudge cake or fresh fruit salad. Traditional Sunday lunch menu also available.
Typical prices Ploughman's £1.75
Home-made steak & kidney pie £2.50

ACCOMMODATION **17 bedrooms £C**
Check-in all day

Pleasant bedrooms, four of which are located in the recently converted stables and eight more in a separate building, are equipped with TVs and tea-makers, and all have pretty duvets and neat modern furniture; one boasts a four-poster. Most offer private facilities; the three without share two functional public bathrooms. Courtyard.

Credit Access, Amex, Diners, Visa

CHIPPING NORTON — Crown & Cushion

B & B High Street
MAP 7 B1 *Oxfordshire*
Chipping Norton (0608) 2533
Parking ample

Landlord Jim Frazer
Free house
Wadworth 6X, IPA; Donnington Best Bitter; Guinness; Kronenbourg.

ACCOMMODATION **18 bedrooms £C**
Check-in all day

At the centre of a small Cotswold town, this handsome coaching inn dates back to 1497. The facade is a mellow honey colour, and there's a splendid bar with original stone walls and oak beams. Good-sized bedrooms, all very neat and tidy, offer TVs, telephones, tea and coffee making facilities and radio-alarms, plus compact modern bathrooms. The residents' lounge has plenty of inviting armchairs and settees. Patio.
Credit Access, Amex, Diners, Visa

CHIPPING NORTON — Fox Hotel

B & B Market Place
MAP 7 B1 *Oxfordshire*
Chipping Norton (0608) 2658
Parking ample

Landlords John & Eileen Finch
Brewery Hook Norton
Hook Norton Best Bitter, Old Hookey; Flowers Best Bitter; Guinness; Heineken; Carlsberg Hof; cider.

ACCOMMODATION **6 bedrooms £C**
Check-in restricted

Splendidly situated in the market place, this old stone inn combines a number of original features and improvements. The large, very attractive main bar has darkwood panelling and a lovely old fireplace. There is a small drinks bar attached to the restaurant. Two of the bedrooms are good-sized family rooms, and one other has its own bathroom. The remaining rooms are small, but newly decorated and have their own TVs, radio-alarms and tea-makers.
Credit Diners, Visa

CHISLEHAMPTON — NEW ENTRY — Coach & Horses

B & B Nr Oxford
MAP 7 B2 *Oxfordshire*
Stadhampton (0865) 890 255
Parking ample

Landlord Mr McPhilips
Free house
Courage Directors, Best Bitter; John Smith's Bitter; Morland Bitter; Carlsberg; Carling Black Label.

ACCOMMODATION **9 bedrooms £B**
Check-in all day

Excellent accommodation is provided in a modern annexe at this much-modernised 16th-century coaching inn situated in a little village on the B480. The nine centrally heated courtyard rooms open on to an attractive flowery patio and enjoy lovely views of the garden and farmland beyond. All have quality furnishings and floral fabrics, plus tea-makers, TVs – and hairdryers in the stylish en suite bathrooms. High standards of housekeeping throughout.
Credit Access, Amex, Diners, Visa

CHORLEYWOOD — Sportsman Hotel

B & B Station Approach
MAP 7 C2 *Hertfordshire*
Chorleywood (092 78) 5155
Parking ample

Landlord Seamus Morgan
Owners Toby Hotels
Bass; Charrington IPA; Stones Bitter; Carling Black Label; Tennent's Pilsner, Extra; cider.

ACCOMMODATION **18 bedrooms £B**
Check-in all day

Situated across the road from Chorleywood underground, this late 19th-century hotel offers very pleasant overnight accommodation. Eighteen comfortable bedrooms with smart built-in units, tea-makers, TVs, trouser presses and radio-alarms; all have carpeted modern bathrooms. There's a traditional oak-panelled public bar in the basement, while the sunny conservatory bar leads to the patio and garden, the latter incorporating a children's playground.
Credit Access, Amex, Diners, Visa

CHRISTOW — Artichoke Inn

B Village Road, Nr Moretonhampstead
MAP 9 C2 *Devon*
Christow (0647) 52387
Parking ample
Landlords Mike & Sue Fox
Brewery Heavitree
Flowers Original, IPA; Whitbread Best Bitter; Guinness; Heineken, Stella Artois; cider.
***ACCOMMODATION* 3 bedrooms £D**
Check-in all day

Tucked away in a tiny village, this ancient thatched pub has rustic charms such as a fern-fringed stream running past the patio, and flagstoned floors, panelling and an old stone fireplace in its characterful bar. The three cottagy bedrooms are clean and pleasant, with white walls, pretty duvet covers, sloping floors and traditional furniture. All have black and white TVs and tea and coffee-makers. A modern bathroom is shared between them. *No dogs.*

CHURCH ENSTONE — Crown Inn

B MAP 7 B2 *Oxfordshire*
Enstone (060 872) 262
Parking ample
Landlords Mr & Mrs G. Wolfe
Freehouse
Hook Norton Bitter; Flowers Best Bitter, Original, Poacher; Guinness; Heineken; Stella Artois; cider.
***ACCOMMODATION* 5 bedrooms £C**
Check-in restricted

Spotless accommodation is the great strength of this attractive old Cotswold-stone pub in a quiet village two miles from the A34. Bedrooms have pretty furnishings, TVs and tea-makers, and all will soon have new en suite bathrooms. There is a good atmosphere in the handsome bar which boasts the exposed stone walls and flagstones typical of the area. There is also a children's area and a pretty garden.

CHURCHSTOW — Church House Inn

D Nr Kingsbridge
MAP 9 B3 *Devon*
Kingsbridge (0548) 2237
Parking ample
Bar Food 12–1.45 & 6.30–9
Landlord Mr H. Nicholson
Free house
Usher Best Bitter, Founder's Ale; Bass; Worthington Best Bitter; Guinness; Carlsberg; cider.

Benedictine monks were the first inhabitants of this 13th-century stone-walled inn. In its heavily beamed, atmospheric long bar, customers can snack on home-made soup (our turkey and vegetable was full of flavour), sandwiches and ploughman's, or have a hearty meal of cottage pie, devilled chicken, grills, or fresh deep-fried haddock. Ice cream or fruit pies for afters.
Typical prices Fish pie £2.25 Local trout £3.25
Credit Access, Amex, Diners, Visa

CIRENCESTER — Crown

D 17 West Market Place
MAP 7 A2 *Gloucestershire*
Cirencester (0285) 3206
Parking difficult
Bar food 12–2.15 & 6.30–10.15, Sun 12–1.45 & 7.30–10
Landlord Graham Williams
Brewery Courage
Courage Best, Directors; John Smith's Yorkshire Bitter, Lager; Kronenbourg; Miller Lite; cider.

Part of the expanding Slug & Lettuce group, this gleaming white pub attracts a lively crowd with its good atmosphere and good food. A blackboard spells out the wide variety of dishes available, from grilled trout with lemon butter to sirloin steak in mustard sauce and lamb's kidneys Amontillado. Sweets include an indulgent but delicious chocolate and rum mousse. Patio.
Typical prices Ratatouille £2.75 Chicken breast with avocado £5.50
Credit Access, Visa

CLANFIELD — Clanfield Tavern

FOOD
B & B

Nr Witney
MAP 7 B2 *Oxfordshire*
Clanfield (036 781) 223
Parking ample

Bar food 11.30–2 & 6–9.45, Sun 12–2 & 7–9.45
Landlords Keith & Susan Nadin
Free house
Arkell BBB; Hook Norton Best Bitter; Morland Bitter; Carlsberg; cider.

Sturdily built and welcoming, this attractive old stone pub has a fine slate roof, thick walls, heavy beams and well-worn flagstones. Susan Nadin offers a delicious selection of imaginative bar snacks, with specials of the day such as smoked pigeon with pistachios and chicken roulade adding variety to familiar sandwiches, salads and pâtés. There are tasty home-made soups, and vegetables are carefully cooked. Appealing sweets like tangy lemon cheesecake to finish. There's a useful snug where children can sit, and a garden. Traditional Sunday lunch menu.

Typical prices Smoked mussel salad £3.85 Stuffed poussin £4.50

ACCOMMODATION **4 bedrooms £D**
Check-in all day

Climb the steep staircase from the main bar to reach the four homely and impeccably kept bedrooms. Excellent linen and ample duvets cover the comfortable beds, the towels are soft and generously sized and each room has a good supply of books. They share a well-fitted modern bathroom. Start the day with a smashing breakfast served in the pretty beamed dining room.

Credit Visa

CLARE — Bell Hotel

B & B

Market Hill
MAP 7 D1 *Suffolk*
Clare (078 727) 7741
Parking ample

Landlords Brian & Gloria Miles
Free house
Nethergate Bitter; Mauldon Bitter; Adnams Bitter; Younger's Tartan Bitter; Webster Yorkshire Bitter; Ruddles County; cider.

ACCOMMODATION **19 bedrooms £C**
Check-in all day

A half-timbered, 16th-century pub in the town centre with beamed bars, one featuring an aquarium and the other a magnificent carved oak fireplace. Eleven of the bedrooms are in a courtyard block; these are traditionally furnished (four have four-posters) and have tea/coffee-makers and private bathrooms. Two of the rooms in the main building have en suite facilities, while the rest share two neat public bathrooms. Garden.

Credit Access, Amex, Diners, Visa

CLEARWELL — Wyndham Arms

B & B

Nr Coleford
MAP 5 A3 *Gloucestershire*
Dean (0594) 33666
Parking ample

Landlords John & Rosemary Stanford
Free house
Doweswell Old spot; Theakston Best Bitter; Flowers Best Bitter; Guinness; Heineken; Stella Artois; cider.

ACCOMMODATION **5 bedrooms £C**
Check-in all day

Dating back to 1340, this whitewashed inn sits in the middle of a pretty village. Inside, the bar is convivial and characterful, with beams, open stonework and lots of brasses. Good sized bedrooms are well-kept and traditionally decorated, with unfussy fabrics and free-standing pine furniture. All have attractive tiled bathrooms and feature TVs, radio-alarms, tea-makers and other useful extras. There are plans to add a further 12 bedrooms this year. Garden.

Credit Access, Visa **LVs**

CLIFTON HAMPDEN — Barley Mow

B

Nr Abingdon
MAP 7 B2 *Oxfordshire*
Clifton Hampden (086 730) 7847
Parking ample

Landlords Mr and Mrs P. Turner
Owner Westward Hosts
Usher PA, Best Bitter, Founder's Ale; Webster Yorkshire Bitter; Guinness; Carlsberg.

***ACCOMMODATION* 4 bedrooms £C**
Check-in all day

Standing near the Thames in a quiet village, this lovely thatched pub has a history that spans seven centuries. Beams and panelling capture a time long past, and bedrooms, too, have real character, with sloping ceilings and pine furnishings. The four rooms, all with TVs and phones, share two modern bathrooms. The double has an en suite shower. Garden. Accommodation closed 1 week Christmas. *No children under five overnight. No dogs.*
Credit Access, Amex, Diners, Visa **LVs**

CLYST HYDON — Five Bells

D

Nr Cullompton
MAP 9 C2 *Devon*
Plymtree (088 47) 288
Parking ample

Bar food 12–2 & 7–9.30

Landlords Barry & Jill Thorne & Olive Dainty
Free house
Hall & Woodhouse Badger Best; Toby Bitter; Bass; Worthington Best Bitter; Courage Directors; Carlsberg; cider.

Take the B3176 to find this peaceful little thatched pub set in a pretty garden. The simple selection ranges from sandwiches, salads and omelettes, all with super local ham, plus scampi or plaice with chips. You can also choose from the restaurant menu to eat in the convivial bar – including nice homely sweets like Bramley apple crumble. Traditional Sunday lunch menu available.
Typical prices Chicken simla £2.75 Lamb daube £2.75
Credit Visa

COCKWOOD — Anchor Inn

D

Starcross, Nr Exeter
MAP 9 C2 *Devon*
Starcross (0626) 890203
Parking limited

Bar food 12–2 & 7–10, Sun 12–1.45 & 7–9.45

Landlord Mr J.D. Endacott
Brewery Heavitree
Flowers IPA, Original; Eldridge Pope Royal Oak; Guinness; Heineken; Stella Artois; cider.

An inlet of the Dart estuary provides an attractive setting for this well-run, atmospheric pub. Local fish is a feature of the bar menu, with mussels and prawns joined by specials like sole or grilled red mullet. Hot pot and cottage pie for carnivores, and some nice puds (apple crumble, sherry trifle). Traditional Sunday lunch in winter. Terrace.
Typical prices Moules marinière £3.95 Steak & kidney pie £3.25
Credit Access, Visa

COCKWOOD — Ship Inn

D

Nr Exeter
MAP 9 C2 *Devon*
Starcross (0626) 890373
Parking ample

Bar food 12–2 & 7–10.30

Landlords Bert & Shirley Hoyle
Brewery Courage
Courage Directors, Best Bitter, Dark Mild; John Smith's Bitter; Guinness; Hofmeister; Kronenbourg; cider.

A former victualler's house, which would have supplied the provisions for seafarers. Eat in the small bar overlooking the Dart estuary or in the compact restaurant. Seafood is the forte here: try the excellent local crab or lobster salad, cockles or oysters. There is also a choice of steaks, chicken, and ham and eggs. Tasty puddings include apple pie and raspberry meringue. Garden.
Typical prices Bouillabaisse £6.25 Moules marinière £1.95
Credit Access, Amex

COGGESHALL — Woolpack Inn

FOOD
B & B

91 Church Street
MAP 6 E2 *Essex*
Coggeshall (0376) 61235
Parking ample

Bar food 12–2 & 7–10
No bar food Sun eve

Landlords Bill & Judith Hutchinson
Brewery Ind Coope
Ind Coope Bitter; Taylor Walker Bitter; Löwenbräu; Skol; cider.

Standing beside the church at the eastern end of historic Coggeshall, this delightful timbered inn dates back to the 15th century. Oak beams, heavy panelling and lovely lattice windows characterise the cosy bars, and there's an atmospheric little restaurant where imaginative and carefully prepared bar snacks can be enjoyed. Flavoursome home-made soups served with garlic bread, pâté and perfectly cooked mushroom omelette are typical light bites, while for something more substantial, there are fresh fish dishes and home-made savoury pies. Leave room for a pleasant sweet like Dutch pear and apple flan.

Typical prices Dover sole £2.95 Chicken & leek pie £2.95

***ACCOMMODATION* 2 bedrooms £D**
Check-in restricted

Upstairs, the larger of the two homely, well-kept bedrooms features beams and sturdily traditional furniture. Both have characterful brass beds, and they share an attractive modern bathroom. Garden. Children under 14 not accommodated overnight. No dogs.

Prices given are as at the time of our research and thus may change.

COLEFORD — Speech House Hotel

B & B

Forest of Dean
MAP 5 A2 *Gloucestershire*
Dean (0594) 22607
Parking ample

Landlord Mr R. Jones
Free house
Bass; Worthington 'E'; Flowers Best Bitter; Ben Truman; Webster Yorkshire Bitter; Carlsberg.

***ACCOMMODATION* 14 bedrooms £A**
Check-in all day

Comfortable accommodation deep in the heart of the Forest of Dean is offered at this 17th-century hunting lodge next to the B4226. The three best bedrooms have intricately carved, antique four-posters, whose period character is echoed in the attractively furnished beamed bars and restaurant. Other bedrooms (three with en suite facilities) are more traditionally styled. All have direct-dial phones, TVs and tea/coffee makers. Garden.

Credit Access, Amex, Diners, Visa **LVs**

COLESBOURNE — Colesbourne Inn

FOOD

Nr Cheltenham
MAP 7 A2 *Gloucestershire*
Coberley (024 287) 376
Parking ample

Bar food 12–2.15 & 6.30–10 (Sun from 7)
Closed Sun lunch

Landlord Eric Bird
Brewery Wadworth
Wadworth 6X, IPA, Farmer's Glory, Old Timer (winter only), Northgate; Guinness; Heineken.

Enjoyable, down-to-earth cooking is served at this listed 17th-century coaching inn. Light snacks range from ploughman's and sandwiches to soup and jacket potatoes, with sizzling platter steaks and a daily blackboard special such as chilli con carne or Cotswold sausages for heartier appetites. Plum crumble to finish. Cold buffet summer lunchtimes. Garden.

Typical prices Fish pie £3.10 Fruit crumble £1.25

Credit Access, Amex, Diners, Visa

COLESHILL — Coleshill Hotel

B 152 High Street
Map 5 B2 *Warwickshire*
Coleshill (0675) 65527
Parking ample

Landlord Stephen Kimbell
Owner Whitbread Coaching Inns
Flowers Best Bitter; Whitbread Best Bitter; Best Mild; Stella Artois; Heineken. *No real ale.*

ACCOMMODATION **15 bedrooms £B**
Check-in all day

The nearby M6 and National Exhibition Centre bring businessmen and visitors to this smart, extremely well-kept, high-street hotel. Quality fitted units and traditional fabrics are used in the bedrooms, which are equipped with many thoughtful extras, from trouser presses and hairdryers to mineral water. Two boast four-posters, and all have attractive tiled bathrooms. The two bars include a basement one with a lively atmosphere. *No dogs.*
Credit Access, Amex, Diners, Visa

COLESHILL — Swan Hotel

B High Street
MAP 5 B2 *Warwickshire*
Coleshill (0675) 64107
Parking ample

Landlords Mr S.A. Narey & Miss V.B. Wright
Brewery Ansells
Tetley Bitter; Ansells Bitter, Mild; Guinness; Castlemaine XXXX; cider.

ACCOMMODATION **32 bedrooms £B**
Check-in all day

Handy for the National Exhibition Centre and the motorways, this modernised 17th-century inn is a popular place with businessmen and motorists. The beamed main bar has a pleasantly rustic feel, and there's another smaller bar. Bedrooms are of a good standard, with modern fitted units, TVs, telephones, hairdryers and trouser presses; all have functional private facilities (showers for annexe rooms). Children welcome overnight. *No dogs.*
Credit Access, Amex, Diners, Visa

COLLYWESTON — Cavalier Inn

B Nr Stamford
MAP 6 D1 *Northamptonshire*
Duddington (078 083) 288
Parking ample

Landlords Noel & Andrew Heigh
Free house
Greene KIng IPA; Ruddles Rutland Bitter, County; Elgood Bitter; Guinness; Fosters; cider.

ACCOMMODATION **7 bedrooms £C**
Check-in restricted

A warm welcome can be guaranteed at this friendly roadside inn. The spacious bars, on three levels, are well-kept, with plenty of plants and flowers and a large open fire. The pub also has its own life-size, model cavalier perched on a barrel in the cellar, which can be seen from the bar. Comfortable, centrally heated bedrooms are unfussy, with well co-ordinated light colour schemes. Terrace. Accommodation closed one week Christmas. *No dogs.*
Credit Access, Diners, Visa

COLN ST ALDWYNS — New Inn

B Nr Cirencester
MAP 7 A2 *Gloucestershire*
Coln St Aldwyns (028 575) 202
Parking limited

Landlord Mr R. Warren
Free house
Morland Viking Pale; Wadworth 6X; Mitchells & Butlers Brew XI; Guinness; Carling Black Label; cider.

ACCOMMODATION **5 bedrooms £C**
Check-in restricted

Much of the original character survives at this 16th-century, village inn, both in the lively public bar and in the lounge bar with its flagstones, beams and huge inglenooks. A narrow winding staircase climbs to the two main-house bedrooms, which share a bathroom. In the cottage annexe are three more modern rooms, with en suite facilities, plus a TV lounge; two self-catering apartments are housed in a converted stable block. Garden and patio. *No dogs.*
Credit Visa

CONGLETON — Lion & Swan Hotel

FOOD
B & B

Swan Bank
MAP 3 C4 *Cheshire*
Congleton (0260) 273115
Parking ample

Bar food 12–2 & 7–9

Landlords Peter & Janet Hudson
Free house
Burtonwood Best Bitter; Marston Pedigree; Burton Bitter; Guinness; Heineken; Stella Artois; cider.

Owners Peter and Janet Hudson are keeping up the high standards associated with this handsome timbered coaching inn, which dates back to the 16th century. The bars exude character and charm, from the cosy little tap room and relaxing cocktail bar to the split-level lounge bar where a tempting lunchtime cold table offers roast meats, salmon mayonnaise, smoked trout and decent fresh salads. Other choices, available both lunchtime and evening, include soup, sandwiches, sirloin steak and grilled fillet of plaice, plus pleasant sweets such as sherry trifle or apple pie. Traditional Sunday lunch menu.
Typical prices Poached sole mornay £2.95 Grilled sirloin steak £5.25

ACCOMMODATION **13 bedrooms £C**
Check-in all day

Bedrooms are smart, comfortable and well appointed. A couple boast fine Jacobean furnishings, while the rest have whitewood pieces; TVs, tea-makers and direct-dial telephones in all rooms, private facilities in ten. There's an inviting beamed resident's lounge and a garden. Accommodation closed one week at Christmas.

Credit Access, Amex, Diners, Visa

CONISTON — NEW ENTRY — Yewdale Hotel

B & B

Yewdale Road
MAP 3 B3 *Cumbria*
Coniston (053 94) 41280
Parking ample

Closed weekday lunches Jan–Feb
Landlords Ken & Barbara Barron
Free house
Hartley XB, Bitter; Tetley Bitter; Guinness; Whitbread Best Mild; Heineken; cider.
ACCOMMODATION **10 bedrooms £D**
Check-in all day

Cumbrian stone and slate went into the building of this solid 19th-century hotel. Originally it housed a bank, and the oak counter still remains in the bar. The newly-completed top floor bedrooms have pink or green themes, with pretty fabrics and carpets; older rooms are spacious, with floral fabrics. All have tea-making facilities and TVs. Many bathrooms are new, with smart tiled showers. Patio. Children are welcome overnight.
Credit Access, Visa

CONSTABLE BURTON — Wyvill Arms

FOOD

Nr Leyburn
MAP 4 D3 *North Yorkshire*
Bedale (0677) 50581
Parking ample

Bar food 12–2 & 7–9.30

Landlord Peter Ingham
Free house
Theakston Best Bitter, XB; John Smith's Bitter, Magnet; Hofmeister; Carlsberg Hof; cider.

Once a farmhouse, this friendly pub enjoys a peaceful country setting. Baguette sandwiches are a favourite light bite, other choices include soup, lasagne, deep-fried cod, and roast pork with crispy crackling and a decent stuffing. To finish, there are gâteaux, ices, fresh fruit salad and good cheeses. Traditional Sunday lunch menu. Patio.
Typical prices Lasagne £2.90 Steak & mushroom pie £2.80
Credit Access

CORSHAM — Methuen Arms Hotel

B High Street
MAP 7 A3 *Wiltshire*
Corsham (0249) 714867
Parking ample

Landlords Mike, Morwenna & Mark Long
Brewery Gibbs Mew
Gibbs Mew Wiltshire, Salisbury Best, Bishop's Tipple; Bass; Wethered SPA; Kronenbourg; cider.

***ACCOMMODATION* 24 bedrooms £B**
Check-in all day

The Georgian facade of this fine old inn masks 15th-century origins, and inside has benefited from extensive restoration. The smart lounge bar is in Laura Ashley style, while splendid beams and stone walls dominate the ancient Long Bar. Bedrooms range from simple beamed rooms to six luxurious rooms in a smart modern style. All have direct-dial telephones and TVs, and most have private bathrooms. Walled garden.
Credit Access, Visa

Changes in data may occur in establishments after the Guide goes to press. Prices should be taken as indications rather than firm quotes.

CORTON — Dove at Corton

D Nr Warminster
MAP 5 B3 *Wiltshire*
Warminster (0985) 50378
Parking limited

Bar food 12–2 (Sun till 1.45) & 7–9.30
Closed Sun eve, Mon (except Bank Hols) & 2 wks Jan

Landlords Jane & Michael Rowse
Brewery Usher
Usher Best Bitter; Webster Yorkshire Bitter; Carlsberg.

True to its name, this charming Victorian pub still has attendant doves. An extensive menu encompasses splendid home-made soups, salmon and prawn pâté, smoked beef; main dishes such as fish curry, and a popular salmon mayonnaise in summer; excellent English cheeses and delicious sweets, plus a vegetarian menu with items like nutty fruity pilaf. Garden.
Typical prices Garlic bread with prawns £2.50 Tipsy cake £1.75
Credit Access, Visa

COUSLEY WOOD — Old Vine

D Nr Wadhurst
MAP 6 E3 *East Sussex*
Wadhurst (089 288) 2271
Parking ample

Bar food 12–2 & 6.45–9.15
No bar food Sun eve

Landlords Tony & Jenny Peel
Brewery Whitbread
Flowers Original; Fremlins Bitter; Whitbread Best Bitter, Poacher; Guinness; Heineken; cider.

A white-painted clapboard pub dating back to the reign of Henry VIII. Decent home-made food is on offer in the cosy bar; you might start with garlic mushrooms or smoked mackerel pâté, and then choose steak and kidney pie, peppered chicken breast or chicken curry, Straightforward desserts include Black Forest gâteau and sherry trifle. Garden.
Typical prices Soft roes on toast £1.20 Pork loin in barbecue sauce £3.25
Credit Access, Diners, Visa

COXWOLD — Fauconberg Arms

FOOD
B & B

MAP 4 D3 *North Yorkshire*
Coxwold (034 76) 214
Parking ample

Bar food 12–2.30
No bar food eves

Landlords Mr & Mrs Goodall
Free house
Younger's Scotch Bitter; Theakston Best; Tetley Bitter; Guinness; Carlsberg, Hof.

The rows of bright, gleaming brass and copper ornaments and the well arranged fresh flowers give a hint of the landlords' scrupulous attention to every detail at this immaculate, old-established 17th-century village pub. Old beams, the splendid stone fireplace and a stone-flagged floor all add to the character and charm. Simple fare is the order of the day: freshly made soup such as tomato or flavoursome onion and Stilton and an excellent choice of sandwiches – turkey, ham, tuna, cheese and the Fauconberg Special: cottage cheese, raisins, apple, celery and nuts in wholemeal bread. There's also an interesting restaurant menu.
Typical prices Vegetable soup £1 Fauconberg Special £1.25

ACCOMMODATION **4 bedrooms £C**
Check-in all day

The four bedrooms show the same high standard of care and attention, with many homely touches (pot pourri, fresh flowers) to welcome the overnight guest. All rooms – one with shower – share a pretty, modern bathroom, and are decorated with floral fabrics and matching wallpapers. *No dogs.*

CRANBORNE — Fleur-de-Lys

B & B

5 Wimborne Street
MAP 5 B4 *Dorset*
Cranborne (072 54) 282
Parking ample

Landlord Mr C.T. Hancock
Brewery Hall & Woodhouse
Hall & Woodhouse Badger Best, Tanglefoot; Worthington 'E'; Guinness; Stella Artois; Carlsberg Hof; cider.

ACCOMMODATION **8 bedrooms £D**
Check-in all day

A characterful building which has been operating as an inn since the 1600s, although parts date back to the 11th century. The attractive bars have exposed beams and brick, bench seating, old fireplaces and corn dollies on the walls. Modest but comfortable bedrooms have functional furniture, TVs and tea-makers; half have baths, the remainder have showers and share two public bathrooms. Garden. Accommodation closed one week Christmas.
Credit Access, Amex, Diners, Visa

CRAWLEY — Fox & Hounds

FOOD

Nr Winchester
MAP 5 C3 *Hampshire*
Sparsholt (096 272) 285
Parking ample

Bar food 12–2 & 6.30–9.30

Landlords Janet & Alan Silsbury
Free house
Gales Best Bitter; Wadworth 6X; Flowers Original; McEwan's Export; Guinness; Stella Artois; cider.

A friendly red-brick pub off the A272 where Janet Silsbury's fine cooking attracts local and passing trade alike. Try the steaks, gammon or cod provençale, or go for a daily special such as tortilla quiche or bacon risotto. Freshly made sandwiches and ploughman's lunch are always on offer. Nice puddings. Limited choice Saturday and Sunday lunchtimes. Patio.
Typical prices Sparsholt smokie £2.15 Buttery garlic chicken £3.80
Credit Amex, Visa

CRAZIES HILL — Horns

)D Nr Wargrave
MAP 7 C3 *Berkshire*
Wargrave (073 522) 3226
Parking ample

Bar food 12.15–2 (Sun 12.30–1.30) & 7–9
No bar food Sun & Mon eves
Landlords Mr & Mrs A. Wheeler
Brewery Brakspear
Brakspear PA, Special; Stella Artois.

Thai and Malaysian dishes are a popular feature of the daily menu at this black and white country pub. Mrs Wheeler's flavoursome touch also extends to moussaka à la grecque, carbonnade of beef, lasagne and a tasty, tender chicken basquaise, while her home-made sweets – such as a superb rhubarb, orange and apple crumble – are not to be missed. Garden.
Typical prices Thai fried rice £1.95 Lasagne verde £2.50

CROSCOMBE — Bull Terrier

B Wells
MAP 9 D1 *Somerset*
Shepton Mallet (0749) 3658
Parking limited

Closed Mon lunch (Nov–Mar)

Landlords Stan & Pam Lea
Free house
Butcombe; Royal Oak; Palmer IPA; Guinness; Stella Artois; cider.
ACCOMMODATION **3 bedrooms £D**
Check-in restricted

This village inn of great character, its oldest part dating from the 15th century, was first granted a licence to sell ale in 1612. The bars abound in rustic charm, and a steep flight of stairs climbs to the bedrooms. The double is tastefully traditional, with spotless en suite bathroom; the other two rooms are in similar style and share a bathroom. Accommodation closed Sunday and Monday November–March. *No children overnight. No dogs.*
Credit Access

CROYDE — Thatched Barn Inn

B Hobbs Hill, Braunton
MAP 9 B1 *Devon*
Croyde (0271) 890349
Parking limited

Landlords Mr T. Pickersgill & Miss E. Barough
Free house
Courage Best Bitter, Directors; John Smith's Yorkshire Bitter; Guinness; Kronenbourg; cider.
ACCOMMODATION **6 bedrooms £D**
Check-in restricted

A 400-year-old thatched barn once used for storage by the monks of nearby St Helen's priory. Its conversion has not spoilt its character, and the spacious bars feature plenty of beams and bare stone walls. The modest bedrooms, some of which have beams and sloping floors, have pretty duvet covers and curtains and provide simple comforts for an overnight stay. Most have TVs. There's a pretty flagstoned patio and a garden at the back for fine weather.
Credit Access, Visa

CROYDON — Windsor Castle

B 415 Brighton Road
MAP 7 D3 *Surrey*
01-680 4559
Parking ample

Landlords Mr & Mrs Wenham
Brewery Bass
Charrington IPA; Stones Bitter; Toby Bitter; Guinness; Carling Black Label; Tennent's Extra.
ACCOMMODATION **30 bedrooms £B**
Check-in all day

Refurbishment has updated the three pleasant bars of this smartly painted pebbledash inn on the A235 Brighton Road. Bedrooms are in a modern extension and offer spacious accommodation, with good working space, fitted units and well-equipped bathrooms, as well as TVs, radio-alarms, trouser presses and tea-makers. Future plans include the addition of 15 new bedrooms. Children are accommodated overnight. Patio. *No dogs.*
Credit Access, Amex, Diners, Visa

CUCKFIELD **NEW ENTRY** King's Head

FOOD
B & B

South Street
MAP 6 D3 *West Sussex*
Haywards Heath (0444) 454006
Parking difficult

Bar food 11–2.30 & 6–10.30

Landlords Martin Lindley & Peter Tolhurst
Free house
King & Barnes Sussex Bitter; Harvey Sussex Keg; King & Barnes Old Ale (in winter), Festive; guest beer (in summer); Holsten; cider.

In the heart of the village, this lemon-painted pub is a highly popular and friendly, local meeting place. Roaring log fires warm the bars decorated with assorted memorabilia, and there's a spacious games room and a popular little rear garden. A big attraction here is the imaginative food served in the cosy restaurant. Chef Jeremy Ashpool takes care with his top-quality ingredients and everything tastes as good as it looks, from simple offerings like asparagus with lemon butter and spiced chicken breast with grapefruit to more elaborate dishes such as spinach ravioli with fresh tomato sauce and superb steamed brill, garnished with scallops and mussels in a creamy sauce. Finish with lovely rich toffee pudding and excellent cheeses. Set menu evenings.
Typical prices Chicken terrine £2.95 Wild rabbit with mushroom sauce £5.95

ACCOMMODATION **9 bedrooms £C**
Check-in all day

Simple, well-kept bedrooms – all but one with private facilities – have TVs, tea-makers and ample writing space.

Credit Access, Visa **LVs**

DAMERHAM Compasses Inn

FOOD
B & B

Nr Fordingbridge
MAP 5 B4 *Hampshire*
Rockbourne (072 53) 231
Parking ample

Bar food 12–2.15 (Sun till 1.45) & 7–10

Landlords Mr & Mrs Reilly
Free house
Ind Coope Burton Ale, John Bull Bitter; Wadworth 6X; Guinness; Skol; Löwenbräu; cider.

A homely red-brick village pub, dating in part back to the 17th century, where Mr and Mrs Reilly have created a warm and friendly atmosphere. The lounge bar boasts an open fire and antique furniture, and a mahogany-built servery bar is a new addition. There is plenty of good home-made fare on offer, ranging from light snacks of sandwiches, pâté, hearty soups and ploughman's to more substantial dishes such as local trout, gammon, sausages and steaks. There are nice straightforward desserts to be had – try baked apple, meringue glacé, ices or else cheese. There is a traditional roast on Sundays.
Typical prices Cottage pie £2.70 Gammon with pineapple £3.80

ACCOMMODATION **4 bedrooms £D**
Check-in restricted

The four neat, spotless bedrooms have matching chintzy curtains and bedcovers and all share a bright, clean, old-fashioned bathroom with a built-in shower cubicle. A good breakfast is served, too, in all making for a pleasant overnight stay. Garden. *No dogs.*

We publish annually so make sure you use the current edition.

DARRINGTON

Darrington Hotel

B Great North Road, Nr Pontefract
MAP 4 D4 *West Yorkshire*
Pontefract (0977) 791458
Parking ample

Landlords Mavis & Robert Kerry
Brewery Younger
Younger's IPA, Scotch; Newcastle Bitter; Harp; Beck's Bier; Kestrel; cider.

ACCOMMODATION **26 bedrooms £B**
Check-in all day

Set back from the A1, this well-equipped hotel, with sauna, solarium and exercise equipment, attracts many business visitors. It has a cheerful residents' lounge/cocktail bar as well as the spacious Tod's Bar. Upgraded bedrooms are most attractive with well co-ordinated colour schemes and modern darkwood units, while older rooms have duvets and laminated units. All have modern bathrooms with coloured suites. Garden. *No dogs.*
Credit Access, Amex, Diners, Visa

DARTINGTON

Cott Inn

D B Nr Totnes
MAP 9 C2 *Devon*
Totnes (0803) 863777
Parking ample

Bar food 12–2 & 7–10

Landlords Mr & Mrs S.G. Culverhouse & Mrs M.C. Yeadon
Free house
Worthington 'E'; Ansells Bitter, Mild; Bass; Carlsberg Export; Skol; cider.

A warm welcome is extended to all visitors at this picture-book thatched inn. Dating from the 14th century, past guests have included Daniel Defoe, said to have written 'Robinson Crusoe' here. The rustic beamed bars have a tremendous atmosphere and there's a pretty patio and garden for summer days. A buffet displays generous portions of cold food together with a bright selection of salads. There's always a roast on, as well as lasagne and steak and kidney pie. In the evening, the blackboard menu is more elaborate and offers choices such as roast duckling with kumquat and lime sauce or breast of chicken with Stilton. Clotted cream, piled high in a bowl, is served with such treats as Dutch apple pie.
Typical prices Fresh brill with cheese sauce £3.95 Poacher's pie £3.95

ACCOMMODATION 6 bedrooms £C
Check-in all day

There are six compact, cottage-style bedrooms, spotlessly clean, simply furnished and with floral bedspreads. All the rooms share two cheerful bathrooms and there's a pleasant TV room. *No children under 10 overnight. No dogs.*

Credit Access, Amex, Diners, Visa

Any person using our name to obtain free hospitality is a fraud.

Proprietors, please inform Egon Ronay's Guides and the police.

DARTMOUTH — Cherub Inn

FOOD

13 Higher Street
MAP 9 C3 *Devon*
Dartmouth (080 43) 2571
Parking difficult

Bar food 12–2 & 7–10
No bar food Sun
Closed Sun eve

Landlords Craig Carew-Wootton, Sally Carew-Comyns & Bob Bennet
Free house
Flowers Original, IPA; Whitbread Best Bitter, Poachers; Guinness; Heineken; cider.

★ This splendid timber-framed inn – the oldest building in Dartmouth – delights both hungry tourists and architectural buffs alike. Wisely no attempt has been made to update the characterful low-beamed bar, where super snacks are served (and also at lunchtime in the first-floor dining room, which becomes a restaurant at night). Local scallops, Salcombe oysters and a seafood pasta feature on the menu, which also includes an appropriate fisherman's lunch of hot smoked mackerel with salad and granary bread. Other tempting items are celery hearts with ham, smoked chicken with broccoli and ham, and a savoury mince thatched pie. Lighter fare ranges from soup and taramasalata to local crab sandwiches and filled jacket potatoes. Mouthwatering sweets like elderflower syllabub, trifle and superb chocolate and mocha gâteau, too. ★

Typical prices Fresh scallops au gratin £3.50 Stilton stuffed mushrooms £2.25 Country style pâté £1.75 Prawn stuffed fillet of sole £4.50

Credit Access, Visa

DARTMOUTH — NEW ENTRY — Royal Castle Hotel

B & B

The Quay
MAP 9 C3 *Devon*
Dartmouth (080 43) 4004
Parking limited

Landlord Nigel Way
Free house
Courage Best Bitter; Bass; Guinness; Stella Artois; Carling Black Label; cider.

ACCOMMODATION **21 bedrooms £A**
Check-in all day

Many period features have been preserved in this sympathetically restored old coaching inn down by the harbour. There are nautical views from both the beamed lounge bar, which boasts two log fires and a stone floor, and upstairs, from the charming residents' lounge. Bedrooms are individually decorated in pastel colours and good quality, country cottage style furnishings; five have four-posters. All have neat, well-equipped bathrooms.
Credit Access, Visa

DEDHAM — Marlborough Head

FOOD
B & B

Mill Lane
MAP 6 E2 *Essex*
Colchester (0206) 323124
Parking limited

Bar food 12–2 & 7–9.30 (till 10 in summer)

Landlords Brian & Jackie Wills
Brewery Ind Coope
Ind Coope Bitter, Burton Ale; John Bull Bitter; Löwenbräu; Castlemaine XXXX; Skol; cider.

Picturesquely set in the heart of Constable country, this well-run pub dates back to the 15th century. Decor within is full of charm and character, with heavy oak beams, rough plaster walls and wheelback chairs. The interesting and extensive range of bar snacks varies daily and includes a selection of well-filled sandwiches, delicious soups and vegetarian dishes like aubergine, tomato and pasta bake. Other choices might include lamb's liver in oats with sherry sauce, roasted bacon steak with

peaches, or Lancashire ploughman's with black pudding. Sweets, perhaps Victoria plum crumble, are tasty too.
Typical prices Breast of chicken stuffed with garlic butter £4.35 Smoked sea trout and shrimp cocktail £3.

ACCOMMODATION **4 bedrooms £C**
Check-in restricted

The four good-sized bedrooms are simple yet characterful, all featuring oak beams, free-standing furniture and comfy armchairs. All rooms now have TVs and en suite bathrooms. Garden. Accommodation closed one week Christmas. *No children overnight.*

DERSINGHAM — Feathers Hotel

B & B

Manor Road
MAP 6 E1 *Norfolk*
Dersingham (0485) 40207
Parking ample

Landlords Tony & Maxine Martin
Brewery Charrington
Adnams Bitter; Charrington IPA; Stones Bitter; Worthington Best Bitter; Guinness; Carling Black Label; cider.

ACCOMMODATION **6 bedrooms £C**
Check-in all day

The Sandringham Estate and lovely woodland walks are within easy reach of the Martins' well-kept stone pub. The oak-panelled Sandringham Bar overlooks a large, attractive garden with a swing and solid wooden tables for summer drinking; the Saddle Bar is cheerful and horsey. The six spacious bedrooms, with modern freestanding furniture, radio alarms, colour TVs and tea and coffee making facilities, share two spotless bathrooms.
Credit Access, Visa

DEVIZES — Bear Hotel

FOOD
B & B

Market Place
MAP 7 A3 *Wiltshire*
Devizes (0380) 2444
Parking ample

Bar food 12–2 & 7–11
Landlords Keith & Jacqueline Dickenson
Brewery Wadworth
Wadworth 6X, IPA, Northgate Bitter; Guinness; Heineken; Löwenbräu; cider.

Rich in history, this renowned West Country coaching inn on the handsome market square is run in splendidly hospitable fashion by long-serving tenants Jacqueline and Keith Dickenson. Fine public areas range from gracious lounges and a formal restaurant to the rustic low-beamed bar where super snacks are served. Choose from freshly cut sandwiches, ploughman's with cheese, ham or sausages, and giant meat rolls, blackboard specials like pork and tarragon pie or boiled beef and carrots. Buffet lunches and waitress-served evening grills. Traditional sweets too, like steamed jam sponge and custard to round things off nicely. There's also a popular Sunday lunch menu available.
Typical prices Devizes pie & salad £2.50 Spotted Dick 85p

ACCOMMODATION **27 bedrooms £B**
Check-in all day

Charmingly old-fashioned bedrooms (three boast four-posters) are sturdily furnished and prettily decorated. All offer TVs, tea-makers and direct-dial telephones, and the majority have simple private facilities. Courtyard.

Credit Access, Amex, Visa **LVs**

DEVIZES — Moonrakers

B & B

29 Nursteed Road
MAP 7 A3 *Wiltshire*
Devizes (0380) 2909
Parking ample

Landlord Mr V.W. Gafney
Brewery Wadworth
Wadworth IPA, 6X, Northgate Bitter; Guinness; Heineken; Löwenbräu.

ACCOMMODATION **5 bedrooms £D**
Check-in all day

Standing less than a mile from the town centre on the Andover road, this mock-Tudor inn provides simple overnight accommodation in five well-kept bedrooms. All offer TVs, tea-makers, duvets and shower cubicles, and there is one modern public bathroom. Downstairs, the refurbished lounge bar is comfortable and welcoming with its plush red seating and open fire, while the more modest public bar has a pool table.

DODDISCOMBSLEIGH — Nobody Inn

FOOD
B & B

Nr Exeter
MAP 9 C2 *Devon*
Christow (0647) 52394
Parking ample

Bar food 11–2 & 7–10

Landlords Mr & Mrs Bolton & Mr Borst-Smith
Free house
Hall and Woodhouse Badger Best; Hancock HB; Stones Bitter; Eldridge Pope Royal Oak; Guinness; Carlsberg Export; cider.

A splendid old place, well worth seeking out, dating in parts from the 16th century. The two beamed bars are traditionally furnished with Windsor chairs and wooden settles and boast an impressive collection of well over 100 malt whiskies. The blackboard menu includes a dozen or so Devon cheeses – a written list gives details of origin, texture and flavour – available with or without locally baked wholemeal bread. There's also home-made spicy bread pudding with local clotted cream.

Typical prices Plate of cheeses £2 One cheese with bread £1.10

ACCOMMODATION **7 bedrooms £C**
Check-in all day

There are four comfortable, old-fashioned rooms at the inn and three larger and more stylish rooms in a nearby Georgian house. These have smart modern bathrooms, splendid country views, and are fully equipped for self-catering breakfasts. The rooms at the inn are well-maintained, two with en suite bathrooms, the other two sharing a spotless and characterful public bathroom. Tea-makers are provided and TVs are available on request. Garden.

Credit Access, Visa

DORCHESTER-ON-THAMES — George Hotel

FOOD
B & B

High Street
MAP 7 B2 *Oxfordshire*
Oxford (0865) 340404
Parking ample

Bar food 12–2
No bar food Sun & eves
Closed 1 wk Xmas

Landlords Brian & Christine Griffin
Free house
Morland Bitter; Brakspear Bitter; Heineken; Stella Artois.

The comfortable bar of this characterful 500-year-old coaching inn has wooden settles and a splendid log fire, and you can either lunch here or in the impressive medieval-style dining hall. A blackboard proclaims a home-made soup of the day and a special dish – perhaps pork cutlet with orange and mustard sauce – while menu choices include steaks, scampi, vegetarian pancakes, toasted sandwiches, cold meats, salads, and smoked salmon or prawn and spicy mayonnaise sandwiches. Best

ACCOMMODATION 17 bedrooms £A
Check-in all day

are the simple dishes and the really excellent English cheeseboard.
Typical prices Beef & kidney pie £3.50 Lasagne £3.20

You can choose between neat modern bedrooms in the converted stable annexe, or more traditional style in the main building (where one room even has a four-poster). All are spotless and warm and have TVs and telephone. All but two have their own modern bathrooms. Patio and garden. Children welcome overnight.

Credit Access, Amex, Diners, Visa

DORNEY — Palmer Arms

OD

Village Road, Nr Windsor
MAP 7 C3 *Buckinghamshire*
Burnham (062 86) 66612
Parking ample

Bar food 12–2 & 6–10

Landlord Mr N. Brookfield
Owner Regent Inns
■ Bass; Charrington IPA; Guinness; Tennent's Extra, Pilsner; Carling Black Label; cider.

Exposed brick, pine and panelling feature throughout this friendly village pub, where blackboard menus offer an appetising choice of daily-changing dishes. Fresh fish is the Tuesday special, and other tasty offerings include pasta in tomato sauce, sautéed lamb's kidneys and lamb cutlets sauced with mint and honey. Fresh fruits with liqueurs make a delicious finale.
Typical prices Garlicky mushrooms £1.95 Chicken suprême £3.95
Credit Access, Visa

DRAGONS GREEN — George & Dragon

A

Nr Shipley, Horsham
MAP 6 D3 *West Sussex*
Coolham (040 387) 320
Parking ample

Landlords Mr & Mrs J. Jenner
Brewery King & Barnes
■ King & Barnes Sussex Bitter, Festive, Mild, Old Ale (winter); Guinness; Holsten Export; cider.

Hidden away down a maze of country lanes in the depths of the lovely Sussex countryside you will find this 17th-century pub with a huge orchard-like garden that makes it a paradise for warm weather drinkers. Beware of very low beams on entering the unpretentious interior, which is simple, clean and very traditional; an immense inglenook fireplace, exposed timbers, gleaming horse brasses and pewter mugs provide plenty of character.

DRIFFIELD — Bell Hotel

& B

Market Place
MAP 4 E3 *Humberside*
Driffield (0377) 46661
Parking ample

Landlords Mr & Mrs G. Riggs
Free house
■ Younger's Scotch; Cameron Strongarm; Webster Yorkshire Bitter; John Smith's Bitter; Guinness; Carlsberg Hof; cider.

ACCOMMODATION 14 bedrooms £B
Check-in all day

Mr and Mrs Riggs run their former coaching inn with pride and care. The lounge bar is elegantly panelled and amenities include squash, billiards and a laundry service. The comfortable bedrooms display a high standard of maintenance; all have antique furniture, light colour schemes and pretty fabrics, hair-dryers, TVs, trouser presses, direct-dial phones and private bathrooms. Accommodation closed one week Christmas. *No children under 12 overnight. No dogs.*
Credit Access, Amex, Diners, Visa

DUDDINGTON **NEW ENTRY** Royal Oak Hotel

B & B

High Street, Nr Stamford
MAP 6 D1 *Northamptonshire*
Duddington (078 083) 267
Parking ample

Landlords William & Rosa Morgado
Free house
Greene King Abbot Ale; Tetley Bitter; Ansells Bitter; Guinness; Skol; Kronenbourg; cider.

***ACCOMMODATION* 5 bedrooms £C**
Check-in all day

Stylishly restored and refurbished by new owners William and Rosa Morgado, this sturdy inn is now a welcoming place to stay. The spacious bar is smart and comfortable, with plush banquet seating and wheelback chairs, as well as a wealth of greenery. Bedrooms, with pretty fabrics and brass bedheads, have been decorated and furnished to a high standard. All offer en suite facilities, central heating, TVs, tea/coffee makers. Excellent housekeeping. Patio.
Credit Access, Visa

DUMMER The Queen

FOOD

Nr Basingstoke
MAP 5 C3 *Hampshire*
Dummer (025 675) 367
Parking limited

Bar food 12–2 & 6.30–10

Landlords John & Jocelyn Holland
Free house
Courage Best Bitter; Fullers ESB; Wadworth 6X; John Smith's Bitter; Guinness; Kronenbourg; cider.

Dating back to 1664 this pebbledash pub in the Duchess of York's former home village is not far from junction 7 of the M3. Bar food is above average, with starters like deep-fried crab claws or grilled grapefruit preceding kebabs, burgers, halibut steak or lasagne. Charcoal grills, too, plus salads. Super wholemeal bread sandwiches are especially noteworthy. Patio.
Typical prices Lasagne £4.95 Ham & Stilton sandwich £1.75
Credit Access, Amex, Diners, Visa

DUNSFOLD Sun

FOOD

The Common
MAP 6 D3 *Surrey*
Dunsfold (048 649) 242
Parking ample

Bar food 10.30–2.15 & 7–10 (Sun till 10.30)
No bar food Sun eve

Landlords B. Greenwood & J. Dunne
Brewery Friary Meux
Friary Meux Bitter, Mild; Ind Coope Burton Ale; John Bull Bitter; Guinness; Skol; cider.

On the village green, a pretty bow-windowed pub which is much older than its Georgian facade. Inside, an exciting choice of eats includes a cooked breakfast, exotic dishes such as chicken suprême stuffed with prawn and lobster as well as steaks, grills, pâtés, home-made soups, ploughman's and filled jacket potatoes. Tasty sweets such as strawberry mousse or cheesecake.
Typical prices Soup of the day £1.10 Sweet & sour pork £3.45
Credit Access, Diners, Visa

DUNWICH **NEW ENTRY** Ship Inn

FOOD
B & B

St James Street
MAP 6 F2 *Suffolk*
Westleton (072 873) 219
Parking ample

Bar food 12–2 & 7.30–9.30

Landlords Stephen & Ann Marshlain
Free house
Adnams Bitter, Old; Greene King Abbot Ale; Guinness; Kronenbourg; Carling Black Label; cider.
No real ale

Stephen and Ann Marshlain have created a warm and friendly atmosphere at their charming pub, where there is a wood-burning stove in the cosy bar, and a conservatory, courtyard and garden for summer days. A blackboard menu offers a pleasing choice of dishes, with a special emphasis on locally caught fish. Start with soup of the day, home-made pâté or marinated kipper, followed by deep-fried fish with home-made tartare sauce, gammon and peaches in brandy sauce, cottage pie, sirloin steak or deep-fried chicken stuffed with ham and cheese. Finish with home-made fruit crumble or pie, sorbet or treacle tart. Ploughman's, sandwiches and quiches are on offer for a lighter snack. ***Typical dishes*** Fresh local fried fish & chips £3 Mushrooms in garlic butter £1.60

ACCOMMODATION **5 bedrooms £D**
Check-in restricted

The five simple bedrooms have traditional furniture, duvets, washbasins and tea and coffee making facilities. They all share a carpeted bath/shower room, and there is a small, neat breakfast room.

EAST CLANDON — Queens Head

OD

The Street
MAP 7 C3 *Surrey*
Guildford (0483) 222332
Parking ample

Bar food 12–2.15 & 7–10.15 (Fri & Sat till 10.45)

Landlord Mr J. Miller
Brewery Friary Meux
Friary Meux Bitter; Ind Coope Burton Ale; John Bull Bitter; Guinness; Löwenbräu; Skol; cider.

Tasty bar snacks can be chosen from a wide-ranging menu at this mellow, red-brick pub of 16th-century origin. Savoury pies of all kinds are the house speciality, while pan haggerty, carpet-bag steak and home-made soups are also firm favourites. Ploughman's and fresh-cut sandwiches are lunchtime extras, and puds include apple crumble and Bakewell tart. Garden with orchard. ***Typical prices*** Raised venison pie in port £4.75 Bakewell tart £1.25
Credit Access, Diners, Visa **LVs**

EAST DEAN — Tiger Inn

A

MAP 6 E4 *East Sussex*
East Dean (032 15) 3209
Parking ample

Landlord James Conroy
Brewery Courage
Courage Directors, Best Bitter; John Smith's Yorkshire Bitter; Guinness; Castlemaine XXXX; Kronenbourg; cider.

The glorious Sussex downland surrounds the pretty village with its cluster of flint cottages around the village green and this unspoilt whitewashed pub is everything you could expect to find in such a setting. Cottagy furniture complements the mellowed, old-world interior, pastoral prints hang on the walls and there is a plethora of knick-knacks such as horse brasses, handbells and mugs hanging above the bar. Patio.

EAST DEREHAM — King's Head Hotel

& B

Norwich Street
MAP 6 E1 *Norfolk*
East Dereham (0362) 693842
Parking ample

Landlords Mr & Mrs R. Black
Brewery Norwich
Norwich Bitter, S&P Bitter, Mild; Guinness; Carlsberg; Fosters; cider.

ACCOMMODATION **15 bedrooms £C**
Check-in all day

Down a side street near the centre of town, this modernised 17th-century inn is run with pride and care by owners Mr and Mrs Black. The bar is roomy and inviting, with doors that open on to a flowery little terrace and the hotel's own bowling green. Comfortable, centrally heated bedrooms, all with colour TVs, direct-dial telephones and en suite facilities, include five modern rooms in a converted stable block.
Credit Access, Amex, Diners, Visa

EAST HADDON — Red Lion

B & B

Nr Northampton
MAP 5 C2 *Northamptonshire*
Northampton (0604) 770223
Parking ample

Landlords Mr & Mrs Ian Kennedy
Brewery Charles Wells
Wells Eagle Bitter, Noggin; Guinness; Kellerbräu; Wells Red Stripe.

***ACCOMMODATION* 5 bedrooms £C**
Check-in all day

In lovely countryside close to Northampton and the M1, this relaxing pub is a welcoming place for a quiet weekend. The bar area is filled with antiques and curios, as well as fresh flowers and a variety of comfy chairs. The bedrooms have a cottagy atmosphere, with pretty floral bedspreads and ornaments, and share two well-kept bathrooms. Good hearty breakfasts. Accommodation closed one week Christmas. Garden and patio. Dogs in kennels only.
Credit Access, Amex, Diners, Visa

EASTERGATE — Wilkes Head

FOOD

Nr Chichester
MAP 6 D4 *West Sussex*
Eastergate (024 368) 3380
Parking ample

Bar food 12–2 & 7–9.30
No bar food Sun & Mon eves
Landlords David & Christine Morris
Brewery Friary Meux
Friary Meux Bitter; Ind Coope Burton Ale; Guinness; Skol; Löwenbräu; cider.

An inglenook fireplace, beams and stone-flagged floors provide a pleasing atmosphere at this 18th-century pub where David and Christine Morris extend a warm welcome. Standard pub fare is on offer in generous portions – sandwiches, ploughman's and filled jacket potatoes, with home-made lasagne, chilli con carne and basket meals catering for larger appetities. Traditional Sunday lunch menu. Garden.
Typical prices Chunky cheese & onion sandwich 90p Cottage pie £1.95

EASTLING — Carpenter's Arms

FOOD
B & B

Nr Faversham
MAP 6 E3 *Kent*
Eastling (079 589) 234
Parking ample

Bar food 12–2.30 & 7.30–10
Landlord Mrs M. J. Wright
Brewery Shepherd Neame
Shepherd Neame Master Brew, Stock Ale (winter only), Abbey Ale, Master Brew Mild; Hurlimann; cider.

The warm and welcoming personality of Mrs Wright fills this delightfully mellow old pub set deep in the Kent countryside. Hop vines hang from heavy beams in the brick-walled bar, where you can sit by the inglenook fireplace and enjoy some excellent home-cooked fare. The extensive menu (less choice on Sunday) ranges from mushroom salad and smoked trout among the starters to chicken casserole, Kentish ham and eggs, pizzas and the splendid beef in ale and mustard – a richly sauced, flavour-packed feast. There are sandwiches and ploughman's, too, and lovely sweets like spicy bread pudding and beautifully glazed apple flan.
Typical prices Hot buttered crab £2.10 Chicken in red wine £4.50

***ACCOMMODATION* 2 bedrooms £D**
Check-in restricted

There are two homely bedrooms, one with simple modern furniture, the other with antique pieces and a full bookshelf. Both are of a good size and share a huge bathroom. Accommodation closed one week at Christmas.

Credit Visa

Our inspectors never book in the name of Egon Ronay's Guides; they disclose their identity only after paying their bills.

EASTON NEW ENTRY Chestnut Horse

OOD

Nr Winchester
MAP 5 C3 *Hampshire*
Itchen Abbas (096 278) 257
Parking ample

Bar food 12–2 & 7–10

Landlords Paul & Roberta Bakes-Bradbury
Free house
Gales HSB; Eldridge Pope Royal Oak; Courage Best Bitter; Guinness; Fosters; Kronenbourg; cider (summer only).

A charming 16th-century inn, standing on the Pilgrim's Way. There's a good choice of hot dishes such as poacher's broth, garlic prawns, and chicken livers, spinach and cheese in wholemeal crêpe for hearty eaters, plus a selection of freshly made sandwiches. Lovely treacle tart or trifle. Traditional Sunday lunch in the restaurant. Patio.
Typical prices Beef curry £2.50 Camembert puffs & gooseberry conserve £1.95
Credit Visa

EASTON White Horse

OOD

Nr Woodbridge
MAP 6 F2 *Suffolk*
Wickham Market (0728) 746456
Parking ample

Bar food 12–2 & 7–9.30

Landlords David & Sally Grimwood
Brewery Tollemache & Cobbold
Tolly Cobbold Bitter, Original, Mild; Guinness; Cameron Hansa; cider.

Thanks to a recent extension, this nice pink-washed pub, overlooking the village green, has added an impressive cold display to its distinguished bar food menu. Choose from smoked fish, cold meats and crispy salads (including red cabbage with peanuts) or try a ploughman's with assorted cheeses. Good hot dishes and a selection of sweets. Traditional Sunday roast. Garden.
Typical prices Steak & oyster pie £3.75 Chicken mozzarella £3.75
Credit Access

EFFINGHAM Plough

OOD

Orestan Lane
MAP 7 C3 *Surrey*
Bookham (0372) 58121
Parking ample

Bar food 12–2 & 6.30–8.30
No bar food Sun

Landlords Lynn & Derek Sutherland
Brewery Courage
Courage Best, Directors; Guinness; Hofmeister; Kronenbourg; cider.

The friendly beamed bar of this spick-and-span white-painted pub features some robust and enjoyable bar snacks, like well-filled turkey pie topped with freshly baked puff pastry, and gooey treacle tart. Regular items – sandwiches, ploughman's, cottage pie – are well supported by daily specials like goujons of plaice and cheese-topped ratatouille, served in generous portions. Garden.
Typical prices Seafood chowder £2.30 Leek & gammon au gratin £2

ELKSTONE Highwayman Inn

OOD

Nr Cheltenham
MAP 7 A2 *Gloucestershire*
Miserden (028 582) 221
Parking ample

Bar food 11–2.15 & 6–10, Sun 12–2 & 7–10

Landlords David & Heather Bucher
Brewery Arkell
Arkell BB, BBB, Kingsdown Ale, Kellar Lager; Guinness; Löwenbräu.

Look for the black and yellow stagecoach in the car park of this 16th-century hostelry on the A417. In the cosy bar – all beams, nooks and rustic stone – a varied menu offers sandwiches, jacket potatoes and pizzas, seafood platter, chilli and the popular Stagecoach pie (steak and mushroom). Simple sweets and a children's menu. Traditional Sunday roast. Garden & patio.
Typical prices Beef & Guinness pie £3.50 Seafood pancakes £3.25
Credit Visa

ELLISFIELD — Fox

FOOD Green Lane, Nr Basingstoke
MAP 5 C3 *Hampshire*
Herriard (025 683) 210
Parking ample

Bar food 12–2 (Sun till 1.30) & 7–10.15
No bar food Mon eve

Landlords Nigel, Lucy & John Moore
Free house
Wadworth 6X; Bunce's Best; Gales HSB; Marston Pedigree; Guinness; Fosters; cider.

Fresh, wholesome and appetising bar snacks are on offer at this pleasant pub, deep in the Hampshire countryside. Baked potatoes come with a wide variety of fillings (Cheddar and spring onion, beef and horseradish, tuna and mayonnaise) and there are sandwiches, salads, and Greek dips with pitta bread. Blackboard specials include steak and kidney casserole, chicken in the pot, and a vegetarian dish.
Typical prices Beef casserole £2.85 Steak sandwich £1.95

ELSLACK — Tempest Arms

FOOD Nr Skipton
MAP 3 C3 *North Yorkshire*
Earby (0282) 842450
Parking ample

Bar food 11–2.15 & 6.30–10, Sun 12–2 & 7–10

Landlord Francis Pierre Boulongne
Free house
Tetley Bitter, Mild; Thwaites Bitter, Mild; Castlemaine XXXX; Carlsberg Hof; cider.

Fresh fish is the speciality at this stone-built pub in a peaceful location near the junction of the A56 and A59. Moules marinière, grilled halibut and tuna provençale are typical treats, while alternatives include steaks, meat pies and vegetable lasagne, with delicious sweets like tipsy trifle to finish. Charcoal grills are also available in the new restaurant.
Typical prices Fish & mushroom pie £1.95 Gammon, egg & chips £3.25

ELSTED — Three Horseshoes

FOOD Nr South Harting
MAP 5 C4 *West Sussex*
Harting (073 085) 746
Parking ample

Bar food 12–2 & 7–10

Landlords S.C. & E.A. Hawkins
Free house
Friary Meux Bitter; Ballard's Best Bitter; Ringwood Old Thumper; Harvey Best Bitter; Adnams Bitter; Dortmunder; cider.

The views of the South Downs are really splendid at this charming country pub, where snacks may be enjoyed in the cosy bars, the dining room or the garden. Jacket potatoes and ploughman's platters come in many tasty variants, and there's soup along with robust main courses and super treacle tart. Sunday lunch brings a buffet in summer and a roast in winter.
Typical prices Steak, mushroom & Guinness pie £3.95 Salmon with mint & cucumber mayonnaise £6.75

ELTERWATER — Britannia Inn

B & B Nr Ambleside
MAP 3 B3 *Cumbria*
Langdale (09667) 210
Parking ample

Landlord David Fry
Free house
Hartley XB; Tetley Bitter; Bass Special; Jennings Bitter; Guinness; Löwenbräu; cider.

ACCOMMODATION **10 bedrooms £B**
Check-in all day

Situated on Elterwater's pretty village green, this smart 400 year-old inn is a typical lakeland hostelry. Popular with locals and walkers alike, the beamed main bar and the slate-floored snug are both welcoming rooms, and there's a chintzy book-stocked lounge for the residents. Modest, clean bedrooms with pretty duvet covers and matching curtains share two smartly tiled bathrooms. Landlord and staff are friendly and helpful. Good breakfast. Terrace.
Credit Access, Visa

ELTISLEY — Leeds Arms

B & B

The Green
MAP 6 D1 *Cambridgeshire*
Croxton (048 087) 283
Parking ample

Landlord Mr G. W. Cottrell
Free house
Greene King IPA; Whitbread Best Bitter, Best Mild; Stones Bitter; Paine EG; Guinness; Carlsberg; Harp. *No real ale.*

ACCOMMODATION **9 bedrooms £C**
Check-in restricted

On the edge of the large village green, this late 18th-century coaching house provides comfortable motel-style accommodation in two single-storey blocks. The twin-bedded rooms have private bathrooms, while the six singles offer showers; all rooms are equipped with TVs and tea-makers. Some of the period flavour remains in the bars with their beams and inglenook. There's a children's outdoor play area. *No dogs.*
Credit Access, Visa

EMPINGHAM — White Horse

FOOD
B & B

2 Main Street, Nr Oakham
MAP 6 D1 *Leicestershire*
Empingham (078 086) 221
Parking ample

Bar food 12–2 & 7.30–9.45 (Sun till 9.30), Fri & Sat 12–2.15 & 7.30–10.15

Landlords Robert, Andrew & Helen Reid
Brewery John Smith
John Smith's Bitter, Chestnut Mild; John Courage Bitter; Guinness; Hofmeister; Kronenbourg; cider.

Close to Rutland Water, this friendly pub is well known for its appetising snacks. In the comfortable main bar there's a fine cold display of meats and salads, while alternative light bites from the menu include potted shrimps, pâté and ploughman's with a range of varied cheeses. For the hungry, tempting main courses such as baked trout, lamb chops with rosemary and fricassée of veal all appeal – and don't forget to leave room for a delicious sweet like lime meringue pie or orange and Cointreau torte. Traditional Sunday lunches also served.
Typical prices Chicken oriental £4.25 Sherry trifle £1.35

ACCOMMODATION **11 bedrooms £B**
Check-in all day

The converted stable block houses eight modern bedrooms featuring pretty floral fabrics and pine furniture (one boasts a four-poster). All rooms have tea-makers, direct-dial telephones and excellent private bathrooms. The three large doubles in the original building are more traditional in style and share two shower-cum-bathrooms. Garden.

Credit Access, Amex, Diners, Visa

ESKDALE — Bower House Inn

FOOD
B & B

Holmrook
MAP 3 B3 *Cumbria*
Eskdale (094 03) 244
Parking ample

Bar food 12–2 & 6.30–9

Landlords Smith family
Free house
Hartley Bitter; McEwan's Scotch Bitter; Guinness; Carlsberg; Fosters; cider.

The friendly Smith family make everyone feel thoroughly at home in this charming slate-roofed inn. The setting, among the peace and beauty of Eskdale, is really delightful, and the beamed bar is warm and inviting. Bar snacks are fresh and appetising: soup, salads and sandwiches are always available or for something more substantial you could start with smoked mackerel pâté and go on to rabbit cooked in ginger ale or succulent poussin with a lemon sauce. Apple crumble is a pop-

ular pud, and there are some good English cheeses.
Typical prices Drunken mallard £3.95 Sticky toffee pudding 80p

ACCOMMODATION **21 bedrooms £C**
Check-in all day

Bedrooms are of two types: six simply and traditionally furnished in the main house and 15 in a converted stable annexe that offer a higher standard of comfort, modern furnishings, colour TVs and good bathrooms. There's a comfortable, chintzy resident's lounge and a pleasant garden. Accommodation closed three days Christmas.

ETON — Christopher Hotel

B

High Street, Nr Windsor
MAP 7 C3 *Berkshire*
Windsor (0753) 852359
Parking limited

Landlords Ron & Barbara France
Free house
Brakspear Bitter; John Smith's Bitter; Courage Best; Younger's Tartan Bitter; Guinness; Kronenbourg; Hofmeister, cider.

ACCOMMODATION **23 bedrooms £B**
Check-in all day

Comfortable overnight accommodation is provided at this high-street hotel that was once a coaching inn. Bedrooms (mostly in a block adjoining the main building) are neat, roomy and modern with TVs and useful extras like hairdryers, trouser presses, fridges and pay phones, plus carpeted bath/shower rooms. Six larger rooms are equipped for families, with bunk beds for the children. There are two bars, one in Victorian style. Patio.
Credit Access, Amex, Diners, Visa

ETTINGTON — Houndshill

OD
B

Banbury Road
MAP 7 B1 *Warwickshire*
Stratford-upon-Avon (0789) 740267
Parking ample

Bar food 12–2 & 7–10

Landlords Mr & Mrs Martin & A. Martin
Free house
Wadworth 6X; Davenports Bitter; McEwan's Export, Tartan Bitter; Guinness; Beck's Bier; McEwan's Lager; cider.

On the Banbury road to Stratford, a mile outside Ettington, this large, white inn makes a useful port of call for the whole family. Children are welcome in the relaxing bar and have their own menu, too, while mum and dad can tuck into soundly prepared and generously served dishes selected from a wide-ranging bill of fare. Soup, pâté and deep-fried mushrooms make tasty starters, perhaps followed by lasagne, chilli con carne, a steak or home-made pizza. There are also omelettes, salads and basket meals, plus sandwiches plain or toasted and simple sweets like apple pie or bakewell tart. There's an à la carte restaurant, too.
Typical prices Moussaka £3.15 Steak & kidney pie £2.80

ACCOMMODATION **8 bedrooms £D**
Check-in all day

Comfortable, spacious bedrooms (including one particularly large room suitable for families) are most attractive with their pretty floral fabrics, wicker chairs and pine bedside furniture. All have modern en suite bathrooms. Garden.

Credit Access, Visa

EVERCREECH JUNCTION — Natterjack

FOOD

Shepton Mallet
MAP 9 D1 *Somerset*
Ditcheat (074 986) 253
Parking ample

Bar food 12–2 & 7–10

Landlords Richard Fensham & Nigel Lea
Free house
Courage Best Bitter; Butcombe Bitter; Double Diamond; John Smith's; Symmonds; Guinness; Hofmeister; Kronenbourg; cider.

The roomy bar is a comfortable spot to take time out for a tasty snack at this sturdy roadside pub. The menu runs an appetising gamut, from sustaining soup and fresh salads to quiche, crab mornay and very decent lasagne in both meat and vegetarian versions. Nice puds, too, like fruit pavlova. Sunday roasts. Garden. Children welcome until 8 pm.

Typical prices Mushrooms in garlic, brandy & cream £3.10 Beef in red wine £3.30
Credit Access, Visa

EWEN — Wild Duck Inn

B & B

Nr Cirencester
MAP 7 A2 *Gloucestershire*
Kemble (028 577) 364
Parking ample

Landlord Kevin Shales
Free house
Wadworth 6X; Archers Best Bitter; Toby Bitter; Guinness; Carling Black Label; Hurlimann; cider.

ACCOMMODATION **10 bedrooms £B**
Check-in all day

Set in a quiet, unspoilt village, this lovely stone inn dates back to 1563, and retains much of its period charm. The bar is a splendid place for a drink, with its beamed ceiling and open fireplace. Most of the bedrooms are in a modern extension, and have practical fitted furniture and traditional fabrics. All have TVs, tea-makers and modern bathrooms. There's also a spacious suite, two splendid four-poster rooms and a residents' lounge. Garden.
Credit Access, Amex, Diners, Visa

EWHURST GREEN — White Dog Inn

B & B

Nr Robertsbridge
MAP 6 E3 *East Sussex*
Staplecross (058 083) 264
Parking ample

Landlords Tina & Richard Hayward
Free house
Charrington IPA, Toby; Bass; Guinness; Tennent's Lager; Carling Black Label; cider.

ACCOMMODATION **6 bedrooms £D**
Check-in restricted

Fine views of the surrounding countryside are a bonus at this tile-hung pub. The six neat, bright bedrooms with plain white furniture all now have private facilities, as well as colour TVs and tea-makers. Downstairs, there's a convivial atmosphere in the beamed and flagstoned bar with its pew seating and inglenook fireplace. Amenities include a heated outdoor swimming pool. Continental breakfast only. Patio and garden.
Credit Amex, Diners, Visa

EXFORD — Crown Hotel

FOOD
B & B

Nr Minehead
MAP 9 C1 *Somerset*
Exford (064 383) 554
Parking ample

Bar food 12–2 & 7–9.30

Landlords John & Marjorie Millward
Brewery Usher
Usher Founder's Ale, Country Bitter; Webster Yorkshire Bitter; Carlsberg Pilsner; cider.

A fully modernised yet characterful pebbledash inn set in an attractive Exmoor village. Inside there are two comfortable lounges featuring velvet sofas and fresh flowers, and warmed by log fires in winter. There's also a simple rustic bar. Honest reliable bar food includes good home-made soup, freshly cut sandwiches, cold meats, salads and well-hung steaks, plus specials like steamed steak and kidney pudding. Sweets, including home-made cheesecake and chocolate mousse, are enjoyable, too.

Traditional roast on Sunday.
Typical prices Steak & mushroom pie £3 Sirloin steak & onion roll £2.95

***ACCOMMODATION* 18 bedrooms £A**
Check-in all day

A glass of sherry on arrival is one of the nice touches that make staying here a pleasure. Individually decorated bedrooms offer a very high standard of accommodation, with many thoughtful extras provided, as well as colour TVs and direct-dial phones. Carpeted en suite bathrooms are excellent, with generous towels and luxury soaps. Outside, a stream runs through the attractive garden.

Credit Access, Amex, Visa

EYAM — Miners Arms

OD
& B

Nr Bakewell
MAP 4 D4 *Derbyshire*
Hope Valley (0433) 30853
Parking ample

Bar food 12–1.30
No bar food eves
Closed Mon lunch

Landlords Mr & Mrs Peter Cooke & Mr & Mrs Paul Morris
Free house
Stones Bitter; Wards Best Bitter; Vaux Mild; Tennent's Lager; cider.

Set in an ancient village within the Peak District National Park, this delightful 17th-century inn has been run with immense warmth and friendliness by the Cookes for over 26 years. The cosily traditional main bar is the place to head for wholesome lunchtime snacks like home-made soup and sandwiches, fresh fish and the day's roast, plus the highly popular chicken in red wine sauce. Traditional Sunday lunch menu also available. Dinners can be enjoyed in the pub's excellent restaurant – where son-in-law Paul Morris is the talented chef – from Tuesday to Saturday.
Typical prices Steak, mushrooms & tomatoes £4.25 Fresh haddock £2.25

***ACCOMMODATION* 6 bedrooms £D**
Check-in all day

Four snug bedrooms in the original inn are equipped with thoughtful extras like tissues and biscuits. One has en suite facilities while the others share the family bathroom. Two superior doubles in the converted stable block have duvets and good modern private facilities. Excellent breakfast. Terrace and garden. *No children under 12 overnight. No dogs.*

EYAM — Rose & Crown

& B

Main Road
MAP 4 D4 *Derbyshire*
Hope Valley (0433) 30858
Parking ample

Closed Mon lunch

Landlords Mason family
Free house
Stones Bitter; Tetley Bitter; Skol; Carling Black Label; cider.

***ACCOMMODATION* 3 bedrooms £D**
Check-in restricted

Three neatly kept bedrooms provide homely overnight accommodation at this little stone pub, run by the efficient Mason family. There are shower cubicles, washbasins and toilets in each room, plus duvets, TVs and tea-makers; there's also a neatly maintained public bathroom. Day rooms include an inviting lounge bar, a very cosy public bar warmed by a coal fire and a games room with pool table and darts. Patio.
Credit Access, Visa

FAIRBOURNE HEATH — Pepper Box

FOOD Harrietsham, Nr Ulcombe
MAP 6 E3 *Kent*
Maidstone (0622) 842558
Parking ample

Bar food 12–2 & 7–10
No bar food Sun eve

Landlord Mr J.D. Wood
Brewery Shepherd Neame
Shepherd Neame Master Brew Bitter, Stock Ale (winter only), Abbey Ale; Hurlimann Sternbrau; cider.

Fish fresh from Dungeness is the speciality of this friendly old pub overlooking the Weald. The split-level bar, festooned with dried hops, is warm and cosy, and if you don't happen to fancy cod, skate, monkfish or huss, there's soup (perhaps curried parsnip), whopper local sausages, stuffed chicken, ploughman's, and freshly-made sandwiches. Garden.
Typical prices Cod cutlets & French fries £3 Lemon sole £4

FAIRFORD — Bull Hotel

B & B Market Place
MAP 7 A2 *Gloucestershire*
Cirencester (0285) 712535
Parking ample

Landlord Mark Gulenserion
Brewery Arkell
John Arkell Bitter, Best Bitter, North Star Bitter; Guinness; Carling Black Label; Stella Artois; cider.

***ACCOMMODATION* 22 bedrooms £C**
Check-in all day

The history of this solid, friendly inn goes back to the 15th century, when it was a monks' chanting house, and the immaculate bars and relaxing residents' lounge retain a strong period feel. The spacious, traditional bedrooms are fitted with practical furniture, floral fabrics and tea-makers; one has a four-poster. Most have bathrooms en suite, and housekeeping is good throughout. The hotel also owns 1½ miles of the trout-stocked river Coln. Terrace.
Credit Access, Amex, Diners, Visa

FALMOUTH — NEW ENTRY — The Pandora Inn

FOOD Restronguet Creek, Mylor Bridge
MAP 9 A3 *Cornwall*
Falmouth (0326) 72678
Parking ample

Bar food 11–3 (winter till 2.30) & 6–11 (winter till 10.30), Sun 12–2 & 7–10.30

Landlords Roger & Helen Hough
Brewery St Austell
Bass; St Austell Tinners Ale, Duchy, Bosun, HSD; Carlsberg Hof; cider.

Turn left off the A39 four miles north of Falmouth and follow signs to Mylor then Restronguet Passage to find this delightful thatched pub. There's a patio and pontoon on the creek for summer drinking, while inside low beamed ceilings and a log fire make for a cosy venue in winter. Super bar food includes excellent sandwiches and a cold buffet at lunchtime, but pride of place must go to the local fish which features strongly on the menu. Start with home-made soup with granary bread, pâté and herb toast or avocado and crab with lemon mayonnaise, then move on to chicken, mushroom and smoked Cheddar pancakes, grilled mackerel with walnut butter or crab thermidor, all served with real chips. Home-made sweets include a luscious lemon meringue pie.
Typical prices Cornish pasty 95p Moules marinière £2.95 Smoked Cornish mackerel salad £2.95 Chocolate fudge cake £1.75

Credit Access, Visa

FARINGDON — Bell Hotel

Market Place
MAP 7 B2 *Oxfordshire*
Faringdon (0367) 20534
Parking limited

Bar food 12–2 & 7–9

Landlord William Dreyer
Brewery Wadworth
Wadworth 6X, Old Timer, Northgate Bitter; Guinness; Harp; Löwenbräu.

Former shipbuilder William Dreyer runs a larger-than-life pub, a 16th-century posting house in the town centre with a real ring of the past. The bar snacks are a popular feature, ranging from salads and sandwiches (traditional or open French) to lasagne, curried chicken and a daily changing special like minced beef pancake, cottage pie, liver and bacon or Friday's fish. Nice home-made sweets, including fresh cream gâteau and lemon meringue pie. An interesting feature in the bar is a fine old bread oven. On Sunday there's a traditional roast.

Typical prices Steak sandwich £3.50 Chilli con carne £2.75

ACCOMMODATION **12 bedrooms £D**
Check-in all day

Overnight guests will find comfort allied to the character that comes from beams and sloping floors. The bedrooms are neatly kept, with pretty floral fabrics and the seven that have TVs also offer good-sized bathrooms. The remaining rooms share a more than adequate public bathroom. Patio.

Credit Access, Amex, Diners, Visa

FAUGH — String of Horses

Heads Hook, Carlisle
MAP 3 C2 *Cumbria*
Hayton (022 870) 297
Parking ample

Bar food 12–2 & 7–10

Landlords Ann & Eric Tasker
Free house
Theakston Best Bitter, Old Peculier; Younger's Scotch; Murphy Stout; Guinness; Carlsberg Hof; Beck's Bier.
No real ale.

A wealth of oak beams, open fires, gleaming brassware and antiques emphasises the period charm of this 17th-century inn, set in a quiet village. A good choice of soundly prepared food is served in the lounge bar, which at lunchtime features an extensive cold buffet backed up by grills, curries, and tasty specials like hearty beef goulash. A range of sandwiches is always available while seafood and salads are the popular evening choices, along with lamb cutlets and Cumberland sausage. Sweets include a delicious chocolate gâteau. There's also a restaurant, and a traditional roast on Sundays.

Typical prices Mushroom & ham on toast with cheese sauce £2 Moussaka £2.20

ACCOMMODATION **13 bedrooms £B**
Check-in all day

The bedrooms, which include three four-poster suites, are furnished in a luxurious, flamboyant style with lots of extras such as fruit and flowers, mini-bars with champagne, and in-house movies. Hollywood-style bathrooms are splendidly ornate. Accommodation closed three days Christmas. Patio.

Credit Access, Amex, Diners, Visa

FELIXSTOWE — Ordnance Hotel

B & B

1 Undercliff Road West
MAP 6 F2 *Suffolk*
Felixstowe (0394) 273427
Parking ample

Landlord James Yeo
Brewery Tollemache & Cobbold
Tolly Cobbold Bitter, Best Bitter, 4X; Guinness; Hansa, Export.

ACCOMMODATION **11 bedrooms £C**
Check-in all day

A friendly pub providing simple but cosy accommodation convenient for the port. A spacious bar leads to a neat terrace and garden, while on the first floor a comfortable residents' lounge provides books and TV to relax with. The bedrooms have period-style furniture, direct-dial telephones, tea-makers and TVs. Four have en suite shower facilities while the rest share two well-maintained modern bathrooms. Children are accommodated overnight. *No dogs.*
Credit Access, Amex, Diners, Visa

FEN DRAYTON — Three Tuns

A

High Street
MAP 6 D2 *Cambridgeshire*
Swavesey (0954) 30242
Parking ample

Landlords Michael & Eileen Nugent
Brewery Greene King
Greene King IPA, Abbot Ale; Guinness; Harp; Kronenbourg; cider.

Pretty window boxes and hanging baskets bedeck the delightful exterior of this 15th-century thatched pub, while inside the bars have oak tables and chairs, polished copperware, old farm implements and assorted bric-a-brac aplenty to add to the charm. Two large inglenook fireplaces provide cheer for cold winter evenings, while there is a neatly maintained garden at the rear for the summer months.

FENNY BENTLEY — Bentley Brook Inn

FOOD
B & B

Nr Ashbourne
MAP 5 B1 *Derbyshire*
Thorpe Cloud (033 529) 278
Parking ample

Bar food 10am–10pm
Landlords David & Jeanne Allingham
Free house
Marston Pedigree; Worthington Bitter; Guinness; Carling Black Label; Marston Pilsner Lager; Tennent's Extra; cider.

This handsome, black and white half-timbered inn is situated two miles north of Ashbourne, set back from the junction of the A515 and B5056. Its extensive acreage includes rough field and woodland with 250 yds of Bentley Brook trout steam. Bay-fronted windows afford good views over the large and attractive gardens for extra pleasure while tucking into the honest and straightforward meals. Start with a hearty home-made soup and follow with lasagne, lamb hot pot, grilled sole or chicken casserole. There are fresh baps filled with roast meat or cheese for a light snack and nice sweets including sherry trifle and Dutch apple tart. Roast available on Sundays.
Typical prices Savoury Derbyshire oatcake £2 Brandied mushrooms in garlic butter £1.90

ACCOMMODATION **8 bedrooms £D**
Check-in all day

The comfortable, airy bedrooms are beamed and characterful; all have duvets, tea-makers, colour TVs and phones. Three have private bathrooms, while the remainder share three well-kept public ones. There is a comfortable lounge on the first floor for residents.

FIDDLEFORD **Fiddleford Inn**

B Sturminster Newton
MAP 9 D1 *Dorset*
Sturminster Newton (0258) 72489
Parking ample
Landlords Joyce, Philip & Valerie Wilson
Free house
Fiddleford Ale; Wadworth 6X; Gales HSB; Old Hookey; Wiltshire Old Devil; Marston Pedigree; cider.
***ACCOMMODATION* 4 bedrooms £D**
Check-in restricted

Once a brewery, this charming, creeper-clad inn keeps the links alive with an excellent selection of real ales. Fires crackle in the cosy beamed bars, while the four cottagy bedrooms have much appeal with their jumble of furnishings, attractive fabrics and numerous thoughtful little extras. One has a TV, and its own bathroom; the others share the three public ones. Excellent housekeeping. The pub is fronted by a pleasant garden with a children's play area.

FINDON **NEW ENTRY** **Snooty Fox Bar**

D Findon Manor, High Street
MAP 6 D4 *West Sussex*
Findon (090 671) 2733
Parking ample
Bar food 11–1.45 & 6–9.45
Closed 1 wk Xmas
Landlords Andrew & Susan Tyrie
Free house
Young Bitter, Special; Hall & Woodhouse Badger Best; Guinness; Carling Black Label; Carlsberg Hof.

Splendid cooking attracts customers to the cosy bar of this converted rectory in the heart of a horsey village. Bites come in all sizes, from sandwiches, salads and jacket potatoes to a mixed grill, curries, and fish and chips. The blackboard special could be a mighty portion of lamb casserole, but leave room for the scrumptious chocolate mousse or pecan pie.
Typical prices Steak sandwich £2.60 Rhubarb crumble £1.50
Credit Acces, Amex, Diners, Visa

FINGEST **Chequers Inn**

D Nr Henley-on-Thames
MAP 7 C2 *Buckinghamshire*
Turville Heath (049 163) 335
Parking ample
Bar food 11.30–2.30 & 6–10, Sun 12–2 & 7–9.30
Landlords Mr & Mrs B.J. Heasman
Brewery Brakspear
Brakspear Bitter, Special, 4X Old; Guinness; Stella Artois.

This 12th-century pub, full of atmosphere, stands opposite an old Norman church. The blackboard menu offers such dishes as hot avocado in cheese sauce or home-made pâté for starters and rump steak, prawn curry or grilled lemon sole for a main course. Delicious sweets include trifle, kiwi-fruit gâteau and banana meringue. Cold buffet only on Sunday evenings. Garden.
Typical prices Steak & kidney pie £3.95 Liver & bacon £3.95
Credit Amex, Visa

FITTLEWORTH **Swan**

B Lower Street, Nr Pulborough
MAP 6 D4 *West Sussex*
Fittleworth (079 882) 429
Parking ample
Landlords James & Helen Crossley
Owners Berni Chef & Brewer Hotels
Webster Yorkshire Bitter; Ruddles County; Watney Special, Mild; Guinness; Holsten Export; Carlsberg; cider.
***ACCOMMODATION* 11 bedrooms £B**
Check-in all day

Study the unique collection of bottle openers as you relax in the beamed bar of this 14th-century hotel. Major refurbishment has transformed the bedrooms; two have exposed timbers, darkwood furniture and four-posters; while the rest have pine furniture and country print wallpapers. All have TVs, telephones, tea-makers and trouser presses. Eight have modern en suite facilities; three share two similarly fitted public bathrooms. Terrace and garden.
Credit Access, Amex, Diners, Visa

FLETCHING — Griffin Inn

FOOD

MAP 6 D3 *East Sussex*
Newick (082 572) 2890
Parking ample

Bar food 12–2.20 & 7–10.30
Landlords Rob & Tina Setchell
Free house
Harvey Best Bitter; King & Barnes Festive; Usher Best Bitter; Hall & Woodhouse Tanglefoot; Holsten Export; Talisman; cider.

A 16th-century pub with a mellow red-brick facade. Inside, oak beams and an open fireplace maintain the old-world charm. Tasty dishes range from smoked salmon pâté and taramasalata to lamb curry and spaghetti carbonara. Sandwiches and ploughman's are available at lunchtime. Nice desserts such as hot chocolate fudge cake. Garden.
Typical prices Spinach & cheese lasagne £3.95 Breast of chicken in champagne sauce £4.25
Credit Access, Amex, Visa

FONTHILL BISHOP — King's Arms

FOOD
B & B

Nr Salisbury
MAP 5 B3 *Wiltshire*
Hindon (074 789) 523
Parking ample

Bar food 12–2 (Sun till 1.30) & 7–10
Landlords Andrew & Sarah MacDonald & Audrey Usherwood
Free house
Wadworth 6X, IPA; Worthington Best Bitter; Guinness; Löwenbräu; Tuborg; cider.

Originally a farm building (vintage 1846) this smart little red-brick pub stands by the roadside with a trim garden to one side. The bar is neat and plush, with old photographs about the walls and a raised area where decent home-prepared snacks may be enjoyed. It's reassuring to be able to see the chef at work in the kitchen, and his lasagne, served with a simple salad garnish, is certainly above average for a pub. Other offerings run from sandwiches, ploughman's and pâté to steak, mushroom and Guinness pie and daily specials like fisherman's pie or full-flavoured tomato and ham soup. Sweets are mainly ice cream variants.
Typical prices Chicken Kiev £3.95 Lasagne £2.95

***ACCOMMODATION* 2 bedrooms £D**
Check-in all day

The two bedrooms are spacious and light, fully carpeted, with white furnishings and pretty wallpaper. Sheets are beautifully ironed, and housekeeping is of a high standard. An equally well-kept bathroom serves the two rooms, and each bedroom also has a washbasin.

Prices given are as at the time of our research and thus may change.

FORD — White Hart at Ford

B & B

Nr Chippenham
MAP 7 A3 *Wiltshire*
Castle Combe (0249) 782213
Parking ample

Landlords Gardner family
Free house
Wadworth 6X; Marston Pedigree; Smiles Exhibition; Fullers ESB; Guinness; Stella Artois; cider.

***ACCOMMODATION* 11 bedrooms £C**
Check-in all day

Tucked away off the A420, beside a trout stream overlooking the Weavern Valley, this fine 16th-century inn offers a high level of comfort and hospitality. A handsome collection of armour is displayed in the low-beamed bar, where a crackling log fire burns in the hearth. Charming bedrooms (six with four-posters) boast excellent private bathrooms; all have colour TVs, tea-makers and writing desks. Closed three days Xmas.
No children under three overnight.
Credit Access

FORTY GREEN — Royal Standard of England

FOOD

Beaconsfield
MAP 7 C2 *Buckinghamshire*
Beaconsfield (049 46) 3382
Parking ample

Bar food 11.30–2.30 & 6–10.30

Landlord Alan Wainwright
Free house
Marston Pedigree, Owd Rodger; Eldridge Pope Royal Oak; Stella Artois; Fosters; Holsten; cider.

Granted its royal title by command of Charles II, who sheltered here after the Battle of Worcester, this splendid hostelry is one of our oldest free houses. Timber and beams from the 11th century make the bar a truly atmospheric setting for an excellent buffet featuring cold meats and pies, fine cheeses, quiches and salads. Finish with memorable fresh fruit salad.
Typical prices Beef salad £3.50 Chocolate fudge cake £1.30

FOSSEBRIDGE — Fossebridge Inn

FOOD & B

Nr Cheltenham
MAP 7 A2 *Gloucestershire*
Fossebridge (028 572) 310
Parking ample

Bar food 12–2 & 6–9.30 (Fri & Sat till 10, Sun from 7)

Landlords Hugh & Suzanne Roberts
Free house
Marston Pedigree, Burton Bitter; Guinness; Carlsberg; Stella Artois; cider.

ACCOMMODATION **13 bedrooms £B**
Check-in all day

★ Hugh and Suzanne Roberts have been busy altering and redecorating this fine old riverside inn centred round a Georgian house. Bar snacks more than match their new, improved surroundings and the frequently changing menu offers such diverse treats as Cornish crab with garlic mayonnaise, potted Wiltshire ham and Guinness-enriched beefsteak pie. Jersey cream accompanies delicious sweets like sticky toffee pudding or fresh fruit, and there are some excellent English farmhouse cheeses. Traditional Sunday lunch menu. ★
Typical prices Cornish monkfish with chive sauce £4.95 Crab with garlic mayonnaise £5.50 Roast pigeon £3.95 Sticky toffee pudding with caramel sauce £2.25

Spacious, attractively refurbished bedrooms in both the main house and annexe provide comfortable overnight accommodation and many rooms enjoy lovely views over the garden and river Coln. All offer TVs, tea-makers and telephones, as well as en suite bath/shower rooms.

Credit Access, Amex, Diners, Visa

FOTHERINGHAY — Falcon Inn

FOOD

Nr Peterborough
MAP 6 D1 *Northamptonshire*
Cotterstock (083 26) 254
Parking ample

Bar food 12.30–2 & 6.45–9.30, Sun 12.30–2 & 7–9
No bar food Mon

Landlord Alan Stewart
Free house
Theakston Bitter; Greene King IPA, Abbot; Elgood Bitter, Greyhound Special; Guinness; Carlsberg; cider.

A cosy, attractive pub in a historic village – Mary Queen of Scots was imprisoned and executed here, and it was also the birthplace of Richard III. Customers come from afar to sample the fine bar meals; the daily-changing menu offers delights such as spiced herring or fresh pear with Stilton and walnut dressing; main courses might be spare ribs or braised venison. Superb sweets. Garden.
Typical prices Braised veal provençale £4.80 Moussaka £2.90

FOVANT — Cross Keys Hotel

B & B

Nr Salisbury
MAP 5 B3 *Wiltshire*
Fovant (072 270) 284
Parking ample

Landlord Pauline Story
Free house
Wadworth 6X; Hall's Harvest Bitter; John Bull Bitter; Carlsberg Hof; Heineken; cider.
***ACCOMMODATION* 4 bedrooms £D**
Check-in all day

Standing on the A30 between Salisbury and Shaftesbury, this nice old stone pub (dating back in parts to the 15th century) is run with warmth and friendliness by Pauline Story. The beamed bars are full of rustic character with their craft bric-a-brac; one boasts a fine old grandfather clock. The four simply furnished bedrooms are bright and fresh. They share a smart public bathroom and new shower room. There's a charming back garden.
Credit Visa

FOVANT — Pembroke Arms

A

Nr Salisbury
MAP 5 B3 *Wiltshire*
Fovant (072 270) 201
Parking ample

Landlords Ron & Joyce Jones
Free house
Marston Pedigree; Wadworth 6X; John Smith's Yorkshire Bitter; Guinness; Carlsberg Hof; Castlemaine XXXX; cider.

Ron and Joyce Jones are the new landlords at this creeper-clad Georgian pub situated on the A30 between Salisbury and Shaftesbury. Once the Earl of Pembroke's shooting lodge – hence the name – it's now known for its collection of World War I memorabilia, and as the headquarters of the Fovant Badges Society. They are the ones responsible for ensuring the upkeep of the remarkable regimental badges carved out of chalk. Garden.

FOWLMERE — Chequers Inn

FOOD

High Street
MAP 7 D1 *Cambridgeshire*
Fowlmere (076 382) 369
Parking ample

Bar food 12–2 & 7–10

Landlord Norman Rushton
Owner Poste Hotels
Tolly Cobbold Original, Bitter; Guinness; Hansa; cider.

A former haunt of Samuel Pepys, this well-kept pub is extremely popular so get there early to make the most of the imaginative bar food. The menu offers such delights as chicken and rosemary soup, with main dishes ranging from grilled herring with salad to pasta with turkey, ham and cream. There's also a cold buffet and sweets are from the restaurant trolley. Garden.
Typical prices Stilton & walnut pâté £2.40 Chicken escalope £4.20
Credit Amex, Amex, Diners, Visa

FOWNHOPE — Green Man

FOOD
B & B

Nr Hereford
MAP 5 A2 *Hereford & Worcester*
Fownhope (043 277) 243
Parking ample

Bar food 11.45–2 & 6.30–10

Landlord Arthur Williams
Free house
Hook Norton Best Bitter; Marston Pedigree; Samuel Smith's Old Brewery Bitter; Guinness; Kronenbourg; Hofmeister; cider.

Charmingly situated in a peaceful village setting close to the river Wye, this pretty black and white timbered inn was once a petty sessions courts. The cosy attractive bars are typically rustic, with open log fires in winter and solid oak beams. Welcoming, too, are the long-serving staff. Familiar dishes in the bar snack menu include soups, pâté, cheese platter, salads and hot dishes such as lasagne, chicken curry and a tasty steak and kidney pie, plus a selection of sandwiches, all enjoyable and

decently prepared. Sunday brings a traditional roast.
Typical prices Home-made steak & kidney pie £3.25 Green Man gammon platter £3.45

ACCOMMODATION **15 bedrooms £D**
Check-in all day

Pretty bedrooms – some with lovely views – are attractively furnished and well-kept. One room has a four-poster and the spacious former Judge's Room is ideally sized for families. All rooms have TVs, tea-makers and compact bath/shower rooms. There's also a comfortable lounge for residents' use and a pretty garden.

FRADLEY — NEW ENTRY — Fradley Arms Hotel

B

Nr Lichfield
MAP 5 B1 *Staffordshire*
Burton-on-Trent (0283) 790186
Parking ample

Landlord Mr R. K. Taylor
Free house
Bass; Worthington Bitter; Carling Black Label; Tennent's Extra; cider.

ACCOMMODATION **6 bedrooms £C**
Check-in all day

The busy A38 runs past this sturdy, family-run white inn, which offers comfortable overnight accommodation. Front rooms are double-glazed, and all are individually furnished with white units or pine furniture and pretty fabrics. All have tiled and carpeted en suite bathrooms. Housekeeping is excellent and the Taylors are welcoming hosts. The small chintzy residents' lounge overlooks the garden and there is a cosy beamed bar.
Credit Access, Amex, Diners, Visa

FRAMFIELD — Barley Mow

OD

Eastbourne Road
MAP 6 E3 *East Sussex*
Framfield (082 582) 234
Parking ample

Bar food 12–2 & 6–9.45, Sun 12–1.30 & 7–9.45
No bar food Mon eve

Landlords Derek & Val Gilbert
Brewery Phoenix
King & Barnes Festive; Webster Yorkshire Bitter; Watney Special; Guinness; Fosters; Budweiser; cider.

A welcoming whitewashed pub with two bars and a pleasant garden. Derek Gilbert's a great enthusiast for his beers, while Val looks to culinary matters, producing real home cooking in generous helpings: vegetable broth, savoury and fruit pies, ham and eggs, quiches, salad platters. Also sandwiches, bangers, jacket potatoes, and an excellent bubble and squeak.
Typical prices Lasagne £3.25 Chilli con carne £3.45

FRAMPTON MANSELL — Crown Inn

B

Stroud
MAP 7 A2 *Gloucestershire*
Frampton Mansell (028 576) 601
Parking ample

Landlord Mrs E. Coley
Free house
Wadworth 6X; Archers Village; Worthington Best Bitter; Younger's Scotch; Guinness; cider.

ACCOMMODATION **12 bedrooms £B**
Check-in all day

Excellent accommodation in a smart 12-room block is a major plus at this Cotswold-stone village pub. Spacious and attractively designed, all the bedrooms feature luxurious carpeting and modular furniture, as well as TVs, tea-makers and direct-dial telephones. En suite bathrooms are equally stylish and well equipped. The beamed and stone-walled bars have an old-fashioned appeal. Garden. Accommodation closed during bad winter weather.
Credit Access, Visa

FRILFORD HEATH — Dog House

B & B Nr Abingdon
MAP 7 B2 *Oxfordshire*
Oxford (0865) 390830
Parking ample

Landlord Mr Hagger
Brewery Morland
Morland Bitter, Best Bitter, Mild; Guinness; Heineken; Stella Artois; cider.

ACCOMMODATION **10 bedrooms £B**
Check-in all day

This modernised 17th-century hotel stands in lovely rural Oxfordshire with views over rich farming land and the Vale of the White Horse. The large bar area with its central fireplace is warm and welcoming, and dog-lovers will lap up the canine posters, pictures and prints. Centrally-heated bedrooms with restrained colour schemes have simple white furnishings; seven have en suite facilities, and all have TVs and tea-makers. Garden. Children's play area.
Credit Access, Amex, Diner, Visa

FRISKNEY — Barley Mow

B & B Sea Lane, Nr Boston
MAP 4 F4 *Lincolnshire*
Friskney (075 484) 483
Parking ample

Landlords Jack & Eileen McCluskie
Brewery Bateman
Bateman Best Bitter, also Triple X and Mild in summer; Guinness; Heineken; cider.

ACCOMMODATION **3 bedrooms £D**
Check-in restricted

A friendly place for an overnight stop, this attractive old pub stands alongside the A52 Boston-Skegness road. Simple, homely comforts are the order of the day, and sloping ceilings add a touch of character to the bedrooms, which are equipped with duvets. Two have wash-basins and all three share the landlords' well-kept bathroom. There are two bars and an outside drinking area. *No children under five overnight. No dogs.*

FULKING — Shepherd & Dog

FOOD Nr Henfield
MAP 6 D4 *West Sussex*
Poynings (079 156) 382
Parking limited

Bar food 12–2 (Sun till 1.45) & 7–9.30 (Mon till 9)
No bar food Sun eve

Landlord Anthony Bradley-Hole
Brewery Phoenix
King & Barnes Festive Ale; Usher Best Bitter; Webster Yorkshire Bitter; Guinness; Holsten; cider.

The situation is a delightful one – tucked into a valley beneath the steepest part of the Sussex Downs, facing a natural spring – and the bar food quite superb at this immensely popular village inn. Find a spot in one of the characterful old bars, in the garden or out on the terrace and tuck into a regularly changing feast – perhaps seafood salad, home-made taramasalata with lovely granary bread, or a perfectly executed lasagne. More hot dishes appear at night (look out for the beef and Guinness pie or the imaginative duck, sage and apple pancakes), and barbecues are a feature of summer Sundays between 7 & 9.30pm. Finish with a perfect, smooth, dark chocolate mousse, passion cake or tangy lemon cheesecake.
Typical prices Beef bourguignon £4.65 Seafood gratin £3.25 Salmon feuilletage £4.95 Steak & kidney pie £3.25

Credit Access, Visa

FYFIELD — White Hart

D

Nr Abingdon
MAP 7 B2 *Oxfordshire*
Frilford Heath (0865) 585
Parking ample

Bar food 12–2.30 & 7–10

Landlord Edward Howard
Free house
Morland Bitter; Wadworth 6X; Ruddles County; Theakston Old Peculier; Guinness; Tennent's Lager; cider.

Flagstones, beams and a gallery are features of this fine old pub with much baronial appeal, and the lovely garden is another attraction. The snacks are a mixture of traditional and a little bit different, with soup, steak, moussaka, pork tropicana and lasagne alongside vegetarian dishes, salads, sandwiches and ploughman's. Bread is home-baked, and sweets are appealing.
Typical prices Steak & kidney pie £3.45 Chicken Strasbourg £4.35
Credit Access, Amex, Diners, Visa

GESTINGTHORPE — Pheasant

D

Nr Halstead
MAP 6 E2 *Essex*
Hedingham (0787) 61196
Parking ample

Bar food 12–2 (Sun till 1.30) & 7–10 (Fri & Sat till 10.30)

Landlords Mike & Jeanne Harwood
Free house
Pheasant Bitter; Greene King IPA, Abbot Ale; Adnams Bitter; Bass; Guinness; cider.

A friendly pub providing a popular rendezvous for the locals. The food is all home-cooked and patrons can choose from a selection of generous sandwiches such as ham, prawn salad or fresh salmon and cucumber for a snack. Main dishes include a fiery chilli, macaroni cheese and boeuf bourguignon, while the daily special might be chicken provençale. Apple pie or treacle tart to finish. Garden.
Typical prices Chicken curry £3.50 Cottage pie £2.50

GIBRALTAR — NEW ENTRY — Bottle & Glass

D

Nr Aylesbury
MAP 7 C2 *Buckinghamshire*
Aylesbury (0296) 748488
Parking ample

Bar food 12–2.15 & 7–10
No bar food Sun eve

Landlords David Berry & Jeremy Davies
Brewery ABC
ABC Bitter; Bass; Burton Ale; Morrell Dark Mild; Skol; Löwenbräu; cider.

On the A418 just outside Aylesbury, this attractive thatched pub started life as a cottage in the 14th century. There are two characterful little bars, and food is served in a couple of panelled dining rooms overlooking the garden. Typically tasty offerings might include celery and Stilton soup, chicken in a creamy cashew nut sauce and roast pork. Salads and open sandwiches, too.
Typical prices Seafood open sandwich £4.25 Steak & oyster pie £4.25
Credit Access, Amex, Diners, Visa **LVs**

GOLDSBOROUGH — Bay Horse Inn

B

Nr Knaresborough
MAP 4 D3 *North Yorkshire*
Harrogate (0423) 862212
Parking ample

Landlord June Manks
Brewery Whitbread
Whitbread Trophy; Castle Eden; Guinness; Stella Artois; Heineken; cider.

***ACCOMMODATION* 5 bedrooms £D**
Check-in all day

This sturdily built inn situated in a quiet village off the A59 offers a warm welcome. The large bar area is full of character and charm, with old beams and an open fireplace. There is also a quiet lounge overlooking an extremely pretty garden. The bedrooms, in a rear extension, are small, neat and tidy, with modern fitted units, washbasins and tea/coffee-makers. They share two well-kept modern bathrooms. *No children under five overnight. No dogs.*
Credit Access, Visa

GOMSHALL — Black Horse

B & B

Station Road
MAP 7 C3 *Surrey*
Shere (048 641) 2242
Parking ample

Landlords Anne & Andrew Brown
Brewery Young
Young Bitter, Special; Beamish; Young Premium, John Young London Lager; cider.

***ACCOMMODATION* 6 bedrooms £C**
Check-in all day

There's a solid dependable air about this 17th-century inn, which stands on the A25 in an area of great natural beauty. Carved antique chairs, sturdy tables and a coal fire give character and warmth to the bar, and bedrooms feature well-chosen fabrics, electric blankets and tea-makers. The residents' TV lounge is large, light and very comfortable. Patio and garden. Children welcome in the bar lunchtime only. *No children under 12 overnight.*
Credit Diners, Visa

We welcome bona fide recommendations or complaints on the tear-out pages for readers' comments.

They are followed up by our professional team but do complain to the management.

GOOSTREY — Olde Red Lion Inn

FOOD

Main Road
MAP 3 C4 *Cheshire*
Holmes Chapel (0477) 32033
Parking ample

Bar food 11.30–3 & 7–11, Sun 12–2 & 7–10
Landlords Mary & Peter Yorke
Brewery Tetley
Tetley Bitter, Mild; Walker Best Bitter; Guinness; Castlemaine XXXX; Oranjeboom; cider.

Log fires keep things cosy at this rambling pub, whose bars feature mock beams, unevenly plastered walls and copper-topped tables. The bar menu offers some very enjoyable eating: cheesy-stuffed mushrooms or grilled sardines for starters or snacks, open and closed butties, home-cooked ham, beef bourguignon, even oysters when available. Traditional Sunday lunch menu.
Typical prices Beef & beer pie £2.95 Prawns in wine & garlic £4.95
Credit Access, Amex, Visa

GOSBERTON — Five Bells

B & B

Spalding Road
MAP 6 D1 *Lincolnshire*
Spalding (0775) 840348
Parking ample

Landlords Mr & Mrs Woodhouse
Brewery Manns
Webster Yorkshire Bitter; Wilson Original Bitter; Manns Best Bitter, Mild; Guinness; Carlsberg.

***ACCOMMODATION* 3 bedrooms £D**
Check-in all day

Simple comforts are offered for an overnight stay in this solid white inn, which stands alongside the A16 Boston-Spalding Road. There are three bedrooms, very clean and well-maintained, with white walls and modern white furnishings, pretty quilt covers, TVs and tea-makers. They all have washbasins and share a functional bathroom. Public rooms include a panelled lounge and a large, simply furnished public bar with a pool table. Garden. *No dogs.*

GREAT CHISHILL — Pheasant Inn

A Nr Royston
MAP 7 D1 *Hertfordshire*
Royston (0763) 838535
Parking ample

Closed Mon lunch

Landlord Denis Ryan
Free house
Younger's IPA, Scotch, Tartan Bitter; Adnams Bitter; McEwan's Lager; Carlsberg.

Ex-jockey Denis Ryan is an exuberant host at his peaceful, 300-year-old pub. Old beams, bricks and a marvellous inglenook fireplace to keep the customers warm in winter provide plenty of character. The bar walls are adorned with stuffed pheasants and racing memorabilia such as signed photographs, prints and paintings of famous jockeys, while antique furniture and horsy bric-a-brac add to the cosy atmosphere overall. Children welcome lunchtimes only.

GREAT RYBURGH — Boar Inn

B Nr Fakenham
MAP 6 E1 *Norfolk*
Great Ryburgh (032 878) 212
Parking ample

Landlords Jim & Margaret Corson
Free house
Tolly Cobbold Original, Wensum Bitter; Adnams Bitter; Guinness; Hansa; Carlsberg; cider.

ACCOMMODATION **4 bedrooms £D**
Check-in all day

Opposite a round-towered Saxon church, this whitewashed pub nestles in a sleepy village. A warm welcome is assured in the low-beamed bar, which has an enormous inglenook fireplace to warm the winter nights. Oak beams and bold floral fabrics give a cottagy appeal to the simple, unfussy bedrooms. All four rooms are compact in size and have their own washbasins, colour TVs and digital alarm clocks. They share a modern shower room. Garden.
Credit Access, Visa

GREAT STAINTON — Kings Arms

D Nr Stockton-on-Tees
MAP 4 D2 *Cleveland*
Sedgefield (0740) 30361
Parking ample

Bar food 12–1.45 & 7–9.45

Landlords Mr & Mrs G. Mitchell
Brewery Whitbread
Castle Eden; Whitbread Trophy; Scotch Bitter; Guinness; Stella Artois; Heineken; cider.

The blackboard menu offers a huge choice of capably prepared food to be enjoyed in the traditional lounge bar of this white-painted village pub. Hearty eaters can tuck into generous portions of main dishes like Hawaiian pork and halibut in seafood sauce, while flavoursome pâté, soup and hot roast meat sandwiches provide tasty lighter bites. Terrace. *No children after 8.30 pm.*
Typical prices Chicken princesse £3.65 Beef stroganoff £3.65
Credit Visa

GREAT TEW — Falkland Arms

A MAP 7 B1 *Oxfordshire*
Great Tew (060 893) 653
Parking ample

Closed Mon lunch

Landlord John Milligan
Free house
Donnington Best Bitter; Wadworth 6X; Hook Norton Best Bitter; Theakston XB; guest beers; cider.

A creeper-clad ancient pub set in a beautiful and historic village, built entirely of golden Cotswold stone. An inglenook fireplace, high-backed settles, oak and elm beams, well-worn flagstones and a huge collection of beer mugs hanging from the ceiling provide a suitably mellow and traditional interior. You can buy country wines, clay pipes filled ready to smoke and some fifty different snuffs. There's also a beer garden for summer drinking.

GREAT WALTHAM **Windmill**

FOOD MAP 7 D2 *Essex*
Chelmsford (0245) 360292
Parking ample

Bar food 12–2 & 7–9.15
No bar food Sat & Sun lunches
Closed Sun eve, Bank Hols & 4 days Xmas

Landlord Martin Ridgewell
Free house
Adnams Bitter; Carling Black Label.

★ The Ridgewells have been maintaining a high standard at their friendly roadside pub on the A130 for some 24 years now and chef Peter Wilson is continuing the tradition of good cooking. Notably fresh produce is handled with care, resulting in some delicious meals. The food ranges from simple bread and cheese and sandwiches to fish and chips and ham off the bone with chips. Weekly-changing specials include wing of skate, lamb chops, poached cod in seafood sauce, pig's liver and bacon and the perennially popular steak, kidney and mushroom pie. Well-chosen vegetables are cooked to perfection and all food is served in extremely generous portions. Finish with one of the simple sweets such as bread and butter pudding or the selection of English cheeses. ★

Typical prices Poached cod with seafood sauce £4.50 Steak & kidney pie £4.50 Dressed crab salad £4.50 Home-made pavlova £1.75

Credit Access, Visa

Changes in data may occur in establishments after the Guide goes to press.

Prices should be taken as indications rather than firm quotes.

GREAT WOLFORD **Fox & Hounds**

B & B Nr Shipston-on-Stour
MAP 7 B1 *Warwickshire*
Barton on the Heath (060 874) 220
Parking ample

Landlords Mr & Mrs C. Olcese
Free house
Flowers IPA, Best Bitter; Whitbread Best Bitter; Guinness; Stella Artois; Heineken; cider. *No real ale.*

ACCOMMODATION **4 bedrooms £B**
Check-in all day

In a quiet village about two miles from the A34, this former 16th-century coaching house is strong on country charm. The bar with its low ceiling, beams and handsome open fireplace is a very popular local meeting place. Four bedrooms in a converted stable block provide comfortable, smartly kept accommodation. Fabrics and furnishings are appealing, and each room has its own spacious, well-fitted bathroom. Garden.
Credit Visa

GRETA BRIDGE — **Morritt Arms Hotel**

Nr Barnard Castle
MAP 4 D2 *Co. Durham*
Teesdale (0833) 27232
Parking ample

Lunch (Sun only) 12–2
Dinner 7.30–9

Landlords John & David Mulley
Free house
Theakston Bitter; William Younger's Scotch; Newcastle Exhibition; Carlsberg; cider.

Charles Dickens stayed at this fine stone-built inn in 1838 and, after visiting Dotheboys Hall at Bowes, wrote *Nicholas Nickleby* here. A delightful mural in the pleasant beamed bar remembers that visit. New owners, the Mulleys, offer an appetising range of food in the handsome panelled restaurant: a typical dinner choice could be herby home-made soup, followed by tender lamb steak in a tasty wine sauce (accompanied by plenty of fresh vegetables), with crème caramel to finish. Snooze it all off beside a roaring winter fire in the comfortable panelled lounge. Traditional Sunday lunch menu.
Typical prices Lasagne £3.50 Steak & mushroom pie £4

ACCOMMODATION **23 bedrooms £B**
Check-in all day

The hotel is well placed for visitors to the beauty spots of Teesdale, High Force, Cauldron Snout and the Lake District. Homely bedrooms, some furnished with sturdy traditional pieces, others more modern in style, all have TVs, tea-makers and trouser presses. Both public and private bathrooms are well maintained. Garden.

Credit Access, Amex, Diners, Visa

GRIMSTHORPE — **Black Horse Inn**

Nr Bourne
MAP 6 D1 *Lincolnshire*
Edenham (077 832) 247
Parking ample

Bar food 12–1.30 & 7–9.30
Closed Sun & Bank Hols

Landlords Mr & Mrs K. S. Fisher
Free house
Samuel Smith Tadcaster Bitter.
No real ale.

ACCOMMODATION **4 bedrooms £B**
Check-in all day

The Fishers have been welcoming folk for over 20 years at their delightful Georgian inn. Traditional English cooking is the mainstay of the nicely varied menu offered in the convivial buttery – which you'll find next to the large, beamed main bar. Everything is prepared with care, from Cornish fish pancakes and pinkly tender rack of lamb to homely sweets like treacle tart and Queen of puddings. A cold buffet is available at lunchtimes.
Typical prices Steak & kidney pie £3.95 Grimsby plaice £3.45 Fish hors d'oeuvre £4.25 Lincolnshire sausages with tomatoes & chutney £2.65

Charmingly cottagy bedrooms offer extras like books and biscuits, as well as tea-makers and radios. Each has a key to its own equally well-equipped, carpeted bathroom. Residents can watch TV in the cosy lounge bar, and there's a patio for summer drinks. *No children under eight overnight.*

Credit Access, Amex, Visa

GRINDLEFORD — Maynard Arms Hotel

FOOD
B & B

Nr Sheffield
MAP 4 D4 *Derbyshire*
Hope Valley (0433) 30321
Parking ample

Bar food 12–2 & 6–9.30 (Sun from 7)

Landlord Robert Lindsay Graham
Brewery Bass (North)
Stones Bitter; Carling Black Label; cider.

The Peak District National Park is the lovely setting for this handsome Victorian hotel, perched on a steep hill a few hundred yards from the river Derwent. Stained-glass windows, wood panelling and a splendid oak staircase characterise public areas, and the bars are a comfortable traditional setting for tasty bar snacks available at all times. The choice includes home-made soup and breakfast-style grills as well as more elaborate offerings like stir-fried prawns and chicken or aubergine and mushroom lasagne. The blackboard menu offers daily specials (roast beef, steak and kidney pie) and there are some simple sweets and well-kept English cheeses.
Typical prices Yorkshireman £2.75 Maynards Special (open sandwich) £1.95

***ACCOMMODATION* 13 bedrooms £B**
Check-in all day

Smart, inviting bedrooms have tea-makers, remote-control TVs, direct-dial phones, and offer good private bath or shower rooms. A number of superior rooms enjoy lovely views of the garden and river. Children welcome overnight.
Credit Access, Amex, Diners, Visa

GUILDFORD — NEW ENTRY — Rats Castle

FOOD

80 Sydenham Road
MAP 7 C3 *Surrey*
Guildford (0483) 572410
Parking difficult

Bar food 11–2 & 6.30–10
No bar food Sun

Landlord Mrs B. Heath
Brewery Friary Meux
Friary Meux Bitter; Ind Coope; Burton Ale; John Bull Bitter; Guinness; Löwenbräu; Skol; cider.

Tucked away in a side street, this Edwardian tile-hung pub offers a wide range of fresh and flavoursome food. There's something to suit everyone, with choices like garlicky pâté, jacket potatoes and mushrooms on toast, cottage pie, bacon and spinach pancake and liver with onions, and a variety of sandwiches. Rattan furniture and marble-topped tables create a stylish setting.
Typical prices Chicken with leeks & Stilton £4.65 Ploughman's £2.45
Credit Access **LVs**

GUISBOROUGH — Fox Inn

B & B

10 Bow Street
MAP 4 E2 *Cleveland*
Guisborough (0287) 32958
Parking limited

Landlords Mr & Mrs Williamson
Brewery Scottish & Newcastle
Scottish & Newcastle Exhibition; Younger's Scotch; McEwan's 80/-; Guinness; McEwan's Lager; cider.
No real ale.

***ACCOMMODATION* 7 bedrooms £C**
Check-in all day

In the centre of a relatively unspoilt market town, this pebbledash pub is run on welcoming lines by the Williamsons. The whole place is kept in apple pie order, and the bedrooms, all of a decent size, offer the comforts of central heating and double glazing, plus colour TVs and tea-makers. There are two bars – one smartly plush, the other with mock beams and a separate area where children may sit. Decent breakfasts. *No dogs.*
Credit Access, Amex, Visa

GUISBOROUGH — Moorcock Hotel

& B

West End
MAP 4 E2 *Cleveland*
Guisborough (0287) 32342
Parking ample

Landlord Alan Mitchell
Brewery Whitbread
Whitbread Trophy; Guinness; Heineken; Stella Artois; cider.
No real ale.

***ACCOMMODATION* 6 bedrooms £D**
Check-in all day

A purpose-built public house on the outskirts of town offering practical comforts for an overnight stay. Bedrooms are centrally heated and each has a modern shower unit, functional fitted furniture and a black and white TV; all share a well-kept public bathroom. There's a large bar, a residents' lounge (colour TV) and a family room where video cartoons are shown at weekends. The roomy beer garden also has a well-equipped area where children can play.

GUNNISLAKE — Cornish Inn

& B

The Square
MAP 9 B2 *Cornwall*
Tavistock (0822) 832475
Parking ample

Landlords Brian & Dawn Marsh
Free house
St Austell Tinners Ale; Hicks Special; Flowers Best Bitter; Worthington Best Bitter; Guinness; Carlsberg Hof.

***ACCOMMODATION* 9 bedrooms £C**
Check-in all day

Brian and Dawn Marsh are the friendly owners of this pub right in the village centre. The whole place is neat and tidy, and the bright bedrooms (six with en suite facilities) offer modest but comfortable overnight accommodation; all have tea/coffee-makers. The bar, with its rustic tables, pew seating and horsy paraphernalia, is a nice spot for a drink, and there's a relaxing residents' lounge. Patio. Children are welcome overnight.
Credit Access, Amex, Diners, Visa

HALFORD — Halford Bridge Inn

& B

Fosse Way
MAP 7 B1 *Warwickshire*
Stratford-upon-Avon (0789) 740382
Parking ample

Landlords Mr & Mrs Westwood
Brewery Northampton
Ruddles County; Wilson Original Bitter; Webster Yorkshire Bitter; Guinness; Fosters; Carlsberg; cider.

***ACCOMMODATION* 6 bedrooms £D**
Check-in all day

On the A429 Fosse Way, this 16th-century coaching inn offers comfortable overnight accommodation in six homely bedrooms. All rooms are double-glazed and are decorated in pastel shades in a mixture of styles. Each has its own TV, and residents have the use of a lounge where tea-making facilities and an ironing board are provided. There are two public bathrooms with showers. Downstairs, an open fire warms the simply furnished bar. Courtyard.
Credit Access

HALLATON — Bewicke Arms

OD

1 Eastgate, Nr Market Harborough
MAP 5 C1 *Leicestershire*
Hallaton (085 889) 217
Parking ample

Bar food 12–1.45 & 7.15–9.45, Sun 12–1.30 & 7–9.30

Landlords Mr & Mrs N.A. Spiers
Free house
Ruddles County, Rutland Bitter; Marston Pedigree; Guinness; Carlsberg; cider.

A 400-year-old white-painted inn with three cosy bars (one bookable as a restaurant) and a hospitable atmosphere. The bar menu, supplemented by blackboard specials, offers a choice of well-prepared dishes. First courses include soup, pâté or smoked mackerel, followed by haddock, roast chicken, lasagne, or seafood pancake. There are ploughman's, salads and sandwiches, and home-made sweets. Garden.
Typical prices Chicken boursin £3.60 Lemon cheesecake £1.30

HAMBLEDEN — Stag & Huntsman Inn

FOOD
B & B

Nr Henley-on-Thames
MAP 7 C3 *Buckinghamshire*
Henley-on-Thames (0491) 571227
Parking ample
Bar food 12–2 & 7–10
No bar food Sun eve
Landlords Mr & Mrs D. Vidgen & Mr N. Vidgen
Free house
Brakspear PA; Flowers Original; Wadworth 6X; Huntsman Royal Oak; Guinness; Stella Artois; cider.

Chef Nick Vidgen's travels have left their mark on the menu of his parents' 17th-century pub in a picturesque village in the Chiltern Hills. At least half the dishes on the blackboard menu are of Mexican origin, with puerco verde – flavoursome pork on a bed of corn chips – a typical example. Cheese nachos, chilli bowl and Colorado chicken are other popular choices. Nearer home there is soup, smooth chicken liver and brandy pâté, salads (smoked trout and rare roast beef), ploughman's, and chicken and mushroom pie. Barbecued steaks are available in the evenings. Tempting sweets include orange cheesecake, chocolate mousse, and a banana split filled with delicious peach ice cream. Most delightful of the atmospheric bars is the cosy snug.
Typical prices Puerco verde £3.20 Mixed tortillas £4.75

ACCOMMODATION **3 bedrooms £D**
Check-in all day

Simple overnight accommodation is available in three bright and airy bedrooms – one with a shower cabinet – that share a spotless bathroom. Good breakfasts. Garden. *No dogs.*
Credit Access, Visa

HAROME — Star Inn

FOOD

Nr Helmsley
MAP 4 E3 *North Yorkshire*
Helmsley (0439) 70397
Parking ample
Bar food 12–2
No bar food eves
Landlords Mr A. D. Bowron & Mr P. Gascoigne-Mullett
Free house
Cameron Lion Bitter; Theakston Best Bitter, Old Peculier; Vaux Samson; Carlsberg Hof.

Character and charm abound at this delightful thatched pub in a quiet village. The very popular lunchtime menu offers home-made soup and delicious sandwiches with tasty fillings ranging from cheese, roast beef and ham to curried chicken and smoked trout pâté; there's also a star special which consists of prawns, cottage cheese, mayonnaise and peppers. Garden.
Typical prices Vegetable soup 75p Prawn curry sandwich £2
Credit Access, Amex, Diners, Visa

HARRIETSHAM — Ringlestone Inn

A

Nr Maidstone
MAP 6 E3 *Kent*
Maidstone (0622) 859207
Parking ample
Landlord Michael Millington-Buck
Free house
Ringlestone Bitter; Fremlins Bitter; Flowers Best Bitter; Wethered Winter Royal; Theakston Old Peculier; Heineken; cider.

Locals are the best guide to the whereabouts of this splendid 400-year-old pub close to the Pilgrims Way. All the bars are knee-deep in character, with blackened beams, brick floors, an inglenook fireplace, and some sturdy 17th-century furnishings. They add up to the perfect setting, with a great sense of history and a very relaxed atmosphere in which to enjoy a good range of traditional beers and fruity country wines. Garden.
Credit Access, Amex, Diners, Visa

HARROGATE — West Park Hotel

B 19 West Park
MAP 4 D3 *North Yorkshire*
Harrogate (0423) 524471
Parking ample

Landlords Mr & Mrs C. A. Gillis
Brewery Tetley
Tetley Bitter, Mild; Marston Burton Bitter; Guinness; Skol; Castlemaine XXXX; cider.

ACCOMMODATION **18 bedrooms £B**
Check-in all day

With its pleasant outlook over the green expanses of the Stray and its proximity to the town's amenities, this up-dated inn is a good stopover for both business visitors and tourists. Bedrooms are all of a decent size, with modern furnishings, light colour schemes and attractive units. Direct-dial telephones and remote-control TVs are standard, and most rooms have private facilities. Note the splendid ornate ceiling in the main bar. *No dogs.*
Credit Access, Amex, Diners, Visa

HASLEMERE — Crowns

OD Weyhill
MAP 6 D3 *Surrey*
Haslemere (0428) 3112
Parking ample

Bar food 12–2 & 7–10.30

Landlord Brenda Heath
Brewery Friary Meux
Friary Meux Bitter; Ind Coope Burton Ale; Crown Special; Guinness; Castlemaine XXXX; Löwenbräu; cider.

★ Huge helpings of good-quality home-cooked food and a warm welcome at the bar make Brenda Heath's substantial pub a winner. In a smart and cheerful pubby atmosphere you can choose from a wide range of dishes written up on blackboards: smoked haddock topped with fresh farm eggs served on a bed of succulent spinach, lamb's kidneys cooked in sherry, lasagne verdi pie and seafood salad are typical offerings. Everything is based on excellent raw materials and simpler items like ploughman's, rump steak, pizza and lemon sole, reach the same high standard. Desserts are enticing and include a really special Bakewell tart. On Thursday, Friday and Saturday evenings part of the pub becomes a restaurant with a separate menu offering dishes like venison in red wine and seafood kebabs. Traditional roast Sunday lunch. Patio and garden. ★

Typical prices Chicken breast stuffed with leeks and Stilton £5.25 Garlic stuffed mussels £2.65 Lamb cutlets in rosemary £5.25 Chocolate rum cake £1.50

Credit Access, Amex, Diners, Visa **LVs**

HASTINGWOOD COMMON — Rainbow & Dove

A Nr Harlow
MAP 7 D2 *Essex*
Harlow (0279) 415419
Parking ample

Landlords Tony & Joyce Bird
Brewery Ind Coope
John Bull Bitter; Tetley Bitter; Guinness; Skol; Löwenbräu; *No real ale.*

You'll find this little pub a short drive from junction 7 of the M11. It has everything you could ask for in a country pub – oak-beamed ceilings, low oak tables, polished horse brasses, pottery, pewter and copper jugs and a variety of bric-a-brac. Outside, hanging baskets spilling over with fuchsias adorn the frontage in summer and the garden contains a putting green for customers in a sporting mood.

HATHERLEIGH — George Hotel

FOOD
B & B

Market Street
MAP 9 B2 *Devon*
Okehampton (0837) 810 454
Parking ample

Bar food 11.30–2.30 & 6–9.30

Landlords Mr & Mrs Andrew Grubb
Free house
Courage Best Bitter; Cornish Original; Wadworth 6X; Guinness; Stella Artois; Tuborg; cider.

This delightful former coaching inn, dating from the 15th century, has a real period flavour. Its thatched roof, cobbled courtyard, and uneven white walls give it a picture-postcard charm. Inside, the theme is continued with big blackened beams, massive inglenook fireplaces and some fine wood panelling in the various bars. Homely snacks are served at the back of the large Jubilee bar. A printed menu offers home-made soup, savoury pancakes, stuffed jacket potatoes and sandwiches, while for the more substantial appetites there are steaks, lasagne, fry-ups and pies. This choice is supplemented by daily blackboard specials, and on Sunday a traditional roast lunch is served.

Typical prices Steak and kidney pie £3 10oz Sirloin steak £4.95

ACCOMMODATION **11 bedrooms £C**
Check-in all day

Rough white walls, deep-set windows and exposed beams give character to the plainly decorated bedrooms, two of which have four-poster beds. Most have neat, basic en suite bathrooms. There's also a large residents' lounge with chintzy armchairs and TV.

Credit Access, Visa

HAWKHURST — Tudor Arms Hotel

FOOD
B & B

Rye Road
MAP 6 E3 *Kent*
Hawkhurst (05805) 2312
Parking ample

Bar food 12–2 & 7–9.30

Landlord Barry Edwards
Owners Sheldon Park Hotels Ltd
Fremlins Bitter; Whitbread Best Bitter; Heineken.

Attractive gardens offer a pleasant summer alternative to the handsome panelled bar at this smart red-brick pub on the A268 Rye road. Well-prepared bar snacks are always available, and the choice ranges from warming home-made soups – perhaps asparagus, carrot or mixed vegetable – omelettes, salads and plain or toasted sandwiches to tasty hot dishes like shepherd's pie, moussaka or things with chips. Spoil-yourself sweets include chocolate mousse and lemon soufflé.

Typical prices Steak & kidney pie £3.20 Leek & potato soup 90p

ACCOMMODATION **14 bedrooms £A**
Check-in all day

Traditional and modern furniture blend well in the spacious, airy and spotlessly maintained bedrooms which have cream decor and flowery furnishings. All have tea-makers, radio alarms and trouser presses (hairdryers on request), and all but two have en suite carpeted bathrooms. Residents can relax in an inviting lounge with an open fire and plenty of leather and chintz sofas and armchairs.

Credit Access, Amex, Diners, Visa

Prices given are as at the time of our research and thus may change.

HAWKSHEAD **Queen's Head**

OD
& B

MAP 3 B3 *Cumbria*
Hawkshead (096 66) 271
Parking ample

Bar food 12–2 & 6.30–9 (in winter from 7)

Landlord Allan Whitehead
Brewery Hartley
Hartley XB, Mild; Guinness; Stella Artois; Heineken; cider.

A traditional family-run pub in a very attractive Lakeland village. The panelled main bar and neighbouring snug provide a fine setting for enjoying some very good bar food, and the promise of the delicious smells wafting from the kitchen is more than fulfilled. Consistency is the keynote throughout the range, from rich creamy mushroom soup and venison pâté to casseroled pheasant, beef curry and some excellent sweets like mocha cheesecake with a super, penetrating coffee taste. Sandwiches are an additional lunchtime offering.
Typical prices Local Cumberland sausage £3.50 Home-made hare casserole with juniper berries £3.95

***ACCOMMODATION* 10 bedrooms £C**
Check-in all day

Beamed ceilings and simple furnishings bestow an old-world charm on the bedrooms, four of which have neat private bathrooms. Recent additions include two new bedrooms in adjacent cottage. Accommodation closed ten days Christmas. *No children under ten overnight. No dogs.*

Credit Access, Amex, Diners, Visa

HAYTOR VALE **Rock Inn**

OD
& B

Nr Newton Abbot
MAP 9 C2 *Devon*
Haytor (036 46) 305
Parking ample

Bar food 11–2 & 6.45–9.45

Landlord Christopher Graves
Free house
Eldridge Pope Royal Oak, Dorset Original IPA, Pope's 1880, Dorchester Bitter; Bass; Guinness; Stella Artois; cider.

In a tiny village nestling below Dartmoor's highest tor, this welcoming 250-year-old pub is an extremely popular eating place. Fresh flowers decorate the mellow, candlelit rooms where every antique table is invariably taken by hungry hordes tucking into a wide variety of tasty snacks. As well as sandwiches, jacket potatoes, Cheddar or Stilton ploughman's, and soup, there are substantial offerings like curry, well-filled pasties, pies, venison in red wine and local trout. Don't forget to leave room for a delicious sweet like tangy lemon tart or bread and butter pudding. Traditional roasts are a feature on Sundays.
Typical prices Steak & kidney pie £3.25 Game pie £3.25

***ACCOMMODATION* 9 bedrooms £C**
Check-in all day

Most of the attractively decorated bedrooms have private bathrooms and one boasts a four-poster. TVs, direct-dial telephones, tea and coffee making facilities, and mini-bars are standard throughout. *No dogs.*

Credit Amex

We publish annually so make sure you use the current edition.

HELFORD — Shipwright's Arms

FOOD

Nr Helston
MAP 9 A3 *Cornwall*
Manaccan (032 623) 235
Parking limited

Bar food 12–2 & 6.30–9.15
No bar food Sun eves in winter

Landlord Brandon Flynn
Brewery Cornish Breweries
Devenish Cornish Bitter, Mild, John Devenish Bitter; Guinness; Heineken; Grünhalle; cider.

A pretty thatched pub on the river where the lunchtime buffet is a great attraction in summer – choose between seafood, Cornish pasty or cold meats. Summer evenings see a blackboard menu with a strong fish bias; don't miss the shellfish platter of lobster, crab claws, prawns and mussels. There are steaks and meaty options too. Hearty, warming dishes in the winter. Terrace.
Typical prices Fresh crab salad £4.50 Home-made apricot and brandy ice cream £1.40

HELMSLEY — Feathers Hotel

B & B

Market Place
MAP 4 E3 *North Yorkshire*
Helmsley (0439) 70275
Parking limited

Landlords Feathers family
Free house
Younger's Tartan Bitter; Theakston Bitter, XB; Cameron Bitter; Bass North Best Mild; Guinness; Beck's Bier; Carlsberg; cider.

ACCOMMODATION **18 bedrooms £C**
Check-in all day

A 15th-century cottage and an 18th-century house make up this friendly, family-run inn overlooking the market square. Comfortable bedrooms are furnished and decorated in a variety of styles; all offer TVs and tea-makers, most have their own modern bathroom. There's a popular, rustic public bar, relaxing lounge bar and a homely residents' lounge. Garden. Accommodation closed from Christmas to the end of January.
Credit Access, Amex, Diners, Visa

HELSTON — Angel Hotel

B & B

Coinagehall Street
MAP 9 A3 *Cornwall*
Helston (0326) 572701
Parking ample

Landlords Mr & Mrs S.W. Hudson
Free house
Flowers Best Bitter; Whitbread Best Bitter, Poacher; Worthington Bitter; Carling Black Label; Heineken; cider. *No real ale.*

ACCOMMODATION **21 bedrooms £D**
Check-in all day

The most striking feature of the public areas at this town centre coaching inn is the illuminated 30-foot well in the lounge bar. Stairs and corridors have been recarpeted and the bedrooms have pleasant wallpaper and upholstery, and well-polished traditional or antique furniture. Most rooms are equipped with colour TVs, tea and coffee-makers, and they share eight fully tiled shower rooms between them. Patio. Accommodation closed two Christmas.
Credit Access, Amex, Diners, Visa

HENLEY-ON-THAMES — Argyll

FOOD

Market Place
MAP 7 C3 *Oxfordshire*
Henley-on-Thames (0491) 573400
Parking ample

Bar food 12–2
No bar food eves
Landlords Ray & Veronica Boswell
Brewery Morland
Morland Best Bitter, Bitter, Mild, Artists; Guinness; Heineken.

Home cooking draws the crowds to this friendly, black and white pub in the centre of town. At lunchtime, the long, split-level bar displays an attractive choice of hot and cold fare. Quiches, hams, stuffed eggs, pâté, beef, chicken and fresh salads are complemented by curries, savoury flan or sausage and mash. Delicious sticky treacle tart or chocolate mousse to follow. Traditional Sunday lunchtime roast. Patio.
Typical prices Chicken, ham & mushroom pie £3 Seafood pie £2.60

HENLEY-ON-THAMES — Little Angel

OD

Remenham Lane, Remenham
MAP 7 C3 *Oxfordshire*
Henley-on-Thames (0491) 574165
Parking ample

Bar food 12–2 & 7–10

Landlord Paul Southwood
Brewery Brakspear
Brakspear Bitter, 4X Old; Guinness; Heineken; cider.

Just over the bridge on the A423 Maidenhead road, this attractive old pub is full of charm and character. The bar food is very popular, and the regularly changing menu tends towards the sea with dishes like lemon sole, sliced Scotch smoked salmon, grilled plaice and soft roes. Meat dishes, too, plus sandwiches, salads, sorbets, and a traditional roast on Sundays. Terrace.
Typical prices Prawn thermidor £4.50 Duck liver & Grand Marnier pâté £3.50
Credit Access, Amex, Diners, Visa

HENTON — Peacock

& B

Nr Chinnor
MAP 7 C2 *Oxfordshire*
Kingston Blount (0844) 53519
Parking ample

Landlord Mr H.S. Good
Free house
Brakspear Bitter; Hook Norton Bitter; Adnams Bitter; Hall & Woodhouse Badger Best; Guinness; cider.

***ACCOMMODATION* 3 bedrooms £C**
Check-in all day

Not just a pretty name, this black and white thatched inn, over 600 years old, has peacocks and ducks roaming the grounds. There is a large spacious bar with a country feel, and three very attractive cottage-style bedrooms with sloping ceilings and beams. Rooms have fitted wardrobes, pretty curtains and duvets as well as TVs and en suite bath or shower rooms. Good breakfast. Garden and patio. Children are welcome overnight. *No dogs.*
Credit Access, Amex, Visa

HEXWORTHY — Forest Inn

OD
& B

Nr Princetown
MAP 9 B2 *Devon*
Poundsgate (036 43) 211
Parking ample

Bar food 12–2 & 6–8.30 (Sun from 7)
Closed eves Nov–Feb & 1 wk Xmas

Landlords Mrs O. Wise & Mr A. Oake
Free house
Worthington Best Bitter; Bass; Guinness; Tennent's Pilsner; cider.

Ideal for walking, fishing or pony trekking holidays, this sturdy Dartmoor inn is set high up in a landscape of rugged, desolate beauty. Plants bring a touch of colour to the spacious courtyard and the homely bars, where a blackboard menu lists daily specials featuring fresh local fish. Also on the menu are hearty soups to warm you after a day on the moors, sandwiches, ploughman's, cold platters, and delicious filling sweets such as steamed sponge pudding topped with clotted cream. There's also a traditional roast served on Sundays.
Typical prices Chicken chasseur £4 Fresh whole lemon sole £5.50

***ACCOMMODATION* 15 bedrooms £C**
Check-in all day

Comfortable beds with crisply laundered sheets ensure a good night's sleep in the simply furnished bedrooms. Four have en suite bathrooms, while the remainder share four old-fashioned bathrooms. Good breakfasts. There's also a garden for summer drinking. Accommodation closed November to February.

Credit Diners, Visa

HIGHCLERE — Yew Tree Inn

B & B

Andover Road, Newbury
MAP 7 B3 *Berkshire*
Highclere (0635) 253360
Parking ample

Landlords Mr & Mrs A.M. Greenwood
Free house
Bunce's Best; Wadworth 6X; guest beers; Guinness; Carlsberg; Löwenbräu. cider.

ACCOMMODATION **4 bedrooms £C**
Check-in all day

Attractively located just outside the village, this old pub has charm and a warm and comfortable bar with inglenook fireplaces. The patio is a splendid spot for summer drinking. Exposed beams and sloping ceilings give the white-walled bedrooms their appeal: all have TV, tea and coffee making facilities and neatly tiled modern bathrooms. There is also one family room. Housekeeping could be improved. Accommodation closed 3 days Xmas.

Credit Access, Amex, Diners, Visa

HILDENBOROUGH — Gate Inn

FOOD

Rings Hill
MAP 7 D3 *Kent*
Hildenborough (0732) 832103
Parking ample

Bar food 12–2 & 7–10
No bar food Sun
Closed Sun eve
Landlord Mr G. R. M. Sankey
Brewery Whitbread
Fremlins Bitter; Flowers Original; Guinness; Stella Artois; Heineken; cider.

Seafood's the name of the game at this substantial pub in Victorian style next to the station. Mullet, conger eel and John Dory are among the ingredients for the excellent fish soup, and you'll also find crab, lobster, mussels, oysters, sole and salmon on the menu. The odd meaty special appears at lunchtime, and there's also a good cheeseboard. Garden.

Typical prices Salmon en croûte with hollandaise sauce £7 Coq crabe £10.50

HINDON — Lamb at Hindon

FOOD
B & B

Nr Salisbury
MAP 5 B3 *Wiltshire*
Hindon (074 789) 573
Parking ample

Bar food 12–2.30 & 7–10
Landlord Bill Stewart
Free house
Wadworth 6X, IPA; McEwan's Export; Webster Yorkshire Bitter; Guinness; Carlsberg Hof; cider.

A bay-windowed, 17th-century stone hostelry which once had an important role as a coaching inn, stabling up to 300 horses. Tasty bar fare includes ploughman's with granary bread, a good selection of sandwiches (toasted too), hot smoked mackerel and home-made pâté as snacks; hot dish of the day might be fried haddock or shepherd's pie. Winter evenings bring a choice of warming dishes such as chicken Kiev or grilled trout. To finish, a few simple sweets or cheese. Less choice on Sunday lunchtimes when a traditional roast is served in the restaurant.

Typical prices Beef curry £3.30 Seasonal fruit pie £1.15

ACCOMMODATION **16 bedrooms £C**
Check-in all day

The style of the bedrooms ranges from sturdy traditional (one with four-poster) to more modern. All are extremely comfortable and well-maintained, with tasteful fabrics and, in some rooms, wildly sloping floors to add atmosphere. Nine have pretty, well-equipped bathrooms. Garden. Accommodation closed three days Christmas. *No dogs.*

Credit Access, Amex, Diners, Visa

HOLT — Old Ham Tree

OD
B

Nr Trowbridge
MAP 7 A3 *Wiltshire*
North Trowbridge (0225) 782581
Parking ample

Bar food 11.30–2.15 & 7–9.45

Landlords John & Carol Francis
Free house
Wadworth 6X; Marston Pedigree; Eldridge Pope Dorset Original IPA; Ben Truman; Usher Country Bitter; Carlsberg Hof; cider.

A friendly, 18th-century whitewashed pub opposite the village green, where traditional no-nonsense cooking is served in the comfortable beamed bar. The bar menu features sandwiches, plain or toasted, salads, ploughman's, and daily blackboard specials such as braised liver, beef bourguignon, or hearty farmhouse-style steak and Guinness pie, mostly served with chips or baked potato and vegetables. Thursday sees a delivery of fresh fish; Cornish lemon sole on the bone is very popular, and other dishes include fresh salmon cutlets, prawn, crab and mussel platter, Cornish scallops and haddock.
Typical prices Steak & Guinness pie £2.75 Strawberry pavlova 85p

ACCOMMODATION **4 bedrooms £D**
Check-in all day

Upstairs are four well-kept and simply furnished rooms with pretty duvets and tea and coffee making facilities. They share one carpeted bathroom with a coloured suite and shower. Residents can watch TV in the small wicker-furnished lounge, and there's also a secluded walled garden.
Credit Access, Diners, Visa

HOLTON — Old Inn

A

Nr Wincanton
MAP 9 D1 *Somerset*
Wincanton (0963) 32002
Parking ample

Landlords Lou & Lin Lupton
Free house
Wadworth 6X; Butcombe Bitter; guest beers; Guinness; Carlsberg Hof; cider.

A peaceful, pleasant pub which is at least 350 years old. Warmed by a bright log fire, the little bar is a cosy and convivial drinking spot. Brick and half-panelled walls, beamed ceiling, paved floor and upholstered settles create that appealing traditional feel which enthusiastic new owners Lou and Lin Lupton plan to preserve carefully in their projected simple improvements. Patio and garden.
Credit Access, Visa

HOLYWELL — Ye Olde Ferry Boat Inn

& B

Nr St Ives, Huntingdon
MAP 6 D2 *Cambridgeshire*
St Ives (0480) 63227
Parking ample

Landlord Mrs J. M. Edwards
Free house
Greene King IPA, Abbot Ale; Adnams Bitter; Bass; Worthington Bitter; cider.

ACCOMMODATION **6 bedrooms £C**
Check-in all day

Records show that this ancient inn on the banks of the Ouse has been retailing drink since AD560, and its heavily beamed and pillared bar is certainly full of old-world character. Upstairs, the two best bedrooms have TVs and their own private facilities and one boasts a four-poster; the others are much more functionally equipped and share two public bathrooms. Morning tea is served in your room. Terrace and garden. *No dogs.*
Credit Access, Amex, Diners, Visa

HOLYWELL GREEN — Rock Hotel

B & B

Nr Halifax
MAP 4 D3 *West Yorkshire*
Elland (0422) 79721
Parking ample

Landlord Robert Vinsen
Free house
Theakston Best Bitter, XB; Younger's IPA; Mitchell's & Butler Mild; Slalom Lager, 'D' International; cider.

ACCOMMODATION **18 bedrooms £B**
Check-in all day

Good accommodation is on offer at this well-modernised inn with a picturesque 17th-century facade and within easy reach of junction 24 of the M62. Cosy, compact bedrooms, with fitted units, alarm-radios and drinks trays, all have private facilities. The bars, on two levels, have beamed ceilings, open fires and a pleasantly traditional character; the public bar includes a popular games room approached by its own narrow staircase. Patio.
Credit Access, Amex, Diner, Visa

HONLEY — Coach & Horses

FOOD

Eastgate, Huddersfield
MAP 4 D4 *West Yorkshire*
Huddersfield (0484) 666135
Parking ample

Bar food 11.30–1.30, Mon eve 6–9.30
No bar food eves (except Mon)
Landlords Mr & Mrs Woodhead
Brewery Bass Yorkshire
Bass Traditional Red, Traditional Light; Stones Bitter; Guinness; Carling Black Label; Tennent's Extra; cider.

A busy village pub offering a good choice of lunchtime bar snacks and a bistro-style menu on Monday evenings. Tagliatelle with spicy meat sauce or crudités with garlic mayonnaise might precede chicken and vegetable crumble, a juicy steak or plaice stuffed with cheese and mushrooms. Super salads, sandwiches and sweets, too.
Typical prices Vegetable hollandaise bake £2 Ham & mushroom pancake with salad & chips £2.20

HOPE — Poachers Arms

FOOD
B & B

Castleton Road
MAP 4 D4 *Derbyshire*
Hope Valley (0433) 20380
Parking ample

Bar food 12–2 & 7–9
Landlords Anton & Barbara Singleton
Free house
Webster Yorkshire Bitter, Dark Mild; Carlsberg; Fosters; cider.

Anton and Barbara Singleton keep things running smoothly and happily at this delightful little hotel by the A625. It's a popular place for bar food, and the menu is much more extensive than average. A mug of soup with a home-baked roll is a good warming starter, which you could follow with anything from cannelloni to curried prawns, from rabbit casserole to roast beef. Snackier items include hot smoked haddock and black pudding in mustard sauce. There's also a good span of vegetarian dishes, along with sorbets, ice creams and sweets from the restaurant trolley. Traditional Sunday roast also available.
Typical prices Rabbit casserole £3.95 Hot smokie £2.25

ACCOMMODATION **7 bedrooms £B**
Check-in all day

The seven bedrooms – each tenanted by a well-dressed teddy bear – are roomy and comfortable, and three of those facing south have the added attraction of large balconies. Direct-dial phones, TVs, clock-radios and tea-makers for all rooms, plus modern carpeted bathrooms. Patio.

Credit Access, Amex, Diners, Visa

HORLEY — Ye Olde Six Bells

FOOD Church Road
MAP 6 D3 *Surrey*
Horley (0293) 782209
Parking ample

Bar food 12–2 & 7–9.30
Landlords David & Karen Beaumont
Owner Vintage Inns
Charrington IPA; Bass; Worthington Bitter; Guinness; Tennent's Pilsner; Carling Black Label; cider.

The gardens of this pub run down to the banks of the river Mole. Parts of the building date back to AD 827 and the Monk's Pantry upstairs has an ancient truss and beam roof. Succulent beef, gammon and pork, smoked mackerel, quiche and salads are on offer here, with daily specials like cottage pie. Evenings bring hot dishes like korma and lamb Marengo. Nice desserts.
Typical prices Porc Normande £4.50 Tagliatelle alla carbonara £2.40
Credit Access, Amex, Diners, Visa

HORNINGSEA — Plough & Fleece

FOOD High Street
MAP 6 D2 *Cambridgeshire*
Cambridge (0223) 860795
Parking limited

Bar food 12–2 & 7–9.30
No bar food Sun & Mon eves
Landlords Joyce & Ken Grimes
Brewery Greene King
Greene King IPA, Abbot Ale; Guinness; Harp; Kronenbourg; cider.

Famous locally for its bar food, the Grimes' friendly pub does a brisk lunchtime trade, so come early. Dishes such as delicious hot garlic cockles, Romany rabbit and cherry cobbler combine imagination with tradition, to complement nice fresh-cut sandwiches. More elaborate evening menus: perhaps exotic vegetarian Eggstravaganza or beef Wellington. No hot food Sunday. Garden.
Typical prices Welsh fish pie £4.75 Devilled crab £1.90
Credit Access, Visa

HORN'S CROSS — Hoops Inn

B & B Nr Bideford
MAP 9 B1 *Devon*
Horn's Cross (023 75) 222
Parking ample

Landlords June & Jimmy Malcolm
Free house
Flowers Original, IPA; Whitbread Best Bitter; Trophy; Guinness; Heineken; Stella Artois; cider.
***ACCOMMODATION* 14 bedrooms £C**
Check-in all day

Picture-postcard material on the outside, this ancient thatched pub is no less appealing within. Beams, oak furnishings and winter fires give real atmosphere to the bar, and there's a cosy, chintzy lounge and pleasant TV room. Main-house bedrooms continue the period charm, while coach house rooms are more modern, with well-fitted private bathrooms. Courtyard. Accommodation closed last 2 weeks November.
No children under 8 overnight. No dogs.
Credit Access, Visa

HORRINGER — Beehive

FOOD The Street
MAP 6 E2 *Suffolk*
Horringer (028 488) 260
Parking ample

Bar food 12.15–2 & 7.15–10
No bar food Sun eve
Landlords Gary & Diane Kingshott
Brewery Greene King
Greene King Abbot Ale, IPA; Kronenbourg; Harp; cider.

Recent improvements have extended this pub, once an old beer house, without sacrificing its cosy rooms and quaint character. The old cellar has been converted into a bar/food area where you can sample the excellently cooked food. Among the hot dishes are burgundy mushrooms on toast and baked avocado with rum, prawns and cream; cold snacks might be gravlax or duck liver partfait. Garden.
Typical prices Lamb vol-au-vent £2.50 Celery & seafood coupe £3

HORTON — Horton Inn

FOOD
B & B

Cranborne, Nr Wimborne
MAP 5 B4 *Dorset*
Witchampton (0258) 840252
Parking ample
Bar food 12–2 & 7–10.30
Landlord Nicholas Caplan
Free house
John Smith's Bitter; Ind Coope Burton Ale; Ringwood Best Bitter; Courage Directors; Whitbread Best Bitter; Ben Truman; cider.

Owner Nicholas Caplan has restored the splendour of former days to this handsome 18th-century inn on the B3078. Refurbished public areas include a roomy but cosy bar lounge and an attractive residents' bar that adjoins the restaurant. The regular bar menu offers a comprehensive variety of enjoyable fare, from sandwiches, ploughman's and salads to fish pie, jumbo sausages and home-cooked gammon. On the blackboard are daily specials like baked crab and succulent pork scallops in a tasty provençale sauce. Leave room for a sweet – hazelnut meringue with raspberry sauce is a winner. Traditional Sunday lunch menu available.

Typical prices Fisherman's pie £2.45 Chocolate cheesecake £1.25

ACCOMMODATION **6 bedrooms £C**
Check-in all day

The six good-sized bedrooms are furnished in traditional style, and a thoughtful list of accessories ranges from TVs to tissues. Two rooms have large, well-equipped bathrooms en suite, the rest share a well-kept public bathroom. Garden. *No dogs.*

Credit Access, Visa

HORTON-IN-RIBBLESDALE — Crown Hotel

B & B

Nr Settle
MAP 3 C3 *North Yorkshire*
Horton-in-Ribblesdale (072 96) 209
Parking ample
Landlords Richard & Norma Hargreaves
Brewery Theakston
Theakston Best Bitter, XB; Matthew Brown Lion Mild; Guinness; Matthew Brown Slalom Lager; cider.

ACCOMMODATION **10 bedrooms £D**
Check-in all day

Its position on the Pennine Way makes this a popular stopping point for walkers, while the proximity of the river Ribble adds to the charm. Two friendly, beamed bars and two homely residents' lounges, both with TV, provide plenty of room for relaxation. The cosy, compact bedrooms have modern furniture, duvets and handbasins. Most have shower units and there are two simple public bathrooms. An early morning cuppa served in your room is a nice touch. Garden.

HOUGHTON — George & Dragon

FOOD

Nr Arundel
MAP 6 D4 *West Sussex*
Bury (079 881) 559
Parking ample
Bar food 12–2 & 7–10
Landlords David & Christine Walters
Free house
King & Barnes Sussex Bitter; Young Special; Harvey Best Bitter; Guinness; Carlsberg; Holsten Export; cider.

Charles II stopped here for a glass of ale while fleeing after the Battle of Worcester. Nowadays, bar food is very popular; full lunch and dinner menus – plus daily specials and cold snacks, and a roast on Sundays. Try delicious Italian melody tagliatelle followed by a traditional English pud. Presentation is excellent, as is service. Booking essential weekends. Garden.

Typical prices Smoked salmon & asparagus £3.75 Beef Wellington £7.45

Credit Access, Visa

HOWDEN — Bowman's Hotel

B

Bridgegate
MAP 4 E3 *Humberside*
Howden (0430) 30805
Parking ample

Landlord Manuel Ucha
Owner Bowman's Hotel Ltd
Cameron Crown, Lion Bitter, Strongarm; Guinness; Cameron Hansa; Dortmunder; cider.
ACCOMMODATION **13 bedrooms £D**
Check-in all day

This pleasant town-centre pub not far from the M62 offers simple overnight accommodation. Well-kept bedrooms with white fitted units and floral furnishings have colour TVs; all but four have compact tiled bathrooms. Young locals make a bee-line for the public bar which has fruit machines and video games; visitors may prefer the comfortable rustic style lounge bar. Patio. Children accommodated overnight. Accommodation closed two days Christmas. *No dogs.*
Credit Access, Amex, Diners, Visa

HUBBERHOLME — George Inn

B

Kirk Gill, Nr Skipton
MAP 3 C3 *North Yorkshire*
Kettlewell (075 676) 223
Parking ample

Landlord John Fredrick
Free house
Younger's IPA, Scotch; Harp; cider.
ACCOMMODATION **5 bedrooms £D**
Check-in all day

The river Wharfe flows alongside this charming, white-painted village pub. Beams made of halved tree trunks, an old stone fireplace and flagstoned floor testify to its antiquity, and beams still remain in some of the neat, well-kept little bedrooms. All have modern furniture; four in the main house share two bathrooms, while the fifth in an adjoining cottage, has private facilities. Patio. *No children under eight overnight.*

HUNTINGDON — Old Bridge Hotel

OD

1 High Street
MAP 6 D2 *Cambridgeshire*
Huntingdon (0480) 52681
Parking ample

Bar food 10.30–2.30 & 6–11
Landlord Raymond Waters
Free house
Ruddles County; James Paine XXX; Tolly Cobbold Bitter; Kestrel.

The mellow panelled bar of this handsome Georgian hotel by the river Ouse has its own appetising menu: home-made soup, pâté, deep-fried sweetbreads, excellent jugged hare or a simple hamburger – all are soundly cooked using fresh ingredients. Finish with some fine gorgonzola or a sweet from the restaurant trolley. Terrace.
Typical prices Gruyère cheese & spinach fritters £3.25 Lamb's sweetbreads & garlic mayonnaise £4.95
Credit Access, Amex, Diners, Visa

ILMINGTON — Howard Arms

OD

Nr Shipston-on-Stour
MAP 7 B1 *Warwickshire*
Ilmington (060 882) 226
Parking ample

Bar food 11.45–2 & 6.30–9.30, Sun 12–1.30 & 7–9
Landlords David & Sarah Russon
Brewery Whitbread
Flowers Best Bitter, IPA; guest beer; Guinness; Stella Artois; Heineken; cider.

A spick-and-span village pub where landlord David Russon is also the chef. The blackboard bar menu changes regularly, listing the likes of horseradish pâté, chicken curry, tasty kidneys in red wine, and fresh fish which could include smoked trout, salmon, swordfish steak or whitebait. Puds like nice gooey chocolate and rum flan round things off. There's a restaurant, too, and a garden.
Typical prices Boeuf bourguignon £3.95 Pigeon breast & rump steak £4.25
Credit Access, Diners, Visa

KENLEY **Wattenden Arms**

FOOD Old Lodge Lane
MAP 7 D3 *Surrey*
01-660 8638
Parking ample
Bar food 12–2 & 7–9

Landlords Joan & Ron Coulston
Brewery Charrington
Charrington IPA; Bass; Worthington Best Bitter; Guinness; Tennent's Extra; Carling Black Label; cider.

An attractive, very patriotic, village pub whose walls are hung with pictures of national heroes and royals past and present. The bar food display includes a good home-cooked ham and cold meats for sandwiches, and there are flavoursome soups and hot snacks such as gammon, egg and chips, scampi platter and salmon steak. Apple pie or spotted dick make appetising afters. On Sundays, sandwiches only.
Typical prices Home-made soup 80p Steak & kidney pudding £3

KERSEY **Bell Inn**

A The Street, Nr Ipswich
MAP 6 E2 *Suffolk*
Hadleigh (0473) 823229
Parking ample

Landlords A. A. & J. R. Fineman
Free house
Strong Country Bitter; Flowers Original; Wethered Bitter; Guinness; Stella Artois; Heineken; cider.

An important ingredient in the picture-postcard prettiness of this delightful Suffolk village, best known for its main-street water ford, is the timbered facade of this fine old inn, which is decorated with attractive flower baskets. In winter, cheerful open fires warm the brass-decked bars, which have exposed brick and oodles of character, while in summer the large attractive garden is the place to be.

KESWICK **Dog & Gun**

FOOD Lake Road
MAP 3 B2 *Cumbria*
Keswick (076 87) 73463
Parking difficult
Bar food 11.30–2 & 6–9.30, Sun 12–1.30 & 7–9.30

Landlord Frank Hughes
Brewery Theakston
Theakston Old Peculier, XB, Best Bitter; Guinness; cider.

Visitors to this characterful town-centre pub will enjoy hearty food in typical old-world surroundings. Cumberland sausage with fried onions in a hot brown loaf is a standing treat, and other favourites include goulash, beef curry and home-roast ham. Lunchtime brings more snack choices – sandwiches, jacket potatoes, and ploughman's with excellent Cheddar.
Typical prices Cumberland sausage £1.80 Prawn salad £3.95

KESWICK **Pheasant Inn**

B & B Crosthwaite Road
MAP 3 B2 *Cumbria*
Keswick (07687) 72219
Parking limited

Landlords D.G. & M. Wright
Brewery Jennings
Jennings Mild; Tetley Bitter; Guinness; Ayingerbräu; cider.

ACCOMMODATION **3 bedrooms £D**
Check-in all day

A favourite with the locals and welcoming all newcomers, this homely old inn stands just off the A66 about a mile from the centre of Keswick. Warm yourself by the cheery fire in the modest bar, where the walls are enlivened with colourful cartoons of open-air enthusiasts, or enjoy a drink on the patio when it's fine. The three simply appointed carpeted bedrooms all have teamakers, washbasins and generous soft towels; they share a modern bathroom.

KETTLEWELL — Racehorses Hotel

B

Nr Skipton
MAP 4 D3 *North Yorkshire*
Kettlewell (075 676) 233
Parking ample

Landlord Clifford Selvus
Free house
McEwan's Tartan Bitter; Tetley Bitter; Wharfedale Goose Eye Bitter; Guinness; Löwenbräu; McEwan's Lager; cider.

ACCOMMODATION **15 bedrooms £C**
Check-in all day

Dating back in part to the 17th century, this hotel stands by the banks of the river Wharfe. The two bars, with their beams, brasses and open fires, have a good deal of traditional charm, and there's a cosy double lounge. Bedrooms are nearly all of a good size, smartly maintained and neatly decorated, with white freestanding furniture and TVs. Improvements under new owner Clifford Selvus include the addition of en suite facilities to all rooms.
Credit Access, Visa

KEYSTON — The Pheasant

FOOD

Nr Huntingdon
MAP 6 D2 *Cambridgeshire*
Bythorn (080 14) 241
Parking ample

Bar food 11.30–2.30 & 6–10.30
Landlord Bill Bennett
Free house
Tolly Cobbold Bitter; Ruddles County, Rutland Bitter; Adnams Bitter; Stella Artois; Carlsberg; cider.

Enterprising chef-patron Bill Bennett provides an interesting and varied menu at this old thatched pub. Garlic bread accompanies good flavoursome soup, and other choices run from prawns and pâté to grilled plaice, Barnsley chop and bread and butter pudding. Free crudités on the bar, with chestnuts (in season) for roasting on the log fire. Traditional roast available on Sundays. Patio.
Typical prices Chicken Thai £3.95 Poached Scotch salmon £4.95
Credit Access, Amex, Diners, Visa

KILVE — Hood Arms

FOOD & B

Nr Bridgwater
MAP 9 C1 *Somerset*
Holford (027 874) 210
Parking ample

Bar food 11.30–2 & 6.30–10

Landlords Robbie Rutt & Neville White
Free house
Flowers Original, IPA; Whitbread Best Bitter; Guinness; Heineken; Stella Artois.

Behind the smart frontage is a civilised, well-run establishment where Robbie Rutt and Neville White are friendly hosts. A delightful landscaped garden and patio caters for sunny day drinking, while the bars are cosy for less clement weather. A good choice of sandwiches, ten different salads, and ploughman's is backed up by the blackboard specials which may be breadcrumbed, herby country style chicken, moussaka or chilli. Fresh vegetables are served in generous portions. The delicious home-made sweets include peach pavlova, a scrumptious apple and mincemeat crumble, treacle tart and lemon meringue pie. Traditional roast on Sundays.
Typical prices Steak & kidney pie £2.75 Bread & butter pudding £1.10

ACCOMMODATION **5 bedrooms £C**
Check-in all day

The smart bedrooms have good quality furniture and attractive floral fabrics. Colour televisions, trouser presses and other thoughtful extras are standard, and all have well-kept modern bathrooms (one not en suite). Accommodation closed two days Christmas. *No children under seven overnight.*

Credit Access, Visa

KINETON **Halfway House**

B & B Nr Guiting Power, Cheltenham
MAP 7 A2 *Gloucestershire*
Guiting Power (045 15) 344
Parking ample

Landlords Mr & Mrs D. Marshall
Brewery Donnington
Donnington Best Bitter, SBA; Carlsberg; cider.

***ACCOMMODATION* 3 bedrooms £D**
Check-in all day

The Windrush valley provides a picturesque setting for the Marshalls' 17th-century stone inn in a hamlet overlooking the valley. The bar is popular with the locals, but the garden provides a pretty summer alternative, especially for children, (only welcome at lunchtime). The three simple bedrooms and main bathroom, though modest, are in excellent order. Accommodation closed four days at Christmas. *No children under 14 overnight. No dogs.*

KINGSCLERE **Crown**

FOOD
B & B Nr Newbury
MAP 7 B3 *Hampshire*
Kingsclere (0635) 298956
Parking ample

Bar food 12–2 (Sun till 1.45) & 7.30–9
No bar food Sun eve

Landlord Mary May
Brewery Courage
Courage Directors, Best; Simonds; Guinness; Hofmeister; cider.

A friendly, unpretentious pub in the centre of the village. The well-frequented main bar has a central brick fireplace to provide cheer in winter and there are plenty of old photographs and decorative plates above the brown dado panelling. Landlady Mary May enjoys cooking a wide variety of dishes and lunchtime offerings on the blackboard menu include pizza, garlic mushrooms, pâté, ravioli, fried sardines, fried chicken livers and beef or cottage cheese salads, broadening to such items as roast guinea fowl, pheasant casserole, steaks and fish dishes in the evenings. Portions are generous. There's always a vegetarian dish, and sandwiches are available for light snacks. Simple puds. Traditional roast only Sunday lunchtimes.
Typical prices Grilled plaice with asparagus £4.75 Chicken livers in garlic butter £3.50

***ACCOMMODATION* 2 bedrooms £D**
Check-in all day

Two modest, clean, traditionally furnished bedrooms, sharing one bathroom, provide simple accommodation for an overnight stay. Patio. Children welcome overnight. *No dogs.*

KINGSCOTE **Hunters Hall Inn**

FOOD Nr Tetbury
MAP 7 A2 *Gloucestershire*
Dursley (0453) 860393
Parking ample

Bar food 12–2 (Sun till 1.45) & 7–10

Landlords Sandra & David Barnett-Roberts
Free house
Bass; Fussel's; Toby Bitter; Guinness; Carling Black Label; Tennent's Extra; cider.

A characterful 16th-century coaching inn on the A4135, five miles from Tetbury, with low beamed ceilings, flagstoned floors and antique furniture. The changing bar menu could include steak and mushroom pie, sweet and sour pork or grilled kidneys. There's also an attractive buffet display at lunchtimes plus tempting sweets. Barbecues in the gardens on summer weekends.
Typical prices Steak & Guinness pie £3.15 Quiche & salad £2.50
Credit Access, Amex, Diners, Visa

KINGSTON — Juggs

ÒOD

Nr Lewes
MAP 6 D4 *East Sussex*
Brighton (0273) 472523
Parking ample

Bar food 12–2 & 6–9.30

Landlords Andrew & Peta Browne
Free house
Harvey Best Bitter; King & Barnes Sussex Bitter, Old Ale, Festive; Guinness; Tennent's Extra; cider.

Flowers smother the tile-hung exterior of this enchantingly pretty 15th-century pub. There's plenty of character inside as well, conveyed by old beams and horsy paraphernalia, but on sunny days the red-brick patio/garden is the great attraction – complete with adventure playground to amuse the kids. The menu ranges from soup, pâté and open sandwiches to steak, sausages and fried fish. Simple, tasty desserts to finish.
Typical dishes Vegetable savoury £1.25 Hot chocolate brownie 85p

KINGSWINFORD — Summerhill House Hotel

& B

Swindon Road
MAP 5 B2 *West Midlands*
Kingswinford (0384) 295254
Parking ample

Landlord Mr R. H. Beatty
Brewery Ansells
Ansells Bitter, Mild; Guinness; Skol; Löwenbräu; Castlemaine XXXX.

ACCOMMODATION **10 bedrooms £D**
Check-in all day

Surrounded by pleasant grounds and trees, this converted Georgian house stands on a hilltop just outside the town centre. The bar is very much in keeping with the building's age, with plenty of space and a fine traditional atmosphere. Bedrooms have a more contemporary feel, with plain colour schemes and furniture of a simple, practical type. All are equipped with TVs, telephones and tea-making facilities. Patio. *No dogs.*
Credit Access, Amex, Diners, Visa

KINTBURY — Dundas Arms

ÒOD
& B

Nr Newbury
MAP 7 B3 *Berkshire*
Kintbury (0488) 58263
Parking ample

Bar food 12–2
No bar food Sun & eves

Landlords Dalzell-Piper family
Free house
Morland Bitter; Arkell BBB; Adnams Bitter; Webster Yorkshire Bitter; Guinness; Carlsberg Hof.

Everything seems just right at this delightful inn beside the Kennet and Avon canal. The Dalzell-Piper family are excellent hosts and the bar, with its cream walls, settles and darkwood, is tasteful without being sombre. Justly popular lunchtime snacks served here include delicious home-made soups, crab au gratin, smoked salmon, quiches, a good mutton pie, and thick, juicy gammon steaks. In summer, tables are put out on the patio, which extends the friendly ambience.
Typical dishes Steak & kidney pie 3.75 Crab au gratin £1.85

ACCOMMODATION **5 bedrooms £B**
Check-in restricted

The pleasing, good-sized bedrooms are in a converted stable block. They have good, solid furniture, bold wallpapers and sliding picture windows leading on to a riverside terrace. All have TVs and tea and coffee making facilities, lots of magazines and pleasant, modern bathrooms en suite. There's an attractive chintzy residents' lounge.

Credit Access, Amex, Diners, Visa

Our inspectors never book in the name of Egon Ronay's Guides; they disclose their identity only after paying their bills.

KINVER — Whittington Inn

A

Nr Stourbridge, West Midlands
MAP 5 B2 Staffordshire
Kinver (0384) 872496
Parking ample

Landlord Miss J. Pike
Free house
Marston Pedigree; Courage Directors; Flowers IPA; Guinness; Stella Artois; Heineken; cider.

History is much in evidence in this grand old pub, originally built in 1310 as the home of Dick Whittington's grandfather. The splendid bars retain the period flavour, with blackened beams and panelled walls, antiques and bric-a-brac. Open fires add a cosy and welcoming touch. The lounge bar is particularly appealing and looks out over the Tudor-style walled garden, with its lawns and fishpond. Barbecues here in the summer.
Credit Access, Amex, Diners, Visa

KIRK LANGLEY — Meynell Arms Hotel

B & B

Nr Derby
MAP 5 B1 *Derbyshire*
Kirk Langley (033 124) 515

Parking ample
Landlord John Richards
Brewery Bass
Bass; Worthington Bitter; Mitchells & Butlers Mild; Tennent's Lager; Carling Black Label; cider.

ACCOMMODATION **10 bedrooms £D**
Check-in all day

A solid, three-storey converted Georgian farmhouse on the A52 to Ashbourne, four miles from Derby, this well-run hotel has two lounge bars and a very simple public bar. The extremely well-maintained and comfortable warm bedrooms (two with four-posters) have homely floral bedspreads and modern facilities such as colour TVs, telephones and tea-makers. Five have modernised private bathrooms. A good breakfast is provided. Garden.
Credit Access, Amex, Diners, Visa

KIRKBY STEPHEN — King's Arms Hotel

FOOD
B & B

Market Street
MAP 3 C2 *Cumbria*
Kirkby Stephen (0930) 71378
Parking ample

Bar food 12–2 & 6.30–9

Landlords Jenny Reed & Keith Simpson
Brewery Whitbread
Whitbread Trophy Cask, Trophy; Heineken; cider.

ACCOMMODATION **9 bedrooms £C**
Check-in all day

★ An attractive and very traditional inn standing at the heart of an unspoilt market town. Chef-partner Keith Simpson is responsible for the bar snacks that are such an outstanding attraction; subtly flavoured cucumber and cheese mousse; home-baked ham; an exemplary steak, kidney and mushroom pie, lovely pear tart served with whipped cream and tiny ratafias. In the evening the food is served in a simple restaurant; the range is similar but includes one or two specials such as game pie or a fresh fish dish. Traditional Sunday lunch. ★
Typical prices Seafood rendezvous £8 Roast duck with spicy orange sauce £6.75 Local salmon with prawns £6 Dover sole £8

Entrance to this fine old hostelry is by a cosy, old-fashioned hall; there are two bars, and a pleasant residents' lounge with TV. Bedrooms are plainish and unpretentious, but with the virtues of sturdy furnishings, soft mattresses and crisply laundered sheets. Two rooms have private facilities.

Credit Access, Visa

KIRKBYMOORSIDE — George & Dragon

OD & B

Market Place
MAP 4 E3 *North Yorkshire*
Kirkbymoorside (0751) 31637
Parking ample

Bar food 12–1.30
No bar food eves

Landlords Mr & Mrs Curtis & Mr & Mrs Austin
Free house
Theakston Best Bitter; Younger's Scotch; Guinness; Carlsberg Hof; cider.

This large, 13th-century coaching inn facing the market square makes a pleasant place to stop for a simple, wholesome lunchtime snack, or more substantial fare. In the traditional beamed bar (with many pictures showing the local passion for racehorses), you'll find soup of the day, plus a good range of open or standard sandwiches packed with a variety of fillings, including prawns, mackerel, ham, turkey or pâté. There's steak and kidney pie, or a roast – and a wide selection of fish dishes from mussels in spicy tomato sauce to local oak-smoked trout. Delicious sweets include an excellent chocolate rum log or mandarin cheesecake.
Typical prices Steak & kidney pie £2.85 Daily roast £2.85

***ACCOMMODATION* 24 bedrooms £C**
Check-in all day

The bedrooms are in a converted granary and old vicarage behind the inn. All have white units, traditional fabrics, direct-dial telephones, TVs and tea-making facilities. Most have bath or shower room en suite. *No children under five overnight. No dogs allowed in the bedrooms.*

Credit Access, Visa

KIRTLING — Queen's Head

OD & B

Nr Newmarket, Suffolk
MAP 7 D1 *Cambridgeshire*
Newmarket (0638) 730253
Parking ample

Bar food 12–1.30 & 7–10
No bar food Thurs eve

Landlord Ann Bailey
Brewery Tolly Cobbold
Tolly Cobbold Original, Bitter, Mild; Guinness; Cameron Hansa; cider.

A real old country pub this, with plenty of rustic character, and ducks and chickens roaming the car park. There's a horsy theme in both bars (both Mrs Bailey's sons-in-law are trainers), and one of the bars overlooks the charming garden. Mrs Bailey does the cooking and the results are very tasty – fresh mushroom soup, sandwiches with excellent ham, omelettes and interesting specials like chicken on a bed of leeks gratinée, fidget pie, and nice home-made puddings including rather special gooey meringues.
Typical prices Stuffed duck with apricot £5 Fidget pie £3.50

***ACCOMMODATION* 5 bedrooms £D**
Check-in restricted

Bedrooms, up a steep staircase, are traditionally furnished with some sturdy old pieces and pretty floral bedspreads. Tea-makers are provided. There are signs of wear but housekeeping is good. Two small simple single rooms are also available. All rooms have pleasing views. *Children are not accommodated overnight.*

Prices given are as at the time of our research and thus may change.

KNAPP — Rising Sun

FOOD

North Curry
MAP 9 C1 *Somerset*
Taunton (0823) 490436
Parking ample

Bar food 12–2 & 7–10
Closed Mon

Landlords Mr & Mrs J. Ord Watt
Free house
Flowers Original, IPA; Whitbread Best Bitter; Guinness; Heineken; cider.

A former cider house with a good deal of rustic charm, where there's a wide choice of dishes, including some for vegetarians. Snacks are home-made soup, freshly made sandwiches, smoked mackerel and herb and brandy pâté; full meals include steak and kidney pie, chicken compote with rich wine sauce, braised duck, grills and curries. Traditional Sunday roast. Patio.
Typical prices Leek and ham bake £2.65 Grilled trout £4.75
Credit Access, Visa

KNIGHTWICK — Talbot Hotel

FOOD
B & B

Nr Worcester
MAP 7 A1 *Hereford & Worcester*
Knightwick (0886) 21235
Parking ample

Bar food 12–2 & 6.30–9.30
Landlords Mr D. Hiles & Mrs J. B. Clift
Free house
Bass; Flowers IPA, Original; Banks's Bitter; Manns Best Bitter; Guinness; cider.

A vast and imaginative blackboard menu and a huge wood-burning stove in the bar make for cosy eating at this friendly, informal pub with a picturesque riverside garden. Fish comes direct from Billingsgate, and if you don't fancy sole, plaice, monkfish or mullet, there are steaks, delicious pasta and ever-changing specials (always a vegetarian choice), as well as sandwiches and ploughman's, which comes with a choice of well-kept cheeses. Home-made sweets abound and include pineapple ice cream and a super strawberry pavlova. On Sunday evenings, bar food is available for non-residents on request only.
Typical prices Steak & kidney pie £4.25 Plaice fillet £4.50

ACCOMMODATION **10 bedrooms £D**
Check-in all day

Plump for the simply furnished bedrooms in the old building if you value character, though those in the modern annexe have the bonus of en suite showers. All rooms are equipped with tea-makers, clock-radios and the like. Prepare to tackle an excellent but massive breakfast!

Credit Access, Visa **LVs**

KNOWL HILL — Bird in Hand

FOOD

Bath Road
MAP 7 C3 *Berkshire*
Littlewick Green (062 882) 2781
Parking ample

Bar food 12–2 & 6–10.30
Landlords Jack & Moira Shone
Free house
Brakspear Bitter; Courage Directors; Young Special; John Smith's Yorkshire Bitter; Guinness; Carlsberg Hof.

On the A4, this popular pub dates back to the 15th century. Lunchtime and summer evenings, the main attraction is an appetising buffet offering cold meats, pies, quiches and interesting salads. Hot dishes available all year round include beef curry, chicken chasseur, lasagne or red mullet, and there's a choice of sweets. Traditional Sunday lunchtime roast. Terrace.
Typical prices Game pie £3.95 Cold table selection £3.95
Credit Access, Amex, Diners, Visa

KNOWLE — Greswolde Arms

B & B

High Street, Nr Solihull
MAP 5 B2 *West Midlands*
Knowle (056 45) 2711
Parking ample
Landlord Mr I.P. Hartley
Brewery Ansells
Ansells Bitter, Mild; Ind Coope Burton Ale; Guinness; Skol; Castlemaine XXXX; cider.

***ACCOMMODATION* 18 bedrooms £C**
Check-in all day

Once a busy coaching inn, this high street hotel now makes an ideal base for visitors to the National Exhibition Centre – just a ten-minute drive away. Comfortable overnight accommodation is provided in well-equipped bedrooms (TVs, radios, trouser presses and direct-dial telephones are standard), all decorated and furnished in simple modern style. There are two bars, one a local favourite. Patio. Accommodation closed three days Christmas. *No dogs.*
Credit Access, Amex, Diners, Visa

LACOCK — Red Lion at Lacock

FOOD
B & B

Nr Chippenham
MAP 7 A3 *Wiltshire*
Lacock (024 973) 456
Parking ample
Bar food 12.15–2 & 7–10
Landlord Mr J.S. Levis
Brewery Wadworth
Wadworth 6X; IPA; Farmers Glory, Northgate Bitter; Guinness; Heineken; cider.

Old-world character is much in evidence in the bars of this fine old coaching inn in the centre of the National Trust village of Lacock. Beams, bare wooden floors, open fires and stuffed game birds in glass cases provide the setting for imaginative, carefully prepared bar food. Snacks include tasty soup of the day – perhaps parsnip and orange – pâté, ploughman's and jacket potatoes, while giant sausages, individual beef pies, home-made rissoles and pork in a mustard seed sauce, all served with vegetables and a jacket potato or bubble and squeak, are typical of the more substantial fare. Finish with a giant meringue and chocolate sauce or delicious home-made ice cream.
Typical prices Smoked mackerel £2.05 Apple & almond crumble £1.40

***ACCOMMODATION* 3 bedrooms £C**
Check-in all day

Antiquarian bric-a-brac lines the staircase leading to three spacious high-ceilinged bedrooms with antique wardrobes; in one there is a splendid brass bed, in another a handsome walnut bedhead. One room has a private bathroom. Garden. *No children under ten overnight.*

LAMBERHURST — George & Dragon Inn

B & B

High Street
MAP 6 E3 *Kent*
Lamberhurst (0892) 890277
Parking ample
Landlord Reg Godward
Free house
Charrington IPA; Bass; Guinness; Tennent's Lager; Carlsberg; cider.

***ACCOMMODATION* 6 bedrooms £D**
Check-in restricted

A garden running down to the river Teise is an attractive feature of this friendly old black and white inn on the A21. There's a pleasant beamed bar and a games room extension. Homely overnight accommodation is provided by six neat, simply furnished bedrooms with candlewick bedspreads and tea-makers (four have TVs). Two have private facilities (one bath, one shower), and the others share a public bathroom. *No dogs.*
Credit Access

LANCASTER — Farmers Arms Hotel

B & B

Penny Street
MAP 3 C3 *Lancashire*
Lancaster (0524) 36368
Parking limited

Owners Mr T. J. & Mrs P. M. Baxter
Brewery Thwaites
Thwaites Bitter, Best Mild; Guinness; Tuborg; Carlsberg Hof.

***ACCOMMODATION* 14 bedrooms £C**
Check-in all day

Nowadays businessmen are more in evidence than farmers at this imposing turn-of-the-century hotel near the centre of town. The lofty lounge bar has French windows opening on to a small beer garden. Comfortable bedrooms, all on the second floor, are equipped with TVs and tea-makers. Five have their own bathrooms; the rest share three well-kept public ones. Patio. Accommodation closed 24, 25 and 31 December and 1 January. *No dogs.*
Credit Access, Visa **LVs**

LANCHESTER — Kings Head

FOOD
B & B

Station Road
MAP 4 D2 *Co. Durham*
Lanchester (0207) 520054
Parking ample

Bar food 12–1.45
No bar food eves & Sun
Landlord Mr H. Bainbridge
Brewery Scottish & Newcastle
Newcastle Exhibition; McEwan's Best Scotch; Harp; Beck's Bier; cider. *No real ale.*

A substantial stone-built pub on the edge of the village green, opposite the parish church. The interior is modernised, and in the bar rough plaster walls and mock beams combine with darkwood furniture and plush banquettes. There's a straightforward choice of lunchtime bar food, the best things being the roasts, the pies (steak and kidney with a good meaty gravy, served with creamed potatoes and mashed swede) and casserole-style dishes such as moussaka. Salads and sandwiches are available for lighter bites and a traditional roast lunch is served in the restaurant on Sunday.
Typical prices Roast of the day £2.35 Steak & kidney pie £2.20

***ACCOMMODATION* 5 bedrooms £D**
Check-in all day

The bedrooms, compact without being cramped, are neat, bright and cheerful, with modern furnishings, tea-makers and large colour TVs. Central heating keeps things snug, and each room has a washbasin; there are two spotlessly kept public bathrooms. Accommodation closed one week Christmas. Patio.

Credit Access, Amex, Diners, Visa

LANCING — Sussex Pad Hotel

FOOD
B & B

Old Shoreham Road
MAP 6 D4 *West Sussex*
Brighton (0273) 454647
Parking ample

Bar food 12–2.30 (Sun till 2) & 7–10
No bar food Sat eves
Landlords Mr & Mrs W. Pack
Free house
Tetley Bitter; John Bull; Guinness; Löwenbräu; Oranjeboom; cider.
No real ale.

Adjacent to Shoreham Airport, this substantial inn, run by the hospitable Packs, stands just off the A27 at the foot of the rolling South Downs. Bar snacks (not Saturday evenings) include some appetising seafood, like the popular mixed fish platter – fresh and smoked salmon, crab, oyster, mussels, herring and prawns – as well as tasty home-made soup, generously filled sandwiches and fresh salads. There are a few hot dishes, too, like spaghetti bolognese, moules marinière and a fine

steak and kidney pie, well-filled with tender meat. Hazelnut gâteau – light meringue layers with hazlenut buttercream – is a delicious sweet.
Typical prices Mixed fish platter £6.75 Gâteau St Honoré £1.25

ACCOMMODATION **6 bedrooms £C**
Check-in all day

Comfortable accommodation is provided in spacious, well-kept bedrooms with simple traditional furnishings. All have en suite bathrooms, TVs, tea and coffee making facilities and direct-dial phones. Garden.

Credit Access, Amex, Diners, Visa

LANGDALE — Pillar Hotel, Hobson's Pub

OOD

Nr Ambleside
MAP 3 B3 *Cumbria*
Langdale (096 67) 302
Parking ample

Bar food 12–2 & 6–9.30

Landlord Yvonne Lee
Free house
Hartley Best Bitter, Mild; Theakston Old Peculier; Marston Merrie Monk; Guinness; Castlemaine XXXX; cider.

Bar food spans a good choice at this modern pub, part of an impressive hotel and country club complex. Cumberland sausage with apple makes a tasty dish, and there's soup, open sandwiches, seafood platters and hot offerings like lamb goulash. Eat in the stone-floored bar or out on the terrace overlooking the waterfall. Live entertainment Saturday night. Traditional Sunday lunch menu.
Typical prices Cold meat selection £3.85 Seafood platter £4.20

LANGHAM — Noel Arms

OOD

Nr Oakham
MAP 5 C1 *Leicestershire*
Oakham (0572) 2931
Parking ample

Bar food 10–2 & 6–10

Landlords Mr & Mrs A. M. Eacott
Free house
Ruddles County Bitter, Rutland Bitter; Marston Pedigree; Tetley Bitter; McEwan's Export; Stella Artois; cider.

North of Oakham on the A606, this handsome, converted farmhouse offers good food in friendly surroundings. Cold meats and salads make an eye-catching buffet, and other dishes, indicated on a blackboard, include pâté, grilled trout, steaks and specials like lasagne or an excellent turkey and ham fricassee. Also sandwiches, burgers, desserts.
Typical prices Home-made steak & kidney pie £3.75 Lasagne £3.50
Credit Access, Amex, Diners, Visa

LANREATH — Punch Bowl Inn

& B

Nr Looe
MAP 9 B2 *Cornwall*
Lanreath (0503) 20218
Parking ample

Landlords Mr & Mrs Frith
Free house
Bass; St Austell Hicks Special; Whitbread Best Bitter; John Smith's Bitter; Guinness; Carling Black Label; cider.

ACCOMMODATION **17 bedrooms £C**
Check-in all day

The building dates back to at least 1620, and gleaming horse brasses, panelling and an inglenook fire in the lounge continue the period feel. There is a children's room and traditional public bar; the residents' lounge overlooks the pretty garden. Bedrooms have solid furniture (three particularly charming, with four-poster beds) and those in the extension have neat fitted units. All have tea-makers and TVs, and all but four have their own bathrooms.
Credit Access, Visa

LEAFIELD — Old George Inn

FOOD

Nr Witney
MAP 7 B2 *Oxfordshire*
Asthall Leigh (099 387) 288
Parking ample

Bar food 12–1.30 (Sun till 1.15) & 7–9.30

Landlords Christine Seymour & Stephen Duckworth
Free house
Marston Pedigree; Stones; Hook Norton Best; Glenny Wychwood Best; Guinness; Tennent's Pilsner; cider.

Run with warmth and enthusiasm, this fine old village inn offers excellent eating in delightful surroundings. French onion soup with croûtons, beef and vegetable curry, and pancakes stuffed with apple, celery, cheese and walnuts typify Christine Seymour's varied repertoire. Delicious open sandwiches and nice sweets, too, like chocolate mousse and meringues. A mini-zoo in the garden keeps the children happy.
Typical prices Prawn sandwich £1.75 Lasagne £2.45

LEDBURY — Feathers Hotel

FOOD
B & B

High Street
MAP 7 A1 *Hereford & Worcester*
Ledbury (0531) 2600
Parking ample

Bar food 12–2 & 7–9.30

Landlord Michael Hester
Free house
Bass; Mitchells & Butlers Brew XI; Springfield Bitter; Guinness; Carling Black Label; Tennent's Extra; cider.

Once a famous coaching inn, this half-timbered Elizabethan building boasts many fine period features. The solid oak beams, wood panelling and open fireplaces combine with the tapestries and many fine antique pieces to create the genuinely traditional feel of an English hostelry. The bar, with its timbered supports and horse-brasses, is particularly atmospheric. The cold table is the centrepiece at lunchtimes, with a selection of cold meats, salads, and a low-calorie slimmer's special, plus an array of home-made sweets. Hot dishes range from beef and venison pie to home-made hamburger with salad, as well as club sandwiches and a fine selection of cheeses. Friendly staff. Traditional Sunday lunch menu.
Typical prices Beef & venison pie £3.40 Hamburger with salad £3.95

***ACCOMMODATION* 11 bedrooms £B**
Check-in all day

The large and charmingly old-fashioned bedrooms all have practical modern bathrooms en suite, as well as tea-makers, direct-dial phones and remote control TVs, and those overlooking the high street are double-glazed.
Credit Access, Amex, Diners

LEDBURY — Verzons Country House Hotel

B & B

Trumpet, Nr Ledbury
MAP 7 A1 *Herefordshire*
Trumpet (053 183) 381
Parking ample

Landlords Edward & Carolyn Henson & Robin Pollock
Free house
Marston Pedigree, John Marston; Hook Norton Best Bitter; Guinness; Carlsberg; cider.

***ACCOMMODATION* 9 bedrooms £C**
Check-in all day

A handsome Georgian farmhouse on the A438 Hereford road three miles from Redbury. The simple, rustic bar has old oak furniture and there's a homely residents' lounge with traditional green velour seating and plenty of reading material. The bright and airy bedrooms are good-sized, with cream modern units, colour TVs and tea-makers. Six bedrooms have en suite facilities; others share a bathroom with separate shower and toilet. Garden.
Credit Access, Amex, Visa

LEDBURY — Ye Olde Talbot Hotel

B New Street
MAP 7 A1 *Hereford & Worcester*
Ledbury (0531) 2963
Parking difficult

Landlords Mr & Mrs Morriss
Free house
Ansells Bitter; Flowers Original, IPA; Ind Coope Burton Ale; Guinness; Skol; cider.

***ACCOMMODATION* 6 bedrooms £D**
Check-in all day

Enter this ancient, half-timbered hotel via a heavy studded oak door. Inside, the bar is equally characterful, with beams and old oak furniture, while the dining room has beautiful linenfold panelling which still bears the scars of a Civil War fight. The quaint bedrooms are simply equipped with old-fashioned furniture and pretty decor; they share neat public bathrooms. There's also a small residents' lounge with TV. Garden. *No dogs.* **LVs**

LEDSHAM — Tudor Rose

OD Two Mills, South Wirral
MAP 3 C4 *Cheshire*
051–339 2399
Parking ample

Bar food 12–2.30 & 6.30–9.45 (Fri & Sat till 10.15)
Landlord Mr F. Fairclough
Brewery Higsons
Higsons Bitter, Mild; Boddingtons Bitter; Guinness; Stella Artois; Kaltenberg; cider.

Mrs Fairclough's home cooking is a good reason for stopping off at this well-kept 1930s red-brick pub on the A540. Robust turkey broth makes a warming starter, followed by a daily special like the lamb-packed Lancashire hot pot or a choice of steaks, curry, lasagne, salads or omelettes. Lighter bites include ploughman's, pâté, and smoked fish. Attractive garden.
Typical prices Gammon & eggs £2.40 Deep fried mushrooms & salad £1.50
Credit Access, Visa

LEDSTON — White Horse

A Main Street, Nr Castleford
MAP 4 D3 *West Yorkshire*
Castleford (0977) 553069
Parking ample

Landlord Graham Bedford
Brewery Whitbread
Castle Eden; Whitbread Trophy, Yorkshire Light; Guinness; Stella Artois; Heineken; cider.

Enjoying a peaceful village setting yet only minutes from the busy A1, this old stone pub fronted by a colourful little garden has been attractively modernised without losing its traditional charm. Landlord Graham Bedford makes everyone welcome in his spacious beamed bar, where a collection of stuffed animals is displayed. Brass plates and copper-topped tables gleam with polish, and there's a cheery fire in winter. Patio. *No children in the evenings.*

LEEK — Three Horseshoes Inn

B Blackshaw Moor
MAP 5 B1 *Staffordshire*
Blackshaw (053 834) 296
Parking ample

Landlord Mr W. R. Kirk
Free house
McEwan's Tartan, 80/-, Export; Guinness; Beck's Bier; McEwan's Lager; cider.

***ACCOMMODATION* 7 bedrooms £D**
Check-in all day

In a beautiful setting on the A53 north of Leek, this spruce former farmhouse dates back some 300 years. Soft lighting makes the beamed lounge bar more intimate than the lively public bar. Cottagy-style bedrooms feature pine furniture and colour TVs, and those at the back have lovely moorland views. All but one have shower cabinets and there are two bathrooms. Garden. Accommodation closed one week Christmas.
Credit Access, Amex, Diners, Visa

LEIGH-ON-MENDIP — Bell Inn

A

Nr Bath
MAP 5 A3 *Somerset*
Mells (0373) 812316
Parking ample

Landlord Mr S. C. M. Taylor
Free house
Bass; Wadworth 6X; Worthington Best Bitter; Devenish Wessex; Guinness; Carling Black Label; cider.

The stone-walled main bar is the great attraction of this 17th-century inn in a peaceful little village set in beautiful countryside. Gleaming brassware, patterned plates and black beams create a cosy and comfortable atmosphere, and you can toast yourself in front of a log fire or bask in the warmth of a wood-burning stove. The skittle alley bar is popular in summer, when drinkers spill out into the delightful garden.
Credit Access, Visa

LEOMINSTER — Royal Oak Hotel

B & B

South Street
MAP 5 A2 *Hereford & Worcester*
Leominster (0568) 2610
Parking ample

Landlords Gregory Surrey & Leonard Eden
Free house
Hook Norton Best; Woods Special; John Smith's Bitter; Bass; Carling Black Label; Tennent's Extra; cider.

***ACCOMMODATION* 18 bedrooms £C**
Check-in all day

A large old coaching inn with a convenient town centre location. Both the lively Oak bar and the smaller Acorn bar are traditional in style, with beams, wheelback chairs and polished wood tables. Bedrooms have simple, modern units, electric blankets and heaters, tea-makers and TVs; some have duvets. All have neat, simple, modern bathrooms. New owners have greatly-improved decor; future plans include upgrading of bedrooms.
Credit Access, Amex, Diners, Visa

LEVINGTON — Ship

FOOD

Nr Ipswich
MAP 6 F2 *Suffolk*
Nacton (047 388) 573
Parking ample

Bar food 12.15–2 & 7–9
No bar food eves in summer

Landlords Len & Jo Wenham
Brewery Tollemache & Cobbold
Tolly Cobbold Bitter, Original; Guinness; Hansa.

A pub with a nautical theme to the beamed bar, as befits the name. The driving force in the kitchen is Jo Wenham, who provides a mouthwatering and imaginative menu with a strong emphasis on healthy eating. A range of salads and ploughman's is complemented by daily specials such as cheese vegetable roast, mushroom stroganoff or lasagne. Delicious sweets. Terrace.
Typical prices Savoury cheesecake £2.75 Spotted dick £1.20

LICKFOLD — Lickfold Inn

FOOD

Nr Petworth
MAP 6 D3 *West Sussex*
Lodsworth (079 85) 285
Parking ample

Bar food 12–2 & 7-9.30
No bar food Mon eve

Landlords Roger Turner & Vivien Moyise
Free house
Fuller ESB, London Pride; Hall & Woodhouse Badger Best, Tanglefoot; Guinness; Fosters; cider.

A charming rural pub dating from 1460. Exposed beams, an inglenook fireplace and attractive panelling grace the bar, where traditional fare such as jacket potatoes, ploughman's and steak and kidney pie are on offer, together with more adventurous dishes such as trout stuffed with avocado, chicken Kiev, or plaice with mussel and prawn sauce. Less choice Sunday evening. Garden.
Typical prices Fillet of lamb £5.25 Pavlova with fresh fruit £1.75
Credit Visa

LIFTON — Arundell Arms

OD & B

MAP 9 B2 *Devon*
Lifton (0566) 84666
Parking ample

Bar food 12–2.30 & 7–10

Landlord Anne Voss-Bark
Free house
Usher Country Bitter, Triple Crown, Founder's Ale; Ben Truman; Guinness; Carlsberg.

A beautiful, creeper-clad hotel with extensive fishing rights, and so a favourite retreat for fisherfolk. Choose between the pleasantly decorated Courthouse bar – snacks comprise sandwiches and dishes like steak and chips – or a split-level cocktail bar, where the lunchtime only menu offers more choice; an attractive buffet display and a menu that includes ploughman's, home-made chicken and pork pâté, soup and a hot dish such as steak and kidney pie. To follow, there's a small selection of sweets, perhaps pineapple and kiwi fruit flan. Choice in the evenings is more limited. Traditional Sunday lunch menu also available.
Typical prices Braised oxtail with prunes £3.75 Chicken & leek pie £3.75

ACCOMMODATION **29 bedrooms £B**
Check-in all day

Comfortable, centrally heated bedrooms have colour TVs, direct-dial phones and smart en suite facilities. All round high standards. Amenities include game fishing, shooting, a games room and skittle alley. Accommodation closed five days Christmas.

Credit Access, Amex, Diners, Visa

LIMPLEY STOKE — Hop Pole Inn

A

Wood Hill, Nr Bath
MAP 7 A3 *Wiltshire*
Limpley Stoke (022 122) 3134
Parking limited

Landlords Mr & Mrs G.C. Titcombe
Brewery Courage
Courage Bitter Ale, Best Bitter, Directors; Guinness; Kronenbourg; Hofmeister; cider.

Once a monks' wine lodge serving travellers from the ancient (now ruined) priory of Hinton Charterhouse en route to nearby Bradford-on-Avon, this characterful old inn built of Bath stone dates from the 14th century. The eponymous hop plant, said to have been planted in 1750, is still growing outside. An unusual entrance porch leads to two cosy bars, warmed by gas log fires, full of atmosphere and ideal for a quiet drink. Garden and patio.

LINCOLN — Wig & Mitre

OD

29 Steep Hill
MAP 4 E4 *Lincolnshire*
Lincoln (0522) 35190
Parking ample

Bar food 8am–midnight

Landlords Valerie & Michael Hope
Brewery Samuel Smith
Samuel Smith's Old Brewery Bitter, Museum Ale; Ayingerbräu; D Pils.

The steep hill up to this cosy pub-cum-wine bar will sharpen your appetite for the very ably prepared food. Blackboard choices (green chalk for vegetarian dishes) could be tasty onion or cauliflower soup, a warming casserole, cheesy courgettes, a pasta dish or home-made pie. There are always sandwiches and ploughman's, and lovely sweets. Traditional Sunday roast. Patio.
Typical prices Lamb's liver £2.65
Beef & mushroom casserole £2.95
Credit Access, Amex, Diners, Visa **LVs**

LINTON — Windmill Inn

FOOD

Nr Wetherby
MAP 4 D3 *West Yorkshire*
Wetherby (0937) 62938
Parking ample

Bar food 11.45–2.30 & 6–10

Landlords Mr & Mrs Toomey
Brewery Younger
Younger's Scotch, No. 3; Guinness; McEwan's Lager; Beck's Bier; cider.

A 200-year-old farmhouse which has been converted into a superb pub. Original stone walls, beams and open fires give a lovely atmosphere and the bar menu enjoyed here or in the new conservatory is equally pleasing. The cooking is excellent, and dishes include crêpes, Windmill chicken, deep-fried Melbury cheese and lasagne. Check for availability of evening meals. Garden with play area.
Typical prices Seafood risotto £2.55 Steak & kidney pie £2.30

LITTLE LANGDALE — Three Shires Inn

FOOD
B & B

Nr Ambleside
MAP 3 B3 *Cumbria*
Langdale (096 67) 215
Parking ample

Bar food 12–2 & 6.30–8.30 (Sun from 7)

Landlords Mr & Mrs Neil Stephenson
Free house
Webster Yorkshire Bitter; Wilsons Original Bitter, Mild; Guinness; Carlsberg; cider.

The Stephensons keep their Lakeland pub in tip-top order, and you can tuck into some enjoyable snacks by the fire in their comfortable slate-walled bar or out in the peaceful garden with its own delightful stream. Lunchtime brings such appetising dishes as Cumberland pie, beef bourguignon and lamb chops with mint sauce, as well as lighter sandwiches, salads with ham or chicken and ploughman's. The choice widens at night (try the tasty home-made tomato soup followed by julienne of chicken and excellent vegetables), and tempting sweets include a delicious strawberry bavarois.
Typical prices Trout with orange & lemon £4.35 Potted shrimps in garlic £2

ACCOMMODATION **11 bedrooms £C**
Check-in all day

Lovely views add to the charm of the light, airy bedrooms with their pretty fabrics and modern white furniture. There's a chintzy TV lounge for residents' use. Accommodation closed Monday to Thursday (November and December) and from Christmas through to the end of January. *No dogs.*

Any person using our name to obtain free hospitality is a fraud.

Proprietors, please inform Egon Ronay's Guides and the police.

LITTLE WALDEN — Crown Inn

Saffron Walden
MAP 7 D1 *Essex*
Saffron Walden (0799) 27175
Parking ample

Bar food 12–1.45 & 7–9.45
No bar food Sun

Landlords Chris & Gillian Oliver
Free house
Ruddles County, Rutland Bitter; Courage Bitter, Directors; Adnams; Mauldon's Bitter; cider.

★ Beer is drawn from the wood in this delightful, friendly little village pub which dates back to 1748. There's just one bar, furnished in a very cosy rural style with old oak furniture and settles – a place of great character. Super bar food tends to follow the seasons, with warming home-made soups in winter and a tempting cold buffet in summer, including salads based on home-cooked beef or ham. Very fresh seafood and fish dishes are justly popular, with choices like local trout, Cromer crab with a huge plate of crisp salad, mussels in garlic butter and grilled Dover sole heading the enterprising menu. Seasonal hot specials range from a venison casserole to game pie and grilled sea bass, and it's as well to leave room for some homely damson crumble, apple pie or chocolate roulade. Garden. ★

Typical prices Plaice stuffed with prawns and mushrooms £6.50 Baked avocado and crab £2.95 Charcoal grilled giant shrimps £3.95 Seafood platter £7.50–£9.95

Credit Access, Visa

LITTLE WASHBOURNE — Hobnails Inn

Nr Tewkesbury
MAP 7 A1 *Gloucestershire*
Alderton (024 262) 237
Parking ample

Bar food 12–2 & 7–10.30

Landlords Mr & Mrs S. Farbrother & Mrs R. C. Fletcher
Brewery Whitbread
Whitbread West Country Pale Ale; Flowers IPA, Original, Best Bitter; Guinness; Stella Artois; cider.

Built in 1474 as a manor house, this friendly roadside inn has been run by the same family since 1743. Savoury baps are the house speciality, and you can fill your fresh round roll with anything from toasted cheese to liver and onions or chicken salad. Don't miss the tempting desserts, including fruit flans, gâteaux and banana rum pudding. Garden.

Typical prices Gamon & mushroom bap £2.10 Steak & mushroom bap £3.10
Credit Access, Visa

LIVERPOOL — Philharmonic Dining Rooms

A

36 Hope Street
TOWN PLAN *Merseyside*
051–709 1163
Parking ample

Landlords Mr & Mrs Smithwick
Brewery Tetley Walker
Tetley Bitter, Mild; Guinness; Skol; Castlemaine XXXX; cider.

A many-splendoured monument to high Victoriana at its most ornate, this is one of Liverpool's most prized landmarks which should not be missed. A preservation order protects its fine moulded ceilings, the stained and engraved glass, the rosewood panelling and mosaics on the floor and around the bar counters. Even the gents is fitted out in pink marble. There are three large bars to choose from and two small snugs, called Brahms and Liszt.

LLANFAIR WATERDINE — Red Lion Inn

FOOD
B & B

Knighton
MAP 5 A2 *Shropshire*
Knighton (0547) 528214
Parking ample

Bar food 12–2 & 7–9.30

Landlords James & June Rhodes
Free house
Ansells Bitter, Pale Ale; John Smith's Yorkshire Bitter; Wrexham Lager; cider.

Turn off the B4355 some three miles north-west of Knighton and cross the river Teme by the tiny stone bridge to reach the Rhodes' welcoming pub in a border country hamlet. Local farmers and parties of walkers are typical patrons of the little quarry-tiled public bar or the delightful lounge bar with its blackened beams and huge inglenook, adorned with hunting prints and copper pans. The bar menu ranges from soup and pâté to savoury flans, grilled gammon with egg and chips or rump steak, with home-made puds or cheese to follow.
Typical prices Home-made soup & roll 85p Cheese & mushroom flan & salad £1.95

***ACCOMMODATION* 3 bedrooms £C**
Check-in restricted

The three simply furnished bedrooms share a shower and bathroom. Their great attraction is the view of the valley through the tiny cottage windows, which amply compensates for the lack of sophisticated comforts. Garden. *No children under 15 overnight. No dogs.*

We welcome complaints and bona fide recommendations on the tear-out pages for readers' comments. They are followed up by our professional team. Please also complain to the management instantly.

LONG COMPTON — Red Lion

B & B

MAP 7 B1 *Warwickshire*
Long Compton (060 884) 221
Parking ample

Landlord Sara McCall
Brewery Mitchells & Butlers
Mitchells & Butlers Brew XI; Bass; Worthington Bitter; Guinness; Carling Black Label; cider.

***ACCOMMODATION* 3 bedrooms £C**
Check-in all day

This characterful village pub stands on the busy A34 Oxford–Stratford road. Flagstoned floors, beams, low ceilings, Cotswold stone walls and open fires give plenty of atmosphere to the long bar area. Three cosy bedrooms with low ceilings and sloping floors offer comfortable accommodation; pretty floral wallpapers and pictures adorn the walls and the furniture is period-style. All have new en suite bathrooms, magazines and radio alarms. Patio and garden.
Credit Amex, Diners, Visa

LONG MELFORD — Crown Inn Hotel

FOOD
B & B

Hall Street
MAP 6 E2 *Suffolk*
Sudbury (0787) 77666
Parking ample

Bar food 12–1.45 & 7–9.30

Landlords Mr & Mrs M. Wright & Mr & Mrs A. Frampton
Free house
Adnams Bitter; Mauldons Bitter; Greene King IPA; Guinness; Carlsberg Export, Hof; cider.

The Wrights and the Framptons (their daughter and son-in-law) have successfully redesigned the interior of this historic inn, in the longest village street in England, without harming its character. The open-plan bar area is spacious and airy, and the chintzy lounge with its unusual stained glass panel is invitingly comfortable. Bar food is simple and home-made, with soup, sandwiches and a summer cold buffet supplemented by popular hot dishes. Locally brewed ales are well represented.

Typical prices Steak & kidney pie £2.60 Chilli con carne £2.45

ACCOMMODATION **13 bedrooms £C**
Check-in all day

Check in for overnight guests is in a well designed reception hall. Main building bedrooms have handsome old furniture (and one four-poster) befitting their characterful charm. Those in the converted coach house are smartly modern. All have TVs and tea-makers, and seven have their own carpeted bathrooms. Public bathrooms are very well kept. Good breakfasts. There's a pretty enclosed garden to the side of the inn.

Credit Access, Amex, Diners, Visa

We welcome bona fide recommendations or complaints on the tear-out pages for readers' comments. They are followed up by our professional team but do complain to the management.

LONG MELFORD — Hare Inn

OD

High Street
MAP 6 E2 *Suffolk*
Sudbury (0787) 310379
Parking ample

Barfood 12–2&6–10 (Sun from 7)

Landlords John & Jill Pipe
Brewery Greene King
Greene King Abbot Ale, IPA, XX Dark Mild; Guinness; Kronenbourg; cider.

The open fires create an atmosphere of warmth and cheer in this traditional inn by the A134. The most interesting choice among the bar snacks is provided by the blackboard specials: tomato, leek and almond soup, moules marinière with garlic bread, stir-fried chicken with bean sprouts, peppers and rice. There's also a roast lunch on Sundays. Garden.
Typical prices Duck galantine £4.25 Plaice paupiettes £3.95
Credit Visa

LONGFRAMLINGTON — Granby Inn

& B

Nr Morpeth
MAP 4 D1 *Northumberland*
Longframlington (066 570) 228
Parking ample

Landlords Hall family
Brewery Bass
Stones Bitter; Worthington Export; Guinness; Carling Black Label; cider. *No real ale.*

ACCOMMODATION **6 bedrooms £C**
Check-in all day

A former coaching inn where old beams, ornaments and a wealth of flowers provide plenty of charm. There are two lively, popular bars and a residents' lounge. Three modern, compact bedrooms in chalets have small sitting areas; those in the main house are more traditional in style. All have TVs and teamakers and four have modern en suite facilities. Garden. Accommodation closed four days Christmas. *No children under five overnight. No dogs.*
Credit Access, Amex, Visa

LONGLEAT — Bath Arms

FOOD
B & B

Horningsham
MAP 5 B3 *Wiltshire*
Maiden Bradley (098 53) 308
Parking ample

Bar food 11.30–2.30 & 6–10 (Sun till 9)

Landlords Joe, Beryl & Paul Lovatt
Free house
Wadworth 6X; Bass; Eldridge Pope Dorchester Bitter; Webster Yorkshire Bitter; Guinness; Holsten.

In the little village of Horningsham within the Longleat estate, this mellow creeper-clad inn was the priory house in the days before the Reformation when Longleat was a monastery. In the friendly, unpretentious main bar decorated with old photos and horse brasses, a short menu supplemented by a list of daily specialities is offered which concentrates on fine, fresh ingredients prepared in a simple, enjoyable fashion. Choices like flavoursome vegetable soup, grilled Dover sole, curries and home-made savoury pies all please, and to finish there's a nicely gingery rhubarb pie. Traditional Sunday lunch menu available.
Typical prices Local trout £3.95 Pasty & chips £1.95

***ACCOMMODATION* 5 bedrooms £B**
Check-in all day

Good-sized bedrooms are modest but well kept, and chintzy soft furnishings add a homely touch. All have TVs and tea-makers, and four offer simple private facilities. There is an attractive little first-floor lounge for residents, and a delightful sheltered garden.

Credit Access, Diners

LONGPARISH — Plough Inn

FOOD

Nr Andover
MAP 5 C3 *Hampshire*
Longparish (026 472) 358
Parking limited

Bar food 12–2 & 7–10
Landlord Trevor Colgate
Brewery Whitbread
Samuel Whitbread; Strong Country Bitter; Flowers Original; Guinness; Heineken.

In a cosy bar hung with dried hops an appealingly wide menu greets visitors to this very popular wisteria-clad pub (early arrival advised). Favourites such as sandwiches and ploughman's (nice choice of cheeses and pickles) are backed up by well-prepared specials including home-made soups, steak sandwiches and snails in garlic butter. Roast on Sundays. Garden and patio.
Typical prices Baked trout with prawns £5.25 Chicken casserole £4.75
Credit Access, Amex, Diners, Visa

LOWDHAM — Springfield Inn

B & B

Old Epperstone Road
MAP 5 C1 *Nottinghamshire*
Nottingham (0602) 663387
Parking ample

Landlords Gordon & Mavis Ferriman
Free house
Marston Pedigree; Home Bitter; Mansfield Bitter; Guinness; Carling Black Label; Skol; cider.

***ACCOMMODATION* 10 bedrooms £C**
Check-in all day

Guests can literally 'drop in' at flying enthusiast Gordon Ferriman's converted private house on the A6097, where parking for helicopters is an unusual amenity. Jimmy the resident parrot is a favourite in the cosy beamed bar, while the relaxing lounge bar offers peace and comfort. Practical overnight accommodation is provided in well-kept bedrooms, all with carpeted facilities, TVs, tea-makers, radio-alarms and direct-dial telephones. Garden.
Credit Access, Amex, Visa

LOWER PEOVER — Bells of Peover

A Nr Knutsford
MAP 3 C4 *Cheshire*
Lower Peover (056 581) 2269
Parking ample

Landlord Goodier Fischer
Brewery Greenall Whitley
Greenall Whitley Local Bitter, Mild; Guinness; Grünhalle; cider.

Down a cobbled lane (off the B5081) and right by the church stands this charming whitewashed and creeper-clad pub, dating back to 1269. Its delightfully traditional interior is reminiscent of an old print. The two cosy bars – a snug with a striking collection of toby jugs, and a lounge furnished with some fine carved settles and a dresser bedecked with blue patterned china – are both warmed by real fires. Garden.
Credit Diners

LOWER WOODFORD — Wheatsheaf Inn

FOOD Salisbury
MAP 5 B3 *Wiltshire*
Middle Woodford (072 273) 203
Parking ample

Bar food 12–2 (Sun till 1.30) & 7–10

Landlord Peter Charlton
Brewery Hall & Woodhouse
Hall & Woodhouse Badger Best, Tanglefoot, Hector's Bitter; Guinness; Carlsberg Hof; Stella Artois; cider.

This popular creeper-clad family pub was once a farmhouse whose beamed barn has become a large lounge bar. A huge choice of food is offered: soups and starters, popular basket meals, salads and baked potatoes; substantial curries, pasta and grills; and daily specials like beef in Guinness. Sunday roast and traditional treacle roly-poly. Special children's menu. Garden.
Typical prices Prawn curry £2.50 Banana split £1.25
Credit Access, Amex, Visa

LOWESWATER — Kirkstile Inn

B & B Nr Cockermouth
MAP 3 B2 *Cumbria*
Lorton (090 085) 219
Parking ample

Landlord Kenneth Gorley
Free house
Jennings Bitter; Younger's Scotch, Tartan Bitter; Guinness; Ayingerbräu Lager; cider.

ACCOMMODATION **10 bedrooms £D**
Check-in all day

Splendid views of a delightful beck and a dominating fell peak provide the picturesque setting for this remote 16th-century inn next to the village church. Bars with wooden settles and a fireplace hewn from local stone are pleasantly rustic, while the simply furnished bedrooms – some with superb views – offer basic comforts for an overnight stay. All but two have private bathrooms. There's also a TV lounge.
Credit Access

LOWICK GREEN — Farmers Arms

FOOD
B & B Nr Ulverston
MAP 3 B3 *Cumbria*
Greenodd (022 986) 376
Parking ample

Bar food 12–2 & 6–10 (Sun from 7)

Landlord Philip Broadley
Brewery Younger
Younger's No 3, Scotch; McEwan's 80/–; Guinness; Harp; Beck's Bier; cider.

A characterful old inn which started life in 1350 as a farmhouse where beer was brewed. Black beams, horse brasses, flagstoned floors and sloping floors in the warren of rooms on several levels make for an atmospheric setting in which to sample the bar fare on offer. Traditional snacks include home-made pâté, smoked mackerel, good sandwiches and specials such as cheese and onion pie. Home-made sweets could include lemon torte or raspberry pavlova as well as the staple fruit pie, sherry

trifle and ice cream. A patio provides for pleasant outdoor eating in summer. At lunchtimes there is also soup and the recent addition of a cold buffet. Sundays bring a traditional roast.
Typical prices Steak & kidney pie £2.50 Fried haddock & chips £2.40

***ACCOMMODATION* 11 bedrooms £C**
Check-in all day

Well-cared-for bedrooms are furnished in simple traditional style, with natural, muted colours and pine furniture. All have TVs, hairdryers, tea-makers and a drinks tray. Seven of them have functional private facilities, the rest sharing one public bathroom.

Credit Access, Amex, Visa

LUDLOW — Angel Hotel

8 Broad Street
MAP 5 A2 *Shropshire*
Ludlow (0584) 2581
Parking ample

Bar food 12–2 & 6–9

Landlord Mr D. Edwards
Free house
Flowers Original, IPA; Whitbread Best Bitter; Guinness; Stella Artois; Heineken; cider.

Standing on one of Ludlow's most elegant streets, this handsome half-timbered inn boasts Lord Nelson as a famous past visitor. The spacious main bar is a comfortably traditional setting for simple snacks like home-made minestrone, jacket potatoes and sandwiches, as well as specials such as spaghetti bolognese and gammon in parsley sauce. Puddings can be chosen from the restaurant menu, and a traditional Sunday lunch is served.
Typical prices Lasagne £3 Beef stroganoff £3

***ACCOMMODATION* 17 bedrooms £B**
Check-in all day

Accommodation is a strong point at the Angel and the 17 handsomely furnished bedrooms are all extremely restful and beautifully warm. The decor is smartly modern, and up-to-date accessories include colour TVs, radio-alarms, hairdryers and tea-makers; bubble bath and generous soft towels feature in the carpeted private bathrooms. Two large, luxurious rooms (one with a four-poster) have their own sitting areas, and there's a relaxing residents' lounge which provides a quiet retreat.

Credit Access, Amex, Diners, Visa

LURGASHALL — Noah's Ark

The Green, Nr Petworth
MAP 6 D3 *West Sussex*
Northchapel (042 878) 346
Parking ample

Bar food 12–2 & 7–10
No bar food Sun

Landlord Barton Edward Swannell
Brewery Friary Meux
Friary Meux Bitter; Ind Cooper Burton Ale; John Bull Bitter; Löwenbräu; Skol; cider.

In a peaceful setting overlooking the village green, this attractive old pub is relaxed, civilised and sparkling clean. Ted Swannell has a welcome for one and all, and his wife prepares tasty bar snacks, from sandwiches and soup to fresh salads, steak and kidney pudding, lasagne and chicken Kiev, plus a few simple sweets – delicious fresh raspberries in season. Garden.
Typical prices English lamb cutlets £3 Calf's liver & bacon £3.25
Credit Diners

LYDDINGTON — Marquess of Exeter

B & B

Nr Uppingham
MAP 5 C1 *Leicestershire*
Uppingham (0572) 822477
Parking ample

Landlords Mr L. Evitt & family
Free house
Ruddles County, Best Bitter; Marston Pedigree; Adnams Bitter; Guinness; Stella Artois; cider.

ACCOMMODATION **20 bedrooms £B**
Check-in all day

Sympathetic updating has preserved considerable period charm at this delightful 16th-century thatched inn. The low-beamed bars particularly appeal, with their inglenook fireplaces and fine cabinet display of ornaments. A modern annexe houses the comfortable, tastefully appointed bedrooms (including two suites), which are all of a good size and offer tea-makers, TVs, radio-alarms and direct-dial telephones. Excellent bathrooms. Patio. *No dogs.*
Credit Access, Amex, Diners, Visa.

LYDFORD — Castle Inn

FOOD
B & B

Nr Okehampton
MAP 9 B2 *Devon*
Lydford (082 282) 242
Parking ample

Bar food 12–2 & 7–9.45 (Sun till 9.30)
Landlords David & Susan Grey
Free house
Usher Best Bitter, Founder's Ale, Triple Crown; Courage Best Bitter; Webster Yorkshire Bitter; Guinness; Carlsberg; cider.

There's no shortage of atmosphere in the Greys' pink-washed pub in a secluded setting on the edge of Dartmoor, next to the castle remains and only a couple of minutes from Lydford Gorge. The beamed bars with their high-backed settles, roaring log fires, and walls lined with prints, daguerrotypes and decorative plates are delightful. Blackboard specials such as leek and potato soup, savoury flans, shepherd's pie with cheese topping and an excellent suet crust steak and kidney pie support the regular grills and basket meals. The lunchtime cold buffet table is available daily, supplemented on Sundays by a choice of two roasts. Good puddings include a rich treacle tart.
Typical prices Steak & kidney pie £2.75 Beef curry £2.95

ACCOMMODATION **7 bedrooms £D**
Check-in all day

A charming staircase leads to the characterful bedrooms, two of which have en suite bathrooms. Four have fine old beds and other period pieces; the rest have reproduction furniture. All have central heating, tea-makers and TVs. Above average breakfast. Garden.

Credit Access, Visa

LYNDHURST — Waterloo Arms

FOOD

Pikes Hill
MAP 5 C4 *Hampshire*
Lyndhurst (042 128) 3333
Parking ample

Bar food 12–2 & 7–9
No bar food Sun–Tues eves
Landlords Nick & Sue Wateridge
Brewery Whitbread
Whitbread Best Bitter; Strong Country Bitter; Flowers Original; Guinness; Stella Artois; Heineken; cider.

Much of this 300-year-old pub's character comes from an extraordinary collection of antiques that includes guns, boomerangs, fishing rods and stuffed crocodiles. Lunchtime brings hearty soup and tasty hot dishes like liver and bacon casserole, plus ploughman's, steak sandwiches, toasties and jacket potatoes. Less choice available evenings and Sunday lunch. Children's adventure playground in the garden.
Typical prices Broccoli quiche £2.50 Beef & beer stew £2.25

LYONSHALL — Royal George Inn

B Nr Kington
MAP 5 A2 *Hereford & Worcester*
Lyonshall (054 48) 210
Parking ample

Landlords Elaine & John Allen
Brewery Whitbread
Flowers Original, IPA; Whitbread Best Bitter, Best Mild; Guinness; Stella Artois; cider.
ACCOMMODATION **3 bedrooms £D**
Check-in all day

This charming black and white inn dating from the 16th century takes its name from the sailing ship whose timbers were used in its construction. It's something of a centre for gliding enthusiasts, and photographs in the rustic bars highlight the sporting theme. There are some attractive period pieces among the assortment of furniture in the bedrooms, which have TVs and tea-makers and share a bathroom and a shower room. Garden.

MADINGLEY — Three Horseshoes

D MAP 7 D1 *Cambridgeshire*
Madingley (0954) 210221
Parking ample
Bar food 12–2 & 7–10

Landlord Dominic Rowsell
Free house
Tolly Cobbold Original, Bitter; Hansa Lager; cider.

Whitewashed walls and a thatched roof give this village inn an attractive and very traditional appearance. The menu is varied and interesting, featuring a good selection of seafood – lobster, grilled sea bass, mussels – and meat dishes include strips of prime Scotch fillet stir fried with vegetables, or succulent, spicy beefburgers. Also baguette sandwiches.
Typical prices Graffam trout £5.85 Bread & butter pudding £1.45
Credit Access, Amex, Diners, Visa

MAIDENSGROVE — Five Horseshoes

D Nr Henley-on-Thames
MAP 7 C2 *Oxfordshire*
Nettlebed (0491) 641282
Parking ample

Bar food 12–2 (Sun till 1.30) & 7–9.30
No bar food Sun eve

Landlords Graham & Mary Cromack
Brewery Brakspear
Brakspear Bitter, Special; Guinness; Heineken; cider.

★ An attractive garden and two characterful bars provide seasonal watering-holes at the friendly Cromacks' cottagy pub, which is set in lovely countryside near Henley. Bar food is of a high standard, with a choice of five home-made pâtés (including avocado, smoked trout), soup or deep-fried mushrooms getting meals off to a tasty start. Equally well-prepared and appetising main dishes range from chicken Kiev, grilled prawns, and first-rate sweet and sour pork to speciality fillet steak in a mustardy cream and brandy sauce and a prize-winning steak and kidney pie. Quick snacks include pancakes, ploughman's and filled jacket potatoes, while any gaps can be filled with super sweets such as a nutty treacle tart or tempting cherry flan. There are no grills on Saturday and Sunday lunchtimes, but barbecues are a feature of Sunday lunch and Thursday evenings. ★
Typical prices Marinated stir-fried spicy beef £5.95 Calf's liver £4.95 Seafood lasagne £4.35 Steak & kidney pie £3.50

MALHAM — Buck Inn

B & B

Nr Skipton
MAP 3 C3 *North Yorkshire*
Airton (072 93) 317
Parking ample

Landlord Mrs R. M. Robinson
Free house
Theakston Best Bitter, XB, Old Peculier; Younger's Scotch, Tartan Bitter, Dark Mild; Guinness; cider.

ACCOMMODATION **10 bedrooms £C**
Check-in all day

Walkers and tourists in the lovely Yorkshire Dales find this sturdy stone inn a good place to pause, whether for a refreshing drink or an overnight stay. Day rooms include a delightful main bar with a real feel of the area, a busy walkers' bar and a TV lounge. Some handsome pieces of period furniture may be found in the bedrooms. All have duvets, tea and coffee making facilities, and four have private bath or shower.

MALMESBURY — Suffolk Arms

FOOD

Tetbury Hill
MAP 7 A3 *Wiltshire*
Malmesbury (066 62) 2271
Parking ample

Bar food 12–2.30 (Sun till 2) & 7–10

Landlords John & Julia Evans
Free house
Wadworth 6X, IPA, Farmers Glory; Guinness; Stella Artois; Kronenbourg; cider.

★ A delightful stone-built pub on the northern outskirts of this pretty Wiltshire town. A wealth of exposed beams and stone, copper pans and cast iron stoves make for atmospheric surroundings in which to enjoy a splendid meal. The fine bar food covers a good range, from lighter bites such as ploughman's and filled jacket potatoes to an aubergine casserole for vegetarians, and for a filling meal perhaps fresh salmon mousse or Suffolk sausages for starters, followed by steak and kidney pie, curry, Moroccan lamb or a blackboard special such as delicious grilled swordfish steak with hollandaise. The exquisite sweets include a plum cheesecake and treacle pie with fresh cream. A traditional menu is on offer at the restaurant, which boasts fine linenfold panelling. Garden. ★

Typical prices Smoked mackerel pâté £2.10 Trout Bretonne £7.95 Casserole of pheasant £8.75 Duckling in black cherry sauce £8.75

Credit Access, Amex, Diners, Visa

MALTON — Green Man Hotel

FOOD
B & B

Market Street
MAP 4 E3 *North Yorkshire*
Malton (0653) 692662
Parking ample

Bar food 12–2 & 7–9
No bar food Sun eve

Landlords John & Liz Barwick
Free house
Cameron Lion Bitter; Wrangham's Original PA; Stowford Press; Guinness; Cameron Hansa; cider.

Both food and accommodation at this town-centre hostelry are thoroughly recommendable. Lunchtime in the comfortable main bar brings a popular buffet of cold meats, quiches and salads; there's also a daily roast during the winter months and a variety of other dishes, from Yorkshire pudding with onion gravy to filled jacket potatoes, grilled gammon and fried Whitby fish. Sandwiches provide lighter bites, and home-made sweets include a nice jam sponge. It's sandwiches only in the

evening except on Friday and Saturday, when hot meals (steak, roast chicken, curry) are also available. Traditional Sunday lunch menu also available.
Typical prices Steak & kidney pie £2.65 Garlic mushrooms £1.30

ACCOMMODATION **25 bedrooms £C**
Check-in all day

Bedrooms are modestly fitted (candlewick bedspreads, simple wooden bedheads); all are kept in apple-pie order. Colour TVs and tea and coffee making facilities are standard, and most rooms have their own shower or bathroom. The remainder share five adequate public bathrooms. Patio.

Credit Access, Amex, Visa **LVs**

MANACCAN — New Inn

D Nr Helston
MAP 9 A3 *Cornwall*
Manaccan (032 623) 323
Parking limited

Bar food 11.30–2 (Sun from 12) & 7–9.30
No bar food Tues eve in winter
Landlord Patrick Cullinan
Brewery Cornish Brewery Company
Devenish Cornish, John Devenish; Guinness; Grünhalle; Stella Artois; cider.

A thatched pub mentioned in Cromwell's dispatches which has retained its simple, unpretentious country atmosphere. There is a constantly changing menu offering a splendid range of home-made food; you might find poussin provençale, savoury beef macaroni and crab salad, with raspberry cheesecake, gooseberry crumble and treacle tart for dessert. More main dishes in the evenings, particularly fish. Garden.
Typical prices Monkfish armoricaine £4.50 Lasagne £4

MARHAMCHURCH — Bullers Arms

B Nr Bude
MAP 9 B2 *Cornwall*
Widemouth Bay (028 885) 277
Parking ample

Landlords Bill and Liz Kneebone
Free house
Devenish Cornish, Wessex; Marston Pedigree; Wadworth 6X; guest beers; Carlsberg; cider.

ACCOMMODATION **24 bedrooms £D**
Check-in all day

Rural tranquillity prevails around this extended and modernised pub, with a fine stained glass entrance door. A roaring log fire increases the welcome of the splendid panelled Hunter's Bar, where the locals gather. Spotlessly clean accommodation is in two bright, well-appointed bedrooms and five self-contained flats (bedroom, sitting room, kitchen, bathroom), serviced or self-catering. All rooms have sweeping pastoral views to the sea. Garden.
Credit Access, Visa

MARKET DRAYTON — Corbet Arms Hotel

B High Street
MAP 5 A1 *Shropshire*
Market Drayton (0630) 2037
Parking ample

Landlord Mr J. Beckett
Free house
Mitchells & Butlers Springfield Bitter; Tetley Mild; Stones Bitter; Guinness; Tennent's Pilsner, Extra; Carling Black Label; cider.

ACCOMMODATION **12 bedrooms £C**
Check-in all day

A substantial creeper-clad inn whose open-plan bars provide a focal point for the local social life, though residents who feel unsociable can retire to their quiet private lounge. Bedrooms are spacious and very comfortable, with functional modern furnishings, colour television and direct-dial phones. All but two have well-maintained private facilities. Stout-hearted males may wish to run the gauntlet of the amorous lady ghost in room 7!
Credit Access, Amex, Diners, Visa.

MARKET WEIGHTON — Londesborough Arms

B & B

High Road
MAP 4 E3 *Humberside*
Market Weighton (0696) 72219
Parking ample

Landlord David Cuckston
Brewery Cameron
Cameron Lion Bitter, Strongarm; Russells Mild; Everards Old Original; Cameron Hansa; cider.

ACCOMMODATION **14 bedrooms £C**
Check-in all day

A handsome Georgian hotel providing good comfort for an overnight stay. Each bedroom is attractively done out in a different colour with white fitted furniture blending well. All rooms have TVs, tea/coffee making facilities, telephones and compact bathrooms. A celebrated local giant of the 18th-century is commemorated in the Bradley's Bar, and you can still see his enormous chair. There's also a second, plusher bar.
Credit Access, Amex, Diners, Visa

MARLBOROUGH — Sun Inn

FOOD
B & B

High Street
MAP 7 B3 *Wiltshire*
Marlborough (0672) 52081
Parking limited

Bar food 11.30–2.15 & 6–10.15 (till 9.45 in winter), Sun 12–1.40 & 7–9.45

Landlords Mr & Mrs G.M. Culver
Brewery Usher
Usher Best, Founder's Ale, Country Bitter; Guinness; Carlsberg; Holsten Export.

Situated opposite a lovely church, this whitewashed inn is one of the few buildings to have survived the Great Fire of Marlborough in 1653. More recently, a fine reputation for food has been established here, the varied menu being supplemented by inventive daily blackboard specials such as fresh local trout with boulangère potatoes, beef and ale casserole, or banana fudge pie. The main menu includes a good selection of snacks, herb sausages with Cumberland sauce, tagliatelle alla carbonara, and open and toasted sandwiches, plus more substantial items such as the simple but delicious breast of chicken baked with avocado and garlic.
Typical prices Pork spare ribs £2.50 Grilled sardines £2.50

ACCOMMODATION **7 bedrooms £D**
Check-in restricted

Narrow winding stairs lead to five low-ceilinged cottagy bedrooms with washbasins, tea and coffee making facilities and colour TVs. There are also two larger bedrooms in a converted coach house. All share two well-equipped, modern shower rooms and a bathroom. Good breakfasts. Patio and garden.
Credit Access, Visa

MARSHSIDE — Gate Inn

FOOD

Nr Canterbury
MAP 6 E3 *Kent*
Chislet (022 786) 498
Parking ample

Bar food 11.30–2.30 & 6–10.30
No bar food Sun lunch

Landlord Christopher John Smith
Brewery Shepherd Neame
Shepherd Neame Invicta Best Bitter, Master Brew Mild, Stock Ale; cider.

Local sports teams and pub games galore are well represented at Christopher Smith's down-to-earth village pub. Doorstep sandwiches of sausage, black pudding or bacon, home-made burgers and enormous bowls of robust soup are just the job after a long walk. Eat in front of a huge log fire in the unspoilt, quarry-tiled bar, or in the garden overlooking a duck pond.
Typical prices Black pudding ploughman's £1.50 Cheesy Gateburger £1.05

MATTINGLEY **Leather Bottle**

D Nr Basingstoke
MAP 7 C3 *Hampshire*
Heckfield (073 583) 371
Parking ample
Bar food 12–2 & 7–10.15
Landlord Richard Moore
Brewery Courage
Courage Best Bitter, Directors; John Smith's Yorkshire Bitter; Guinness; Hofmeister; Kronenbourg; cider.

Quite an attractive old pub, partly creeper-clad, and with a pretty little garden. Inside it's warm and comfortable, a good spot in which to enjoy a sandwich, a salad or something more serious like ham, egg and chips, chicken curry or a steak. Spicy sausages are a popular choice, and there are pleasant sweets.
Typical prices Chicken fillets with barbecue sauce £4 Roast guinea fowl Madeira £5
Credit Access, Amex, Diners, Visa

MAYFIELD **Rose & Crown**

D Fletching Street
MAP 6 E3 *East Sussex*
Mayfield (0435) 872200
Parking ample
Bar food 12–1.55 & 7–10 (Mon & Tues till 9.30, Sun till 9)
Landlords Richard & Claudette Leet
Free house
Everards Tiger; Adnams Bitter; Marston Albion Mild; Tennent's Lager; Faust; cider.

Tubs and baskets of flowers decorate the exterior of this neat, white-painted weatherboarded pub, while inside is an attractive beamed bar. Claudette Leet does all the cooking, and her daily changing menu offers many delights, including country broth, game pie and grilled pork with barbecue sauce. Vegetarian dishes are always featured and filled savoury crêpes are a speciality. Garden.
Typical prices Seafood pancake £2.60 T-bone steak £6.15

MELLOR **Millstone Hotel**

B Church Lane, Nr Blackburn
MAP 3 C3 *Lancashire*
Mellor (025 481) 3333
Parking ample
Landlord Richard Robinson
Free house
Thwaites Best Bitter, Mild; Guinness; Carlsberg; Tuborg.
***ACCOMMODATION* 16 bedrooms £A**
Check-in all day

Situated just off the A59, ten minutes' drive from junction 31 of the M6, this roadside inn has a comfortable, well-cared for air. Attractively decorated bedrooms have handsome furnishings and are equipped with TVs, tea-makers, radio-alarms and trouser presses; all have modern, carpeted bathrooms. Executive rooms offer extras like fruit, dressing gowns and teletext TVs. The spacious lounge-bar is smartly rustic in style.
Credit Access, Amex, Diners, Visa

MELMERBY **Shepherds Inn**

D Nr Penrith
MAP 3 C2 *Cumbria*
Langwathby (076 881) 217
Parking ample
Bar food 11–2.30 & 6–9.45, Sun 12–2 & 7–9.45
Landlords Martin & Christine Baucutt
Brewery Marston
Marston Burton Bitter, Pedigree, Merrie Monk, Owd Rodger, Pilsner Lager; cider.

Opposite the village green, this pleasant pub offers some highly enjoyable eating in its open-plan bar. Daily specials like Cumberland sausage hot pot and beef bourguignon are notably good, while lighter bites include tasty soups, pâté, ploughman's and really crisp salads. Nice home-made sweets and an excellent cheeseboard (Wensleydale, Yorkshire goat's cheese, blue Cheshire). Patio.
Typical prices Chicken leoni £4.10 Vegetable lasagne £3.50
Credit Access

MERE — Old Ship Hotel

B & B Castle Street
MAP 5 B3 *Wiltshire*
Mere (0747) 860258
Parking ample

Landlord Philip Johnson
Brewery Hall & Woodhouse
Hall & Woodhouse Badger Best, Badger Export; Worthington Dark; Guinness; Hall & Woodhouse Brock Lager; cider.

***ACCOMMODATION* 24 bedrooms £C**
Check-in all day/restricted

Log fires in winter make things really snug at this sturdy, 17th-century coaching inn near the town centre. The bars offer panelled walls and beamed ceilings, or residents can sample the charm of the cosy lounge. The ten annexe bedrooms have practical units and modern bathrooms, while those in the main building – seven of which have bathrooms en suite – are more traditional in style (one boasts a four-poster). All have tea-makers and TVs. Patio.
Credit Access, Visa

METAL BRIDGE — Metal Bridge Inn

B & B Nr Gretna
MAP 3 B2 *Cumbria*
Rockcliffe (022 874) 206
Parking ample

Brewery Younger
Younger's Export, Tartan, Scotch, IPA; Beck's Bier; Harp.

***ACCOMMODATION* 5 bedrooms £C**
Check-in restricted

Excellent overnight accommodation in recently refurbished bedrooms is the reward for travellers stopping at this white-painted old pub alongside the A74. All the pretty, pine-furnished bedrooms offer TVs, trouser presses, hairdryers and tea-makers, while four out of the five have smart modern bathrooms. The split-level bar with its cane-furnished conservatory overlooking the river Esk is an attractive setting for a quiet drink. Patio.
Credit Access, Amex, Visa

METHERELL — Carpenters Arms

B & B Nr Callington
MAP 9 B2 *Cornwall*
Liskeard (0579) 50242
Parking limited

Landlords Douglas & Jill Brace
Free house
Worthington Best; Bass; Wadworth 6X; Theakston Old Peculier; Ben Truman; Guinness; cider.

***ACCOMMODATION* 3 bedrooms £D**
Check-in restricted

A flower-bedecked terrace catches the eye in front of this delightfully unspoilt old inn just south of the A390 Gunnislake–Liskeard road. Within are several very convivial interconnecting bars with rough stone walls and a wealth of black beams. In contrast, the three cheerful bedrooms are in a modern extension; they share a spacious carpeted shower room and offer modest comforts including tea-makers.

MIDDLEHAM — Black Swan

B & B Market Place
MAP 4 D3 *North Yorkshire*
Wensleydale (0969) 22221
Parking ample

Landlords Kenneth & Margaret Burton
Free house
Theakston Best Bitter, Old Peculier; John Smith's Bitter, Tawny Light; Guinness; Carlsberg; cider. *No real ale.*

***ACCOMMODATION* 7 bedrooms £D**
Check-in all day

Middleham is a long-established centre of racehorse training, so the pictures and paraphernalia in the charming bar of this 17th-century inn are appropriately horsy. Bedrooms, all with en suite facilities, are very neat and tidy; four have original beams (two with four-posters) and furnishings vary from traditional to modern. Summer sipping can be enjoyed in a pleasant garden. Accommodation closed three days Christmas. *No children under five overnight.*

MIDDLETON STONEY **Jersey Arms**

B Nr Bicester
MAP 7 B2 *Oxfordshire*
Middleton Stoney (086 989) 234
Parking ample

Landlords Donald & Helen Livingstone
Free house
Courage Best Bitter, Directors.

ACCOMMODATION **14 bedrooms £C**
Check-in all day

Overnight accommodation is a strong point at this handsome, 16th-century Cotswold-stone inn, which stands at the junction of the A43 and B4030. Bedrooms are very comfortable, with well-sprung beds, carpeted en suite bathrooms, direct-dial telephones and colour TVs. Four spacious suites in the courtyard boast stained-glass windows and heavy oak doors. There's a delightful beamed bar and an elegant lounge. Good breakfasts. Garden. *No dogs.*
Credit Access, Amex, Diners, Visa

MIDHURST **Angel Hotel**

B North Street
MAP 6 D3 *West Sussex*
Midhurst (073 081) 2421
Parking ample

Landlord Mr N. Gibson
Owner Lyons Catering Ltd
Gales HSB, BBB; Guinness; Carlsberg; cider.

ACCOMMODATION **17 bedrooms £B**
Check-in all day

A delightful rose garden and two fine beamed bars offer an attractive choice of venues for a quiet drink at this friendly old coaching inn. Some of the excellent bedrooms boast smart pine furnishings, while a few larger rooms have handsome antiques. Colour TVs and tea-makers are standard, and all except one have private facilities. There's a comfortable residents' lounge on the first floor. Good breakfast.
Credit Access, Amex, Diners, Visa

Changes in data may occur in establishments after the Guide goes to press. Prices should be taken as indications rather than firm quotes.

MILDENHALL **Bell Hotel**

B High Street
MAP 6 E2 *Suffolk*
Mildenhall (0638) 717272
Parking ample

Landlords John & Carolyn Child
Free house
Greene King Abbot Ale; Adnams Bitter; Younger's Scotch; Guinness; Carlsberg Hof, Pilsner; cider.

ACCOMMODATION **18 bedrooms £C**
Check-in all day

For more than half a century the Child family have been in charge of this busy town-centre pub with a delightful old coaching inn character. The spacious beamed L-shaped bar is a popular local meeting place, and there is a pleasant patio for outdoor drinking and useful family room for children. Bright, attractive bedrooms (most with private bathrooms) have neat modern furnishings, direct-dial telephones and tea-makers.
Credit Access, Amex, Diners, Visa

MILTON ABBAS **Hambro Arms**

FOOD
B & B

Nr Blandford Forum
MAP 5 B4 *Dorset*
Milton Abbas (0258) 880233
Parking ample

Bar food 12–2 & 7–10 (till 9.30 in winter)

Landlord Ken Baines
Brewery Devenish
John Devenish Dry Hop, Wessex Stud; Guinness; Holsten Export; Carlsberg; cider.

Built around 1780, this fine thatched pub stands at the top of an exceptionally pretty Dorset village. The bar snacks stay in good form under landlord Ken Baines, and a blackboard declares the day's choice. Sandwiches, ploughman's and slices of quiche provide good light bites, and main courses run from lasagne and lamb cutlets to sautéed chicken and a very enjoyable pork curry with rice and poppadoms. Traditional puds include apple pie and baked jam roll with custard, and a popular Sunday extra is the roast beef lunch served in the restaurant.

Typical prices Beef & oyster pie £3.95 Ploughman's from £1.55

ACCOMMODATION **2 bedrooms £C**
Check-in all day

There are only two bedrooms, both with plenty of space and plenty of character; one has a four-poster, the other a handsome period wardrobe and Victorian spoonback chairs. Comfortable, smartly kept and well heated, they have little shower cubicles in the corner. Patio. Children are welcome overnight. *No dogs.*

Credit Diners, Visa

MILTON COMBE **Who'd Have Thought It**

FOOD

Nr Yelverton
MAP 9 B2 *Devon*
Yelverton (0822) 853313
Parking ample

Bar food 12–2 & 7–9.45

Landlords Gary Rager & Keith Yeo
Free house
Wadworth 6X; Flowers Best Bitter; Golden Hill Exmoor Ale; Eldridge Pope Royal Oak; Fosters; Heineken; cider.

The good bar food brings customers from miles around to this 16th-century pebbledash pub. Almost all the snacks are home-produced, and the list is quite extensive, from chunky sandwiches and cold platters to basket meals (super chips), steaks and specials like sweet and sour pork, chilli con carne, fresh trout, or chicken and ham pie. Apple and blackberry crumble is a nice pud.

Typical prices Jumbo sausages & chips £2 Ploughman's lunch £1.85

MINSTER LOVELL **Old Swan Hotel**

FOOD
B & B

Nr Witney
MAP 7 B2 *Oxfordshire*
Minster Lovell (0993) 75614
Parking ample

Bar food 12–2
No bar food eves & all Sun

Landlords Mr & Mrs Tim Turner
Brewery Hall's
Hall's Harvest Bitter; Ind Coope Burton Ale; Löwenbräu; cider.

This distinctive creeper-clad inn some 600 years old stands in the pretty and peaceful Cotswold village of Minster Lovell. A log fire warmly welcomes visitors making for the neat and simple flagstoned bar, where a small but imaginative selection of lunchtime snacks awaits. Besides traditional home-made soups, ploughman's and sandwiches, there's a weekly-changing menu of hot food, perhaps tasty breaded mussels, casseroled rabbit and chicken curry, as well as vegetarian dishes, all carefully

cooked and nicely presented. Garden.
Typical prices Smoked mackerel mousse £2 Old Swan country pâté £2 ⊜

ACCOMMODATION **10 bedrooms £B**
Check-in all day

Accommodation in this charming, atmospheric inn is of a high standard. Comfortable, tastefully furnished rooms all have excellent bathrooms with plenty of thoughtful extras, and all are equipped with direct-dial phones, TVs, hairdryers and trouser presses. Singles, in cottagy style, make good use of limited space. One room features a four-poster under a fine beamed ceiling. *No children under 12 overnight. No dogs.*

Credit Access, Amex, Diners, Visa

MOLESWORTH — Cross Keys

B Nr Huntingdon
MAP 6 D2 *Cambridgeshire*
Bythorn (080 14) 283
Parking ample

Landlord Frances Mary Bettsworth
Free house
Adnams Bitter; Younger's Tartan Bitter; McEwan's Export; Guinness; Carlsberg; cider.

ACCOMMODATION **10 bedrooms £D**
Check-in all day

There's a friendly feel about this unpretentious pub, and the accommodation side is doing very well. Four rooms are in the pub itself, while a further six are in a well-designed single-storey block to the rear. All rooms are centrally heated, and tea-makers are provided; most have en suite facilities. In the bar there's a local version of skittles, or you can try your hand at billiards in an adjoining room. Garden.

MONKSILVER — Notley Arms

OD Taunton
MAP 9 C1 *Somerset*
Stogumber (0984) 56217
Parking ample

Bar food 12–2 & 7–9.30, Sun 12–1.30 & 7–9

Landlords Alistair & Sarah Cade
Brewery Usher
Usher Triple Crown, Founder's Ale, Best Bitter, Country Bitter; Guinness; Carlsberg; cider.

★ A stream-bordered garden, rustic bar and pleasant family room provide an inviting setting for chef Sally Wardell's excellent food. She concentrates on fresh, top-quality produce, and the results range from a delicately spiced vegetable soup and whole wheat pittas stuffed with hot garlic lamb or beef to jacket potatoes, imaginative salads, and haymaker's lunches (cheese with granary bread and home-made chutney). Daily specials could be home-made pasta, a superb vegetable curry, or chicken breast in pastry, with steaks and local trout in the evenings. Treacle tart is the favourite sweet, but the lemon meringue pie would take some beating. Winter brings a traditional roast for Sunday lunch. ★

Typical prices Pasta with ham & mushrooms £2.25 Cidered chicken breast in a puff pastry case £3.85 Trout in almonds £4.95 Home-made ice cream £1.15 ⊜

MONKTON COMBE — Wheelwrights Arms

B & B

Nr Bath
MAP 7 A3 *Avon*
Limpley Stoke (022 122) 2287
Parking ample

Landlords Mr & Mrs R.J. Gillespie
Free house
Wadworth 6X; Whitbread Pale Ale; Butcombe Bitter; Flowers IPA; Guinness; Stella Artois; cider.

***ACCOMMODATION* 8 bedrooms £C**
Check-in all day

A lovely setting in the Midford Valley is one of the attractions here. The bar has rustic charm and there is a quaint snug. The bedrooms, in a converted barn, are comfortable and pretty, with co-ordinated fabrics and modern facilities such as shower rooms, TVs, hairdryers and direct-dial telephones. Note that every item must be paid for when ordering. Patio and garden. Accommodation closed two weeks January. *No children under 14 overnight. No dogs.*
Credit Access, Visa

MONTACUTE — King's Arms Inn

FOOD
B & B

MAP 5 A4 *Somerset*
Martock (0935) 822513
Parking ample

Bar food 12–2.30 & 7.30–10

Landlords Jean & Roger Skipper
Free house
Bass; Gibbs Mew Salisbury Best; Guinness; Carlsberg; cider.

Old-fashioned standards of service and housekeeping combine with modern-day comforts at this mellow 16th-century inn opposite the village church. The open-plan bar area is divided into three sections – an elegant lounge with chintzy sofas, the tiny Pickwick Bar and the street-facing front bar where the lunchtime buffet is a popular feature: cold meats, quiches, cheeses and pâtés to accompany imaginative salads. Alternatives on the menu might include cottage pie or plaice florentine, and there are tempting sweets like sherry trifle and pavlova. The choice of hot dishes is increased at night, or you can dine more formally in the Abbey Room restaurant.
Typical prices Chicken chasseur £3.95 Steak & kidney pie £3.95

***ACCOMMODATION* 11 bedrooms £B**
Check-in all day

Among the stylish bedrooms are an executive de luxe with its own sitting area, and a four-poster room. Most of the rooms are housed in the converted skittle alley and all rooms have teamakers, radio-alarms and drinks trays, plus carpeted modern bathrooms. Patio.
Credit Access, Visa

MORETON-IN-MARSH — Redesdale Arms Hotel

B & B

High Street
MAP 7 B1 *Gloucestershire*
Moreton-in-Marsh (0608) 50308
Parking ample

Landlords Michael C. Elvis & Patricia M. Seedhouse
Free house
Bass; Courage Best Bitter, Directors; Guinness; Carlsberg Export; Tennent's Extra; cider.

***ACCOMMODATION* 18 bedrooms £B**
Check-in all day

Charm and character are much in evidence in the public areas of this fine 18th-century coaching inn with a beamed and panelled lounge bar and cosy first-floor residents' lounge. Spacious bedrooms, including six in cottagy extensions, have attractively stylish furnishings and reflect the good housekeeping. Standard facilities include teamakers, trouser presses, hairdryers and radio alarms, with extra comforts in the three luxury suites. Patio. *No dogs.*
Credit Access, Amex, Visa

MORETONHAMPSTEAD — White Hart Hotel

B The Square
MAP 9 C2 *Devon*
Moretonhampstead (0647) 40406
Parking limited

Landlord Peter Morgan
Free house
Bass; Flowers IPA; Whitbread Trophy; Tetley Bitter; Ansells Bitter; Guinness; Skol; Carlsberg; cider.

***ACCOMMODATION* 22 bedrooms £C**
Check-in all day

A flowery courtyard, cosy beamed bar and relaxing lounge set the tone of this well-maintained Georgian posting house, run with professionalism by landlord Peter Morgan. Bedrooms, which differ in size and style, are most appealing, with quality furniture and many thoughtful extras including TVs, hairdryers and tea and coffee making facilities. All have their own smartly decorated bathrooms. *No children under ten overnight.*
Credit Access, Amex, Diners, Visa

MORVAL — Snooty Fox Hotel

B Nr Looe
MAP 9 B2 *Cornwall*
Widegates (050 34) 233
Parking ample

Landlords Tony & Lyn Hayward
Free house
Whitbread Best Bitter, Poacher; Flowers Original, Best Bitter; Guinness; Stella Artois; cider.

***ACCOMMODATION* 8 bedrooms £B**
Check-in restricted

About three miles outside of Looe, this tile-hung hotel is set in three acres of landscaped garden with waterfall and children's play park complete with a huge rustic climbing frame. There's a comfortable, roomy lounge and a large games room with pool tables and juke-box. The functional bedrooms are clean and pleasant, with woodchip walls, simple fitted units and good modern en suite bathrooms. All are equipped with colour TVs and tea-makers.
Credit Access, Visa

MOULTON — Black Bull Inn

D Nr Richmond
MAP 4 D3 *North Yorkshire*
Barton (032 577) 289
Parking ample

Bar food 12–2
No bar food eves & all Sun

Landlords Mr & Mrs G. Pagendam
Free house
Theakston Best Bitter, Old Peculier; McEwan's 80/-; Guinness; Carlsberg Hof.

★ A justly popular pub drawing the crowds from far around. The attractive bar has an open fire (with a large wooden chest to contain the logs), wooden banquettes, brasses and potted plants, while there is a variety of small dining rooms ranging from a conservatory to a Pullman coach! For snacks, there are home-made soups, avocado with prawns, mushrooms in garlic butter, barbecued spare ribs, smoked salmon pâté or sandwiches; a short selection of hot main dishes includes steaks, sole mornay and scallop and bacon brochette. Of the cold meals, pride of place must go to the mixed cheese salad, featuring prime local and English cheeses. To finish, try brandy snaps, orange liqueur pan-cakes or ice cream with raisins in Madeira. There is also a fortnightly-changing fixed price menu. Garden. ★
Typical prices Seafood pancake £3 Welsh rarebit £2.50 Mixed cheese salad £2.50 Lemon sole £7.25

Credit Access, Amex, Visa

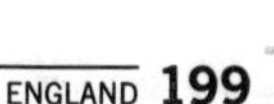

MURCOTT — Nut Tree Inn

FOOD

Nr Islip
MAP 7 B2 *Oxfordshire*
Charlton-on-Otmoor (086 733) 253
Parking ample

Bar food 12–2 & 7–9.30
No bar food Sun
Landlords Gordon & Diane Evans
Free house
Wadworth 6X, Farmers Glory; Wychwood; Guinness; Löwenbräu; Ind Coope Burton Ale; cider.

The archetypal English pub, complete with its own duckpond in the garden, not to mention ponies, donkeys and pheasants. On offer at the bar is a good choice of tasty fare, ranging from sandwiches, ploughman's and salads to a variety of Scottish steaks, breaded plaice or chicken in apricot sauce. Home-made desserts include treacle tart, meringues and lemon cheesecake.
Typical prices Steaks from £6.95 Chilli con carne £3.90

NANTWICH — Lamb Hotel

FOOD
B & B

Hospital Street
MAP 3 C4 *Cheshire*
Nantwich (0270) 625286
Parking limited

Bar food 12–2 & 6–10 (Sun from 7)
Landlord Ronald Jones
Brewery Greenall Whitley
Greenall Whitley Original Bitter, Mild; Wem Best Bitter; Guinness; Grünhalle Export Gold; cider.

In the heart of an attractive little town, this solidly built old coaching inn offers a good range of lunchtime and evening snacks in its comfortably traditional bars. Flavoursome home-made soups, pâté and sandwiches (both plain and toasted) are all popular light bites, which the hungry can supplement with appetising main dishes such as a tasty turkey and ham pie served with a simple, fresh salad, chilli con carne, deep-fried clams or favourites like cottage pie and savoury stuffed mushrooms. There's also a traditional Sunday lunch menu available.
Typical prices Cottage pie £1.75 Steak & kidney pie £2.95

ACCOMMODATION **16 bedroom £C**
Check-in all day

You can hear the nearby church clock chiming the hours from the spacious bedrooms. All rooms are furnished with sturdy freestanding pieces. Half have functional private facilities and colour TVs, the rest share two public bathrooms. *No dogs.*

Credit Access, Visa

NASSINGTON — Black Horse Inn

FOOD

Nr Peterborough
MAP 6 D1 *Northamptonshire*
Stamford (0780) 782324
Parking ample

Bar food 12–1.30 & 7–9.45
Landlord Tom Guy
Free house
Greene King IPA; Adnams Bitter; Flowers Original; Guinness; Harp; Kronenbourg; cider.

Dating back to the 17th century, this carefully maintained pub is a charming place to enjoy good interesting food. Fresh fish dishes such as braised octopus or cod and shrimp pie are listed on the blackboard, and the main menu includes devilled crab, mussel and bacon brochettes, and a choice of steaks as well as popular pasta dishes. Traditional Sunday lunch. Garden.
Typical prices Poacher's pie £5.95 Lasagne £3.65
Credit Access, Amex, Diners, Visa

NAUNTON **Black Horse**

OD
& B

Nr Cheltenham
MAP 7 A2 *Gloucestershire*
Guiting Power (045 15) 378
Parking ample

Bar food 12–2 & 6–10

Landlords Adrian & Jennie Bowen-Jones
Brewery Donnington
Donnington Best Bitter, Special Bitter Ale; Carlsberg; cider.

Well situated in a delightful Cotswold village, this pleasant hostelry has two most amicable hosts in Adrian and Jennie Bowen-Jones. Bar food is also a big draw – the menu features tried and trusted favourites like pâté, wholesome soups, lasagne, or the ever-popular ploughman's. More interesting dishes include deep-fried duck, while the blackboard lists the day's specials, perhaps carbonnade of beef, smoked trout fillets, pork in cider or marinated herring fillets. Finish with a really tasty apple flan, cheesecake or chocolate roulade. Eat in either the spacious and airy flagstoned public bar or the more intimate lounge bar.
Typical prices Carbonnade of beef £3.50 Double lamb chop in port & orange sauce £4

***ACCOMMODATION* 3 bedrooms £D**
Check-in restricted

The cosy, homely bedrooms provide comfortable overnight accommodation. Practically furnished and unfussily decorated, each has its own washbasin and tea-maker, and they all share one functional bathroom. A good breakfast sends you on your way. Patio. *No children under 14. No dogs.*

NEEDHAM MARKET **Limes Hotel**

OD
& B

High Street
MAP 6 E2 *Suffolk*
Needham Market (0449) 720305
Parking ample

Bar food 12–2 & 6.30–10

Landlords Terry & Stephanie Watts
Free house
Adnams Bitter; Webster Yorkshire Bitter; Guinness; Holsten; Carlsberg Pilsner; Fosters; cider.

Even older than its handsome Georgian facade suggests, this sturdy inn standing on the high street of an unspoilt county town has origins going back some 500 years. There's a neat cocktail bar as well as the attractive Bugs Bar with its impressive timbers, Tudor brickwork and open fires, which provides a cosy setting for a tempting lunchtime buffet of cold meats – including good home-cooked ham carved from the bone – pies and salads, with some hot dishes. In the evening there are burgers, savoury pancakes, steak and mushroom pie, and other well-prepared dishes. Traditional Sunday lunch menu. A handsome panelled oak room is ideal for private functions.
Typical prices Steak & mushroom pie £2.60 Rissoles in bacon £2.50

***ACCOMMODATION* 11 bedrooms £B**
Check-in all day

Double glazing on the front bedrooms makes for a quiet overnight stay. The 11 nicely furnished bedrooms – some with sloping and beamed ceilings – are spacious and comfortable, with TVs, radio-alarms, phones and tea-makers. All have compact en suite bathrooms.

Credit Access, Amex, Diners, Visa

NEEDINGWORTH — Pike & Eel

B & B Overcote Ferry, Nr St Ives
MAP 6 D2 *Cambridgeshire*
St Ives (0480) 63336
Parking ample

Landlords John & Nicola Stafferton
Free house
Bass; Adnams Bitter; Greene King IPA, Abbot Ale; Worthington Best Bitter; Stones Bitter; Carling Black Label; Kronenbourg; cider.

ACCOMMODATION **10 bedrooms £C**
Check-in all day

The location on the banks of the river Ouse makes the garden of this much extended 17th-century inn a popular spot for summer drinking. Indoors there's a pleasant spacious bar divided into several areas, two cosy lounges in the oldest part of the inn, and a residents' lounge upstairs. The best bedrooms are those with en suite bathrooms, but all are neat and decorated in traditional style. Accommodation closed three days Christmas. *No dogs.*
Credit Access, Amex, Diners, Visa

NETLEY — Prince Consort

FOOD Victoria Road, Nr Southampton
MAP 5 C4 *Hampshire*
Southampton (0703) 452676
Parking ample

Bar food 12–2 & 6–10.30
Landlord Mr K. Lockstone
Brewery Whitbread
Whitbread Best Bitter, Samuel Whitbread Strong; Flowers Original; Guinness; Stella Artois; cider.

Excellent fresh seafood – salmon, cockles, mussels, crab – tops the menu at this busy, turn-of-the-century pub. There are also grills, home-made pies, tasty quiches and lighter bites. Vegetarians are well catered for, and so are children (who might choose a thunderburger washed down by a Terror Hawks milkshake). Traditional Sunday lunch menu also available. Patio.
Typical prices Pork teriaki & rice £2.50 Seafood & lobster thermidor £2.95
Credit Access, Amex, Visa

NETTLECOMBE — Marquis of Lorne

B & B Bridport
MAP 5 A4 *Dorset*
Powerstock (030 885) 236
Parking ample

Landlords Bob & Philippa Bone
Brewery Palmer
Palmer IPA, BB; Guinness; Eldridge Pope Faust Pilsner.

ACCOMMODATION **8 bedrooms £D**
Check-in all day

Set amidst rolling hills, this idyllic country pub is nearly 500 years old. Stop for a pint in the old-world atmosphere of the bar (lounge or public), why not stay a couple of days. Comfortable bedrooms, some with their own bathrooms, are brightly decorated with modern furnishings and have teamakers. Two rooms have extra beds for families with children. The cosy TV lounge with open fireplace is an added attraction, and the large garden includes a children's play area. *No dogs.*

NEWARK — Robin Hood Hotel

B & B Lombard Street
MAP 4 E4 *Nottinghamshire*
Newark (0636) 703858
Parking ample

Landlord Mr Gatenby
Free house
John Smith's Yorkshire Bitter; Robinson Old Tom; Guinness; Stella Artois; Kronenbourg; John Smith's Lager; cider.

ACCOMMODATION **21 bedrooms £A**
Check-in all day

A converted coaching inn with a town centre location which makes it popular with conferences and business visitors. The convivial bar, with oak beams and plush burgundy seating, has a good atmosphere, while upstairs the bedrooms have all been attractively refurbished using pretty fabrics and wallcoverings and freestanding lightwood units. All have TVs, telephones and teamakers, and offer private facilities upgraded to a similar standard. *No dogs.*
Credit Access, Amex, Diners, Visa

NEWENDEN **White Hart**

A MAP 6 E3 *Kent*
Northiam (079 74) 2166
Parking ample

Landlord Mr A.E. Faulkner
Brewery Courage
Courage Best Bitter, Directors, John Courage; Guinness; Hofmeister; Kronenbourg; cider.

The beer garden runs down to a little river at this charming, 16th-century clapperboard pub, making it a popular spot for summer drinks. On cooler days, the mellow beamed bar with its fine old inglenook and burnished brassware has a warm, inviting feel. Note the bundles of hop stalks surrounding a second fireplace, in traditional Kentish style. Mr Faulkner is the most amiable of hosts.
Credit Access

NEWTON **Queens Head**

D Nr Cambridge
MAP 7 D1 *Cambridgeshire*
Cambridge (0223) 870436
Parking ample

Bar food 11.30–2.30 & 6–10.30, Sun 12–2 & 7–10

Landlord David Short
Free house
Adnams Bitter, Old (winter only); Palmer Tally Ho (summer only); Guinness; cider.

★ Nostalgia rules in this charming, welcoming pub which revels in its truly old-fashioned atmosphere. There are no pretensions: the public bar has its darts and bar skittles while the comfortable saloon bar, with its bare brick walls and large open fireplace, has no aspirations to trendiness. It's just friendly, honest 'pubbiness' throughout. Bar snacks are straightforward too – soup and sandwiches lunchtimes and soup, cold buffet and cheeseboard evenings – but the standard is first class. Served in a mug with a hunk of bread, the chunky soup smells delicious and tastes even better. Sandwiches are made to order and rely on top quality components – good, fresh wholemeal bread, excellent roast beef with a hint of horseradish, freshly carved ham, smoked salmon – and you'll get no fussy garnishings. Everything is so simple yet so good. Terrace. ★
Typical prices Plate of smoked salmon £2 Wholemeal pâté sandwich £1 Soup of the day 90p Cheddar ploughman's £1.65

NEWTON **Red Lion Inn**

A Nr Sleaford
MAP 6 D1 *Lincolnshire*
Folkingham (052 97) 256
Parking ample

Landlords Bill & Gaenor Power
Free house
Bateman XB; Webster Yorkshire Bitter; Guinness; Carlsberg; Holsten; cider.

Visitors who seek out this lovely little old pub in a remote rural setting off the A52 can be sure of a warm welcome from long-standing owners Bill and Gaenor Power. The main bar is full of atmosphere with its rough brick walls, antiques, stuffed animals and country artefacts. Equally appealing is the smaller, second bar where Bill displays his collection of nautical objects, and there's an attractive garden for summer drinks.

NEWTON — Saracen's Head

B & B

Nr Sudbury
MAP 6 E2 *Suffolk*
Sudbury (0787) 79036
Parking ample

Landlords Mr & Mrs J. Eglin
Brewery Tollemache & Cobbold
Tolly Cobbold 4X, Original, Best Bitter; Guinness; Hansa, Hansa Export; cider.

***ACCOMMODATION* 2 bedrooms £D**
Check-in all day

A warm welcome is extended to guests at this 16th-century coaching inn. There is a beamed saloon bar with oak tables and settles, a public bar and, for summer drinking, a garden with mature fruit trees and small pond. Two homely bedrooms are simply furnished and have washbasins, tea/coffee-makers and black and white TVs. They share a neat bathroom. Accommodation closed 25 and 31 December. *No dogs.*
Credit Access, Visa

NEWTON-IN-BOWLAND — Parkers Arms Hotel

FOOD
B & B

Nr Clitheroe
MAP 3 C3 *Lancashire*
Slaidburn (020 06) 236
Parking ample

Bar food 12–2 & 7–10.30, Sun 12–10.30

Landlord Henry Rhodes
Brewery Whitbread
Whitbread Trophy, Best Mild, Best Bitter; Guinness; Heineken; cider.
No real ale.

Once a deer-keeper's house, this welcoming inn enjoys a village setting in the heart of the lovely Hodder Valley. Henry Rhodes is a splendid host and the comfortably mellow lounge bar – warmed by a roaring fire in winter – is an excellent spot for tucking into some honest, straightforward fare. Delicious fresh local salmon served with a crisp salad is a real treat in season, and other choices include flavour-packed soups, hearty home-made steak and kidney pie, sandwiches, some decent English cheeses (Stilton and a flavoursome Cheddar are always available) and a few simple sweets.
Typical prices Steak & kidney pie £2.85 Fresh salmon £4.95

***ACCOMMODATION* 3 bedrooms £D**
Check-in restricted

The three fully carpeted bedrooms provide adequate overnight comforts and are neatly kept. All have tea-makers and share a well-equipped bathroom. Guests can watch TV in the cosy residents' lounge, and there's a decent cooked breakfast in the morning. Garden. *No dogs.*

NORTH BOVEY — Ring of Bells

FOOD
B & B

Moretonhampstead, Newton Abbot
MAP 9 B2 *Devon*
Moretonhampstead (0647) 40375
Parking limited

Bar food 12–2.30 (Sun till 2) & 7–9.30
Landlords Mr & Mrs Batcock
Free house
Wadworth 6X; Bass; Hall & Woodhouse Tanglefoot; Eldridge Pope Royal Oak; Golden Hill Exmoor Ale; Guinness; Heineken; cider.

The Batcocks are justly proud of their delightful old thatched pub in one of Devon's prettiest villages. The beamed bars with their rough stone walls and sturdy settles provide a splendidly atmospheric setting for a popular summer cold table offering rare roast beef, ham off the bone and tasty meat pies. Winter brings warming fare such as soups, casseroles and moussaka. Afters include sherry trifle and Bakewell tart.
Typical prices Hot pot £2.85 Meringues with cream £1 **LVs**

***ACCOMMODATION* 5 bedrooms £C**
Check-in all day

A separate paved entrance of obvious antiquity leads to steep stairs up to the spacious, simply furnished bedrooms which all have spotless en suite bathrooms. Exposed beams and impressively thick walls pierced by tiny windows overlooking the moors give the rooms plenty of character; two of them are furnished with four-posters. Gardens back and front cater for summer drinking, and there is also a swimming pool. Accommodation closed January.

Our inspectors never book in the name of Egon Ronay's Guides; they disclose their identity only after paying their bills.

NORTH CERNEY — Bathurst Arms

OOD
& B

Nr Gloucester
MAP 7 A2 *Gloucestershire*
North Cerney (028 583) 281
Parking ample

Bar food 11–2.30 & 6.30–9.30, Sun 12–2 & 7–9.30
Landlords Freddie & Caroline Seward
Free house
Gibbs Mew Bishop's Tipple; Hook Norton; Wadworth 6X; Archers Best Bitter; Flowers Original; Guinness; cider.

Freddie and Caroline Seward are the owners of this 17th-century pink-washed former farmhouse which has three characterful bars and a most attractive riverside garden. Bar food includes quiche, ploughman's and chicken in a basket, along with Arbroath smokies, lasagne and filled hot croissants. It's worth going for one of the daily-changing blackboard specials, at lunchtime with an oriental slant (satay, nasi goreng), in the evening with more of a traditional English ring (beef Wellington, casseroles, juicy lamb cutlets with mint butter). Classic puds to follow, and in summer there's a cold table. Traditional roast for Sunday lunch. An à la carte menu is available in the restaurant.
Typical prices Chicken & cider pie £3.75 Lasagne verde £2.95

***ACCOMMODATION* 7 bedrooms £C**
Check-in restricted

Upstairs, seven delightful bedrooms provide excellent overnight accommodation. Attractive cane furniture complements the pastel shades, prints and duvets. The bathrooms, four en suite, are modern and kept immaculate.

Credit Visa

NORTH DALTON — Star Inn

OOD

Nr Driffield
MAP 4 E3 *Humberside*
Middleton-on-the-Wolds (037 781) 688
Parking ample

Bar food 12–2 & 7–10 (Sun till 9.30)
Landlords Marie & Nick Cragg
Free house
Tetley Bitter; John Smith's Yorkshire Bitter, Midlands Mild, Tawny Light; Carlsberg; Hofmeister; cider.

A pondside village pub deservedly popular for its good bar food and friendly atmosphere. Deliciously creamy fish pie, vegetarian curry and beef olives are supplemented by good steaks, as well as an exciting daily menu. Sweets are irresistible – try the apple and pear sponge. Sunday roast is served in the restaurant. Future plans include accommodation. Patio and garden.
Typical prices Steak & mushroom pie £3.25 Vegetarian lasagne £2.95
Credit Access, Visa

NORTH PETHERTON — Walnut Tree Inn

B & B

Fore Street, Nr Bridgwater
MAP 9 C1 *Somerset*
North Petherton (0278) 662255
Parking ample

Closed *1 wk Xmas*

Landlords Mr & Mrs Goulden
Free house
Wadworth 6X, Northgate; John Smith's; Guinness; Heineken; Tuborg Gold.

ACCOMMODATION **20 bedrooms £C**
Check-in all day

Gleaming brasses and a gas log fire give a pleasing traditional look to the relaxing, well-appointed bars of this extended coaching inn just off junction 24 of the M5. Check in at the smart reception area for excellent accommodation: standard rooms have good quality wood furniture and tea and coffee making facilities, and ten more spacious executive rooms are individually decorated in striking colour schemes. *No dogs.*
Credit Access, Amex, Diners, Visa

NORTH WOOTTON — Crossways Inn

FOOD
B & B

Nr Shepton Mallet
MAP 9 D1 *Somerset*
Pilton (074 989) 237
Parking ample

Bar food 12–2.30 & 6.45–10.45, Sun 12–2 & 7–10.15

Landlords John & Cynthia Kirkham
Free house
Wadworth 6X; Bass; Usher Triple Crown; Courage Best Bitter; Guinness; Löwenbräu; cider. *No real ale.*

The peaceful Somerset countryside is the setting for this agreeable inn, the pubby nature of which has not been spoilt by extensions over the years. John and Cynthia Kirkham are the most welcoming hosts you could wish for and the food, although mainly standard pub fare, is good quality and pleasingly cooked. Choose from freshly-cut sandwiches or salads of turkey, beef and ham or a hot dish such as a filled jacket potato, cottage pie or chicken curry. A vegetarian dish is always available and simple sweets include cheesecake, apple pie, gâteau and fresh cream trifle. Traditional roast on Sundays.
Typical prices Steak & kidney pie £3 Vegetarian lasagne £2.50

ACCOMMODATION **7 bedrooms £D**
Check-in all day

The comfortable bedrooms are of a decent size, centrally heated and fully carpeted. Two have compact shower rooms, while the remaining five share a well-kept public bathroom. All have TVs. There is a cosy and homely lounge for residents. Patio. *No dogs.*

Credit Access, Visa

NORTHIAM — Six Bells

FOOD

MAP 6 E3 *East Sussex*
Northiam (079 74) 2570
Parking ample

Bar food 12–2 & 7–10
No bar food Sun eves and all Mons in winter

Landlords Mr W.S. Tipples & Miss J.A. Lilley
Free house
Fremlins Bitter; Adnams Bitter; Flowers Original; King & Barnes Festive; Stella Artois; cider.

A welcoming old pub in the centre of a pretty village. The bars are full of character and provide a focal point for village social life. The imaginative bar food is well-prepared; soups, salads and steaks, plus daily specials, with pasta and local fresh fish making important contributions. Nice sweets, too. Traditional roast on Sundays. Garden.
Typical prices Sole in white wine £3.95 Spinach crêpe £2.75
Credit Access, Amex, Diners, Visa

NOTTINGHAM — Ye Olde Trip to Jerusalem Inn

A

Brewhouse Yard, Castle Road
MAP 5 C1 *Nottinghamshire*
Nottingham (0602) 473171
Parking difficult

Landlords Janet & Ernie Marshall
Free house
■ Marston Pedigree, Border Mild; Samuel Smith's Old Brewery Bitter; Ruddles Best Bitter; Wards Sheffield Best Bitter; Carling Black Label; cider.

A public house since 1189 (and a brewhouse for Nottingham Castle even before that) this celebrated inn is said to have been frequented by Crusaders on their way to the holy wars. Its 16th-century facade leads into an extraordinary bar, a maze of cellars, rooms and passages that have been adapted from natural caverns or scooped out of the porous rock on which the castle stands. A very characterful spot in which to enjoy a pint of well-kept ale.

NUNNEY — George Inn

OOD
& B

11 Church Street, Nr Frome
MAP 9 D1 *Somerset*
Nunney (037 384) 458
Parking ample

Bar food 12–2 & 7–9.45

Landlord John Lewis
Free house
■ Butcombe Bitter; Oakhill Farmer's Ale; Bass; Guinness; Holsten; Carling Black Label; cider.

Rustic character abounds in the bars of this white-painted, 14th-century inn, which stands in a picturesque village opposite the ruins of a Norman castle. Bar snacks are based on good fresh ingredients and cover a span from soup, pâté and sandwiches to seafood pancakes and the always popular steak and kidney pie. Daily specials such as moules marinière and sautéed kidneys introduce further choice, and there are some nice puds like apple pie or chocolate brandy mousse. Traditional Sunday lunch menu.
Typical prices Steak & kidney pie £2.95 Lasagne £2.75

ACCOMMODATION **13 bedrooms £C**
Check-in all day

Overnight accommodation ranges from a fine four-poster room with a commodious bathroom through charming rooms under the eaves to smartly modernised ones featuring much natural wood (these are in a converted skittles alley). Almost all rooms have bath or shower en suite. There's a pleasant residents' lounge, and a stone-walled dining room where a decent breakfast may be had. Garden. Children welcome overnight.

Credit Access, Amex, Diners, Visa

OAKWOODHILL — Punchbowl Inn

OOD

Nr Ockley
MAP 6 D3 *Surrey*
Oakwoodhill (030 679) 249
Parking ample

Bar food 12–2 & 7–10

Landlords Rob & Shirley Chambers
Free house
■ King & Barnes Sussex Bitter; Young Special; Hall & Woodhouse Badger Best, Tanglefoot; Guinness; Carlsberg; cider.

Shirley Chambers' super cooking is a great attraction at this ancient, tile-hung pub. Sweet and sour crispy duck, lasagne, chicken curry and flavoursome soup are typical treats, while summer brings a weekday lunchtime cold buffet, and barbecues at both sessions. There's a traditional Sunday lunch, and it's soup and sandwiches only on Sunday and Monday evenings. Garden.
Typical prices Soup £1 Steak & kidney pie £3.50
Credit Diners, Visa

OCKLEY — King's Arms

FOOD
B & B

Stane Street
MAP 6 D3 *Surrey*
Dorking (0306) 711224
Parking ample
Bar food 12–2 & 7–10 (Sun till 9.30)
Landlords Mary Doyle & family
Free house
King & Barnes Sussex Bitter; Hall & Woodhouse Badger Best; Ruddles Rutland Bitter; Guinness; Fosters; Carlsberg; cider.

Dating back to the 17th century, this friendly tile-hung roadside pub is kept in spick-and-span order by Mary Doyle and her two daughters. They offer the warmest of welcomes in the cosy beamed bar, where highly polished brass and copper pieces gleam above the inglenook, and fresh flower arrangements add a delightfully homely touch. Here you can enjoy wholesome snacks that range from flavoursome soups, sandwiches, cold meat salads and pâté to hearty casseroles and curries, with simple sweets like fruit pie to finish. Traditional Sunday lunch menu available.

Typical prices Prawn curry £3.85 Ploughman's £1.45

ACCOMMODATION **6 bedrooms £C**
Check-in all day

The six neat bedrooms (including three in a recent extension with their own private facilities) are furnished in traditional style and all have radio-alarms plus tea-making facilities. Also in the extension is a new multi-purpose room that acts as bar extension, lounge and children's room, as required. Garden.

Credit Access, Amex, Visa **LVs**

ODIHAM — George Hotel

FOOD
B & B

High Street
MAP 7 C3 *Hampshire*
Odiham (025 671) 2081
Parking ample
Bar food 10.30–2.30 & 5.30–11, Sun 12–2 & 7–10.30
Landlords Peter & Moira Kelsey
Brewery Courage
Courage Best Bitter, Directors; John Smith's Bitter; Guinness; Hofmeister; Kronenbourg. *No real ale.*

Sympathetic renovation has both preserved and enhanced the appeal of this picture-postcard pub in the heart of a pretty village. The original building dates back to the late 14th century, while the annexe – once used as the local assizes court, now an attractive restaurant – is 16th century. In the comfortable, traditional bars the carefully prepared selection of snacks inludes flavoursome home-made pâté, sandwiches filled with super ham or prawn and asparagus, chicken curry and satisfying meat pies. Simple puddings. Traditional Sunday lunch also available.

Typical prices Beefsteak & Guinness pie £2.50 Lasagne £1.95

ACCOMMODATION **8 bedrooms £C**
Check-in all day

Mind your head upstairs – some of the solidly furnished bedrooms feature low original beams. Colour TVs, direct-dial telephones and tea-makers add a 20th-century touch, while effective central heating and double glazing make for a snug stay. All rooms have private facilities. There's a splendid residents' lounge featuring exposed stonework, and a garden.

Credit Access, Diners, Visa

OFFCHURCH
Stag's Head

FOOD Nr Leamington Spa
MAP 5 C2 *Warwickshire*
Leamington (0926) 25801
Parking ample

Bar food 11.30–2.30 & 7–10, Sun 12–2 & 7–10

Landlords Mr & Mrs Owen
Brewery Ansells
Tetley Bitter; Ansells Bitter, Mild; Guinness; Skol; Löwenbräu; cider.

In the heart of the village, this attractive black and white inn with its low-beamed bars makes a cheerful setting for the landlord's robust, reliable cooking. Try crispy mushrooms or flavoursome taramasalata and houmus to start, followed perhaps by herby beef casserole, vegetarian moussaka or a speciality steak. Ploughman's and salads, too. Garden.
Typical prices Fillet kebab £4.95 Beef in red wine £3.95

OLD BASING
Bolton Arms

FOOD The Street
MAP 7 B3 *Hampshire*
Basingstoke (0256) 22085
Parking ample

Bar food 12–2 & 7.30–9.30

Landlord Peter Kent
Brewery Courage
Courage Best, Directors, John Courage; Guinness; Hofmeister; Kronenbourg; cider

A pleasant and popular 16th-century timbered inn with beams in abundance and a cosy rustic feel. The menu offers a choice of a dozen or so dishes such as chicken pancakes, steak in pitta bread or an excellent fisherman's hot pot. Also sandwiches and ploughman's, which are the only things available on Tuesday evening and all day Sunday. No starters or sweets. Garden.
Typical prices Seafood pancakes £2.95 Pitta bread with fillet steak & mixed salad £2.95

OLD DALBY
Crown Inn

FOOD Nr Melton Mowbray
MAP 5 C1 *Leicestershire*
Melton Mowbray (0664) 823134
Parking ample

Bar food 12–1.45 & 6.30–9.45
No bar food Sun & Mon eves in winter 

Landlords Salvatore Inguanta & Lynne Bryan
Free house
Adnams Bitter; Marston Pedigree; Ruddles County, Rutland Bitter; Hook Norton BB; Theakston XB, Old Peculier; Wadsworth 6X.

★ It's best to check directions to this charming and characterful 200-year-old, village-centre inn, which was formerly a farmhouse. Cosy public rooms dotted with antique furniture, and a large garden provide equally pleasant settings for some delicious, expertly prepared food. The tempting menu offers plenty of choice, from a plate of peeled prawns on a nest of coleslaw in a Madras sauce to Yorkshire sausage with onion sauce. Other faultlessly prepared options are tasty stuffed mushrooms, baked avocado with tuna and prawns, black pudding, a liver and sausage kebab, and chicken in a spicy curry sauce. Lighter bites include home-made soup, filled rolls and a bookmaker's sandwich of sirloin steak. One tip from any bookmaker: the rich rum truffle cake should definitely not be missed. ★
Typical prices: Welsh rarebit £1.75 Seafood pasta salad £3.95 Carbonnade of beef £3.95 Game in a red wine sauce and pastry case £4.95

OLDBURY-ON-SEVERN — **Anchor Inn**

FOOD

Church Road
MAP 5 A3 *Avon*
Thornbury (0454) 413331
Parking ample

Bar food 11.30–2.30 & 6.30–9.30

Landlord Michael J. Dowdeswell
Free house
Marston Pedigree; Theakston Best Bitter, Old Peculier; Butcombe Bitter; Guinness; Harlech Lager; cider.

A characterful 16th-century pub which once served ale to passing trading barges. Nowadays its fine food draws the crowds; among the cold items is locally-caught salmon, while hot dishes include appetising turbot and pasta in a bubbling cream and tarragon sauce, a popular beef curry and steak and kidney pie. Delicious sweets and excellent cheeses. Garden.

Typical prices Salmon & prawn vol-au-vent £2.65 Shoo-fly pie 95p

OLLERTON — **Dun Cow**

FOOD

Chelford Road, Nr Knutsford
MAP 3 C4 *Cheshire*
Knutsford (0565) 3093
Parking ample

Bar food 12–2 (Sun till 1.45) & 6–9.30
No bar food Tues & Sun eves in winter

Landlord Mr G. Tilling
Brewery Greenall Whitley
Greenall Whitley Local; Watney Export Gold; Guinness; Grünhalle; cider.

An unassuming little pub, its pebble-dash exterior hiding a 300-year history that includes long service as an assize court. A pleasant, homely atmosphere is fostered by the kindly landlord, and tasty, home-cooked snacks are served on attractive floral china. Cauliflower soup, Cornish pasty, meatloaf and damson crumble show the range. Traditional Sunday lunch available in the restaurant. Terrace.

Typical prices Steak & kidney pie £1.80 Damson crumble 80p

OMBERSLEY — **Kings Arms**

FOOD

Nr Worcester
MAP 7 A1 *Hereford & Worcester*
Worcester (0905) 620142
Parking ample

Bar food 12.15–2.15 & 6–9.30
No bar food Sun

Landlords Judy & Chris Blundell
Brewery Mitchells & Butlers
Bass; Mitchells & Butlers Brew XI, Mild, Springfield Bitter; Guinness; Carling Black Label; cider.

Built around 1411, there's a marvellous atmosphere at this crooked, black and white inn, whose cosy beamed bars are filled with bric-a-brac. All the snacks are home-made, generously served and well presented: try turkey and leek pie, smokies in a creamy fish sauce, chilli beef chowder, the super cold meat salads and tempting sweets. Garden.

Typical prices Seafood crumble £3.65 Wholewheat macaroni cheese £3.45

ONECOTE — **Jervis Arms**

FOOD

Nr Leek
MAP 5 B1 *Staffordshire*
Onecote (053 88) 206
Parking ample

Bar food 12–2 & 7–10

Landlords Peter & Julie Elizabeth Wilkinson
Free house
Theakston Best Bitter, Old Peculier; Bass; Marston Pedigree; McEwan's 70/–; Ruddles County; cider.

Stroll over a picturesque wooden bridge spanning the river and through the pretty garden to reach the pub from the car park. Inside, the atmosphere is cosy and friendly. Simple home cooking, with freshly made specials, results in some satisfying dishes such as roasts of beef, chicken and ham, plus a popular vegetarian menu and roast on Sundays. Children have their own room and menu. Garden.

Typical prices Shepherd's pie £1.30 Nut roast £3.15

ORFORD — King's Head Inn

B Front Street, Nr Woodbridge
MAP 6 F2 *Suffolk*
Orford (0394) 450271
Parking ample

Landlords Phyllis & Alistair Shaw
Brewery Adnams
Adnams Bitter; Skol; cider.

***ACCOMMODATION* 5 bedrooms £D**
Check-in restricted

Nowadays visitors far outnumber any smugglers at the friendly Shaw family's characterful 13th-century village pub. A handsome fireplace (with a cheery fire in winter) provides the focal point of the popular beamed bar, which is decorated with old prints and well-polished brassware. The homely bedrooms nestling under the eaves are equally delightful. Simply furnished and spotless, they share two well-kept bathrooms. Patio. Accommodation closed January.
Credit Diners

OSWALDKIRK — Malt Shovel Inn

D
B Nr Helmsley
MAP 4 E3 *North Yorkshire*
Ampleforth (043 93) 461
Parking ample

Bar food 11.30–2 (Sun 12–1.30) & 7–9.30 (Fri & Sat till 10)
No bar food Mon eves (except Bank Hols)

Landlords Ian & Carol Pickering
Brewery Samuel Smith
Samuel Smith's Old Brewery Bitter, Museum Ale; cider.

A most unusual pub, converted from a 17th-century manor house, oozing character and atmosphere. The lounge bar is subtly lit and decked out with paintings and plenty of greenery, with an open fire for the winter months. The beamed public bar, though simpler, is just as welcoming. The bar menu is full of interesting snacks, such as black pudding with Dijon mustard, spinach and cheese roulade, and mushrooms and prawns in garlic butter, as well as a selection of tasty open sandwiches on granary bread. For larger appetites, there's the popular 'Shovel Bun' (a cottage loaf filled with curried chicken) chicken suprême in an orange sauce, or lamb chops with mint butter. Tasty sweets might include chocolate and coffee roulade.
Typical prices Lamb's liver in red wine £4.10 Ham & leek pancake £3.15

***ACCOMMODATION* 3 bedrooms £D**
Check-in restricted

The three bedrooms, all sharing a well-kept bathroom, are simple yet homely and comfortable, with lovely views over surrounding countryside. Patio and garden. *No dogs.*

OVINGTON — Bush Inn

A Nr Alresford
MAP 5 C3 *Hampshire*
Alresford (096 273) 2764
Parking ample

Landlords Mr & Mrs G. M. Draper
Free house
Wadworth 6X; Strong Country Bitter; Flowers Original; Samuel Whitbread Strong Ale; Guinness; Stella Artois; cider.

A delightful rose-covered pub in a picturesque setting by the river Itchen, favourite haunt of trout fishermen. Tucked away down a quiet country lane off the A31, if offers the visitor a relaxing retreat from the bustle of the modern world. The bars have low ceilings, copper and brassware, a large log fire, subtle lighting and plenty of rustic charm. Charming landlord and staff. Children welcome in the bar lunchtime only. Garden.
Credit Access, Amex, Visa

OXFORD — Perch

FOOD

Binsey
TOWN PLAN *Oxfordshire*
Oxford (0865) 240386
Parking ample

Bar food 12–2 (Sun till 1.45) & 6.30–9
No bar food Sun & Mon eves in winter
Landlords Vaughan & Sue Jagger
Brewery Hall's
Hall's Harvest; Burton Ale; Arkell BBB; Guinness; Skol; Löwenbräu; cider.

Found down a turning off the A420, this charming old thatched pub is linked by a path to the river Thames. In the beamed and flagstoned bars you can tuck into appetising blackboard dishes like beef curry, vegetarian harvest pie, Cumberland sausages in French bread and creamy soups. There's a cold buffet at both sessions, and jacket potatoes lunchtimes only. Garden.
Typical prices Stuffed trout £3.25 Somerset pork £2.95

PAGLESHAM — Plough & Sail

FOOD

East End, Nr Rochford
MAP 6 E3 *Essex*
Canewdon (037 06) 242
Parking ample

Bar food 12–2 & 7–9
Landlord Kenneth Oliver
Brewery Watneys
Combes Bitter; John Smith's Yorkshire Bitter; Ben Truman Bitter; Watney PA; Fosters; Carlsberg; cider.

Check directions when leaving the B1013 for this delightful old timbered pub near the river Roach. Splendid local oysters are the undisputed stars of the menu, along with other seasonal treats like mussels and poached salmon. Appetising alternatives include sandwiches, salads and hot dishes such as liver and bacon. Strawberry pavlova is a favourite summer sweet. Garden.
Typical prices Scampi £3.80 Meat pie £3.95
Credit Access, Visa

PELYNT — Jubilee Inn

B & B

Nr Looe
MAP 9 B3 *Cornwall*
Lanreath (0503) 20312
Parking ample

Landlord Mr F.E. Williams
Free house
Flowers Original; Whitbread Best Bitter, Poacher; Guinness; Stella Artois; Heineken; cider.

ACCOMMODATION **10 bedrooms £D**
Check-in all day

A pretty, pink-washed pebbledash pub whose friendly appearance is more than matched by the welcome inside. Old, carved settles, a handsome stone fireplace and a collection of Victorian china in the lounge bar all add to the warm atmosphere. Bedrooms, most of them traditionally furnished, are of a good size with TVs and radios. Six have impeccably kept, en suite bathrooms. Other facilities include a residents' lounge, children's play area and garden.
Credit Access, Visa

PEMBRIDGE — New Inn

FOOD
B & B

Market Square
MAP 5 A2 *Hereford & Worcester*
Pembridge (054 47) 427
Parking ample

Bar food 12–2 & 6.30–9.45
Landlord Jane Melvin
Brewery Whitbread
Flowers Original, IPA, PA; Guinness; Stella Artois; cider.

Built in 1311, this black and white inn has been a regular stop for travellers down the centuries. It's a good place to choose for a snack in traditional surroundings, and Jane Melvin's menu changes with the seasons. She manages to offer something to suit everyone, from garlic mushrooms and variants on ploughman's to seafood vol-au-vent, chicken pancakes, crunchy aubergine bake and succulent pork fillet in a deliciously creamy sauce flavoured with apples, pears and cider; plus, a traditional roast on Sunday. Treacle tart and cider-baked bananas are tasty sweets. The bars are agreeably rustic, and a little cobbled terrace overlooks the market place.

Typical prices Seafood pancakes £2.95 Pitta bread with lamb £2

***ACCOMMODATION* 7 bedrooms £D**
Check-in all day

Modest but comfortable bedrooms (one with TV) have plenty of character, with traditional furnishings, good old-fashioned beds and a notable lack of right angles. They share an adequate bathroom and separate shower.

PENDOGGETT — Cornish Arms

FOOD
B & B

St Kew, Bodmin
MAP 9 B2 *Cornwall*
Bodmin (0208) 880263
Parking ample

Bar food 12.30–2 & 7–10

Landlords Nigel Pickstone & Margaret & Alan Wainwright
Free house
Bass; Pendoggett Special; Guinness; Carlsberg Hof; cider.

This delightful, well-run old inn has an almost rustic appeal: its shiny slate-floored bars, with exposed beams and gleaming brass, are full of atmosphere. The chintzy public bar is justly popular, and there's also a large residents' lounge with TV. The main lunchtime attraction is a magnificent buffet – cold meats, crab, prawns, cheeses, salads – backed up by excellent home-made pies like steak and kidney or salmon. To follow, try the lovely locally made ice cream. On Sunday there's a traditional roast. Evening choice is limited to soup, sandwiches, salads, grills and puddings.

Typical prices Liver, bacon & fried onions £2.75 Smoked mackerel salad £2.50

***ACCOMMODATION* 7 bedrooms £C**
Check-in all day

Bedrooms are wonderfully warm and cosy, with good, solid, old-fashioned furniture in white Regency style. En suite bathrooms are neat and functional and the public bathroom is spotless. Willing service by cheerful staff. Garden. *No children under 14 overnight. No dogs.*

Credit Access, Amex, Diners, Visa

PENSAX — Bell Inn

FOOD

Nr Abberley
MAP 5 A2 *Hereford & Worcester*
Great Witley (029 921) 677
Parking ample

Bar food 12–2 & 7–10

Landlords John & Christine Stroulger
Free house
Hook Norton Best Bitter, Old Hookey; Timothy Taylor Landlord; Bass; Tennent's Pilsner, Extra; cider.

Inside this attractive pub you will find a cosy, wooden-floored bar where you can sample highly enjoyable and filling pub fare. Starters include garlic mushrooms, grilled sardines and home-made pâté; main dishes might be grilled trout, kebabs, chicken in wine sauce or chilli con carne, served in lavish portions with excellent fresh vegetables. Finish with blackcurrant meringue. Garden.

Typical prices Lasagne £3.25 Beef in Guinness £4.25

PENSHURST — NEW ENTRY — Spotted Dog

FOOD

Smarts Hill
MAP 6 E3 *Kent*
Penshurst (0892) 870253
Parking ample

Bar food 12–2 & 7–10

Landlord Ian Buchanan
Brewery Whitbread
Fremlins Bitter; Pompey Royal; Wethered Bitter; Flowers Original; Whitbread Best Mild; Stella Artois; cider.

Stunning views across the Weald of Kent make the sloping terrace of this ancient clapboard pub a popular summer venue. The beamed bar is an inviting setting for imaginative snacks like deep-fried Brie with fig conserve or hot avocado, as well as more substantial specials – perhaps chicken breast with peppercorns, or salmon mayonnaise. Traditional Sunday lunch. Restaurant.
Typical prices Speldhurst sausage £2.50 Steak sandwich £2.95
Credit Access, Visa

PEPPARD COMMON — Red Lion

FOOD

Nr Henley
MAP 7 B3 *Oxfordshire*
Rotherfield Greys (049 17) 329
Parking ample

Bar food 12–2 & 7–9.30, Sun 12–1.30 & 7.30–9

Landlords Ian & Pauline Wadham
Brewery Brakspear
Brakspear Mild, Bitter, Special; Guinness; Heineken; Stella Artois; cider.

An unpretentious little pub with a very friendly atmosphere. There are three bars, in one of which children are allowed. The specialities here are nine varieties of jacket potato filled with anything from prawns to beef goulash, and there are plenty of snacks ranging from home-made soup to individual pot meals such as moussaka and seafood gratin. Garden.
Typical prices Swiss steak-filled jacket potato £2.45 Crispy duck £5.75

PETER TAVY — NEW ENTRY — Peter Tavy Inn

FOOD

Nr Tavistock
MAP 9 B2 *Devon*
Mary Tavy (082 281) 348
Parking ample

Bar food 12–2 & 7–10

Landlords Janice & Phil Hawkins
Free house
Blackawton Bitter; Courage Directors; guest beers; Guinness; Hofmeister; Kronenbourg; cider.

Built in the 15th century as a home for masons working on the church, this country inn became a blacksmiths and a coaching house along the way. The imaginative menu has a wholefood emphasis – choose from vegetable lasagne, homity pie, cauliflower croustade as well as cold meats and local fish in season. Evening menu extends to dishes such as pork fillet, plaice stuffed with prawns. Nice sweets. Garden.
Typical prices Vegetable lasagne £2.85 Beef pepper pot £3.85

PETT BOTTOM — Duck Inn

FOOD

Bridge, Nr Canterbury
MAP 6 F3 *Kent*
Canterbury (0227) 830354
Parking ample

Bar food 11.30–2 & 7–10
Closed Mon

Landlords Mr & Mrs L. C. Boothright
Free house
Marston Pedigree; Wem Best Bitter; Fullers London Pride; Shepherd Neame Master Brew Bitter; Hurlimann Sternbrau; cider.

The pace is leisurely at this charming old pub in the depths of the country, but the popular bar snacks are worth the wait. Much in demand are jacket potatoes (with a choice of 12 fillings), the house pâté, steak and kidney pie, and local spiced sausages. Also on the menu are home-made soup, salads, and garlic mushrooms topped with cheese. Garden.
Typical prices Cauliflower cheese with crispy bacon £2.45 Steak & kidney pie £3.95
Credit Access, Amex

PETWORTH — Angel

B

Angel Street
MAP 6 D3 *West Sussex*
Petworth (0798) 42153
Parking ample

Landlords Brian & Anne Pellant
Free house
Flowers Best Bitter; Whitbread Best Bitter; Courage Best Bitter; Guinness; Stella Artois; Heineken; cider.

ACCOMMODATION **4 bedrooms £D**
Check-in all day

A charming old inn near to the centre of pretty Petworth. The beamed bar is spacious, with a log fire, plenty of knick-knacks and a homely atmosphere. The characterful bedrooms also boast black beams, teamed with white plasterwork walls and pretty soft furnishings providing a touch of colour. The four rooms share two public bathrooms, which have carpets and immaculate modern suites. Garden. *No dogs.*
Credit Access, Diners, Visa

PETWORTH — Welldiggers Arms

OD

Pulborough Road
MAP 6 D3 *West Sussex*
Petworth (0798) 42287
Parking ample

Bar food 12–2 & 6–10

Landlord Mr E.H. Whitcomb
Free house
Young Bitter, Special; Guinness; Carlsberg; Budweiser; cider.

East of Petworth on the A283, this pleasantly rustic pub specialises in robust home cooking, with an emphasis on seafood and local game. There's a regular printed menu, plus blackboard specials like salade niçoise, grilled halibut, roast partridge and oxtail casserole. Leave room for a nice sweet, perhaps ice cream or chocolate gâteau. Traditional Sunday lunch menu. Patio.
Typical prices Roast partridge £6.95 French onion soup £2.20
Credit Access, Amex, Diners, Visa

PHILLEIGH — Roseland Inn

OD

Nr Truro
MAP 9 A3 *Cornwall*
Portscatho (087 258) 254
Parking ample

Bar food 12–2 & 7–9
No bar food winter eves

Landlord Desmond Sinnott
Brewery Cornish Brewery Company
John Devenish Dry Hop, Cornish Original; Guinness; Grünhalle Export Gold; Heineken; cider.

Off the beaten track, this 17th-century inn has abundant rustic charm. Most of the snacks served in the beamed bar are home made, with local crab and seafood mornay two popular items. Other choices include sandwiches, chicken liver pâté, smoked mackerel, quiches, good cheeses and a nice chocolate biscuit cake served with clotted cream. Garden.
Typical prices Steak & kidney pie £1 Asparagus & tuna salad £2.75

PICKHILL — Nag's Head

B

Nr Thirsk
MAP 4 D3 *North Yorkshire*
Thirsk (0845) 567391
Parking ample

Landlords Raymond & Edward Boynton
Free house
Theakston Best Bitter, Old Peculier; Tetley Bitter; Guinness; Löwenbräu; Carlsberg Hof; cider.

ACCOMMODATION **10 bedrooms £C**
Check-in all day

Run in a friendly, helpful fashion by the Boynton brothers, this popular inn is situated in a village near the A1. Eight of the bedrooms are in the main building, the other two in a separate cottage. All have pine units, duvets, radio-alarms, tea-makers and good modern bath/shower rooms. A cosy and traditional atmosphere prevails in the main bar with its open fire, and the simpler public bar features a fine display of neckties. Garden.
Credit Access, Visa

PIN MILL — Butt & Oyster

A Nr Chelmondiston, Ipswich
MAP 6 F2 *Suffolk*
Woolverstone (0473) 84764
Parking ample

Landlords Mr & Mrs Mainwaring
Brewery Tollemache & Cobbold
Tolly Cobbold Bitter, Mild, Original, Old Strong; Hansa; cider.

The seafaring locals love this splendid old inn standing right on the banks of the river Orwell. On fine days the sunny terrace is a favourite spot for taking the sea air, or you can join the throng in the characterful main bar for a pint drawn from wooden barrels behind the bar. Yellowing walls, sturdy wooden furniture and nautical bric-a-brac – from photographs to models of barges in glass cases – all add to the atmosphere.

PINNER — Queen's Head

A 31 High Street
MAP 7 C2 *Middlesex*
01-868 4607
Parking ample

Landlords Derek & Susie Passey
Brewery Benskins
Ind Coope Burton Ale; Benskins Strong Ale; John Bull Bitter; Castlemaine XXXX; Löwenbräu; Skol; cider.

The sign dates this black and white, timber-constructed pub, in the middle of the high street, as 1705 and its age shows in beamed ceilings and dark wood-panelled walls. The leaded windows add to the mellowed atmosphere. There is comfortable seating in which to relax, a cosy red carpet and a real fire burns in the deeply recessed fireplace to keep the customers warm on nippy days. **LVs**

PITTON — Silver Plough

FOOD Salisbury
MAP 5 B3 *Wiltshire*
Farley (0722 72) 266
Parking ample

Bar food 12–2 & 6.30–10 (Sun from 7) 

Landlord Michael Beckett
Free house
Wadworth 6X; Hook Norton; Usher Best Bitter; Webster Yorkshire Bitter; Guinness; Carlsberg Hof; cider.

★ Seafood and game are star attractions on the ambitious menu at this attractively converted farmhouse. Bouillabaisse, monkfish in a rich crab, tomato and cream sauce or Red Sea bream marinated in fresh herbs are typical exciting options, while pheasant in a whisky, shallot and red wine sauce makes a splendid seasonal treat. The regular menu embraces soup and pâté, spare ribs and steaks, and vegetables and salads are of excellent quality. Home-made ice creams and plum tart feature among tempting desserts, and there's a fine English cheeseboard. Traditional Sunday lunches also served. Beams, open fires, paintings and antiques characterise the two cosy bars and restaurant, and there's a fine display of engraved Bristol glass rolling pins. Garden. ★

Typical prices Mussels in cream & white wine £3.25 Duck in pink peppercorn sauce £8.25 Seafood pasta with cream sauce £3.75 Gâteau St Honoré £1.60

Credit Access, Amex, Diners, Visa

PLUMLEY — Smoker Inn

D Nr Knutsford
MAP 3 C4 *Cheshire*
Lower Peover (056 581) 2338
Parking ample

Bar food 11–2.45 & 5.30–11, Sun 12–2 & 7–10

Landlord Jorge Masso
Brewery Robinson
Robinson Best Bitter, Best Mild; Guinness; Robinson Einhorn Lager.

Decent home cooking in a mellow thatched pub by the A556. The menu spans sandwiches, salads and hot dishes like liver and onions, fresh plaice and moussaka, plus sweets such as sherry trifle or crème brûlée. Sandwiches are the only choice Saturday evening and all day Sunday, though a traditional Sunday lunch is served in the restaurant. Garden. Children welcome lunchtime only.
Typical prices Home-made steak & kidney pie £2.95 Kofta curry £2.25

PLYMOUTH — Unity

D Eastlake Street
MAP 9 B2 *Devon*
Plymouth (0752) 262622
Parking ample

Bar food 12–2
No bar food eves
Closed Sun

Landlord Mr Bibby
Brewery Hall's
Hall's Plympton Pride; John Bull Bitter; Tetley Bitter; Skol; Löwenbräu; Castlemaine XXXX; cider.

The honest, enjoyable bar food continues to draw lunchtime support for this bustling modern pub in the city centre. Cold cuts (ham, pork, beef) and prawns are the basis of fresh salads and granary bread sandwiches, and there are a couple of hot daily specials like lasagne, hot pot or shepherd's pie. The Stilton is well-kept and makes a tasty sandwich. Patio.
Typical prices Shepherd's pie £1.80 Chilli con carne with rice £2

POCKLINGTON — Feathers Hotel

B 56 Market Place
MAP 4 E3 *Humberside*
Pocklington (0759) 303155
Parking ample

Landlord K.F. Suttle
Brewery Younger
Younger's Scotch, No.3, IPA; Beck's Bier; Kestrel; McEwan's Lager; cider.

***ACCOMMODATION* 12 bedrooms £C**
Check-in all day

Simple overnight accommodation is offered at this pebbledash hotel in the market place. Six rooms in the main building have a fairly traditional look, with darkwood furniture; the other six, which are in a motel-style block across the car park, are in tasteful modern style, using light colour schemes and fitted units. All rooms offer TVs, telephones, tea-makers, trouser presses and private facilities. Staff could be more enthusiastic. Garden. *No dogs.*
Credit Access, Amex, Diners, Visa

POOLE — Inn in the Park

B Pinewood Road, Branksome Park
MAP 5 B4 *Dorset*
Bournemouth (0202) 761318
Parking limited

Landlords Alan & Paula Potter
Free house
Wadworth 6X, IPA; Younger's Tartan Bitter; Guinness; Stella Artois; cider.

***ACCOMMODATION* 5 bedrooms £D**
Check-in all day

Just a short walk from Branksome Dene Chine and the sea, this converted Victorian house has been much modernised. The Potters work hard to keep standards high, and the bedrooms are bright and practical, with TVs and tea-makers; three have private facilities, while the other two share a spotless bathroom. The large open-plan bar features a fine collection of stamps, and there's a patio for fine-weather drinking. Children welcome in the bar lunchtime only.

POOLEY BRIDGE — Crown Hotel

B & B

Nr Penrith
MAP 3 C2 *Cumbria*
Pooley Bridge (085 36) 217
Parking ample

Landlord James Haddart
Brewery Whitbread
Whitbread Trophy; Guinness; Heineken; Stella Artois; cider.
No real ale.

***ACCOMMODATION* 5 bedrooms £D**
Check-in all day

A friendly village inn offering simple, but pleasant accommodation. Its popularity as a pub attracts both locals and hikers, who often congregate in the bars or in the gardens that extend to the banks of the river Earmont. Good-sized, old-fashioned bedrooms share a common bathroom, and are all equipped with tea-makers. You can expect a good breakfast in the morning. There is a comfortable TV lounge for residents. Garden. *No dogs.*

PORLOCK WEIR — Anchor Hotel & Ship Inn

B & B

Nr Minehead
MAP 9 C1 *Somerset*
Porlock (0643) 862636
Parking ample

Landlords Pandy Sechiari & Donald Wade
Free house
Usher Best Bitter, Triple Crown; Golden Hill Exmoor Ale; Guinness; Fosters; Holsten; cider.

***ACCOMMODATION* 30 bedrooms £A**
Check-in all day

The thatched 16th-century Ship Inn, the 19th-century Anchor Hotel and a recently converted annexe enjoy a delightful setting overlooking the pretty harbour, with views across the Bristol Channel to the Welsh coast. All the bedrooms have TVs and tea and coffee making facilities; 20 have private facilities and many enjoy sea vistas. There are a number of lounge areas and several bars. Accommodation closed two weeks January. Patio.
Credit Access, Amex, Visa

PORT GAVERNE — Port Gaverne Hotel

B & B

Nr Port Isaac
MAP 9 B2 *Cornwall*
Bodmin (0208) 880244
Parking limited

Closed 15 Jan–28 Feb

Landlords Mr & Mrs F. P. Ross
Free house
Flowers Best Bitter, IPA; Whitbread Best Bitter; St Austell Hicks Special; Stella Artois; Guinness; cider.
***ACCOMMODATION* 19 bedrooms £B**
Check-in all day

Charm is in plentiful supply at this early 17th-century inn set in a rugged cove half a mile from Port Isaac. The three cosy bars – decorated with old photographs and watercolours – are full of character, and the pleasant little lounge with antique furniture has a seaview balcony. Pretty, spotless bedrooms – all with modern bathrooms – have thoughtful extras like books, magazines and quality soap. There's also a TV lounge and a garden.
Credit Access, Amex, Diners, Visa

POWERSTOCK — Three Horseshoes Inn

FOOD
B & B

Bridport
MAP 5 A4 *Dorset*
Powerstock (030 885) 328
Parking ample

Bar food 12–2 & 7–11
No bar food Sun eve & all Mon (Nov–Feb except Bank Hol Mons)

Landlords Pat & Diana Ferguson
Brewery Palmer
Palmer BB, IPA; Guinness; Eldridge Pope Faust Pilsener; cider.

Imaginative dishes on an adventurous menu are on offer at this handsome Victorian pub known locally as 'The Shoes'. Fresh seafood includes salmon and scallop salad, mussels and sea bass with fennel; other choices could include roast pork with apples or lamb's kidneys with Dijon mustard, all served with a good selection of nicely cooked vegetables. Also, each month there's a selection of dishes cooked with the minimum of fat, salt and sugar – perhaps chicken and spinach terrine

with watercress sauce, lamb fillet in a rosemary crust and a fresh fruit sorbet to finish. Excellent sandwiches and snacks, plus a Sunday roast lunch. Recent improvements include the addition of a new restaurant.
Typical prices Moules marinière £2.95 Grilled fresh plaice £4.25

ACCOMMODATION **3 bedrooms £C**
Check-in restricted

Bedrooms are simple and homely, with central heating to keep things cosy. Furniture is traditional, and the rooms enjoy lovely views of the surrounding countryside. Two have carpeted bathrooms; all have duvets, and tea-makers.

Credit Access, Visa

PRIORS HARDWICK — Butchers Arms

A Nr Southam
MAP 7 B1 *Warwickshire*
Byfield (0327) 60504
Parking ample

Landlords Pires family
Free house
Bass; Mitchells & Butlers Springfield Bitter, Brew XI; Carling Black Label; Carlsberg Hof; Tennent's Lager.
No real ale.

A village inn since 1375, this solid stone building stands just off the old Welsh road, amid 4½ acres of lovely gardens designed by welcoming Portuguese owners the Pires. The interior is rather splendid, with flagstone floors, beams and large, handsome fireplaces, and it features some fine antiques and period furnishings. The delightful village of Priors Hardwick was a Royalist stronghold during the Civil War. A wonderful stop for a drink in quiet and historic surroundings.

PULBOROUGH — Waters Edge

D Station Road
MAP 6 D4 *West Sussex*
Pulborough (079 82) 2451
Parking ample

Bar food 12–2.30 & 6.30–10
Landlords John & Margaret Salmon
Brewery Friary Meux
Marston Burton Bitter; Friary Meux Bitter; John Bull Bitter; Guinness; Löwenbräu; Skol; cider.

A splendid range of food and a beautiful view of the river Arun are the attractions here. There is an excellent carvery of roast meats (the exclusive choice in the evenings) accompanied by a good choice of crisp fresh vegetables. Other lunchtime dishes include vegetable quiche and beef hot pot, and a good variety of salads and sandwiches. Home-made sweets. Garden.
Typical prices Game pie £3.75 Bread & butter pudding £1.10
Credit Access, Amex, Diners, Visa **LVs**

PULVERBATCH — White Horse

D Nr Shrewsbury
MAP 5 A1 *Shropshire*
Dorrington (074 373) 247
Parking ample

Bar food 12–2 & 7–10

Landlords Margaret & Hamish MacGregor
Brewery Whitbread
Flowers Original; Whitbread Best Bitter; guest beer; Guinness; Heineken; Stella Artois; cider.

Winding country lanes lead from the A49 at Dorrington to this thriving, old timbered inn. The MacGregors' pride in Scotland is evident everywhere – from the tartan decor to the popular Rob Roy sandwich (roast beef and melted cheese in hot French bread). Other choices from the vast selection include home-made burgers, soups, curries, grills and salads. Children's menu. Patio.
Typical prices Chicken & prawn curry £3.50 Rob Roy sandwich £1.10

PYRTON — Plough Inn

FOOD

Nr Watlington
MAP 7 B2 *Oxfordshire*
Watlington (049 161) 2003
Parking ample

Bar food 11–2.30 & 6–11
No bar food Sun eve

Landlords Jackie & Jeremy Hunt
Free house
Adnams Bitter, Extra Special; Theakston XB; Carlsberg Hof; Talisman non-alcoholic; cider.

Visitors and locals alike receive a cheery welcome from enthusiastic hosts at this idyllic, old thatched pub. By the log fire, under the low-beamed ceiling, you can enjoy jacket potatoes, garlic prawns or mushrooms, chicken Kiev or locally cooked ham. A blackboard menu offers daily specials, and there's a selection of good English cheeses and lovely home-made puds, too. Garden.
Typical prices Fresh salmon in white wine £6.95 Pork Marsala £5.95
Credit Access, Visa

RAMSBURY — Bell at Ramsbury

FOOD

The Square
MAP 7 B3 *Wiltshire*
Marlborough (0672) 20230
Parking ample

Bar food 12–2 & 7–9.30
No bar food Sat eve

Landlord Michael Benjamin
Free house
Wadworth IPA, 6X; Younger's Tartan Bitter; Guinness; Carlsberg Hof, Pilsner; cider.

A 16th-century pub with a comfortable bar and a log fire in winter. The main feature of the food is the range of unusual pies, such as scrumpy (pork and apple) and gobble and grunt (turkey and pork). Also on offer are kedgeree, taramasalata, pâté and, at lunchtimes, ploughman's and steak sandwich. Delicious sweets. A traditional roast is available on Sundays. Garden.
Typical prices Fondue pie £2.80 Mariners pie £2.95

RINGMORE — Journey's End Inn

FOOD
B & B

Kingsbridge, Bigbury-on-Sea
MAP 9 B3 *Devon*
Bigbury-on-Sea (0548) 810205
Parking ample

Bar food 12–2 & 7–10

Landlords Robert & Tessa Dunkley
Free house
Hall's Plympton Best, Plympton Pride; Golden Hill Exmoor Ale; Guinness; Carlsberg; cider.

Licensed as an ale house under Elizabeth I, but taking its name from the play R. C. Sherriff wrote while staying here, this rambling old tavern with its blackened beams and narrow corridors is full of nooks and crannies and rich in historic atmosphere. An open fire warms the simple, old-world bar where they serve soup – perhaps celery or leek and potato – salads, sandwiches (lunchtime only) and tasty home-made dishes like cottage pie, fish pie, lentil and mushroom lasagne and sometimes a tasty rabbit casserole. Puddings are suitably old-fashioned, with steamed chocolate pudding or a delicious pear and walnut crumble taking care of any gaps.
Typical prices Steak & kidney pie £2 Pavlova 90p

***ACCOMMODATION* 3 bedrooms £C**
Check-in all day

The three bedrooms are small and cottagy. Two have en suite facilities, the other a bathroom across the corridor. The rooms are quiet, simply furnished and spotless, with radio alarms, TVs and tea-makers. Improvements are planned by the new young owners. Patio.
Credit Access, Visa

RINGWOOD — Original White Hart

B

Market Place
MAP 5 B4 *Hampshire*
Ringwood (042 54) 3313
Parking ample

Landlords Mary & Terry Eales
Brewery Eldridge Pope
Eldridge Pope Royal Oak, Dorset Original IPA, Dorchester Bitter, Pope's 1880; Faust Pilsener, Export Lager; cider.

ACCOMMODATION **10 bedrooms £D**
Check-in all day

This cheerful old inn at the centre of town claims to be the first by that name, harking back to the time of Henry VII. Recent improvements have created more space without sacrificing any of the ancient character. There's a choice of four very agreeable bars, each with a real fire and a distinctive theme. Simple bedrooms, three with en suite shower rooms, are traditionally furnished and have colour TVs and tea/coffee makers. Two public bathrooms. Patio.
Credit Access, Amex, Visa

RIPLEY — Anchor

OD

High Street
MAP 7 C3 *Surrey*
Guildford (0483) 224120
Parking ample

Bar food 12–2
No bar food eves

Landlord Christine Beale
Brewery Friary Meux
Friary Meux Bitter; Ind Coope Burton Ale; John Bull Bitter; Guinness; Skol; Löwenbräu; cider.

This mellow village pub is over 700 years old, and its cosy, low-beamed bars are filled with burnished brass and pretty porcelain. Christine Beale's tasty, savoury pies are the favourite choice at lunchtime, with soup, sandwiches and ploughman's providing lighter bites. Chilli con carne or spaghetti bolognese are typical daily specials and there's a roast on Sunday. Patio.
Typical prices Cottage pie with vegetables £2.10 Jacket potato with prawn filling £1.60

RIPLEY — Seven Stars

OD

Newark Lane
MAP 7 C3 *Surrey*
Guildford (0483) 225128
Parking ample

Bar food 12–2 & 7–9, Sun 12–1.30 & 7.30–9
Landlord Rodney Dean
Brewery Friary Meux
Friary Meux Bitter; Ind Coope Bitter, Burton Ale; Benskins Bitter; Guinness; Löwenbräu; cider.

Prize-winning pizzas are among the tasty home-prepared snacks served in this cheerful pub, which stands by the B367 just north of Ripley. Other dishes marked up on the blackboard could include chilli con carne with rice, beef and dumplings in ale, trout or lemon sole, with apricot crumble, a splendid trifle, or cheese and biscuits to finish. Also sandwiches, winter soup and a cold buffet.
Typical prices Goulash & jacket potato £3.85 Vegetarian pizza £2.30

RIPON — Unicorn Hotel

B

Market Place
MAP 4 D3 *North Yorkshire*
Ripon (0765) 2202
Parking ample

Landlords Mr & Mrs D.T. Small
Free house
Taylor Landlord; John Smith's Yorkshire Bitter; Tetley Bitter; Younger's Scotch; Guinness; Carlsberg Export; cider.

ACCOMMODATION **27 bedrooms £B**
Check-in all day

Enjoy an overnight stop at this nice old posting house in the market place of a historic, 9th-century town. There's a choice of a rustic public bar, popular with the locals, and a large, comfortable lounge, as well as a residents' lounge. Light, spacious bedrooms, with modern or attractive period furnishings, have private bathrooms or showers, TVs, direct-dial phones and tea and coffee making facilities. Children are welcome overnight.
Credit Access, Amex, Diners, Visa **LVs**

RISPLITH — Black-a-Moor Inn

B & B Sawley, Nr Ripon
MAP 4 D3 *North Yorkshire*
Sawley (076 586) 214
Parking ample
Landlords David & Joyce Beckett
Free house
William Younger's Scotch, No 3, IPA; Beck's Bier; McEwan's Lager; cider.

ACCOMMODATION **3 bedrooms £D**
Check-in restricted

Perched up on the moors west of Ripon, this homely stone-built pub is right on the B6265 and a good spot for an overnight stop. The single bar is divided between a plushy lounge area and a more informal public end with wooden furniture and a jukebox. Pretty floral bedrooms have duvets and freestanding furniture, and share a bathroom. All the bedrooms have colour TVs, coffee and tea-making facilities and washbasins. *No dogs.*
Credit Access, Visa

ROCHESTER — Redesdale Arms Hotel

FOOD
B & B Nr Otterburn
MAP 3 C1 *Northumberland*
Otterburn (0830) 20668
Parking ample
Bar food 12–3 & 7–10
Landlords Hilda & Johnny Wright
Free house
Drybrough Heavy, Scotch; Tetley Bitter; Carlsberg; cider. *No real ale*

For many years the first or last hotel in England (and known locally as 'The First and Last'), this mellow old coaching inn stands just 12 miles from the Scottish border, alongside the A68. Part of the Northumbrian National Park, it makes a good base for exploring the region – and home-made snacks served in the two simple, rustic bars are a welcome prospect on return. Nourishing ham and lentil soup with lovely wholemeal bread, cheese scones and well-filled sandwiches (plain and toasted) are all popular light bites. There are more substantial dishes like chilli con carne, too, and few can resist the lure of home-made chocolate fudge cake, served hot, for dessert.
Typical prices Soup & stottie 85p Steak & kidney pie £3.65

ACCOMMODATION **12 bedrooms £D**
Check-in all day

Traditionally furnished bedrooms (three with four-posters) all have TVs, teamakers and easy chairs (there is no residents' lounge). Three are equipped with shower cabinets, and the carpeted bathrooms also offer showers. Patio and garden.
Credit Access, Visa

ROCKCLIFFE — Crown & Thistle

FOOD Nr Carlisle
MAP 3 B2 *Cumbria*
Rockcliffe (022 874) 378
Parking ample
Bar food 12–2 (Sun till 1.30) & 7–9 (Sat till 9.30)
Landlords Kevin & Joanne Dempsey
Brewery Scottish & Newcastle
McEwan's 70/-; Younger's IPA; Guinness; Harp; Beck's Bier; cider.

If the choice on the bar menu of this pleasant old pub on the outskirts of the village looks ordinary, the preparation certainly isn't. Succulent home-cooked ham heads the list, and the steaks are good, too. Other offerings include soup and sandwiches and the popular hot pot. The favourite sweet is a creamy apple gâteau. Children welcome in the bar every evening till 8pm, except Saturday. Garden.
Typical prices Gammon with pineapple £3 Squire's lunch £2

ROMALDKIRK — Rose & Crown Hotel

OD
& B

Teesdale
MAP 4 D2 *Durham*
Teesdale (0833) 50213
Parking ample

Bar food 12–2 & 7–9.30

Landlords David & Jill Jackson
Free house
Theakston Best Bitter; Matthew Brown Lion Bitter, Slalom Lager, Slalom 'D'.

Once a major coaching house, this 18th-century inn stands next to the ancient church overlooking the green. Hospitality's still the name of the game, and both the food and the accommodation are excellent. The lunchtime bill of fare includes a popular cold buffet (summer only), along with pâté, soup, sandwiches and hot dishes like fish and chips or chilli con carne. In the evening a wider choice of main courses could include gammon, sirloin steak, pan-fried trout and barbecue-sauced breast of chicken. Roast lunch available on Sundays.
Typical prices Seafood platter £5.50 Meat & potato pie £2.25

ACCOMMODATION **11 bedrooms £C**
Check-in all day

Comfortable bedrooms in the main building are traditionally furnished and have either a settee or a couple of armchairs each and a choice of duvets or sheets and blankets. Smart chalet-style rooms in the courtyard block include a honeymoon room complete with four-poster. Private bathrooms and lots of little extras throughout. Patio. *No babies under six months overnight.*

Credit Access, Diners, Visa

ROSEDALE ABBEY — Blacksmiths Arms Hotel

& B

Hartoft End, Nr Pickering
MAP 4 E3 *North Yorkshire*
Lastingham (075 15) 331
Parking ample

Landlords M. P. & J. K. Barrie
Free house
Younger's Scotch; John Smith's Bitter; Newcastle Exhibition; Guinness; Carlsberg; cider.

ACCOMMODATION **12 bedrooms £C**
Check-in all day

At the foot of Rosedale in the North Yorkshire Moors National Park, this 16th-century farmhouse – built with stone from the nearby Abbey – makes a comfortable and welcoming place to stay. Attractively decorated bedrooms, most with private facilities, have simple modern furniture and tea-making facilities. The two cottagy bars are full of charm and character, with their homely bric-a-brac, and there's a splendid garden. Children accommodated.
Credit Access, Visa

ROSEDALE ABBEY — White Horse Farm Hotel

& B

Nr Pickering
MAP 4 E3 *North Yorkshire*
Lastingham (075 15) 239
Parking ample

Landlords Mr & Mrs D. C. Wilcock
Free house
Tetley Bitter, Mild; Cameron Lion Bitter; Strongarm, Hansa; Skol; cider.

ACCOMMODATION **15 bedrooms £C**
Check-in all day

Stunning moorland views are a bonus of this sturdy stone pub, well placed as a base for a touring holiday. The stone-walled bar with its wealth of old beams and church pew seating is splendidly rustic. Bedrooms are spacious with pleasing colour schemes, modern attractive fitted units and very comfortable armchairs. All have tea and coffee making facilities, radio-alarms, colour TVs, and compact bath or shower rooms. Patio and garden.
Credit Amex, Diners

ROTHERWICK — Coach & Horses

FOOD

The Street, Nr Hook
MAP 7 C3 *Hampshire*
Hook (025 672) 2542
Parking ample

Bar food 12–2.15 & 7–10.30, Sun 12–2 & 7–9
Landlord Mrs Terry Williams
Free house
Hall & Woodhouse Badger Best, Tanglefoot; Eldridge Pope Royal Oak; Arkell Kingsdown; Ringwood Old Thumper; guest beer; cider.

The owner's son Liam prepares the tasty bar fare in this agreeable pub that features an excellent selection of real ales. His pizzas and meaty burgers are particularly popular, and there are sandwiches, quiches and heartier dishes like roast duck or mixed grill. A cold buffet in summer and carvery in winter, which run from Thursday to Sunday, provide appetising fare. Sunday lunch menu offers carvery only. Patio.
Typical prices Hamburger £1.75 Carvery or cold table £5.75

ROWHOOK — Chequers Inn

FOOD

Nr Horsham
MAP 6 D3 *West Sussex*
Sinfold (0403) 790480
Parking ample

Bar food 12–2 (Sun till 1.30) & 7–10
No bar food Sun eve
Landlord Mr P.A. Barrs
Brewery Whitbread
Flowers Original; Whitbread Strong Country Bitter, Samuel Whitbread; guest beer; cider.

An unpretentious 15th-century inn whose snack menu changes daily, with home-made pies and casseroles among the regular favourites. There are also sandwiches and ploughman's, home-cooked ham, grilled sole and a particularly good toad-in-the-hole. Evening extras could include rainbow trout and chicken Kiev. Traditional Sunday lunch menu also available.
Typical prices Game casserole £2.50 Steak & kidney pudding £2.50
Credit Visa

ROYDON **NEW ENTRY** — Three Horseshoes

FOOD

Lynn Road, Nr Kings Lynn
MAP 6 E1 *Norfolk*
Hillingdon (0485) 600362
Parking ample

Bar food 12.30–2 & 7–10
No bar food Sat & Sun eves
Landlord Michael Mansfield
Brewery Norwich
Ruddles County; Webster Yorkshire Bitter; Norwich Bitter; Guinness; Carlsberg; Holsten Export; cider.

A popular local haunt dating back to the 15th century, whose beamed bar or informal restaurant are convivial places in which to enjoy a range of simple yet excellently prepared dishes. The choice extends from a perfect Welsh rarebit through omelettes, soups, pâté and pitta bread sandwiches to specials on the blackboard such as Cromer crab. More choice available in the restaurant.
Typical prices Potted Norfolk beef & toast £1 Sussex smokies £1.50
Credit Access

RUNNING WATERS — Three Horse Shoes

B & B

Sherburn House, Nr Durham
MAP 4 D2 *Co. Durham*
Durham (0385) 720286
Parking ample

Landlords Derek & Lesley Crehan
Free house
Vaux Samson; Lorimer Best Scotch; Wards Sheffield Best Bitter; Guinness; Tuborg; Stella Artois; cider.
No real ale.
ACCOMMODATION **4 bedrooms £C**
Check-in all day

In a tiny hamlet high up on the A181 between Durham and Hartlepool, this cream-painted pub is run with warmth and pride by the charming Crehans. The two bars, where children are welcome at lunchtime, have a cosy, rustic appeal and the bedrooms are roomy and comfortable. Three have shower cabinets and washbasins, and tea and coffee making facilities, TVs and duvets are standard throughout. Garden. Accommodation closed 1 week Xmas.
Credit Access, Visa

RUSTHALL — Red Lion

OD

Nr Tunbridge Wells
MAP 6 E3 *Kent*
Tunbridge Wells (0892) 20086
Parking ample

Bar food 12.30–2 & 7.30–10.45

Landlords Mr and Mrs B Cooter
Brewery Whitbread
Whitbread Best Bitter, Mild; Fremlins Bitter; Guinness; Stella Artois; Heineken; cider.

Two bars – one plushly comfortable, the other beamed and full of character – provide a choice of venue for enjoying the Cooters' appetising snacks. Stick to old favourites such as soup, salads, sausages and steaks, or opt for something more unusual like savoury meatballs in a vegetable-packed curry sauce. Less choice in the evening. Garden.
Typical prices Kidneys in red wine sauce £1.45 Chicken and ham Mexicano £1.45

SAFFRON WALDEN — Eight Bells

OD
& B

Bridge Street
MAP 7 D1 *Essex*
Saffron Walden (0799) 22790
Parking ample

Bar food 12–2 & 6.30–9.30 (Sat till 10), Sun 12–1.45 & 7–9.30

Landlord Robin Moore
Brewery Benskins
John Bull Bitter; Benskins Best Bitter; Burton Ale; Guinness; Skol; Oranjeboom; cider.

Polished oak furniture, beamed walls hung with old prints and candlelight at night make this 500-year-old inn a particularly appealing place for a thoroughly enjoyable snack. The imaginative selection of dishes suits all tastes, from guacamole and farmhouse cheese ploughman's to surf 'n' turf (rump steak and giant prawns), fried plaice and Stilton-topped mushrooms baked in cider and thyme. Daily specials such as fresh crab and chicken in champagne sauce expand the choice, and delicious sweets from Greek yoghurt with honey and toasted almonds to home-made blackberry and apple crumble. There's a cold buffet in summer, and a thoughtful children's menu too.
Typical prices Prawn thermidor with garlic bread and salad £4.95 Lasagne with salad £3.50

ACCOMMODATION **2 bedrooms £C**
Check-in all day

Upstairs the two beamed, good-sized bedrooms have a comfortable, homely appeal. Both offer televisions, tea and coffee making facilities and share a carpeted bathroom. Garden.

Credit Access, Amex, Diners, Visa **LVs**

Any person using our name to obtain free hospitality is a fraud.

Proprietors, please inform Egon Ronay's Guides and the police.

SAFFRON WALDEN — Saffron Hotel

FOOD
B & B

High Street
MAP 7 D1 *Essex*
Saffron Walden (0799) 22676
Parking limited

Bar food 12–2 & 6.30–9.30
No bar food Sun
Landlords Craddock family
Free house
Greene King IPA; John Smith's Yorkshire Bitter; Younger's Tartan Bitter; Guinness; Carlsberg; Kronenbourg; cider.

The Craddock family offer a friendly welcome and high standards at their town-centre hotel (the African grey parrot in the foyer also extends a cheery greeting). There is a cosy panelled bar and a beautifully secluded patio for al fresco eating and drinking. The extensive menu offers a range of ploughman's, sandwiches, jacket potatoes, salads and omelettes for snacks, while for a hearty meal you might tuck into the soup of the day followed by grilled trout or spaghetti bolognese. Finish with apple and orange pie, caramelised oranges in brandy with cream or bread and butter pudding.
Typical prices Steak & onion ale pie £3.95 Chicken tandoori & curried vegetables £3.35

ACCOMMODATION **22 bedrooms £C**
Check-in all day

The comfortable bedrooms vary in size from compact singles to spacious doubles. Most have tea-making facilities, all have direct-dial telephones and colour TVs. Twelve have en suite bathrooms; six have shower cubicles and there are neat public bathrooms for the remainder. Children welcome overnight.

Credit Access, Visa **LVs**

ST DOMINICK — Who'd Have Thought It Inn

FOOD

Saltash
MAP 9 B2 *Cornwall*
Liskeard (0579) 50214
Parking ample

Bar food 12–1.45 & 7.30–10.30 (till 11 in summer)
Landlords Potter family
Free house
Courage Directors; Bass; Worthington Best Bitter; Guinness; Hofmeister; Carling Black Label; cider.

The courteous Potter family put their hearts into this charming inn, which is spotlessly kept and lovingly cared for. Drawn by the homely atmosphere, people rendezvous for drinks and bar snacks: best are the simple items like fresh sandwiches of excellent ham and silverside – or try mature cheddar with pickle – ploughman's, jacket potatoes and very good salad platters.
Typical prices Silverside of beef sandwich £1.25 Ham platter with jacket potato £2.90

ST MARGARET'S AT CLIFFE — Cliffe Tavern

B & B

High Street, Nr Dover
MAP 6 F3 *Kent*
Dover (0304) 852749
Parking ample

Landlord Mr C. J. Waring Westby
Free house
Shepherd Neame Master Brew XX; Fremlins Bitter; Webster Yorkshire Bitter; guest beer; Carlsberg Hof; Fosters; cider.

ACCOMMODATION **12 bedrooms £C**
Check-in all day

Owned and run by the friendly Westby family, this white-painted clapboard pub in a pretty village just outside Dover offers convenient overnight accommodation for ferry passengers. Bedrooms in the main building and two adjacent cottages all have prettily coordinated soft furnishings, writing desks, TVs, teamakers and neat modern bathrooms. There are two convivial bars – one with mock beams and polished wooden tables – and a peaceful walled garden.
Credit Access, Amex, Diners, Visa

ST MAWES — NEW ENTRY — Rising Sun Inn

& B

The Square
MAP 9 A3 *Cornwall*
St Mawes (0326) 270233
Parking difficult

Landlords R. J. Milan & F. N. B. Atherley
Brewery St Austell
St Austell BB, Hicks Special, Extra; Guinness; Carlsberg Hof, Pilsner.

***ACCOMMODATION* 12 bedrooms £B**
Check-in all day

Completely refurbished, this villagey pub has blossomed under new tenants. In the restful residents' lounge overlooking the harbour there are comfy sofas and armchairs, and the warm, convivial main bar adjoins a flower-bordered terrace. Bedrooms with TVs, phones and tea/coffee makers, look well in soft colours and quality furnishings. Nine have neat private facilities, others share one spotless bathroom. *No children under nine overnight.*
Credit Access, Amex, Diners, Visa

ST MAWGAN — Falcon Inn

& B

Nr Newquay
MAP 9 A2 *Cornwall*
St Mawgan (0637) 860225
Parking ample

Landlords Mr & Mrs P. Joyce
Free house
St Austell Bosun, Pinner's Ale; Devenish Cornish Best; Worthington Bitter; Guinness; Carlsberg; cider.

***ACCOMMODATION* 4 bedrooms £D**
Check-in all day

A beautiful scenic drive through the wooded Lanherne valley followed by a drink in the large garden or neat bar are two good reasons for a detour to the Joyces' charming little pub. Spend the night in one of the pretty pink bedrooms, simply furnished and absolutely spotless. The rooms share an immaculate bathroom with the family. Residents also have a pleasantly homely lounge. *No children overnight in July and August.*

ST NEOTS — Chequers Inn

OOD

St Mary's Street, Eynesbury
MAP 7 C1 *Cambridgeshire*
Huntingdon (0480) 72116
Parking ample
Bar food 12–2 & 7–10

Landlords David James & Ann Elizabeth Taylor
Free house
Paine XXX, EG; Webster Yorkshire Bitter; Stones Bitter; Carlsberg; Carling Black Label. *No real ale.*

Low-beamed ceilings, an old oak rocking chair and an inglenook fireplace give this 16th-century pub tremendous atmosphere. Lunchtime is busy, with customers making the most of daily specials which always include two fish choices. Favourites are French onion soup and steak and kidney pie. Tempting sweets and a selection of cheeses. Patio and garden.
Typical prices Fillet of plaice £6.25 Chicken Stanley & rice £3.85
Credit Access, Amex, Diners, Visa

ST NEOTS — Rocket

& B

Crosshall Road, Eaton Ford
MAP 7 C1 *Cambridgeshire*
Huntingdon (0480) 72773
Parking ample

Landlord Mrs V. Stephenson
Free house
Adnams Bitter; Greene King IPA; Paine 3X; Wells Gold Eagle; Guinness; Kellerbräu;

***ACCOMMODATION* 9 bedrooms £C**
Check-in all day

Named after the famous old steam engine, this converted farmhouse inn at the junction of the A1 and A45 is smartly run by the inventor's distant relatives. The main building houses a panelled bar, while a separate modern block provides comfortable overnight accommodation. Large, centrally heated bedrooms, all with nicely fitted bathrooms en suite, have direct-dial phones, colour TVs and tea-makers. Patio. Children are welcome overnight. *No dogs.*
Credit Access, Amex, Diners, Visa

SALISBURY — Haunch of Venison

A

1 Minster Street
MAP 5 B3 *Wiltshire*
Salisbury (0722) 22024
Parking difficult

Landlords Mr & Mrs Leroy
Brewery Courage
Courage Directors, Best Bitter; Guinness; Hofmeister; Holsten Export; cider.

The date 1320 is painted into the exterior wall of this fine half-timbered pub and inside, the intimate little bar has polished panelling and a beautiful mahogany and brass wine and spirit dispenser. Three tiny rooms off the bar – The House of Lords (once a discreet watering hole for Victorian churchmen), The Horse Box (a real cubby hole for a quiet noggin), and The Cloisters (open summer only) – engender a particular charm. Patio.
Credit Access, Amex, Diners, Visa **LVs**

SALISBURY — King's Arms

B & B

9 St John Street
MAP 5 B3 *Wiltshire*
Salisbury (0722) 27629
Parking limited

Landlord Anthony Wilkinson
Owner Westward Hosts
Usher Best Bitter, Founder's Ale, Triple Crown; Webster Yorkshire Bitter; Holsten; Carlsberg; cider.
ACCOMMODATION **15 bedrooms £B**
Check-in all day

Charles II was once a guest at this fine half-timbered inn near the cathedral, and would feel quite at home today in the oak-panelled residents' lounge and two atmospheric beamed bars. The bedrooms, however, while full of period charm (two boast handsome four-posters) are splendidly up-to-date after their recent refurbishment and offer direct-dial phones, TVs, hairdryers and trouser presses. Excellent new bathrooms. Courtyard.
Credit Access, Amex, Diner, Visa

SANDON BANK — Seven Stars Inn

FOOD

Nr Stafford
MAP 5 B1 *Staffordshire*
Sandon (088 97) 316
Parking ample

Bar food 11.30–2 & 6.30–10, Sun 12–1.30 & 7–9.30
Landlords Jill & Ron Roestenburg
Brewery Burtonwood
Burtonwood Best Bitter, Dark Mild. Top Hat Strong Ale; Guinness; Skol; Castlemaine XXXX; cider.

A popular family pub with five cosy bar-food areas, a cocktail bar, an 80-seat restaurant and a large garden. Ploughman's lunches, steak and kidney pie, steaks and curries are served in bumper portions, along with specials like seafood mornay, chicken à la king or beef mexicana. There's a weekday cold buffet in summer and a traditional Sunday lunch menu in the restaurant.
Typical prices Beef in red wine £4 Sweet & sour pork £4
Credit Access, Visa

SANDSIDE — Ship Inn

B & B

Nr Milnthorpe
MAP 3 C3 *Cumbria*
Milnthorpe (044 82) 3113
Parking ample

Landlord John Nancarrow
Brewery William Younger's Inns
Younger's No 3, Scotch; McEwan's 70/-, Lager; Beck's Bier; cider.
ACCOMMODATION **6 bedrooms £D**
Check-in all day

Morecambe Bay and the Lakeland hills make a most attractive backdrop for this cheerful inn, which is less than ten minutes' drive from the M6 (junction 36). The bedrooms, all with TVs and tea-makers, have attractive pine wardrobes and chests of drawers; one double has an en suite bathroom, and the rest share a public one. Children are not accommodated overnight, but they are admitted to the pub, and there's a play area. Garden. *No dogs.*
Credit Access, Visa

SANDWICH — Fleur-de-Lis

B&B

Delf Street
MAP 6 F3 *Kent*
Sandwich (0304) 611131
Parking limited

Landlord Mr R. J. Tillings
Brewery Whitbread
Fremlins Bitter; Flowers Original; guest beer; Guinness; Stella Artois; Heineken; cider.

ACCOMMODATION **8 bedrooms £C**
Check-in restricted

Oil lamps light one of the three pleasant bars at this mellow old red-brick pub. There's also a well-equipped games room with two pool tables and a juke box. Comfortable bedrooms are furnished in traditional style (one has a half-tester) and all provide TVs and tea-makers. Those in the main building share a modern bathroom, while annexe rooms have shower cubicles. Breakfast is served in a vaulted room that was once the old corn exchange.
Credit Access, Amex, Diners, Visa

SANDYGATE — Blue Ball Inn

FOOD

Old Rydon Lane
MAP 9 C2 *Devon*
Topsham (039 287) 3401
Parking ample

Bar food 12–2 & 6.30–10
No bar food Sun eve

Landlords Mike & Linda Ward
Brewery Whitbread
Whitbread Best Bitter, Samuel Whitbread Strong; Flowers IPA, Original; Guinness; Stella Artois; cider.

The large garden is a major attraction at this thatched-roof pub dating from the 16th century but now extensively modernised. (Follow signs for Topsham after leaving junction 30 of the M5.) Bar snacks are a mixture of fresh produce and convenience foods, and concentrate on popular items such as pâtés, quiches, salads, meat pies, and ham, egg and chips. Home-made puds include apple pie and fudge cake.
Typical prices Lasagne £2.75 Chicken Madras curry £2.75

SAUNDERTON — Rose & Crown Inn

B&B

Wycombe Road, Nr Princes Risborough
MAP 7 C2 *Buckinghamshire*
Princes Risborough (084 44) 5299
Parking ample

Landlords Robert & John Watson
Free house
Morland Bitter; Wethered Bitter; Morrell Varsity; Stella Artois; Heineken.

ACCOMMODATION **15 bedrooms £A**
Check-in all day

Both modern and period styles grace the pretty bedrooms of this large white-painted inn on the A4010. All are spacious and attractively furnished, with colour TVs, direct-dial telephones and tea-makers, and most have neat private bathrooms. Housekeeping is excellent. Guests can relax in the cosy bow-windowed bar, or enjoy the large beer garden at the rear. Accommodation closed one week Christmas. *No children under eight overnight. No dogs.*
Credit Access, Amex, Diners, Visa

SCOLE — Crossways Inn

B&B

Nr Diss
MAP 6 F2 *Norfolk*
Diss (0379) 740638
Parking ample

Landlord Peter Black
Free house
Adnams Bitter; Tolly Cobbold Original; Cameron Hansa; Dortmunder; cider.

ACCOMMODATION **5 bedrooms £B**
Check-in restricted

A 16th-century pub which has been largely modernised, with the beamed bars retaining the most character. Three acres of well-tended gardens at the rear offer a delightful setting for summer drinking. Bedrooms are of a good size, and are attractively decorated in cream, with salmon pink velour chairs; all have radios, and potted plants create a homely atmosphere. Three have modern en suite bathrooms while all have hand basins and toilets.
Credit Access, Visa

SCOLE — Scole Inn

B & B

Nr Diss
MAP 6 F2 *Norfolk*
Diss (0379) 740481
Parking ample

Landlord Bob Nylk
Free house
Adnams Bitter; Greene King Abbot Ale; Webster Yorkshire Bitter; Worthington Best Bitter; Tennent's Lager; Carling Black Label; cider.

***ACCOMMODATION* 23 bedrooms £B**
Check-in all day

A former coaching inn and now a listed building, this impressive inn boasts plenty of atmosphere and character. The main bar has sturdy oak furniture and an enormous inglenook fireplace. Four of the spacious main house bedrooms have four-posters, and all have solid antique furniture as well as modern accessories and well-appointed bathrooms. To the rear, a converted stable block houses a dozen more compact but no less well equipped rooms.
Credit Access, Amex, Diners, Visa

SEAHOUSES — Olde Ship Hotel

B & B

Seahouses
MAP 4 D1 *Northumberland*
Seahouses (0665) 720200
Parking ample

Landlords Alan & Jean Glen
Free house
McEwan's Scotch Bitter, 80/–; Newcastle Exhibition, Bitter; Guinness; McEwan's Lager; cider.

***ACCOMMODATION* 12 bedrooms £C**
Check-in all day

Overlooking the picturesque harbour, this family-run inn caters for both visitors and the local fishermen, who can often be heard placing their orders over the shortwave radio in the splendidly nautical main bar. There's also an intimate little cocktail bar and a homely traditional residents' lounge. Bedrooms are cosy and simply furnished. Most have their own neat bathrooms and all have TVs. Accommodation is closed November to March. *No dogs.*

SEDGEFIELD — Dun Cow Inn

B & B

43 Front Street
MAP 4 D2 *Co. Durham*
Sedgefield (0740) 20894
Parking ample

Landlord Geoff Rayner
Free house
McEwan's 80/-, Scotch; Younger's No 3; Newcastle Exhibition; Guinness; Carlsberg; cider.

***ACCOMMODATION* 6 bedrooms £C**
Check-in all day

Colourful window boxes and hanging baskets festoon this white-painted old pub in summer, and it's just as inviting within. Burgundy banquettes, pretty drapes and photographs of old Sedgefield lend a cosy, homely air to the main bar. Spacious bedrooms in mock rustic style have darkwood furniture, brass light fittings and thoughtful extras like fruit, sweets, tea-makers and TVs. Smart, carpeted public bath/shower rooms. Terrace.
Credit Access, Amex, Diners, Visa

SELLACK — Lough Pool Inn

FOOD

Ross-on-Wye
MAP 5 A2 *Hereford & Worcester*
Harewood End (098 987) 236
Parking ample

Bar food 12–1.30 & 7–9.30
Landlords Paul & Karen Whitford
Free house
Bass; Mitchells & Butlers Springfield Bitter; Hereford Bitter; Guinness; Tennent's Lager; Carling Black Label; cider.

Situated in a dip on the Hoarwithy-Bridstow road, this 16th-century former cider house oozes old-world charm. Under the beams in the bar you can enjoy traditional and more elaborate snacks, from deep-fried Brie or Stilton and port pâté to seafood lasagne and trout stuffed with crab, spinach and almonds. Sweets include ice creams, sorbets and fruit pies. Garden.
Typical prices Mushrooms with garlic mayonnaise £1.85 Garlic chicken £4.20

SEMLEY — Benett Arms

FOOD
B & B

Nr Shaftesbury
MAP 5 B3 *Wiltshire*
East Knoyle (074 783) 221
Parking ample

Bar food 12–2 (Sun till 1.30) & 7–10

Landlord Joseph Duthie
Brewery Gibbs Mew
Gibbs Mew Salisbury Best; Godson Chudley Bitter, Black Horse; Guinness; Harp; Carlsberg Export; cider.

An old-fashioned pub in rolling countryside run by welcoming hosts Joe and Annie Duthie. Open fires and rustic furniture create a pleasing atmosphere in the bar, where a good variety of food is on offer. Home-made soup, ploughman's, sandwiches (on request), omelettes and assorted salads cater for lighter appetites, while hungrier customers can tuck into steak and kidney pie, Wiltshire ham, egg and chips, trout, gammon, rump or sirloin steak and chilli con carne. There are home-made sweets such as Benett sundae, chocolate mousse and apple pie, together with a selection of Loseley ice creams and sorbets. Traditional roast available on Sundays.
Typical prices Venison pie £3 Banana split £1.60

ACCOMMODATION **5 bedrooms £C**
Check-in all day

A modern annexe contains bedrooms with correspondingly modern units, while those in the main house are traditionally furnished. All are well-kept and equipped with colour TVs, tea and coffee making facilities and up-to-date bathrooms, some with shower only.

Credit Access, Amex, Diners, Visa

SENNEN COVE — Old Success Inn

B & B

Land's End
MAP 9 A3 *Cornwall*
Sennen (073 687) 232
Parking ample

Landlord Mr F. Carroll
Free house
Bass; Worthington Bitter; Guinness; Carling Black Label; Tennent's Lager; cider.

Recent refurbishment has raised accommodation to new high standards at this 17th-century fisherman's inn on the sea front. Many of the bedrooms enjoy fine views and all now have modern private facilities as well as quality pine furniture (one has a four-poster). Duvets, hairdryers and tea-makers are provided. The bar and spacious residents' lounge have also been stylishly updated. Patio. Children are accommodated overnight. *No dogs.*
Credit Visa

ACCOMMODATION **11 bedrooms £C**
Check-in all day

SEVENOAKS — NEW ENTRY — Royal Oak

FOOD
B & B

Upper High Street
MAP 7 D3 *Kent*
Sevenoaks (0732) 451109
Parking limited

Bar food 12–2 & 6.30–10

Landlords Mr & Mrs M. R. Rix
Free house
Fremlins Bitter; Trophy Bitter; Heineken; Carling Black Label.

Visitors to nearby Knowle get a friendly welcome at this handsome Georgian pub with a cosy bar furnished with stripped antique pine tables and chairs. The menu, written on a blackboard changes regularly. You can snack on a ploughman's, home-made pâtés and quiches, tagliatelle, or the very popular steak sandwich; or tuck into simple grills, excellent chargrilled pork steaks or a generous portion of succulent skate wings served with a crisp salad. Enjoyable sweets include crème brûlée, apple

ACCOMMODATION **21 bedrooms £C**
Check-in all day

strudel and hazelnut meringue.
Typical prices Skate wing & tomato £2 Smoked chicken & bacon £4.25

The hotel is popular with overnight visitors. Individually furnished bedrooms with designer fabrics and free-standing furniture range from compact singles to bright, spacious doubles. Beds all have duvets, and standard features include clock-radios, teamakers, and carpeted bathrooms (two singles have showers). There is a small conservatory-style lounge. Accommodation closed three days Christmas.

Credit Access, Diners, Visa

SHALFLEET **New Inn**

OD

Yarmouth Road
MAP 5 C4 *Isle of Wight*
Isle of Wight (0983) 78314
Parking ample

Bar food 12–2.30 (till 2 in winter) & 7–9.30, Sun 12–1.30 & 7–9.30

Landlord Nigel Simpson
Brewery Whitbread
Whitbread Pompey Royal, Strong Country; Wethered Bitter; Flowers Original; Guinness; Stella Artois; cider.

Marine delights like garlic mussels, a shellfish cocktail or a pint of prawns in the shell get you off to a good start at this characterful country pub. All sorts of local fish including conger eels turn up on ex-fisherman Nigel Simpson's menu, but there are also meat pies and pasties, ploughman's, sandwiches, and a traditional Sunday roast. Expect to share a table with fellow fish-lovers. Garden.
Typical prices Moules marinière £2 Poacher's meat pie £3.95

SHAMLEY GREEN **Red Lion**

OD
& B

Nr Guildford
MAP 6 D3 *Surrey*
Guildford (0483) 892202
Parking ample

Bar food 12–2.30 & 7–10.30

Landlord Mr P. Yates
Brewery Friary Meux
Friary Meux Bitter; Red Lion Bitter; Ind Coope Burton Ale; Guinness; Löwenbräu; cider.

ACCOMMODATION **4 bedrooms £D**
Check-in restricted

★ ★

Now under new management, this appealing white pebbledash pub on the village green has the added attraction of some tasteful redecoration in its welcoming bar. An imaginative bar menu includes baguettes filled with delicious fresh crab, unusual toasted sandwiches like Camembert and cranberries or Brie and salami, salad niçoise, and a well flavoured tomato soup, made with onions and cream. Bigger appetites can enjoy a plateful of stuffed mussels, or tender lamb cutlets with rosemary. Everything is home-made and portions are generous. Nice desserts range from raspberry romanoff to treacle tart. Traditional Sunday roast. There's also a little bistro-style restaurant. Garden.
Typical prices Chicken indienne £3.45 Lemon sole £4.95 Chicken & ham pie salad £3.25 Cherry & banana pie £1.75

Spacious, bright rooms have pretty fabrics, duvets and antique furniture. They share a large modern bathroom. Children accommodated overnight. *No dogs.*

Credit Access, Amex, Diners, Visa

SHAVE CROSS — Shave Cross Inn

FOOD

Marshwood Vale, Nr Bridport
MAP 9 C2 *Dorset*
Broadwindsor (0308) 68358
Parking ample

Bar food 12–1.45 (Sun till 1.30) & 7–9.30
Closed Mon (except Bank Hols)

Landlords Mr & Mrs Slade
Free house
Hall & Woodhouse Badger Best; Bass; Royal Oak; Guinness; Carlsberg; Carling Black Label; cider.

Set in the beautiful Marshwood Vale, this thatched, 14th-century inn exudes period charm; the beamed bars have exposed stone, rustic furniture and an inglenook fireplace. A simple range of cold bar snacks includes a variety of ploughman's, salads (fresh lobster and salmon in season), and basket meals in the evenings. Sweets include traditional Dorset apple cake. Garden and adventure playground for children.
Typical prices Ploughman's £1.05 Lobster with salad from £5.50

SHELLEY — Three Acres Inn

B & B

Roydhouse, Nr Huddersfield
MAP 4 D4 *West Yorkshire*
Huddersfield (0484) 602606
Parking ample

Landlords Derrick & Neil Truelove & Brian Orme
Free house
Tetley Bitter, Mild; Younger's IPA, No 3, Scotch; Beck's Bier; cider.

ACCOMMODATION **10 bedrooms £B**
Check-in all day

The nearby Cemley television mast provides a useful guide to this stone-built, family-run pub high up in the Pennines above Huddersfield. The homely bedrooms with pine furniture have teamakers, TVs, radio-alarms and neat, carpeted bathrooms. Some have showers. The beamed bar is in a comfortable, traditional style, and there are plans to extend the residents' lounge. Terrace. *No dogs.*
Credit Access, Amex, Visa

SHENINGTON — Bell

FOOD
B & B

Nr Banbury
MAP 7 B1 *Oxfordshire*
Edge Hill (029 587) 274
Parking ample

Bar food 12–2.30 & 7–11

Landlords Mr & Mrs K. Brewer
Free house
Flowers Original, IPA, Best Bitter; Whitbread Poacher; Stella Artois; Heineken; cider.

ACCOMMODATION **4 bedrooms £D**
Check-in all day

Keith and Vanessa Brewer offer guests the friendliest welcome to their attractive 18th-century pub near the village green. Mrs Brewer's menus are full of invention and interest and her cooking is to a consistently high standard. From the daily-changing menu you might choose creamy onion soup or mixed seafood pâté for a starter, followed by bobotie, kidneys à la crème, shrimps Phoebe or creamy spiced chicken. Finish with a first-class peach and almond tart. The freshest ingredients are used and vegetables and rice are cooked to perfection.
Typical prices Mixed seafood casserole £4.75 Chicken & broccoli divan £4.25 Sausages in red wine £4 Fruit pavlova £1.95

The four bedrooms are decorated in country style, with floral wallcoverings and pine furniture. Sloping ceilings accentuate the warm and cosy atmosphere. One has its own shower and toilet; the other three share a simple bathroom.

SHEPPERTON — Anchor Hotel

B&B

Church Square
MAP 7 C3 *Middlesex*
Walton-on-Thames (0932) 221618
Parking limited

Landlord Mr Goddard
Free house
Flowers Original; Whitbread Trophy; Eldridge Pope Dorset Original IPA, Royal Oak; Faust Pilsner; cider.

ACCOMMODATION **24 bedrooms £B**
Check-in all day

Overlooking a square once notorious for its bare-knuckle prize fights, this sturdy old Thames-side inn has 400 years of history behind it. The bar, much friendlier today, still retains some of its original beams and lovely carved oak paneling. Double-glazed bedrooms, most furnished in modern style with simple colour schemes, all have compact shower rooms. Standard accessories include direct-dial phones, TVs and teamakers. Patio.
Credit Access, Amex, Diners, Visa

SHEPPERTON — King's Head

A

Church Square
MAP 7 C3 *Middlesex*
Walton-on-Thames (0932) 221910
Parking ample

Landlord Mr D.K. Longhurst
Brewery Courage
Courage Directors, Best Bitter, JC, Bitter, Ale; Guinness; Kronenbourg; cider.

A 300-year-old inn which apparently once provided accommodation for Nell Gwyn. Its position facing on to a quaint little square close to the Thames gives it immediate appeal, and once you get inside, the cosy main bar with an inglenook fireplace is a welcoming spot. This is deservedly popular and often crowded but you can hunt out a quiet corner in one of the tiny rooms that lead off from the main bar. There's a patio and garden, too, for when the weather's fine. **LVs**

SHEPPERTON — Thames Court

FOOD

Towpath
MAP 7 C3 *Middlesex*
Walton-on-Thames (0932) 221957
Parking ample

Bar food 12–2.15 (Sun 12–2) & May–Sept only 6–9.30 (Sun 7–9.30)

Landlords Jim & Matthew Negus
Free house
Bass; Charrington IPA; Stones Bitter; Guinness; Tennent's Extra; Carling Black Label; cider.

This handsome brick-built pub enjoys a garden setting by the Thames. In the food area – now attractively refurbished using antique Delft tiles – a tempting cold buffet is laid out. There's always a couple of hot dishes – perhaps beef curry and delicious roast pork – plus jacket potatoes, sandwiches and several sweets. Restaurant meals, too.
Typical prices Wholemeal quiche lorraine £1.15 Roast beef & Yorkshire pudding £3
Credit Access, Visa

SHEPPERTON — Warren Lodge

B&B

Church Square
MAP 7 C3 *Middlesex*
Walton-on-Thames (0932) 42972
Parking limited

Landlord Douglas Gordon
Free house
Whitbread Tankard; Heineken.
No real ale.

ACCOMMODATION **45 bedrooms £A**
Check-in all day

Enthusiastic owners add to the appeal of this 18th-century house in a lovely riverside setting. The simple bar offers warm surroundings, while there's a terrace and garden for al fresco summer drinking. The bedrooms, housed in two modern wings, are generally of a good size, with modern fitted furniture and light colour schemes. All are supplied with hairdryers, direct-dial phones, tea/coffee-makers, drinks' fridges and en suite bathrooms. *No dogs.*
Credit Access, Amex, Diners, Visa

SHEPTON MALLET — Kings Arms

B & B Leg Square
MAP 9 D1 *Somerset*
Shepton Mallet (0749) 3781
Parking ample

Landlords Mr and Mrs P.W. Swan
Brewery Hall
Hall's Harvest Bitter, Barleycorn; Wadworth 6X; Ind Coope Burton Ale; Gibbs Mew Bishop's Tipple; Guinness, cider.
ACCOMMODATION **3 bedrooms £D**
Check-in all day

Built in the 17th century from local stone, this handsome pub became a favourite of nearby quarry workers and is still affectionately known to many as the 'Dusthole'. Today's visitors can be sure of spotlessly clean accommodation in three comfortable, traditionally furnished bedrooms which share a modern carpeted bathroom. There is a relaxing residents' lounge with TV, too, and the three beamed bars are full of character. Good breakfasts. Patio. *No children under ten overnight.*

We welcome bona fide recommendations or complaints on the tear-out pages for readers' comments.

They are followed up by our professional team but do complain to the management.

SHIPLAKE — Baskerville Arms

B & B Station Road, Nr Henley
MAP 7 C3 *Oxfordshire*
Wargrave (073 522) 3332
Parking ample

Landlords Mr & Mrs D. J. Tomlin
Brewery Whitbread
Wethered Bitter, Spa, Winter Royal (in season); Flowers Original; Guinness; Heineken; cider.
ACCOMMODATION **3 bedrooms £D**
Check-in restricted

Having recently chalked up its 50 years, this friendly inn, next to Shiplake station, offers a traditional pint and clean, but simple accommodation. Downstairs is one big bar with conventional decor and furniture and a lively pub atmosphere. Upstairs, where the noise sometimes carries, the three neat bedrooms have old-fashioned furnishings with washbasins, and a shared bathroom and shower. All rooms have own TVs. Terrace.

SHIPSTON-ON-STOUR — Bell Inn

B & B Sheep Street
MAP 7 B1 *Warwickshire*
Shipston-on-Stour (0608) 61443
Parking ample

Landlords Mr & Mrs Edward Fila
Brewery Whitbread
Flowers Original; Whitbread Best Bitter; guest beer; Guinness; Stella Artois; Heineken; cider.
ACCOMMODATION **7 bedrooms £D**
Check-in all day

Comfortable overnight accommodation is provided at this town-centre inn, which dates from 1730. Large floral print fabrics are pleasing in the bedrooms, which are centrally heated and have tea-makers, trouser presses and TVs with free in-house movies; three have their own spacious bathrooms. There are two bars, the public one in simple traditional style, the lounge with exposed stonework and a log fire in winter. Patio.
Credit Amex, Diners, Visa

SHIPSTON-ON-STOUR **White Bear**

FOOD
B & B

High Street
MAP 7 B1 *Warwickshire*
Shipston-on-Stour (0608) 61558
Parking ample

Bar food 12–2 & 6.30–9.30
No bar food Sun

Landlords Suzanne & Hugh Roberts
Free house
Bass; Mitchells & Butlers Brew XI, Springfield Bitter; Guinness; Carling Black Label; Tennent's Pilsner; cider.

Under the expert direction of Suzanne and Hugh Roberts this town centre pub has become a very popular eating place over the years. The busy bar with its pine furnishings and rural feel offers a tempting array of above average bar food. Starters like tasty tomato and basil soup or coronation chicken herald in home-made dishes of the day – perhaps carbonnade of beef, Stilton and walnut quiche or moussaka, all competently cooked and enjoyable. The regular menu features salads and steaks and additional lunchtime bites are well filled baguettes and sandwiches. Delicious sweets, too.
Typical prices Beef & Guinness pie £3.95 Chicken stuffed with spinach £3.75 **LVs**

***ACCOMMODATION* 10 bedrooms £C**
Check-in all day

Sloping ceilings and creaking floors add character to the pretty bedrooms, which have a cottagy appeal. All are individually decorated with attractive fabrics and wallpapers, some with modern furniture, some with period pieces. Each has its own bathroom, TV and tea/coffee making facilities. Patio.

Our inspectors never book in the name of Egon Ronay's Guides; they disclose their identity only after paying their bills.

SHIPTON-UNDER-WYCHWOOD **Lamb Inn**

FOOD
B & B

High Street
MAP 7 B2 *Oxfordshire*
Shipton-under-Wychwood (0993) 830465
Parking ample

Bar food 12.15–2 & 7–10, Sun 12–1.30 & 7.30–9.30

Landlords Hugh & Lynne Wainwright
Free house
Hook Norton Best Bitter, Old Hookey (winter only); Wadworth 6X; Guinness; cider.

You can depend on good-quality bar food cooked to a high standard at this delightful old inn on the edge of the village. The handsome beamed bar with its bare walls of Cotswold stone is furnished with wooden settles and Windsor chairs, and burns a welcoming log fire – a most agreeable setting for a snack. Tasty starters include hot buttered shrimps on toast and a soup of the day. Then its hard to choose between local pink trout with new potatoes, perfectly cooked ham and eggs, and the chef's ever popular Cotswold pie. In summer there's a lunchtime cold table. Sunday's traditional roast is served in the restaurant and there's only a limited choice in the bar. Terrace.
Typical prices George's Cotswold pie £3.50 Scandinavian hash £3

***ACCOMMODATION* 5 bedrooms £C**
Check-in all day

Light, airy and impeccably-kept cottage-style bedrooms at the top of a steep staircase are blissfully quiet. All have en suite carpeted bathrooms, TVs, radios and tea-makers. Accommodation closed one week Christmas. *No children under 14 overnight. No dogs.*
Credit Access, Amex, Diners, Visa

SHIPTON-UNDER-WYCHWOOD **Shaven Crown Hotel**

FOOD
B & B

High Street
MAP 7 B2 *Oxfordshire*
Shipton-under-Wychwood (0993) 830330
Parking ample

Bar food 12–2 & 7–9.30, Sun 12–1.30 & 7–9
Landlords Brookes family
Free house
Hook Norton Best Bitter; Flowers Original, Best Bitter; Heineken; Tuborg Gold; cider.

A strong sense of history pervades this lovely 14th century inn where once the monks played host. Perhaps the most impressive room is the medieval hall, now the reception/lounge. Today, in the hospitable Buttery bar across from the lounge bar, a blackboard menu offers a thoughtful variety of snacks, including a nicely prepared babouti (South African curried meat loaf) as well as whitebait, steaks, garlic mushrooms, chicken and mushroom pie, and spinach and bacon lasagne. Also available are traditional favourites like pâté, soups, ploughman's and sandwiches. Sweets include a good choice of home-made ices and fruit pies. Patio.

Typical prices Mushroom & walnut pancake £2.65 Ice cream from 85p

ACCOMMODATION **8 bedrooms £B**
Check-in all day

Cottage-style bedrooms, of different sizes, are traditionally furnished and spotlessly clean. There's one huge family room that was once the monks' chapel. Most rooms have en suite carpeted bathrooms and there are two public bathrooms. TVs and tea-makers in all rooms. *No dogs.*

Credit Access, Visa

SHIRLEY **Saracens Head Hotel**

B & B

Stratford Road
MAP 5 B2 *West Midlands*
021-744 1016
Parking ample

Landlord Michael Stevens
Brewery Ansells
Ansells Bitter, Mild; Tetley Bitter; Guinness; Castlemaine XXXX; Skol; cider.

ACCOMMODATION **34 bedrooms £B**
Check-in all day

On the A34 Birmingham–Stratford road, this substantial hostelry has comfortable, well-equipped modern bedrooms. Attractive pastel colour schemes, brass lamps, prints and lightwood units are common to all rooms, along with double glazing, direct-dial phones, TVs and good private facilities. There are two pleasant bars – a cocktail bar with rattan-backed chairs and another in Victorian style, as well as a patio for summer drinking. Children are welcome overnight. *No dogs.*

Credit Access, Amex, Diners, Visa

SHOREHAM-BY-SEA **Red Lion**

FOOD

Old Shoreham
MAP 6 D4 *West Sussex*
Shoreham (0273) 453171
Parking limited

Bar food 12–2 & 7–9
No bar food Mon eve & all Sun
Landlord Norman Stevens
Brewery Phoenix
Gales HSB; Usher Best Bitter; Webster Yorkshire Bitter; Watney Mild, Special Bitter; Guinness; cider.

This low, white-painted pub was originally a Saxon burial chapel. Things have livened up since then, and there are now two bars (one for non-smokers) with a good range of bar snacks – ploughman's, prawn or chicken salads or freshly made sandwiches – and a choice of hot dishes from chilli con carne to smoked haddock pasta. Try the perennially popular spiced apple cake with walnuts. Garden.

Typical prices Fisherman's pie £2.50 Garlic prawns £3.25

SILK WILLOUGHBY — Horseshoes

FOOD

Nr Sleaford
MAP 6 D1 *Lincolnshire*
Sleaford (0529) 303153
Parking ample

Bar food 12–2 (Sun till 1.45) & 7–10
No bar food Sun eve

Landlord Francisco Cuñago
Brewery John Smith
John Smith's Bitter; Guinness; Kronenbourg; Hofmeister; cider. *No real ale.*

A plush and attractively decorated pub alongside the A15, with subdued lighting and comfortable banquette seating in its roomy bar. The menu changes daily, offering a good variety of well-prepared and satisfying dishes, from cream of cauliflower soup to steak and oyster pie, roast turkey and poached haddock with prawn sauce. Traditional Sunday lunch menu. Garden.
Typical prices Chicken à la crème £3.25 Grilled trout (pair) £3.25
Credit Access, Visa

SINDLESHAM — Walter Arms

FOOD
& B

Bearwood Road
MAP 7 C3 *Berkshire*
Wokingham (0734) 780260
Parking ample

Bar food 12–2 & 7–10

Landlord Ronald William Ballard
Brewery Courage
Courage Best Bitter, Directors, John Courage; Guinness; Kronenbourg; Hofmeister.

Housekeeping is exemplary at this sturdy Victorian roadside pub. Every wooden surface and piece of brassware gleams with polish in the three bars, and open fires contribute to the feeling of homely comfort. The food is hearty and wholesome here, with choices like cold roast pork with a jacket potato, pickle and coleslaw, beef in burgundy and baked haddock florentine, as well as simpler sandwiches, soups, pâté and ploughman's. Particularly good, if decidedly indulgent, sweets include chocolate fudge cake, vicar's delight (ice cream with stem ginger) and lovely sticky treacle tart.
Typical prices Chicken in the pot £2.95 Baked ham £2.25 **LVs**

ACCOMMODATION **4 bedrooms £C**
Check-in restricted

The four spotless bedrooms share a large old-fashioned bathroom and all have TVs. The first-floor twin offers an en suite shower and washbasin, while second-floor rooms are particularly charming with their sloping raftered ceilings and pretty fabrics. Terrace. *No children overnight. No dogs.*

Prices given are as at the time of our research and thus may change.

SKIDBY — Half Moon Inn

FOOD

16 Main Street
MAP 4 E3 *Humberside*
Hull (0482) 843403
Parking ample

Bar food 12–2 & 7–10

Landlord Peter Madeley
Brewery John Smith
John Smith's Bitter, Chestnut Mild; Guinness; Hofmeister; Kronenbourg; cider.

They're ready for healthy appetites at this smart, white-painted pub, where the bar snacks are tasty and satisfying. Giant Yorkshire puddings are the speciality, served in various ways – with onion gravy, chilli, curry or traditional roast beef. Toad and lamb-in-the-hole are other variants, and there are burgers, ploughman's and steak and kidney pie. Large beer garden.
Typical prices Lamb-in-the-hole £2.80 Vegetarian ragout £2
Credit Access, Visa, **LVs**

SLAIDBURN — Hark to Bounty Inn

B & B

Nr Clitheroe
MAP 3 C3 *Lancashire*
Slaidburn (020 06) 246
Parking ample

Landlord Phillip Mason
Free house
John Smith's Bitter, Chestnut; Moorhouses Pendle Witches Brew; Guinness; Hofmeister; Kronenbourg; cider.

***ACCOMMODATION* 8 bedrooms £D**
Check-in all day

Bounty was a particularly vocal member of the local pack of hounds, and this ancient stone pub was renamed after him in Victorian times. The spacious bar has a welcoming air with its open fire, oak furniture and burnished brassware, and there's a homely TV lounge for residents. TVs are provided in the cosy beamed bedrooms, together with radios and tea-makers. All except one have modern private facilities. Garden.
Credit Access, Amex, Diners, Visa

SLEIGHTS — Salmon Leap

B & B

Coach Road, Nr Whitby
MAP 4 E2 *North Yorkshire*
Whitby (0947) 810233
Parking ample

Landlords Adrian Linford Mee
Brewery Cameron
Lion Bitter; Strongarm, Mild; Guinness; Cameron Hansa; cider.

***ACCOMMODATION* 10 bedrooms £D**
Check-in all day

Close to the river Esk and four miles inland from Whitby, this is an ideal stopping place for fishermen and walkers. There are three simple bars with a preponderance of laminate and vinyl, as well as a homely residents' lounge with sofas and easy chairs on the first floor. The compact bedrooms have laminate units, vinyl headboards and tea and coffee making facilities. They share three small, simple bathrooms. Garden.

SMARDEN — Bell

FOOD
B & B

Bell Lane, Nr Ashford
MAP 6 E3 *Kent*
Smarden (023 377) 283
Parking ample

Bar food 12–2 & 6.30–10
Landlord Mr I. J. Turner
Free house
Fremlins Bitter; Shepherd Neame Master Brew Bitter; Goacher's 1066; Theakston Best Bitter, Old Peculier; Young Special; Heineken; cider.

Chequered brickwork overhung with scalloped tiles gives a picturesque charm to this 15th-century inn in a pretty corner of Kent. All three bars have flagstones and beams garlanded with hops and two have inglenook fireplaces. They provide a characterful setting for homely bar food, with a popular choice of grills, pizzas and basket meals, as well as sandwiches, soup and home-made pâté. Evenings are busy, but the Greek shepherd's pie made from prime quality mince is well worth a wait – and tastes even better by candlelight. Limited choice Sunday lunch.
Typical prices Steak & kidney pie £2.95 Clam fries £1.60

***ACCOMMODATION* 4 bedrooms £D**
Check-in restricted

An outside spiral staircase leads to the simply furnished bedrooms over the pub, which have white brick walls and darkwood furniture and ceilings. Floral fabrics provide a welcome splash of colour, and all rooms are equipped with TVs and tea-makers. Continental breakfast is served in the rooms. Garden.
Credit Access, Visa

We publish annually so make sure you use the current edition.

SMARDEN — Chequers Inn

D Nr Ashford
MAP 6 E3 *Kent*
Smarden (023 377) 217
Parking ample

Bar food 10–2.30 & 6–10.45, Sun 12–2 & 7–10.30

Landlord Frank Stevens
Brewery Courage
Courage Best Bitter, Directors; Guinness; Hofmeister; Kronenbourg; cider.

A weatherboarded pub of great character where Frank Stevens exercises his considerable cooking talents. Delicious soups, including French onion, courgette and tomato and celery and cauliflower; main courses range from beef carbonnade to ham and eggs, fresh fish and vegetarian dishes. Pâtés, cold meats and salads, too. Puddings include an excellent raspberry pavlova.
Typical prices Bouillabaisse £2.65 Fillet of pork normande £4.25
Credit Access, Visa

SNAINTON — Coachman Inn

B Nr Scarborough
MAP 4 E3 *North Yorkshire*
Scarborough (0723) 85231
Parking ample

Landlord Mr G. Senior
Brewery Cameron
Cameron Lion Bitter, Strongarm, Hansa; cider.

***ACCOMMODATION* 12 bedrooms £C**
Check-in all day

A jolly landlord and comfortable, well-kept accommodation keep up the tradition of hospitality at this 200-year-old coaching inn in pleasant gardens and paddocks set back from the A170. Neat, good-sized bedrooms – most with their own bath/shower rooms – have modern white free-standing units and floral curtains and bedspreads. There are two bars, and a cosy TV lounge well stocked with flowers and magazines.
Credit Access, Amex, Diners, Visa

Changes in data may occur in establishments after the Guide goes to press. Prices should be taken as indications rather than firm quotes.

SNETTISHAM — Rose & Crown Inn

A Old Church Road, Nr King's Lynn
MAP 6 E1 *Norfolk*
Dersingham (0485) 41382
Parking ample

Landlord Margaret Trafford
Free house
Adnams Bitter; Greene King, Abbot Ale, IPA; Woodforde Norfolk Pride; Webster Yorkshire Bitter; Guinness; cider.

Near to the royal estate at Sandringham, this convivial country pub enjoys a delightfully secluded village setting. Among its three atmospheric bars is one with dark old beams, flagstoned floor and large inglenook fireplace. To the rear, there's a well-maintained walled garden with plenty of wooden tables and bench seating for alfresco drinking – try the freshly squeezed orange or pineapple juices. Staff are friendly and smartly turned out.
Credit Access, Visa

SONNING-ON-THAMES — Bull Inn

FOOD
B & B

High Street
MAP 7 C3 *Berkshire*
Reading (0734) 693901
Parking ample

Bar food 12–2
No bar food eves

Landlord Mr D. T. Catton
Brewery Wethered
Wethered Bitter, SPA, Winter Royal (seasonal); Flowers Original; Heineken; Stella Artois; cider.

Set next to the village church, this 600-year-old inn, its smart black and white facade covered in climbing wistaria, is steeped in picture-postcard charm. Inside, every surface, every glass is spotlessly clean and gleaming; the heavily beamed main bar has a striking inglenook – flower-filled in summer, fire-filled in winter. Here a delicious cold buffet awaits lunchtime visitors: veal and ham pie, Chesham pie, cold meats, Scotch eggs, cheeses and a good selection of salads – rice, pasta, coleslaw plus others – are on display, as well as nice gâteaux and cheesecakes. In winter, there is always home-made soup and a hot dish offered. Patio.
Typical prices Quiche & salad £2.60 Mixed meat salad £3.80

ACCOMMODATION **5 bedrooms £A**
Check-in restricted

Simple, old-fashioned furnishings match the homely feel of the timbered, white-walled bedrooms with tiny paned windows. All rooms are nice and warm with TVs and share a modest but spick-and-span bathroom. Accommodation closed for one week at Christmas. *No children overnight. No dogs.*

SOUTH DALTON — Pipe & Glass

FOOD

West End
MAP 4 E3 *Humberside*
Dalton Holme (069 64) 246
Parking ample

Bar food 12–2 & 7.30–10

Landlord Mr M. A. Crease
Free house
Webster Choice; Ruddles County; Stones Bitter; Guinness; Fosters; Carlsberg; cider.

Three bars cater for different moods and styles at this friendly pub, and there's also a restaurant and a lovely beer garden. A blackboard lists the day's bar fare, which ranges from burgundy mushrooms or Yorkshire pudding with onion gravy to hot smoked mackerel and pork chop in mustard sauce. Also sandwiches, a summer cold table and some sweets. Traditional Sunday lunch.
Typical prices Pheasant pie with vegetables £3 Chicken piri-piri £2.85
Credit Access, Visa

SOUTH LEIGH — Mason Arms

FOOD

Nr Witney
MAP 7 B2 *Oxfordshire*
Witney (0993) 2485
Parking ample

Bar food 12–2 & 7–10
No bar food Mon
Closed Mon
Landlords Ferguson family
Free house
Glenny Witney Bitter; Younger's Scotch; Newcastle Bitter; Guinness; Beck's Bier.

Two flagstoned bars with log fires provide a cosy setting for sandwiches of delicious locally-cured salt beef or a tasty snack of seafood pancakes or savoury pie. A good fresh fruit salad and Black Forest gâteau are sweet choices, and there's a roast lunch on Sunday. The Ferguson's spick-and-span 400-year-old thatched pub has a patio and a delightful garden with peacocks.
Typical prices Steak & kidney pie £3.90 Salt-beef salad £3.90
Credit Access, Visa **LVs**

SOUTH ZEAL — Oxenham Arms

& B

Nr Okehampton
MAP 9 B2 *Devon*
Okehampton (0837) 840244
Parking ample

Landlords Mr & Mrs J. H. Henry
Free house
St Austell Tinners Ale; Hicks Special; Guinness; Stella Artois; Kronenbourg; cider.

***ACCOMMODATION* 8 bedrooms £C**
Check-in all day

Full of mellow charm, this creeper-clad inn (first licensed in 1477) enjoys a quiet village setting just off the A30. The beamed bar is cosy and welcoming, and there's a delightful lounge with comfortable armchairs and the odd antique. Bedrooms, too, mainly feature black beams and antiques with chintzy curtains, combining homeliness with modern amenities like direct-dial phones and colour TVs; six have their own bathrooms. Pretty garden.
Credit Access, Amex, Diners, Visa

SOUTHWOLD — The Crown

OOD & B

High Street
MAP 6 F2 *Suffolk*
Southwold (0502) 722275
Parking ample

Bar food 12.30–2 & 7.30–9.45

Landlord Stephen Bournes
Brewery Adnams
Adnams Bitter, Mild, Old (winter only); Guinness; Stella Artois; Skol.

The handsome front bar of this sympathetically restored 18th-century inn makes a pleasant setting for a pot of coffee or tea, or imaginative bar snacks, which can be enjoyed with a glass of wine from the excellent range on the Cruover machine. The daily-changing menu of very nicely cooked dishes shows a distinct fondness for fish, with Southwold fish soup, poached cod and conger eel, but tasty alternatives include a flavoursome fresh mushroom soup, carefully cooked kidneys in red wine, and confit of duck. Chocolate marquise is a popular sweet. Patio.
Typical prices Warm salad of pigeon breast, soy sauce £2.95 Southwold fish soup £1.20

***ACCOMMODATION* 12 bedrooms £C**
Check-in all day

Quality refurbishment has given a new look to the twelve compact bedrooms. All have pine furniture, TVs, alarm radios and direct-dial telephones. Adnams flamboyant wine list – thoughtfully provided – makes intoxicating bedside reading. Of the neat private bathrooms, nine are en suite, the others are across the corridor.

Credit Access, Amex, Visa

Any person using our name
to obtain free hospitality is a fraud.
Proprietors, please inform
Egon Ronay's Guides and the police.

SPEEN NEW ENTRY Old Plow Inn

FOOD
B & B

Flowers Bottom
MAP 7 C2 *Buckinghamshire*
Hampden Row (024 028) 300
Parking ample

Bar food 12–2
No bar food eves

Landlords Bill & Frances Atkins
Free house
Fullers London Pride, ESB, Morland Bitter; Brakspear Bitter; Guinness; Carlsberg; cider.

***ACCOMMODATION* 3 bedrooms £A**
Check-in all day

★ Built as a forge in 1620, this welcoming inn is run on friendly, professional lines by Bill and Frances Atkins. Original stone tiles, exposed beams and timbers are a feature of the stylish little bar, where uniformed young staff serve the excellent snacks on offer with efficiency and a smile. Frances Atkins' training as a chef shines throughout every dish on the sensibly short lunchtime menu – from thick and creamy mushroom soup, pâtés and terrines to deliciously light turkey pancakes, succulent ham off the bone and superb salads enhanced by fresh herbs. Full evening meals are available in the restaurant. ★

Typical prices Spinach soup £2 Salmon roulade £4 Vegetable moussaka £4 Beef & mushroom casserole £4

Three comfortable bedrooms (two with en suite facilities) are beautifully kept and offer thoughtful extras like fresh flowers, mineral water and magazines. There's a beamed and prettily furnished residents' lounge with TV. Garden.

Credit Access, Amex, Diners, Visa

STAFFORD Swan Hotel

B & B

46 Greengate Street
MAP 5 B1 *Staffordshire*
Stafford (0785) 58142
Parking ample

Landlord John Fiddler
Brewery Ansells
Ind Coope Burton Ale; Ansells Bitter, Mild; Guinness; Skol; Castlemaine XXXX; cider. *No real ale.*

***ACCOMMODATION* 32 bedrooms £B**
Check-in all day

This town centre hotel offers pleasant overnight accommodation. There are two bars, one encompassing a covered, quarry-tiled courtyard, the other with comfortable green plush seating. Bedrooms are decent-sized and have recently been refurbished with attractive pine freestanding furniture and warm decor. All have remote control TVs, trouser presses, tea/coffee-makers and bathrooms with shower facilities. Patio. *No dogs.*
Credit Access, Amex, Diners, Visa

STAMFORD Bull & Swan Inn

B & B

St Martins
MAP 6 D1 *Lincolnshire*
Stamford (0780) 63558
Parking ample

Landlords William & Rosa Morgado
Brewery Melbourn
Samuel Smith's Old Brewery Bitter, Mild, Sovereign; Guinness; Diät Pils; Ayingerbräu; cider.

***ACCOMMODATION* 6 bedrooms £D**
Check-in all day

Parts of this charming coaching inn to the south of the town centre date back to the 12th century, and the interior is suitably atmospheric, with its highly polished brass and copper pieces adorning the spacious beamed bar. Smart burgundy velour seating and three open fires add to the cosy, welcoming effect. Simply furnished bedrooms (front ones are double glazed) all have washbasins and TVs and share two carpeted public bathrooms.
Credit Visa

STAMFORD — Crown Hotel

B

All Saints Place
MAP 6 D1 *Lincolnshire*
Stamford (0780) 63136
Parking ample
Landlords R. D. & E. W. McGahon
Free house
Ruddles County; Ind Coope Burton Ale; Ansells Bitter; Guinness; Heineken; Stella Artois; cider.

ACCOMMODATION **18 bedrooms £C**
Check-in all day

Dating back to 1678, this handsome hotel stands in the heart of town overlooking All Saints Church. Fresh flowers add a homely, welcoming touch to public areas like the comfortable bar and stone-walled lounge. Spacious, neatly kept bedrooms – most with private bathrooms – are furnished in simple, modern style and all have TVs, telephones and tea-makers. Excellent nearby fishing facilities – including instruction.
Credit Access, Amex, Diners, Visa

STAMFORD — George of Stamford

OD
B

71 St Martin's High Street
MAP 6 D1 *Lincolnshire*
Stamford (0780) 55171
Parking ample
Bar food 12–2 & 7–10
Landlord Jolyon Gough
Free house
Samuel Smith's Old Brewery Bitter; Ruddles Rutland Bitter; Beck's Bier; Carlsberg; Kestrel. *No real ale.*

The airy garden lounge with its exotic plants and summery white furniture is a delightful setting in which to enjoy the first-class snacks served at this renowned 16th-century coaching inn. A fine display of roast meats, poached salmon, salads, good cheeses and delicious sweets makes up the magnificent cold buffet, while hot choices include minestrone, ravioli in a creamy mushroom sauce and seafood pancakes. Alternative eating venues include the elegant lounge with its open log fire, and the pretty walled garden. An excellent restaurant offers a traditional roast on Sundays.
Typical prices Chicken winglets in a barbecue sauce £3.95 Skate wings in a brown butter lemon sauce £4.95

ACCOMMODATION **47 bedrooms £A**
Check-in all day

Stunning bedrooms (including four with four-posters) are individually decorated to a very high standard and feature stylish fabrics, quality furniture and modern accessories such as hairdryers, trouser presses and digital radio-alarms. All have TVs, phones and well-equipped private bathrooms.
Credit Access, Amex, Diners, Visa

STANFORD DINGLEY — Old Boot Inn

OD

Nr Bradfield
MAP 7 B3 *Berkshire*
Bradfield (0734) 744292
Parking ample
Bar food 12–2 & 6–9.30
Landlords Mr & Mrs J.M. Pratt
Free house
John Arkell Bitter; Theakston Best Bitter; Fullers London Pride; Ruddles County; Guinness; Stella Artois.

Slightly off the beaten track, this well-kept 18th-century pub in a pretty village offers some enjoyable eating in its welcoming beamed bar. The simple choice includes grills, liver and bacon braised in Guinness, roast beef salad, snacks like garlicky mushrooms and bacon on toast and pleasant home-made sweets. More elaborate evening meals Wed–Sat. Traditional Sunday lunch menu also available. Garden.
Typical prices Jambon à la crème £3.75 Steak & kidney pie £3.95

STANTON HARCOURT — Harcourt Arms

FOOD
B & B

Nr Eynsham
MAP 7 B2 *Oxfordshire*
Oxford (0865) 882192
Parking ample

Bar food 12–2.30 & 6–10.30

Landlord George Dailey
Free house
Wadworth 6X; Harvey Best Bitter; Castlemaine XXXX; Löwenbräu; cider.

ACCOMMODATION **10 bedrooms £B**
Check-in all day

★ You're just as welcome popping in for a quick bowl of steaming mussels or a sandwich as you are for a full meal in George Dailey's friendly 18th-century pub. His excellent food, based on good fresh ingredients, is now all served in the extended bistro-style restaurant: snacks, set meals, specials and à la carte. Firm favourites are Indonesian satay, steaks, good fish and chips, and a hard-to-resist seafood pie packed with prawns, scallops and firm white fish. Go for the excellent crème brûlée if offered. Traditional Sunday lunch available. ★

Typical prices Reverend Mee's smoked haddock crumble £5.50 King prawns £2.95 Steak & kidney pie £5.95 Raw spinach salad with bacon & croûtons £2.75

In cottages just a few steps away, ten bedrooms with sloping ceilings, floral wallpapers and nice furnishings, provide comfortable accommodation (one has a four-poster). All have warm, modern bathrooms. Patio. *No children under ten overnight.*

Credit Access, Amex, Diners, Visa

We welcome bona fide recommendations or complaints on the tear-out pages for readers' comments.

They are followed up by our professional team but do complain to the management.

STAPLE FITZPAINE — Greyhound Inn

FOOD

Nr Taunton
MAP 9 C1 *Somerset*
Hatch Beauchamp (0823) 480227
Parking ample

Bar food 11.30–2 & 6.30–10, Sun 12–2 & 7–10

Landlords David Townsend & Paul Aiston
Free house
Golden Hill Exmoor Ale; Wadworth 6X; Eldridge Pope Royal Oak; Guinness; Carlsberg; Stella Artois; cider.

Winding lanes lead from the A358 to this creeper-clad pub. Wholemeal bread and pasta, steamed vegetables and many vegetarian specialities feature on the enterprising menu, where you'll find some unusual combinations. There are a few meat dishes, too, plus excellent cheeses and sweets. Outdoor adventure play area. Terrace.

Typical prices Pasta with a bacon and cream sauce £2.90 Breaded mushrooms £1.95

Credit Access, Visa

STAPLETON — Bridge Inn

●D Nr Darlington
MAP 4 D2 *Co. Durham*
Darlington (0325) 50106
Parking ample

Bar food 12–2.30 & 7–9.30
No bar food Sun & Mon eves

Landlords Nicholas & Catherine Young
Brewery Vaux
Vaux Samson; Lorimer Best Scotch; Guinness; Stella Artois; cider.

★ A relaxed, unpretentious pub where landlord Nick Young gratifies his love of cooking to the delight of his appreciative customers. The usual ploughman's, sandwiches and salads are on offer for light snacks, as well as a popular home-made beefburger, and black pudding to add a regional flavour. The daily-changing blackboard menu is strong on fish – brill, turbot and sole are favourites. You might start with an excellent chicken terrine with Cognac before moving on to lamb's kidney with Dijon mustard, wine and cream, accompanied by delicious crisp vegetables. Finish with mouthwatering chocolate brandy cake. A good selection of English cheeses is frequently available. Traditional Sunday lunch menu also available. ★

Typical prices Roast leg of lamb with garlic & thyme £4.25 Braised ham with sage & onion sauce £2.75 Breast of lamb with crispy onion crust & tomato sauce £3.25 Peach with raspberry & port purée £2

Credit Access, Amex, Diners, Visa

STARBOTTON — Fox & Hounds

A Nr Kettlewell, Upper Wharfdale
MAP 3 C3 *North Yorkshire*
Kettlewell (075 676) 269
Parking ample
Landlord Ann Wilkinson
Free house
Theakston Best Bitter, Old Peculier, XB; Carlsberg; cider.

This smart, white-painted little pub is in a lovely village in the heart of the Yorkshire Dales. Inside there's a tiny bar; the stone-flagged floor, rough walls and splendid, old open fireplace all add to the air of sturdy, rural charm. Simple, wooden chairs and tables furnish the bar – which is especially cosy in winter – and you can drink outdoors on the patio on warmer days.

Credit Access, Visa

STAVELEY — Royal Oak

●D Nr Knaresborough
MAP 4 D3 *North Yorkshire*
Copgrove (090 14) 267
Parking ample

Bar food 12–2
No bar food eves

Landlords Mr & Mrs P. Gallagher
Brewery Younger
Younger's Scotch; McEwan's Lager; cider.

The Gallaghers put a lot of love into the running of their village pub and it shows in the welcoming atmosphere and delicious food. From the daily-changing menu you could choose pâté, followed perhaps by a flavour-filled game pie with perfect pastry. Lighter snacks include a selection of salads and sandwiches. Traditional roast on Sundays, plus an interesting restaurant menu.

Typical prices Smoked trout salad £3.45 Steak & kidney pie £3.50

Credit Access

STAVERTON — Sea Trout Inn

B & B

Nr Totnes
MAP 9 C2 *Devon*
Staverton (080 426) 274
Parking ample
Landlord Andrew M. Mogford
Free house
Hall's Plympton Pride, Harvest Bitter; Bass; Guinness; Castlemaine XXXX; Löwenbräu; cider.
***ACCOMMODATION* 6 bedrooms £C**
Check-in restricted

Displays of mounted fish, fishing flies and stags' heads give a huntin', shootin', fishin' touch to this modernised old roadside inn. The lounge bar is plush, with red banquette seating, while the Village bar is the place for darts and fruit machines. Bedrooms, which share two modern bathrooms, are furnished in simple, cottagy style and have wash-basins and tea-makers. Andrew Mogford keeps the inn spotless and is planning re-decoration. Patio.
Credit Access, Amex, Diners, Visa

STEEP — Harrow Inn

FOOD

Nr Petersfield
MAP 5 C3 *Hampshire*
Petersfield (0730) 62685
Parking limited
Bar food 12–2 & 6.15–10
Landlord Eddie McCutcheon
Brewery Whitbread
Samuel Whitbread, West Country Pale Ale; Stella Artois; Heineken; cider.

The McCutcheon family take great pride in the running of their friendly village pub, from the pretty wild flower arrangements that adorn the cosy beamed bars to the top-quality, home-made bar food served there. Tender roast beef, ham or cheese, with fresh salads, can be enjoyed in sandwiches or as a ploughman's with hunks of fresh crusty bread. Excellent soup and other hot dishes are also available. Garden.
Typical prices Ham ploughman's £3.50 Home-made soup £1.20

STEEPLE ASTON — NEW ENTRY — Red Lion

FOOD

Oxford
MAP 7 B1 *Oxfordshire*
Steeple Aston (0869) 40225
Parking limited
Bar food 12–2
No bar food eves & all Sun
Landlords Colin & Margaret Mead
Free house
Hook Norton Best Bitter; Hall & Woodhouse Tanglefoot; Wadworth 6X; Tuborg Gold, Pilsner.

A delightfully traditional pub nestling in a handsome Oxfordshire village, and a lovely setting in which to enjoy Margaret Mead's accomplished home cooking. Creamy onion soup and pâté stuffed mushrooms are both enjoyable and popular choices, and there's also a tasty selection of sandwiches. There's usually a fresh fish dish and a well prepared casserole. Good puddings, too.
Typical prices Rare beef sandwich £1.15 Pork & bean hot pot £2.20
Credit Access, Visa

STEWKLEY — Swan

FOOD

Nr Leighton Buzzard
MAP 7 C1 *Buckinghamshire*
Stewkley (052 524) 285
Parking ample
Bar food 12–2 & 7–9.30
No bar food Fri & Sat eves & all Sun
Landlords Colin & Carole Anderson
Brewery Courage
Courage Directors, Best Bitter, John Courage; Guinness; Kronenbourg; Hofmeister; cider.

The Andersons run this rustic village pub with great enthusiasm. Carole's splendid bar snacks include Cumberland sausages with home-made coleslaw and chicken in butter sauce supplemented by a winter-warming broth and salmon mayonnaise in summer. Charcoal grills and fish dishes available in the restaurant at night, delicious desserts. Garden.
Typical prices Smoked salmon sandwich £3.50 Kidney turbigo £2.95
Credit Access, Amex **LVs**

STOCKBRIDGE NEW ENTRY Grosvenor Hotel

B & B

High Street
MAP 5 C3 *Hampshire*
Andover (0264) 810606
Parking ample

Landlords Linda & Graham Atkins
Brewery Whitbread
Strong Country Bitter; Whitbread Best Bitter; Heineken; Stella Artois; cider.

***ACCOMMODATION* 25 bedrooms £B**
Check-in all day

The world's most exclusive fishing club has its headquarters at this refurbished Georgian-style hotel near the River Test. Pictures of racehorses decorate the cosy bar, and there is a small first-floor residents' lounge. Bedrooms – half in a converted stable block – have pastel decor and mahogany furniture. Modern comforts include alarm-radios, hairdryers, trouser presses and tea-makers, as well as well-equipped carpeted bathrooms. Garden. *No dogs.*
Credit Access, Amex, Diners, Visa

STOCKBRIDGE Vine

FOOD
B & B

High Street
MAP 5 C3 *Hampshire*
Andover (0264) 810652
Parking ample

Bar food 12–2 & 7–10
No bar food Sun eve

Landlords Mike & Vanessa Harding
Brewery Whitbread
Flowers Original; Whitbread Strong Country Bitter, Best Bitter; Guinness; Heineken; Stella Artois; cider.

This friendly high street pub of 16th-century origin, with a trout steam running through its garden, is a pleasant spot to enjoy some accomplished home cooking. Fish features extensively on the menu – local trout, plaice, Dover sole, moules marinière, and even salmon quiche – together with steaks, gammon, turkey in a lovely fruity curry sauce, lasagne and salads. Tasty quick bites include deep-fried Camembert and to finish there's a choice of delicious sweets, perhaps passion fruit ice cream.
Typical prices Grilled local trout £3 Lasagne £3.25

***ACCOMMODATION* 3 bedrooms £D**
Check-in all day

Three cosy bedrooms sharing a large well-kept bathroom comprise the overnight accommodation. Two of the rooms are attractively furnished with natural pine fittings whilst the other room has more traditional pieces. All have colour TVs. In the morning, a large, good quality breakfast will set you up for the day. Children are welcome overnight. Accommodation closed one week Christmas.
Credit Access, Amex, Diners, Visa

STOKE-BY-NAYLAND Angel Inn

FOOD
B & B

MAP 6 E2 *Suffolk*
Colchester (0206) 263245
Parking ample

Bar food 12–2 & 6.30–9.30

Landlords Richard E. Wright & Peter G. Smith
Free house
Greene King Abbot, IPA; Adnams Bitter; Mauldon's Bitter; Kronenbourg; cider.

A village inn of style and character, with beams, exposed brickwork and good-quality furnishings. The blackboard menu features a wide variety of carefully prepared dishes, from simple avocado with prawns and a superb smooth-as-velvet lentil soup to mushrooms in Madeira, poacher's pie and sesame-fried chicken pieces with a barbecue sauce. Fish is a speciality, with four or five dishes usually being available. Excellent chips, crisp salads and some interesting sweets like pear and almond

strudel or pineapple St Moritz. There's also a pleasant restaurant.
Typical prices Braised oxtail in Madeira sauce £4.75 Mixed meat brochette £5.50

***ACCOMMODATION* 3 bedrooms £C**
Check-in all day

Bedrooms run from the handsome gallery above the restaurant, and are comfortable and nicely furnished, with well-upholstered armchairs and antiques. Modern facilities include telephones, tea-makers and remote control TVs. All have modern en suite bathrooms. Children are welcome overnight. Patio. *No dogs.*

Credit Access, Amex, Diners, Visa

STOKE LACY — Plough Inn

OD

Nr Bromyard
MAP 5 A2 *Hereford & Worcester*
Munderfield (088 53) 658
Parking ample

Bar food 12–2 & 7–10

Landlords Norman & Janet Whittall
Brewery Greenall Whitley
Greenall Whitley Local Bitter, Festival, Wem Special; Davenports Traditional; Guinness; Grünhalle Export Gold; cider.

A smart, white-painted pub on the A465 in cider country. Apple pie order is kept in the bay-windowed bar, where Norman Whittall dispenses good beer and bonhomie. Janet turns her hand to tasty dishes like rabbit pie, cidery chicken or the popular salmon tart. Also sandwiches and grills, with lovely home-made ice-creams and traditional puds. Sunday roast also available. Garden.
Typical prices Pigeon with apricots & ginger £2.50 Stuffed aubergine £2
Credit Access, Visa

STOKE ST GREGORY — Rose & Crown Inn

OD
& B

Nr Taunton
MAP 5 A3 *Somerset*
North Curry (0823) 490296
Parking ample

Bar food 12–2.30 & 7–10.30

Landlords Ron & Irene Browning
Free house
Eldridge Pope Royal Oak, Dorchester Bitter; Golden Hill Exmoor Ale; Guinness; Faust; Tennent's Extra; cider.

The route to this quaint little 18th-century pub winds down narrow lanes off the A361. Nooks and crannies, horse brasses and an illuminated well, 60 feet deep, give plenty of atmosphere to the beamed bar, where blackboards list the day's tasty fare. This might be smoked trout or soup to start, followed by hearty scrumpy chicken, duckling à l'orange, grilled steaks or delicious plaice stuffed with chicken and asparagus. Ploughman's, omelettes, cold meat salads and sandwiches are also available for those with lighter appetites. There's an extensive choice of delicious sweets, including home-made gâteaux, meringue glacé, cheesecake, crème caramel and pear belle Hélène. Traditional roast available on Sundays.
Typical prices Plaice stuffed with broccoli & cheese £3.50 Chocolate mousse cake £1.15

***ACCOMMODATION* 3 bedrooms £D**
Check-in all day

Upstairs, three simple bedrooms offer adequate accommodation. All have modern fitted units, pretty coordinated fabrics and TVs. They share a smart bathroom with shower. Patio. *No dogs.*

Credit Access, Visa

STONY STRATFORD — Bull Hotel

B & B 64 High Street
MAP 7 C1 *Buckinghamshire*
Milton Keynes (0908) 567104
Parking ample
Landlords Everett Johnson & Paul Waring
Brewery Aylesbury Brewery
ABC Bitter; Everards Tiger; Bass; Marston Pedigree; Guinness; Castlemaine XXXX; Skol; cider.
ACCOMMODATION **13 bedrooms £C**
Check-in all day

The phrase 'cock and bull story' originated in Stony Stratford, as travellers here swopped tall tales with patrons of the Cock Inn next door. There are several bars, the nicest being the Vaults Bar which has flagstones and pine settles. The bedrooms are generally good-sized and very clean, with TVs and tea-makers. Four have private bathrooms, while the rest share two well-maintained public ones. Decent cooked breakfast. *No dogs.*
Credit Access, Visa **LVs**

STONY STRATFORD — The Cock Hotel

B & B 72 High Street
MAP 7 C1 *Buckinghamshire*
Milton Keynes (0908) 562109
Parking ample
Landlord James Higgins
Free house
Adnams Bitter; Younger's Tartan; Courage Directors; Beck's Bier; Carlsberg.
ACCOMMODATION **19 bedrooms £B**
Check-in all day

Like its close neighbour the Bull, this hostelry is still a cosy place for a yarn and a comfortable one for an overnight stop. The best bedrooms are smartly furnished and have en suite facilities. The rest have more ordinary decor and share half a dozen public bathrooms. All rooms have TVs and tea-makers. The bar area opens on to an attractive walled garden. Accommodation closed one week at Christmas. *No dogs.*
Credit Access, Amex, Visa

STOURBRIDGE — Talbot Hotel

B & B High Street
MAP 5 B2 *West Midlands*
Stourbridge (0384) 394350
Parking limited
Landlords Mr & Mrs M. Chatterton
Brewery Wolverhampton & Dudley
Banks's Bitter; Holden Black Country Bitter, Mild; Guinness; Stella Artois; Harp Extra; cider.
ACCOMMODATION **25 bedrooms £B**
Check-in all day

Accommodation is spotless at this 500-year-old coaching inn. Standard and de luxe rooms have attractive freestanding pine units, plus TVs, direct-dial phones and hairdryers. Executive rooms are a lot larger, with period or antique furnishings, and all categories have their own attractive modern bathrooms. Re-styled public rooms include a spacious, comfortable lounge bar, coffee lounge and cocktail bar. Patio. Children welcome overnight.
Credit Access, Amex, Visa **LVs**

STOW BARDOLPH — Hare Arms

FOOD King's Lynn
MAP 6 E1 *Norfolk*
Downham Market (0366) 382229
Parking ample
Bar food 12–2 & 7–10
No bar food Sun
Landlords David & Tricia McManus
Brewery Greene King
Greene King Abbot Ale, IPA, Mild; Guinness; Kronenbourg; Harp; cider.

The McManuses are rightly proud of their homely inn and the food they produce. Local fish, shellfish and game find their seasonal way on to the blackboard menu, and there's often lobster in summer. Soups, curries and individual pies are other appealing choices, with sandwiches for quicker snacks and a selection of sweets. Recent refurbishment has made room for a new conservatory. Garden.
Typical prices Fresh Torbay sole £3.75 Steak & oyster pie £2.95

STOW-ON-THE-WOLD **Royalist Hotel**

& B

Digbeth Street
MAP 7 A2 *Gloucestershire*
Cotswold (0451) 30670
Parking ample

Landlords Mr & Mrs L. Bellorini
Free house
Worthington Best Bitter; Wadworth 6X; Flowers Original; Whitbread Best Bitter; Heineken.

ACCOMMODATION **15 bedrooms £C**
Check-in all day

Behind the 17th-century Cotswold-stone facade are timbers dating back over a thousand years at this cosy hostelry. New curtains and carpets have brightened many of the bedrooms, which include characterful main-building rooms, four in the annexe with a modern, spacious appeal, and a luxury suite. Most have private facilities and all offer TVs and tea-makers. There's a popular bar. Accommodation closed January. Patio and garden.
Credit Access, Amex, Visa

STRATFORD-UPON-AVON **Slug & Lettuce**

OOD

38 Guild Street
TOWN PLAN *Warwickshire*
Stratford-upon-Avon (0789) 299700
Parking difficult

Bar food 12–2 & 6–10, Sun 12–1.30 & 7–9.30

Landlords Mr & Mrs Harris
Brewery Ansells
Ind Coope Burton Ale; Tetley Bitter; Wiltshire Traditional; Guinness; Löwenbräu; cider.

Although this lively pub/bistro has changed hands, the style and quality of the bar food hasn't altered. Good fresh produce is used in a tempting array of dishes like sardines provençale, duck and orange terrine, soups, filet mignon au poivre and kidneys Amontillado. Good flavours and seasonings. Blackcurrant roulade, syllabub and crumbles are typical sweets. Patio.
Typical prices Chicken breast & avocado £5 Blue Brie & fresh fruit £2
Credit Access, Visa

STRETTON **Ram Jam Inn**

OOD
& B

Great North Road, Nr Oakham
MAP 6 D1 *Leicestershire*
Castle Bytham (078 081) 776
Parking ample

Bar food 7 am–11 pm

Landlord Lucy Goldthorp
Free house
Ruddles County, Rutland Bitter; Stella Artois; Carlsberg.

Travellers on the A1 will find this smart, informal motel a very convenient stopping-off point. Snacks – available from 7 am onwards – range from a breakfast time choice that includes muesli, yoghurt and local sausages to nourishing soup, huge wholemeal baps, prawns, salads, excellent cheeses and hot dishes like freshly made fettuccine with parmesan and garlic bread-crumbs or with mushrooms. The snack counter menu is also available in the elegant bar, while the restaurant offers additional hot dishes, and there's a children's menu, too. Try the deliciously rich treacle and nut tart for afters.
Typical prices Rutland sausage with sweet & sour onions £3 Cream cheese & smoked salmon bap £2.70

ACCOMMODATION **8 bedrooms £C**
Check-in all day

Spacious bedrooms (including two family rooms) facing away from the road, are attractively furnished with rustic-style pine and pleasing colour schemes. Facilities include telephones, remote control TVs, clock radios and tea-makers as well as superior, well-equipped bathrooms.
Credit Access, Amex, Diners, Visa

STUCKTON — Three Lions

FOOD Stuckton Road, Fordingbridge
MAP 5 B4 *Hampshire*
Fordingbridge (0425) 52489
Parking ample

Bar food 12.15–1.30 (Sun from 12) & 7.15–9.30
No bar food Sun eve
Closed 2 wks Feb, 1st wk Aug & 1 wk Xmas

Landlords Karl & June Wadsack
Free house
Wadworth 6X; Marston Burton Bitter; Hall's Harvest Bitter; Guinness; Castlemaine XXXX; Löwenbräu.

★ Major refurbishment has created a smart, comfortable dining area and separate bar lounge in rustic Austrian/Scandinavian style as befits the respective nationalities of Karl and June Wadsack; the feel is that of a restaurant rather than a pub. Karl is a dedicated and talented chef and his daily-changing blackboard menus would delight even the most jaded palate. His quest for prime produce even extends to importing fish from the Seychelles, while winter brings New Forest game such as pheasant and venison. Starters might be gravad lax with mustard sauce, sweet cured herring fillets or moules marinère, with calf's kidneys moutarde de Meaux, duck with hazelnut stuffing or breast of chicken with crab and brandy sauce to follow. Superb sweets. Traditional Sunday lunch menu. Patio. ★

Typical prices Cucumber & cream cheese mousse £2.80 Plaice stuffed with salmon mousse in white wine £6.80 Wing of skate beurre noir £5.40 Crème brûlée £2.50

Credit Access, Visa

SURBITON — Oak

FOOD Maple Road
MAP 7 C3 *Surrey*
01-399 1662
Parking ample

Bar food 12–2.30
No bar food eves & all Sun

Landlord Robert Mahon
Brewery Charrington
Charrington IPA; Bass; Guinness; Tennent's Extra, Pilsner; Carling Black Label; cider.

On a corner site in a tree-lined road, this is a pleasant, roomy place for enjoying a lunchtime snack. There's an appetising display of ham, beef and pâté, coronation turkey and salads, plus a choice of hot dishes – perhaps stuffed peppers, freshly baked quiche and Lancashire lamb pie (there's always a vegetarian dish, too). To round things off, cheese or the day's pud such as apple and orange flan. Garden.

Typical prices Dijon pork hot pot £2.20 Salmon mousse £1.95

SUTTON — Anne Arms

FOOD Suttonfield Road, Nr Doncaster
MAP 4 E4 *South Yorkshire*
Doncaster (0302) 700500
Parking ample

Bar food 12–2 & 7.30–9.30
No bar food Sun

Landlords Mr and Mrs J.R. Simm
Brewery John Smith
John Smith's Bitter; Guinness; John Smith's Lager; Hofmeister; cider.
No real ale.

Toby jugs, porcelain statues and polished copperware fill the beamed bars of this ivy-clad pub – but it's not just the homely decor that draws the crowds. Mrs Simm is a splendid cook, and all of her specialities – including superb pies, a daily roast, liver and onions – are priced at £2. Tasty home-made sweets too. Garden. *No children under five.*

Typical prices Joint of the day £2 Rabbit pie £2

SUTTON — Sutton Hall

OOD
& B

Bullocks Lane, Nr Macclesfield
MAP 4 D4 *Cheshire*
Sutton (02605) 3211
Parking ample

Bar food 12–2.30 & 7–10.15, Sun 12–2 & 7–10

Landlords Robert & Phyllida Bradshaw
Free house
Bass, 4X Mild; Stones Bitter; Marston Burton Bitter; Guinness; Tennent's Lager; cider.

Once the baronial residence of the Sutton family, and more recently a convent, this fine establishment is today a splendid inn oozing old-world charm. Open fires warm the heavily beamed bar, where a suit of armour and a grandfather clock add to the atmosphere. Here you can tuck into leek and potato soup, chicken liver pâté and roast beef baps, together with such appetising daily specials as grilled lamb chops or ham and asparagus pancake. There's a traditional roast lunch on Sundays, and more formal meals are served in the dining room. Children welcome in the bar weekends only.
Typical prices Seafood pancake £3.55 Pot-roast pigeon £3.25.

ACCOMMODATION **10 bedrooms £A**
Check-in all day

Very comfortable accommodation is provided in spacious, characterful bedrooms, reached by a handsome carved staircase. All boast four-posters and good-quality oak furniture. TVs, direct-dial telephones and tea-makers are standard, and each room has its own carpeted modern bathroom. Garden.

Credit Access, Amex, Visa

SUTTON HOWGRAVE — White Dog Inn

OOD

Nr Ripon
MAP 4 D3 *North Yorkshire*
Melmerby (076 584) 404
Parking ample

Bar food 12–2.15 (Sun till 1.45)
No bar food eves
Closed Sun eve & all Mon
Landlords Mr & Mrs Bagnall
Free house
Webster Pennine Bitter; Carlsberg Hof. *No real ale.*

Lunchtime snacks are full of variety at this pleasant village pub named in memory of a beloved bull terrier. Cooking is robust and dependable, with things like venison pie, mariner's hot pot and chicken casserole among the stalwarts. Also sandwiches and salads, omelettes, steaks and sweets. Restaurant meals in the evening. There's also a garden.
Typical prices Seafood hot pot £2.50 Steak & kidney pie £3.50

SUTTON-UPON-DERWENT — St Vincent Arms

OOD

York
MAP 4 E3 *Humberside*
Elvington (090 485) 349
Parking ample

Bar food 12–2 & 7–10

Landlords Max & Kate Royds
Free house
Theakston Best Bitter, Old Peculier; Tetley Bitter; Younger's Scotch; Guinness; Carlsberg; cider.

Parts of this timbered pub date back more than 300 years, and the whole place has a warm, welcoming air. Tasty snacks to suit all appetites can be enjoyed in the cosy bars, whether your preference is for a light bite – soup, a salad or freshly made sandwich – or for something more robust like roast chicken, haddock, gammon or a steak. Garden.
Typical prices Home-made pâté £1.40 Beef & Guinness casserole £3.95

SYMONDS YAT WEST — Old Court Hotel

B & B

Nr Ross-on-Wye
MAP 5 A2 *Hereford & Worcester*
Monmouth (0600) 890367
Parking ample
Landlords Mr & Mrs John Slade
Free house
Wadworth 6X; Flowers Original, Best Bitter; Heineken; Stella Artois; cider.

***ACCOMMODATION* 17 bedrooms £C**
Check-in all day

An impressive mansion near the river Wye. The main building dates from about 1570, and it's here that you'll find the lofty dining room, the oak-panelled bar and the lounge. Here, too, is the roomiest accommodation – six pleasant, chintzy rooms, two with ingeniously fitted bathrooms. The other rooms are in a modern wing, compact and simply furnished. Children welcome in the bar till early evening. Garden, swimming pool & play area. ***Credit*** Access, Amex, Diners, Visa

TALKIN VILLAGE — Hare & Hounds Inn

FOOD
B & B

Nr Brampton
MAP 3 C2 *Cumbria*
Brampton (069 77) 3456
Parking ample
Bar food 12–2 & 7–9
Closed weekday lunches (except during school or Bank Hols)
Landlords Joan & Les Stewart
Free house
Theakston Best Bitter, Old Peculier, XB; Hartley XB; Younger's Scotch; Carlsberg; cider.

Standing in the heart of a peaceful Cumbrian village, this homely 200-year-old inn is run with tremendous warmth and hospitality by Joan and Les Stewart. It's first-name terms for everyone in the convivial, traditional bars, where soundly prepared snacks of the popular variety can be enjoyed. Filled jacket potatoes (Talkin tatties) and generous layered sandwiches are regular favourites, along with pizzas, steaks and plaice with ratatouille. Daily specials like chilli con carne or spaghetti bolognese extend the choice, and there's a special menu for jokily named dishes for the children. Sweets tend to be ice cream based.

Typical prices Barbecued bangers £1.85 Rainbow trout £3.45

***ACCOMMODATION* 4 bedrooms £D**
Check-in all day

Two of the bedrooms boast handsome old wardrobes, splendid beds and private bathrooms, while the other two are more modern and functional in style. All four have washbasins and there's a TV in the upstairs residents' lounge. Garden. *No dogs.*

Prices given are as at the time of our research and thus may change.

TARRANT MONKTON — Langton Arms

FOOD
B & B

Blandford Forum
MAP 9 D1 *Dorset*
Tarrant Monkton (025 889) 225
Parking ample
Bar food 11.30–2.30 & 6–10.30, Sun 12–2 & 7–10.30
Landlords Diane & Chris Goodinge
Free house
Bass; Wadworth 6X; Toby Bitter; Worthington Best Bitter; Guinness; Carling Black Label; cider.

An unspoilt village in Hardy country is home for this 17th-century thatched pub, where sound home-cooked snacks are served in its cosy beamed bar. Soup, sandwiches, pâté and ploughman's are staples, as well as favourite hot dishes like shepherd's pie and steak and kidney pudding. Consult the blackboard for daily specials like seafood lasagne or seasonal game, and remember to leave room for a pleasant sweet like gooseberry fool or orange sorbet. Evenings bring grills, and special themes for different nights of the week: French on Monday, for example, Chinese on Thursday. The popular restaurant is open every night and for Sunday lunch. Garden and large skittles alley.

Typical prices Mushroom florentine £2.10 Gammon steak £3.75 ⓔ

***ACCOMMODATION* 6 bedrooms £C**
Check-in all day

The six pine-furnished bedrooms in a modern block overlook the beautiful countryside. All have pretty duvets and curtains, and en suite bathrooms. Tea-makers and colour TVs are standard. Some rooms can be converted into family suites.

Credit Access, Amex, Diners, Visa

TEDDINGTON — Clarence Hotel

& B

19 Park Road
MAP 7 C3 *Middlesex*
01-977 8025
Parking ample

Landlords Ron & Rose Currall
Free house
Webster Yorkshire Bitter; Marston Pedigree; Wadworth 6X; Young Special; Guinness; Holsten Export; cider.

***ACCOMMODATION* 15 bedrooms £C**
Check-in all day

Hanging plants and pot plants adorn the large bar of this friendly pub. Together with leather-look Chesterfields they give a pleasing atmosphere and a video jukebox attracts a lively young crowd. The bedrooms are large and furnished with freestanding furniture – some period pieces and some more modern. Most rooms have duvets and all have spacious, simply fitted modern bathrooms and tea-makers. TVs are available on request.

Credit Access, Amex, Diners, Visa

TEMPLE GRAFTON — Blue Boar

OOD

Nr Alcester
MAP 7 A1 *Warwickshire*
Stratford-upon-Avon (0789) 750010
Parking ample

Bar food 12–2 & 6.30–10 (Sun 7–9.30)

Landlords Mr G. Ponzi
Free house
Whitbread Best Mild, Poacher; Flowers IPA, Original, Best Bitter; Stella Artois; cider.

A very popular pub in a village just off the A422 Stratford-Alcester road. The central bar is surrounded by cosy seating areas where hungry folk can enjoy anything from a ham sandwich or ploughman's platter to fish soup or poached salmon. Plentiful vegetables accompany main courses and there are some tasty home-made sweets. Traditional Sunday lunch.

Typical prices Cannelloni £1.95 Fresh sardines provençale £1.90 ⓔ

Credit Access, Visa

TERRINGTON — Bay Horse Inn

& B

Nr York
MAP 4 E3 *North Yorkshire*
Coneysthorpe (065 384) 255
Parking ample

Closed Mon lunch (except Bank Hols)

Landlord Grace Hoggard
Free house
John Smith's; Younger's Scotch; Tetley; Guinness; Hofmeister; Carlsberg Hof; cider. *No real ale.*

***ACCOMMODATION* 4 bedrooms £C**
Check-in restricted

Kept in pristine condition throughout, this smart black and white village inn hung with pretty window boxes has a genuinely hospitable air. Roaring fires warm the two cosy bars, while central heating and hot-water bottles keep overnight guests snug in the cheerful little bedrooms. All have pretty, soft furnishings, washbasins, black and white TVs, tea and coffee making facilities, and radio-alarms. They share two public bathrooms. Patio.

TESTCOMBE — Mayfly

FOOD
Nr Stockbridge
MAP 5 C3 *Hampshire*
Chilbolton (026 474) 283
Parking ample

Bar food 12–2 & 7–9

Landlord Barry Lane
Brewery Whitbread
Flowers Original; Strong Country Bitter; Wadworth 6X; Wethered Winter Royal (winter only); Heineken; Stella Artois; cider.

A conservatory provides an attractive alternative to the popular garden of this red-brick pub beside the river Test. A splendid display offers 20 or 30 cheeses, plus tempting cold meats, quiche and imaginative salads, like mushroom and apple or cabbage and raisin. Curries, steak and mushroom pie and trout lead the blackboard specials with puds like treacle tart for any gaps.
Typical prices Hot chicken tandoori £2.90 Selection of cheeses £1.95
Credit Access, Visa

THAMES DITTON — Albany

FOOD
Queens Road
MAP 7 C3 Surrey
01-398 7031
Parking ample

Bar food 12–2.30
No bar food eves & all Sun

Landlord Mr A. R. Christie
Brewery Charrington
Bass; Charrington IPA; Guinness; Tennent's Extra, Pilsner; Carling Black Label; cider.

You can admire Hampton Court from the riverside terrace of this spacious Victorian pub with an appetising lunchtime buffet. Cold items range from home-cooked ham and beef to Cumberland pie, salmon mousse and pâté with crisp salads, while hot fare includes boeuf berlinoise pie, jacket potatoes, sausages, and soup (in winter). Finish with cheese or ice cream.
Typical prices Frenchman's cassoulet £2.40 Vegetable terrine £1.95

THETFORD — Historical Thomas Paine Hotel

B & B
White Hart Street
MAP 6 E2 *Norfolk*
Thetford (0842) 5631
Parking ample

Landlord Thomas Muir
Free house
Adnams Bitter; Stones Bitter; McEwan's Export; Guinness; Carlsberg Hof; Fosters; cider.

ACCOMMODATION **14 bedrooms £C**
Check-in all day

Named after a political pamphleteer who was reputedly born here in 1737, this attractive white-painted hotel is a good place for an overnight stop. The bedrooms – double-glazed when appropriate – have individual colour schemes and well-chosen modern furnishings, plus TVs, telephones and tea-makers. Day rooms include a comfortable bar which has recently been refurbished, a relaxing residents' lounge and a strikingly decorated breakfast room. Garden.
Credit Access, Amex, Diners, Visa

TICHBORNE — Tichborne Arms

FOOD
Nr Alresford
MAP 5 C3 *Hampshire*
Alresford (096 273) 3760
Parking ample

Bar food 11.30–2 & 6.30–10

Landlord Lynn O'Callaghan
Free house
Wadworth 6X; Courage Best Bitter; Flowers Original; Eldridge Pope Royal Oak; Guinness; Heineken; cider.

Simple home cooking (by local ladies) can be enjoyed in the pleasant bar of this redbrick thatched pub or in its delightfully peaceful garden. Choice ranges from soup, sandwiches, salads and jacket potatoes to daily specials like a mild chicken curry, paella or mixed grill. Save room for a delicious – and filling – syrup sponge, bread pudding, or crunchy fruit crumble.
Typical prices Lasagne with salad £3.25 Chicken, ham & mushroom pie £3.25

TIMPERLEY — Hare & Hounds

OD

1 Wood Lane, Nr Altrincham
MAP 3 C4 *Cheshire*
061-980 5299
Parking ample

Bar food 12–2
No bar food eves

Landlords Jim & Fran Cunningham
Brewery Marston Thompson & Evershed
Marston Burton Bitter, Mercian Mild, Pedigree; Guinness; Marston Pilsner Lager; Stella Artois; cider.

Lunchtime visitors to this popular roadside pub can choose from an impressive cold buffet – roast meats, smoked fish, quiches and salads – served in the main bar, or plump for a hot dish such as spicy Cumberland sausage or succulent roast lamb in the small bar. On summer evenings there's sometimes a barbecue. No cold buffet on Sundays. Patio and terrace. *No children in the evenings.*
Typical prices Chicken & leek pie £2.75 Cod fillet in chive sauce £2.75
LVs

TORMARTON — Compass Inn

& B

Nr Badminton
MAP 7 A3 *Avon*
Badminton (045 421) 242
Parking ample

Landlords Monyard family
Free house
Wadworth 6X; Bass; Archers Village; Younger's Tartan Bitter; Beck's Bier; Carlsberg Hof; cider.
ACCOMMODATION **19 bedrooms £B**
Check-in all day

Conveniently placed for both the M4 and M5, this creeper-clad coaching inn, with its characterful, Cotswold-stone bars, offers a friendly welcome and comfortable overnight accommodation. Two extensions house the majority of rooms, which offer TVs, tea-makers and direct-dial telephones. All except four in the main building have private facilities. Children welcome in the bar lunchtime only. Delightful enclosed orangery, patio and garden.
Credit Access, Amex, Diners, Visa

TOWERSEY — Three Horseshoes

OOD

Chinnor Road, Nr Thame
MAP 7 C2 *Oxfordshire*
Thame (084 421) 2322
Parking ample

Bar food 12–2 & 7–10
Landlords Mr & Mrs Worsdell
Brewery Aylesbury
ABC Bitter; Beechwood; Everards Tiger; Guinness; Skol; Castlemaine XXXX; cider.

Once a milking parlour, this much-modernised pub dates back in parts to the 13th century and is run in cheerful, friendly fashion by the Worsdells. In the beer garden, flagstoned bar or pleasant restaurant you can enjoy favourites like soup, jacket potatoes and excellent lasagne, or tuck into something more substantial – perhaps kidney turbigo or vegetarian split pea cutlets.
Typical prices Two-in-one pie £2.95 Ice cream £1.40
Credit Access, Visa

TREBARWITH — Mill House Inn

& B

Nr Tintagel
MAP 9 B2 *Cornwall*
Camelford (0840) 770200
Parking ample

Landlords Jennifer & David Liddiard-Jenkin
Free house
Flowers Original, IPA; Whitbread Best Bitter; Guinness; Stella Artois; cider.
ACCOMMODATION **9 bedrooms £C**
Check-in restricted

A slate-built corn mill which has been transformed into a characterful inn. The rustic, flagstoned bar has a children's/games room leading off it and there's a cosy bar and lounge for residents. The pretty bedrooms have pine furniture and modern bathrooms (three not en suite). All have colour TVs, tea-makers, hairdryers and radio intercoms. Refurbishment underway in bedrooms. Accommodation closed three days Christmas. *No children under ten overnight*
Credit Access, Visa

TROUTBECK **Mortal Man**

B & B Nr Windermere
MAP 3 C3 *Cumbria*
Ambleside (0966) 33193
Parking ample
Landlords Annette & Christopher Poulsom
Free house
Younger's Scotch; McEwan's Export; Guinness; McEwan's Lager; cider.
***ACCOMMODATION* 13 bedrooms £B**
Check-in all day

Overlooking Lake Windermere from its hillside position, this famous old inn offers peace and comfort in idyllic surroundings. Double-glazed bedrooms (eight with their own bathrooms) are neatly kept and provide easy chairs and washbasins. There's a TV lounge and bar for residents' use, as well as an oak-furnished main bar decorated with fresh flowers and warmed by an open fire. Terrace and garden. Accommodation closed mid-November to mid-February. *No children under five overnight.*

TURVILLE **Bull & Butcher**

FOOD Nr Henley-on-Thames
MAP 7 C2 *Buckinghamshire*
Turville Heath (049 163) 283
Parking ample
Bar food 12–2 & 7.30–10.15
Landlord Peter David Wright
Brewery Brakspear
Brakspear Bitter, Special, Old; Guinness; Stella Artois; cider.

Now under new management, this pretty little black and white timbered pub still serves up scrumptious bar snacks in a friendly atmosphere. Choices on an imaginatively cosmopolitan menu include spicy chilli con carne, taramasalata, mediterranean prawns and pork fillet provençale, as well as traditional grills, salads, soups and pâtés. Home-made puds, too. Garden.
Typical prices Vegetarian lasagne £2.95 Beef & Guinness casserole £3.75

TUTBURY **Ye Olde Dog & Partridge**

FOOD
B & B High Street
MAP 5 B1 *Staffordshire*
Burton on Trent (0283) 813030
Parking ample
Bar food 12.15–2 & 7.15–10
Landlord Mr D. J. Martindale
Free house
Marston Pedigree, John Marston, Border Mild; Worthington Bitter; Marston Pilsner Lager; Stella Artois; cider. *No real ale.*

A splendid choice of bar food, cheerful, welcoming staff and a lovely relaxed atmosphere (aided by a pianist evenings and weekends) tempts the crowds to this half-timbered, 15th-century pub in the town centre. Arrive early to be first in the queue at the carvery, which offers an excellent choice of cold meats, about a dozen imaginative salads (pasta and peppers, bulgar wheat and peanuts) – all very fresh and well presented – and a popular selection of hot dishes from roast beef to chilli con carne and turkey curry. There are hot puddings too, as well as sweets like chocolate fudge cake and charlotte russe, and a range of ice cream coupes.
Typical prices Roast beef £4.50 Spotted dick and custard £1.20

***ACCOMMODATION* 18 bedrooms £B**
Check-in all day

Best bedrooms (with four-posters) are in an adjacent Georgian house, but main building rooms, up steep, rickety stairs, have the charm of beams and sloping floors. All have colour TVs, tea-makers, hairdryers and bedside controls, and most have well-supplied modern bathrooms. Patio and garden.

Credit Access, Amex, Diners, Visa

TWICKENHAM — Prince Albert

OD

30 Hampton Road
MAP 7 C3 *Middlesex*
01-894 3963
Parking limited

Bar food 12–2.30
No bar food Sun
Landlords Elizabeth & Bruce Lunn
Brewery Fullers
Fullers London Pride, ESB, Chiswick Bitter; Guinness; Tennent's Extra; Heineken.

A really delightful Victorian pub, with excellent food and a real feeling of the country in town. Elizabeth Lunn puts a lot of effort into her lunchtime menus, which offer delights as diverse as mussels bretonne, liver and bacon, seafood grill and tasty pork casserole with wine and mushrooms. Pancakes are a popular pud. Toasted sandwiches are available evenings on request. Patio and garden.
Typical prices Suffolk hot pot £3.40 Cumberland pie £2.90 **LVs**

TWICKENHAM — White Swan

OD

Riverside
MAP 7 C3 *Middlesex*
01–892 2166
Parking ample
Bar food 1–2.45 & 6–9.30
No bar food Sun

Landlord Shirley Sutton
Brewery Watney Combe Reid
Watney Special Bitter, Combes Bitter; Webster Yorkshire Bitter; Guinness; Carlsberg; Fosters; cider.

A friendly riverside pub whose modest appearance somewhat belies the high quality of the home-cooked bar food. Selections such as creamy courgette and potato soup, ploughman's and rolls made with fresh granary bread, jacket potatoes, grilled gammon and cold roast beef make up a good lunchtime menu. Tasty toasted sandwiches in the evenings. Attractive terrace and garden. Children welcome lunchtime only.
Typical prices Beef & veg hot pot £2.50 Toasted cheese sandwich 60p

UMBERLEIGH — Rising Sun

B

MAP 9 B1 *Devon*
High Bickington (0769) 60447
Parking ample

Landlord Peter Gardner
Owner Westward Hosts
Usher Country Bitter, Triple Crown; Holsten. *No real ale.*

***ACCOMMODATION* 8 bedrooms £C**
Check in all day

Fishing is very much the theme of this historic inn – it has local fishing rights and a rod room as well as a lounge bar decked out in angling regalia. There's also a flagstoned bar and a refurbished lounge with a log fire and relaxing armchairs. Bedrooms, also recently upgraded, feature quality pine furniture, strikingly contrasted with salmon pink to give a cottage feel. Most have well-equipped, en suite bathrooms.
Credit Access, Amex, Diners, Visa

UPPER ODDINGTON — Horse & Groom Inn

B

Nr Stow-on-the-Wold
MAP 7 B2 *Gloucestershire*
Cotswold (0451) 30584
Parking ample

Landlords Mr & Mrs Howarth & Mr & Mrs Evans
Free house
Wadworth 6X, IPA; John Smith's Yorkshire Bitter; Guinness; Tuborg Gold; Heineken; cider.

***ACCOMMODATION* 7 bedrooms £C**
Check-in all day

In a delightful village not far from Stow-on-the-Wold, this 16th-century, Cotswold-stone inn makes a super place for the whole family to stay. Seven centrally heated bedrooms – including two in a separate cottage – are spotlessly kept and all have tea-makers plus carpeted private facilities (mainly showers). Stone walls, beams and flagstone floors characterise the cosy bars, and the garden includes a children's paddock and playground. Accommodation closed three days Christmas.

UPTON GREY — Hoddington Arms

FOOD

Nr Basingstoke
MAP 5 C3 *Hampshire*
Basingstoke (0256) 862371
Parking ample

Bar food 12–2 & 7–10, Sun 12–1.30 & 7–9.30

Landlords Ian & Irene Fisher
Brewery Courage
Courage Best, Directors; John Smith's Yorkshire Bitter; Guinness; Kronenbourg; Hofmeister; cider.

Enjoyable home cooking in an 18th-century village pub. The lunchtime menu offers ploughman's, sandwiches, summer salads and hot dishes like corn chowder, garlicky prawns, lemon chicken and mixed grill. Similar, but slightly more expensive, evening choice of starters and mains (seafood platter a speciality). Clafoutis is an unusual pub pud. Patio and garden.
Typical prices Steak & kidney pie £3 Lemon chicken £3.65
Credit Access, Visa

UTTOXETER — White Hart Hotel

B & B

Carter Street
MAP 5 B1 *Staffordshire*
Uttoxeter (088 93) 2437
Parking ample
Landlord Vera Porteous
Brewery Allied Lyons
Ind Coope Burton Ale, Bitter; Guinness; Castlemaine XXXX; Löwenbräu; Skol; cider.

***ACCOMMODATION* 28 bedrooms £B**
Check-in all day

Supporters of Bonnie Prince Charlie were earlier guests at this beamed and panelled, 16th-century coaching inn in the town centre. Many of the spacious bedrooms have antique furniture – one boasts a four-poster and splendid panelling. Most have private bathrooms, and all are equipped with tea-makers and TVs. The split-level lounge bar is warm and welcoming, and staff are very friendly and helpful. Patio.
Credit Access, Amex, Diners, Visa

WALKERN — White Lion

FOOD

High Street
MAP 7 D1 *Hertfordshire*
Walkern (043 886) 251
Parking ample

Bar food 12–2 (Sun till 1.30) & 7–9.30
No bar food Sun & Mon eves

Landlords Mike & Jenny Windebank
Brewery Greene King
Greene King Abbot Ale, IPA, Dark Mild; KK Light, Mild; Guinness; Kronenbourg; Harp; cider.

The Windebanks have been here 18 years, the building itself more than 400. In the cosy bar they offer a varied selection of enjoyable snacks from celery and Stilton soup to three-bean stew and chicken curry. Fresh fish features on Tuesday and Thursday, and the cold table includes home-made pâté and a reasonable cheeseboard. Sunday roast lunch available. Garden.
Typical prices Beef in red wine £5.95 Kidneys in cream, mushrooms & wine £3

WALL — Hadrian Hotel

B & B

Nr Hexham
MAP 3 C2 *Northumberland*
Humshaugh (043 481) 232
Parking ample

Landlords Mr & Mrs Malcolm Mellors
Brewery Vaux
Vaux Samson; Lorimer's Best Scotch; Guinness; Stella Artois; Tuborg; cider.

***ACCOMMODATION* 9 bedrooms £C**
Check-in all day

The Mellors make everyone feel welcome at their well-kept roadside inn set in a peaceful village named after Hadrian's Wall. The newly enlarged bar and pleasantly traditional foyer-lounge have a warm, inviting air. Two of the bedrooms boast half-testers and some enjoy fine country views. Tea-makers and fresh fruit are provided, and the carpeted bathrooms have simple, modern units. Garden. *No children under 12 overnight.*
Credit Access

WALTHAM ON THE WOLDS — Royal Horseshoes

B & B

Melton Road, Nr Melton Mowbray
MAP 5 C1 *Leicestershire*
Waltham (066 478) 289
Parking ample

Landlords Mr & Mrs M. A. Wigglesworth
Brewery John Smith
John Smith's Bitter, Chestnut; John Courage; Kronenbourg; Hofmeister; cider.

ACCOMMODATION **4 bedrooms £C**
Check-in restricted

Standing in the heart of the village on the A607, this friendly thatched pub has a history dating back nearly 500 years. Despite much modernisation, its charm and character are intact, with beams and brass plates providing a touch of tradition in the welcoming bar. Light, airy bedrooms in a converted stable block have good light-wood furniture, duvets and tea-makers. Immaculate bathrooms reflect the high standard of housekeeping throughout. Accommodation closed 1 week August.

WALTHAM ST LAWRENCE — Bell

FOOD

Nr Reading
MAP 7 C3 *Berkshire*
Twyford (0734) 341788
Parking limited

Bar food 12–2 & 7–9.45
No bar food All Sun & Mon eve

Landlords Mr & Mrs L. A. G. Hall
Free house
Brakspear Bitter; Wadworth 6X, Farmer's Glory; guest beers; Löwenbräu; Stella Artois; cider.

In a quiet village setting, next to the church, this delightful little 600-year-old pub offers highly enjoyable eating in its two cosily rustic beamed bars. Consult the blackboard for choices like splendid home-made liver pâté, prawn and asparagus pancake, seafood platter and beef curry – and don't miss super puds like apple and blackcurrant pie or jam roly-poly. Garden.
Typical prices Nut roast £2.85 Trawlerman's pie £2.55
Credit Access, Amex, Diners, Visa

WALTHAM ST LAWRENCE — Plough Inn

FOOD

West End
MAP 7 C3 *Berkshire*
Twyford (0734) 340015
Parking ample

Bar food 10.30–2.30 & 6–9
No bar food Sun & Mon

Landlord Mrs B. Boulton-Taylor
Brewery Morland
Morland Best Bitter, Pale Ale; Heineken.

Good farmhouse-style food, carefully prepared, is a big draw at this comfortable old pub where Mrs Boulton-Taylor has been doing visitors proud for more than 35 years. The lunchtime cold table displays her excellent veal pie alongside ham on the bone, beef sirloin, pâtés and salads. Tasty home-made soup is much in demand and your steak and kidney pie or chops come with home-grown vegetables. Book at night. Terrace.
Typical prices Calf's liver & bacon £3.50 Treacle tart £1.20

WANSFORD — Haycock Hotel

FOOD
B & B

Nr Peterborough
MAP 6 D1 *Cambridgeshire*
Stamford (0780) 782223
Parking ample

Bar food 12–2.30 & 6–10.30, Sun 12–2 & 7–10

Landlord Richard Neale
Free house
Ruddles County, Rutland Bitter; Bass; Younger's Scotch; Carling Black Label; Tennent's Extra; Carlsberg; cider.

Six acres of grounds reaching down to the river Nene surround this lively 17th-century hotel in a picturesque village just off the A1. A splendid cold buffet is laid out in the River Lounge – a pleasant spot overlooking the walled garden – and snacks can also be eaten by the fireside in the comfortable bar (with friendly waitress service available in both rooms). Hot choices from a varied selection might include home-made soup and granary bread, garlicky baked mushrooms, a seasonal game casserole

and vegetarian offerings such as wild rice risotto with hazelnuts. Enjoyable sweets like chocolate brandy mousse to finish. Traditional Sunday lunch menu.
Typical prices Courgettes & prawns £4.75 Stir-fried pork £3.95 ⊜

ACCOMMODATION **25 bedrooms £A**
Check-in all day

Accommodation is of an extremely high standard: all the bedrooms are individually decorated and boast fine reproduction furniture, with four-posters in some. Direct-dial phones, remote-control TVs, hairdryers and trouser presses are among the many accessories, and all the bathrooms are en suite.

Credit Access, Amex, Diners, Visa

WANSTROW — King William IV

FOOD

Shepton Mallet
MAP 9 D1 *Somerset*
Upton Noble (074 985) 247
Parking limited

Bar food 12–2 & 7–9.30, Sun 12–1.30 & 7–9

Landlords Kathy & John Geen
Brewery Usher
Usher Best Bitter, Triple Crown; Webster Yorkshire Bitter; Watney Special Mild; Guinness; Carlsberg.
No real ale.

Good, sound bar snacks are the speciality of the Geens' neatly kept, unpretentious pub. Traditional favourites such as grilled gammon or steak, ploughman's and salads are backed up by daily specials, which include a delicious, lightly spiced chicken curry or a beef and mushroom casserole. The lounge bar displays an interesting collection of tools, and there's a skittle alley for the energetic. Patio.
Typical prices Chilli con carne £3.25 Home-cured ham salad £2.95 ⊜

WARBOROUGH — Six Bells

FOOD

The Green South
MAP 7 B2 *Oxfordshire*
Warborough (086 732) 8265
Parking ample

Bar food 12–2 & 7.30–9.30
Landlords Mr & Mrs Bethell
Brewery Brakspear
Brakspear Pale Ale, Special, Old Ale; Guinness; Heineken.

Next to the village green, this thatched 17th-century pub has real old-world charm with its low ceilings, beams and exposed stonework. Tasty, robust food includes lasagne and steak chasseur as well as simpler items like winter soups and lunchtime open sandwiches. Restaurant meals available Friday and Saturday evenings, traditional Sunday roasts in winter. Garden.
Typical prices Mushroom dip £2.95 Steak & kidney pie £2.95 ⊜
Credit Access, Visa

WARENFORD — Warenford Lodge

FOOD

Nr Belford
MAP 4 D1 *Northumberland*
Belford (066 83) 453
Parking ample

Bar food 12–1.30 & 7–9.30
Closed Mon lunch (except Bank Hols) & Mon eve (Oct–Easter)

Landlord Ray Matthewman
Free house
McEwan's Best Scotch; Newcastle Exhibition; Drybrough Heavy; Carlsberg; cider.

Off the A1, a friendly village pub offering a nice variety of seasonal snacks and generous main course dishes. The summer menu includes delicacies such as mussels steamed in wine, curried prawns on poori and croques parisiens, while heartier appetites can tackle a fine Northumberland fish soup or deep-fried Georgian chicken in whisky. Good puds, too.
Typical prices Cheese & asparagus £1.95 Poached salmon £4.90 ⊜
Credit Diners, Visa

WARK — Battlesteads Hotel

B & B

Nr Hexham
MAP 3 C2 *Northumberland*
Bellingham (0660) 30209
Parking ample

Landlords Robert & Jane Dodd
Free house
Drybrough Heavy, Scotch; Tetley Bitter; Guinness; Castlemaine XXXX; cider.

ACCOMMODATION 7 bedrooms £D
Check-in all day

A peaceful setting five miles to the north of Hadrian's Wall is the location for this characterful and friendly roadside pub dating back to 1690. The cosy bar boasts an ancient carved oak dresser and open fireplace. The homely bedrooms have a mellow decor and simple furnishings; early morning tea is brought in. There are two well-maintained public bathrooms and a first-floor residents' lounge with pretty views. Garden.

WARMINGTON — Wobbly Wheel Inn

FOOD

Nr Banbury
MAP 7 B1 *Warwickshire*
Farnborough (029 589) 214
Parking ample

Bar food 12–2.30 (Sun 12–2) & 7–10

Landlord Mike Hayden
Free house
Younger's Scotch; Wilson Original Bitter; Webster Yorkshire Bitter; Guinness; Carlsberg; Holsten.

This sturdy, Cotswold-stone pub stands alongside the busy A41. Two characterful beamed bars are the setting for robust, dependably prepared snacks that range from favourite sandwiches, jacket potatoes, pâtés and salads to more exotic fare – perhaps deep-fried Camembert or roast pheasant with Madeira sauce. There's a restaurant, too. Garden.

Typical prices Lasagne £3.65 Ploughman's £2.10

Credit Access, Diners, Visa

WARMINSTER — Old Bell Hotel

FOOD
B & B

Market Place
MAP 5 B3 *Wiltshire*
Warminster (0985) 216611
Parking ample

Bar food 12–2.30

Landlord Howard Astbury
Brewery Wadworth
Wadworth 6X, Devizes Bitter; Bass; Guinness; Harp; Heineken; Stella Artois.

A splendid old building with a colonnaded facade in Warminster's handsome market place. A former coaching inn, its courtyard is now a delightful place to enjoy some honest home cooking in warmer weather. Inside, choose between the traditional lounge bar or the beamed Chimes bar with its excellent cold buffet. The changing menu could include steak and kidney pie, Wiltshire special (various meats in a cheesy sauce), bubble and squeak, liver and bacon, or devilled kidneys. Finish with a good traditional pudding such as baked jam roll, sherry trifle or bread and butter pudding. Soup, sandwiches and salads are available on request in the evening, and there's always a traditional roast on Sundays.

Typical prices Chilli con carne £1.60 Beef curry £1.60

ACCOMMODATION 16 bedrooms £C
Check-in all day

Neat bedrooms (ten with their own functional bath or shower rooms) have practical wood veneer fitted units, colour TVs and tea-makers.

Credit Access, Amex, Diners, Visa

Prices given are as at the time of our research and thus may change.

WARREN STREET **Harrow Inn**

OD & B

Nr Lenham
MAP 6 E3 *Kent*
Maidstone (0622) 858727
Parking ample

Bar food 12–2 & 7–10

Landlord Mark Watson
Free house
Shepherd Neame Master Brew Bitter; Goacher Maidstone Ale; guest beer; Guinness; Beck's Bier; Hurlimann Sternbrau; cider.

Just off the A20 and close to the M2 this carefully converted inn was once the forge and rest house for travellers to Canterbury along the Pilgrim's Way. There's plenty of room in the comfortable lounge bar, or you can sit out in the tranquil garden. Imaginative bar food makes good use of local produce, with venison in a cherry and wine sauce, baked whiting and a tasty seafood pancake, as well as lighter snacks such as soup and sandwiches. Puds are splendidly traditional, with queen of puddings, spicy bread and butter pudding and fruit crumbles.

Typical prices Crab & tomato quiche £2.65 Beef & pheasant casserole £4.95

ACCOMMODATION **7 bedrooms £C**
Check-in restricted

Well-kept bedrooms are in a modern style, with darkwood furniture and fitted units and luxurious furnishings. Four have en suite facilities and the public bathroom, too, is spotless. Residents can watch TV in a cosy chintzy lounge with a wood-burning stove. Good breakfasts. Children are welcome overnight. *No dogs.*

Credit Access, Visa

WARRINGTON **Barley Mow**

A

Golden Square
MAP 3 C4 *Cheshire*
Warrington (0295) 31153
Parking difficult

Landlord Susan Haskey
Brewery Tetley Walker
Ind Coope Burton Ale; Tetley Bitter, Mild; Guinness; Castlemaine XXXX; Skol; cider.

A splendid genuine Tudor facade graces this handsome pub, which stands on the corner of a smart shopping precinct. Inside, it has been sensitively revamped so as to preserve its historic character and there is a wealth of panelling and oak beams set off by old prints. Literary-minded toppers will particularly enjoy the book-lined 'library' room. The atmosphere is jolly, and the beers are well-kept. Patio.

WARWICK-ON-EDEN **Queen's Arms Inn**

& B

Nr Carlisle
MAP 3 C2 *Cumbria*
Wetheral (0228) 60699
Parking ample

Landlords John & Joyce Jenkins
Free house
Tetley Bitter, Drum Bitter, Mild; Guinness; Castlemaine XXXX; Oranjeboom; cider.

ACCOMMODATION **8 bedrooms £C**
Check-in all day

Just a few minutes' drive from junction 43 of the M6, this white-painted 18th-century inn offers a friendly welcome and pleasant overnight accommodation. Neatly kept bedrooms (including three in a separate cottage) all have TVs, radio-alarms and tea-makers, as well as practical little bathrooms, mostly with showers only. There's a convivial bar and a well-equipped children's playground next to the beer garden.

Credit Access, Amex, Diners, Visa

WASDALE HEAD — Wasdale Head Inn

FOOD
B & B

Nr Gosforth
MAP 3 B2 *Cumbria*
Wasdale (094 06) 229
Parking ample

Bar food 11–3 & 6–10
Closed Mon–Fri (mid Jan–mid Mar & mid Nov–28 Dec)
Landlord Mr J. R. M. Carr
Free house
Jennings Bitter; Theakston Best Bitter, Old Peculier, Slalom 'D'; cider.

ACCOMMODATION **11 bedrooms £A**
Check-in all day

Walking and climbing are favourite pastimes around this splendid inn, which stands in a secluded position at the head of one of Lakeland's unspoilt valleys. The panelled bars have a very straightforward choice of appetising fare (there's also a restaurant). Chicken liver pâté is fresh and well flavoured, and main courses include cheese and onion flan, chicken casserole and tasty pies. The platter of local smoked meats is a popular choice, and a daily-changing choice of sweets nearly always includes a fruit pie.
Typical prices Smoked meat platter £3.60 Shepherd's pie £2.10

Overnight accommodation (half-board only) comprises eleven comfortable, cosy bedrooms, all with practical tiled bath/shower rooms and most with lovely views. Day rooms include a delightful residents' lounge featuring a restored Victorian fireplace. Good management. Accommodation closed mid-January to mid-March and mid-November to 28 December.

Credit Access, Visa

WASHBROOK — Brook Inn

FOOD

Back Lane, Nr Ipswich
MAP 6 E2 *Suffolk*
Copdock (047 386) 455
Parking ample

Bar food 12–2
No bar food eves & Sun
Landlords William & Nicky Freeth
Brewery Tollemache & Cobbold
Tolly Cobbold Original, 4X, Mild; Guinness; Dortmunder Lager; cider.

Homely lunchtime snacks are served in this comfortable village pub. The menu is shortish and quite simple, and the day's savoury pie is always one of the most popular dishes. Other choices might be warming leek soup, sirloin steak, smoked trout and grilled duck breast. There's also a good selection of cheeses and a sweet of the day. Patio.
Typical prices Fish pie £2.75 Stilton soup 95p
Credit Access, Visa **LVs**

WASHINGTON — Frankland Arms

FOOD

Nr Storrington
MAP 6 D4 *West Sussex*
Ashington (0903) 892220
Parking ample

Bar food 12–2.15 & 7–9.30 (Sat till 10)
Landlords Bob & Jane Carey
Brewery Whitbread
Whitbread Best Bitter; Flowers Original; Strong Country Bitter; Guinness; Stella Artois; Heineken; cider.

The blackboard specials provide the pick of the eating in this whitewashed pub just off the A24. Puff pastry pies (lamb and apricot, steak and kidney, chicken with leeks and sweetcorn) are the house speciality, and other favourites include lasagne, game casserole and a roast every Sunday and Wednesday. Ploughman's and open granary sandwiches for quick bites. Garden.
Typical prices Lamb, apricot & almond pie £2.85 Seaford lasagne £3.25
Credit Access, Visa

WATERINGBURY NEW ENTRY Wateringbury Hotel

& B

Tonbridge Road, Nr Maidstone
MAP 7 D3 *Kent*
Maidstone (0622) 812632
Parking ample

Landlord Mr Wylie
Owner Whitbread Coaching Inns
Whitbread Best Bitter; Flowers Original; Fremlins Bitter; Guinness; Stella Artois; Heineken; cider.

***ACCOMMODATION* 28 bedrooms £B**
Check-in all day

Standards of accommodation are high at this roadside hotel overlooking hopfields and orchards. Bedrooms are a decent size and all have tiled and carpeted bathrooms and a full range of modern comforts from alarm-radios and tea and coffee making facilities to hairdryers and trouser presses. The public areas include a residents' lounge in contemporary style and a cosy public bar with live music on Friday nights. Friendly staff. Garden. *No dogs.*
Credit Access, Amex, Diners, Visa **LVs**

WATERLEY BOTTOM New Inn

& B

North Nibley, Dursley
MAP 7 A2 *Gloucestershire*
Dursley (0453) 3659
Parking ample

Landlord Ruby Sainty
Free house
Greene King Abbot Ale; Theakston Old Peculier; Smiles Best, Exhibition; Cotleigh Tawny, WB; Guinness; Stella Artois; cider.

***ACCOMMODATION* 2 bedrooms £D**
Check-in restricted

Ruby Sainty's friendly inn – a veritable haven for real ale drinkers – nestles in a beautiful secluded valley. Ask for directions. The stonework and rustic character of the beamed bars contrasts with the equally attractive modern style furnishings of the two bedrooms. Bright and comfortable, with duvets, teamakers and TVs, they share a well-kept bathroom, and also offer a fine view of the surrounding countryside. Children are welcome overnight. *No dogs.*

WATH-IN-NIDDERDALE Sportsman's Arms

OD
& B

Pateley Bridge, Nr Harrogate
MAP 4 D3 *North Yorkshire*
Harrogate (0423) 711306
Parking ample

Bar food 12–2
No bar food eves

Landlords Ray & Jane Carter
Free house
Younger's Scotch; McEwan's Export; Guinness; Carlsberg Hof; Harp; Beck's Bier; cider.

The river Nidd runs not a hundred yards from this handsome sandstone hotel, which stands in an area of great natural beauty just a quarter of a mile from Gouthwaite Reservoir, famous for its birdlife. Enjoyable lunchtime snacks may be ordered in the bar and there's also a restaurant with à la carte and fixed price menus. Soup, chicken liver pâté and ploughman's, avocado with prawns, rarebit and pasta are typical snacks, or you can push the boat out with the day's fish special, perhaps monkfish with Chablis sauce, or a sirloin steak. Traditional Sunday lunch menu also available.
Typical prices Nidderdale trout £3.60 Wath rarebit £2.60

***ACCOMMODATION* 6 bedrooms £C**
Check-in all day

Bedrooms, all of a decent size, are kept very neat and tidy. Attractive pine furnishings and pretty floral fabrics take the eye, and all now have colour TVs. Two rooms have their own bathrooms. Besides the simply appointed bar there's a comfortable lounge and a homely TV room. Garden. Accommodation closed four days Christmas.

Credit Access, Amex, Diners, Visa

WATTON-AT-STONE — George & Dragon

FOOD

MAP 7 D2 *Hertfordshire*
Ware (0920) 830285
Parking ample

Bar food 12–2 & 7.15–10
No bar food Sun
Landlords Christine & Kevin Dinnin
Brewery Greene King
Greene King IPA, Abbot Ale, KK Light Mild; Harp; Kronenbourg. *No real ale.*

A Millionaire bun – tender fillet steak with salad garnish in a toasted roll – is just one of the delights on the menu at this mellow redbrick pub, which was first licensed in 1603. Others include tasty duck in red wine (a dish of the day), quails' eggs in lemon mayonnaise, Japanese oysters and king prawns on skewers. Traditional snacks and nice puds are also on offer. Garden.
Typical prices George & Dragon smokey £2.75 Ploughman's £2
Credit Access, Amex, Diners, Visa

WELFORD-ON-AVON — Shakespeare Inn

FOOD

Chapel Street
MAP 7 A1 *Warwickshire*
Stratford-upon-Avon (0789) 750443
Parking limited

Bar food 12–2 (Sun till 1.30) & 7–9.30
No bar food Sun eve (mid Oct–Easter)
Landlords Mr & Mrs J.M. Shaw
Brewery Whitbread
Flowers Original, IPA; Guinness; Stella Artois; Heineken; cider.

Lovely hot home-made pies topped with excellent flaky pastry attract the customers to this charming village pub, whose homely bar is well-stocked with paperbacks. Other choices include pâté, a variety of ploughman's, sandwiches and jacket potatoes, with more elaborate evening options such as trout, steak and mixed grills. Garden.
Typical prices Steak & kidney pie £2.85 Gammon steak & pineapple £2.85
Credit Access, Visa

WELL — Chequers

A

Nr Odiham
MAP 5 C3 *Hampshire*
Basingstoke (0256) 862605
Parking ample

Closed Mon
Landlord Maurice Bernard
Free house
Hall & Woodhouse Badger Best, Tanglefoot; Guinness; Stella Artois; cider.

A French landlord and staff lend a Gallic flavour to the convivial atmosphere at this delightfully unspoilt 17th-century pub. Panelled walls, a low ceiling, lots of old carving, horse brasses, candle holders and assorted bric-a-brac make the bar an atmospheric spot for a quiet drink, while in summer the pretty patio covered by a flourishing vine is especially popular. There's a garden, too.
Credit Access, Diners, Visa

WENDRON — New Inn

B & B

Nr Helston
MAP 9 A3 *Cornwall*
Helston (032 65) 2683
Parking ample

Landlord Bill & Gloria Standcumbe
Brewery Cornish Brewery Company
Devenish, Cornish, Falmouth Bitter; Guinness; Grünhalle; Heineken; cider.

***ACCOMMODATION* 2 bedrooms £D**
Check-in all day

The exterior of this pleasant little stone pub opposite the churchyard is bedecked with flowers, while polished horse brasses, bridles and posting horns adorn the spotless and appealing stone-walled interior. Upstairs, two modest but comfortable bedrooms have traditional furnishings and colour TVs; they share a neat modern bathroom. Patio. Accommodation closed one week Christmas. *No children under 14 overnight. No dogs.*

WENTWORTH — George & Dragon

OOD

Main Street
MAP 4 D4 *South Yorkshire*
Barnsley (0226) 742440
Parking ample

Bar food 12–2.15 & 7–9
Landlord Margaret Dickinson
Free house
Theakston Old Peculier, XB; Taylor Bitter Ale; Oak Double Dagger; Löwenbräu; cider.

The old-fashioned bar of this pub in the attractive stone village of Wentworth is a genuinely comfortable place to eat and drink. A small menu of good wholesome food offers an excellent ploughman's, sandwiches and salads to complement the three or so hot dishes available daily – perhaps fidget pie or tasty onion surprise. Splendid moist ale and fruit cake to finish. Sandwiches only evenings. Courtyard.

Typical prices Wholewheat pasta salad £1.65 Beef & veg roll £2.20

WEOBLEY — Red Lion Hotel

OOD & B

MAP 5 A2 *Hereford & Worcester*
Weobley (0544) 318220
Parking ample

Bar food 12–2 & 7–9.30
Landlord E.J. Townley-Berry
Free house
Usher Founder's Ale; Webster Yorkshire Bitter; Guinness; Carlsberg Hof; cider.

There are many historic buildings in the village and this delightful half-timbered pub, where Mr Townley-Berry offers a genial welcome to his guests, dates from the 14th century. At the bar there are sandwiches, toasties, a cold buffet and home-made hot dishes (including vegetarian meals), as well as a new carvery. A bistro has also been added, serving à la carte French meals. In the comfortable dining room hearty appetites can be satisfied by a wider range of dishes. There are home-made desserts and an excellent cheeseboard serving well-kept English cheeses to round off a good meal. Sunday lunch is table d'hôte at £8.95.

Typical prices Chicken chasseur £3.75 Kidneys turbigo £3.75

***ACCOMMODATION* 7 bedrooms £C**
Check-in all day

The seven bedrooms offer smart, comfortable accommodation. Furnishings are simple, providing plenty of storage and writing space, and there are spotless bath or shower rooms en suite. All have TVs and telephones. Amenities include a patio, garden and bowling green.

Credit Access, Visa

WEST ADDERBURY — White Hart

OOD

Tanners Lane, Nr Banbury
MAP 7 B1 *Oxfordshire*
Banbury (0295) 810406
Parking limited

Bar food 12–2.15 & 7.30–9.30
No bar food Sun & Mon eves
Landlords Andrina & Frank Coroon
Free house
Hook Norton Best Bitter; Webster Yorkshire Bitter; Fosters; Tennent's Special.

In a peaceful village just off the A423 Banbury–Oxford road, this attractive Cotswold-stone pub offers the warmest of welcomes. Excellent cooked meats, quiches, prawns and salads make up the appetising cold table, while hot choices might include curry, lasagne, savoury pancakes or Malaysian fried noodles. Nice sweets, too, like chocolate pots or home-made bakewell tart. Garden.

Typical prices Chicken & ham pancakes £4 Belgian chocolate cake £1

WEST ILSLEY — Harrow

FOOD

Nr Newbury
MAP 7 B3 *Berkshire*
East Ilsley (063 528) 260
Parking ample
Bar food 12–2 & 7–9.30

Landlord Heather Humphreys
Brewery Morland
Morland Mild, Bitter, Best Bitter; Guinness; Heineken; cider.

This attractive pub opposite the village pond has an interesting and varied bar menu – spinach and mushroom roulade or baked trout stuffed with cucumber are typical delights. There's traditional fare, too, like steak and kidney pie and brown bread sandwiches. Home-made sweets include a terrine of cheesecake and summer fruits. Traditional Sunday roast.
Typical prices Rabbit pie £2.30 Treacle tart with cream £1.50
Credit Access, Visa

WEST LAVINGTON — Wheatsheaf Inn

B & B

Nr Devizes
MAP 7 A3 *Wiltshire*
Devizes (038 081) 3392
Parking ample
Landlord Trevor Emery
Free house
Wadworth 6X, IPA; Tetley Bitter; Guinness; Castlemaine XXXX; Löwenbräu; cider.

ACCOMMODATION **10 bedrooms £D**
Check-in restricted

Improvements have recently taken place at this black and white village pub on the A360. Stables have been converted into a smartly comfortable lounge bar extension, and there's also a rustic public bar with pool table, a function room and skittle alley. Bedrooms range from modern, with contemporary furniture, pretty fabrics and bedside consoles, to more traditional. All have teamakers and colour TVs: seven have en suite facilities. Garden.

WEST LULWORTH — Castle Inn

B & B

MAP 9 D2 *Dorset*
West Lulworth (092 941) 311
Parking ample
Landlords Pat & Graham Halliday
Brewery Devenish
Devenish Dark Mild, John Groves, Great British Heavy, Wessex; Guinness; Holsten Export; Fosters.

ACCOMMODATION **13 bedrooms £D**
Check-in all day

A terraced garden is among the charms of this 17th-century thatched pub. Long, low and picture-postcard-pretty, it has numerous cosy corners in the country-style bars, while the bedrooms benefit from delightfully homely touches like books, sweets, biscuits and ornaments. Five are in a newer extension and one room on the ground floor is suitable for the disabled. All but two rooms have private facilities; in addition there are two public bathrooms.
Credit Access, Amex, Diners, Visa

WEST WITTON — Wensleydale Heifer

B & B

Nr Leyburn
MAP 4 D3 *North Yorkshire*
Wensleydale (0969) 22322
Parking ample
Landlords Major & Mrs Sharp
Free house
John Smith's Bitter; Tetley Bitter; McEwan's Export; Castlemaine XXXX; Stella Artois.

ACCOMMODATION **20 bedrooms £B**
Check-in all day

Set among splendid scenery, on the A684 Leyburn-Hawes road, this 17th-century inn is a comfortable base for tourists and walkers. Half the bedrooms are in the main building, the rest in adjacent premises; decor is quietly appealing, and furnishings range from modern lightwood fitted units to attractive period pieces. TVs and tea-makers are standard, and all rooms have neat en suite shower or bathroom. Charming bar, inviting lounge.
Credit Access, Amex, Visa

WESTBURY — Reindeer Inn

OOD

Nr Brackley
MAP 7 B1 *Buckinghamshire*
Brackley (0280) 704934
Parking ample
Bar food 12–2 & 7.30–9.30
No bar food Sun & Mon eves

Landlord Joanne Hicks
Brewery Manns
Manns; Wilson Original Mild; Webster Yorkshire Bitter; Guinness; Holsten Export; Fosters; cider.

A sturdy, stone-built pub where a fine beer garden draws the crowds on sunny days. Beams and an open fireplace create a rustic atmosphere in the bar, where a simple menu covers a range of tasty snacks; choose from smoked mackerel, Brixworth pâté, chicken Kiev, steak, burgers, salads and open sandwiches. There is a very popular hot chocolate fudge cake and ice cream.
Typical prices Lasagne & salad £2 Banana split £1.20

WESTON — White Lion

OOD
& B

Nr Crewe
MAP 3 C4 *Cheshire*
Crewe (0270) 587011
Parking ample
Bar food 12–2.15 & 7–9.45
Landlords Alison & Gordon Davies
Brewery Ind Coope
Tetley Bitter; Ind Coope Burton Ale, Bitter, Mild; Guinness; Löwenbräu; cider.

There's a comfortable, mellow atmosphere at Alison and Gordon Davies' friendly black and white village pub that dates back to 1652. Old settles, brassware and horsy bric-a-brac characterise the beamed bar, and the garden has a bowling green for those keen to work up a thirst – and appetite. The extensive choice of dishes ranges from soup, pâtés and toasted sandwiches (note the Lionheart version, featuring chicken, bacon, lettuce and mayonnaise) to meat and fish platters, grilled entrecôte steak and the daily-changing weekday roast. Fresh strawberry roulade, apple layer cake and trifle are typical of the enjoyable sweets on offer.
Typical prices Toasted steak sandwich £3.25 Roast of the day £2.50

ACCOMMODATION **16 bedrooms £B**
Check-in all day

A sympathetically designed extension has added 16 brand new bedrooms to the White Lion's attractions. Each room has an en suite bath or shower room, together with a colour TV and direct-dial telephone. Accommodation closed five days over Christmas and New Year. Garden. *No dogs.*

WESTWOOD — New Inn

OOD

Nr Bradford-on-Avon
MAP 7 A3 *Wiltshire*
Bradford-on-Avon (022 16) 3123
Parking ample
Bar food 12–2 & 6–10, Sun 12–1.30 & 7–10
Landlords Mr and Mrs F. McFadden
Brewery Usher
Usher Best Bitter, Founder's Ale, PA; Webster Yorkshire Bitter; Carlsberg; Holsten; cider.

There's an impressive choice of bar food at this cosy village pub, where local ladies produce anything from a quick bite to a slap-up meal. Fish chowder, lasagne and shepherd's pie are popular one-course orders, and other goodies range from hot smoked mackerel to scampi, gammon, and mushroom and prawn stuffed plaice. Puds include a really super treacle tart. Patio.
Typical prices Roast duckling £5.50 Home-made beef casserole £2.40

WETHERBY — Alpine Inn

FOOD

MAP 4 D3 *North Yorkshire*
Wetherby (0937) 62501
Parking ample

Bar food 11–2.30 & 6–10.30, Sun 12–2 & 7–10.30

Landlord Alan Gillam
Brewery Samuel Smith
Samuel Smith's Old Brewery Bitter; Ayingerbräu; cider.

On the southbound carriageway of the A1, this Alpine-style inn is a handy stopping place for the hungry motorist. Everything in the food line is home-made, the house speciality being a fillet steak sandwich served on a sizzling platter. Burgers, ploughman's and jacket potatoes are other options, with apple pie and gâteau among the sweets; plus a roast on Sundays. Garden.
Typical prices Alpine salad £3.50 Fillet steak sandwich £4.30
Credit Access, Visa

WHATCOTE — Royal Oak

A

Nr Shipston-on-Stour
MAP 7 B1 *Warwickshire*
Tysoe (029 588) 319
Parking ample

Landlords Matthews family
Free house
Hook Norton Best Bitter; Flowers Best Bitter; Guinness; Heineken; Stella Artois; cider.

A delightful village pub with the remains of the oak in its name outside. Built in 1168 as an ale house for the workers building churches in the area, it also features a large chimney with iron rungs leading up to a hideaway used by Oliver Cromwell during the Battle of Edge Hill. Today, the bar, with its beams and low ceilings, offers an atmosphere full of character in which to enjoy a convivial drink. Genial hosts. Garden.

WHITEWELL — Inn at Whitewell

B & B

Forest of Bowland, Nr Clitheroe
MAP 3 C3 *Lancashire*
Dunsop Bridge (020 08) 222
Parking ample

Landlords Bowman family
Free house
Moorhouses Burnley Bitter, Pendle Witches Brew; Webster Yorkshire Bitter; Wilson Special Mild; Guinness; Carlsberg; cider.

ACCOMMODATION **12 bedrooms £B**
Check-in all day

A winding stretch of a tributary of the Ribble makes a delightfully peaceful setting for this friendly old inn. The pleasantly rustic bars are warmed by open fires and a quiet residents' lounge also serves as an art gallery. The cosy bedrooms are tastefully furnished with nice wallpapers and some period pieces. Half have their own facilities; the rest share two modern carpeted bathrooms. Patio and garden.
Credit Access, Amex, Diners, Visa

WHITNEY-ON-WYE — Rhydspence Inn

FOOD
B & B

MAP 5 A2 *Hereford & Worcester*
Clifford (049 73) 262
Parking ample

Bar food 12–1.30 & 7–9.30

Landlords Peter & Pam Glover
Free house
Robinson Bitter; Hook Norton Best Bitter; Mitchells & Butlers DPA; Bass Special; Guinness; Carling Black Label; cider.

A stunning view over the Wye Valley and the Black Mountains is just one of the bonuses of this half-timbered, 16th-century inn by the A438. The fine old bar, complete with beams and old oak furniture, fairly oozes character, and here you can tuck into a variety of delicious dishes. The standard menu offers Devon farm sausages, smoked mackerel, beef pasties, fried whitebait, home-made pâté, grilled fresh sardines, ploughman's and sandwiches, while from the blackboard menu you could

start with avocado with crab or ogen melon with blackcurrant sorbet; then move on to guinea fowl forestière or Wye salmon hollandaise. Don't miss the selection of 14 English cheeses.
Typical prices Prawns in white wine & garlic £3.75 Grilled rack of lamb £6.95

ACCOMMODATION **5 bedrooms £C**
Check-in all day

The homely bedrooms have pine furniture, an armchair, tea and coffee making facilities and colour TVs. Sloping floors, warm colour schemes, books and fresh flowers all create a delightful atmosphere. Garden. *No dogs.*

Credit Access, Amex, Visa

WICKHAM — Five Bells

B & B

MAP 7 B3 *Berkshire*
Boxford (048 838) 242
Parking ample

Landlord Mrs D.A. Channing-Williams
Brewery Usher
Usher Best Bitter; Webster Yorkshire Bitter; Guinness; Fosters; Carlsberg; cider.

ACCOMMODATION **4 bedrooms £C**
Check-in all day

Dottie Channing-Williams and her delightful staff run this attractive thatched country pub in a warm and friendly fashion. A log fire warms the cosy, low-beamed bar, which opens on to a large garden with a children's swimming pool. Four neat bedrooms in an adjoining stable block are simple and spotless and share a good-sized bathroom; all have washbasins, colour TVs and tea and coffee making facilities.
Credit Visa

WILMCOTE — Swan House Hotel

B & B

Nr Stratford-on-Avon
MAP 7 A1 *Warwickshire*
Stratford (0789) 67030
Parking ample

Landlords Ian & Diana Sykes
Free house
Wadworth 6X; Marston Pedigree; Hook Norton Best Bitter; Carlsberg Hof; Carlsberg; cider.

ACCOMMODATION **11 bedrooms £B**
Check-in all day

This welcoming white-painted hotel is in the heart of Shakespeare country (the Bard's mother, Mary Arden, lived in Wilmcote). The attractive bar is a popular rendezvous for real ale drinkers. Well-kept bedrooms have light colour schemes, and white furniture. All have tea/coffee-makers; eight in the main house have en suite facilities, while three in an annexe share one spotless bathroom. Accommodation closed four days Christmas. *No dogs.*
Credit Access, Amex, Visa

Changes in data may occur in establishments after the Guide goes to press. Prices should be taken as indications rather than firm quotes.

WIMBORNE ST GILES — Bull Inn

FOOD
B & B

MAP 5 B4 *Dorset*
Cranborne (072 54) 284
Parking ample

Bar food 12–2 & 7–10
Landlord Mr A. D. Sharp
Brewery Hall & Woodhouse
Hall & Woodhouse Badger Best, Badger Export; Guinness; Hall & Woodhouse Brock Lager; Carlsberg Hof; Stella Artois; cider.

Standing peacefully in the middle of the Shaftesbury Estate, this charming little place is worth seeking out whether for an overnight stop or just a bar snack. Charcoal-grilled steaks are the house speciality, and other main courses include basket meals, steak and kidney pie, vegetarian bake and, when the season's right, crab and lobster from Poole. Daily specials like stuffed vine leaves add to the interest, and for lighter bites there are salads and ploughmans' platters (cheese or meat). Kiddies' dishes, too, and a nice Bakewell tart or locally made chocolate trifle gâteau are among the sweets.
Typical prices Steak & kidney pie £3.25 Fresh porky crab £7.50

ACCOMMODATION **3 bedrooms £D**
Check-in restricted

Three simply furnished bedrooms with pretty fabrics and pleasing views are kept in tip-top condition and share an equally spotless modern bathroom. Washbasins and tea-makers in each room. There's a pleasant garden. Accommodation closed two weeks Christmas. *No children overnight. No dogs.*

Our inspectors never book in the name of Egon Ronay's Guides; they disclose their identity only after paying their bills.

WINCHAM — Black Greyhound Hotel

FOOD

Hall Lane, Nr Northwich
MAP 3 C4 *Cheshire*
Northwich (0606) 3053
Parking ample

Bar food 12–2 & 7.30–10
Landlords David & Janet Buckley
Brewery Greenall Whitley
Greenall Whitley Local Bitter, Mild; Watney Export Gold; Guinness; Grünhalle; cider.

A friendly welcome and good food are on offer at this large roadhouse-style pub. There is a comprehensive range of imaginative dishes: steak and kidney pie, vegetarian lasagne, grilled gammon and pineapple and a variety of fish dishes from fried plaice to cod with prawns. Delicious sweets such as cabinet pudding. Traditional roast available on Sundays. Garden.
Typical prices Beef stroganoff £3 Tagliatelle £2.75
Credit Access, Visa **LVs**

WINCHCOMBE — George Inn

B & B

High Street
MAP 7 A1 *Gloucestershire*
Winchcombe (0242) 602331
Parking limited

Landlord Mr S. Smith
Brewery Whitbread
Flowers IPA, Original, Best Bitter; Stella Artois; Heineken.

ACCOMMODATION **8 bedrooms £C**
Check-in all day

Benedictine monks used this half-timbered inn as a hostelry over 700 years ago, and it remains a comfortable, welcoming place to stay. Spacious, pine-furnished bedrooms offer tea-makers, TVs, trouser presses and direct-dial telephones; all but one have modern carpeted bathrooms. The beamed and flagstoned bars are full of character and the handsome residents' lounge features a magnificent Tudor inglenook and mullioned windows. Gardens. *No dogs.*
Credit Access, Amex, Diners, Visa

WINCHELSEA — Winchelsea Lodge Motel

& B

Sandrock, Hastings Road
MAP 6 E3 *East Sussex*
Rye (0797) 226211
Parking ample

Landlord George Morgan
Free house
Harvey Best Bitter; King & Barnes Festive; Webster Yorkshire Bitter; Fosters; Holsten; Carlsberg.

***ACCOMMODATION* 24 bedrooms £C**
Check-in all day

This modern motel complex on the A259 provides a sharp contrast to Winchelsea's imposing medieval gate, nearby. Bedroom blocks are grouped round the striking split level bar-lounge reception area and offer identical accommodation for the overnight traveller. Bedrooms have neat units, cheerful fabrics, TVs and tea-makers. All have tiled shower rooms, but there are two new ground floor bedrooms with baths. Garden facilities for children.
Credit Access, Amex, Diners, Visa

WINCHESTER — Wykeham Arms

OOD
& B

75 Kingsgate Street
MAP 5 C3 *Hampshire*
Winchester (0962) 53834
Parking ample

Bar food 12–2 & 6.45–8.45
No bar food Mon eve & all Sun

Landlords Graeme & Anne Jameson
Brewery Eldridge Pope
Eldridge Pope Royal Oak, Original IPA, Dorchester Bitter; Guinness; Faust Pilsner; cider.

***ACCOMMODATION* 7 bedrooms £B**
Check-in all day

★ A 17th-century pub near the cathedral which has the combined appeal of a delightful atmosphere and delicious food. Graeme and Anne Jameson make guests as welcome as could be and their attention to detail is commendable. The three convivial bars have log fires in winter, while a pretty garden makes an ideal spot for summer drinking and for sampling the luscious meals. First course might be tuna and bean antipasto or courgette and carrot soup, with escalope of venison au poivre or honey spiced chicken to follow. Mouthwatering sweets such as pear and chocolate flan or blackcurrant fool. ★
Typical prices Stilton & quince pâté £1.95 Pork in cider sauce £4.95 Alresford trout £4.95 Garlic mushrooms £1.95

The centrally heated bedrooms have stylish decor, pine furniture, tea-makers, TVs and mini-bars; five have spotless modern bathrooms. There's a panelled lounge, breakfast room and sauna. *No children under 14 overnight.*

WINFORTON — Sun Inn

OOD

MAP 5 A2 *Hereford & Worcester*
Eardisley (054 46) 677
Parking ample

Bar food 12–2 & 7–9.45, Sun 12–1.30 & 7–9.30
Closed Tues in winter

Landlords Brian & Wendy Hibbard
Free house
Felinfoel Double Dragon; Whitbread Best Bitter; Wadworth 6X; Guinness; Heineken; cider.

Wendy Hibbard is responsible for the constantly changing variety of delicious snacks offered at this charming pub on the A438. Horses brasses and old farm tools decorate the single bar, where you can tackle favourites like cheese mushroom puffs, pizzas, hearty stockpot soup and vegetarian lasagne. Try tipsy pear in pastry to finish. Garden.
Typical prices Devilled crab au gratin £2.30 Pork with brandy & apricots £4.25

WINFRITH NEWBURGH — Red Lion

B & B

Dorchester
MAP 9 D2 *Dorset*
Warmwell (0305) 852814
Parking ample

Landlords Mike & Libby Smeaton
Brewery Hall & Woodhouse
Hall & Woodhouse Tanglefoot, Badger Best; Worthington 'E'; Guinness; Stella Artois; Carlsberg; cider.
***ACCOMMODATION* 4 bedrooms £D**
Check-in all day

An immaculate roadside inn which has been in the care of the Smeaton family for over 40 years. Extensive rebuilding after a fire has not spoilt the charm of the flagstoned public bar, while the wood-panelled lounge bar is relaxing and friendly. There's a small residents' lounge and four simple bedrooms high in comfort and cleanliness. All have colour TVs and tea/coffee-makers and share a spotless bathroom. Garden.
Credit Visa

WINKFIELD — Olde Hatchet

FOOD

Hatchet Lane, Nr Windsor
MAP 7 C3 *Berkshire*
Bracknell (0344) 882303
Parking ample

Bar food 12–2 & 7.30–9.30

Landlord Enrico Pires
Brewery Bass Charrington
Charrington IPA; Bass; Guinness; Carling Black Label; Tennent's Extra, Pilsner. *No real ale.*

There's a fine country feel to this attractive black and white inn with 16th-century origins. Bar snacks are tasty and enjoyable: ploughman's and rolls for quick bites; home-made pâtés; salads; hot dishes like lasagne, chilli or beef marengo. Simple sweets include ice cream and apple bake. A traditional roast is available on Sundays. Garden and patio.
Typical prices Lasagne £3.60 Lamb chop with chasseur sauce £3.95
Credit Access, Amex, Visa

WINKLEIGH — King's Arms

FOOD

MAP 9 B2 *Devon*
Winkleigh (083 783) 384
Parking ample

Bar food 11.30–2.30 & 6–10.30
Closed Mon lunch (except Bank Hols)

Landlord Nigel Hammond Rickard
Free house
Usher Best Bitter, Triple Crown; Webster Yorkshire Bitter; Carlsberg; cider.

A charming, 16th-century village pub where new owner, Nigel Hammond Rickard has not wavered from the previous high standards in both food and hospitality. A cold buffet displays a range of salads, as well as turkey pie, quiches and pasties; also daily hot specials – perhaps roast Devon chicken – and a hearty soup. Tempting sweets include crème caramel and rum chocolate pots.
Typical prices Cod and prawn cobbler £2.25 Poacher's pie £1.40
Credit Access, Amex, Visa

WINKTON — Fisherman's Haunt Hotel

B & B

Salisbury Road, Christchurch
MAP 5 B4 *Dorset*
Christchurch (0202) 484071
Parking ample

Landlords James & Isobel Bochan
Free house
Bass; Ringwood Best Bitter; Guinness; Carling Black Label; Tennent's Export; Carlsberg.
***ACCOMMODATION* 20 bedrooms £C**
Check-in all day

A friendly 17th-century inn by the river Avon. Two beamed bars offer comfortable seating and, more surprisingly, an old well with running spring water. There is a conservatory and a cosy TV lounge. The attractive bedrooms in the stable block have white furniture, pretty fabrics and extras such as direct-dial phones and tea and coffee-makers. Bedrooms in the main building are larger and more traditional. Spotless tiled bathrooms. Garden.
Credit Access, Amex, Diners, Visa

WINSFORD — Royal Oak Inn

& B Exmoor National Park
MAP 9 C1 *Somerset*
Winsford (064 385) 455
Parking ample

Landlord Charles Steven
Free house
Flowers Original, IPA; Whitbread Best Bitter; Guinness; Stella Artois; cider.

ACCOMMODATION **13 bedrooms £A**
Check-in all day

Colourful hanging baskets festoon this picturesque, old thatched inn by the village green. Refurbishment has given first-floor bedrooms a delightfully cottagy look: they include a luxurious suite with big brass bed, dressing room and super bathroom. Modern annexe rooms are equally attractive, and all rooms have TVs, tea-makers and excellent private facilities. Downstairs, the relaxing lounges have been stylishly revamped and there are two rustic bars. Patio.
Credit Access, Amex, Diners, Visa

WINSLOW — Bell Hotel

& B 1 Sheep Street, Market Square
MAP 7 C1 *Buckinghamshire*
Winslow (029 671) 2741
Parking ample

Landlords Mr & Mrs William Alston
Free house
Hook Norton Old Hookey; Adnams Bitter; Marston Pedigree; Samuel Smith's Old Brewery Bitter; Carlsberg; Fosters.

ACCOMMODATION **15 bedrooms £B**
Check-in all day

On the market square in the centre of town, this fine old coaching inn is run with pride and care by the charming Alstons. There's a good choice of convivial drinking areas, including a cosy snug and a beer garden. Attractively decorated bedrooms of a decent size have white freestanding units and offer TVs, tea and coffee making facilities and telephones. All except one have their own well-kept bath/shower room.
Credit Access, Visa

WINTERTON-ON-SEA — Fisherman's Return

& B The Lane
MAP 6 F1 *Norfolk*
Winterton-on-Sea (049 376) 305
Parking ample

Landlords John & Kate Findlay
Brewery Norwich
Norwich S&P Bitter; Webster Yorkshire Bitter; Ruddles County; Guinness; Carlsberg; Fosters; cider.

ACCOMMODATION **4 bedrooms £D**
Check-in restricted

A traditional Norfolk building of brick and flint, this village pub stands just a short walk from the dunes and sea. The panelled bars have a cosy, friendly character, and the first-floor hallway serves as a little lounge area with TV. Neat bedrooms vary in style with modern built-in units or traditional oak furniture. All have sloping ceilings and one has its own charming sitting room. Garden.

WISBECH — Rose & Crown Hotel

& B Market Place
MAP 6 D1 *Cambridgeshire*
Wisbech (0945) 583187
Parking limited

Landlords John Martin & David Owen
Brewery Greene King
Greene King IPA, Abbot Ale; Guest beer; Guinness; Harp Special; Kronenbourg; cider.

ACCOMMODATION **21 bedrooms £C**
Check-in all day

Major refurbishment to the public areas of this town centre hotel has resulted in a sophisticated atmosphere, with cool, modern colour schemes and a collection of contemporary art lining the walls. Bedrooms range from compact with basic furnishings and functional bathrooms to more spacious rooms with modern four-posters and carpeted bathrooms with smart corner baths. All have tea/coffee-makers, colour TVs and telephones. Children welcome overnight.
Credit Access, Amex, Diners, Visa **LVs**

WITHINGTON — Mill Inn

B & B

Nr Cheltenham
MAP 7 A2 *Gloucestershire*
Withington (024 289) 204
Parking ample

Landlord Mr G. P. Stourton
Brewery Samuel Smith
Samuel Smith's Old Brewery Bitter, Museum Ale; Flowers IPA, Best Bitter; Carlsberg; cider.

***ACCOMMODATION* 3 bedrooms £C**
Check-in restricted

Originally built to accommodate workers at the nearby mill, this marvellously traditional inn has a history going back 500 years. The flagstones, beams, yellowed walls and rustic furnishings ooze charm, and the garden which flanks the river Coln is a model of rural tranquillity. Upstairs, to three equally delightful bedrooms with pretty fabrics and sturdy oak pieces, that offer simple but comfortable overnight accommodation.
Credit Access, Visa

WITHYBROOK — Pheasant

FOOD

Main Street, Nr Coventry
MAP 5 C2 *Warwickshire*
Hinckley (0455) 220 480
Parking ample

Bar food 12–2 & 6.30–10 (Sun from 7)
Landlords Mr & Mrs D. Guy & Mr & Mrs A. H. Bean
Free house
Courage Dark Mild, Directors; Everards Old Original; John Smith's Bitter; Hofmeister; Miller Lite; cider.

A busy brookside pub with a bar adorned with rural artefacts and stuffed pheasants. The bar menu is long and varied, with soup and assorted pâtés preceding anything from liver and bacon to lasagne, stuffed plaice to sweetbreads, moules marinière to a mixed grill. Also sandwiches, omelettes, simple sweets. Traditional Sunday lunch served in bar and restaurant.
Typical prices Pheasant in Madeira £4.50 Steak & kidney pie £2.95
Credit Access, Visa

WITHYPOOL — Royal Oak Inn

FOOD
B & B

Nr Minehead
MAP 9 C1 *Somerset*
Exford (064 383) 236
Parking ample

Bar food 12–2 & 7–9.30, Sun 12–1.30 & 7–9
Landlords Mr & Mrs Bradley & Mr & Mrs Lucas
Free house
Usher Best Bitter, Country Bitter, Founder's Ale; Webster Yorkshire Bitter; Guinness; Carlsberg; cider.

Lovers of the great outdoors find both the surroundings and the friendly welcome at this well-maintained 300-year-old inn very much to their liking. When all that fresh air has roused an appetite, rest assured that some suitably hearty snacks await in the rustic bars warmed by open fires. Choose from giant filled rolls, ploughman's and pâté, home-cooked gammon and eggs, locally baked pasties, salads and steaks. In addition, weekends and winter months see a warming special such as a substantial beef stew with herb dumplings, and there are pleasant sweets to finish. There's also a restaurant.
Typical prices Farmhouse pork and herb sausages, salad & chips £3.30 Somerset Brie ploughman's £2.10

***ACCOMMODATION* 8 bedrooms £B**
Check-in all day

A glass of sherry is a typically thoughtful touch in the charming beamed bedrooms, many of which enjoy lovely views. Six now have en suite facilities, and all are equipped with direct-dial phones, hair-dryers, tea-makers and radio-alarms. Patio. *No children under ten overnight.*

Credit Access, Amex, Diners, Visa

WITNEY — Red Lion Hotel

FOOD
B & B

Corn Street,
MAP 7 B2 *Oxfordshire*
Witney (0993) 3149
Parking ample

Bar food 12–2 & 6–10 (Sun from 7)
Landlords Mr & Mrs R. Tams
Brewery Morrell
Morrell Bitter, Friar's Ale; Guinness; Harp; cider.

A convivial crowd gathers in the friendly bars of this homely pub standing at one end of the main road through town. There's something on the menu here to suit all tastes, from hearty main dishes like curry, steak and kidney pie, chilli and corned beef hash to lighter bites such as pâté, pasties, ploughman's and rarebits. Sandwiches include the popular brunch muffin filled with soft cheese, smoked ham and a poached egg, and there's apple pie or treacle tart to finish. A traditional roast is served on Sundays.
Typical prices Wiltshire gammon £2.95 Cauliflower cheese £1.85

ACCOMMODATION **2 bedrooms £B**
Check-in restricted

Accommodation is still in the process of being increased here, and the two first rooms are most agreeable with their pretty fabrics, attractive furnishings and central heating. TVs and tea and coffee making facilities are provided, and each room has its own modern bathroom (en suite). Terrace. *No smoking in bedrooms.*

Any person using our name to obtain free hospitality is a fraud.

Proprietors, please inform Egon Ronay's Guides and the police.

WIXFORD — Three Horseshoes

FOOD

Nr Alcester
MAP 7 A1 *Warwickshire*
Stratford (0789) 773443
Parking ample

Bar food 12–2 & 6.30–9.45
No bar food Mon (except Bank Hols)
Landlords Mr & Mrs Crumpton
Brewery Flowers
Flowers Original, IPA, Best Bitter; Guinness; Stella Artois; Heineken; cider.

This large country inn stands in its own grounds by a pretty little stream. Inside, there's warmth and character a-plenty, plus tasty bar snacks ranging from soup and pâté to grilled plaice, prawn curry, poussin and steaks, as well as sandwiches (lunchtime only). Sweets like apple and blackcurrant pie or gâteau round things off. Traditional Sunday lunch menu. Garden.
Typical prices Baby chicken in herbs & garlic £3.90 Fresh trout £3.20
Credit Access, Visa

WOBURN — NEW ENTRY — Bell Inn

FOOD
B & B

21 Bedford Street
MAP 7 C1 *Bedfordshire*
Woburn (052 525) 280
Parking ample

Bar food 12–2.15 & 6-9.30
No bar food Sun eve

Landlords Tim Chilton & Andrew Wadham
Brewery Greene King
Greene King Abbot Ale, IPA; Guinness; Harp; Kronenbourg; cider.

The main part of this attractive cream pebbledash pub in the main street is 17th century with accordingly gnarled beams and period fireplaces, although the upmarket bar, which has a wine bar atmosphere, is a Victorian addition. The cold food available includes good rare beef, quiche and a wide selection of salads, while for a hot meal there is a variety of offerings such as lasagne and jacket potatoes filled with cheese or prawns, all well-prepared. Desserts – cheesecake, gâteau St Honoré, grasshopper pie, bavarois and home-made ice cream – are particularly delicious. There is a courtyard for sunny days.
Typical prices Seafood pancake £2.95 Walnut roulade £1.20

ACCOMMODATION **6 bedrooms £C**
Check-in all day

The six bedrooms, several of which are beamed, are extremely pretty and welcoming, with floral wallpaper and matching fabrics. Half have nice old pine furniture, while the rest have traditional pieces. Four have smart new bathrooms (one with shower only). Children are welcome overnight. *No dogs.*

Credit Access, Amex, Diners, Visa

WOBURN — Black Horse Inn

FOOD

Bedford Street
MAP 7 C1 *Bedfordshire*
Woburn (052 525) 210
Parking ample

Bar food 12–2.30 & 6–10.30

Landlord Mr T. Aldous
Free house
Marston Burton Bitter, Pedigree; Guinness; Oranjeboom; Castlemaine XXXX; Löwenbräu; cider.

Close to Woburn Abbey, this former coaching inn is a popular haunt for both locals and tourists. Choose between the mellow traditional bar, the comfortable food bar with plenty of tables, or the attractive walled garden on summer days. A good range of bar food includes jumbo steak sandwiches, salads, and a savoury dish of the day, as well as soups and a vegetarian lasagne.
Typical prices Steak & kidney pie £1.85 Coq au vin £1.85
Credit Access, Visa

WOLVEY — Axe & Compass

FOOD

Nr Hinckley
MAP 5 C2 *Warwickshire*
Hinckley (0455) 220240
Parking ample

Bar food 12–2 & 6.30–10

Landlords Jones family
Brewery Mitchells & Butlers
Bass; Mitchells & Butlers Brew XI, Highgate Mild; Guinness; Carling Black Label; Tennent's Pilsner, Extra; cider.

Excellent bar snacks attract the crowds in droves to the Joneses family-run pub, where the landlord's son cooks and his daughter runs the restaurant. The constantly changing selection embraces simple soup, sandwiches and salads as well as more elaborate blackboard specials like chicken and prawn indienne and kidneys turbigo. There's a traditional roast on Sunday. Garden.
Typical prices Coquilles St Jacques £3.50 Lamb & courgette bake £2.50
Credit Access, Visa

WONERSH — Grantley Arms

OD

The Street
MAP 6 D3 *Surrey*
Guildford (0483) 893351
Parking ample

Bar food 12–2 & 7–10
No bar food Sun eve

Landlord John Davidson
Brewery Friary Meux
Friary Meux Bitter; Ind Coope Burton Ale; Tetley Bitter; Guinness; Skol; Löwenbräu.

On the pilgrims' route to Canterbury, this old black and white timbered inn is still offering refreshment to travellers in its mellow bar. Decent rare beef goes down well with salad, and other options are home-made seafood quiche or steak and Guinness pie; there's also the daily special – perhaps chicken in mustard sauce – and home-made sweets. No cold buffet evenings. Patio.
Typical prices Sauté of chicken chasseur £2.75 Apple pie 85p
Credit Access, Amex, Diners, Visa

WOODBRIDGE — Bull Hotel

& B

Market Hill
MAP 6 F2 *Suffolk*
Woodbridge (039 43) 2089
Parking limited

Landlords Neville & Anne Allen
Free house
Adnams Bitter; Younger's Tartan Bitter; John Bull Bitter; Tolly Cobbold Original; Tennent's Lager; Heineken; cider.

ACCOMMODATION **25 bedrooms £B**
Check-in all day

A former coaching inn in the bustling town centre, opposite the fine Tudor shire hall. There are two bars, one very popular with locals and the other more peaceful; also a residents' lounge and a family room. Bedrooms vary in size, facilities and decor. Best ones have antique-style pine furniture, colour TVs and trouser presses; all have tea/coffee-makers. Fourteen bedrooms offer neat, modern en suite bathrooms; the rest share four public bathrooms.
Credit Access, Amex, Diners, Visa

WOODHALL SPA — Abbey Lodge Inn

A

Tattershall Road, Kirkstead
MAP 6 D1 *Lincolnshire*
Woodhall Spa (0526) 52538
Parking ample

Landlords Tom & Eileen Sloan
Brewery John Smith
John Smith's Bitter; Guinness; Hofmeister; cider.

Take the road for Tattershall Castle to reach this cosy, friendly pub which stands in open fields about a mile out of Woodhall Spa. The single long bar, decorated in a rich, warm burgundy red, boasts two central back-to-back fireplaces that provide welcome cheer in winter. Lovingly polished furniture and a mixture of hunting prints and Air Force photographs complete a most inviting and homely atmosphere.
Credit Visa

WOOLER — Tankerville Arms

& B

Cottage Road
MAP 3 C1 *Northumberland*
Wooler (0668) 81581
Parking ample

Landlords Park & Morton families
Free house
McEwan's 80/-, Best Scotch; Drybrough Heavy; Harp; McEwan's Lager; cider.

ACCOMMODATION **15 bedrooms £C**
Check-in all day

Originally built to accommodate the overspill of guests at nearby Chillingham Castle, this welcoming old coaching inn on the A697, overlooking Wooler's livestock market, remains a comfortable overnight stopping place. Spacious, centrally heated bedrooms all offer tea-makers and radios; eight have private facilities, the rest share four well-kept public bathrooms. There's a choice of three bars and a quiet residents' TV lounge. Garden.
Credit Access, Visa

WOOLHOPE — Butchers Arms

FOOD
B & B

Nr Hereford
MAP 5 A2 *Hereford & Worcester*
Fownhope (043 277) 281
Parking ample

Bar food 11.30–2.15 (Sun 12–1.45) & 7–10 (Fri & Sat till 10.30)

Landlords Mrs M. Bailey & Mr W. Griffiths
Free house
Younger's Tartan, Bitter; Hook Norton Best Bitter, Old Hookey; Marston Pedigree; Carlsberg; cider.

In a quiet lane surrounded by meadows and wooded hills, this black and white 14th-century pub has the friendly, informal atmosphere of a proper country pub. Open log fires warm both low-beamed bars in winter, while the patio garden with its flowering shrubs and little stream makes a delightful spot for a peaceful summer's drink. Tasty snacks range from sandwiches, salads and ploughman's with home-made apple chutney to full meals: mushroom and walnut soup or prawn pot with garlic mayonnaise, followed by vegetable lasagne or rabbit and bacon pie cooked in local cider. Finish with scrumptious almond and apple strudel or frozen ginger and coffee meringue cake. Children welcome lunchtimes only.

Typical prices Woolhope pie £3.35 Mushroom biriani with dahl £3.35

ACCOMMODATION 3 bedrooms £D
Check-in all day

Three bright, airy bedrooms with duvets, TVs and tea-makers share a thoughtfully equipped bathroom. *No children under 14 overnight. No dogs.*

We welcome complaints and bona fide recommendations on the tear-out pages for readers' comments. They are followed up by our professional team. Please also complain to the management instantly.

WOOLVERTON — Red Lion

FOOD

Nr Bath
MAP 5 B3 *Somerset*
Frome (0373) 830350
Parking ample

Bar food 12–2 (Sun till 1.15) & 7–10

Landlord Mr B. A. Lander
Brewery Wadworth
Wadworth 6X, IPA; Bass; Guinness; Stella Artois; Harp; cider.

This well-run pub by the A36 draws a loyal following with its highly successful bar food formula. The choice centres on jacket potatoes with a variety of tasty fillings such as cooked tomato and onion topped wtih melted Stilton, and an impressive list of salads ranging from smoked sausage, cheese and garlic croûtons to pâté-filled cornets of ham and prawns in curried mayonnaise. Garden.

Typical prices Antillaise (seafood salad) £3.20 Jacket potatoes £2

WORCESTER — Slug & Lettuce

FOOD

12 The Cornmarket
MAP 7 A1 *Hereford & Worcester*
Worcester (0905) 28362
Parking ample

Bar food 11.45–2 & 6.30–9.30
No bar food Sun
Closed Sun lunch

Landlord Brian Hulme
Brewery Ansells
Ind Coope Burton Ale; Gibbs Mew Wiltshire Bitter; Guinness; Löwenbräu; Castlemaine XXXX; cider.

One of a small chain of pubs, all putting the emphasis firmly on food. A blackboard in the roomy bar proclaims the day's selection, which includes interesting starters (or snacks) like hot tuna melt or herring roes in mustard cream. Main dishes aplenty (pasta, pies, steaks, vegetarian) and tempting sweets like gooseberry fool or banana flambé.

Typical prices Cream of mushroom soup 85p Beef bourguignon £2.50

WORTHING — Far Post

OOD

Wigmore Road
MAP 6 D4 *West Sussex*
Worthing (0903) 39561
Parking ample

Bar food 11–2 (Sun 12–1.30) & 5.30–10
No bar food Sun eve

Landlords Nicky & Malcolm MacDonald
Brewery Whitbread
Whitbread Best Bitter; guest beers; Guinness; Stella Artois; Heineken; cider.

Malcolm MacDonald, former England football star, is winning new fans as the amiable and hardworking landlord of this smartly appointed pub. His wife Nicky tackles the food side of things, pleasing the crowds with her omelettes, burgers, baguette sandwiches and tasty chilli con carne. The dish of the day, usually a savoury pie, is also a winner.
Typical prices Home-made steak & kidney pie £2.65 Prawn baguette with salad £1.65

WYE — New Flying Horse Inn

& B

Upper Bridge Street
MAP 6 E3 *Kent*
Wye (0233) 812297
Parking ample

Landlords Barry & Anita Law
Brewery Shepherd Neame
Shepherd Neame Masterbrew Bitter, Invicta Best Bitter; Hurlimann Sternbrau; Steinbock Lager; cider.

***ACCOMMODATION* 11 bedrooms £C**
Check-in all day

There's a particularly cheerful and inviting bar here, with gleaming horse brasses and copper plates, dark beams and an old rustic brick fireplace. Bedrooms have modern decor and assorted furniture of various styles; seven rooms in the main house share two public bathrooms, while four remaining rooms in a separate stable block have functional en suite facilities. Telephones, TVs and tea and coffee makers are standard. Garden and patio.
Credit Access, Amex, Diners, Visa

WYKEHAM — Downe Arms

& B

Pickering Road, Nr Scarborough
MAP 4 E3 *North Yorkshire*
Scarborough (0723) 862471
Parking ample

Landlord Mr P. Mort
Free house
Younger's Scotch; Newcastle Exhibition; Cameron Bitter; Tetley Bitter; Carlsberg; McEwan's Lager; cider.

***ACCOMMODATION* 9 bedrooms £C**
Check-in all day

An old coaching inn, restored and extended, has generated this pleasant roadside pub with conference facilities. The spacious, popular public bar gives plenty of scope for spreading out or finding a quiet corner, while the cocktail bar is tiny and intimate. Bright bedrooms with freestanding white furniture are of good size and have carpeted bathrooms (some shower only) and tea/coffee making facilities. Garden.
Credit Access, Amex, Diners, Visa

YARDE DOWN — Poltimore Arms

OOD

Nr South Moulton
MAP 9 B1 *Devon*
Brayford (059 88) 381
Parking ample

Bar food 11.30–2 & 6–9.30, Sun 12–1.30 & 7–9.30

Landlords Mike & Mella Wright
Free house
Usher Best Bitter, Triple Crown, Country Bitter; Guinness; Carlsberg; cider.

The setting, halfway between South Moulton and Simonsbath, may be remote, but this 300-year-old pub attracts plenty of trade. Chief reason for this is Mella Wright's tasty bar food: there's something for everyone, from sandwiches to steaks, vegetarian specials, children's dishes and pies both sweet and savoury. Super chunky chips. There's a wider evening choice. Garden.
Typical prices Lasagne £1.50 Savoury nut roast £2

YARMOUTH — Bugle Hotel

B & B

The Square
MAP 5 C4 *Isle of Wight*
Isle of Wight (0983) 760272
Parking limited

Landlords Karen & David Fleetwood
Brewery Whitbread
Whitbread Best Mild; Flowers Original; Guinness; Stella Artois; Heineken; cider.

ACCOMMODATION **10 bedrooms £C**
Check-in all day

Standing in the town square, this attractive 300-year-old inn has plenty of old-world character. Mellow panelling, beams and highly polished brassware characterise the cosy Wagon Wheel Bar, while the Galleon Bar (which includes a family room that opens on to a pretty courtyard) is suitably rustic in style. Cheerful bedrooms (four have showers) offer simple modern comforts. Overnight guests can watch TV in the residents' lounge.
Credit Access, Visa

YATTENDON — Royal Oak

FOOD
B & B

The Square, Nr Newbury
MAP 7 B3 *Berkshire*
Hermitage (0635) 201325
Parking ample

Bar food 12–2 & 7.30–9.30

Landlords Richard & Kate Smith
Free house
Wadworth 6X; Charrington IPA; Bass; Stella Artois; cider.

ACCOMMODATION **5 Bedrooms £B**
Check-in all day

Full of charm and style, Kate and Richard Smith's creeper-clad 16th-century village pub is an absolute delight. Log fires warm the snug bars, where some superlative snacks are served. The imaginative menu changes daily and might offer such treats as smoked duck with blackcurrant sauce followed by fresh tuna with herb butter sauce or lamb steak with red pepper mustard. To finish, try homely rice pudding or an elegant loganberry and passion fruit sorbet. More elaborate meals in the pretty little restaurant.
Typical bar prices Chicken suprême with oyster mushrooms in a creamy curry sauce £6.85 Calf's liver & bacon £6.25 Avocado with smoked chicken and prawns £4.85 Venison pie £4.75

Immaculate bedrooms with fine fabrics and antique furniture are equipped with thoughtful extras such as mineral water, books and magazines. Splendid bathrooms offer huge fluffy towels and dressing gowns. Excellent breakfasts. Garden.

Credit Amex, Visa

SCOTLAND

AIRDRIE — Staging Post

B & B

8 Anderson Street
MAP 2 C5 *Strathclyde*
Airdrie (0236) 67525
Parking limited

Landlord Mr D. Barr
Brewery Scottish & Newcastle
■ McEwan's 80/-, Tartan Special; Guinness; Beck's Bier; McEwan's Lager; cider. *No real ale.*

In a quiet back street near the town centre, this pale green-painted pub offers practical, up-to-date accommodation in its nine rooms. Similarly appointed with good darkwood units and pretty soft furnishings, all the rooms are neatly kept and have TVs, radios, teamakers and telephones; six offer smartly tiled private facilities. The split-level public bar has been attractively refurbished and there's a cosy, mock-rustic cocktail bar too.

ACCOMMODATION **9 bedrooms £B**
Check-in all day

Credit Access, Amex, Diners, Visa

ANSTRUTHER — Craw's Nest Hotel

FOOD
B & B

Bankwell Road
MAP 2 C4 *Fife*
Anstruther (0333) 310691
Parking ample

Bar food 12.15–2 & 6.30–10.30

Landlords Clarke family
Free house
■ McEwan's Export, Tartan Special; Guinness; Carlsberg Pilsner, Hof; cider. *No real ale.*

Overlooking the Firth of Forth, this much-modernised Scottish manse offers enjoyable snacks in both its cosy little cocktail bar and spacious, contemporary lounge bar. Locally caught seafood is always popular – look out for fried haddock, lemon sole and Tay salmon in salads and sandwiches. Leek and potato soup makes an appetising start, and for meat-lovers there are choices like shepherd's pie, ham and tongue salad and pork chop garni. Simple sweets like chocolate gâteau and cream-filled brandy snaps to finish.
Typical prices Haddock & chips £3.30 Salmon salad £4.25

ACCOMMODATION **50 bedrooms £A**
Check-in all day

Best of the bedrooms are in a new wing and boast thick carpets, attractive darkwood units and pretty, soft furnishings. Main-house bedrooms are being progressively upgraded to this same high standard. All offer colour TVs, radio-alarms, direct-dial telephones and teamakers, and private bath/shower rooms are spotlessly kept. Garden. *No dogs.*

Credit Access, Amex, Diners, Visa

Prices given are as at the time of our research and thus may change.

ANSTRUTHER — Smugglers Inn

A

High Street
MAP 2 C4 *Fife*
Anstruther (0333) 310506
Parking limited

Landlords Mr & Mrs Michael McSharry
Free House
■ McEwan's Export, 80/-; Younger's Tartan Bitter; Guinness; McEwan's Lager; cider.

Fine views of the harbour can be enjoyed from both bars of this fine old town-centre inn which was once the home of the Earl of Strathmore, who made the proclamation for the Pretender at nearby Anster Cross during the rising of 1715. The public bar has a pool table and is popular with locals. The upstairs cocktail lounge with its warming log fire, barrel chairs and nautical bric-a-brac is full of character.

ARDENTINNY — Ardentinny Hotel

)OD & B

Loch Long, Argyll
MAP 2 B4 *Strathclyde*
Ardentinny (036 981) 209
Parking ample

Bar food 12–2.30 (Sat till 3) & 6.30–9.30

Landlords John & Thyrza Horn & Hazel Hall
Free house
McEwan's Export; Webster Yorkshire Bitter; Guinness; Fosters; Holsten; cider. *No real ale.*

With its pretty garden running down to the shores of Loch Long, and with its own private moorings, this white-painted inn is a popular base for fishing and yachting. Inside there's a friendly atmosphere in the three cosy bars, one of which has a nautical theme. The honest, enjoyable, bar food makes extensive use of fresh fish and shellfish from nearby lochs, and will cater for most appetites – hearty home-made soup with granary bread, pâté with oatcakes, marinated herrings, omelettes, and lasagne. Finish off with a tasty sweet, perhaps chocolate and raspberry roulade or coffee gâteau. The evening menu includes steaks, chicken chasseur and veal scaloppina.
Typical prices Pâté & oatcakes £1.65 Chicken & mushroom pie £3.35

ACCOMMODATION **11 bedrooms £B**
Check-in all day

Bedrooms, varying in style from the solidly traditional to the agreeably modern, have pretty fabrics and wallcoverings. All have en suite facilities, and there's a comfortable residents' lounge. Accommodation closed from November to mid-March.

Credit Access, Amex, Diners, Visa

BUSBY — Busby Hotel

OOD & B

2 Field Road, Clarkston, Glasgow
MAP 2 C5 *Strathclyde*
041-644 2661
Parking ample

Bar food 12–2 & 6–9 (Sun 6.30–9)

Landlord John Hebditch
Free house
McEwan's 80/-, Tartan Special; Guinness; McEwan's Lager; Beck's Bier; cider.

In a tree-lined road off the A726, overlooking the river Cart, this purpose-built modern hotel is a popular overnight stop with business visitors (20 minutes to Glasgow city centre). There's a smartly contemporary cocktail bar on the first floor, together with a number of function suites, plus a large and very busy lounge bar where simple, satisfying snacks are served. Standard favourites like lasagne, steak and kidney, chilli con carne and chicken curry are supplemented by such tasty daily specials as fisherman's pie and roast lamb. Filled rolls and salad platters are available, as is a traditional roast on Sundays.
Typical prices Gammon steak £2.50 Scampi £2.50

ACCOMMODATION **14 bedrooms £C**
Check-in all day

Comfortable, centrally heated bedrooms with pretty duvets and matching fabrics have good modern furniture and up-to-date accessories like direct-dial telephones, colour TVs and tea and coffee making facilities. Excellent private bath/shower rooms.

Credit Access, Amex, Diners, Visa

CANONBIE — Riverside Inn

FOOD
B & B

MAP 2 C6 *Dumfries & Galloway*
Canonbie (054 15) 295
Parking ample

Bar food 12–2 & 7–9
No bar food Sun lunch
Closed last 2 wks Feb

Landlords Robert & Susan Phillips
Free house
Theakston Best Bitter; Tennent's 70/-; Merlin (in summer); Guinness; Tennent's Lager.

The river Esk flows past this white-painted inn and salmon and trout from its well-stocked waters feature on the snack menu offered in the welcoming main bar. Caring hosts Robert and Susan Phillips share the cooking and use local produce wherever possible, including vegetables from their own garden. The choice ranges from soup, pâté, ploughman's and salads to meat, fish or chicken main dishes. Lovely puddings, too, like butterscotch profiteroles and home-made damson ice cream.

Typical prices Potted pigeon £2.65 Salmon with watercress hollandaise £4.25

ACCOMMODATION **6 bedrooms £B**
Check-in all day

Charming bedrooms (including two in a delightful cottage annexe overlooking the river) all have TVs and tea-makers, together with thoughtful touches like potted plants, fresh fruit and home-made biscuits. Private bathrooms – two with shower only – are smart and well equipped. A tastefully decorated lounge with a homely feel has been added for residents' use. Garden. *No dogs.*

Credit Access, Visa

CASTLE DOUGLAS — King's Arms Hotel

B & B

St Andrew Street
MAP 2 C6 *Dumfries & Galloway*
Castle Douglas (0556) 2626
Parking ample

Landlord Iain MacDonald
Free house
Younger's Tartan, Scotch; Guinness; Carlsberg Hof; cider. *No real ale.*

ACCOMMODATION **15 bedrooms £C**
Check-in all day

A leafy, sheltered patio is an appealing feature of this former coaching inn near the heart of a bustling market town. Inside, the tartan-carpeted bars are cosy and welcoming, and there's a traditionally styled residents' lounge and a modest TV room for overnight guests. Centrally heated bedrooms (double-glazed at the front of the building) are well-kept and comfortable; eight have their own bath/shower room. Accommodation closed 1 January.

Credit Access, Amex, Diners, Visa

COMRIE — Royal Hotel

B & B

Melville Square
MAP 2 C4 *Tayside*
Comrie (0764) 70200
Parking ample

Landlord Margaret Gordon
Free house
McEwan's Tartan, 80/–, Pale Ale; Harp; cider.

ACCOMMODATION **14 bedrooms £B**
Check-in all day

An attractive L-shaped inn on the main square of this pretty village. The hub of activity is the smart cocktail bar, decorated in the owner's tartan and stocked with a fine selection of malt whiskies. Pride of the bedrooms is one with a four-poster and royal coat of arms commemorating a visit by Queen Victoria. The rest have modern practical units and plenty of extras. All have splendid bathrooms. Garden.

Credit Access, Amex, Diners, Visa

DYSART — Old Rectory Inn

OOD West Quality Street
MAP 2 C4 *Fife*
Kirkcaldy (0592) 51211
Parking ample
Bar food 12–2 & 6.30–9.30
Closed Sun
Landlords Stuart & Kay Nelson
Free House
Alloa Export; Skol; cider.
No real ale.

North of Kirkcaldy in a pretty coastal village, this agreeable Georgian inn provides a good range of bar food. The cold table, set in a bar overlooking the walled garden, is a popular lunchtime feature, and other dishes could be anything from subtle celery and pineapple soup to beef and onion casserole, seafood vol-au-vents and Dutch apple pie.
Typical prices Chilli con carne £2.50 Beef bourguignon £2.50
Credit Access, Amex, Diners, Visa

EDDLESTON — Horse Shoe Inn

OOD MAP 2 C5 *Borders*
Eddleston (072 13) 225
Parking ample
Bar food 11.30–2 & 5–10, Sun 12.30–2.15 & 6.30–10
Landlord C. A. McIntosh-Reid
Free house
McEwan's 80/-; Greenmantle; Murphy Stout; Theakston Best Bitter; Belhaven 70/- Heavy; Carlsberg; cider.

Once the village smithy, this white-painted inn offers a particularly wide range of bar snacks (there's a restaurant, too). Sandwiches and salads are popular light bites, while hot dishes run from Stilton soup to lemon sole, chicken curry and steak and kidney pie. If you've left room for a sweet, try the deliciously indulgent butterscotch pear concoction. Traditional Sunday lunch.
Typical prices Stilton soup £1.10 Smoked fish pie £2.85
Credit Access, Amex, Diners, Visa

EDINBURGH — Cramond Inn

OOD Cramond Glebe Road
TOWN PLAN *Lothian*
031-336 2035
Parking ample
Bar food 12–2.15
No bar food eves
Closed Sun eves (beg. Oct–Mar)
Landlord Gordan Duncan
Free house
Lorimer & Clark 80/-; McEwan's Tartan Bitter; Carlsberg; cider.

Robert Louis Stevenson was a former patron of this white-washed inn overlooking the Firth of Forth. Come at lunchtime to enjoy simple, homely food with a distinctly Scottish flavour. Expect to find vegetable-packed Scotch broth, home-cooked ham and cold meat pie with attractive salads, and – if you're lucky – haggis with traditional neeps and tatties. Terrace.
Typical prices Game pie £2.45 Pavlova 95p
Credit Access, Amex, Diners, Visa

EDINBURGH — Rutland Hotel

& B 3 Rutland Street
TOWN PLAN *Lothian*
031-229 3402
Parking difficult
Landlord Mr M. McIlwraith
Brewery Scottish & Newcastle
Younger's Tartan Bitter; McEwan's 80/-; Beck's Bier; Guinness; McEwan's Lager; cider.
***ACCOMMODATION* 18 bedrooms £B**
Check-in all day

Ideally placed for visitors who want a central location, this friendly hotel offers a complete contrast between its lively bars and its quiet, peaceful accommodation. Decor in the bars is heavy Victorian, and they are popular especially with the young. The double-glazed bedrooms are comfortable and well-equipped, with TVs, tea-makers, trouser presses and hairdryers. Half have en suite facilities while the rest share four spotless public bathrooms.
Credit Access, Amex, Diners, Visa

FOCHABERS — Gordon Arms Hotel

B & B

High Street
MAP 1 C2 *Grampian*
Fochabers (0343) 820508
Parking ample

Landlord Iain MacKinnon
Free house
Younger's 80/-; McEwan's Export, Tartan Bitter; Guinness; Harp; cider.

ACCOMMODATION **12 bedrooms £B**
Check-in all day

On the high street of Fochabers, this former coaching inn has a white-painted facade adorned with antlers. Inside, the public rooms include a comfortable cocktail bar with a good collection of malt whiskies. Upstairs there is a large, comfortable residents' lounge. The real strength here is the overnight accommodation – 12 well-laid-out rooms with fitted furniture, direct-dial phones, TVs and hairdryers. All but one have their own good carpeted bathrooms. Garden.
Credit Access, Amex, Visa

GLAMIS — Strathmore Arms

FOOD

The Square
MAP 2 C4 *Tayside*
Glamis (030 784) 248
Parking ample

Bar food 12.15–2 & 7–9.45
No bar food Sat eve
Closed Mon (Jan–Mar) & 1–8 Jan

Landlords Messrs Benton & Henderson
Free house
Alloa Export; Skol; cider.
No real ale.

A friendly village pub serving a popular range of reasonably priced snacks and meals. Lunchtime in the main dining room brings soup, pâté, a fish dish or two, simple roasts and seasonal game. There's a cold buffet, too, and sweets include a delightful steamed syrup sponge. Evening bar food comprises pâté, grills and steaks. Traditional Sunday roast.
Typical prices Gamekeeper's casserole £2.95 Fisherman's pie £2.85
Credit Access, Amex, Diners, Visa

GLASGOW — Babbity Bowster

FOOD
B & B

16 Blackfriars Street
TOWN PLAN *Strathclyde*
041–552 5055
Parking limited

Bar food 11am–11pm

Landlords Fraser & Tom Laurie
Free house
Maclay 70/–, 80/–; Murphy Stout; Tennent's Lager; Fürstenberg.

Deep in the heart of the city's old merchant district this handsome town house (circa 1790) combines café, bar, restaurant and hotel. Snacks and a lavish breakfast start proceedings at 8am, and the complete bar service is available from 11. This includes both lighter items – scones, wheaten rolls, traditional Scottish cheeses with oatcakes – and more substantial fare such as lasagne, casseroles (meat, fish and vegetarian), smoked sausage and, at lunchtime only, wholewheat pancakes, both savoury and sweet. Live music is a regular feature.
Typical prices Ham & mushroom lasagne £3.45 Cauliflower moussaka £2.95

ACCOMMODATION **6 bedrooms £B**
Check-in all day

Six compact, neatly designed bedrooms are decorated in pine and pastel blue; furnishings are modern, stylish and of good quality. Each features an original print or lithograph, and all have carpeted shower rooms en suite. Besides the restaurant and bar there's a little patio for when the sun shines. Children are accommodated overnight. *No dogs.*
Credit Access, Amex, Visa

GLENDEVON — Tormaukin Hotel

& B Nr Dollar
MAP 2 C4 *Tayside*
Muckhart (025 981) 252
Parking ample

Closed 25 Dec–1 Jan
Landlords Mr & Mrs R. Worthy
Free house
Ind Coope Burton Ale; Alloa Diamond Heavy, Export; Guinness; Skol; cider.
ACCOMMODATION **6 bedrooms £C**
Check-in all day

A warm welcome awaits visitors to this cheerful black and white roadside inn, pleasantly set in hilly terrain. Good-sized bedrooms with tasteful decor and handsome stripped pine furniture offer a comfortable night's stay, and there's a choice of beamed bars – one with a lovely stone fireplace – for enjoying a drink. Bedrooms have private bathrooms or shower facilities (all except one are en suite) and colour TVs. Patio. *No dogs.*
Credit Access, Amex, Visa

GLENFINNAN — Stage House Inn

& B MAP 1 B3 *Highland*
Kinlocheil (039 783) 246
Parking ample

Closed end Oct–mid March
Landlords Helen & Andrew Brooks
Free house
Younger's Tartan; Guinness; Tennent's Lager.
ACCOMMODATION **9 bedrooms £C**
Check-in all day

Extensive fishing rights and seven boats on lovely Loch Shiel are added attractions at this spick-and-span old coaching inn. There are two pine-raftered bars, a separate pool and darts room, and two conservatory-style lounges for residents which afford stunning views. Spotless bedrooms offer simple comforts, with pretty duvet covers, tea/coffee-makers and electric blankets. All rooms have neat bathrooms, six with showers only. Garden.
Credit Access, Diners, Visa

INGLISTON — NEW ENTRY — Norton Tavern

OOD Edinburgh
MAP 2 C5 *Lothian*
031–333 1275
Parking ample

Bar food 12–2.30 & 6.30–9.30
Landlords Forbes Crawford & Sam Foggin
Free house
McEwan's 80/-, Export; Tennent's Special; Murphy Irish Stout; Tennent's Lager; Carlsberg; cider.

Imaginative food draws customers from miles around to this former stables whose clever conversion provides a stylish setting for American-inspired dishes like a Frisco Bay mussel stew, burgers and steaks. Make your own open sandwiches at the buffet, or choose from pâtés and salads. Mississippi mud pie makes a rich and delicious sweet. Cold food available all day. Garden.
Typical prices Teriyaki lamb kebab £2.25 New York Strip steak £3.95
Credit Access, Amex, Diners, Visa

We welcome bona fide recommendations or complaints on the tear-out pages for readers' comments.
They are followed up by our professional team but do complain to the management.

INVERMORISTON — Glenmoriston Arms

FOOD
B & B

MAP 1 B3 *Highland*
Glenmoriston (0320) 51206
Parking ample

Bar food 11.30–2.15
Closed 1 & 2 Jan & 25 Dec

Landlords Mr & Mrs R. Shepherd
Free house
McEwan's 80/–; Younger's Tartan; Guinness; Harp; Carlsberg; cider.
No real ale.

A smart white-painted inn conveniently located at the junction of the A82 and the A887 – a good stopping-off point for some hearty and tasty lunches. Apart from the usual ploughman's lunch there's fisherman's (with prawns), crofter's (with ham), and ghillie's (with smoked trout). Add to that haggis with 'chappit neeps and tatties', good home-made soup, plus freshly cut sandwiches and a selection of tasty sweets and you have a most appetising choice. The bar is sportily decked out with old fishing rods, flies and flintlock guns.
Typical prices Crofter's lunch £2.95 Apple pie 95p

ACCOMMODATION **8 bedrooms £C**
Check-in all day

The best of the bedrooms have good antique furniture and pretty wallpaper and curtains. Others are simply and traditionally furnished but all are neat and well-kept. Both public and private bathrooms are well-equipped, most are part-tiled and prettily decorated. There's also a pleasant residents' TV lounge. Terrace and garden.

Credit Access, Amex, Diners, Visa

We publish annually so make sure you use the current edition.

KILLIN — Clachaig Hotel

B & B

Falls of Dochart, Gray Street
MAP 2 C4 *Central*
Killin (056 72) 270
Parking ample

Landlord John Mallinson
Free house
McEwan's 80/–; Guinness; Tennent's Special, Lager; cider.

ACCOMMODATION **5 bedrooms £D**
Check-in all day

Spectacular views over the Falls of Dochart are the main reason for stopping at this rambling old inn. Housekeeping is another strong point, with every room kept spotlessly clean. Neat bedrooms are full of character, featuring unusual artefacts and woodwork taken from a broken-up liner. One room has private facilities; the others share two comfortable bathrooms. Future plans include much needed refurbishment of residents' lounge and bar.
Credit Visa

KIPPEN — Cross Keys Inn

FOOD
B & B

By Stirling
MAP 2 C4 *Central*
Kippen (078 687) 293
Parking ample

Bar food 12.15–2 & 7.15–9
No bar food Mon eve & limited choice Mon lunch

Landlords Richard & Penny Miller
Free house
Mc Ewan's 80/-; Younger's No 3; Broughton Greenmantle Ale; Guinness; McEwan's Lager; cider.

In the heart of an unspoilt village, this gem of a place run by friendly couple Richard and Penny Miller has masses of traditional charm. There are old wooden settles in the atmospheric public bar, and a cheery open fire warms the stone-walled main bar, where honest, straightforward food with plenty of flavour is served. Look out for the excellent, daily-changing soups, salads based on prawns or honey-roast ham, traditional mutton pie and tasty roasts. A recently added, separate dining area specialises

in steaks, grills and kebabs, and there are pleasant home-made sweets like apple pie, ice creams and sorbets to finish.
Typical prices Roast chicken with lemon & rosemary £2.95 Tomato soup 60p

ACCOMMODATION **2 bedrooms £D**
Check-in restricted

Lovely views are enjoyed by the two warm, fully carpeted bedrooms, where bright duvets and attractive bedside lamps add a nice homely touch. They share an equally spotless bathroom. Patio and garden. Accommodation closed 25 Dec–1 Jan. *No dogs.*

LEWISTON — Lewiston Arms

& B

Nr Drumnadrochit
MAP 1 B3 *Highland*
Drumnadrochit (045 62) 225
Parking ample
Landlords Mr & Mrs N. Quinn
Free house
Younger's Tartan; McEwan's Export, Lager; cider. *No real ale.*

ACCOMMODATION **8 bedrooms £D**
Check-in all day

The Quinns offer a relaxed and friendly welcome at their 15th-century pub just a mile from Loch Ness. There's a simple public bar, a lounge bar overlooking the pretty garden, a cosy residents' lounge with open fire and a TV lounge. Modest bedrooms (half in the garden cottage) have traditional furniture, candlewick bedspreads and pleasant wallpaper. All have tea/coffee-makers and electric blankets. Garden. Accommodation closed mid-January to mid-March.
Credit Visa

LINLITHGOW — Champany Inn

OOD

Philipstown
MAP 2 C5 *Lothian*
Philipstown (050 683) 4532
Parking ample
Bar food 12–2.30 (Sun from 12.30) & 6.30–10
Landlords Anne & Clive Davidson
Free house
Belhaven 80/-; Skol; cider.

Food is central to the operation at the inn's chop house, where it's brought to your table with the drinks by efficient waitresses. Prime quality meat and sausages, simply and well prepared, are the main attractions: beef sirloin, T-bone steak, lamb cutlets and veal T-bone, burgers and boerewors served with salad and chips. Home-made soup, starters and fish dishes, too.
Typical prices Charcoal grilled steak £5.95 Boerewors £3
Credit Access, Amex, Diners, Visa

LOCH ECK — Coylet Inn

OOD

By Dunoon
MAP 2 B4 *Strathclyde*
Kilmun (036 984) 426
Parking ample
Bar food 11.30–2 & 5.30–10, Sun 12.30–2 & 6.30–10
Landlords Richard & Helen Addis
Free house
McEwan's 80/-, Tartan Special; Younger's No. 3; Guinness; Tennent's Lager.

Satisfying, home-made food is offered in the cheerful bar of this long, low dormer-windowed pub enjoying a lovely setting opposite the loch. As well as familiar sandwiches, salads and grills, there are appetising daily specials like chicken broth and smoked haddock and egg pie. There's a traditional lounge bar and a pleasant garden.
Typical prices Grilled rainbow trout with jacket potato £2.75 Mussels and crusty bread £2.20

LOCHGAIR — Lochgair Hotel

FOOD
B & B

Nr Lochgilphead
MAP 2 B4 *Strathclyde*
Minard (0546) 86333
Parking ample

Bar food 12–2.30 & 6–9

Landlords Craig & Susan Whale
Free house
McEwan's Export, Tartan Special; Guinness; Tennent's Lager; McEwan's Lager; cider. *No real ale.*

Its position just across the A83 from Loch Gair makes this white-painted hotel a popular place for fishermen and there is plenty on the menu to satisfy a hearty appetite gained from the fresh-air life. The choice of good bar food, available in both the cosy cocktail bar and the panelled bar, ranges from sandwiches and salads to the ever-popular steak and kidney pie, and the excellent local catch contributes to grilled langoustines, poached trout, haddock and salmon. Healthy eaters are well catered for, with fare such as vegetarian curry, wholemeal bread and fresh fruit salad being available.
Typical prices Poached trout £3.50 Ham salad £2.45

***ACCOMMODATION* 18 bedrooms £C**
Check-in all day

The bedrooms, some of which have balconies, are simple and bright, with practical fitted units, duvets and tea-makers; ten have private bathrooms, but more are planned. There's also a residents' lounge with TV. Amenities include a garden, game and sea fishing, sailing, pony trekking, a hotel boat, mooring and a laundry room.
Credit Access, Amex, Visa

LYBSTER — Bayview Hotel

B & B

Russel Street
Map 1 C1 *Highland*
Lybster (059 32) 346
Parking ample
Closed 1 & 2 Jan

Landlords Ranald & Norma Hutton
Free house
Murphy Irish Stout; Younger's Tartan; McEwan's 80/–; Harp; cider.
No real ale.

***ACCOMMODATION* 3 bedrooms £D**
Check-in all day

A tiny, red and white painted inn tucked away in a side street a short walk from the town's harbour. Three bright, clean and simple bedrooms comprise the accommodation, each with plain painted walls, pretty duvets and matching curtains. Furniture is traditional, and each room has a radio and electric blankets. All share a pretty, modern bathroom. There's also a comfortable pine-panelled TV lounge and a pleasant sun room.
Credit Access, Amex, Diners, Visa

MAIDENS — NEW ENTRY — Bruce Hotel

FOOD
B & B

Harbour Road, by Turnberry
MAP 2 B5 *Strathclyde*
Turnberry (0655) 31401
Parking ample

Bar food 12–2

Landlord Brian Sage
Free house
McEwan's 80/-, Tartan Bitter, Export; Guinness; McEwan's Lager; Carlsberg; cider. *No real ale.*

Built 14 years ago, this pleasant, modern hotel has fine views out to sea and over the tiny harbour of Maidens. The tartan-carpeted lounge bar has red plush seating and copper-topped tables. The lunchtime blackboard menu changes daily according to market availability; you'll find good home-cooked food like hearty pea soup, well-flavoured chicken liver pâté, entrecôte chasseur and fried fillet of plaice, and to finish maybe a crunchy topped apple crumble or chocolate fudge cake. In summer you can watch the world go by from under a parasol on the patio.

Typical prices Pea soup 60p Lamb's liver & bacon £2.95 **LVs**

***ACCOMMODATION* 9 bedrooms £D**
Check-in all day

Immaculately clean bedrooms have pretty fabrics and lightwood fitted units, and all have tea and coffee making facilities, TVs, and well-kept bathrooms (some shower only). Most have sea views. Children are welcome overnight only. Accommodation closed two weeks Christmas.

Prices given are as at the time of our research and thus may change.

MELROSE — Burts Hotel

FOOD
B & B

Market Square
MAP 2 C5 *Borders*
Melrose (089 682) 2285
Parking ample
Bar food 12–2 & 7–9.30
Landlords Graham & Anne Henderson
Free house
Belhaven 80/-, 70/-; Guinness; Hofmeister; Kronenbourg; cider.

Standing in the centre of town on the market square, this distinctive old black and white hotel offers an appetising selection of snacks in its spacious main bar. Garlicky prawns, bacon and mushrooms, home-made soups and pâtés are all favourite starters, while main dishes range from familiar roasts and grills to duck and ham pie with salad, baked fillet of cod with banana and devil sauce or spiced vegetables and rice wrapped in a cabbage leaf; plus a roast on Sundays. Rich sweets like chocolate pudding and custard to finish. Dinner can be taken in Burts restaurant.

Typical prices Baked mullet £3.25 Poached chicken with prawn & lemon sauce £3

***ACCOMMODATION* 21 bedrooms £C**
Check-in all day

Over half the bedrooms have been smartly refurbished with good-quality darkwood furniture, attractively coordinated fabrics and equally smart bathrooms. Remaining rooms are in simpler style and most have private facilities. Direct-dial telephones, TVs and teamakers are standard throughout. Decent breakfasts. Garden. *No dogs.*

Credit Access, Amex, Diners, Visa

MELROSE — George & Abbotsford Hotel

B & B

High Street
MAP 2 C5 *Borders*
Melrose (089 682) 2308
Parking ample
Landlord John Brown
Free house
McEwan's 80/-, Tartan Bitter, Pale Ale; Carlsberg; Harp; cider.

***ACCOMMODATION* 32 bedrooms £C**
Check-in all day

Handy for visitors to the Border country and Sir Walter Scott's home (two miles away), this handsome town-centre hotel offers simple overnight accommodation. Rooms in the main building are plain and old-fashioned, those in the new wing modern and functional. Most have bath/shower rooms, and TVs are supplied on request. The large public bar is a pleasant place to unwind, and there is also a residents' lounge overlooking a pretty rose garden.

Credit Access, Amex, Diners, Visa

MOFFAT — Balmoral Hotel

B & B

High Street
MAP 2 C5 *Dumfries & Galloway*
Moffat (0683) 20288
Parking ample

Landlords Chris Bingham & John Graham
Free house
Younger's Tartan; Tennent's 80/–; Greenmantle; Guinness; Tennent's Lager; Carlsberg Hof; cider.

ACCOMMODATION **15 bedrooms £C**
Check-in all day

A white pebbledash inn located right in the town centre. Mock olde-worlde features such as exposed beams in the bars create a cheerful, welcoming feel. Bedrooms have matching floral wallpaper and curtains and mostly whitewood furniture; six have en suite bathrooms, while the rest share four public ones. All have TVs and tea-making facilities. There is a children's room and a lounge for residents on the first floor. Patio.
Credit Access, Amex, Visa

MOFFAT — Black Bull

FOOD
B & B

1 Station Road
MAP 2 C5 *Dumfries & Galloway*
Moffat (0683) 20206
Parking limited

Bar food 12–2 & 7–9
No bar food Sun eve

Landlord Mrs Hughes
Free house
McEwan's 80/-; Younger's No. 3, Tartan Scotch; Guinness; Carlsberg; cider.

Dating from the 16th century, this historic pub has been smartened up by its new owner. Once the haunt of Robbie Burns (an epigram scratched by him on a window pane can still be seen), the main bar has a truly welcoming atmosphere, as does the pleasant little restaurant (non-smoking). There's also a public bar converted from the old stables, which has taken the Caledonian Railway as its theme. Food remains as good as ever. Haggis is justifiably still one of the favourites, and there's also tasty hot dishes such as hot pot, fish pie and roast beef, and a good selection of salads and cooked meats, with delicious apple pie to follow.
Typical prices Haggis £2.45 Quiche & salad £2.10

ACCOMMODATION **3 bedrooms £D**
Check-in all day

Neat, compact and very clean accommodation is on offer in the three bedrooms, which share one spotless bathroom. All rooms have washbasins, teamakers and crisp new bed linen. Plug-in heating supplements the central heating. *No dogs.*

Credit Visa

MUIR OF ORD — Ord Arms Hotel

B & B

Great North Road
MAP 1 B2 *Highland*
Inverness (0463) 870286
Parking ample

Landlords Mr & Mrs D. Nairn
Free house
McEwan's Export, Light, Tartan; Harp; cider. *No real ale.*

ACCOMMODATION **15 bedrooms £C**
Check-in all day

Redecoration and improvements are afoot at this mellow, stone-built inn just outside the town on the A862. There are two bars and a pleasant dining room; upstairs, the bright, clean bedrooms mainly have pretty wallpaper, matching fabrics and fitted furniture. All have TVs and tea/coffee making facilities. Eight have private bathrooms, while the remaining seven share three public ones, all well-maintained. Garden.
Credit Access **LVs**

Our inspectors never book in the name of Egon Ronay's Guides; they disclose their identity only after paying their bills.

NEW ABBEY — Criffel Inn

OD B

Dumfries
MAP 2 C6 *Dumfries & Galloway*
New Abbey (038 785) 305
Parking ample

Bar food 12–2 & 4.30–11

Landlords Jenny & Herries McCulloch
Free house
Younger's No. 3; Tennent's Heriot Brewery 80/-; McEwan's 70/-; Guinness; Tennent's Lager; cider.

There's a really warm welcome awaiting all-comers to the McCullochs' homely little inn. Jenny loves cooking and it shows in the splendidly wholesome and appetising home-cooked food to be enjoyed here. There's always a daily soup – maybe well flavoured chicken broth – and a special like minced beef pie, plus a sweet like super-duper steamed sultana pudding or fruit pie. The regular menu offers good choices like home-cooked ham and fresh Solway salmon salad, and a children's section of beefburgers and things with chips. From 4.30 to 6 pm high tea is served, when home-made cakes and scones are added to the menu. Sandwiches are the only choice after 7 pm.
Typical prices Pork fillet in tomato & onion sauce £2.95 Steamed pudding 95p

***ACCOMMODATION* 4 bedrooms £C**
Check-in all day

Four spick-and-span bedrooms – three with shower cabinets – have pretty duvet covers and practical laminated fitted units. All have colour TVs and tea/coffee making facilities and share a modern bathroom. Patio.

Changes in data may occur in establishments after the Guide goes to press. Prices should be taken as indications rather than firm quotes.

SPEAN BRIDGE — Letterfinlay Lodge Hotel

B

MAP 1 B3 *Highland*
Spean Bridge (039 781) 622
Parking ample

Landlords Forsyth family
Free house
Alloa Export; Löwenbräu; cider.
No real ale.

***ACCOMMODATION* 15 bedrooms £D**
Check-in all day

The friendly Forsyth family own and run this welcoming, traditional hotel, which stands some seven miles north of Spean Bridge by lovely Loch Lochy. Picture windows in the lounge enhance the scenic setting, and there's a cosy bar. Spotless bedrooms provide modest, but very comfortable accommodation; five have private facilities, the rest share old-fashioned bathrooms with splendid Victorian fittings. Terrace. Accommodation closed November to February.
Credit Access, Amex, Diners, Visa

TARBERT — West Loch Hotel

FOOD
B & B

Loch Fyne
MAP 2 B5 *Strathclyde*
Tarbert (088 02) 283
Parking ample

Bar food 12–2
No bar food eves
Closed Nov

Landlords Thom family
Free house
McEwan's Export; Younger's Pale Ale; Guinness; Carlsberg; cider.
No real ale.

ACCOMMODATION **6 Bedrooms £C**
Check-in all day

★ A charming, creeper-clad inn on the shores of West Loch where the Thoms offer a warm welcome and splendid home cooking. At lunchtime the menu is on the blackboard in the small, rustic bar; try the satisfying home-made soup or tuna pâté for a starter, then guinea fowl in light curry sauce, honey-roast duckling with walnut stuffing, trout fillet fried in oatmeal or grilled salmon steak with béarnaise sauce to follow. Finish with a lovely angel pie (lemon curd on a meringue base). In the evenings meals are served in the restaurant only, from a prix fixe menu with similar dishes to those at lunchtime. Children welcome lunchtime only. ★

Typical prices Sweet & sour pork £4.75 Local Dublin Bay prawns £6.90 Tagliatelle Alfredo £3.75 Strawberry & coffee gâteau £1.75

The simple bedrooms are fresh and bright, with traditional furniture, floral duvets and washbasins; they share two public bathrooms. Most rooms have views across the loch. There's also a pleasant residents' lounge and a garden.

Credit Access

TAYVALLICH — Tayvallich Inn

FOOD

Nr Lochgilphead
MAP 2 B4 *Strathclyde*
Tayvallich (054 67) 282
Parking ample

Bar food 12–2 & 6–7
Closed 1 wk in winter

Landlords Pat & John Grafton
Free house
Alloa Export, Diamond Heavy, Arrol's 70/–; Guinness; Castlemaine XXXX; cider.

John Grafton is in charge of the cooking at this simple little pebbledash pub on the shores of Loch Sween. Local seafood looks good and is popular, but John's home-made soup and succulent burgers are well worth sampling, too. His wholesome fare also includes salads and he prides himself on home-made puds. In summer food tastes even better on the terrace.

Typical prices Moules marinière £2.50 Sweet & sour stir-fried chicken £3
Credit Access, visa

TURRIFF — NEW ENTRY — Towie Tavern

FOOD

Auchterless
MAP 1 D2 *Grampian*
Turriff (088 84) 201
Parking ample

Bar food 12–2 & 6–9.30
No bar food Sun & Mon eves

Landlords Mr & Mrs Rattray
Free house
Alice Ale; McEwan's Special, Export, Lager; Carlsberg Export, Special; Beck's Bier; cider.

A pebbledash pub on the A943 to which Mrs Rattray's imaginative menus draw the crowds, so booking is a must at weekends. Excellent local produce is cooked with an eye to healthy eating and vegetarian tastes: lentil, nut and wholemeal pâté, seafood and broccoli lasagne, breast of chicken stuffed with Brie or excellent local fish. Children's room and menu.

Typical prices Mussels au gratin £3.45 Lentil & nut ratatouille £3.95
Credit Visa

ULLAPOOL — Argyll Hotel

B

Argyle Street
MAP 1 B2 *Highland*
Ullapool (0854) 2422
Parking ample

Landlord Ian Matheson
Free house
McEwan's Export 80/-; Guinness; Harp; McEwan's Lager; cider.

ACCOMMODATION **8 bedrooms £D**
Check-in all day

One street up from the harbour stands this unpretentious white-painted hotel. It's a friendly place, and in the evening the bars frequently ring with the sound of chatter, laughter and music (the residents' lounge with TV is a quieter retreat). Spotlessly kept bedrooms share four bathrooms – one newly converted – that are also spick and span. Whopping breakfasts are served in a pleasant dining room. Accommodation closed 24 December–3 January.
Credit Amex

WEEM — Ailean Chraggan Hotel

OD
B

Nr Aberfeldy
MAP 2 C4 *Tayside*
Aberfeldy (0887) 20346
Parking ample

Bar food 12–2 & 6.30–10

Landlords Gillespie family
Free house
Younger's Tartan Scotch; Carlsberg Export; cider. *No real ale.*

A friendly pebbledash pub where the Gillespie family have been offering a warm welcome, good food and excellent accommodation for over 20 years. The traditional cosy bar opens on to a picture-windowed eating area with delightful country views. The daily specials, notably the seafood, are the highlight of the good selection offered – these could include fresh salmon or a vast seafood platter made up of jumbo prawns, mussels and salmon. The standard menu features well-hung steaks, soups, salads, casseroles and a popular home-made lasagne.
Typical prices Sirloin steak £7.25
Lasagne £2.65

ACCOMMODATION **3 bedrooms £C**
Check-in all day

Accommodation here is of an extremely high standard. The three bedrooms are stylishly furnished and decorated and boast some fine antique pieces. All rooms have good en suite facilities, plus TVs and tea-makers supplied with fresh milk. Two have separate dressing rooms and the third room is a family room as well. Garden.

Our inspectors never book in the name of Egon Ronay's Guides; they disclose their identity only after paying their bills.

WESTER HOWGATE — Old Howgate Inn

OD

Nr Penicuik
MAP 2 C5 *Lothian*
Penicuik (0968) 74244
Parking ample

Bar food 11.30–2.30 & 6–10

Landlord Robert Allan
Free house
McEwan's 80/-; Belhaven 80/-; Greenmantle; Theakston Best Bitter; Guinness; Carlsberg; cider.

Alongside the A6094, the handsome little bar of this former coaching inn is the place to head for an elegant snack. Dainty finger sandwiches and quail's eggs are the only choice, and the seven different varieties of open sandwiches include prawns and lemon mayonnaise, Danish herring on rye, and a gourmet plate which offers a taste of each. Garden.
Typical prices Gravad lax £1.85
Chicken & curry mayonnaise £1.40
Credit Access, Amex, Diners, Visa

WALES

ABERGAVENNY **Crowfield**

FOOD
B & B

Ross Road
MAP 8 C3 *Gwent*
Abergavenny (0873) 5048
Parking ample

Bar food 12–2 & 7–9.30
No bar food Sun

Landlords Crabb family
Free house
Bass; Worthington Best Bitter; Carlsberg Hof.

The Crabb family have made their home in this delightful farmhouse, now converted to a peaceful inn, where daughter Lucy's cooking is a definite attraction. Food is served in a chintzy lounge off the stone-flagged bar, and home-made soup can be followed by a spicy beef casserole or tender kidneys in a creamy mushroom and sherry sauce with freshly cooked pasta. Don't miss the delicious home-made sweets – like chocolate cream pie or chocolate slice – and ice creams.
Typical prices Chicken escalope £5.75 Lemon sole £6.85

ACCOMMODATION **5 bedrooms £C**
Check-in restricted

An old stone-walled barn with a Welsh slate roof houses the five spacious bedrooms, a sitting room (with TV) and an elegant breakfast room. The atmosphere is quiet, cosy and cottagy, with comfortable beds, armchairs, and carpeted bathrooms well stocked with towels. Accommodation is closed from 23 to 30 December. *No children. No dogs.*

We welcome complaints and bona fide recommendations on the tear-out pages for readers' comments. They are followed up by our professional team. Please also complain to the management instantly.

ABERGAVENNY **Llanwenarth Arms Hotel**

FOOD
B & B

Brecon Road, Llanwenarth
MAP 8 C3 *Gwent*
Abergavenny (0873) 810550
Parking ample

Bar food 11–2 & 6–10

Landlords D'Arcy & Angela McGregor
Free house
Robinson Best Bitter; Wadworth 6X; Worthington Best Bitter; McEwan's Export; Kronenbourg; Miller Lite; cider.

Perched above the river Usk, where it owns two stretches of salmon and trout fishing, this smartly modernised old inn offers fine views of mountain scenery and the Usk valley below. In the two traditional bars, the stone-built restaurant area and the newly built conservatory on the terrace, the same appealingly wide menu is available. There are trusty standards such as soup, chilli con carne, steaks, and chicken curry, as well as fresh salmon, halibut and pork normandy. A supplementary weekly-changing menu offers specials like garlicky mushrooms provençale and ham, asparagus and cheese flan. Good home-made desserts too. Terrace.
Typical prices Chicken and mushroom pie £4.75 Pineapple prawn indienne £5.95

ACCOMMODATION **18 bedrooms £C**
Check-in all day

Most rooms are built chalet-style into the hillside, overlooking the Usk valley, and the remaining three view the Sugarloaf Mountain. All have bold soft furnishings, quality furniture, TVs, tea makers and en suite bathrooms. Good housekeeping. *No dogs.*

Credit Access, Amex, Diners, Visa

BABELL — Black Lion Inn

OD

Nr Holywell
MAP 8 C1 *Clwyd*
Caerwys (0352) 720239
Parking ample

Bar food 12.15–2 & 7.30–10
No bar food Sat lunch & Sun

Landlords Mr & Mrs H.G.E. Foster
Free house
Stones Best Bitter; Carling Black Label; Holsten Export; cider.
No real ale.

Tucked away in the hills, this leisurely old pub of 13th-century origin has just clocked up its 21 years under the Fosters' meticulous management. The bar menu featuring hot dishes is as good as ever. Start with delicious home-made mushroom soup or pâté followed by tender fried lamb's liver and bacon, rounded off by an irresistible pud. Well-kept cheeses. Book in advance.
Typical prices Casserole of guinea fowl £5.50 Spring lamb chop £4.75
Credit Amex, Diners, Visa **LVs**

Any person using our name to obtain free hospitality is a fraud.
Proprietors, please inform Egon Ronay's Guides and the police.

BEAUMARIS — Liverpool Arms

OD
& B

Castle Street, Anglesey
MAP 8 B1 *Gwynedd*
Beaumaris (0248) 810362
Parking limited

Bar food 12–2 & 6–9.30 (Sun from 7)

Landlords Allan & Margaret Jones
Free house
Younger's IPA, Scotch; Guinness; McEwan's Lager; cider.

A nautical theme runs through this delightful hotel, which Allan and Margaret Jones have renovated with loving care. Among the mass of marine memorabilia in the bar you can enjoy some tasty, satisfying snacks, from soup and sandwiches to prawn curry, roast chicken and a very good steak and kidney pie served with jacket potatoes and a generous salad garnish. Daily specials like chicken and mushroom pancakes provide further choice, and there are some simple sweets.
Typical prices Prawns & mushrooms in cream & garlic sauce £3.25 Fresh plaice in parsley sauce £2.95

ACCOMMODATION **10 bedrooms £B**
Check-in all day

An original staircase, preserved by Ancient Monuments of Anglesey, leads up to ten spotless bedrooms, each named after an admiral and each with a skilfully designed private bathroom. Colour TVs, direct-dial phones and hairdryers are standard accessories, and one particularly nice room boasts a four-poster. Lots of choice for breakfast. *No children overnight. No dogs.*

Credit Access, Diners, Visa

BEAUMARIS **NEW ENTRY** Ye Olde Bull's Head

FOOD
B & B

Castle Street, Anglesey
MAP 8 B1 *Gwynedd*
Beaumaris (0248) 810329
Parking limited

Bar food 12–2.30
No bar food eves & Sun

Landlords Keith Rothwell & David Robertson
Free house
Bass; Worthington Best Bitter; Stones Bitter; Younger's Scotch; Guinness; Carlsberg Export; cider.

Just a stone's throw from Beaumaris Castle stands this characterful, 16th-century black and white timber-fronted inn, now thriving under caring new owners, Keith Rothwell and David Robertson. A wonderful old world atmosphere prevails within: the black-painted beams are very low, the oak stairs and landings creak inexorably, and there's an abundance of Welsh dressers, copper pans, brass candlesticks, swords, bayonets and memorabilia everywhere. The residents' lounge, in pure chintz, is a veritable museum piece! A simple lunchtime bar menu offers soup with hot bread, sandwiches, ploughman's, salads and one or two hot options, like deep-fried strips of sea trout and halibut. Desserts like almond pie, and well-kept cheeses.
Typical prices Curried lamb £2.75 Mediterranean salad £2.95

ACCOMMODATION **17 bedrooms £D**
Check-in all day

Beamed bedrooms have traditional free-standing furniture, lacy white bedspreads and spotless linen and towels. Some rooms have been redecorated and bathrooms, too, have been pleasantly spruced up. Accommodation closed last two weeks October. *No dogs.*

BETWYS-YN RHOS Ffarm Hotel

FOOD

Nr Abergele
MAP 8 B1 *Clwyd*
Dolwen (049 260) 287
Parking ample

Bar food 7pm–10pm
No bar food lunches
Closed Sun & Mon (Oct–mid-Mar)

Landlords Lomax family
Free house
Ind Coope Bitter; Tetley Bitter; Mild; Wrexham Lager; cider.

A castellated stone building in spacious grounds which is only open in the evenings, when satisfying bar meals are on offer. The blackboard menu displays such dishes as celery and almond soup, with spiced beef silverside, local trout or veal marengo to follow. Sweets include blackberry and apple pie, lemon meringue and chocolate fudge cake.
Typical prices Chicken breast in lemon & cream sauce £4.95 Steak in the pot £4.25

BODFARI Dinorben Arms

FOOD

Nr Denbigh
MAP 8 C1 *Clwyd*
Bodfari (074 575) 309
Parking ample

Bar food 12–2.30 & 6–10.15

Landlord Mr R. Sandland
Free house
Webster Yorkshire Bitter, Younger's Scotch; Guinness; Fosters; Wrexham Lager; cider.

This substantial 17th-century pub has much to offer: a pretty hillside location, a children's playground, attractive bars and terraces as well as an interesting menu. The lunchtime house-speciality is self-service smörgåsbord – plenty of crisp salads – with roast on Sundays. More traditional fare includes home-made soups, sandwiches, or pâté with fresh fish, meat or poultry to follow.
Typical prices Poached salmon £5 Chicken curry £3.55
Credit Access, Visa

CARDIGAN — Black Lion Hotel

& B

High Street
MAP 8 A3 *Dyfed*
Cardigan (0239) 612532
Parking limited

Closed Sun

Landlord Mr J. Baxter
Free house
Flowers IPA; Whitbread Best; Welsh; Heineken; Stella Artois; cider.

ACCOMMODATION **11 bedrooms £C**
Check-in all day

Visitors were first welcomed on this site in 1105, and this much-enlarged inn later became an important coaching stop. Now, a red-brick Georgian facade hides a wealth of beams and rustic charm in the bars, one of which boasts some linenfold panelling. Upstairs, there's a comfortable TV room and a quaint little writing room. Bedrooms, all with private bath or shower, colour TVs and tea and coffee making facilities, have attractive pine fittings.
Credit Access, Amex, Diners **LVs**

CENARTH — White Hart

OOD

Nr Newcastle Emlyn
MAP 8 A3 *Dyfed*
Newcastle Emlyn (0239) 710305
Parking ample

Bar food 12–2.30 & 6.30–9.30, Sun 12–1.30 & 7–9.30

Landlord Terry & Linda Parsons
Free house
Buckley Best Bitter; Courage Best Bitter, Directors, Dark Mild; Hofmeister; Kronenbourg; cider.

An agreeable old inn near the river Teifi where Terry and Linda Parsons offer an appetising range of food in their appealing bars. Typical choices might include Welsh broth, locally-caught salmon and Anglesey eggs (served au gratin with leeks and potatoes). There are vegetarian choices, too, with sandwiches and salads for lighter bites and nice sweets like sherry trifle. Garden.
Typical prices Chicken curry £3.80 Lasagne £3.60

CHEPSTOW — Castle View Hotel

OOD
& B

16 Bridge Street
MAP 8 C3 *Gwent*
Chepstow (029 12) 70349
Parking ample

Bar food 12–2 & 7–9.30

Landlords Mervyn & Lucia Gillett
Free house
Marston Pedigree; John Smith's Yorkshire Bitter; Kronenbourg.

A popular hotel where a vast range of food can be enjoyed in the bar lounge or the restaurant. Lucia Gillett uses as much fresh produce as possible and takes particular pride in her extensive vegetarian menu. Snacks include home-made soup, ploughman's, sandwiches, home-made pâté, Gloucester sausage and garlic prawns; for a hot meal, you could begin with tasty chicken liver pâté, followed by vegetarian pasta shells in a rich celery, pepper and walnut sauce. Finish with a mouth-watering lemon syllabub. Traditional Sunday lunch menu.
Typical prices Lentil bolognese £3.50 Rabbit & mushroom pie £4.10

ACCOMMODATION **11 bedrooms £B**
Check-in all day

A recent expansion into an adjoining cottage has allowed for a new well-furnished residents' lounge with TV and a spacious suite upstairs. Older rooms in the main house and more modern rooms in an annexe are all spotless and well-equipped with tea-makers, TVs, radios, hairdryers and mini-bars. All have en suite facilities. Rear rooms look over a lovely garden.

Credit Access, Amex, Diners, Visa

COWBRIDGE — Bear Hotel

B & B

High Street
MAP 8 C4 *South Glamorgan*
Cowbridge (044 63) 4814
Parking ample

Landlord John Davies
Free house
Brains SA, Red Dragon; Worthington Best Bitter; Allbright Bitter; Hancock HB; Stella Artois; cider.

ACCOMMODATION **37 bedrooms £C**
Check-in all day

A lovely old coaching inn with wood and stonework dating back to the 17th century. The plush comfort of the lounge bar contrasts with the more homely charm of the timbered floors and ceilings in the public bar. Modern bedrooms in a courtyard annexe have direct-dial phones, TVs and bathrooms with hairdryers. Bedrooms in the old building are more traditional; most have their own bathrooms. Housekeeping could be improved.
Credit Access, Amex, Diners, Visa

CRICKHOWELL — Bear Hotel

FOOD
B & B

MAP 8C3 *Powys*
Crickhowell (0873) 810408
Parking ample

Bar food 12–2 & 6–10, Sun 12–1.30 & 6–9.30
Landlord Steve Sims
Free house
Bass Best Mild; Flowers Original; Worthington Best; Allbright Bitter; Stella Artois; Heineken; cider.

This tremendously characterful inn, over 500 years old, has recently been extended to provide extra accommodation and dining room facilities. The heavy-beamed main bar features some handsome antique furniture. A varied bar menu offers a range of tasty dishes including home-made soups and pâtés, pancakes, garlicky mussels, deep-fried squid and bouillabaisse. Favourites like omelettes, steaks and trout are served with sauté potatoes and side salads, while venison in red wine or vegetarian parmigiana are other options. Fresh-cream gâteaux, ice creams, and sorbets and parfaits round things off nicely. Traditional Sunday lunch. Garden.
Typical prices Pear & Stilton cocotte £2.25 Pepperpot beef £4.95

ACCOMMODATION **13 bedrooms £C**
Check-in all day

Creaky stairs and uneven landings with little alcoves and skylights lead to comfortable bedrooms of varying size, most with bathroom or shower. Rooms in the new annexe have en suite bathrooms and are more modern. All rooms have phones, TVs and coffee-makers and housekeeping standards are good.

Credit Access, Visa

CRICKHOWELL — Nantyffin Cider Mill Inn

FOOD

MAP 8 C3 *Powys*
Crickhowell (0873) 810775
Parking ample

Bar food 11.30–2.30 & 6–10.30, Sun 12–1.30 & 7–10
Landlord John Flynn
Free house
Marston Pedigree; Worthington Best Bitter; John Smith's Bitter; Carlsberg Export; cider.

Pork and cider pie and cider syllabub are two of the highly appropriate specialities offered at this former cider mill. The imaginative menu also embraces devilled prawns, flavoursome terrine and honey-barbecued chicken, cold meats and salads; as well as regular grills and a fresh fish dish. Puds also include lovely old-fashioned apple or treacle tarts.
Typical prices Pork & cider pie £3.05 Steak & kidney pie £3.05
Credit Access, Visa

EAST ABERTHAW — Blue Anchor

A

Nr Barry
MAP 8 C4 *South Glamorgan*
St Athaw (0446) 750329
Parking ample

Landlords John & Jeremy Coleman
Free house
Theakston Old Peculier; Brains SA; Wadworth 6X; Robinson Best Bitter; Marston Pedigree; Guinness; cider.

Turn your back firmly on the power station opposite and drink in the charm of this ancient, thatched inn hung with creepers and ivy. It's tiny inside, with thick old stone walls everywhere: squeeze down narrow passageways and stoop under low lintels to reach the maze of bars and drinking alcoves. Landlord John Coleman has been here for over 40 years, and with son Jeremy has created a marvellous medieval atmosphere. Patio.

FELINDRE FARCHOG — Salutation Inn

OD
& B

Crymych
MAP 8 A3 *Dyfed*
Newport (0239) 820564
Parking ample

Bar food 12–2.30 & 6.30–10
Landlords Richard & Valerie Harden
Free house
Bass; Worthington Best Bitter; Welsh Brewers Allbright; Guinness; Tennent's Extra; Carlsberg.

The Hardens have made substantial improvements to their delightful white-washed pub on the A487 Cardigan–Fishguard road. The beamed bars, one chintzy and the other tile-floored and practical (and popular with the local farmers) are full of character, and there you can tuck into a pleasing range of bar food. Cold snacks include pâté, salads, quiches and delicious ham sandwiches, while for a hot meal you might go for soup, with steak and kidney pie or the popular chicken paprika to follow. Home-made desserts include a tasty lemon cheesecake. Children's menu. *No smoking in the dining room.*
Typical prices Lasagne £2.80 Roast chicken breast £3.20

***ACCOMMODATION* 8 bedrooms £C**
Check-in all day

Bedrooms are in a modern annexe wing. All have recently been recarpeted and redecorated and have duvets, TVs, radio-alarms, tea-makers and practical modern bathrooms. There's a peaceful lounge for residents. Fishermen will appreciate the 3½ miles of fishing rights on the river Nevern, which flows past the bottom of the garden.

Credit Access, Visa

We welcome bona fide recommendations or complaints on the tear-out pages for readers' comments. They are followed up by our professional team but do complain to the management.

FELINGWM UCHAF — Plough Inn

FOOD
B & B

Nantgaredig, Carmarthen
MAP 8 B3 *Dyfed*
Nantgaredig (0267 88) 220
Parking ample

Bar food 12–2 & 7–10
Landlord Leon Hickman
Free house
Felinfoel Double Dragon, Bitter; Buckley Mild, Bitter; Guinness; Löwenbräu; cider.

The pub and restaurant are set in linked 16th-century buildings on a steep incline. It's a serious eating place, and the owner once worked for Robert Carrier at Hintlesham Hall. The bar meal menu provides sandwiches, ploughman's, salads and hot dishes like trout, chicken and gammon steak. You can also eat from the restaurant menu in the bar: this widens the choice considerably, with lots of starters, crab (fresh-dressed or au gratin), salmon and steaks, plus daily specials such as lobster Thermidor, duck en croûte or beef curry. There's a good cheeseboard, and sweets include home-made ice cream and a splendid liqueur gâteau.

Typical prices Fresh dressed crab £3.35 Fillet steak £8.75

***ACCOMMODATION* 5 bedrooms £B**
Check-in all day

Five spacious, attractively decorated bedrooms, one a family room, are in a house across the street. Two have their own bathrooms, and all rooms have TVs. There's a panelled reception area, plus kitchen and breakfast room. Garden. *No dogs.*

Credit Access, Amex, Diners, Visa **LVs**

FFAIRFACH — Torbay Inn

FOOD

Llandeilo
MAP 8 B3 *Dyfed*
Llandeilo (0558) 822029
Parking ample

Bar food 12–1.45 & 6.30–9.30 (Mon till 9, Tues till 8)
No bar food Sun lunch
Closed Sun eve
Landlords Callum & Vera Mackay
Free house
Buckley Best; Whitbread Mild; Welsh Bitter; Flowers IPA; Heineken; cider.

A really tiny pub, built of stone, painted pink and frequently bursting at the seams with contented quaffers and snackers. The bar food is very good and varied, with local fish, savoury pies and casseroles among the robust favourites. Our vegetable soup, served piping hot in a huge crockpot, was excellent. Garden and children's room.

Typical prices Turbot in prawn sauce £3.95 Chicken chasseur £2.25

GLANWYDDEN — Queen's Head

FOOD

Llandudno Junction, Nr Penrhyn Bay
MAP 8 B1 *Gwynedd*
Llandudno (0492) 46570
Parking limited

Bar food 12–2.15 (Sun till 1.45) & 7–9
No bar food Sun eve in winter
Landlords Robert & Sally Cureton
Brewery Ansells
Ind Coope Burton Ale, Bitter; Tetley Bitter; Guinness; Skol Special; cider.

The kitchen is in full view at this stone-walled, beamed pub reached by country lanes off the A546. Daily specials such as fresh salmon salad increase the scope of ever-changing menus of traditional favourites. More adventurous dishes at night might include veal in a tomato and basil sauce. Luscious sweets. Traditional Sunday lunch. Patio.

Typical prices Chicken in mushroom & tarragon £4.50 Conway crab £4.75

Credit Access, Visa

HAY-ON-WYE — Old Black Lion

ɔOD
& B

Lion Street
MAP 8 C3 *Powys*
Hay-on-Wye (0497) 820841
Parking ample

Bar food 12–2.30 & 7.30–9.30

Landlords Paul & Ann Andrews
Free house
Davenports Traditional Draught Bitter, Drum Bitter; Greenall Local Bitter; Wem Local Bitter; Davenports Continental Lager; Carlsberg Hof; cider.

Welcoming landlords Paul and Ann Andrews plan lots of improvements at this ancient coaching inn straddling the border between Wales and England. The two lounges (one with TV, for residents' use only) have already been spruced up and a new bar created, where a good selection of simple but appetising snacks is available. The choice includes home-made soup and pâté, exotic Polynesian-style meatballs served on a bed of noodles, vegetarian specials like nut roast with horseradish, and pleasant sweets – look out for the fresh and fruity apple pie.
Typical prices Steak & kidney pudding £3.95 Moussaka £2.25

ACCOMMODATION **10 bedrooms £C**
Check-in all day

Comfortable bedrooms of varying size range from traditional to smartly refurbished (pastel colour schemes, mahogany reproduction furniture, and bright duvets) in the annexe. Eight rooms have neat private facilities and all offer wall-mounted TVs and direct-dial telephones. Patio.

Credit Access, Amex, Diners, Visa

LLANARMON DYFFRYN CEIRIOG — West Arms Hotel

& B

Nr Llangollen
MAP 8 C2 *Clwyd*
Llanarmon Dyffryn Ceiriog
(069 176) 665
Parking ample

Landlord Mary Wildon
Free house
Tetley Bitter, Mild; Wrexham Lager; Castlemaine XXXX. *No real ale.*

ACCOMMODATION **12 bedrooms £B**
Check-in all day

Now under new management, this substantial 400-year old stone inn is being renovated, but will retain all its former charm and character. Log fires warm the reception area and welcome the visitor to a handsome oak-beamed lounge, next to which a huge second lounge overlooks gardens stretching down to the banks of the river Ceiriog. Accommodation is being transformed and upgraded: eight rooms will have private facilities when complete.
Credit Access, Amex, Diners, Visa

LLANDISSILIO — Bush Inn

ɔOD

MAP 8 A3 *Dyfed*
Clynderwen (099 12) 626
Parking ample

Bar food 11–2.30 & 6.30–9.30, Sun 12–1.30 & 7–10

Landlords Ken & Joyce Honeker
Free house
Crown Bitter; Webster Yorkshire Bitter; Guinness; Harp; Holsten Export; cider.

Home-made salads – potato, coleslaw, pickled cauliflower, mushrooms à la grecque – steal the show at this simple little pub on the A478. Try them with tasty turkey or smoked trout, or go for something warming like casserole or curry. Soup comes in a generous portion that's a meal in itself, and there are prime English cheeses or apple pie and cream for afters.
Typical prices Quiche £2.55 Rump steak £5.50
Credit Amex, Diners, Visa

LLANDOGO — Sloop Inn

B & B Nr Monmouth
MAP 8 C3 *Gwent*
Dean (0594) 530291
Parking ample

Landlords Grace Evans & George Morgan
Free house
Smiles Best Bitter; Wadworth 6X; Worthington Best Bitter; Guinness; Carlsberg; Stella Artois; cider.

ACCOMMODATION **4 bedrooms £C**
Check-in all day

Grace Evans and George Morgan are the friendliest and most jovial of hosts at this modernised inn, which takes its name from the barges that once sailed here from Bristol. Homely bedrooms are spotlessly clean and offer TVs and tea-makers, plus tidy modern bathrooms. Good breakfasts, too. There are two bars; public with pool table, darts and jukebox, lounge with a more restful ambience and some lovely views. Garden.
Credit Access, Amex, Diners, Visa

LLANDOVERY — King's Head Inn

B & B Market Square
MAP 8 B3 *Dyfed*
Llandovery (0550) 20393
Parking ample

Landlords Mr & Mrs D.P. Madeira-Cole
Free house
Worthington Dark Mild, Best Bitter; Hancock Bitter; Welsh Brewers Allbright; Guinness; Carling Black Label; cider.

ACCOMMODATION **4 bedrooms £C**
Check-in all day

The Madeira-Coles are welcoming hosts at this pleasant little inn on the market square. Dating back in parts to the early 17th century, its delightful rustic bar is a particularly cosy and convivial spot and there's a comfortable lounge bar as well as a spacious first-floor residents' lounge. The four bedrooms have a bright, modern appeal, with neat fitted furniture and all have tiled bathrooms en suite.

LLANFIHANGEL CRUCORNEY — Skirrid Inn

FOOD Nr Abergavenny
MAP 8 C3 *Gwent*
Crucorney (0873) 890258
Parking ample

Bar food 12–2 & 7–9.30

Landlords Foster Family
Free house
Wadworth 6X; Robinson Best Bitter; Felinfoel Bitter; Allbright Bitter; Guinness; Carlsberg Export; cider.

★ Certainly the oldest pub in Wales and a contender for the oldest pub in Great Britain, the Skirrid dates back to the 12th century and is steeped in history: medieval stone walls, mullion windows and beams there are in abundance. It's said there's even a ghost – drawn, no doubt, by the tantalising smell of the daily Skirrid pie baking: a delectable item full of venison, mushrooms and vegetables and served to corporeal souls in huge platefuls with real mash. There's lots of other genuine home-cooked food to choose from: spinach and Stilton pancake, rabbit casserole, dressed crab, pork fillet Dijon, and some good old-fashioned puds like jam roly-poly and figgy duff to finish. There's also a traditional Sunday lunch menu available. Eat out on the terrace in summer and enjoy the view up to Skirrid mountain or the valley below. ★
Typical prices The Skirrid pie £4.20 Vegetable mornay £2.95 Pork fillet in Dijon sauce £4.45 Fish pot in cream sauce £4.30

Credit Amex, Diners

LLANFRYNACH — White Swan

OOD

Nr Brecon
MAP 8 C3 *Powys*
Brecon (0874) 86276
Parking ample

Bar food 12–2.30 & 7–10.30, Sun 12–1.30 & 7–9.30
No bar food all Mon & eves last 3 wks Jan

Landlords David & Susan Bell
Free house
Brains; Flowers IPA; Whitbread Best; Guinness; Stella Artois; cider.

Look for this ancient, appealing pub opposite the largest graveyard in Wales. The spacious, beamed bar is full of character and here you can sample Susan Bell's tasty meat and fish pies, her casseroles, curries and juicy steaks. Lighter alternatives include French onion soup, garlic mushrooms, ploughman's and lasagne. Nice sweets, too. Pretty garden. Closed for lunches Monday and last three weeks January.
Typical prices Cottage pie £3.80 Chocolate cream mousse £1.50

LLANGOLLEN — Britannia Inn

& B

Horseshoe Pass
MAP 8 C2 *Clwyd*
Llangollen (0978) 860144
Parking ample

Landlords Mr & Mrs M. Callaghan
Free house
Webster Yorkshire Bitter, Green Label; Guinness; Carlsberg; Fosters; cider. *No real ale.*

ACCOMMODATION **7 bedrooms £C**
Check-in all day

A delightful 15th-century inn at the foot of the Horseshoe Pass with mountain views and terraced gardens among its charms. Nicely appointed bedrooms, nestling under eaves, have fitted units, colour TVs, tea and coffee making facilities, and share three modern bath/shower rooms. The low-beamed, rustic bars with their massive fireplace are a popular meeting place, and there's a patio and garden for summer drinking.
Credit Access, Amex, Diners, Visa

LLANGORSE — Red Lion

& B

Nr Brecon
MAP 8 C3 *Powys*
Llangorse (087 484) 238
Parking ample

Landlords Mr & Mrs C. Cocker
Free house
Flowers IPA; Marston Pedigree; Whitbread Best Bitter, Welsh Bitter; Guinness; Stella Artois; Heineken; cider.

ACCOMMODATION **10 bedrooms £D**
Check-in all day

Standing opposite the village church, with its own pretty stream and a rear garden that looks down the valley towards Llangorse Lake, this friendly little pub is run in cheerful fashion by the Cockers. There's a maze of passageways to the bedrooms which have been attractively refurbished; all have private bath /shower rooms, as well as TVs, teamakers and radio-alarms. Darts, pool and dominoes are popular in the stone-walled bars. Patio. *No dogs.*

LLANGURIG — Blue Bell

& B

Nr Llanidloes
MAP 8 B2 *Powys*
Llangurig (055 15) 254
Parking ample

Landlords Bill & Diana Mills
Free house
Samuel Powell Best Bitter; Welsh Bitter; Flowers Original; Whitbread Best Bitter; Stella Artois; Heineken.

ACCOMMODATION **10 bedrooms £D**
Check-in restricted

Bill and Diana Mills are friendly, welcoming hosts at this charming old roadside inn, whose cosy bar is very much the centre of village life. There's a pool room, the games room has darts and skittles, and next to it is a residents' lounge with TV. Steep stairs and narrow corridors give a cottagy feel, and the bedrooms (front ones with views of the church) are neat, simple and homely. One has an en suite bathroom. *No dogs.*
Credit Access, Visa

LLANNEFYDD

Hawk & Buckle Inn

B & B Nr Denbigh
MAP 8 B1 *Clwyd*
Llannefydd (074 579) 249
Parking ample

Landlords Bob & Barbara Pearson
Free house
Wilson Original Bitter, Mild; Guinness; Fosters; Carlsberg; cider. *No real ale.*

***ACCOMMODATION* 10 bedrooms £C**
Check-in all day

Winding country lanes lead to this old stone-built village inn opposite the Saxon church. There are two bars, one with a pool table, the other with two lovely settles before a large open hearth. The smartly carpeted residents' area affords some splendid views and well-kept bedrooms, seven in a ground floor extension, provide comfortable en suite accommodation, with TVs, radios, telephones and tea-makers. Patio. *No children under eight overnight.*
Credit Access, Visa

Changes in data may occur in establishments after the Guide goes to press. Prices should be taken as indications rather than firm quotes.

LLANTILIO CROSSENNY

Hostry Inn

B & B Nr Monmouth
MAP 8 C3 *Gwent*
Llantilio (060 085) 278
Parking ample

Landlords Mike & Pauline Parker
Free house
Usher Best Bitter; Webster Yorkshire Bitter; Tate Traditional Maiden-over; Worthington Best Bitter; Holsten Export.

***ACCOMMODATION* 2 bedrooms £D**
Check-in all day

The Parkers are proving enterprising hosts at this delightful little black and white inn on the B4233 between Monmouth and Abergavenny. They've converted an old barn into a function room and hire out a splendid vintage Rolls Royce for wedding receptions held there. The tiny bar and lounge are full of character, and you have to bend double when climbing the stairs to the bedrooms – a simple double and twin that share a shower and separate toilet. Garden.

LLANTRISSENT

Royal Oak Inn

B & B Nr Usk
MAP 8 C3 *Gwent*
Usk (029 13) 3317
Parking ample

Landlord D. W. H. T. Gascoigne
Free house
Flowers Best Bitter, Original; Wadworth 6X; Felinfoel Double Dragon; Stella Artois; Heineken; cider.

***ACCOMMODATION* 23 bedrooms £C**
Check-in all day

It's worth asking the way to this 15th-century inn overlooking the Usk valley. The old beamed bar, with stone fireplace, is full of character, which is reproduced in the cosy bedrooms above. The eight rooms in the modern motel block are more compact and have showers only. In a converted cottage nearby are four larger, traditionally furnished rooms. Accessories include direct-dial phones, tea/coffee-makers and TVs. Patio and garden. *No dogs.*
Credit Access, Amex, Visa

LLOWES — Radnor Arms

OD Nr Hay-on-Wye
MAP 8 C3 *Powys*
Glasbury (049 74) 460
Parking ample

Bar food 12–3 & 6.30–10 (Sun from 7)

Landlords Brian & Tina Gorringe
Free house
Felinfoel Double Dragon; Everards Tiger; Marston Burton Bitter; Guinness; Löwenbräu; cider.

★ Brian Gorringe received an MBE for his catering for Whitehall chiefs during the Falklands War and his customers would no doubt like to award him another for the delicious food he provides at his pretty pub in the Golden Valley. There are over 150 choices to suit all palates and pockets, all home-prepared and cooked from the freshest ingredients. You might start with carrot and orange soup or pigeon and walnut pâté; follow with lemon sole in cream, white wine and brandy, or kidneys in red wine omelette; then tackle the treacle and walnut tart or profiteroles with orange cream to round off a splendid meal. For snacks, there are quiches, ploughman's and salads, and a traditional roast lunch is available on Sundays. Children welcome lunchtime only. ★

Typical Prices Veal escalope provençale £7.50 Duck in Amaretto sauce £7.50 Smoked quail & walnuts £3.95 Home-made raspberry sorbet £1.90

LLYSWEN — Griffin Inn

OOD
& B

MAP 8 C3 *Powys*
Llyswen (087 485) 241
Parking ample

Bar food 12–2 & 7–9
No bar food Sun eve
Landlords Richard & Di Stockton
Free house
Flowers Original; Brains Bitter; Whitbread Best Bitter; Welsh Bitter; Guinness; cider.

Consistently high standards make this an ever-delightful place to visit. An old inn on the A470, its black-beamed bar has a stone fireplace, well-stocked with logs, pictures and gleaming horse brasses. The blackboard menu, which changes every few weeks, offers tasty dishes such as vegetarian minestrone, home-made pâté, Griffin curry, mushrooms in garlic, haddock and prawn cheese, mutton pie and vegetarian paella. Delicious puddings include treacle tart, fruit pie, raspberry pavlova and crème brûlée. A good choice of 'healthy' and vegetarian dishes is always to be had, and the cheeseboard is excellent. There is also a smart dining room offering an impressive evening menu.

Typical prices Fresh salmon £4.95 Mussels in garlic £2.25

ACCOMMODATION **6 bedrooms £D**
Check-in all day

The airy and attractive bedrooms, individually named rather than numbered, all have private facilities, tea-makers, radios and hairdryers, and there is a small lounge for residents. Amenities include salmon and trout fishing. Patio.

Credit Access, Amex, Diners, Visa

MENAI BRIDGE — Gazelle Hotel

B & B Glyn Garth
MAP 8 B1 *Gwynedd*
Menai Bridge (0248) 713364
Parking ample

Landlords Mr & Mrs J.M. Clark
Brewery Robinson
Robinson Best Bitter, Cock Robin, Three Shires Mild, Old Tom; Guinness; Einhorn; cider.

ACCOMMODATION **13 bedrooms £C**
Check-in all day

This is a splendid spot for a pub, down by the water's edge looking across the Menai Strait to Bangor and up the narrows to Telford's road bridge. Temporary moorings enable seafarers to quench their thirst in the cheerful bar. Five front bedrooms enjoy this fine view while smaller en suite rear rooms overlook the attractive, steeply rising garden. All are freshly painted, neat and bright with TVs, telephones and tea-making facilities. An annexe provides popular family accommodation. Patio.

MONMOUTH — Queen's Head Hotel

B & B St James' Street
MAP 8 C3 *Gwent*
Monmouth (0600) 2767
Parking limited

Landlords Margaret & Alan Statham
Free house
Flowers Original, IPA; Boddingtons Bitter; Samuel Smith's Old Brewery Bitter; Guinness; Tennent's Extra; cider.

ACCOMMODATION **3 bedrooms £D**
Check-in all day

One of the few pubs that can boast its own brewery, this splendid black-and-white timbered building stands by the A40 near the town centre. The characterful lounge bar is well furnished and traditional, and there's a little public bar. Comfortable overnight accommodation is provided in three simply but attractively furnished and centrally heated bedrooms with TVs, tea-makers and hairdryers. All have en suite facilities. Cot available.
Credit Access, Visa

MUMBLES — NEW ENTRY — Langland Court Hotel

B & B 31 Langland Court Road, Landland, Swansea
MAP 8 B4 *West Glamorgan*
Swansea (0792) 361545
Parking ample

Landlord Mr C. R. Birt
Free house
Worthington Best Bitter, Dark Mild; Allbright Bitter; Carling Black Label; Tennent's Extra.

ACCOMMODATION **21 bedrooms £C**
Check-in all day

Bedrooms are most attractive at this clifftop hotel facing the Bristol Channel. Some have large bow windows and four-posters; others are tucked up under the eaves; others still are in a converted coach house. All have excellent colour coordinated furnishings with matching duvets and offer phones, TVs, hairdryers, trouser presses, tea-makers, and good bathrooms. There's a tasteful cocktail bar overlooking the garden, and a more informal locals bar.
Credit Access, Amex, Diners, Visa

NOTTAGE — Rose & Crown

B & B Nr Porthcawl
MAP 8 B4 *Mid Glamorgan*
Porthcawl (065 671) 4850
Parking limited

Landlord Chris Rout
Owner Westward Hosts
Usher Best Bitter, Triple Crown; Webster Yorkshire Bitter; Ruddles County; Guinness; Holsten Export; cider.

ACCOMMODATION **8 bedrooms £B**
Check-in all day

An attractive old Welsh-stone pub with a whitewashed frontage and a bright display of window boxes. Inside, three cosy, carpeted bars and a huge stone fireplace give a pleasing rustic feel. The eight bedrooms (most in a more recent extension) are airy and comfortable and have been recently refurbished in modern style; all have en suite bathrooms, TVs and tea-makers. Garden. *No dogs.*
Credit Access, Amex, Diners, Visa

PANT MAWR — Glansevern Arms

& B Nr Llangurig
MAP 8 B2 *Powys*
Llangurig (055 15) 240
Parking ample
Landlord Mr W.T.O. Edwards
Free house
Bass; Worthington Dark Mild; Guinness; Carlsberg Export; cider.
***ACCOMMODATION* 8 bedrooms £B**
Check-in all day

This spotless little inn on the A44 Aberystwyth road four miles from Llangurig is surrounded by the superb scenery of the Plynlimon range. Mr Edwards is a welcoming host, and makes guests feel really at home in the characterful little bar and relaxing cottagy lounge, which has lovely Wye Valley views. Neat, traditionally furnished bedrooms have colour TVs and smart bath/shower rooms. Accommodation closed ten days Christmas. *No dogs.*
Credit Access, Visa

PEMBROKE — Old King's Arms Hotel

& B Main Street
MAP 8 A3 *Dyfed*
Pembroke (0646) 683611
Parking limited
Landlords Mr & Mrs Wheeler
Free house
Courage Directors; Worthington Best Bitter; Guinness; Carlsberg Hof, Pilsner; Miller Lite; cider.
***ACCOMMODATION* 21 bedrooms £C**
Check-in all day

Flagstones, a splendid fireplace and historic artefacts give the Wheelers' old coaching inn plenty of character. Main house bedrooms are delightful, with those on the top floor nestling right up under the eaves. The annexe rooms are small and less interesting, but all have telephones, TVs and modern bathrooms. Residents have a chintzy TV lounge upstairs, and there are two bars. Housekeeping could be improved. Patio.
Credit Access, Amex, Visa

PENLLYN — The Fox at Penllyn

OOD Nr Cowbridge
MAP 8 C4 *South Glamorgan*
Cowbridge (044 63) 2352
Parking ample
Bar food 12–2 & 6.30–10
Closed Sun & 3 days Xmas
Landlords Sarah & Nigel Collett
Free house
Felinfoel Double Dragon; Crown Special; Worthington Best Bitter; Carling Black Label; Kronenbourg.

A friendly, white-shuttered pub serving splendid cooked-to-order bar lunches, plus restaurant dinners. In the bar you eat at gingham-clothed tables; fresh fish is a speciality (the grilled sardines are superb), and there's soup, home-baked wholemeal bread, pasta and pancakes, steaks and chicken, with a chocolate mousse for sweet. Garden.
Typical prices Prawns on rye bread £2.95 Slices of salmon in a cream and watercress sauce £6.95
Credit Access, Visa

PENMAENPOOL — George III Hotel

& B Nr Dolgellau
MAP 8 B2 *Gwynedd*
Dolgellau (0341) 422525
Parking ample
Landlord Gail Hall
Free house
Younger's Tartan Bitter; John Marston Premium; Welsh Bitter; Guinness; Carlsberg Hof; cider.
No real ale.
***ACCOMMODATION* 14 bedrooms £C**
Check-in all day

Superbly situated at the head of the Mawddach estuary, this inn has its own moorings and fishing, too. Prints and brassware create a homely atmosphere in one bar, while the cellar bar is quaintly rustic. There's also a cosy lounge. Seven compact, main-house bedrooms share two bathrooms; smart, spacious rooms in the nearby lodge have en suite facilities. All have TVs, telephones and tea-makers. Patio. Accommodation closed 2 weeks Christmas
Credit Access, Amex, Diners, Visa

PENTWYNMAWR — Three Horseshoes

High Street
MAP 8 C3 *Gwent*
Newbridge (0495) 243436
Parking ample

Bar food 12–2 & 8–10 (Sat from 7.30)
No bar food Sun eve

Landlords Ann & Porter Reynish
Brewery Whitbread
Flowers Original; Whitbread Best Bitter; Guinness; Stella Artois; Heineken; cider. *No real ale.*

Lovingly restored by the Reynish family, this splendid village pub on the A472 offers a friendly welcome and some excellent bar snacks. A crusty sandwich filled with pâté, Cheddar and ham, French ploughman's, crispy mushroom corn bake and shepherd's pie with lentils are typical of the tasty range. Lovely rhubarb pie to finish, and there's also a traditional Sunday lunch menu available. Garden.
Typical prices Steak & kidney pie £2.95 Vegetable lasagne £3.95

PENYBONT — Severn Arms

Nr Llandrindod Wells
MAP 8 C3 *Powys*
Penybont (059 787) 224
Parking ample

Landlords Geoff & Tessa Lloyd
Free house
Bass; Whitbread Best Bitter; Worthington Best; Guinness; Tennent's Extra; Carling Black Label; cider.

ACCOMMODATION **10 bedrooms £D**
Check-in all day

Geoff and Tessa Lloyd are the friendly hosts at this old whitewashed inn on the A44. Two characterful bars provide a choice for the thirsty, and there is also a residents' lounge with TV and a games room. Spacious, comfortable bedrooms have tea-makers and good bathrooms; all ten now have colour TVs. Across the garden is a sports field where ponytrotting races are a regular feature. Accommodation closed one week Christmas.
Credit Access, Visa

RAGLAN — Beaufort Arms Hotel

High Street
MAP 8 C3 *Gwent*
Raglan (0291) 690412
Parking ample

Bar food 12–2.30 & 7–10
Landlords Jeanes family
Free house
Smiles Best Bitter; Ansells Bitter; John Bull Bitter; Guinness; Carlsberg Export; Skol; cider.

Loving restoration by the Jeanes family has preserved and embellished the period charm of this historic inn, in the centre of the village. There are some wonderful antiques here, including a fireplace from Raglan Castle, looking much as it did in the 14th century. The bar boasts some Tudor beams – and appetising food prepared by Julian Lunnon. Choice includes tasty home-made soup, pâté, devilled whitebait, with perhaps steak, a roast, a curry or a really juicy beefburger with freshly cooked chips to follow. Nice home-made puds like fruit fool and raspberry meringue nests, too.
Typical prices Fried mushrooms with pâté £2.60 Beef mexicaine £3

ACCOMMODATION **10 bedrooms £C**
Check-in all day

Spacious double bedrooms (and one single) have been ingeniously fitted into 17th-century unevenness. Rooms have attractive individual decor, with fitted units leaving space for an easy chair, dressing table and small desk. All have TVs, telephones, tea-makers, and spacious tiled bathrooms. There's also a residents' lounge. Patio. *No dogs.*

Credit Access, Amex, Diners, Visa

SHIRENEWTON — NEW ENTRY — Carpenter's Arms

OD

Lisk Road, Nr Chepstow
MAP 8 C3 *Gwent*
Shirenewton (029 17) 231
Parking ample

Bar food 12–2.15 & 6.30–10.15

Landlords Rob & Val Edwards
Free house
Theakston Old Peculier; Wadworth 6X; Marston Pedigree; Ruddles County; Hook Norton Best Bitter; Murphy Irish Stout; cider.

A popular pub on the B4235 four miles from Chepstow. Formed from a row of cottages bounded by a smithy and a carpenter's, its ancestry is betrayed by a huge bellows and coach wheels. The blackboard menu offers a variety of delicious meals, including garlic mushrooms with curry, steaks or gammon to follow. Home-made sweets include rhubarb crumble. Traditional Sunday lunch menu. Patio.
Typical prices Beef & mushroom pie £3.20 Chicken chasseur £3.95

TRECASTLE — Castle Hotel

OD
& B

Nr Sennybridge
MAP 8 B3 *Powys*
Sennybridge (087 482) 354
Parking ample

Bar food 12–2.30 & 6.30–9.30

Landlords Dick & Joan Ward
Free house
Ruddles County; Usher Best Bitter; Webster Yorkshire Bitter; Guinness; Holsten Export; Carlsberg; cider.

A welcoming fire burns in the appealing bar of this sturdy grey-painted inn at the heart of a village on the A40. Snacks can also be enjoyed in a summery conservatory, a comfortable lounge where children are welcome, or in the garden. Dick and Joan Ward are friendly hosts, and their wholesome, tasty bar food is much appreciated. Soup, pâté, sandwiches and salads provide light bites, while lamb or chicken curry, an excellent lasagne and spaghetti bolognese are among the hot dishes. Traditional roast lunch is a feature on Sundays.
Typical prices Chicken breast in barbecue sauce £2.90 Shepherd's pie £2.10

ACCOMMODATION **6 bedrooms £D**
Check-in all day

Six attractive, spacious bedrooms, with pretty, floral wallpaper and practical modern furniture, share three well-equipped bathrooms (only one has its own bathroom en suite). All rooms have TVs and tea and coffee making facilities.

Credit Access, Visa

USK — NEW ENTRY — Olway Inn

OD

Old Chepstow Road
MAP 8 C3 *Gwent*
Usk (029 13) 2047
Parking ample

Bar food 12–2 & 7–10

Landlords John & Jan Murray
Free house
Felinfoel Bitter; Davenports Bitter; Samuel Smith's Old Brewery Bitter; Worthington Best Bitter; Tennent's Export; Davenports Continental Lager; cider.

The low-ceilinged, beamed bar with its huge log fire makes a homely setting for the Murray family's good food. The lunch-time accent is on imaginative open sandwiches, while Hangover Breakfast tops the choice of daily specials. Evening prices include vegetables or salad, with quails, chicken curry or mullet on the menu. Traditional Sunday lunch menu also available. Garden.
Typical prices Lamb kebabs £2.50 Sirloin with Stilton, cream & port £6.50

WHITEBROOK — The Crown at Whitebrook

FOOD
B & B

Nr Monmouth
MAP 8 C3 *Gwent*
Monmouth (0600) 860254
Parking ample

Bar food 12–2 & 7–10

Landlords John & David Jackson
Free house
Flowers IPA; Heineken.

Three miles up a valley off the A466 Monmouth–Chepstow road you'll find this pub where peaceful accommodation in lovely surroundings and serious wining and dining are to be had. Relax in a deep armchair in the spacious and chintzy lounge (there is no bar) while David Jackson creates your meal to order. Sandwiches are not available and bar snacks are exotic – for example truffled duck terrine with port and marc de Bourgogne – while for a full meal you might go for a lovely crème Dubarry, followed by sautéed chicken and pork in two sauces. Delicious sweets. *No smoking in dining room.*
Typical prices Cucumber & cheese mousse £2.30 Artichoke heart with chicken livers and brioche £3.25

ACCOMMODATION **12 bedrooms £B**
Check-in all day

Bedrooms are equipped to a high standard, with matching fabrics, good fitted furniture, easy chairs, direct-dial telephones, TVs and spotless bathrooms. For luxury, choose the Manor Room, which has a four-poster and whirlpool bath. Breakfast in bed is a popular feature. Terrace.

Credit Access, Amex, Diners, Visa

WOLF'S CASTLE — Wolfe Inn

FOOD
B & B

Nr Haverfordwest
MAP 8 A3 *Dyfed*
Treffgarne (043 787) 662
Parking ample

Bar food 12–2 & 7–10
No bar food Sun eves & all Mon in winter
Closed Mon lunch in winter

Landlords Mr & Mrs Fritz Neumann
Free house
Felinfoel Bitter; Ansells Bitter; Worthington Best Bitter; Guinness; Löwenbräu; Carlsberg Export; cider.

You'll find this deceptively small inn some seven miles out of Fishguard on the A40, ideally situated for an early lunch before the afternoon ferry. Inside, it's very smart and welcoming and the experienced Neumanns know just how to tempt you with satisfying snacks. Home-made turkey and vegetable soup, smoked trout pâté and ploughman's vie with daily specials like chicken Kiev, veal cordon bleu and trout with almonds, as well as steaks and (summer only) an inviting cold buffet. Good sweets, too, like raspberry charlotte and Tia Maria syllabub. Patio.
Typical prices Local smoked trout with brown bread £2.50 Fresh crab salad in mayonnaise £4.25

ACCOMMODATION **1 bedroom £D**
Check-in restricted

In a converted outbuilding attached to the inn there is a spacious twin-bedded room (with space for a child's bed). It has its own private bathroom and kitchen and TV. Breakfast of fresh orange juice and scrambled egg is served in the room.

Credit Access, Visa

CHANNEL ISLANDS

ST ANNE — NEW ENTRY — Georgian House

D B

Victoria Street
MAP 9 D3 *Alderney*
Alderney (048 182) 2471
Parking ample

Bar food 12–2.30 (Sun till 2) & 7.30–9.30

Landlords Elizabeth & Stephen Hope
Free house
Guernsey Best Bitter; Guinness; Breda. *No real ale*

A cobbled shopping street is the picturesque setting for this handsome whitewashed Georgian town house run by the cheerful and friendly Hopes. Lunchtime snacks at the bar include home-made lasagne, steak and mushroom pie and sandwiches, but for a slap-up meal head for the dining room where an à la carte menu offers such seasonal delights as potted game with Cumberland sauce, Alderney crab and chicken with asparagus and paprika sauce, followed by traditional sweets like treacle tart. There's a lavish barbecue in the garden in summer, and Wednesday evenings and Sunday lunchtimes bring a carvery with a choice of roasts.

Typical prices Pork, apricot & mead pie £6.50 Fresh fruit pavlova £1.50

ACCOMMODATION **4 bedrooms £C**
Check-in all day

Comfortable accommodation is provided by the airy bedrooms, all of which have well-kept en suite bathrooms, remote-control colour TVs, tea-makers and radio-alarms. Residents have a TV lounge, breakfast room and bar. *No children under eight overnight. No dogs.*

Credit Access, Diners, Visa

PLEINMONT — Imperial Hotel

B

Torteval
MAP 9 C3 *Guernsey*
Guernsey (0481) 64044
Parking ample

Landlord Mr J.W. Hobbs
Brewery Randall
Randall Best Bitter; Worthington 'E'; Guinness; Breda; cider.
No real ale.

ACCOMMODATION **16 bedrooms £C**
Check-in all day

Splendid views of the rugged coastline are a feature of many bedrooms at this friendly inn; a popular base for family holidays. There are two residents' lounges, and a popular locals' bar. Comfortable bedrooms, some with balconies, have functional modern units, pretty duvets and bedcovers, TVs and tea-makers. All rooms have neat private bathrooms, most are en suite. Accommodation closed November to March. Patio and garden.

Credit Access, Visa

ST AUBIN'S HARBOUR — Old Court House Inn

FOOD
B & B

The Bulwarks
MAP 9 D3 *Jersey*
Jersey (0534) 46433
Parking limited

Bar food 12.30–2.30 & 7.30–10.30

Landlords Jonty & Vicky Sharp
Free house
Mary Ann Special; John Smith's Yorkshire Bitter; Guinness; Stella Artois; cider. *No real ale.*

A 15th-century inn occupying a prime position overlooking the bustling harbour. The bars are full of atmosphere and character, from the cellar bars with exposed beams and bricks (and even a floodlit well) to the teak-lined Mizzen Mast bar upstairs. Daily specials on the blackboard menu feature fresh local fish, and game in winter, while sweets offer seasonal fruits and hearty, warming puds in winter. You might start with salmon mayonnaise, king-size prawns or turtle soup, followed by crayfish salad or fillet steak with Stilton sauce, finishing perhaps with a superb fruit salad or chocolate mousse. The inn's restaurant is closed February.
Typical prices Sea bass farcie £6.75 Seasonal fruits £2.75

ACCOMMODATION **9 bedrooms £A**
Check-in all day

The delightful bedrooms couldn't be more welcoming, with their lovely old beds, antique pine furniture and harmonious paintwork and fabrics. Many, including the penthouse suite, have fabulous views and all are well-equipped with modern conveniences and stylish bathrooms. *No dogs.*

Credit Access, Visa

ISLE OF MAN

PEEL **Creek Inn**

ÞD The Quayside
MAP 3 A3 *Isle of Man*
Peel (062484) 2216
Parking ample

Bar food noon–11

Landlords Robert & Jean McAleer
Brewery Okells
Okell Bitter, Mild; Guinness; Holsten Export; Harp; cider.

Robert and Jean McAleer bring a sense of character and fun to their pub on the busy harbour. There's an appropriately nautical theme to the lounge bar where the light, simple snacks include open, closed and toasted sandwiches, pizzas, salads and delicious kipper pâté. Daily specials such as herring and scallop dishes are capably cooked, and there's apple pie or gâteau to finish.
Typical prices Lasagne £1.95 Seafood platter £3.95

BATH

Town plan opposite

Population 84,000

The Romans settled in Bath because of the waters and built baths used for therapy and recreation. In the 18th century spa treatment reached the peak of fashion and Bath was greatly enlarged at this time. Being wholly built within the space of a century, all its buildings are of the same classic, elegant style. Its Georgian character and charm remained unchanged until very recently. Yet Bath has become the centre of much environmental controversy: should the face of Bath be gradually eroded to develop it as a 20th-century commercial city, or should it be enshrined for ever as a masterpiece of urban architecture?

Annual Events
Bath Festival (music and drama)
22nd May–7th June
Royal Bath and West Show

Sights Outside City
Cheddar Gorge, Wooky Hole Caves, Wells Cathedral, Glastonbury Abbey, Longleat House and Safari Park, Castle Combe Village, Lacock Abbey and Village, Stourhead House and gardens, Avebury Circles, Corsham Court

Tourist Information Centre
Abbey Church Yard
Telephone Enquiries Bath 62831

Fiat Dealer
Motor Services (Bath) Ltd
Margaret's Buildings
Circus Place
Bath
Avon BA1 2PW
Tel. Bath 27328
Map reference 2A

1 Abbey *15th c* B4
2 American Museum at Claverton Manor *$2\frac{1}{2}$ miles, life in the New World from 17th c to 1860* C3
3 Assembly Rooms *Finely restored Georgian suite, also houses world-famous Museum of Costume* A2
4 Bath Industrial Heritage Centre A2
5 Bath Spa Station B5
6 Botanical Gardens in Victoria Park A2
7 Burrows Toy Museum B4
8 The Circus, Royal Crescent and Lansdown Crescent *superb examples of Georgian town-planning* A1 & A2
9 Guildhall Banqueting Room *fine Adam-style room* B3
10 Herschel House A3
11 Holburne of Menstrie Museum *paintings, silver, objects d'art* C2
12 Huntingdon Centre B2
13 Lansdown Race-course A1
14 Museum of Bookbinding B4
15 National Museum of Photography B3
16 Postal Museum B3
17 Pulteney Bridge *Adam bridge lined with shops* B3
18 Pump Room and Roman Baths *the heart of Bath, includes Britain's finest Roman remains* B4
19 Sham Castle *18th-c folly and viewpoint* C2
20 Theatre Royal A3
21 Tourist Information Centre B4
22 University C3
23 Victoria Art Gallery *works by mainly West Country artists; glass; Delft; horology* B3

For your local dealers see pages 50-53

Bath FIAT

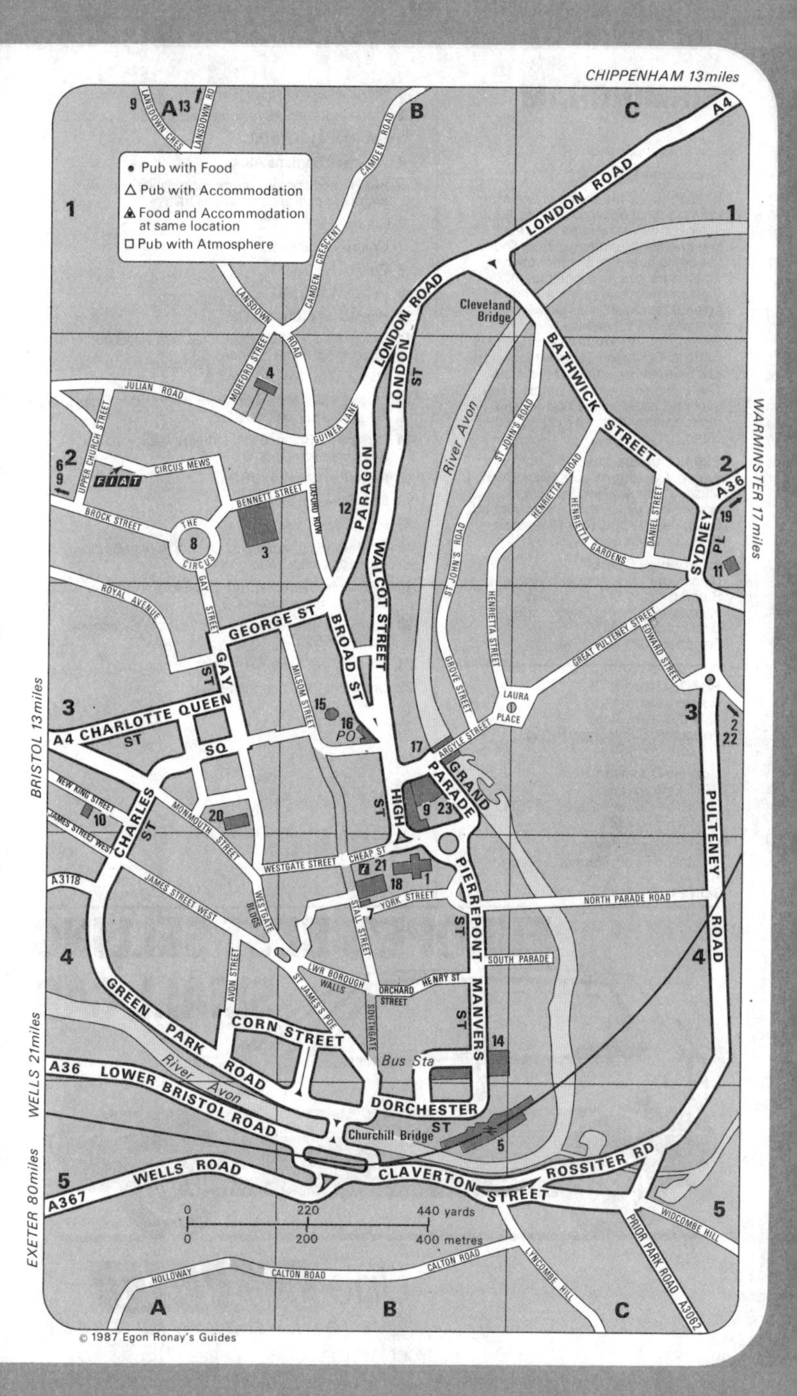

CHIPPENHAM 13 miles
WARMINSTER 17 miles
BRISTOL 13 miles
WELLS 21 miles
EXETER 80 miles
• Pub with Food
△ Pub with Accommodation
Food and Accommodation at same location
□ Pub with Atmosphere
LONDON ROAD
BATHWICK STREET
River Avon
Cleveland Bridge
PARAGON
WALCOT STREET
BROAD ST
GEORGE ST
GAY ST
QUEEN SQ
CHARLOTTE ST
CHARLES ST
HIGH ST
GRAND PARADE
PIERREPONT ST
MANVERS ST
SYDNEY PL
PULTENEY ROAD
GREAT PULTENEY STREET
LAURA PLACE
NORTH PARADE ROAD
SOUTH PARADE
CORN STREET
GREEN PARK ROAD
LOWER BRISTOL ROAD
DORCHESTER ST
Churchill Bridge
Bus Sta
PO
WELLS ROAD
CLAVERTON STREET
ROSSITER RD
PRIOR PARK ROAD
WIDCOMBE HILL
LYNCOMBE HILL
CALTON ROAD
HOLLOWAY
0 220 440 yards
0 200 400 metres

GUIDE TO SIGHTS

BIRMINGHAM

Town plan opposite

Population 1,006,000

Birmingham is the centre of one of Britain's most dynamic regions. It achieved industrial fame as a result of a fine tradition of craftsmanship. Today the city is noted for its production of motor cars, electrical equipment, machine tools and plastics. It has a splendid tradition in metal ware, including gold and silver work. Birmingham sponsored the £20m plus National Exhibition Centre at Bickenhill, just nine miles south-east of the city. This exhibition centre is Britain's first ever purpose-designed centre and ranks among the most modern in the world.

Sights Outside City
Airport, Coughton Court, Black Country Museum, Ragley Hall, Packwood House, Warwick Castle, West Midland Safari Park, Arbury Hall, Charlecote Park, Stratford-upon-Avon

Information Office
Birmingham Convention & Visitor Bureau, Ticket Shop & Tourist Information Centre, City Arcade, Birmingham B2 4TX
Telephone 021-643 2514

1 Alexandra Theatre C3
2 Aston Hall *Jacobean masterpiece open to public* D1
3 Baskerville House B2
4 Botanical Gardens A3
5 Bull Ring Shopping Centre *rotunda, multi-level shopping centre and market* C/D3
6 Cannon Hill Park C3
7 Central Libraries B2
8 Council House B2
9 Hall of Memory B2
10 Hippodrome Theatre C3
11 Lickey Hills *500 beautiful acres with views from Beacon Hill of ten counties* C3
12 Midland Red Bus Station C3
13 Museum and Art Gallery *from Veronese to Picasso via Hogarth and Constable* B2
14 Museum of Science and Industry *a link with the Industrial Revolution* B1
15 Repertory Theatre A/B2
16 New Street Station C3
17 Post Office Tower B1
18 St Chad's Cathedral *first English Roman Catholic Cathedral since Reformation* C1
19 St Philip's Cathedral *18th-c Palladian with later Burne-Jones windows* C2
20 Town Hall *meeting-place and home of Symphony orchestra* B2
21 University of Aston D1
22 University of Birmingham C3

For your local dealers see pages 50-53

Birmingham
FIAT

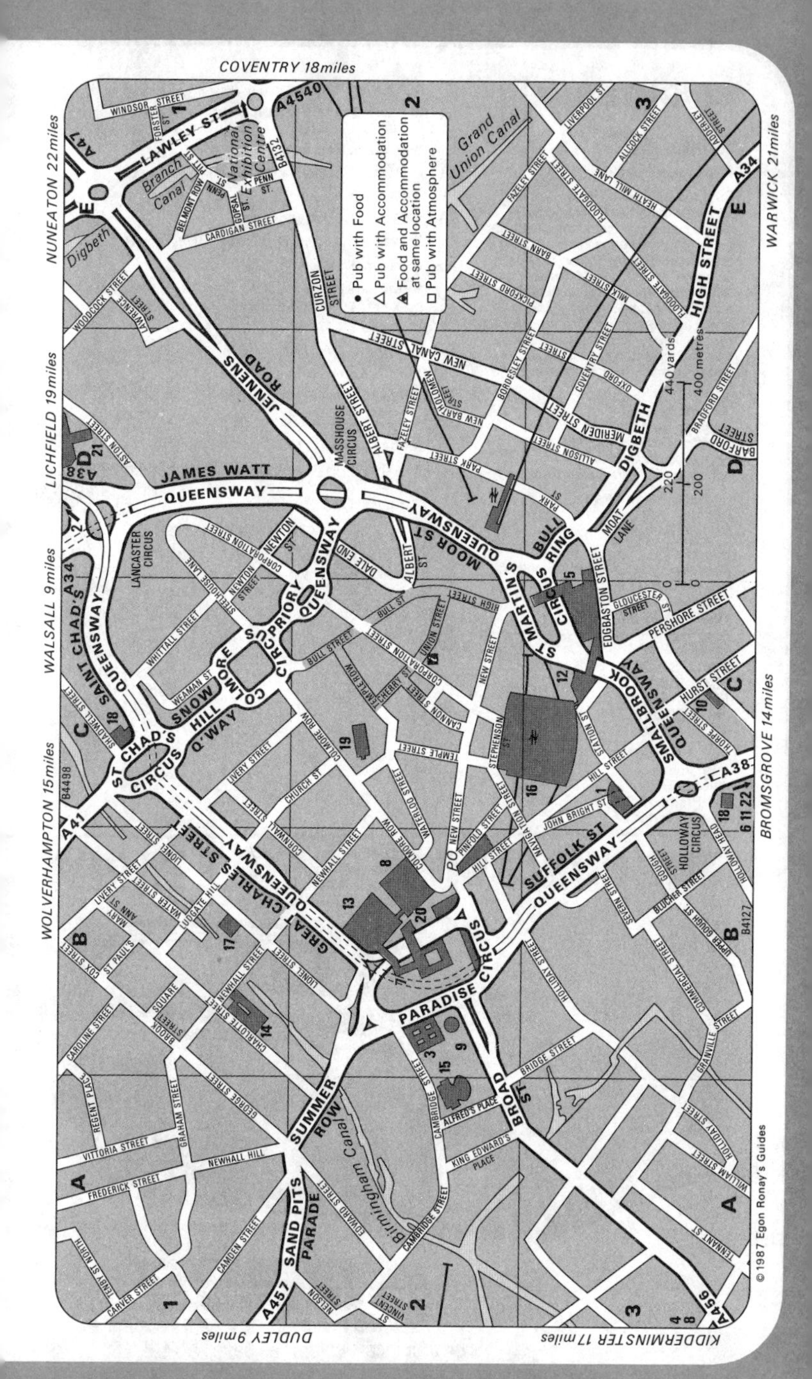
COVENTRY 18 miles
NUNEATON 22 miles
LICHFIELD 19 miles
WALSALL 9 miles
WOLVERHAMPTON 15 miles
DUDLEY 9 miles
KIDDERMINSTER 17 miles
BROMSGROVE 14 miles
WARWICK 21 miles
● Pub with Food
△ Pub with Accommodation
▲ Food and Accommodation at same location
□ Pub with Atmosphere
440 yards
400 metres
National Exhibition Centre
Grand Union Canal
Birmingham Canal
JAMES WATT QUEENSWAY
ST CHAD'S CIRCUS
PARADISE CIRCUS
ST MARTIN'S CIRCUS
BULL RING
HIGH STREET
DIGBETH
BROAD ST
SUMMER ROW
SAND PITS PARADE
SUFFOLK ST QUEENSWAY
SMALLBROOK QUEENSWAY
GREAT CHARLES STREET QUEENSWAY
MOOR ST QUEENSWAY
JENNENS ROAD
LAWLEY ST
© 1987 Egon Ronay's Guides

BRIGHTON

Town plan opposite

Population 153,700

Brighton is Regency squares and terraces, the maze of art and junk shops called the Lanes, the beach and piers, the conferences and entertainments, the milling crowds in Brighton, and the quiet lawns of Hove, a day out for Londoners, a holiday and retirement centre, a commuter's town and a university town. The person most responsible for all this was George IV, who made it the vogue and commissioned his unique palace, the Royal Pavilion.

Annual Events
Brighton Boat Show *May*
Brighton Festival *May*
Glyndebourne *May–Aug*
London to Brighton veteran car run *Nov*

Sights Outside Town
Arundel Castle, Petworth House, Bluebell Railway

Information Centres
Marlborough House, Old Steine and Sea-front opp. West Street
Telephone Brighton 23755
Weekends Brighton 26450

Fiat Dealers
Tilleys (Sussex) Ltd
100 Lewes Road
Brighton BN2 3QA
Tel. Brighton 603244
Map reference 1D

Tilleys (Sussex) Ltd
2 Church Road
Hove BN3 2FL
Tel. Brighton 738949
Map reference 2A

1 Aquarium and Dolphinarium D3
2 Booth Bird Museum *British birds in natural surroundings* B1
3 Brighton & Hove Albion F.C. A1
4 Brighton Conference & Exhibition Centre C3
5 Churchill Square C3
6 County Cricket Ground A2
7 Devil's Dyke *4 miles, Sussex beauty spot* B1
8 Information Centres C3
9 The Lanes *network of old fisherman's cottages, now world centre for antiques* C3
10 Marina E3
11 Museum & Art Gallery C/D3
12 Palace Pier D3
13 Preston Park and Preston Manor *18th c* C1
14 Race-course E1
15 Rottingdean *2$\frac{1}{2}$ miles, toy museum* E3
16 Royal Pavilion *Regency exhibition, art gallery and museum* C/D3
17 Station C2
18 Sussex University *4 miles* E1
19 Theatre Royal C3
20 Volks Railway *first electric railway, on seafront* D3

Brighton

FIAT

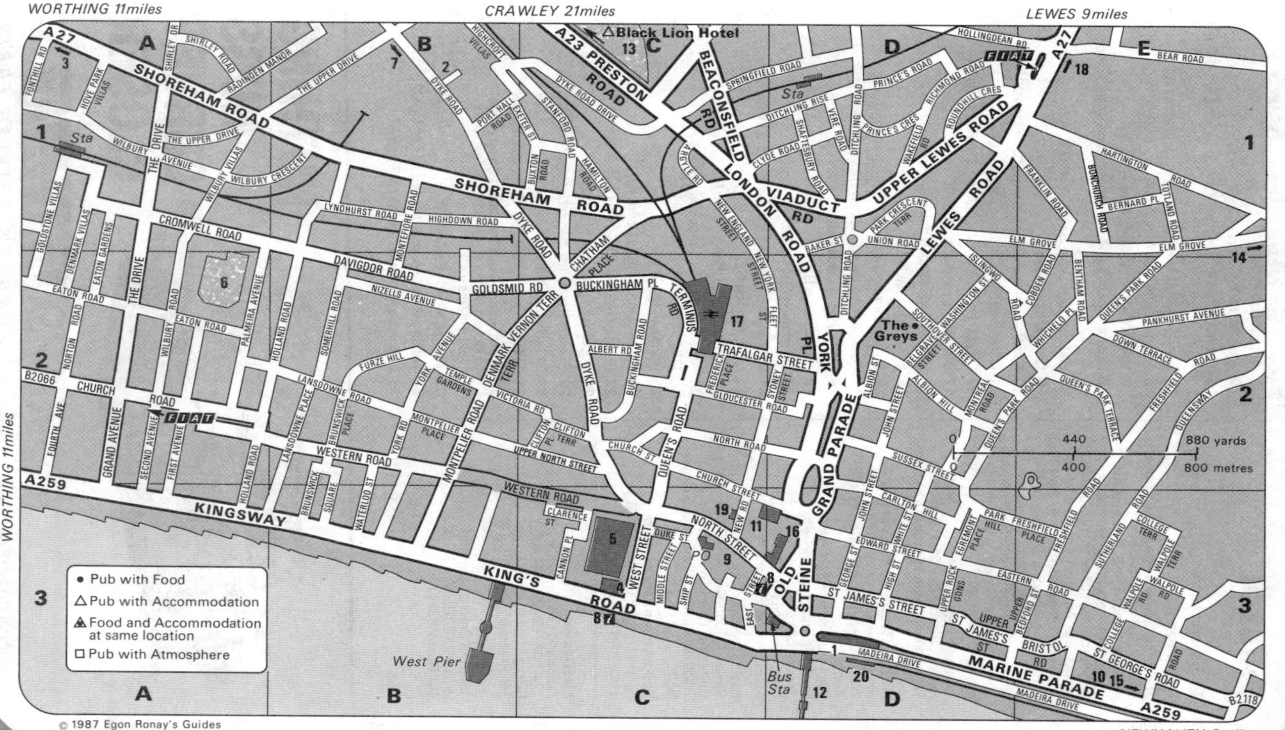

WORTHING 11miles
CRAWLEY 21miles
LEWES 9miles
NEWHAVEN 9miles
Black Lion Hotel
The Greys
West Pier
Bus Sta
Sta
880 yards
800 metres
440
400
A27
A23 PRESTON ROAD
A259
B2066
B2118
SHOREHAM ROAD
LEWES ROAD
UPPER LEWES ROAD
LONDON ROAD
BEACONSFIELD RD
VIADUCT RD
YORK PL
GRAND PARADE
OLD STEINE
MARINE PARADE
KING'S ROAD
KINGSWAY
DYKE ROAD
WEST STREET
NORTH STREET
QUEEN'S ROAD
WESTERN ROAD
CHURCH ROAD
CROMWELL ROAD
DAVIGDOR ROAD
GOLDSMID RD
BUCKINGHAM PL
TERMINUS RD
TRAFALGAR STREET
ST JAMES'S STREET
EASTERN ROAD
EDWARD STREET
DITCHLING ROAD
ELM GROVE
THE DRIVE
GRAND AVENUE
HOLLAND ROAD
PALMEIRA AVENUE
MONTPELIER ROAD
FIAT
• Pub with Food
△ Pub with Accommodation
▲ Food and Accommodation at same location
□ Pub with Atmosphere

BRISTOL

Town plan opposite

Population 401,100

The Birthplace of America–the Cabots sailed from here to discover Newfoundland in 1497. This and later voyages brought Bristol prosperity, largely in sugar, tobacco, rum and the slave trade. Architecture surviving the 1940 war damage ranges over the 13th-century Lord Mayor's Chapel, St Mary Redcliffe Church, England's oldest working theatre (Theatre-Royal–now completely renovated), and Clifton's Georgian terraces.

Annual Events
Senior Citizens' Day *21st June*
World Wine Fair and Festival *10th–19th July*
Harbour Regatta and Rally of Boats *8th–9th August*
International Balloon Fiesta *14th–16th August*
Maritime Carnival *31st August*
Bristol Flower Show *2nd–4th September*
Christmas Illuminated Water Carnival *19th–20th December*

Sights Outside City
Severn Bridge, Berkeley Castle, Wells Cathedral, Cheddar Gorge, Severn Wildfowl Trust, Castle Combe Village, Bath

Tourist Information Centre
Colston House, Colston Street
Telephone Bristol 659491

Fiat Dealers
Autotrend Ltd
724–726 Fishponds Road
Bristol BS16 3UE
Tel. Bristol 657247

Bawns Ltd
168–176 Coronation Road
Bristol BS3 1RG
Tel. Bristol 631101

1 Airport *6 miles* A3
2 Arnolfini (Arts Centre) C3
3 Ashton Court Estate and Mansion *beautiful parklands* A1
4 Blaise Castle House Folk Museum *Henbury* A1
5 National Lifeboat Museum C3
6 Bristol Cathedral *dates from 12th c* B3
7 Bristol Tapestry and Permanent Planning Exhibition D1
8 Cabot Tower *Brandon Hill, built 1897* A2
9 Central Library B3
10 Chatterton House *Chatterton's birthplace* D3
11 Christmas Steps *antique shops* C1
12 City Museum & Art Gallery *fine & applied arts* B1
13 Clifton suspension bridge A1
14 Colston Hall concert hall B2
15 Council House B2
16 Entertainment Centre B2
17 Georgian House *late 18th-c showpiece* B2
18 Harveys Wine Museum B2
19 Hippodrome B2
20 Information Centre B2
21 John Wesley Chapel *first Methodist Chapel* D1
22 Little Theatre C2
23 Lord Mayor's Chapel *13th c* B2
24 Nails and the Exchange *'pay on the nail' originated here* C2
25 Norman Arch B3
26 Observatory, Clifton Down A1
27 Red Lodge *late 16th-c showpiece* B2
28 Royal York Crescent *Regency* A2
29 St Mary Redcliffe Church *dates from 13th c* D3
30 St Nicholas Church Museum C2
31 St Peter and St Paul *R.C. Cathedral* A1
32 S.S. 'Great Britain' *first ocean-going propeller ship, launched Bristol 1843, Great Britain Dock, Gasferry Road* A3
33 Temple Meads Station E3
34 Theatre Royal *home of the Bristol Old Vic* C2
35 Zoo *including flowers and rare trees* A1

For local dealers see pages 50-53

Bristol
FIAT

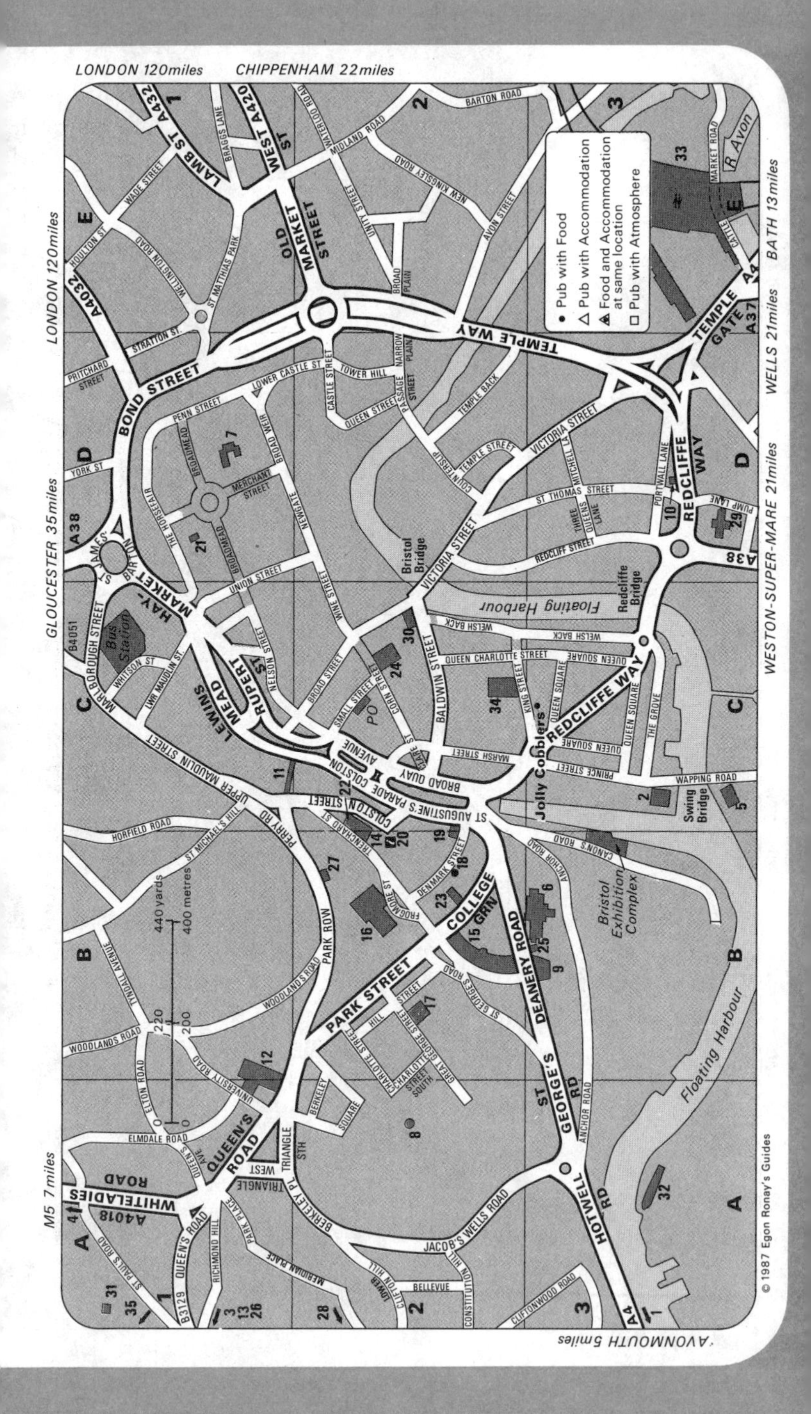
LONDON 120miles
CHIPPENHAM 22miles
GLOUCESTER 35miles
M5 7miles
AVONMOUTH 5miles
WESTON-SUPER-MARE 21miles
WELLS 21miles
BATH 13miles
• Pub with Food
△ Pub with Accommodation
▲ Food and Accommodation at same location
□ Pub with Atmosphere
440 yards
400 metres
TEMPLE WAY
OLD MARKET STREET
BOND STREET
REDCLIFFE WAY
VICTORIA STREET
BALDWIN STREET
PARK STREET
COLLEGE GRN
DEANERY ROAD
ST GEORGE'S RD
HOTWELL RD
QUEEN'S ROAD
WHITELADIES ROAD
Floating Harbour
Bristol Bridge
Redcliffe Bridge
Swing Bridge
Bristol Exhibition Complex
Bus Station
Jolly Cobblers
R. Avon
© 1987 Egon Ronay's Guides

Edinburgh

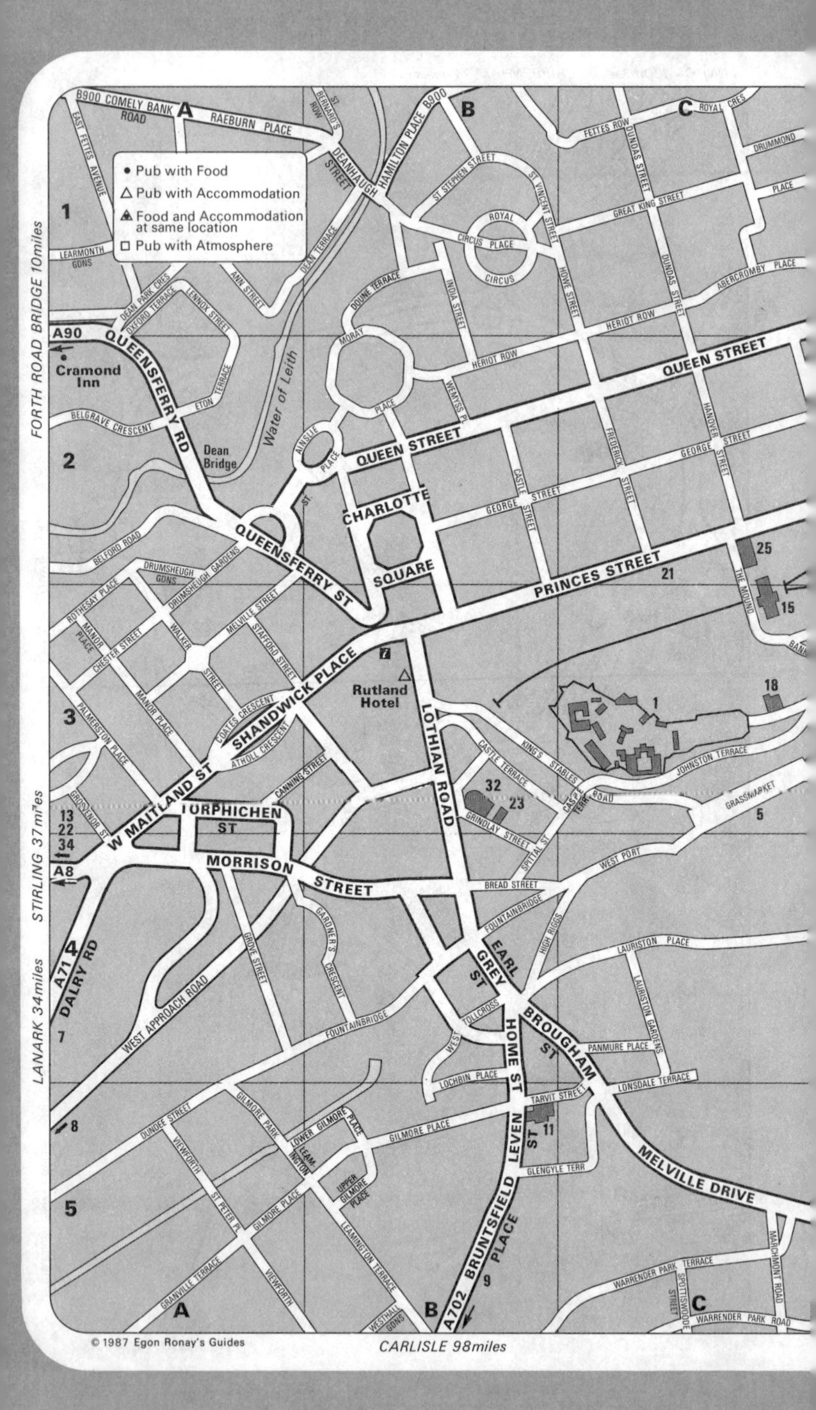

• Pub with Food
△ Pub with Accommodation
Food and Accommodation at same location
□ Pub with Atmosphere
A
B
C
1
2
3
4
5
FORTH ROAD BRIDGE 10miles
STIRLING 37 miles
LANARK 34miles
CARLISLE 98miles
A90
A8
A71
A702
B900
Cramond Inn
Rutland Hotel
Dean Bridge
Water of Leith
COMELY BANK ROAD
RAEBURN PLACE
EAST FETTES AVENUE
LEARMONTH GDNS
DEANHAUGH STREET
HAMILTON PLACE
ST STEPHEN STREET
ST VINCENT STREET
ROYAL CIRCUS
CIRCUS PLACE
FETTES ROW
ROYAL CRES
DUNDAS STREET
DRUMMOND PLACE
GREAT KING STREET
ABERCROMBY PLACE
HERIOT ROW
QUEEN STREET
INDIA STREET
DOUNE TERRACE
MORAY PLACE
DEAN TERRACE
ANN STREET
DEAN PARK CRES
OXFORD TERRACE
LENNOX STREET
QUEENSFERRY RD
ETON TERRACE
BELGRAVE CRESCENT
AINSLIE PLACE
WEMYSS PL
HOWE STREET
FREDERICK STREET
HANOVER STREET
GEORGE STREET
CASTLE STREET
CHARLOTTE SQUARE
PRINCES STREET
THE MOUND
QUEENSFERRY ST
BELFORD ROAD
DRUMSHEUGH GDNS
DRUMSHEUGH GARDENS
ROTHESAY PLACE
MANOR PLACE
CHESTER STREET
WALKER STREET
MELVILLE STREET
STAFFORD STREET
SHANDWICK PLACE
COATES CRESCENT
ATHOLL CRESCENT
PALMERSTON PLACE
GROSVENOR ST
W MAITLAND ST
TORPHICHEN ST
CANNING STREET
LOTHIAN ROAD
CASTLE TERRACE
KING'S STABLES ROAD
JOHNSTON TERRACE
GRASSMARKET
GRINDLAY STREET
SPITTAL ST
WEST PORT
MORRISON STREET
BREAD STREET
FOUNTAINBRIDGE
HIGH RIGGS
EARL GREY ST
LAURISTON PLACE
LAURISTON GARDENS
DALRY RD
GROVE STREET
GARDNER'S CRESCENT
WEST APPROACH ROAD
TOLLCROSS
HOME ST
BROUGHAM ST
PANMURE PLACE
LONSDALE TERRACE
LOCHRIN PLACE
TARVIT STREET
LEVEN ST
GLENGYLE TERR
MELVILLE DRIVE
DUNDEE STREET
GILMORE PARK
LOWER GILMORE PLACE
GILMORE PLACE
UPPER GILMORE PLACE
LEAMINGTON TERRACE
VIEWFORTH
ST PETER PL
GRANVILLE TERRACE
WESTHALL GDNS
BRUNTSFIELD PLACE
WARRENDER PARK TERRACE
SPOTTISWOODE STREET
WARRENDER PARK ROAD
MARCHMONT ROAD
1
5
7
8
9
11
13
15
18
21
22
23
25
32
34

FIAT

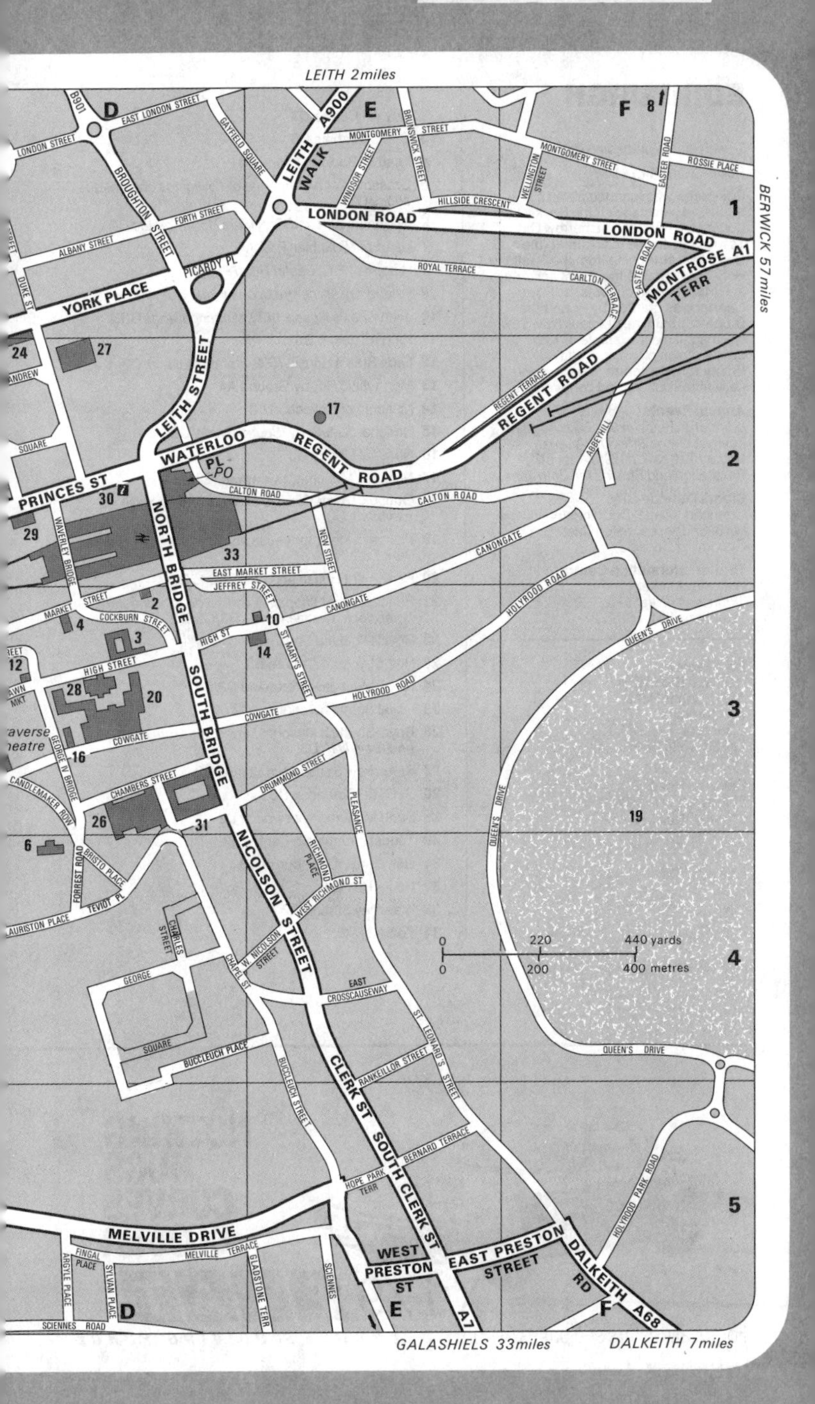

LEITH 2 miles
BERWICK 57 miles
GALASHIELS 33 miles
DALKEITH 7 miles
LEITH WALK
A900
LONDON ROAD
MONTGOMERY STREET
BRUNSWICK STREET
WINDSOR STREET
HILLSIDE CRESCENT
WELLINGTON STREET
EASTER ROAD
ROSSIE PLACE
EAST LONDON STREET
LONDON STREET
GAYFIELD SQUARE
BROUGHTON STREET
FORTH STREET
ALBANY STREET
DUKE ST
PICARDY PL
YORK PLACE
ROYAL TERRACE
CARLTON TERRACE
MONTROSE TERR
A1
REGENT TERRACE
REGENT ROAD
LEITH STREET
WATERLOO PL
PO
ABBEYHILL
PRINCES ST
CALTON ROAD
NORTH BRIDGE
WAVERLEY BRIDGE
NEW STREET
CANONGATE
EAST MARKET STREET
JEFFREY STREET
MARKET STREET
COCKBURN STREET
HIGH ST
HIGH STREET
HOLYROOD ROAD
QUEEN'S DRIVE
ST MARY'S STREET
SOUTH BRIDGE
COWGATE
Traverse Theatre
GEORGE IV BRIDGE
CANDLEMAKER ROW
CHAMBERS STREET
DRUMMOND STREET
PLEASANCE
NICOLSON STREET
RICHMOND PLACE
WEST RICHMOND ST
BRISTO PLACE
FORREST ROAD
TEVIOT PL
LAURISTON PLACE
CHARLES STREET
W. NICOLSON STREET
CHAPEL ST
GEORGE SQUARE
EAST CROSSCAUSEWAY
ST LEONARD'S STREET
RANKEILLOR STREET
BUCCLEUCH PLACE
BUCCLEUCH STREET
CLERK ST
SOUTH CLERK ST
BERNARD TERRACE
HOPE PARK TERR
HOLYROOD PARK ROAD
MELVILLE DRIVE
MELVILLE TERRACE
FINGAL PLACE
ARGYLE PLACE
SYLVAN PLACE
GLADSTONE TERR
SCIENNES
SCIENNES ROAD
WEST PRESTON ST
EAST PRESTON STREET
DALKEITH RD
A68
A7
B901
0 220 440 yards
0 200 400 metres
D E F
1 2 3 4 5
2 3 4 6 8 10 12 14 16 17 19 20 24 26 27 28 29 30 31 33

EDINBURGH

Town plan on preceding page

Population 444,741

Edinburgh was founded about a thousand years ago on the Rock which dominates the city. The narrow Old Town, with its one main street (the Royal Mile stretching from the Castle to Holyroodhouse) is the city of John Knox and Mary Queen of Scots. Its Royal Charter was granted by Robert the Bruce in 1329. The gracious New Town is a magnificient example of 18th-century town planning. Today Edinburgh is a centre of festival and pageantry, culture and conferences.

Annual Events
Edinburgh Festival *9th–30th August*
Festival Fringe *9th–30th August*
Military Tattoo *7th–29th August*
Royal Highland Show *21st–24th June*

Sights Outside City
Cramond Village, Duddingston Village, Forth Bridge, Lauriston Castle, Craigmillar Castle

Tourist Information Centre
Waverley Market
3 Princess Street EH2 2QP
Telephone 031–557 2727

Fiat Dealers
Hamilton Bros. (Edinburgh) Ltd
162 St Johns Road
Corstorphine
Edinburgh EH12 8AZ
Tel. 031–334 6248

Croall & Croall
Glenogle Road
Edinburgh EH3 5HW
Telephone 031–556 6404

1 Castle **C3**
2 City Art Centre **D3**
3 City Chambers **D3**
4 Festival Booking Office **D3**
5 Grassmarket *picturesque old buildings and antique shops* **C3**
6 Greyfriars Kirk *and Greyfriars Bobby statue* **D4**
7 Heart of Midlothian F.C. **A4**
8 Hibernian F.C. *Easter Road Park* **F1**
9 Hillend *dry ski centre open all year* **B5**
10 John Knox's House *1490, timber galleries* **D/E3**
11 King's Theatre **B5**
12 Lady Stair's House *1692, literary museum* **D3**
13 Murrayfield Rugby Ground **A4**
14 Museum of Childhood **E3**
15 National Gallery *try 'Sound Guide'* **C3**
16 National Library **D3**
17 Nelson's Monument *viewpoint* **E2**
18 Outlook Tower *Camera obscura and Scottish life exhibition* **C3**
19 Palace of Holyroodhouse and Arthur's Seat and the Park **F3**
20 Parliament House and Law Courts **D3**
21 Princes Street *shopping and gardens, bandstand, floral clock, war memorials* **B3/C2/D2**
22 Royal Highland Showground **A3**
23 Royal Lyceum Theatre **B3**
24 Royal Museum of Scotland **D2**
25 Royal Scottish Academy **C2**
26 Royal Scottish Museum *largest museum of science and art in U.K.* **D3**
27 St Andrew Square Bus Station **D2**
28 St Giles' Cathedral **D3**
29 Scott Monument *viewpoint* **D2**
30 Tourist Information Centre **D2**
31 University of Edinburgh **D3**
32 Usher Hall **B3**
33 Waverley Station **D2**
34 Zoo **A3**

GLASGOW

Town plan on preceding page

Population 755,429

Prime factors in Glasgow's history were the River Clyde and the Industrial Revolution (helped by the Lowland genius for shipbuilding and engineering). Glasgow is the home of Scottish Opera, Scottish Ballet and the Scottish National Orchestra. The city has a fine collection of museums, most notably that at Kelvingrove and the Burrell Gallery. Famous for learning (two universities), sport (soccer), shops, and art galleries, the city boasts over seventy parks and the Scottish Exhibition and Conference Centre.

Annual Events
Mayfest, Paisley Festival *May*
Horse Show and Country Fair *July*
Glasgow Marathon *September*

Sights Outside City
Paisley Abbey, Forth and Clyde Canal at Kirkintilloch, Clyde Muirshiel Park at Lochwinnoch, Weavers Cottage (Kilbarchan)

Tourist Information Offices
35/39 St Vincent Place, Glasgow G1 2ER. Open June–Sept Mon–Sat 9am–9pm Sun 10am–6pm. Open Oct–May Mon–Sat 9am–5pm Sun Closed
Telephone 041–227 4880.
Telex 779504
Town Hall, Abbey Close, Paisley PA1 1JS. Open June–Sept Mon–Fri 9am–6pm, Sat 9am–5pm, Oct–May Mon–Fri 9am–5pm
Telephone 041–889 0711

Fiat Dealers
Peat Road Motors (Jordanhill) Ltd
120 Whittingehame Drive
Jordanhill, Glasgow GL12 0YJ
Tel. 041–357 1939

Ritchie's
393 Shields Road, Glasgow G41 1 NZ
Tel. 041–429 5611

Currie of Shettleston
85–89 Amulree Street
Glasgow G32 7UN
Tel. 041–778 1295

1 Airport **A5**
2 Art Gallery and Museum *paintings, ceramics, silver, costumes, etc.* **A2**
3 The Barrows *weekend street market* **F5**
4 Botanic Gardens **A1**
5 Briggait **D5**
6 Burrell Gallery *paintings, stained glass, tapestries, ceramics* **C5**
7 Central Station **C4**
8 Citizens' Theatre **D5**
9 City Chambers *fine loggia* **D3**
10 City Hall **E4**
11 Clyde Tunnel **A4**
12 Glasgow Cathedral *impressive Gothic* **F3**
13 Glasgow Cross *1626 Tolbooth Steeple* **E5**
14 Glasgow Green *city's oldest riverside park* **F5**
15 Glasgow Zoo **F5**
16 Haggs Castle—children **C5**
17 Hunterian Museum & Art Gallery (Glasgow University) *early books, archaeology* **A2**
18 King's Theatre **A2**
19 Mitchell Library and Theatre **A2**
20 Museum of Transport *comprehensive collection. Also engineering, shipbuilding* **C5**
21 People's Palace *local history* **F5**
22 Pollok House *Spanish paintings, English furniture, rare silver, in Adam building amid parkland* **C5**
23 Queen Street Station **D3**
24 Scottish Exhibition and Conference Centre **A4**
25 Tenement House **B1**
26 Theatre Royal **C2**
27 Tourist Information Centre **C3**

FIAT **Glasgow**

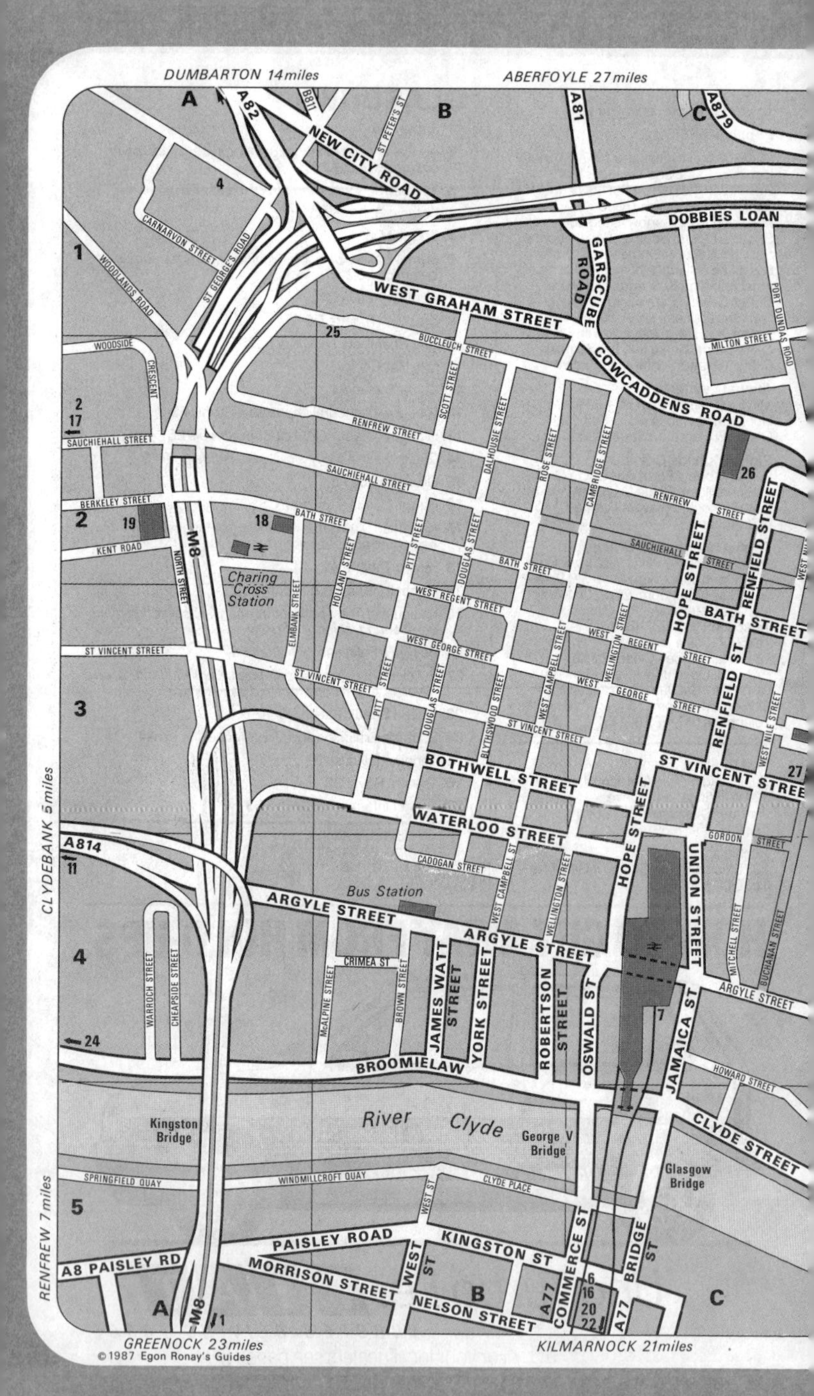

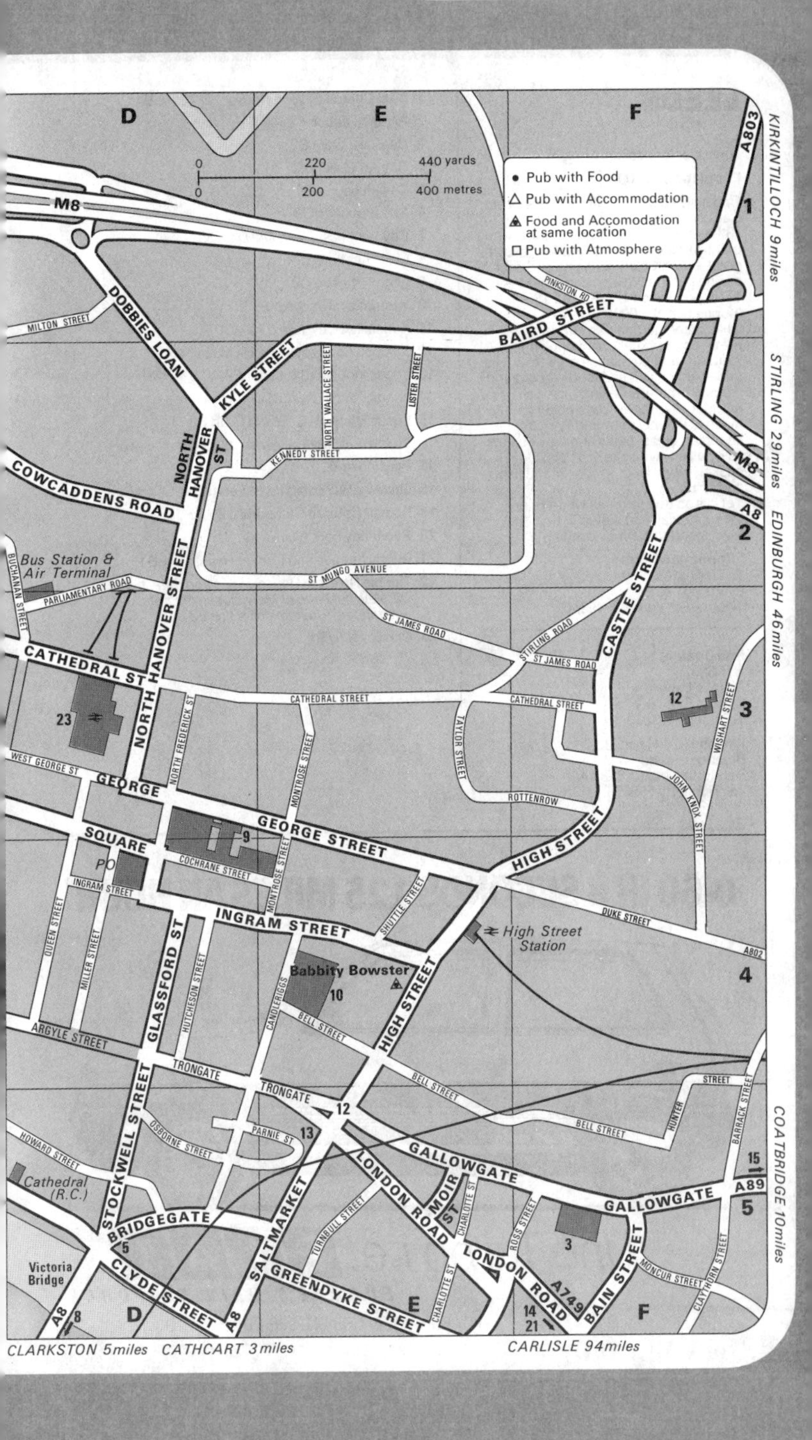
D
E
F
0
220
440 yards
0
200
400 metres
• Pub with Food
△ Pub with Accommodation
▲ Food and Accomodation at same location
□ Pub with Atmosphere
M8
A803
1
KIRKINTILLOCH 9miles
PINKSTON RD
BAIRD STREET
MILTON STREET
DOBBIES LOAN
KYLE STREET
NORTH WALLACE STREET
LISTER STREET
STIRLING 29miles
NORTH HANOVER ST
KENNEDY STREET
M8
COWCADDENS ROAD
A8
2
EDINBURGH 46miles
Bus Station & Air Terminal
BUCHANAN STREET
PARLIAMENTARY ROAD
ST MUNGO AVENUE
CASTLE STREET
ST JAMES ROAD
STIRLING ROAD
ST JAMES ROAD
CATHEDRAL ST
NORTH HANOVER STREET
CATHEDRAL STREET
CATHEDRAL STREET
12
3
WISHART STREET
23
NORTH FREDERICK ST
MONTROSE STREET
TAYLOR STREET
WEST GEORGE ST
GEORGE
JOHN KNOX STREET
ROTTENROW
GEORGE STREET
9
SQUARE
HIGH STREET
PO
COCHRANE STREET
MONTROSE STREET
INGRAM STREET
SHUTTLE STREET
DUKE STREET
INGRAM STREET
High Street Station
A802
4
QUEEN STREET
MILLER STREET
GLASSFORD ST
HUTCHESON STREET
Babbity Bowster
10
CANDLERIGGS
HIGH STREET
BELL STREET
ARGYLE STREET
TRONGATE
TRONGATE
BELL STREET
STREET
HUNTER
BARRACK STREET
12
BELL STREET
STOCKWELL STREET
OSBORNE STREET
PARNIE ST
13
HOWARD STREET
GALLOWGATE
15
COATBRIDGE 10miles
Cathedral (R.C.)
LONDON ROAD
MOIR ST
CHARLOTTE ST
GALLOWGATE
A89
5
BRIDGEGATE
TURNBULL STREET
ROSS STREET
3
5
SALTMARKET
LONDON ROAD
A749
BAIN STREET
MONCUR STREET
CLAYTHORN STREET
Victoria Bridge
CLYDE STREET
GREENDYKE STREET
E
CHARLOTTE ST
F
A8
8
D
A8
14
21
CLARKSTON 5miles
CATHCART 3miles
CARLISLE 94miles

LEEDS

Town plan opposite

Population 748,000

Originally Loidis, a Celtic settlement, it was given its industrial send-off by a 13th-century community of monks, who practised the crafts that made the town great–notably cloth-spinning and coal-mining but the big leap came between 1775 (population 17,000) and 1831 (population 123,000).
It has taken gargantuan efforts to eliminate the excesses of unplanned industrial and population growth, but its post-war housing and roads record and industrial mix are making Leeds a prouder city. Today it can boast as much of its University and Poly, its shopping areas, parks and new estates as it has always done of its choir, cricket, rubgy league, soccer and fish and chips.
Yet it is as true today as when Henry VIII's Librarian first stated it, that 'the town stondith most by clothing'.

Information Centre
19 Wellington Street
Leeds LS1 4DE
Telephone Leeds 462453/4

Fiat Dealers
JCT 600
Spence Lane
Leeds LS12 1AG
Tel. Leeds 431843

Whitehead & Hinch Ltd
Broadgate Lane
Horsforth, Leeds LS18 4AG
Tel. Horsforth 585056

1 Adel Church *St John the Baptist 12th c* B1
2 Airport *Yeadon 8 miles* B1
3 Central Library C2
4 City Art Gallery C2
5 City Museum C2
6 City Station B/C3
7 City Varieties *'Good Old Days'* C2
8 Civil Theatre C2
9 Grand Theatre C2
10 International Pool A2
11 Kirkstall Abbey *12th c* A2
12 Kirkstall Abbey House Folk Museum A2
13 Leeds Industrial Museum A2
14 Leeds Parish Church D3
15 Leeds United F.C. *Elland Road* C3
16 Middleton Colliery Railway *1785, oldest in world* C3
17 Playhouse B1
18 Queen's Hall *Exhibitions* (Leeds Exhibition Centre) C3
19 Roman Catholic Cathedral C2
20 Roundhay Park E1
21 Rugby League and Cricket *Headingley* B1
22 Temple Newsam House *15th c and Park, home of Darnley, husband of Mary Queen of Scots; outstanding furniture collection* E2
23 University A/B1

For your local dealers see pages 50-53

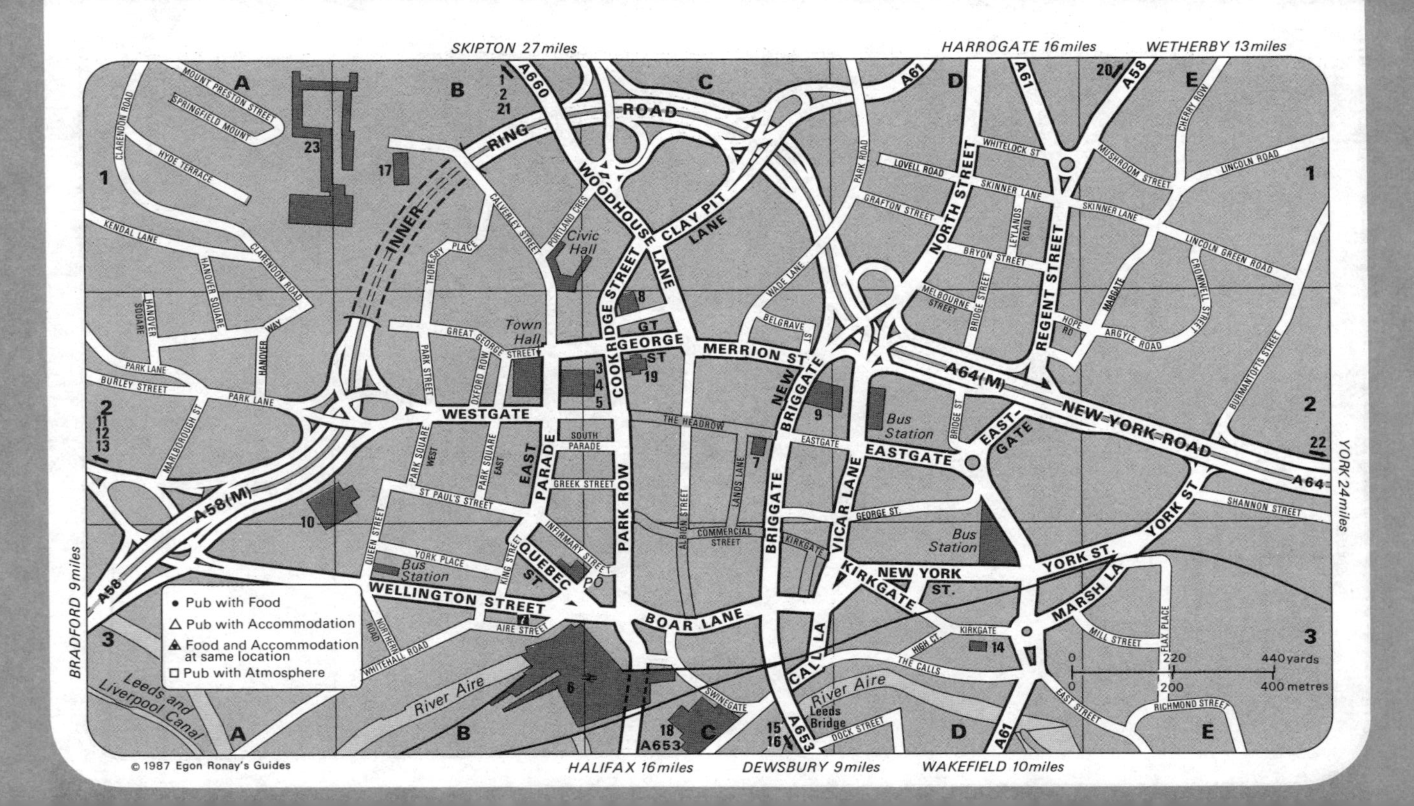

SKIPTON 27 miles
HARROGATE 16 miles
WETHERBY 13 miles
YORK 24 miles
BRADFORD 9 miles
HALIFAX 16 miles
DEWSBURY 9 miles
WAKEFIELD 10 miles
RING ROAD
INNER
WOODHOUSE LANE
CLAY PIT LANE
COOKRIDGE STREET
GEORGE ST
MERRION ST
NEW BRIGGATE
BRIGGATE
VICAR LANE
EASTGATE
NEW YORK ROAD
A64(M)
REGENT STREET
NORTH STREET
YORK ST
MARSH LA
KIRKGATE
NEW YORK ST.
BOAR LANE
CALL LA
PARK ROW
EAST PARADE
WESTGATE
QUEBEC ST
WELLINGTON STREET
A58(M)
Civic Hall
Town Hall
Bus Station
River Aire
Leeds Bridge
Leeds and Liverpool Canal
440 yards
400 metres
● Pub with Food
△ Pub with Accommodation
▲ Food and Accommodation at same location
□ Pub with Atmosphere
© 1987 Egon Ronay's Guides

Leeds

FIAT

FIAT Liverpool

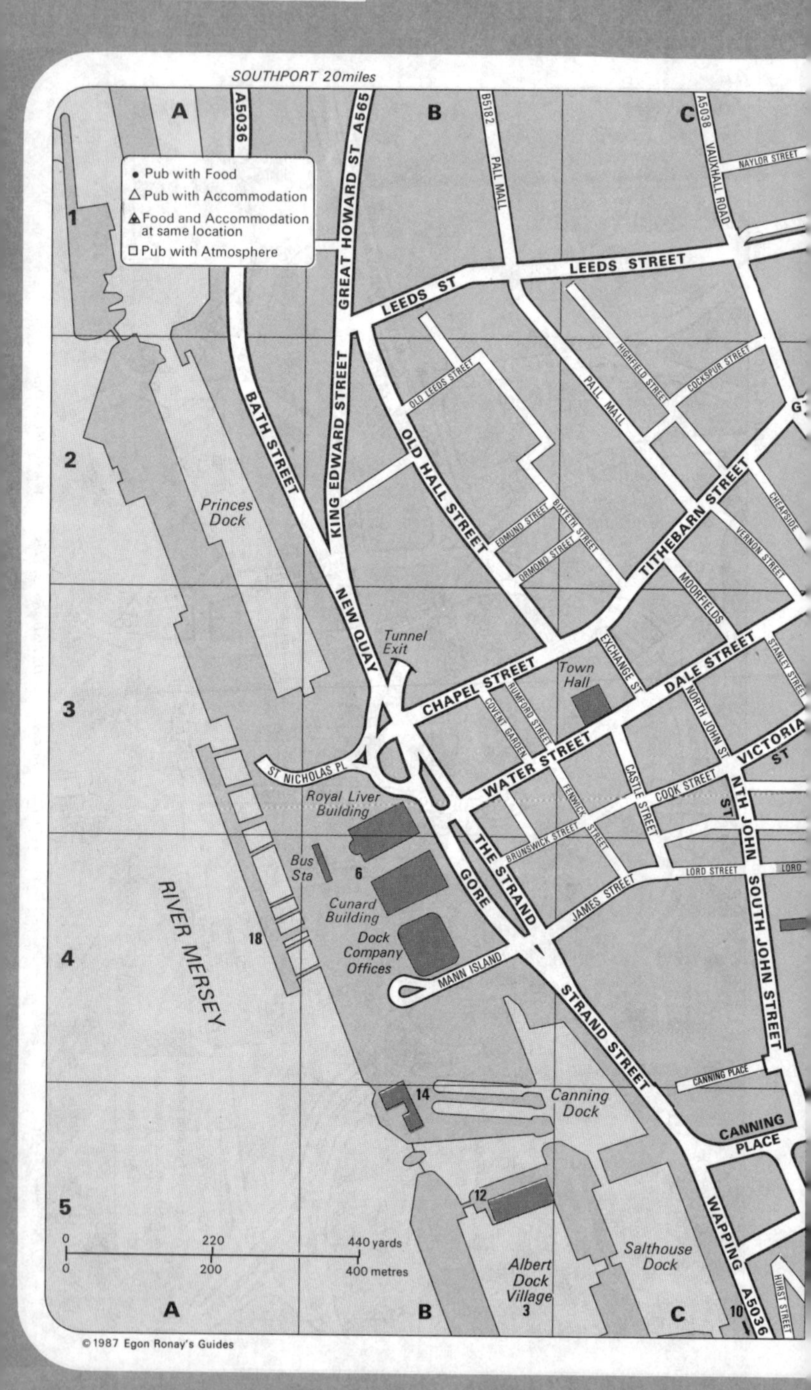

FIAT

PRESTON 30miles
MANCHESTER 36miles
M62 11miles
WARRINGTON 18miles
WIDNES 12miles
WIDNES 12miles
BANASTRE STREET
SCOTLAND ROAD
BYROM STREET
CHRISTIAN STREET
ST ANNE STREET
ISLINGTON
HUNTER ST
CHURCHILL WAY NORTH
WILLIAM BROWN STREET
LONDON ROAD
LIME STREET
NORTON ST
PRESCOT ST
PEMBROKE PLACE A5047
VICTORIA STREET
LORD NELSON STREET
SKELHORNE STREET
Coach Sta
COPPERAS HILL
BROWNLOW HILL
RANELAGH STREET
MOUNT PLEASANT
RENSHAW STREET
BOLD STREET
WOOD STREET
SEEL STREET
HANOVER STREET
DUKE STREET
PARADISE ST
PARK LANE A561
BERRY STREET A5038
LEECE STREET A5039
Philarmonic Dining Rooms

LIVERPOOL

Town plan on preceding page

Population 509,981

Since King John granted its Charter in 1207. Liverpool has taken increasing advantage of its sheltered Merseyside position to become England's leading Atlantic port and an industrial magnet, while the Arts are as vigorously pursued as football. The Royal Liverpool Philharmonic Orchestra, the Walker Art Gallery, the University's music-making, and the city's five theatres are at least as important to it as pop.

Annual Events
Grand National at Aintree
City of Liverpool Parade
Orange Day Parade *July*

Sights Outside City
Aintree, Hoylake, Chester, New Brighton, Southport

Information Office
Lime Street
Liverpool 1
Telephone 051–709 3631

Fiat Dealers
Stanley Motors Ltd
243 East Prescot Road
Liverpool L14 5NA
Tel. 051–228 9151

Crosby Park Garage Ltd
2 Coronation Road
Crosby
Liverpool L23 3BJ
Tel. 051–924 9101

Lambert Autos Ltd
Custom House
Brunswick Business Park
Liverpool L3 4BJ
Tel. 051–708 8224

1. Aintree Race-course E1
2. Airport D5
3. Albert Dock, *Shopping, business, conference centre* B5
4. Anglican Cathedral *20th-c Gothic, complete after 75 years* F5
5. Birkenhead Tunnel Entrance D2
6. Cunard Building, Dock Board office and Royal Liver Building *waterfront landmarks* B4
7. Empire Theatre E2
8. Everton Football Club E1
9. Everyman Theatre F4
10. Festival Gardens and Otterspool Promenade C5
11. Library and Museum *Hornby library has outstanding prints and first editions. Museum houses aquarium, ivories, jewellery, birds, shipping gallery* E2
12. Lime Street Station E/F3
13. Liverpool Football Club E1
14. Maritime Museum B4/5
15. Museum of Labour History E2
16. Neptune Theatre D4
17. Philharmonic Hall F5
18. Pier Head A4
19. Playhouse Theatre D3
20. Roman Catholic Cathedral *space-age architecture* F4
21. St George's Hall Former Assize Courts and Concert Hall E3
22. Speke Hall *Elizabethan house with beautiful gardens on the Mersey* D5
23. Walker Art Gallery *England's largest collection outside London* E2

MANCHESTER

Town plan on preceding page

Population 458,600

Established 38 BC as Mancenion, the 'place of tents', a Roman fortification centre. Became a free market town in 1301. Opened Manchester Ship Canal in 1894 leading to Manchester becoming Britain's third inland seaport. The textile trade prepared it for the Industrial Revolution and the city prospered with engineering skills brought to its cotton industry. Apart from night-spot entertainment the city is noted for the Hallé Orchestra.

Annual Events
Manchester Parade *June*
Hallé Summer Proms *June–July*
Manchester Show *August*
Manchester Festival *September*
Northern Motor Show *April*

Sights Outside City
Jodrell Bank, Tatton Hall, Chatsworth House, Haddon Hall, Little Moreton Hall, Bramall Hall

City of Manchester Public Relations Office St James's Buildings, Oxford Street, Manchester M1 6FL
Telephone 061–234 1343

Tourist Information Offices
PO Box 532, Town Hall, Manchester M60 2LA
Telephone 061–234 3157/8

Theatre Information
Telephone 061–234 3156

Fiat Dealers
Knibbs (Manchester) Ltd
Midland Street Garage
Ashton Old Road
Manchester M12 6LB
Tel. 061–273 4411

1 Abraham Moss Centre *leisure facilities* D1
2 Airport *8 miles* C5
3 Barton Aqueduct *swing trough bridge* A4
4 Cathedral *mainly 15th-c. fine carvings* C1
5 Central Library *houses 11 libraries* C3
6 City Art Gallery *mostly early British art* D3
7 Cornerhouse Art Gallery & Cinema D4
8 Fletcher Moss Museum & Art Gallery E5
9 Free Trade Hall *home of Hallé Orchestra* C3
10 G-Mex Centre C3/4
11 Greater Manchester Museum of Science & Industry A3
12 Heaton Hall *Georgian museum* D1
13 John Rylands Library *rare books* C3
14 Manchester Air & Space Gallery B3
15 Manchester City F.C. D5
16 Manchester Craft Village E1
17 Manchester Museum *Egyptology, natural history; coins; stamps* E5
18 Manchester United F.C. A5
19 Old Trafford Cricket Ground A5
20 Opera House B3
21 Oxford Road Station D4
22 Palace Theatre D4
23 Piccadilly Station F3
24 Platt Hall *Gallery of English Costume* E5
25 Schools Library *Europe's oldest public library; part of the 13th-c Chetham Hospital School* D1
26 Tourist Information Centre C3
27 Town Hall *Gothic revival* C3
28 University Theatre E5
29 Victoria Station D1
30 Whitworth Art Gallery *paintings; textiles* E5
31 Wythenshawe Forum *leisure facilities* A5
32 Wythenshawe Hall *Elizabethan manor and art gallery* A5

FIAT
Manchester

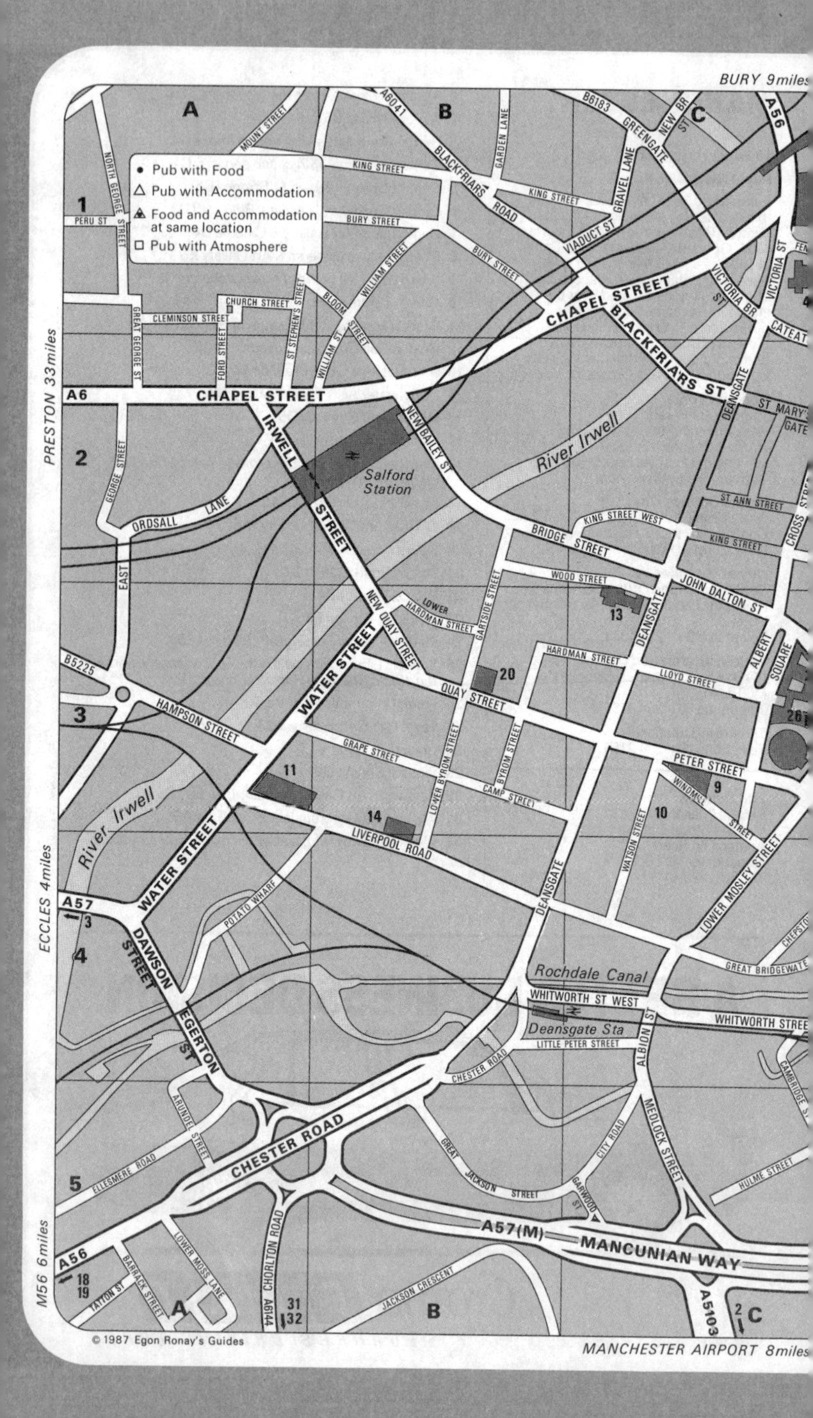
BURY 9miles
PRESTON 33miles
ECCLES 4miles
M56 6miles
MANCHESTER AIRPORT 8miles
A
B
C
1
2
3
4
5
• Pub with Food
△ Pub with Accommodation
Food and Accommodation at same location
□ Pub with Atmosphere
MOUNT STREET
A6041
B6183
GREENGATE
NEW BR ST
A56
KING STREET
BLACKFRIARS ROAD
GARDEN LANE
GRAVEL LANE
NORTH GEORGE STREET
PERU ST
BURY STREET
VIADUCT ST
WILLIAM STREET
BLOOM STREET
CHURCH STREET
CLEMINSON STREET
GREAT GEORGE ST
FORD STREET
ST STEPHEN'S STREET
WILLIAM ST
CHAPEL STREET
BLACKFRIARS ST
VICTORIA BR ST
VICTORIA ST
CATEATON
DEANSGATE
ST MARY'S GATE
A6
IRWELL STREET
NEW BAILEY ST
River Irwell
Salford Station
GEORGE STREET
ORDSALL LANE
ST ANN STREET
KING STREET WEST
BRIDGE STREET
KING STREET
CROSS STREET
EAST
WOOD STREET
JOHN DALTON ST
GARTSIDE STREET
LOWER HARDMAN STREET
NEW QUAY STREET
13
HARDMAN STREET
ALBERT SQUARE
B5225
WATER STREET
20
QUAY STREET
LLOYD STREET
HAMPSON STREET
26
GRAPE STREET
LOWER BYROM STREET
BYROM STREET
PETER STREET
11
9
WINDMILL STREET
CAMP STREET
10
14
WATSON STREET
LIVERPOOL ROAD
LOWER MOSLEY STREET
A57
3
POTATO WHARF
DAWSON STREET
GREAT BRIDGEWATER
Rochdale Canal
WHITWORTH ST WEST
WHITWORTH STREET
Deansgate Sta
LITTLE PETER STREET
ALBION ST
EGERTON ST
CHESTER ROAD
CAMBRIDGE ST
ARUNDEL STREET
GREAT JACKSON STREET
CITY ROAD
MEDLOCK STREET
ELLESMERE ROAD
GARWOOD ST
HULME STREET
A57(M)
MANCUNIAN WAY
LOWER MOSS LANE
CHORLTON ROAD
A56
18
19
TATTON ST
BARRACK STREET
A6144
31
32
JACKSON CRESCENT
A5103
2

ROCHDALE 14 miles
OLDHAM 7 miles
STOCKPORT 7 miles
ASHTON-UNDER-LYNE 7 miles
STOCKPORT 7 miles
WILMSLOW 12 miles
D
E
F
1
2
3
4
5
A665 MILLER STREET
A664
ROCHDALE ROAD
ANGEL STREET
DANTZIC STREET
THOMPSON STREET
CROSS KEYS ST
ADDINGTON ST
SWAN STREET
OLDHAM ROAD
A62
POLAND STREET
RADIUM STREET
GEORGE LEIGH STREET
JERSEY STREET
NEW UNION ST
HANOVER STREET
SHUDEHILL
CORPORATION STREET
WITHY GROVE
SHUDE HILL
DANTZIC STREET
THOMAS STREET
HIGH ST
16
HENRY STREET
REDHILL STREET
Rochdale Canal
GREAT ANCOATS STREET
CANNON STREET
HIGH STREET
HILTON STREET
TIB STREET
OLDHAM STREET
LEVER STREET
NEWTON STREET
CHURCH STREET
MARKET STREET
PO
BROWN STREET
SPRING GARDENS
FOUNTAIN STREET
DALE STREET
PICCADILLY
TARIFF STREET
LAYSTALL STREET
CANNEL STREET
A665
Bus Station
PARKER STREET
DUCIE STREET
STORE STREET
YORK ST
MOSLEY STREET
CHARLOTTE ST
COOPER STREET
PORTLAND STREET
AYTOUN STREET
LONDON ROAD
DUCIE ST
STATION APPROACH
CHAPELTOWN STREET
SPARKLE ST
BROAD STREET
6
PRINCESS STREET
GEORGE STREET
BLOOM STREET
CHORLTON STREET
23
SHEFFIELD STREET
TRAVIS STREET
DICKINSON STREET
PORTLAND STREET
Coach Sta
SACKVILLE STREET
PRINCESS STREET
FAIRFIELD STREET
B6469
OXFORD STREET
WHITWORTH STREET
Rochdale Canal
ALTRINCHAM STREET
22
River Medlock
SACKVILLE STREET
CHARLES ST
21
OXFORD ST
MANCUNIAN WAY
A635
A57(M)
CHARLES STREET
MANOR ST
DOWNING ST
HULME STREET
ARDWICK GREEN NORTH
ARDWICK GREEN STH
A6
MANCUNIAN WAY
OXFORD ROAD
BROOK ST
GROSVENOR STREET
WADESON ROAD
CAMBRIDGE ST
KINCARDINE ROAD
UPPER BROOK ST
A34
0 220 440 yards
0 200 400 metres
B5117
8 17 30 28 24
15

NEWCASTLE UPON TYNE

Town plan opposite

Population 272,914

Newcastle was founded in Roman times and later became a fortress against the Scots. Its commercial influence began with the mining of coal, but today rests on engineering and other industries. The coast and hinterland of Northumberland are areas of outstanding natural beauty. The theatres, Northern Sinfonia Orchestra, and the University, provide some of the many cultural activities.

Annual Events
The Hoppings (travelling fair) *last full week in June*
Tyneside Summer Exhibition *End July–beginning August*

Sights Outside City
Hadrian's Wall, Hexham Abbey, Durham Cathedral, Alnwick, Seaton Delaval, Northumberland National Park

City Information Service
Central Library, PO Box 1DX, Princess Square
Newcastle upon Tyne NE99 1DX
Telephone Tyneside 2610691

Fiat Dealer
Benfield Motors Ltd
Railway Street
Newcastle upon Tyne
NE4 7AD
Tel. Tyneside 2732131

1 Airport **A1**
2 Bessie Surtees House *fine 17th-c timbered house* **B5**
3 Blackfriars Heritage and Interpretation Centre **A4**
4 Castle, Black Gate Museum **B5**
5 Central Library and Information Bureau **B3**
6 Central Station **A5**
7 Civic Centre *outstanding modern architecture including Carillon Tower* **B2**
8 Gosforth Park Race-course **B1**
9 Grey Monument **B3**
10 Guildhall *17th-c with Georgian facade* **B5**
11 Hancock Museum *natural history of area* **B1/2**
12 Jesmond Dene Park **C1**
13 John George Joicey Museum *history, furniture, Northumberland Fusiliers Museum* **C4**
14 Laing Art Gallery **B3**
15 Museum of Science and Engineering *exhibits of Newcastle's great engineers* **A5**
16 Newcastle Playhouse Theatre **A2**
17 Newcastle United F.C. *St James's Park* **A3**
18 Northumberland County C.C. **B1**
19 Plummer Tower *museum in rebuilt tower of old walls* **B3**
20 Quayside *open-air market on Sunday mornings* **C4/5**
21 St Nicholas's Cathedral *mainly 14th & 15th c* **B4**
22 Theatre Royal **B4**
23 Town Moor *nearly 1,000 acres of free grazing, sport and recreation* **A1**
24 Tyne Bridge **C5**
25 University and Museum of Antiquities **A2**

Newcastle upon Tyne
FIAT

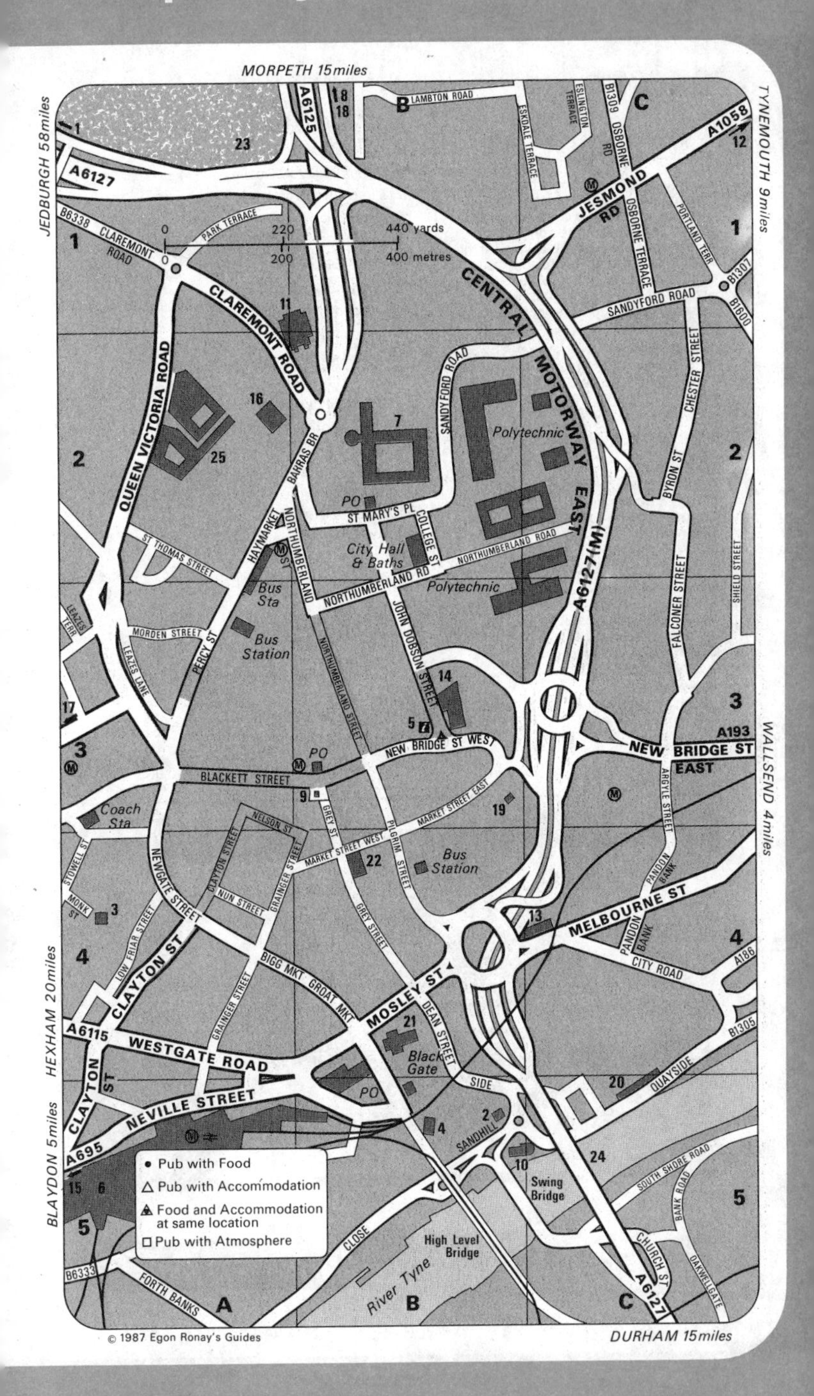
MORPETH 15miles
JEDBURGH 58miles
TYNEMOUTH 9miles
WALLSEND 4miles
HEXHAM 20miles
BLAYDON 5miles
DURHAM 15miles
LAMBTON ROAD
ESKDALE TERRACE
ESLINGTON TERRACE
OSBORNE RD
JESMOND RD
OSBORNE TERRACE
PORTLAND TERR
SANDYFORD ROAD
CENTRAL MOTORWAY EAST
A6127(M)
PARK TERRACE
CLAREMONT ROAD
QUEEN VICTORIA ROAD
BARRAS BR
HAYMARKET
NORTHUMBERLAND ST
ST MARY'S PL
COLLEGE ST
City Hall & Baths
NORTHUMBERLAND RD
NORTHUMBERLAND ROAD
Polytechnic
CHESTER STREET
BYRON ST
FALCONER STREET
SHIELD STREET
ST THOMAS STREET
Bus Sta
Bus Station
MORDEN STREET
LEAZES TERR
LEAZES LANE
PERCY ST
JOHN DOBSON STREET
NORTHUMBERLAND STREET
NEW BRIDGE ST WEST
NEW BRIDGE ST EAST
BLACKETT STREET
PO
Coach Sta
NELSON ST
CLAYTON STREET
GRAINGER STREET
MARKET STREET WEST
MARKET STREET EAST
GREY ST
PILGRIM STREET
ARGYLE STREET
PANDON BANK
MELBOURNE ST
CITY ROAD
STOWELL ST
MONK ST
NEWGATE STREET
NUN STREET
LOW FRIAR STREET
CLAYTON ST
BIGG MKT
GROAT MKT
MOSLEY ST
DEAN STREET
WESTGATE ROAD
NEVILLE STREET
Black Gate
SIDE
SANDHILL
QUAYSIDE
Swing Bridge
SOUTH SHORE ROAD
BANK ROAD
CHURCH ST
OAKWELLGATE
CLOSE
High Level Bridge
River Tyne
FORTH BANKS
A6127
A6125
A1058
A193
A186
B1305
B1307
B1600
B1309
B6338
A6115
A695
B6333
0 220 440 yards
0 200 400 metres
● Pub with Food
△ Pub with Accommodation
Food and Accommodation at same location
□ Pub with Atmosphere

OXFORD

Town plan opposite

Population 114,200

Despite the encroachment of industry, Oxford remains incomparable–except with Cambridge–as a centre of learning for 800 years, interrupted only by the disturbance of the Civil War siege in the 1640s. No city has more to offer the sightseer in its own architectural glories and the beauty of its surroundings–the Thames Valley, the Cotswolds and so much besides.

Annual Events
St Giles Fair *September*
Eights Week (5th week of University term)
Sheriff's Races *summer*

Sights Outside City
Blenheim Palace
Burford Village
Dorchester-on-Thames
Chipping Campden
Cogges Farm Museum
Cotswold Wild Life Park
Sulgrave Park
Waddesdon Manor

Information Centre
St Aldate's, Oxford OX1 1DY
Telephone Oxford 726871
Accommodation 726871
Guided Walking Tours 726871

Fiat Dealer
J. D. Barclay Ltd
Barclay House
Botley Road
Oxford OX2 0HQ
Tel. Oxford 722444

1. Apollo Theatre B3
2. Ashmolean Museum *art and archaeology treasures* B3
3. Bate Collection of Historical Musical Instruments B4
4. Botanic Garden *one of the oldest in the country* C4
5. Carfax Tower *viewpoint open in summer* B4
6. Christ Church Meadow C5
7. Coach Park A4
8. Divinity School *15th-c fine vaulted ceiling* B3
9. Folly Bridge B5
10. Martyrs' Memorial B3
11. Museum of History of Science B3
12. Museum of Oxford B4
13. Oxford Ice Rink A4
14. Oxford Information Centre B4
15. Oxford Story B3
16. Pitt Rivers Museum of Ethnology B1/C2
17. Playhouse B3
18. Sheldonian Theatre *Wren building for conferment of degrees* B3
19. Station A3
20. Town Hall B4
21. University Museum B2
22. University Parks B/C1/2

For your local dealers see pages 50-53

Oxford

FIAT

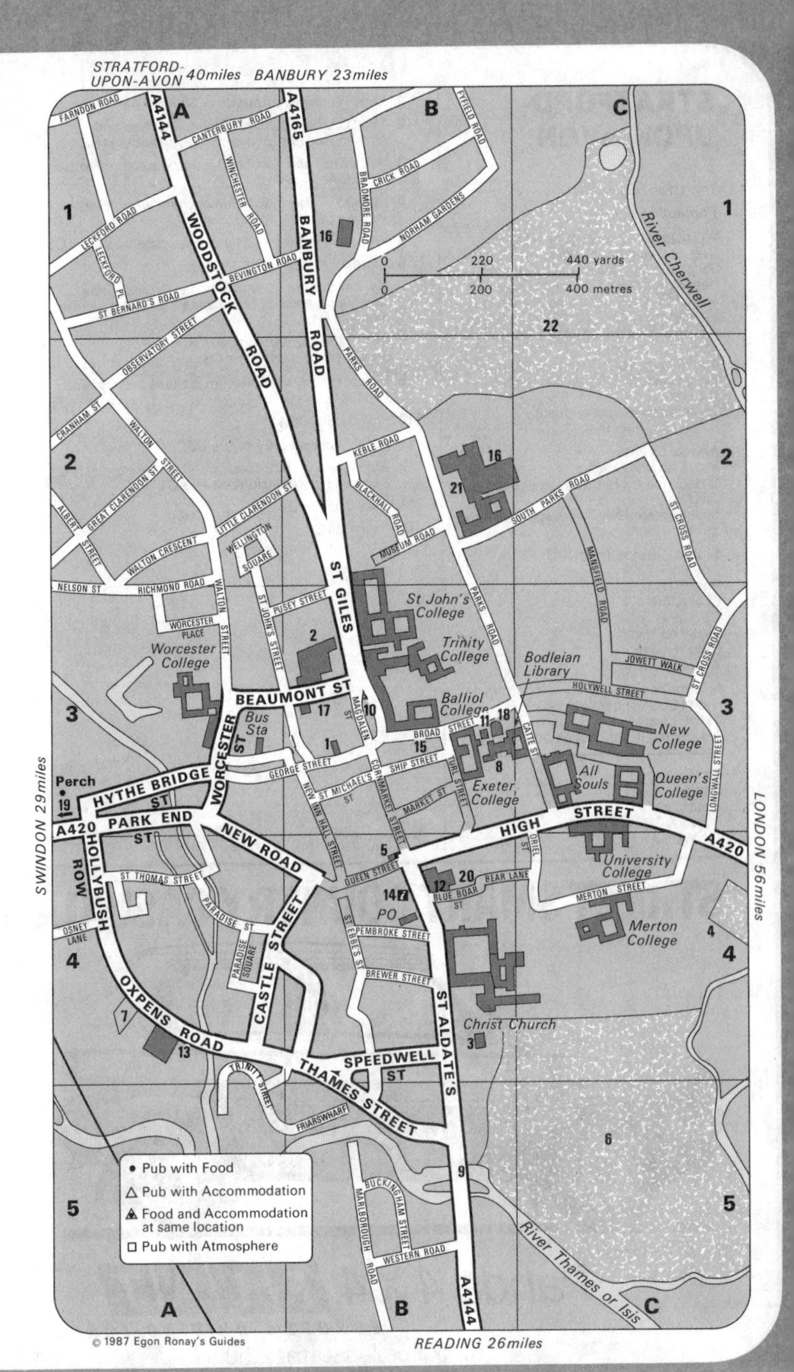
STRATFORD-UPON-AVON 40miles
BANBURY 23miles
SWINDON 29miles
LONDON 56miles
READING 26miles
0 220 440 yards
0 200 400 metres
Pub with Food
Pub with Accommodation
Food and Accommodation at same location
Pub with Atmosphere
St John's College
Trinity College
Balliol College
Bodleian Library
New College
All Souls
Queen's College
Exeter College
University College
Merton College
Christ Church
Worcester College
Bus Sta
PO
Perch
River Cherwell
River Thames or Isis
WOODSTOCK ROAD
BANBURY ROAD
ST GILES
PARKS ROAD
SOUTH PARKS ROAD
HIGH STREET
BROAD STREET
BEAUMONT ST
HYTHE BRIDGE ST
PARK END ST
NEW ROAD
CASTLE STREET
OXPENS ROAD
SPEEDWELL ST
THAMES STREET
ST ALDATE'S
WORCESTER ST
HOLLYBUSH ROW
GEORGE STREET
CORNMARKET STREET
QUEEN STREET
MERTON STREET
HOLYWELL STREET
ST CROSS ROAD
LONGWALL STREET
KEBLE ROAD
MUSEUM ROAD
WALTON STREET
A4144
A4165
A420

STRATFORD-UPON-AVON

Town plan opposite

Population 21,675

A prosperous market-town on a lovely river site, with good Tudor and Jacobean architecture, would be a fair description of Stratford-upon-Avon–if it wasn't for the Bard. It took 200 years after Shakespeare's birth for proper tribute to be paid to him in a festival staged by David Garrick. The first Theatre was not built until 1879; it was burnt down in 1926 and succeeded by the present theatre in 1932, built with large overseas subscriptions, particularly from the U.S.

Annual Events
Map Fair *12th October*
Shakespeare's Birthday Celebration *23rd April*
Shakespeare Theatre Season *from April*
Stratford Festival *July*

Sights Outside Town
Coughton Court
Ragley Hall
Charlecote
Coventry Cathedral
Packwood House
Upton House
Warwick Castle

Information Centre
Judith Shakespeare's House
1 High Street
Telephone Stratford-upon-Avon 293127

Fiat Dealer
Grays Garage Ltd
Wharf Stroot
Warwick CV34 4PA
Tel. Warwick 496231

1. Anne Hathaway's cottage *at Shottery* A3
2. Guild Chapel, Guildhall, Grammar School and Almshouses *exceptional medieval buildings* C3
3. Hall's Croft *fine Tudor house and walled garden, also houses Festival Club* C3
4. Harvard House *1596 home of grandfather of Harvard's founder* C2
5. Holy Trinity Church *contains Shakespeare's tomb* C3
6. Information Centre C2
7. Mary Arden's house *at Wilmcote, 3 miles. Tudor farmhouse, home of Shakespeare's mother, farming museum* B1
8. New Place *Elizabethan garden on site of Shakespeare's last home* C3
9. Picture Gallery and Museum *pictures and relics of famous actors* D3
10. Railway Station A1
11. Royal Shakespeare Theatre D3
12. Shakespeare's birthplace *architectural interest and museum of rare Shakespeariana* C1
13. Swan Theatre D3
14. Town Hall C2

Stratford-upon-Avon
FIAT

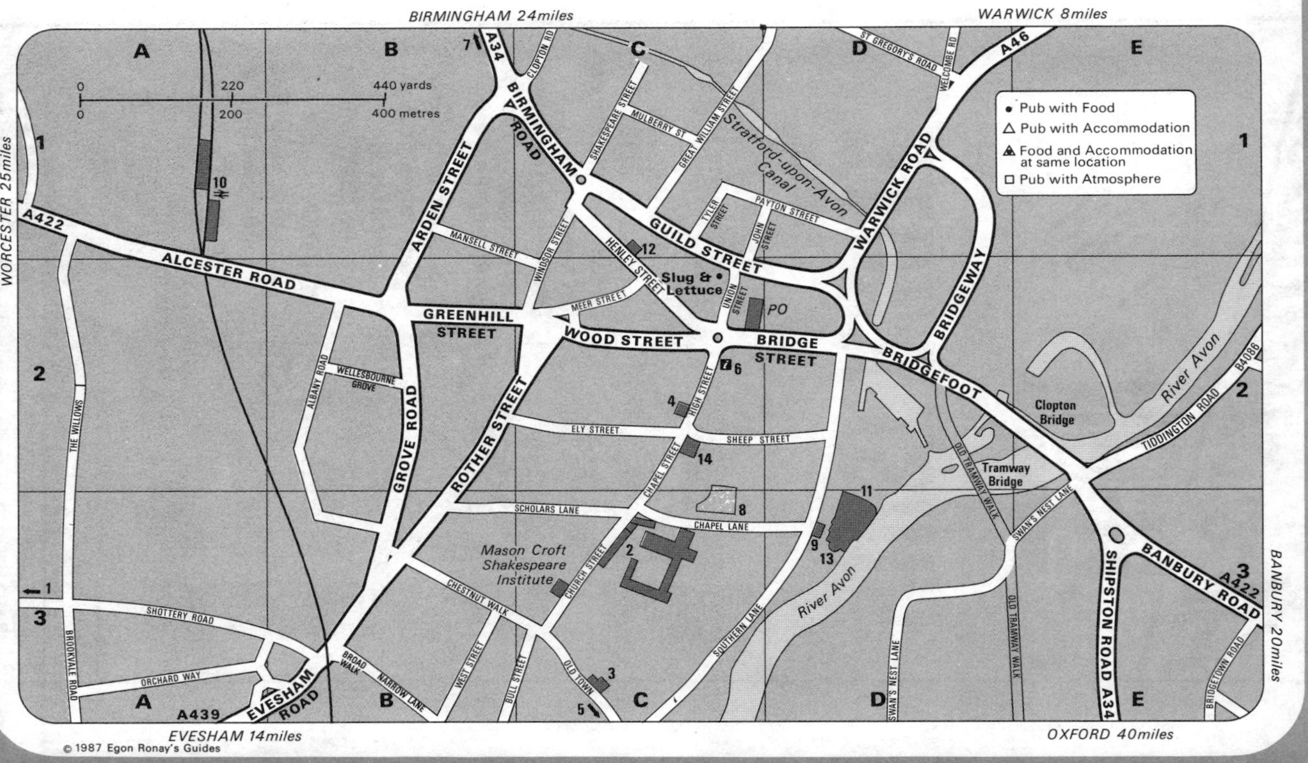
BIRMINGHAM 24miles
WARWICK 8miles
WORCESTER 25miles
BANBURY 20miles
EVESHAM 14miles
OXFORD 40miles
Pub with Food
Pub with Accommodation
Food and Accommodation at same location
Pub with Atmosphere
440 yards
400 metres
Stratford-upon-Avon Canal
River Avon
Clopton Bridge
Tramway Bridge
Mason Croft Shakespeare Institute
Slug & Lettuce
PO
ALCESTER ROAD
ARDEN STREET
BIRMINGHAM ROAD
CLOPTON RD
SHAKESPEARE STREET
MULBERRY ST
GREAT WILLIAM STREET
TYLER STREET
PAYTON STREET
JOHN STREET
GUILD STREET
WARWICK ROAD
BRIDGEWAY
ST GREGORY'S ROAD
WELCOMBE RD
MANSELL STREET
WINDSOR STREET
HENLEY STREET
UNION STREET
MEER STREET
GREENHILL STREET
WOOD STREET
BRIDGE STREET
BRIDGEFOOT
TIDDINGTON ROAD
ALBANY ROAD
WELLESBOURNE GROVE
GROVE ROAD
ROTHER STREET
HIGH STREET
ELY STREET
SHEEP STREET
CHAPEL STREET
SCHOLARS LANE
CHAPEL LANE
CHURCH STREET
CHESTNUT WALK
WEST STREET
BULL STREET
OLD TOWN
SOUTHERN LANE
OLD TRAMWAY WALK
SWAN'S NEST LANE
SHIPSTON ROAD A34
BANBURY ROAD
BRIDGETOWN ROAD
THE WILLOWS
SHOTTERY ROAD
ORCHARD WAY
BROOKVALE ROAD
BROAD WALK
NARROW LANE
EVESHAM ROAD
A422
A34
A46
A439
B4086
© 1987 Egon Ronay's Guides

·MAP·SECTION·

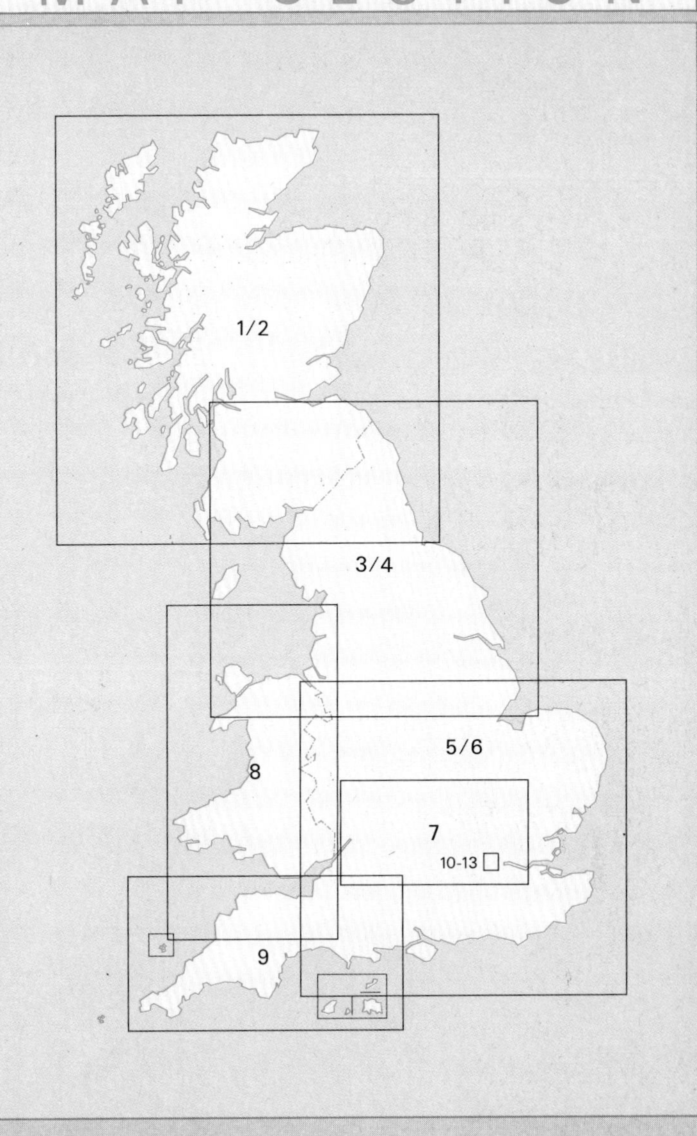

Key to Maps

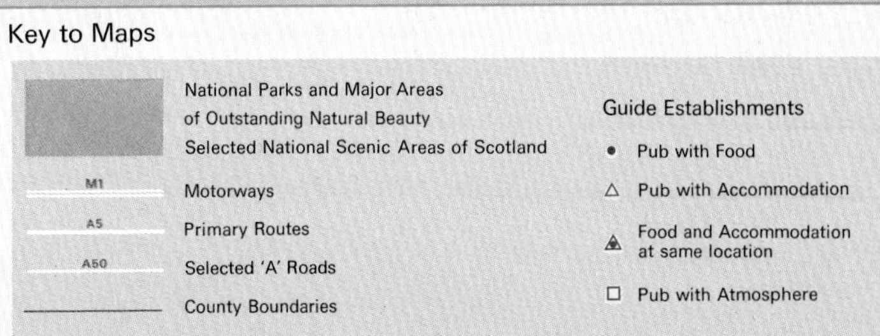

National Parks and Major Areas of Outstanding Natural Beauty
Selected National Scenic Areas of Scotland

Motorways

Primary Routes

Selected 'A' Roads

County Boundaries

Guide Establishments

- Pub with Food
- Pub with Accommodation
- Food and Accommodation at same location
- Pub with Atmosphere

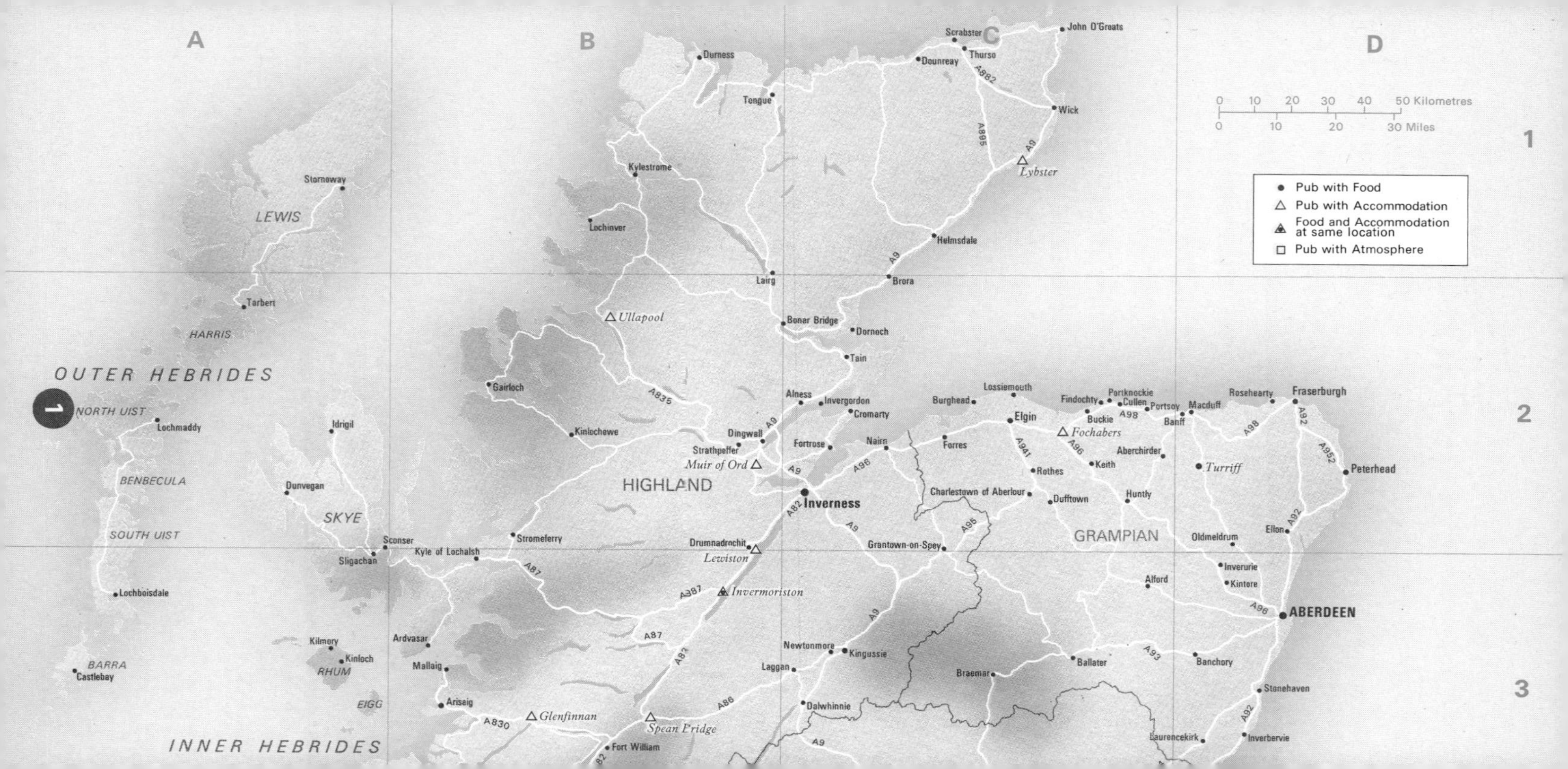

1
A
B
C
D
1
2
3
0 10 20 30 40 50 Kilometres
0 10 20 30 Miles
Pub with Food
Pub with Accommodation
Food and Accommodation at same location
Pub with Atmosphere
OUTER HEBRIDES
LEWIS
HARRIS
NORTH UIST
BENBECULA
SOUTH UIST
BARRA
INNER HEBRIDES
SKYE
RHUM
EIGG
HIGHLAND
GRAMPIAN
Stornoway
Tarbert
Lochmaddy
Lochboisdale
Castlebay
Idrigil
Dunvegan
Sconser
Sligachan
Kilmory
Kinloch
Ardvasar
Mallaig
Arisaig
Glenfinnan
Fort William
Spean Bridge
Durness
Tongue
Kylestrome
Lochinver
Ullapool
Gairloch
Kinlochewe
Stromeferry
Kyle of Lochalsh
Lairg
Bonar Bridge
Dornoch
Tain
Alness
Invergordon
Cromarty
Dingwall
Strathpeffer
Muir of Ord
Fortrose
Nairn
Inverness
Drumnadrochit
Lewiston
Invermoriston
Laggan
Newtonmore
Kingussie
Dalwhinnie
Grantown-on-Spey
Scrabster
Thurso
Dounreay
John O'Groats
Wick
Lybster
Helmsdale
Brora
Burghead
Lossiemouth
Forres
Elgin
Charlestown of Aberlour
Rothes
Dufftown
Findochty
Buckie
Portknockie
Cullen
Portsoy
Fochabers
Keith
Aberchirder
Huntly
Banff
Macduff
Rosehearty
Fraserburgh
Turriff
Peterhead
Oldmeldrum
Ellon
Inverurie
Kintore
Alford
ABERDEEN
Ballater
Banchory
Braemar
Stonehaven
Laurencekirk
Inverbervie
A9
A882
A895
A835
A96
A941
A98
A92
A952
A82
A87
A887
A86
A830
A93

SCOTLAND
2
4
5
6
3/4
TIREE
MULL
COLONSAY
JURA
ISLAY
ARRAN
BUTE
CENTRAL
FIFE
STRATHCLYDE
LOTHIAN
BORDERS
DUMFRIES AND GALLOWAY
NORTHUMBERLAND
TYNE AND WEAR
DURHAM
CUMBRIA
HOLY ISLAND
Craignure
Oban
Connel
Tyndrum
Crianlarich
Dalmally
Killin
Lochearnhead
Comrie
Crieff
Perth
DUNDEE
Monifieth
Carnoustie
Coupar Angus
Newport-on-Tay
Tayport
Newburgh
Cupar
Auchtermuchty
Auchterarder
Inveraray
Arrochar
Strachur
Kilmartin
Lochgair
Lochgilphead
Tayvallich
Loch Eck
Ardentinny
Kilcreggan
Garelochhead
Helensburgh
Drymen
Callander
Glendevon
Milnathort
Kinross
Falkland
Ladybank
Kilrenny
Crail
Pittenweem
Anstruther
St Monance
Earlsferry
Elie
Leven
Methil
Buckhaven
Leslie
Markinch
Glenrothes
Dysart
Kirkcaldy
Lochgelly
Cowdenbeath
Kinghorn
Burntisland
Doune
Dunblane
Alva
Dollar
Bridge of Allan
Kippen
Stirling
Alloa
Tillicoultry
Kincardine
Dunfermline
Culross
North Berwick
East Linton
Dunbar
Larbert
Denny
Grangemouth
Falkirk
Bo'ness
Inverkeithing
Queensferry
Kilsyth
Linlithgow
Edinburgh
Prestonpans
Cockenzie
Tranent
Haddington
Musselburgh
Dalkeith
Alexandria
Dunoon
Gourock
Dumbarton
Colintraive
Greenock
Port Glasgow
Wemyss Bay
Rothesay
Bearsden
Kirkintilloch
Cumbernauld
Clydebank
Coatbridge
Airdrie
Armadale
Bathgate
Ingliston
Livingston
Whitburn
Glasgow
Shotts
Paisley
Johnstone
Barrhead
Rutherglen
Hamilton
Motherwell
Wishaw
Busby
East Kilbride
Larkhall
Carluke
Penicuik
Wester Howgate
Eddleston
Peebles
Innerleithen
Lauder
Galashiels
Melrose
Selkirk
Greenlaw
Duns
Eyemouth
Berwick-upon-Tweed
Coldstream
Kelso
Jedburgh
Hawick
Belford
Seahouses
Warenford
Wooler
Alnwick
Amble
Rothbury
Longframlington
Rochester
Tarbert
Whitehouse
Claonaig
Lochranza
Kingarth
Largs
Millport
Port Askaig
Feolin Ferry
Portnahaven
Ardbeg
Port Ellen
Killean
Brodick
Lamlash
Campbeltown
Kilwinning
Ardrossan
Saltcoats
Stevenston
Irvine
Kilmarnock
Stewarton
Newmilns
Darvel
Galston
Strathaven
Kirkmuirhill
Lanark
Biggar
Abington
Troon
Prestwick
Ayr
Mauchline
Cumnock
Sanquhar
Maidens
Maybole
Girvan
Moffat
Thornhill
Langholm
Lochmaben
Lockerbie
Canonbie
New Galloway
Dumfries
New Abbey
Annan
Gretna
Metal Bridge
Rockcliffe
Warwick-on-Eden
Carlisle
Talkin
Faugh
Armathwaite
Alston
Melmerby
Newton Stewart
Castle Douglas
Dalbeattie
Kirkbean
Gatehouse of Fleet
Stranraer
Glenluce
Wigtown
Whithorn
Silloth
Maryport
Cockermouth
Workington
Bassenthwaite Lake
Pooley Bridge
Penrith
Ashington
Newbiggin-by-the-Sea
Morpeth
Bedlington
Blyth
Cramlington
Seaton Delaval
Belsay
Wark
Wall
Ponteland
Longbenton
Tynemouth
Gosforth
Wallsend
NEWCASTLE UPON TYNE
SOUTH SHIELDS
Jarrow
Gateshead
Haydon Bridge
Haltwhistle
Corbridge
Hexham
Washington
SUNDERLAND
Consett
Stanley
Chester-le-Street
Hetton-le-Hole
Seaham
Easington
Lanchester
Durham
Peterlee
Tow Law
Brandon
Running Waters
Crook
Willington
Spennymoor
Sedgefield
Hartlepool
Bishop Auckland
Newton Aycliffe
Billingham
Shildon
A85
A82
A816
A83
A84
A9
A94
A914
A91
A915
A977
M90
M9
A8
A80
M8
M74
A71
A77
A736
A78
A726
A721
A73
A74
A702
A703
A72
A7
A68
A697
A1
A1068
A696
A69
A189
A19
A76
A701
A713
A75
A596
A6
M6
A66
© Egon Ronay's Guides Crown Copyright Reserved

A
B
C
2
3
8
5
Kirkintilloch
Cumbernauld
Linlithgow
Edinburgh
Tranent
Haddington
Port Glasgow
Bearsden
Clydebank
Bishopbriggs
Armadale
Bathgate
Ingliston
Musselburgh
Renfrew
Glasgow
Airdrie
Livingston
Dalkeith
Paisley
Coatbridge
Whitburn
LOTHIAN
Johnstone
Busby
Rutherglen
Shotts
Penicuik
Barrhead
Hamilton
Motherwell
Wishaw
Wester Howgate
Duns
East Kilbride
Berwick-upon
Carluke
Larkhall
Lauder
Greenlaw
Eddleston
Stewarton
Strathaven
Kirkmuirhill
Lanark
Coldstream
Kilwinning
Stevenston
Peebles
Biggar
Galashiels
Newmilns
Darvel
Innerleithen
Melrose
Kelso
Irvine
Kilmarnock
Galston
BORDERS
Troon
Selkirk
Mauchline
Prestwick
Abington
Jedburgh
Ayr
Cumnock
Hawick
Sanquhar
Maybole
Maidens
Moffat
Rochester
NORTHUMBER
Thornhill
DUMFRIES AND GALLOWAY
Langholm
Lochmaben
Lockerbie
Wark
Canonbie
New Galloway
Dumfries
Annan
Metal Bridge
Gretna
Haydon Bridge
New Abbey
Rockcliffe
Haltwhistle
Newton Stewart
Castle Douglas
Warwick-on-Eden
Talkin
Dalbeattie
Kirkbean
Carlisle
Faugh
Gatehouse of Fleet
Glenluce
Wigtown
Silloth
Armathwaite
Alston
Melmerby
Whithorn
Maryport
Bassenthwaite Lake
Penrith
Workington
Cockermouth
Pooley Bridge
Askham
Keswick
Appleby
Lowesweater
Whitehaven
CUMBRIA
Cleator Moor
Shap
Brough
Egremont
Wasdale Head
Kirkby Stephen
Elterwater
Langdale
Troutbeck
Boot
Little Langdale
Ambleside
Hawkshead
Eskdale
Coniston
Windermere
Ramsey
Bowland Bridge
Kendal
Cartmell Fell
Lowick Green
Peel
Sandside
Beetham
Barbon
ISLE OF MAN
Millom
Casterton
Ulverston
Grange-over-Sands
Kirkby Lonsdale
Douglas
Dalton-in-Furness
Horton-in-Ribbles
Barrow-in-Furness
Carnforth
Castletown
Morecambe
Heysham
Lancaster
Slaidburn
Newton-in-Bowland
Fleetwood
Preesall
Whitewell
Cleveleys
Thornton
Clitheroe
Nelson
Eccleston
LANCASHIRE
Blackpool
Longridge
Mellor
Great Harwood
Kirkham
Preston
Lytham St Anne's
BLACKBURN
Rawtenstall
Leyland
Darwen
Haslingden
Southport
Chorley
Ainsworth
Horwich
Bury
Burscough
Formby
Ormskirk
BOLTON
GREATER
Skelmersdale
Wigan
Farnworth
Atherton
Maghull
Rainford
Leigh
MANCHES
Crosby
Kirkby
Newton-le-Willows
Eccles
Bootle
ST HELENS
Urmston
Burtonwood
Wallasey
Liverpool
Prescot
Timperley
Hoylake
MERSEYSIDE
Altrincham
Birkenhead
Bowdon
West Kirby
Warrington
Widnes
Runcorn
Amlwch
Llandudno
Glanwydden
Prestatyn
Heswall
Bebington
Knutsford
Holyhead
ANGLESEY
Beaumaris
Conwy
Colwyn Bay
Rhyl
Frodsham
Plumley
Abergele
Holywell
Neston
Wincham
Llangefni
Penmaenmawr
Llanfairfechan
Betws-yn-Rhos
Flint
Ellesmere Port
Northwich
Menai Bridge
Bangor
Babell
Ledsham
Bodfari
Connah's Quay
Queensferry
CHESHIRE
Middlewich
Llannefydd
Bethesda
Chester
Winsford
Denbigh
Mold
Buckley
Brereton Green
Caernarfon
Llanrwst
Sandbach
Crewe
Alsager
Ruthin
Betws-y-Coed
CLWYD
Wrexham
Nantwich
Weston
STOKE-ON-T
GWYNEDD
Rhosllanerchrugog
Newcastle-under-Lyme
Blaenau Ffestiniog
Llangollen
Ffestiniog
M8
M74
M6
M55
M65
M58
M62
M56
M53
M61
M66
A82
A8
A73
A71
A702
A703
A68
A7
A697
A736
A77
A726
A721
A72
A74
A71
A76
A713
A76
A701
A75
A69
A6
A596
A66
A591
A595
A592
A590
A685
A683
A585
A583
A59
A570
A565
A5
A55
A470
A487
A494
A51
A56
A41
A34
A483
A525
© Egon Ronay's Guides
Crown Copyright Reserved

D
E
F
0 10 20 30 40 50 Kilometres
0 10 20 30 Miles
HOLY ISLAND
1
Pub with Food
Pub with Accommodation
Food and Accommodation at same location
Pub with Atmosphere
Seahouses
Warenford
Alnwick
Amble
Longframlington
A1068
Ashington
Newbiggin-by-the-Sea
Morpeth
Bedlington
Blyth
Cramlington
A189
Seaton Delaval
Longbenton
Tynemouth
Gosforth
Wallsend
SOUTH SHIELDS
Jarrow
Blaydon
Whickham
Gateshead
TYNE AND WEAR
Stanley
Washington
SUNDERLAND
Chester-le-Street
Houghton le Spring
Seaham
Hetton-le-Hole
A19
Easington
Durham
Brandon
Running Waters
Peterlee
Crook
Willington
Spennymoor
Hartlepool
Sedgefield
Newton Aycliffe
Great Stainton
Billingham
Redcar
Marske-by-the-Sea
Saltburn-by-the-Sea
Shildon
MIDDLESBROUGH
Eston
Brotton
Loftus
Barnard Castle
Stockton-on-Tees
CLEVELAND
Guisborough
Thornaby-on-Tees
Stapleton
A66
Darlington
Whitby
Castleton
Sleights
2
Scotch Corner
Moulton
A172
A171
Richmond
Rosedale Abbey
Constable Burton
Northallerton
Scalby
Scarborough
Middleham
A19
Kirkbymoorside
Wykeham
Pickhill
Helmsley
A170
Pickering
Snainton
A165
Filey
Carthorpe
Thirsk
Harome
Sutton Howgrave
Coxwold
Oswaldkirk
A64
NORTH
YORKSHIRE
Malton
Norton
Risplith
Ripon
Terrington
Bridlington
Boroughbridge
Staveley
A166
Appletreewick
Bishop Wilton
Driffield
3
Knaresborough
Goldsborough
A166
Harrogate
North Dalton
A661
Pocklington
Hornsea
Ilkley
Wetherby
YORK
A64
A163
Otley
A658
A1079
South Dalton
Sutton-upon-Derwent
Linton
Beverley
Guiseley
A165
Bingley
Tadcaster
Market Weighton
Horsforth
HUMBERSIDE
Shipley
Pudsey
LEEDS
Selby
Skidby
Cottingham
Garforth
A63
Howden
M62
Hedon
Withernsea
WEST YORKSHIRE
Rothwell
Ledston
A63
Hessle
KINGSTON UPON HULL
Halifax
Castleford
Batley
Morley
Knottingley
Goole
Barton-upon-Humber
Ossett
M62
Pontefract
Dewsbury
Wakefield
Darrington
M18
A15
Elland
Horbury
Thorne
Immingham
A160
A180
HUDDERSFIELD
Hemsworth
Stainforth
Grimsby
Darton
Askern
A18
Scunthorpe
Royston
Sutton
Cleethorpes
Shelley
Honley
Barnsley
Thurnscoe
Adwick le Street
Brigg
A18
M180
Worsbrough
Wombwell
Doncaster
Penistone
A629
SOUTH
Mexborough
Caistor
A46
Conisbrough
A614
A15
A16
Stocksbridge
Wentworth
Rawmarsh
Rotherham
A631
A1(M)
Bawtry
A631
Glossop
M18
Market Rasen
Louth
YORKSHIRE
Maltby
Gainsborough
Mablethorpe
SHEFFIELD
A156
Castleton
Bamford
A57
M1
A1
Hope
Dronfield
Killamarsh
Chapel-en-le-Frith
Grindleford
Staveley
Clowne
Worksop
East Retford
A57
A46
A158
4
Buxton
Eyam
A619
Creswell
A614
A1
Lincoln
Chesterfield
A60
Bakewell
Bolsover
Horncastle
A158
Skegness
A515
A61
NOTTINGHAMSHIRE
Woodhall Spa
Clay Cross
Mansfield
Matlock
Sutton in Ashfield
Newark
LINCOLNSHIRE
Friskney
Onecote
DERBYSHIRE
A617
A17
A15
A16
Wirksworth
Alfreton
Kirkby in Ashfield
Blidworth
Southwell
A523
Lowdham
Hucknall
Kenny Bentley
Ripley
Boston
A46
4
Sleaford
Belper
Heanor
Eastwood
Arnold
Silk Willoughby
6
Hunstanton
Ashbourne
A38
A17
Ilkeston
Carlton
A52
A52
Aswarby

WE STILL HOLD POLL POSITION.

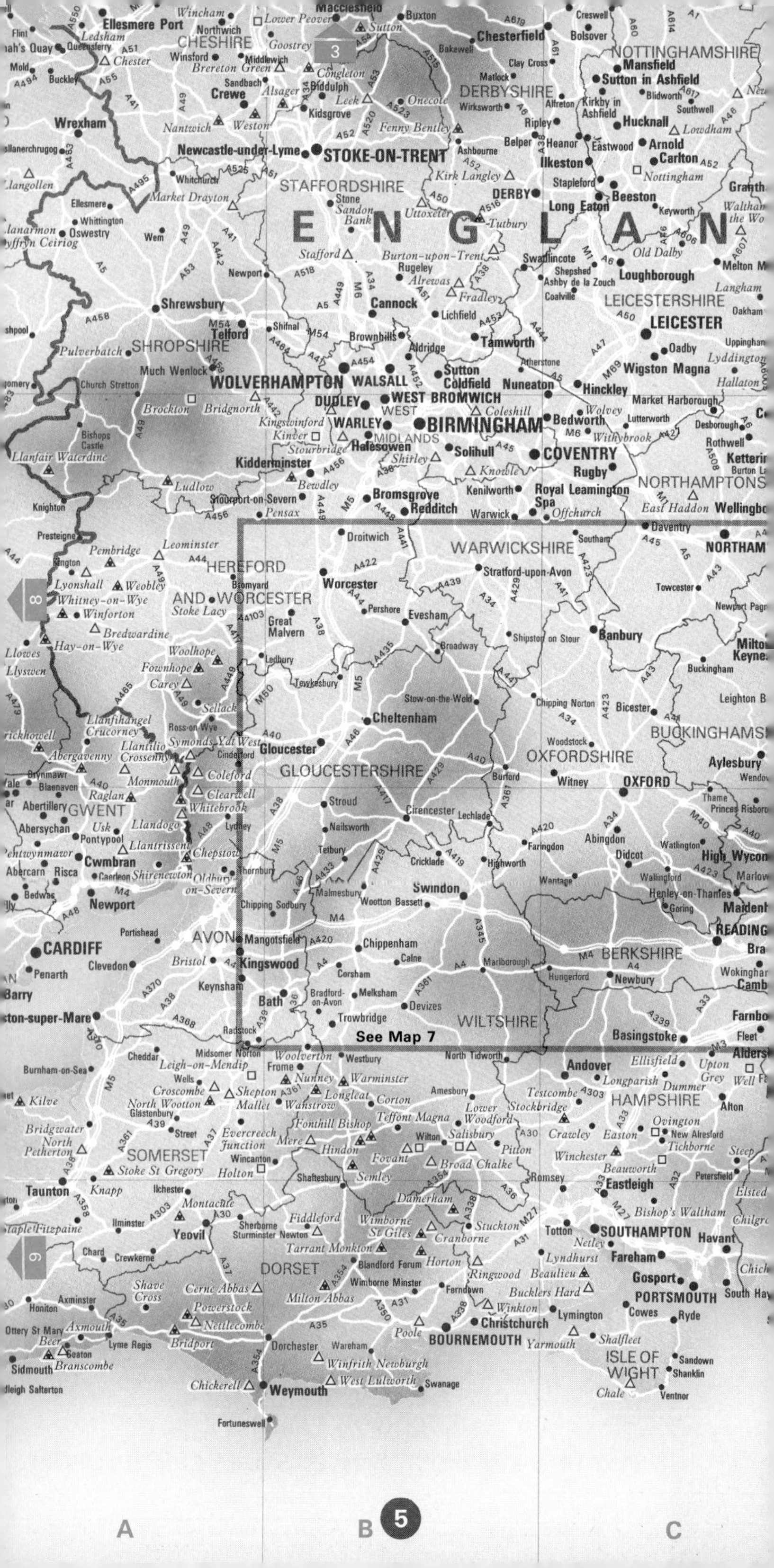

3
8
9
See Map 7
ENGLAND
CHESHIRE
NOTTINGHAMSHIRE
DERBYSHIRE
STAFFORDSHIRE
SHROPSHIRE
LEICESTERSHIRE
WEST MIDLANDS
NORTHAMPTONSHIRE
WARWICKSHIRE
HEREFORD AND WORCESTER
GWENT
GLOUCESTERSHIRE
OXFORDSHIRE
BUCKINGHAMSHIRE
AVON
BERKSHIRE
WILTSHIRE
HAMPSHIRE
SOMERSET
DORSET
ISLE OF WIGHT
Ellesmere Port
Wincham
Lower Peover
Macclesfield
Buxton
Creswell
Flint
Ledsham
Queensferry
Northwich
Sutton
Chesterfield
Bolsover
Chester
Goostrey
Bakewell
Mansfield
Mold
Buckley
Winsford
Middlewich
Congleton
Clay Cross
Sutton in Ashfield
Brereton Green
Matlock
Sandbach
Biddulph
Crewe
Alsager
Leek
Onecote
Wirksworth
Alfreton
Kirkby in Ashfield
Bildworth
Southwell
Kidsgrove
Ripley
Wrexham
Nantwich
Weston
Fenny Bentley
Hucknall
Lowdham
Belper
Heanor
Arnold
Newcastle-under-Lyme
STOKE-ON-TRENT
Ashbourne
Eastwood
Ilkeston
Carlton
Llangollen
Whitchurch
Kirk Langley
Nottingham
Stapleford
Grantham
Market Drayton
Stone
DERBY
Beeston
Ellesmere
Sandon Bank
Uttoxeter
Long Eaton
Keyworth
Whittington
Tutbury
Oswestry
Wem
Old Dalby
Llanarmon Dyffryn Ceiriog
Stafford
Burton-upon-Trent
Swadlincote
Loughborough
Melton Mowbray
Newport
Rugeley
Shepshed
Alrewas
Ashby de la Zouch
Langham
Fradley
Coalville
Oakham
Shrewsbury
Cannock
Lichfield
LEICESTER
Telford
Shifnal
Brownhills
Tamworth
Uppingham
Aldridge
Oadby
Lyddington
Pulverbatch
Atherstone
Wigston Magna
Much Wenlock
WOLVERHAMPTON
WALSALL
Sutton Coldfield
Nuneaton
Hinckley
Hallaton
Church Stretton
DUDLEY
WEST BROMWICH
Brockton
Bridgnorth
Coleshill
Market Harborough
Kingswinford
WARLEY
BIRMINGHAM
Bedworth
Wolvey
Lutterworth
Desborough
Bishops Castle
Kinver
Withybrook
Stourbridge
Halesowen
Rothwell
Kettering
Llanfair Waterdine
Shirley
Solihull
COVENTRY
Burton Latimer
Kidderminster
Knowle
Rugby
Ludlow
Bewdley
Kenilworth
Royal Leamington Spa
East Haddon
Wellingborough
Knighton
Stourport-on-Severn
Bromsgrove
Redditch
Pensax
Warwick
Offchurch
Daventry
Presteigne
Droitwich
Southam
NORTHAMPTON
Leominster
Pembridge
Kington
Weobley
Bromyard
Worcester
Stratford-upon-Avon
Towcester
Lyonshall
Whitney-on-Wye
Winforton
Stoke Lacy
Pershore
Evesham
Newport Pagnell
Bredwardine
Great Malvern
Shipston on Stour
Banbury
Hay-on-Wye
Broadway
Milton Keynes
Llowes
Woolhope
Llyswen
Fownhope
Ledbury
Buckingham
Carey
Tewkesbury
Stow-on-the-Wold
Chipping Norton
Leighton Buzzard
Sellack
Bicester
Llanfihangel Crucorney
Cheltenham
Ross-on-Wye
Crickhowell
Llantilio Crossenny
Symonds Yat West
Woodstock
Abergavenny
Cinderford
Gloucester
Aylesbury
Brynmawr
Coleford
Burford
Witney
OXFORD
Wendover
Blaenavon
Monmouth
Raglan
Clearwell
Stroud
Thame
Princes Risborough
Abertillery
Whitebrook
Cirencester
Lechlade
Usk
Llandogo
Lydney
Nailsworth
Faringdon
Abingdon
Watlington
Abersychan
Pontypool
High Wycombe
Pentwynmawr
Llantrissent
Chepstow
Tetbury
Didcot
Cwmbran
Cricklade
Highworth
Wallingford
Marlow
Abercarn
Risca
Caerleon
Shirenewton
Thornbury
Wantage
Oldbury-on-Severn
Malmesbury
Swindon
Henley-on-Thames
Bedwas
Wootton Bassett
Goring
Maidenhead
Newport
Chipping Sodbury
READING
Portishead
Mangotsfield
Chippenham
CARDIFF
Calne
Clevedon
Bristol
Kingswood
Marlborough
Penarth
Corsham
Hungerford
Newbury
Wokingham
Camberley
Barry
Keynsham
Melksham
Bath
Bradford-on-Avon
Devizes
Weston-super-Mare
Trowbridge
Farnborough
Radstock
Basingstoke
Fleet
Midsomer Norton
Woolverton
Westbury
North Tidworth
Aldershot
Cheddar
Andover
Ellisfield
Leigh-on-Mendip
Frome
Upton Grey
Burnham-on-Sea
Wells
Nunney
Warminster
Longparish
Dummer
Well
Croscombe
Shepton Mallet
Longleat
Corton
Amesbury
Testcombe
Kilve
North Wootton
Wanstrow
Lower Woodford
Stockbridge
Alton
Glastonbury
Fonthill Bishop
Teffont Magna
Bridgwater
Street
Evercreech Junction
Ovington
North Petherton
Mere
Wilton
Salisbury
Crawley
Easton
New Alresford
Tichborne
Hindon
Pitton
Wincanton
Fovant
Winchester
Steep
Holton
Stoke St Gregory
Broad Chalke
Beauworth
Shaftesbury
Semley
Romsey
Petersfield
Taunton
Knapp
Eastleigh
Elsted
Ilchester
Damerham
Montacute
Bishop's Waltham
Chilgrove
Ilminster
Yeovil
Sherborne
Fiddleford
Wimborne St Giles
Stuckton
Totton
SOUTHAMPTON
Havant
Staple Fitzpaine
Sturminster Newton
Cranborne
Netley
Chard
Crewkerne
Tarrant Monkton
Horton
Lyndhurst
Fareham
Blandford Forum
Ringwood
Beaulieu
Gosport
Chichester
Shave Cross
Cerne Abbas
Wimborne Minster
Ferndown
Bucklers Hard
PORTSMOUTH
South Hayling
Honiton
Axminster
Milton Abbas
Powerstock
Winkton
Lymington
Cowes
Christchurch
Ryde
Ottery St Mary
Axmouth
Nettlecombe
Poole
BOURNEMOUTH
Yarmouth
Beer
Lyme Regis
Bridport
Dorchester
Wareham
Shalfleet
Seaton
Sandown
Sidmouth
Branscombe
Winfrith Newburgh
Shanklin
West Lulworth
Swanage
Chale
Budleigh Salterton
Chickerell
Weymouth
Ventnor
Fortuneswell
A
B
C

4
Horncastle
Skegness
Friskney
Boston
Gosberton
Spalding
Holbeach
Bourne
King's Lynn
Wisbech
PETERBOROUGH
Old Fletton
Whittlesey
March
Wansford
Nassington
Chatteris
Ramsey
CAMBRIDGESHIRE
Molesworth
Needingworth
St Ives
Holywell
Huntingdon
Godmanchester
Fen Drayton
Horningsea
Ely
Soham
Littleport
Newmarket
Hunstanton
Snettisham
Dersingham
Wells-next-the-Sea
Sheringham
Cromer
Holt
Fakenham
Great Ryburgh
Blickling
North Walsham
Roydon
East Dereham
Swaffham
Stow Bardolph
Downham Market
NORFOLK
NORWICH
Wymondham
Winterton-on-Sea
Caister-on-Sea
Great Yarmouth
Lowestoft
Beccles
Bungay
Harleston
Brandon
Thetford
Mildenhall
Diss
Scole
Brome
Eye
Southwold
Halesworth
Dunwich
Bury St Edmunds
Horringer
SUFFOLK
Saxmundham
Leiston
Aldeburgh
Easton
Wickham Market
Stowmarket
Needham Market
Woodbridge
Orford
Long Melford
Chelsworth
Cavendish
Kersey
Sudbury
Newton
Washbrook
IPSWICH
Hadleigh
Levington
Pin Mill
Felixstowe
Gestingthorpe
Stoke-by-Nayland
Dedham
Harwich
Halstead
Colchester
Coggeshall
Wivenhoe
Walton on the Naze
Frinton-on-Sea
Brightlingsea
Clacton-on-Sea
West Mersea
Braintree
Witham
Maldon
St Neots
Cambridge
Sawston
Bedford
Sandy
Biggleswade
Haverhill
Royston
Saffron Walden
Letchworth
Baldock
Hitchin
Stevenage
Puckeridge
Stansted Mountfitchet
Great Dunmow
LUTON
Bishop's Stortford
HERTFORDSHIRE
ESSEX
Ware
Sawbridgeworth
Hertford
Harlow
Hatfield
Hoddesdon
Chelmsford
St Albans
Cheshunt
Epping
Waltham Abbey
Potters Bar
ENFIELD
Brentwood
Wickford
BASILDON
Rayleigh
Paglesham
FOULNESS
Burnham-on-Crouch
SOUTHEND-ON-SEA
Shoeburyness
Watford
Rickmansworth
BARNET
REDBRIDGE
HAVERING
HARROW
GREATER LONDON
LONDON
Benfleet
Canvey
Grays
Tilbury
Swanscombe
RICHMOND
BEXLEY
Dartford
Gravesend
Staines
BROMLEY
KINGSTON
Chertsey
SUTTON
CROYDON
Epsom
Banstead
Caterham
Leatherhead
Oxted
Sevenoaks
SURREY
Redhill
Reigate
Dorking
Sheerness
Minster
SHEPPEY
Gillingham
Chatham
Sittingbourne
Herne Bay
Whitstable
Margate
Broadstairs
Ramsgate
Marshside
Faversham
Canterbury
Sandwich
Harrietsham
Eastling
Maidstone
Warren Street
Chilham
Pett Bottom
Deal
Wye
Kennington
St Margaret's at Cliffe
Fairbourne Heath
Smarden
KENT
Ashford
Dover
Folkestone
Hythe
Tonbridge
Penhurst
Southborough
Royal Tunbridge Wells
Lamberhurst
Biddenden
Benenden
Tenterden
Rusthall
East Grinstead
Cousley Wood
Crowborough
Hawkhurst
Newenden
Burwash
Mayfield
Ewhurst Green
Northiam
Rye
New Romney
Lydd
Winchelsea
Horley
Shamley Green
Ockley
Oakwoodhill
Rowhook
Crawley
Horsham
Dragons Green
Haywards Heath
Fletching
WEST SUSSEX
Cuckfield
Burgess
Brightling
Framfield
Battle
EAST SUSSEX
Pulborough
Washington
Lewes
Fulking
Kingston
Hailsham
Polegate
Hastings
Bexhill
Findon
Shoreham-by-Sea
Hove
Lancing
Southwick
Brighton
Worthing
Alfriston
Newhaven
Seaford
Eastbourne
East Dean
Pub with Food
Pub with Accommodation
Food and Accommodation at same location
Pub with Atmosphere
0 10 20 30 40 50 Kilometres
0 10 20 30 Miles
1
2
3
4
D
E
F
6
© Egon Ronay's Guides Crown Copyright Reserved

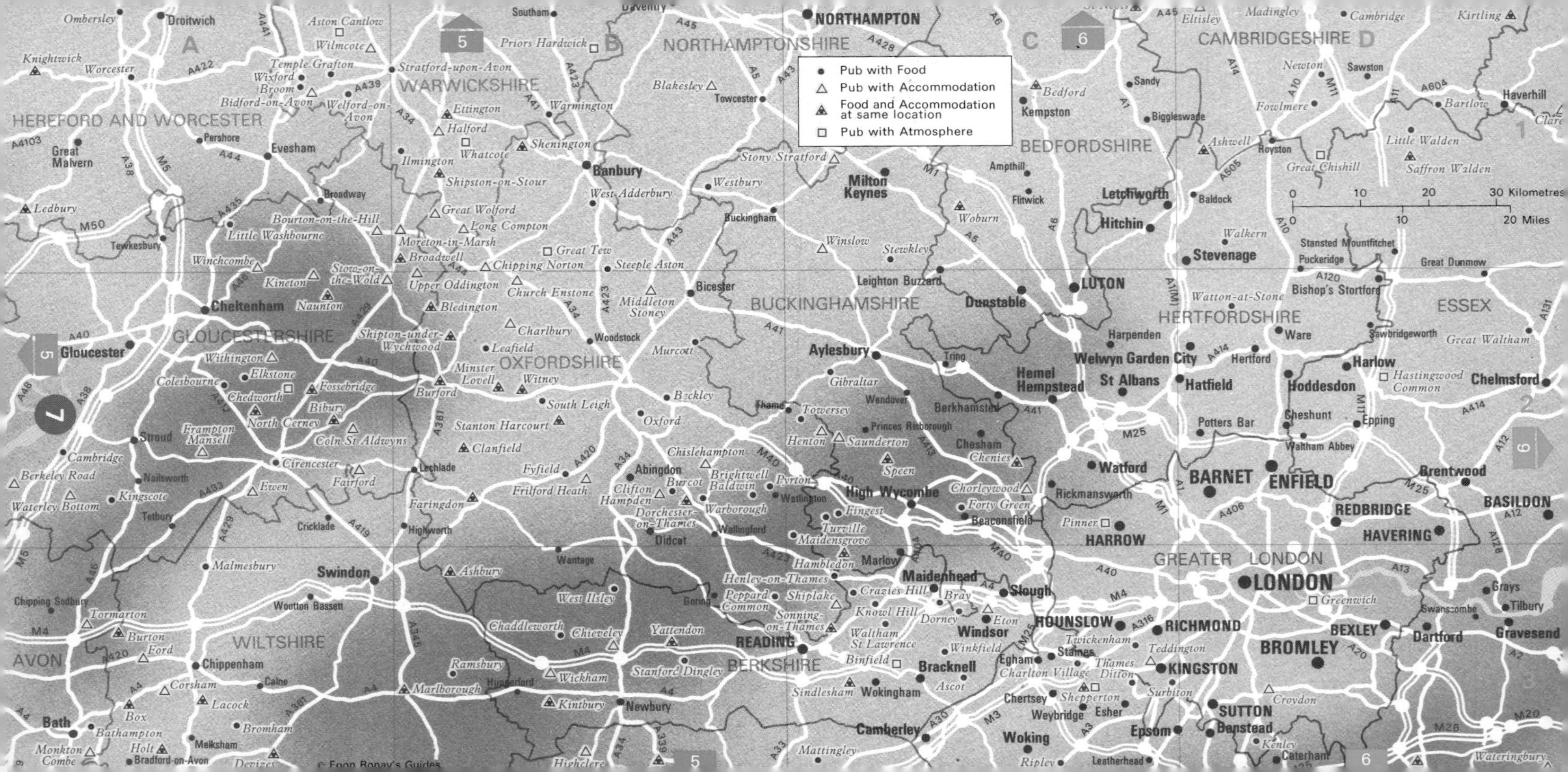

Pub with Food
Pub with Accommodation
Food and Accommodation at same location
Pub with Atmosphere
0 10 20 30 Kilometres
0 10 20 Miles
A
B
C
D
1
2
3
5
6
7
HEREFORD AND WORCESTER
WARWICKSHIRE
NORTHAMPTONSHIRE
CAMBRIDGESHIRE
BEDFORDSHIRE
BUCKINGHAMSHIRE
HERTFORDSHIRE
ESSEX
GLOUCESTERSHIRE
OXFORDSHIRE
GREATER LONDON
BERKSHIRE
WILTSHIRE
AVON
NORTHAMPTON
Milton Keynes
LUTON
LONDON
BARNET
ENFIELD
REDBRIDGE
HAVERING
HARROW
HOUNSLOW
RICHMOND
KINGSTON
SUTTON
BEXLEY
BROMLEY
BASILDON
READING
Droitwich
Ombersley
Worcester
Knightwick
Great Malvern
Ledbury
Tewkesbury
Pershore
Evesham
Cheltenham
Gloucester
Stroud
Cambridge
Berkeley Road
Waterley Bottom
Kingscote
Nailsworth
Tetbury
Cirencester
Chippenham
Bath
Swindon
Banbury
Bicester
Oxford
Abingdon
Aylesbury
High Wycombe
Maidenhead
Slough
Windsor
Bracknell
Wokingham
Camberley
Newbury
Stratford-upon-Avon
Chipping Norton
Woodstock
Burford
Witney
Wantage
Didcot
Wallingford
Henley-on-Thames
Marlow
Dunstable
Leighton Buzzard
Hemel Hempstead
St Albans
Welwyn Garden City
Hatfield
Hitchin
Letchworth
Stevenage
Watford
Hertford
Ware
Harlow
Bishop's Stortford
Chelmsford
Brentwood
Epping
Hoddesdon
Cheshunt
Waltham Abbey
Potters Bar
Royston
Baldock
Biggleswade
Sandy
Kempston
Bedford
Ampthill
Flitwick
Woburn
Towcester
Buckingham
Stony Stratford
Winslow
Tring
Berkhamsted
Chesham
Wendover
Princes Risborough
Thame
Beaconsfield
Rickmansworth
Pinner
Egham
Staines
Chertsey
Weybridge
Esher
Woking
Epsom
Banstead
Croydon
Caterham
Dartford
Gravesend
Grays
Tilbury
Sawbridgeworth
Great Dunmow
Saffron Walden
Haverhill
Sawston
Marlborough
Hungerford
Lechlade
Highworth
Faringdon
Cricklade
Malmesbury
Calne
Melksham
Devizes
Bradford-on-Avon
Chipping Sodbury
© Egon Ronay's Guides

A
B
C
3
0 10 20 30 40 50 Kilometres
0 10 20 30 Miles
Pub with Food
Pub with Accommodation
Food and Accommodation at same location
Pub with Atmosphere
1
2
3
4
Fleetwood
Preesall
Cleveleys
Thornton
Eccleston
Blackpool
Kirkham
Lytham St Anne's
Leyland
Southport
Formby
Ormskirk
Burscough
Skelmersdale
Maghull
Crosby
Kirkby
Bootle
ST HELENS
MERSEYSIDE
Wallasey
Liverpool
Hoylake
Birkenhead
West Kirby
Widnes
Heswall
Bebington
Neston
Ellesmere
Ledsham
Chester
Amlwch
ANGLESEY
Holyhead
Llangefni
Beaumaris
Menai Bridge
Bangor
Llandudno
Glanwydden
Colwyn Bay
Conwy
Penmaenmawr
Llanfairfechan
Abergele
Betwys-yn-Rhos
Bodfari
Llannefydd
Prestatyn
Rhyl
Holywell
Babell
Flint
Connah's Quay
Queensferry
Denbigh
Mold
Buckley
Bethesda
Caernarfon
Llanrwst
Ruthin
Betws-y-Coed
CLWYD
Wrexham
GWYNEDD
Blaenau Ffestiniog
Ffestiniog
Rhosllanerchrugog
Llangollen
Porthmadog
Criccieth
Pwllheli
Bala
Ellesmere
Whittington
Oswestry
Harlech
Llanarmon Dyffryn Ceiriog
Llanfyllin
Penmaenpool
Dolgellau
Barmouth
Shrewsbury
Welshpool
SHROPS
Pulverbatch
Montgomery
Church Stretton
Machynlleth
Aberdovey
Newtown
Bishops Castle
Llanidloes
Llangurig
POWYS
Llanfair Waterdine
Aberystwyth
WALES
Knighton
Rhayader
Penybont
Presteigne
Llandrindod Wells
Pembridge
Aberaeron
New Quay
Kington
Lyonshall
Builth Wells
Winforton
Whitney-on-Wye
Bredwardine
Lampeter
Llanwrtyd Wells
Llowes
Hay-on-Wye
Cardigan
DYFED
Llyswen
Felindre Farchog
Cenarth
Newcastle Emlyn
Fishguard
Llandovery
Llangorse
Brecon
Trecastle
St David's
Wolf's Castle
Felingwm Uchaf
Llandeilo
Llanfrynach
Llanfihangel Crucorney
Llantilio Crossenny
Llandissilio
Carmarthen
Ffairfach
Crickhowell
Abergavenny
Haverfordwest
Brynmawr
Narberth
Ammanford
Ebbw Vale
Blaenavon
Ystradgynlais
Merthyr Tydfil
Tredegar
GWENT
Milford Haven
Neyland
Kidwelly
Abertillery
Usk
Aberdare
Abersychan
WEST GLAMORGAN
Pentwynmawr
Pembroke
Tenby
Mountain Ash
Llantrissent
Llanelli
Gorseinon
Neath
MID
Abercarn
Cwmbran
SWANSEA
Briton Ferry
Rhondda
Pontypridd
Risca
Caerleon
Maesteg
GLAMORGAN
Bedwas
Newport
Port Talbot
Mumbles
Llantrisant
Caerphilly
Nottage
Bridgend
Penllyn
SOUTH
Portishead
CARDIFF
Porthcawl
Cowbridge
Penarth
Clevedon
GLAMORGAN
Barry
Llantwit Major
East Aberthaw
Weston-super-Mare
Burnham-on-Sea
Lynton
Porlock Weir
Minehead
Ilfracombe
Brendon
Watchet
Kilve
Exford
Williton
Monksilver
Bridgwater
Croyde
Yard Down
Winsford
North Petherton
Barnstaple
Withypool
SOMERSET
Northam
South Molton
Taunton
Knapp
Horn's Cross
Bideford
Umberleigh
Wellington
Alswear
Ilminster
Tiverton
Staple Fitzpaine
9
8
Chard
© Egon Ronay's Guides
Crown Copyright Reserved
Bude
Stratton
Winkleigh
DEVON

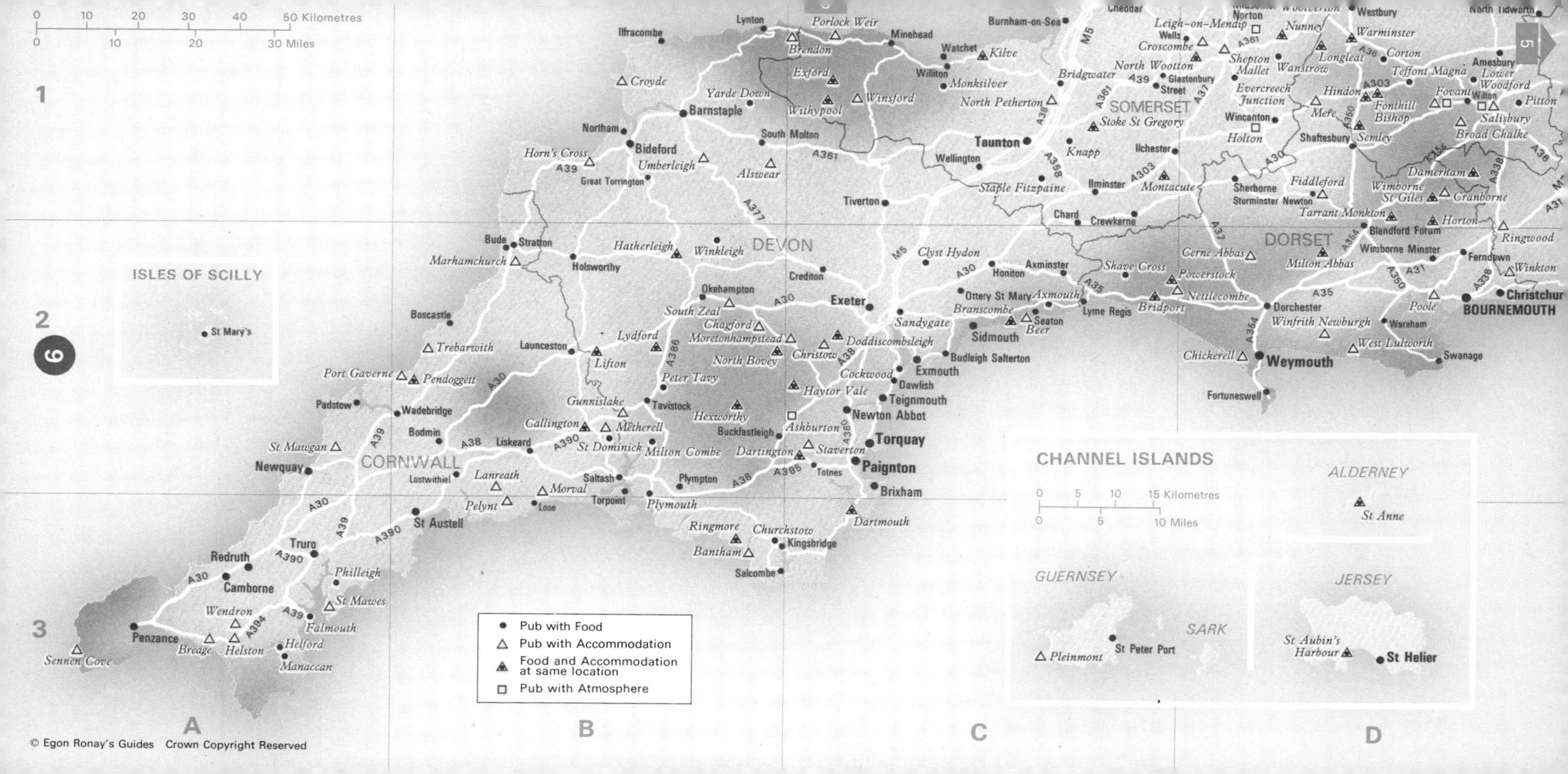

0 10 20 30 40 50 Kilometres
0 10 20 30 Miles
ISLES OF SCILLY
St Mary's
CHANNEL ISLANDS
0 5 10 15 Kilometres
0 5 10 Miles
ALDERNEY
St Anne
GUERNSEY
SARK
Pleinmont
St Peter Port
JERSEY
St Aubin's Harbour
St Helier
Pub with Food
Pub with Accommodation
Food and Accommodation at same location
Pub with Atmosphere
CORNWALL
DEVON
SOMERSET
DORSET
Penzance
Sennen Cove
Breage
Helston
Wendron
Helford
Manaccan
Falmouth
St Mawes
Philleigh
Camborne
Redruth
Truro
Newquay
St Mawgan
Padstow
Port Gaverne
Pendoggett
Wadebridge
Bodmin
Lostwithiel
St Austell
Lanreath
Pelynt
Looe
Morval
Liskeard
Trebarwith
Boscastle
Bude
Stratton
Marhamchurch
Launceston
Lifton
Lydford
Gunnislake
Callington
Metherell
St Dominick
Saltash
Torpoint
Plymouth
Plympton
Milton Combe
Tavistock
Peter Tavy
Holsworthy
Hatherleigh
Winkleigh
Okehampton
South Zeal
Chagford
Moretonhampstead
North Bovey
Hexworthy
Buckfastleigh
Ashburton
Dartington
Staverton
Totnes
Ringmore
Bantham
Churchstow
Kingsbridge
Salcombe
Dartmouth
Brixham
Paignton
Torquay
Newton Abbot
Teignmouth
Dawlish
Cockwood
Haytor Vale
Christow
Doddiscombsleigh
Exeter
Crediton
Exmouth
Budleigh Salterton
Sidmouth
Sandygate
Branscombe
Beer
Seaton
Axmouth
Lyme Regis
Ottery St Mary
Honiton
Axminster
Clyst Hydon
Tiverton
South Molton
Alswear
Umberleigh
Great Torrington
Horn's Cross
Bideford
Northam
Barnstaple
Croyde
Ilfracombe
Yarde Down
Lynton
Brendon
Porlock Weir
Exford
Withypool
Winsford
Minehead
Watchet
Williton
Monksilver
Kilve
Wellington
Taunton
North Petherton
Bridgwater
Burnham-on-Sea
Staple Fitzpaine
Chard
Crewkerne
Ilminster
Knapp
Stoke St Gregory
Ilchester
Montacute
Shave Cross
Powerstock
Bridport
Nettlecombe
Cerne Abbas
Chickerell
Weymouth
Fortuneswell
Dorchester
Winfrith Newburgh
West Lulworth
Wareham
Swanage
Poole
BOURNEMOUTH
Ferndown
Winkton
Ringwood
Wimborne Minster
Milton Abbas
Blandford Forum
Tarrant Monkton
Horton
Wimborne St Giles
Cranborne
Damerham
Sherborne
Sturminster Newton
Fiddleford
Holton
Wincanton
Shaftesbury
Semley
Mere
Hindon
Fonthill Bishop
Evercreech Junction
Shepton Mallet
Wanstrow
Nunney
Longleat
Warminster
Corton
Teffont Magna
Fovant
Wilton
Salisbury
Broad Chalke
Lower Woodford
Amesbury
Pitton
Westbury
Norton
Leigh-on-Mendip
Wells
Croscombe
North Wootton
Glastonbury
Street
Cheddar
North Tidworth
© Egon Ronay's Guides Crown Copyright Reserved

Fish Lovers!

Everlasting!

BEER OFFER

THIS remarkable fish, a distant relative of the infamous Japanese Lager-Sipper, thought until recently to be extinct, was discovered by Turkish explorer O'my-O'my.

He writes: *"On a recent field trip to the Amazon, I noticed the presence of the Amazing Amazonian Drinking-Fish in my glass of cold* **Gold Label Very Strong Special Beer.** *We had chosen the* **Gold Label VSSB** *because of its unique compact proportions. (Although only 180ml,* **Gold Label** *is Britain's strongest nationally available beer. Brewed twice as long and matured six times as long as ordinary beers.)*

Incredibly, each time I drank from the glass, the Amazing Amazonian Drinking-Fish was able to regenerate the exact amount of **Gold Label** *I had drunk."*

WARNING

Although the fish leave the factory in perfect condition, we take no responsibility for evaporation during posting.

THIS remarkable ability to regenerate **Gold Label Beer** remains an unexplained mystery – even to scientists!!! However, we have been able to obtain a small number of these remarkable fish, which we can offer to you at a chance of a lifetime price of 50p for 1,000.

A
B
C
D
1
2
3
10
Spaniards Inn
Flask
Jack Straw's Castle
Eagle
Hampstead Heath
Regent's Park
Gladstone Park
Brent Reservoir
Barn Hill
Alexandra Park
Finsbury Park
Lockwood Reservoir
Warwick Reservoir West
HARINGEY
HACKNEY
ISLINGTON
BRENT
NORTH CIRCULAR ROAD
A1 GREAT NORTH WAY
WATFORD WAY
HENDON WAY
HENDON LANE
FINCHLEY ROAD
FALLODEN WAY
LYTTELTON FOAD
AYLMER RD
ARCHWAY RD
GREAT NORTH RD
EAST END ROAD
FORTIS GREEN
MUSWELL HILL
PRIORY ROAD
HIGH ST
TURNPIKE LA
WESTBURY AVE
LORDSHIP LANE
GREEN LANES
SEVEN SISTERS ROAD
STAMFORD HILL
STOKE NEWINGTON ROAD
KINGSLAND ROAD
HOLLOWAY ROAD
CAMDEN ROAD
CALEDONIAN ROAD
FORTRESS ROAD
JUNCTION RD
HIGHGATE HILL
HIGHGATE WEST HILL
HAMPSTEAD LANE
SPANIARDS ROAD
NORTH END ROAD
GOLDERS GREEN ROAD
EDGWARE ROAD
CRICKLEWOOD LANE
WILLESDEN LANE
NEW NORTH RD
UPPER ST
CITY ROAD
EDGWARE ROAD
KINGSBURY ROAD
FRYENT WAY
NEASDEN LA
DUDDEN HILL LANE
HIGH ROAD
CHURCH ROAD
HARROW RD

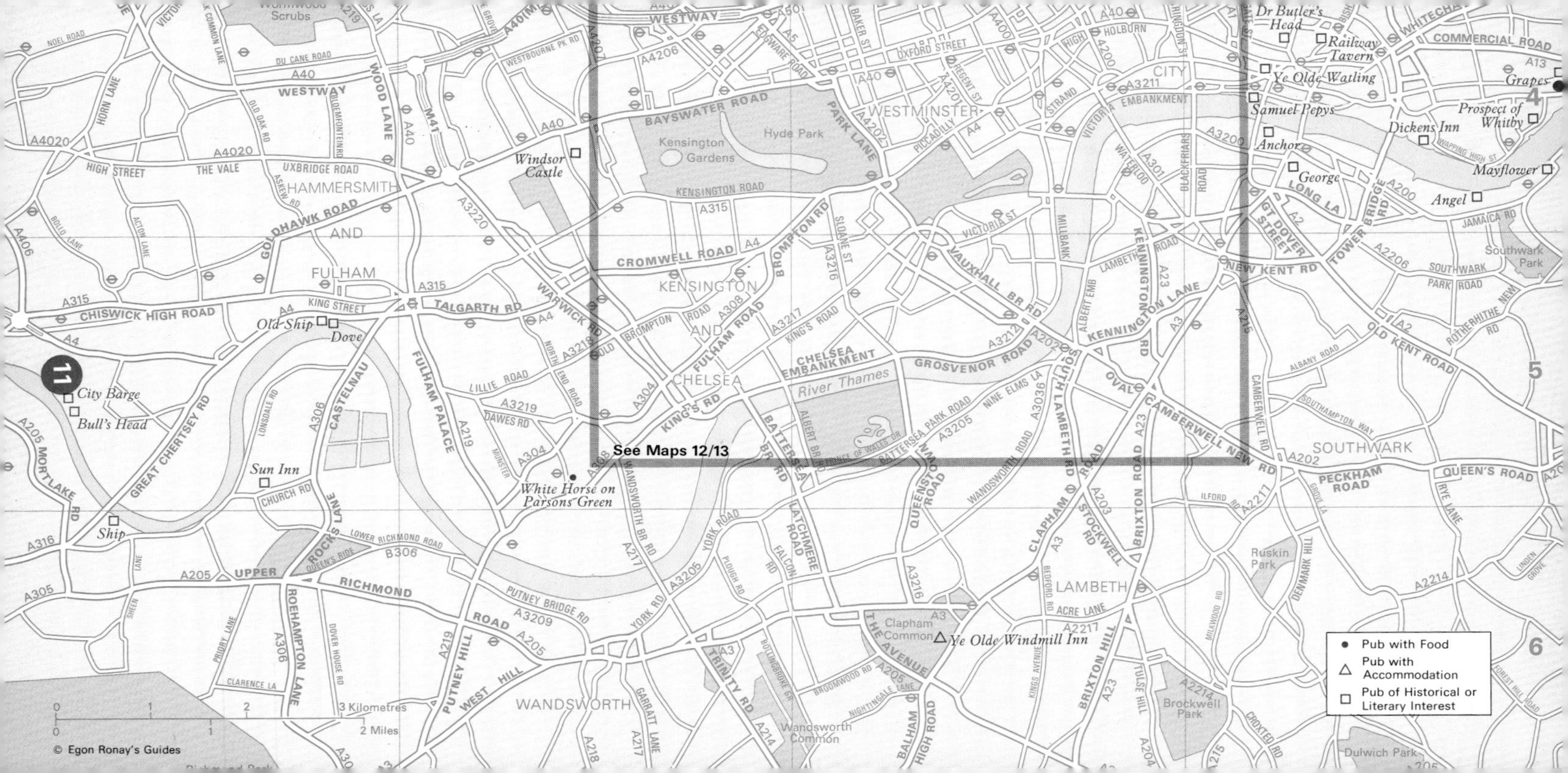

Pub with Food
Pub with Accommodation
Pub of Historical or Literary Interest
See Maps 12/13
4
5
6
11
Dr Butler's Head
Railway Tavern
Ye Olde Watling
Grapes
Samuel Pepys
Prospect of Whitby
Dickens Inn
Anchor
George
Mayflower
Angel
Windsor Castle
Old Ship
Dove
City Barge
Bull's Head
Sun Inn
Ship
White Horse on Parsons Green
Ye Olde Windmill Inn
WESTMINSTER
CITY
HAMMERSMITH AND FULHAM
KENSINGTON AND CHELSEA
SOUTHWARK
LAMBETH
WANDSWORTH
Hyde Park
Kensington Gardens
River Thames
Clapham Common
Wandsworth Common
Brockwell Park
Ruskin Park
Southwark Park
Dulwich Park
Wormwood Scrubs
0 1 2 3 Kilometres
0 1 2 Miles
© Egon Ronay's Guides

Pub with Food
Pub of Historical or Literary Interest
A
B
C
D
1
2
3
Primrose Hill
Regent's Park
Boating Lake
King's Cross Station
St Pancras Station
Euston Station
Paddington Station
British Museum
St Paul's Cathedral
Somerset House
Albion
Slug & Lettuce
Lamb
Prince Regent
Fox & Anchor
Hand & Shears
Cock Tavern
Ye Olde Mitre Tavern
Museum Tavern
Printer's Devil
Princess Louise
Seven Stars
Ye Olde Cheshire Cheese
Nell of Old Drury
Old Bell Tavern
Ye Olde Cock Tavern
Black Friar
Nag's Head
Lamb & Flag
Salisbury
Glasshouse Stores
Victoria
Swan Tavern
Slug & Lettuce
FINCHLEY ROAD
WELLINGTON ROAD
MAIDA VALE
A5 KILBURN HIGH RD
ST JOHN'S WOOD ROAD
EDGWARE ROAD
PARK ROAD
PRINCE ALBERT ROAD
ALBANY STREET
PARKWAY
CAMDEN HIGH ST
CAMDEN ST
ROYAL COLLEGE STREET
ST PANCRAS WAY
HAMPSTEAD ROAD
EVERSHOT ROAD
EUSTON ROAD
PANCRAS ROAD
YORK WAY
CALEDONIAN ROAD
PENTONVILLE ROAD
UPPER STREET
ESSEX ROAD
CITY ROAD
GOSWELL ROAD
ALDERSGATE STREET
ROSEBERY AVENUE
ROSEBERY AVE
FARRINGDON ROAD
KINGS CROSS ROAD
GRAY'S INN ROAD
CLERKENWELL ROAD
THEOBALD'S ROAD
WOBURN PLACE
RUSSELL SQUARE
SOUTHAMPTON ROW
GOWER STREET
TOTTENHAM COURT RD
PORTLAND PLACE
MARYLEBONE ROAD
BAKER STREET
GLOUCESTER PLACE
A40(M) HARROW ROAD
BISHOP'S BRIDGE ROAD
EASTBOURNE TERR
PRAED STREET
SUSSEX GARDENS
WESTBOURNE GROVE
BAYSWATER ROAD
PARK
SEYMOUR ST
OXFORD STREET
WIGMORE STREET
REGENT ST
OXFORD ST
REGENT
SHAFTESBURY
CHARING CROSS RD
AVENUE
HIGH HOLBORN
KINGSWAY
HOLBORN
SHOE LANE
HOLBORN VIADUCT
LUDGATE HILL
FLEET STREET
STRAND
VICTORIA EMBANKMENT
12

13
4
5
6
Kensington Gardens
Kensington Palace
The Serpentine
Goat
Greyhound
Paxton's Head
Grenadier
Shepherd's Tavern
Red Lion
Two Chairmen
Two Chairmen
Charing Cross Station
Green Park
St James's Palace
St James's Park
Buckingham Palace Gardens
Buckingham Palace
The Royal Mews
Horse Guards Parade
Cask & Glass
Albert
Westminster Abbey
Houses of Parliament
Science Museum
Admiral Codrington
Victoria Station
Slug & Lettuce
Victoria Coach Station
Waterloo Station
Imperial War Museum
Kennington Park
Battersea Park
Boating Lake
RIVER THAMES
KENSINGTON ROAD
KENSINGTON HIGH ST
KENSINGTON CHURCH ST
KNIGHTSBRIDGE
CROMWELL ROAD
BROMPTON ROAD
OLD BROMPTON ROAD
FULHAM ROAD
FULHAM RD
KINGS ROAD
KINGS RD
SLOANE STREET
LOWER SLOANE STREET
GROSVENOR PL
HOBART PL
ECCLESTON ST
BUCKINGHAM PALACE ROAD
VAUXHALL BRIDGE ROAD
BELGRAVE ROAD
PIMLICO ROAD
CHELSEA BRIDGE ROAD
CHELSEA BR
CHELSEA EMBANKMENT
GROSVENOR ROAD
VICTORIA STREET
MILLBANK
LAMBETH BRIDGE
WESTMINSTER BRIDGE
WESTMINSTER BRIDGE RD
VICTORIA EMBANKMENT
WHITEHALL
PALL MALL
PICCADILLY
LAMBETH PALACE ROAD
LAMBETH ROAD
ALBERT EMBANKMENT
KENNINGTON ROAD
KENNINGTON LANE
KENNINGTON PARK ROAD
HARLEYFORD ROAD
SOUTH LAMBETH ROAD
WANDSWORTH ROAD
NINE ELMS LANE
CLAPHAM ROAD
BRIXTON ROAD
CAMBERWELL NEW ROAD
YORK ROAD
WATERLOO ROAD
BLACKFRIARS ROAD
SOUTHWARK BRIDGE ROAD
BOROUGH RD
BOROUGH HIGH ST
LONDON RD
ST GEORGE'S RD
WALWORTH ROAD
EARL'S COURT RD
REDCLIFFE GDNS
FINBOROUGH ROAD
EDITH GROVE
ALBERT BRIDGE
ALBERT BRIDGE ROAD
BATTERSEA BRIDGE RD
QUEENSTOWN RD
BATTERSEA PARK ROAD
A315
A3220
A3218
A304
A308
A3216
A3205
A3036
A203
A3
A23
A202
0
400
800 Metres
440
880 Yards
© Egon Ronay's Guides

AN OFFER FOR ANSWERS

▪ A DISCOUNT ON THE NEXT GUIDE ▪

(FOR UK RESIDENTS ONLY)

Readers' answers to questionnaires included in the Guide prove invaluable to us in planning future editions, either through their reactions to the contents of the current Guide, or through the tastes and inclinations indicated. Please send this tear-out page to us *after you have used the Guide for some time*, addressing the envelope to:

Egon Ronay's Coca Cola Pub Guide
Second Floor, Greencoat House,
Francis Street
London SW1P 1DH,
United Kingdom

As a token of thanks for your help, we will enable respondents resident in the UK to obtain the 1989 Guide post free from us at a 33⅓% discount off the retail price. We will send you an order form before publication, and answering the questionnaire imposes no obligation to purchase. All answers will be treated in confidence.

This offer closes 30 June 1988 and is limited to addresses within the United Kingdom.

Please tick

1. Are you

male?	☐	Under 21?	☐	31–45?	☐
female?	☐	21–30?	☐	46–65?	☐
				over 65?	☐

2. Your occupation ....

3. Do you have any children? Yes ☐ No ☐

4. Do you have any previous editions of this Guide?
1985 ☐ 1986 ☐ 1987 ☐

5. Do you refer to this Guide

four times a week?	☐	once a week?	☐
three times a week?	☐	once a fortnight?	☐
twice a week?	☐	once a month?	☐

6. How many people, apart from yourself, are likely to consult this Guide (including those in your home and place of work)?

male .... female ....

7. Do you have our Hotel & Restaurant Guide?
1986 ☐ 1987 ☐ 1988 ☐

8. Do you have our Just a Bite Guide?
1986 ☐ 1987 ☐ 1988 ☐

9. Do you have our Healthy Eating Out Guide?
1987 ☐

10. How many times have you travelled overseas in the past year?

....

11. How many nights have you spent in hotels during the past year?

....

12. Do you occupy more than one home? Yes ☐ No ☐

Do you own the house you live in? Yes ☐ No ☐

13. Your car
type .... year ....

14. What is your daily newspaper? ....

15. Which of the following cards do you use?

Access ☐ Diners ☐
American Express ☐ Visa ☐

16. What fields would you like us to survey or what improvements do you suggest?

....
....
....
....
....
....
....
....
....
....
....
....
....
....

Please *print* your name and address here if you would like us to send you a pre-publication order form for the next Guide.

Name ....

Address ....

....

.... **Postcode** ....

► READER'S COMMENTS ◄

Please use this sheet to recommend bar snacks or inn accommodation of very high quality – *not* full restaurant or hotel facilities. Your complaints about any of the Guide's entries are also welcome.

Please post to: PUB GUIDE 1988
Egon Ronay's Guides Greencoat House, Francis Street, London SW1P 1DH

Name and address of establishment
(Please state whether food or accommodation)

PUB

Your recommendation or complaint

NB We regret that owing to the enormous volume of readers' communications received each year, we will be unable to acknowledge these forms but they will certainly be seriously considered.

NAME OF SENDER
(in block letters)

ADDRESS OF SENDER
(in block letters)

► READER'S COMMENTS ◄

Please use this sheet to recommend bar snacks or inn accommodation of very high quality – *not* full restaurant or hotel facilities. Your complaints about any of the Guide's entries are also welcome.

Please post to: PUB GUIDE 1988
Egon Ronay's Guides Greencoat House, Francis Street, London SW1P 1DH

Name and address of establishment
(Please state whether food or accommodation)

Your recommendation or complaint

NB We regret that owing to the enormous volume of readers' communications received each year, we will be unable to acknowledge these forms but they will certainly be seriously considered.

NAME OF SENDER
(in block letters)

ADDRESS OF SENDER
(in block letters)

► READER'S COMMENTS ◄

Please use this sheet to recommend bar snacks or inn accommodation of very high quality – *not* full restaurant or hotel facilities. Your complaints about any of the Guide's entries are also welcome.

Please post to: PUB GUIDE 1988
Egon Ronay's Guides Greencoat House, Francis Street, London SW1P 1DH

Name and address of establishment
(Please state whether food or accommodation)

Your recommendation or complaint

NB We regret that owing to the enormous volume of readers' communications received each year, we will be unable to acknowledge these forms but they will certainly be seriously considered.

NAME OF SENDER
(in block letters)

ADDRESS OF SENDER
(in block letters)

► READER'S COMMENTS ◄

Please use this sheet to recommend bar snacks or inn accommodation of very high quality – *not* full restaurant or hotel facilities. Your complaints about any of the Guide's entries are also welcome.

Please post to: PUB GUIDE 1988
Egon Ronay's Guides Greencoat House, Francis Street, London SW1P 1DH

Name and address of establishment
(Please state whether food or accommodation)

Your recommendation or complaint

PUB

NB We regret that owing to the enormous volume of readers' communications received each year, we will be unable to acknowledge these forms but they will certainly be seriously considered.

NAME OF SENDER
(in block letters)

ADDRESS OF SENDER
(in block letters)

► READER'S COMMENTS ◄

Please use this sheet to recommend bar snacks or inn accommodation of very high quality – *not* full restaurant or hotel facilities. Your complaints about any of the Guide's entries are also welcome.

Please post to: PUB GUIDE 1988
Egon Ronay's Guides Greencoat House, Francis Street, London SW1P 1DH

Name and address of establishment
(Please state whether food or accommodation)

Your recommendation or complaint

NB We regret that owing to the enormous volume of readers' communications received each year, we will be unable to acknowledge these forms but they will certainly be seriously considered.

NAME OF SENDER
(in block letters)

ADDRESS OF SENDER
(in block letters)

► READER'S COMMENTS ◄

Please use this sheet to recommend bar snacks or inn accommodation of very high quality – *not* full restaurant or hotel facilities. Your complaints about any of the Guide's entries are also welcome.

Please post to: PUB GUIDE 1988
Egon Ronay's Guides Greencoat House, Francis Street, London SW1P 1DH

Name and address of establishment
(Please state whether food or accommodation)

Your recommendation or complaint

PUB

NB We regret that owing to the enormous volume of readers' communications received each year, we will be unable to acknowledge these forms but they will certainly be seriously considered.

NAME OF SENDER
(in block letters)

ADDRESS OF SENDER
(in block letters)

► READER'S COMMENTS ◄

Please use this sheet to recommend bar snacks or inn accommodation of very high quality – *not* full restaurant or hotel facilities. Your complaints about any of the Guide's entries are also welcome.

Please post to: PUB GUIDE 1988
Egon Ronay's Guides Greencoat House, Francis Street, London SW1P 1DH

Name and address of establishment
(Please state whether food or accommodation)

Your recommendation or complaint

NB We regret that owing to the enormous volume of readers' communications received each year, we will be unable to acknowledge these forms but they will certainly be seriously considered.

NAME OF SENDER
(in block letters)

ADDRESS OF SENDER
(in block letters)

► READER'S COMMENTS ◄

Please use this sheet to recommend bar snacks or inn accommodation of very high quality – *not* full restaurant or hotel facilities. Your complaints about any of the Guide's entries are also welcome.

Please post to: PUB GUIDE 1988
Egon Ronay's Guides Greencoat House, Francis Street, London SW1P 1DH

Name and address of establishment
(Please state whether food or accommodation)

Your recommendation or complaint

NB We regret that owing to the enormous volume of readers' communications received each year, we will be unable to acknowledge these forms but they will certainly be seriously considered.

NAME OF SENDER
(in block letters)

ADDRESS OF SENDER
(in block letters)

Coca-Cola

REGISTERED TRADE MARK

Coca-Cola is the ideal drink for all the family, and complements all kinds of meals and snacks. Every day more than 350 million servings of Coca-Cola are sold in 155 countries throughout the world, and nowadays the world's most famous trade mark is advertised in over 80 languages.

Early Coca-Cola Advertising

The world's best known taste sprang from humble beginnings, formulated in a back yard in Atlanta, Georgia in 1886. Pharmacist Dr. John Styth Pemberton carried his new product down the street and put it on sale at Jacobs' Pharmacy for 5 cents a glass. His partner, Frank M. Robinson named the dark brown liquid Coca-Cola, he wrote it in the flowing Spencerian script of the day and added the rejoinder 'Delicious and Refreshing'. Coca-Cola was to become one of the world's greatest success stories.

Jacob's Pharmacy where Coca-Cola was first sold.